Production and operations management

A life cycle approach

Irwin Series in Quantitative Analysis for Business

Consulting Editor   ROBERT B. FETTER   *Yale University*

Production and operations management

A life cycle approach

RICHARD B. CHASE

NICHOLAS J. AQUILANO

Both of the
University of Arizona

Revised edition 1977

RICHARD D. IRWIN, INC. Homewood, Illinois 60430
Irwin-Dorsey Limited Georgetown, Ontario L7G 4B3

© RICHARD D. IRWIN, INC., 1973 and 1977

Revised Edition

5 6 7 8 9 0 K 5 4 3 2 1 0 9 8

ISBN 0-256-01919-3
Library of Congress Catalog Card No. 76–28892
Printed in the United States of America

To HARRIET and NINA

Preface

Since the first edition of this book was published a great many schools have adopted it to satisfy the requirement of the American Assembly of Collegiate Schools of Business that member schools must include production management in their undergraduate core. We were very pleased by this, of course, since it was our intent in the design of the text that it be used in courses developed to meet this requirement, as well as for introductory upper-division production management courses currently being offered in schools of business and engineering. The book has also been widely adopted at the graduate level both as the only text and also in conjunction with other material.

This revised edition still maintains the main distinctive features of the first edition that set it apart from other books in the field:

1. The life cycle approach to studying productive systems and decisions. Existing production management texts, though dealing with time problems affecting the product being made by the productive system, ignore the basic problem—how the system itself develops over time. Crucial questions of how the system arises, how it evolves, and where it is going are never considered in depth, yet they are vital to the understanding of the subject as it applies to real-world operations. The life cycle approach used in this text takes the reader from the origins of the system (the selection of the product), to the design of the system and processes, manning of the system, installing and starting the system, examination of the daily decision problems of the system in steady state, revisions, and, finally, termination of the system.

2. Broadening of the field. As a result of following the life cycle approach, complete sections not usually treated in other basic texts are provided. For example, Section II, "The Product Decision," deals with how the product or service is selected; Section IV, "Start-up of the System," deals with the unique problems of installation and implementation of a new productive system; Section V, "The System in Steady State," examines the day-to-day operating problems and decisions faced by the production manager; Section VI, "Revision of the System," deals with production policy evaluation and significant system adaptations to environmental changes; Section VII, "Termination of the System," deals with the causes and effects of the system ceasing as an entity. Because of the innovative life cycle approach, these topics can be treated more effectively in their relevant time context.

3. Extensive treatment of nonmanufacturing activities. Production management in many schools is now termed "operations management" in order to emphasize its applicability to any type of productive system. Despite this explicit recognition, the general conception of production or operations management is, at best, that it is limited to dealing with factory operations; and at worst, that it is the business school equivalent of industrial engineering. This misconception results in large measure from the "traditional" orientation of existing textbooks. While noting the value of operations management concepts in solving problems arising in, say, service industries, these books present the subject in the context of manufacturing. This orientation is certainly understandable, since the factory environment was the proving ground for most of the techniques encompassed by the field, and abounds in good shop-floor examples. Nevertheless, we feel that it is high time that writers in the area addressed themselves directly to the specific applications of production management in nonmanufacturing organizations such as hospitals, department stores, and banks. This text attempts to meet this goal in every chapter by casting both descriptive and quantitative material in the context of nonmanufacturing, as well as manufacturing activities.

4. Presentation of the latest developments in the field. Production management is a dynamic area and unquestionably even basic texts should draw heavily upon recent research findings. The authors of this text are research oriented; we have done extensive work in job design and are currently developing new approaches to project layout, assembly line balancing, and inventory systems. Part of the impetus to writing this book derives from the desire to disseminate recent research findings—our own and those of others —to beginning students so that they will find the field as interesting and rewarding as we have.

5. Logical development of the material. Production management, being a blend of operations research, economics, and industrial engineering, presents substantial problems in textbook organization. We feel that by virtue of the life cycle approach we have managed to integrate this diverse material in such a way that the student can readily visualize the field in its entirety. He can even fit into the broad framework of production management those topics that may not be covered by lectures or class discussion. With respect to quantitative methods, we have attempted to bring them in at the most logical point of application. Where a technique warrants a good deal of discussion, such as linear programming and queueing theory, a supplement is presented at the conclusion of the chapter where it is most appropriate. This approach enables the instructor either to treat the topic in depth at that point or to bypass it, without losing continuity of topical coverage. If he does elect to treat the supplements in detail, the book readily lends itself to a two-semester sequence.

While this edition retains the life cycle structure as before, and our intent to present the basic concepts of contemporary production and operations management in a logical and interesting manner, the text has been extensively revised in a number of ways:

1. Inclusion of 56 propositions that contrast service and manufacturing systems from the point of view of the operations manager.
2. Introduction of a complete chapter on Materials Requirements Planning (MRP) and a reorganizing of inventory material according to independent and dependent demand concepts.
3. Introduction of what we believe to be an innovative chapter—"Evaluation of Production Policies"—which includes original manufacturing and service policy questionnaires and short cases to which they are applied. (This chapter takes the place of the research and development chapter presented in the original edition, although many of the concepts from the R&D chapter have been integrated into other parts of the book.)
4. Inclusion of recent applications of production and operations management concepts in a variety of organizational settings (see for example, Chapters 2, 3, and 7).
5. Additional discussion of a variety of topics including: location of service facilities; strategic and tactical decisions and techniques in quality control; computer programs for maintenance, line balancing and MRP; and ongoing experiments in work structuring.
6. Introduction of new discussion questions and problems, and of course, updating of bibliographical references and textual material in light of changes in the field since 1973.

ACKNOWLEDGMENTS

We would like to thank the following individuals who provided reviews at various stages of the revision: Everett E. Adam, Jr., University of Missouri-Columbia; John G. Carlson, University of Southern California; Lawrence J. Chase, California State University at Sacramento; Robert B. Fetter, Yale University; William A. Fischer, Clarkson College; Dale R. Flowers, Texas Tech University; Stanley T. Hardy, Ohio State University; and John R. Matthews, University of Wisconsin-Madison.

We would again like to thank the reviewers of the first edition: William J. Abernathy and Lawrence A. Bennigson, Harvard University; Joel Corman, Suffolk University; Stanley J. Garstka, University of Chicago; Oliver Galbraith III, California State University at San Diego; Michael P. Hottenstein, Penn State University; Trevor Sainsbury, University of Pittsburgh.

We would also like to thank our colleagues in operations management who have gone out of their way to share with us their views on the first edition as well as on new developments in the field. Both types of input were of great value in our writing of this revision.

Last, but certainly not least, we would like to thank our families who, once again, let the life cycle of the book disrupt theirs.

January 1977

RICHARD B. CHASE
NICHOLAS J. AQUILANO

Contents

Section six   REVISION OF THE SYSTEM

Section seven   TERMINATION OF THE SYSTEM

Appendixes

Indexes

**Production and
operations management**

A life cycle approach

1

Introduction

C harles Dickens' classic phrase "It was the best of times, it was the worst of times" aptly illuminates the state in which organizations find themselves today. The promise of boundless growth due to ever-expanding demand is countered by changes in value systems that reject many of the products and by-products of a consumer-oriented economy. Now more than ever before in our history, organizational goals are challenged to be more responsive to the needs of minority groups, labor, and the ecosystem. The productive system and its management ultimately feel these pressures. Thus the operations manager must be wary of contributing to environmental pollution when designing the physical productive system; he must account for the changing mix of the labor force when manning the system; and he must keep his labor and other costs down when operating the system. Naturally, these problems vary in severity and complexity from one system to the next; yet they all exist to some degree regardless of the function of the organization. It is the purpose of this book to convey some of the concepts and techniques that are of proven value in helping the manager cope with these and related problems.

Since this text is intended as an introduction to the field, the student is not expected to become an expert in operations management simply by reading it. We do hope, however, to achieve three goals: (1) to impart a knowledge of the standard tools and techniques used in the field; (2) to develop an appreciation for the interaction of operations management with other management systems of the organization; and (3) to develop an appreciation of the field as a totality. With respect to the latter goal, we intend to show that operations management is not just a loosely knit aggregation of tools but rather a *synthesis* of concepts and techniques which relate directly to, and enhance the management of, productive systems. This point is important because operations management, like its environment, is in a state of flux that generates some confusion as to the boundaries and content of the field itself—a problem we will consider later in this chapter. This confusion has not been eased by the variety of appellations used to denote the discipline: "production management," "production and operations management," and, of course, "operations management." Nevertheless, the field is a distinct entity, and viewing it as such is essential to understanding its full range of application.

Before considering the historical evolution of operations management, a clarification of the aforementioned "name problem" is in order. Our subject matter has its origins in the factory environment, and therefore the term *production management* has been, and still is, widely used to denote it. Within the past few years, however, it has become more apparent that the value of production management concepts and techniques extends far beyond the shop floor—that it encompasses virtually all types of productive enterprise. Hence the need for a broader and more appropriate title, such as *operations management,* to describe the discipline—a fact that has been recognized by a number of writers and practitioners. Nevertheless, we feel that, at this time in the development of the subject, the transitional term *production and operations management* most readily conveys the nature of the material to the uninitiated reader. This term therefore is used in the title of this book. However, for ease of presentation, "operations management," "production management," and "production and operations management" will be used interchangeably throughout the text.[1]

HISTORICAL DEVELOPMENT

Operations management has existed as a function since man first organized to hunt and gather food, and later to farm, trade, and build. His degree of sophistication in performing this function, however, has varied enormously, and the procedures have been developed in a far from direct course of evolution. Clearly, the Egyptians must have had a high degree of coordinative ability to construct the pyramids, the Chinese to build the Great Wall, the Romans to build their aqueducts, the Incas to build their temples, and so forth. It seems fair to say that most of the great civilizations enjoyed a "golden age" of master works in which early project managers had to contend with such operations management questions as job design, production control, materials handling, and inventory control. Completing these great projects no doubt tested the skills and technologies of the ancients much as the space exploration program challenges their present-day counterparts. Indeed, archaeologists and historians have provided us with evidence of some of the concepts and techniques used by earlier societies, indicating that insight into work organization and management is not strictly a twentieth-century phenomenon.

We may begin our history survey with the writings of Mencius (circa 372–289 B.C.). This Chinese philosopher not only dealt with the concepts of systems and models in an almost contemporary fashion, but pointed out the advantages to the individual and society of a division of labor. The ancient Greeks certainly were aware of the value of uniform work methods, as we find noted in an army manual that detailed how soldiers should arrange their clothes and weapons in encampments to enable dressing and arming at a moment's notice.[2] In attempting to make trying or monotonous jobs more palatable, the inventive Greeks also employed songs and standard motions to achieve a smooth work tempo—concepts basic to current-day industrial psychology. Plato (circa 427–347 B.C.), in *The Republic,* acknowledged the merits of division of labor, stating that "a man whose work is confined to such a limited task [e.g., shoe stitching] must necessarily excel at it."[3] Work specialization was in fact so extensive in Greece that stonemasons didn't even sharpen their own cutting tools, relying instead upon a specialist supporting staff.

---

[1] For an interesting pair of articles on "the name problem," see R. T. Schonberger, "The Resources Management Movement," *Academy of Management Journal,* vol. 15, no. 1, 1972, pp. 382–85, and E. E. Burch and W. R. Henry, "Production Management is Alive and Well," *Academy of Management Journal,* vol. 17, no. 1, 1974, pp. 144–49.

[2] Claude S. George, Jr., *The History of Management Thought* (Englewood Cliffs, N.J.: Prentice-Hall, 1968), pp. 12–13.

[3] Ibid., p. 15.

The dominance of feudalism in the period between the fall of the Roman Empire and the Renaissance (roughly from the fourth into the fifteenth century) inhibited the development of new technological and managerial ideas. Only toward the end of the fourteenth century do we find a development of major significance: the mechanical clock (see Table 1.1). This device, by enabling precise coordination of man's activities, led historian Louis Mumford to state: "The clock, not the steam engine, is the key machine of the modern industrial age. For every phase of its development the clock is both the outstanding fact and typical symbol of the machine: even today no other machine is so ubiquitous."[4]

By the fifteenth century the value of standardization of parts was fairly widely recognized. The Arsenal of Venice planning committee was now requiring that bows be made to accommodate all types of arrows, all stern-parts of ships be of identical design so that rudders would not have to be specially fitted, and all rigging and deck furnishings be uniform.

The work of Adam Smith and Eli Whitney dominates the historical developments of the 1700s. In his classic *Wealth of Nations,* Smith noted with respect to pin manufacture that division of labor increases output for three reasons: (1) increased dexterity on the part of each worker, (2) avoidance of lost time due to handling, and (3) "the invention of a great number of machines which facilitate and abridge labor, and enable one man to do the work of many."[5] These observations were of particular significance since they laid the groundwork for the subsequent development of modern work simplification, process analysis, and time study.[6] Eli Whitney's use of interchangeable parts in the making of guns paved the way for rapid production of other multicomponent assembled items. Whitney also employed cost accounting concepts and quality control procedures at his musket factory.[7]

An arresting historical anomaly in the development of production and general management concepts is found in the application of highly advanced techniques by the Soho Engineering foundry in England at the beginning of the 1800s. According to Claude George, Jr., this remarkable firm left "concrete evidences of market research and forecasting, planned site location, machine layout study . . . , established production standards, production planning, standardized components, cost control applications, cost accounting, employee training, work study and incentives, and an employee welfare program." If these practices did in fact exist, it would be difficult to dispute Professor George's claim that the Soho foundry was "a century ahead of its time."[8]

In 1832 the gifted engineer, philosopher, and mathematician Charles

---

[4] Lewis Mumford, *Technics and Civilization* (New York: Harcourt Brace Jovanovich, 1934), p. 13.

[5] Adam Smith, *An Inquiry into the Nature and Causes of the Wealth of Nations* (London: A. Strahan & T. Cadell, 1776), Vol. 1, pp. 7–8.

[6] Not everybody waited for Adam Smith. By 1496 Leonardo da Vinci had developed a machine that could make 400 needles per hour—automatically!

[7] George, *History of Management Thought,* p. 63.

[8] Ibid., p. 60.

TABLE 1.1

Historical summary

Year	Concept or tool	Originator or developer
1370	Mechanical clock	Heinrich von Wyck (Paris)
Circa 1430	Assembly line outfitting of ships at the Arsenal of Venice	Venetian shipbuilders
1776	Economic benefits from division of labor	Adam Smith (England)
1798	Interchangeable parts	Eli Whitney (U.S.)
1832	Skill differentials in wage payment; general concepts of time study	Charles Babbage (England)
1911	*Principles of Scientific Management;* formalized time study and work study concepts	Frederick W. Taylor (U.S.)
1911	Motion study; basic concepts of industrial psychology	Frank and Lillian Gilbreth (U.S.)
1913	Moving assembly line	Henry Ford (U.S.)
1914	Activity scheduling chart	Henry L. Gantt (U.S.)
1917	Application of economic lot size model for inventory control	F. W. Harris (U.S.)
1931	Sampling inspection and statistical tables for quality control	Walter Shewhart, H. F. Dodge, and H. G. Romig (U.S.)
1927–33	Hawthorne studies' new light on worker motivation	Elton Mayo (U.S.)
1934	Activity sampling for work analysis	L. H. C. Tippett (England)
1940	Team approaches to complex system problems	Operations research groups (England)
1947	Simplex method of linear programming	George B. Dantzig (U.S.)
Since 1950	Extensive development and application of simulation theory, decision theory, mathematical programming, computer hardware and software, project scheduling techniques of PERT and CPM	U.S. and Western Europe
1970s	Development of a variety of computer software packages to deal with routine problems of shop scheduling, inventory, layout, forecasting, and project management	Computer manufacturers and users in the United States and Western Europe

Babbage published *On the Economy of Machines and Manufactures,* in which he advocated the use of the scientific method in analyzing business problems, the use of time study, the performance of research and development activities, the location of factories on the basis of economic analysis, the use of bonus payment plans, and a number of other concepts that are standard practice today. As we shall see, much of what Babbage recommended was proposed and widely applied some 75 years later in the context of the scientific management movement headed by Frederick W. Taylor. Besides being an avant-gardist on matters of organization, Babbage was also the designer of the first digital computer. One could speculate that Taylor might have received his time study records on a computer printout if the British government had not withdrawn funds needed by Babbage to complete his final prototype.[9]

With the advent of scientific management around the turn of the century, the field of production and operations management began to assume the form it has today. As we have said, the concept of scientific management was developed by Taylor, who, like Babbage, was an imaginative engineer and insightful observer of organizational activities. Unlike Babbage, however, Taylor was a shrewd promotor of his own ideas and synthesizer of the ideas of others. Here, perhaps, his great talents shone most brilliantly. A good historical case can be made that Taylor did not *discover* any of the major concepts or tools that are associated with his development of scientific management. Time study, methods analysis, bonus payment plans, and the advisability of the scientific method in solving production problems were all known and applied—some many centuries before—yet it remained for Taylor truly to amalgamate these concepts and tools into a philosophy that could be broadly applied throughout industry.

The essence of Taylor's philosophy was that scientific laws govern how much a man could produce per day and that it is the function of management to discover and use these laws in the operation of productive systems. This philosophy, however, was not greeted with approval by all his contemporaries. On the contrary, there were unions that resented or feared scientific management, and with some justification. In too many instances, managers of the day were quick to embrace the "mechanisms" of Taylor's philosophy—time study, incentive plans, etc.—but they ignored their responsibility to organize and standardize the work to be done. Hence there were numerous cases of rate cutting (reducing the payment per piece if the production rate were deemed too high), overwork of labor, and poorly designed work methods. Such abuses resulted in overreaction—leading even to the introduction of a bill in Congress in 1913 to prohibit the use of time study and incentive plans in federal government operations. The unions advocating the legislation claimed that Taylor's subject in several of his time study experiments—a steelworker designated "Schmidt"—had died from

---

[9] The Chancellor of the Exchequer found Babbage's project "indefinitely expensive. . . . The ultimate success problematical. . . . The expenditure utterly incapable of being calculated." Edward C. Bursk, Donald T. Clark, and Ralph W. Hidy, *The World of Business* (New York: Simon & Schuster, 1962), Vol. IV, p. 2310.

overwork as a result of following Taylor's methods (in evidence whereof they even distributed pictures of Schmidt's "grave"). It was later discovered that Schmidt (whose real name was Henry Nolle) was alive and well and working as a teamster.[10] Ultimately, the bill was defeated.

Notable contemporaries and co-workers of Taylor were Frank and Lillian Gilbreth (motion study, industrial psychology) and Henry L. Gantt (scheduling, wage payment plans). We will discuss their contributions in somewhat more detail later.

The year 1913 also saw the introduction of one of the machine age's greatest technological innovations—the moving assembly line for the manufacture of Ford automobiles.[11] Before the line was introduced, in August of that year, each auto chassis was assembled by one man in about 12½ hours. Eight months later, when the line was in its final form, with each worker performing a small unit of work and the chassis being moved mechanically, the average labor time per unit was 93 minutes. This technological breakthrough, coupled with the concepts of scientific management, signaled both the promise and the problems of the machine age. Workers were now able to achieve unheard-of levels of output—or, conversely, they were now able to become consumers on a scale never before dreamed of. But, unfortunately, thanks to this same technological advance they were also to become de-skilled and made subservient to the machine. This issue is still far from resolved today, as we shall see in Chapter 10, "Job Design."

Mathematical and statistical developments dominated the evolution of operations management from Taylor's time up to around the 1940s. An exception was the Hawthorne studies, conducted in the 1930s by a research team from the Harvard Graduate School of Business Administration and supervised by the sociologist Elton Mayo. These experiments were designed to study the effects of certain environmental changes on the output of assembly workers at the Western Electric plant in Hawthorne, Illinois. The unexpected findings, reported in *Management and the Worker* (1939) by F. J. Roethlisberger and W. J. Dickson, intrigued sociologists and students of "traditional" scientific management alike. To the surprise of the researchers, changing the level of illumination (for example) had much less effect on output than the way in which the changes were introduced to the workers. Discoveries such as these had tremendous implications for work design and motivation and ultimately led to the establishment of personnel management and human relations departments in most organizations. They also played a major part in the development of new academic disciplines in schools of business administration.

World War II, with its complex problems of logistics control and weapons systems design, provided the impetus for the development of the interdisciplinary, mathematically oriented field of operations research. "OR," as it is often termed, brings together practitioners in such diverse fields as

---

[10] Milton J. Nadworny, "Schmidt and Stakhanov: Work Heroes in Two Systems," *California Management Review*, Vol. 6, No. 4 (Summer 1964), pp. 69–76.

[11] Ford is said to have gotten the idea for an assembly line from observing a Swiss watch manufacturer's use of the technology.

mathematics, psychology, and economics. Specialists in these disciplines customarily form a team to structure and analyze a problem in quantitative terms so that a mathematically optimal solution can be obtained. Operations research, or its approximate synonym "management science," now provides many of the quantitative tools used in operations management as well as in such basic business functions as marketing, finance, and accounting.

The development and application of quantitative methods continued in the physical sciences through the late 1940s and early 1950s. In the late 1950s and early 1960s, scholars began to write texts dealing specifically with production management as opposed to industrial engineering or manufacturing management, which, as their names imply, are heavily oriented toward factory problems. Two books especially had significant impact on the coalescing of the field: E. H. Bowman's and R. B. Fetter's *Analysis for Production Management* (1957) and E. S. Buffa's *Modern Production Management* (1961). Although other texts on the topic had been published earlier, these two texts clearly noted the commonality of problems faced by all productive systems and emphasized the importance of viewing the production function as a system rather than as an agglomerate of vaguely related activities. In addition, they stressed the useful applications of waiting line theory, simulation, and linear programming, which are now standard topics in the field.

Undoubtedly the major development of the past 15 years is the application of the high-speed digital computer to the multidimensional problems encountered in production systems. Problems that, because of sheer size, had previously all but defied solution now are solved in moments by the computer. While virtually every aspect of operations management has been touched by this tool, the areas of scheduling and inventory management seem to have been most ardently subjected to computer programming. One of the more striking aspects of the growth in computers is the associated growth in commercial programming packages for use in these areas. A perusal of an IBM catalog, for example, will quickly indicate the tremendous variety of "canned" programs available, especially for manufacturing applications. (We will discuss several of these software packages in this book.)

However, despite the potency of the computer there remain many problems that, from the standpoint of mathematical optimality, obstinately resist any satisfactory solution. In general, these fall under the heading "combinatorial problems" and are most often encountered in the areas of job shop scheduling and facilities layout. The basic characteristic of these problems is that the number of alternative solutions is so great that complete enumeration of possible answers is impractical or impossible. In an attempt to deal with problems of this type, researchers have resorted to rules of thumb, termed *heuristics*, that greatly reduce the number of alternatives to be evaluated and hence the number of computations to be made. These empiricisms vary from simple prescriptions, such as "Exclude from inventory calculations those items that cost less than 50 cents," to highly sophisticated directives based upon particular mathematical properties of the problem structure. An examination of the recent literature shows that heuristic methods represent a major development in the field and that their full range of application is far from exhausted.

In concluding our historical survey, we must mention that we have yet to satisfactorily answer a question that has been considered in myriad ways throughout the evolution of operations management. That question is, simply, What is man's place in the productive system? Certainly, from a human engineering standpoint, we know in what ways a man surpasses a machine in performing certain tasks; however, stopping here treats man as simply an odd kind of machine that has variable performance characteristics, talks back to the manager, and goes home every night for dinner. While man is something more than this, by the testimony of our still primitive notions of job design we have really failed to take full advantage of man's unique attributes of perception, flexibility, and emotion—in a word, humanness. Harnessing these attributes to achieve maximum benefit to the productive system and to the individual clearly is the great challenge facing operations management.

OPERATIONS MANAGEMENT DEFINED

Operations management may be defined as the performance of the managerial activities entailed in selecting, designing, operating, controlling, and updating productive systems. These activities are in turn defined as follows.

Selecting: the strategic decision of choosing the process by which some good or service is to be made or performed. In a steel mill producing railway wheels, the primary process decision might be whether the wheels will be forged or cast; in a restaurant, the decision might be between cafeteria or table service.

Designing: the tactical decisions involved in the creation of methods of carrying out a productive operation. In both the steel mill and the restaurant, tactical decisions would be made with regard to the form and content of jobs to be performed and to the type of service and control activities needed to assure smooth operation.

Operating: the decisions of planning long-term output levels in the light of forecast demand and the short-term decisions of scheduling jobs and allocating workers. In the railway wheel factory, this activity would range from forecasting the growth in rail cars for the next five years to determining which order to process first out of the array of orders on hand. In the cafeteria-style restaurant, this activity would range from monitoring community growth and competition to determine whether a new culinary specialty should be introduced to positioning busboys at various stations in the dining area.

Controlling: the procedures involved in taking corrective action as the product or service is created. In the steel company, control activities would range from monitoring and adjusting the metallurgical characteristics of heats of steel to the expediting of orders to meet delivery deadlines. In the restaurant, control would range from the inspection of incoming food and linen to ensuring speed and hospitality on the part of its staff and waiters.

Updating: the implementation of major revisions of the productive system in the light of changes in demand, organizational goals, technology, and management. In the steel company, updating might take the form of installing new capital equipment to produce a new alloy or the introduction of a computer-based production control system. In the restaurant, updating might range from the addition of car-service facilities to offering complete home-service catering.

In summary, it should be noted that, in practice, separating the foregoing activities into five discrete elements is rarely as straightforward as implied here. Still, all productive systems must engage in these functions, and the operations manager will ultimately be judged on how well they are executed and integrated.

With respect to the term *managerial*, it should be emphasized that this definition is really more normative than descriptive. "Managerial" usually implies the function of guiding and supervising subordinates who actually perform the detailed data gathering and analysis required by the aforementioned activities. However, if we are to cover the range of operational systems we must take cognizance of the fact that many managers must do some data gathering and make some calculations using the same tools and techniques of such a subordinate. In addition, and most importantly, "managerial" often connotes that the individual performing this function need not have any particular skill in using the analytical tools and concepts required in the execution of these activities. This is far from the truth in most real-world situations.

Indeed, the operations manager must have a very good understanding of the available tools and how they are manipulated, even if he does not directly apply them. This is requisite for at least three reasons: (1) so that he may intelligently ask questions or challenge the findings brought to him by his subordinates; (2) so that he may be able to coordinate activities on overlapping projects (i.e., to knowledgeably transfer skills between departments); and (3) so that he can suggest to his subordinates which tools are most appropriate in analyzing a given problem. By way of analogy, we don't expect a manager to do the bookkeeping in order to make sound financial decisions, but we can reasonably expect him to understand how ledger entries that provide the basis for his analysis are derived and interpreted.

A NOTE ABOUT PRODUCTIVE SYSTEMS

As previously defined, operations management is directly concerned with productive systems, and we shall now elaborate on this concept. For our purposes, a productive system may be thought of as *a set of components whose function is to transform a set of inputs into some desired output.* A component may be a machine, a man, a tool, or a part of the environment of the system. An input may be a raw material, a person, or a finished product emanating from another system, which is to be acted upon. Some transformations that take place are:

a. Physical, as in manufacturing.
b. Locational, as in transportation.
c. Exchange, as in retailing.
d. Storage, as in warehousing.

In addition, there are physiological transformations—making a sick person well—and attitudinal or gratificational transformations—entertainment or reading for pleasure. These phenomena, of course, are not mutually exclusive. For example, a department store is set up to enable shoppers to compare prices and quality (informational) and to hold items in inventory until needed (storage), as well as to sell goods (exchange). Table 1.2

TABLE 1.2

Input–transformation–output relationships for typical systems

System	Primary inputs	Components	Primary function(s)	Desired output
Hospital	Patients	MDs, nurses, medical supplies, equipment	Health care (physical)	Healthy individuals
Restaurant	Hungry customers	Food, chef, waitress, environment	Well-prepared food, well served; agreeable environment (physical and exchange)	Satisfied customers
Automobile factory	Raw materials	Tools, equipment, workers	Fabrication and assembly of cars (physical)	Complete automobiles
College or university	High school graduates	Teachers, books, classrooms	Imparting knowledge and skills (informational)	Educated individuals
Department store	Shoppers	Displays, stock of goods, sales clerks	Attract shoppers, promote products, fill orders (exchange)	Sales to satisfied customers

presents sample input–transportation–output relationships for some typical kinds of systems.

It should be emphasized that the table lists only the direct production components of these systems; a complete system description would, of course, require inclusion of managerial and support functions as well. In addition, the desired outputs specified are merely indicative of the nature and specificity of actual outputs and are presented from the point of view of society in general, rather than that of management or labor. Finally, no mention is made of cost or profit requirements, or the extent of satisfaction with services rendered—factors that, as we shall see, are of pivotal importance in operations management.

THE LIFE CYCLE APPROACH

Two common complaints from students in beginning production and operations management courses are that (1) the presentation of the subject matter in most texts lacks continuity, jumping from topic to topic, and (2) it is difficult to visualize the "big picture" of the discipline. In consequence, students often walk away from such courses with the impression that production and operations management is merely a convenient way of denoting a set of tools, such as linear programming, time study, PERT, and economic lot size models, rather than a distinct discipline. The structure we have adopted in this book was developed specifically to overcome this misconception. This structure, which we have termed "the life cycle approach," follows the progress of a productive system from its inception to its termination—a concept that we feel reflects the true breadth of the area. The following discussion illustrates how a productive system evolves through its life cycle.

At the onset, let us assume that some idea for a product or service is proposed. This product or service must be examined as to its marketability, its producibility, its capital requirements, and so on. If the decision is made to produce this good or service, then the final form of the product, the location of the producing facility, the building, and the floor layout all must be specified. The required equipment must be purchased and the production, inventory, and quality control systems designed. The particular tasks to be done must be designed, the functional groups manned, and production initiated. Quite likely there will be problems in this startup phase requiring design changes, relayout, and personnel adjustments. Once the facility is in operation, problems become more of the day-to-day type, requiring decisions on scheduling priorities, minor changes to remove inefficiencies, and maintenance to assure continued operation. We term this operation stage the *steady state* of the system.

This steady-state operating condition may be perturbed in a number of ways: new products may come into the system or a new service may be offered; new developments may cause significant changes in the present methods; markets may shift, or even cease to exist. If these changes are moderate, a slight revision may be all that is necessary to bring the system into line. At times, though, the needed revisions may be of such magnitude that certain phases of the life cycle must be repeated, probably calling for new designs, more or less extensive restaffing, and restarting the revised system. *If the system cannot adjust to the stimulus that has generated the need for revision, then, in the extreme case, the enterprise will die (through liquidation) or cease to exist as a separate entity (through sale or merger).*

In reality, most enterprises operate within this dynamic life cycle. A system, whether it is a manufacturing firm, service facility, or government agency, is born of an idea, passes through a growth stage, and continuously changes to meet new demands. And sometimes, of course, it is deliberately terminated.

Some of the key decision areas at the various stages in a system's life cycle are shown in Figure 1.1. It must be emphasized that this is a dynamic process, one in which a number of phases in the life cycle may be occurring concurrently. Indeed, many firms allocate a large portion of their resources to foster a continuous rebirth or rejuvenation program through the medium of research and development staffs. Further, no interconnections are shown in the illustration. In actuality, the introduction of a new product, for example, would cause the system to loop back to basic product design, followed by the activities of process selection, new system design, staffing, and startup.

It should also be emphasized that this text is not built around the life cycle of any one system. On the contrary, we have intentionally sought

FIGURE 1.1

Key decisions in the life of a productive system

BIRTH of the System	What are the goals of the firm? What product or service will be offered?
PRODUCT DESIGN and PROCESS SELECTION	What is the form and appearance of the product? Technologically, how should the product be made?
DESIGN of the System	Where should the facility be located? What physical arrangement is best to use? How do you maintain desired quality? How do you determine demand for the product or service?
MANNING the System	What job is each worker to perform? How will the job be performed, measured; how will the workers be compensated?
STARTUP of the System	How do you get the system into operation? How long will it take to reach desired rate of output?
The System in STEADY STATE	How do you run the system? How can you improve the system? How do you deal with day-to-day problems?
REVISION of the System	How do you revise the system in light of external changes?
TERMINATION of the System	How does a system die? What can be done to salvage resources?

illustrations from a variety of products and services. By doing this we hope to emphasize the fact that production and operations management is essential in such diverse systems as hospitals, supermarkets, banks, universities—and, of course, factories.[12]

MANUFACTURING VERSUS SERVICE SYSTEM EMPHASIS

The "name problem" mentioned earlier in this chapter relates to a low-key debate centering on how much of the production and operations management subject matter should be presented in the context of "operations" with particular emphasis on services, and how much should be presented in the context of "production," with its traditional emphasis on manufacturing. If it is reasonable to base one's argument on employment trends, both sides of the issue have a case. Figure 1.2, based on employment trends from the U.S. Department of Labor, shows an average 26 percent growth in services (broadly defined as all industries on the chart except construction, manufacturing, mining, and agriculture). In contrast, while manufacturing will grow a lesser rate in percentage terms (11 percent), it will still have the highest employment of all industries in 1980.

Looking at the service versus manufacturing setting from a different perspective, advocates of service systems point out that students are more familiar with services and therefore couching concepts in service settings would be more desirable. However, there are three counter arguments to this position. Firstly, service systems are so diverse in their operations that it would be difficult to distill a cohesive view of the field even after analyzing a significant number of service systems. Secondly, most production and operations management concepts were derived from manufacturing, and they are still best illustrated in manufacturing settings. (While many topics and concepts can be translated from manufacturing applications to service applications, important subtleties will be lost since the concepts, like good wine, do not always travel well.) Finally, and we believe most importantly, the field lacks a "theory of services" that would enable the development of a unified set of concepts having general application across a variety of service systems. While manufacturing also lacks a unifying theory, it does have an extensive and generally agreed-upon language that can be used to describe and analyze manufacturing systems and subsystems in an efficient way.

---

[12] It is worthy of note that weapons systems acquisitions by the U.S. Air Force follow a similar "life cycle" approach, which includes the following phases: Conception (examining such things as feasibility and risk), Validation (source selection and production planning), Full-scale development (producibility and methods), Production (with emphasis on improvement and control), and Transition and phase-down (essentially delivering the weapons system to the Air Force Logistics Command and ceasing production). (For further development of the parallelism between the two life cycle concepts, see W. K. Goss and L. W. Lockwood, "Acquisition Program Management Tasks: A Program Office/AFPRO Comparison of Relative Task Size and Priority," Department of Research and Communicative Studies, Air Force Institute of Technology, 1975.)

FIGURE 1.2

Employment trends in various industry sectors, 1968–1980

Employment (millions) 1968	1980	Industry	Percent change
80.8	99.6	All Industries	23
9.1	13.8	State and Local Government	52
15.1	21.1	Services, Personal, Professional, Business	40
4.0	5.5	Construction	35
3.7	4.6	Finance, Insurance, and Real Estate	24
16.6	20.5	Trade	23
20.1	22.4	Manufacturing	11
4.5	4.9	Transportation, Communication, and Public Utilities	10
2.7	3.0	Federal Government	10
0.6	0.6	Mining	-9
4.2	3.2	Agriculture	-23

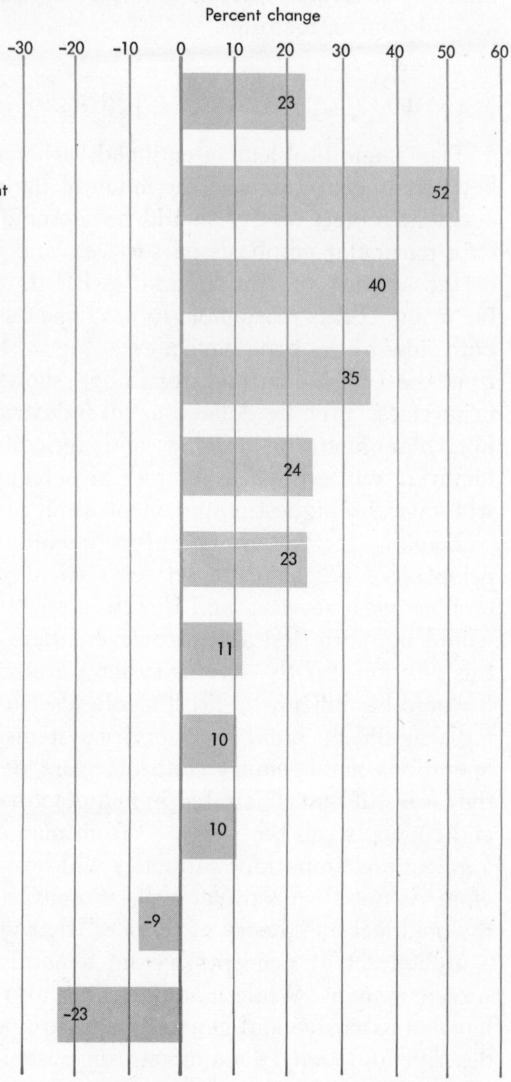

Source: U.S. Department of Labor.

In summary, reviewing both sides of the issue has led us to the following approach in dealing with the subject matter in the remainder of the book: Most of the topics and problem-solving techniques will be introduced in the context of manufacturing; most chapters will then provide specific examples of applications in a variety of service systems; and end-of-chapter assignments and problems will include both manufacturing and service system situations.

CLASSIFICATION OF SERVICE SYSTEMS RELATIVE TO MANUFACTURING SYSTEMS

Our treatment of service systems in this book is predicated on two basic ideas: First, *that the operations management requirements in managing service systems can best be understood by contrasting them with manufacturing systems;* and second, *that only certain types of service systems are significantly different from manufacturing when viewed from an operations management perspective.*

Taking the second idea first, we assert that the main feature that sets a service system apart from a manufacturing system (again, from the *operations management perspective*) is the extent to which the customer must be in direct contact with the service system during the creation of the service product. Operationally, we measure "extent of contact" as that percentage of the total service creation time that the average customer spends in direct contact with the service system. To the extent that the service can be created in the absence of the customer, the greater the likelihood that the service system can operate according to traditional manufacturing management concepts. Based upon this distinction, it is possible to develop three categories of service systems: "pure services"—those that typically require a high ratio of customer contact time to the total service creation time; "mixed services"—those that typically require a medium ratio of customer contact time to the total service creation time; and "quasi-manufacturing" —those that typically require a low ratio of customer contact time to the total service creation time. A listing of some of the various service systems that fall under each category is presented in Table 1.3.

TABLE 1.3

Classification of various service systems by extent of required customer contact in the creation of the service product

Pure services (typically high contact)	Mixed services (typically medium contact)	Quasi-manufacturing (typically low contact)
Entertainment centers	"Branch" offices of: financial institutions	"Home" offices of: financial institutions
Health centers	government computer firms	government computer firms
Hotels	law firms ad agencies	law firms ad agencies
Public transportation	real estate firms etc.	real estate firms etc.
Retail establishments		
	Park service	Wholesale establishments
Schools	Police and fire departments	Postal service
Personal services	Janitoral services	Mail order services
Jails	Moving companies	News syndicates
	Repair shops	Research laboratories
	Funeral homes	

Increasing freedom in designing efficient production procedures

Relative to the first idea mentioned, we will present the contrasts between manufacturing and services [13] through the use of propositional statements. In most chapters, we will present four propositions relating directly to one of four general areas of concern in operations management decision making. These areas are:

1. Product—That combination of goods and services provided by the productive system.
2. Technology of transformation—The physical steps by which a productive system creates goods and services.
3. Operating-control system—The management and support systems required to coordinate the transformation process.
4. Workforce—The employees who have the responsibility of carrying out the steps of the transformation process.

We believe that each of the propositions to be presented is valid in contrasting pure service systems with manufacturing systems. We believe that they are generally valid in contrasting specific organizations in the mixed services category with manufacturing systems. By definition, we do not believe the propositions pertain in contrasting quasi-manufacturing service systems and manufacturing systems. In any case, the reader is cautioned that the propositions await scientific validation, and hence are subject to challenge and refutation. We are convinced, however, that careful consideration of them will add another dimension to one's study and understanding of the field of operations management.

REVIEW AND DISCUSSION QUESTIONS

1. Compare the definition of production and operations managment given here with definitions found in one or two other production management texts. What similarities and differences do you find?
2. Using Table 1.2 as a model, describe the input—transformation—output relationships found in the following types of systems: (1) an airline, (2) a state penitentiary, (3) a branch bank, (4) a "home" office of a major banking firm.
3. Compare the concept of a system life cycle with that of a product life cycle as used in marketing. (A product life cycle is described in Chapter 17.)
4. Who was Schmidt? What was his role in emergent production management?
5. How would Frederick W. Taylor fare as a plant manager in today's industrial environment?
6. Why is *production* management usually associated with *factory* management?

---

[13] We have omitted the third category of production—continuous process industries —because, with the exception of two major characteristics, they are analogous to manufacturing. These characteristics are: (1) the workflow is built into the equipment itself, and the worker does not handle the material, except possibly for running an occasional test; and (2) the job of the worker is to monitor this workflow.

7. Relate the definition of production and operations management to the key decisions in the life of a productive system.

8. What is a heuristic rule? What heuristics do you use in obtaining a book from the library? In your personal finances? In studying for examinations?

9. Based upon your other courses or your own experience, how is the factory worker perceived by management?

SELECTED BIBLIOGRAPHY

Ansoff, Igor H.   *Corporate Strategy.* New York: McGraw-Hill, 1965.

Buffa, Elwood S.   *Modern Production Management.* 3d ed. New York: John Wiley & Sons, 1969.

Bursk, Edward C.; Clark, Donald T.; and Hidy, Ralph W.   *The World of Business.* Vols. 3 and 4. New York: Simon & Schuster, 1962.

George, Claude S.   *The History of Management Thought.* Englewood Cliffs, N.J.: Prentice-Hall, 1968.

Groff, Gene K., and Muth, John F.   *Operations Management: Analysis for Decisions.* Homewood, Ill.: Richard D. Irwin, Inc., 1972.

Moore, Franklin G.   *Production Management.* 6th ed. Homewood, Ill.: Richard D. Irwin, Inc., 1973.

Mumford, Lewis   *Technics and Civilization.* New York: Harcourt Brace Jovanovich, 1934.

Nadworny, Milton J.   "Schmidt and Stakhanov: Work Heroes in Two Systems," *California Management Review,* Vol. 6, No. 4 (Summer 1964), pp. 69–75.

Smith, Adam   *An Inquiry into the Nature and Causes of the Wealth of Nations.* London: A. Strahan & T. Cadell, 1776.

Steade, Richard D.   *Business and Society in Transition: Issues and Concepts.* San Francisco: Canfield Press, 1975.

Taylor, Frederick W.   *The Principles of Scientific Managment.* New York: Harper & Bros., 1911.

Walker, Charles R.   *Technology, Industry, and Man: The Age of Acceleration.* New York: McGraw-Hill, 1968.

Section one

Selection of the product

2

The product decision and the design of the production function

A productive system is designed to produce a product that originally derived from an idea. Before this idea can become the basis for a productive system or reach fruition in the form of a marketable product, it is subjected to careful analysis, which culminates in one of the most difficult of managerial decisions. Selecting the product, termed the *product decision,* entails the systematic gathering of a number of ideas and choosing those that, when translated into a tangible product, will meet the objectives of the firm. The first part of this chapter examines the product decision from the point of view of organization and subsystem objectives and discusses some of the tools and procedures commonly used to make the decision.

The second part of the chapter is concerned with the productive system that must produce the product selected. Initial focus is on the activities, objectives, and organization of the production function as they relate to the definition of operations management given in Chapter 1. Next, the relationship between the product and the production organization is considered in the context of their common meeting ground, technology. Then, the role of production policy in corporate strategy is discussed, highlighting some important tradeoff decisions encountered during product selection. Finally, facility location is considered and a heuristic method is applied to the problem of locating service facilities.

THE PRODUCT DECISION

Objectives of the functional subsystems and their influence on the product decision

A few basic activities are necessary in every business organization, whether it is large or small, specialized or diversified, or engaged in providing goods or offering services to consumers. These activities, often termed the *functional* areas of business, include, at a minimum, production, finance, marketing, and general management. In small corporations or proprietorships, all these activities may be performed by one or a few persons; in large firms they are organized as divisions or departments and are headed by an individual who typically is directly responsible to the chief executive officer.

Each specialized function or subsystem of the firm tends to pursue goals peculiar to its own objective. These goals have significant bearing on the product decisions made by the firm. Figure 2.1 illustrates some general objectives of four primary subsystems and indicates the variety of outcomes desired from the product decision.

The potential for conflict among the various functional areas is apparent. Marketing departments tend to be innovative and aggressive. This leads to a higher willingness on their part to take greater risks in the marketplace than are desired by managers of finance departments, who tend to be more conservative, preferring to rely on currently successful products to expand sales. Marketing's advocacy of broad, deep, and multiple product lines can

FIGURE 2.1

Goals of the functional subsystems and their influence on the product decision

Subsystem	General subsystem goals	Desired product policy
Production	1. Use simple manufacturing methods 2. Minimize costs 3. Stabilize demand and output 4. Maintain quality standards	1. Make few products 2. Make similar products 3. Make products that are easily and inexpensively modified
Marketing	1. Promote innovation 2. Raise sales volume 3. Increase market share 4. Maintain flexibility in the marketplace 5. Enter new markets 6. Maximize revenue 7. Orient products to consumers 8. Perform consumer research	1. Broaden product lines 2. Introduce new products 3. Modify existing products and lines frequently 4. Balance product lines
Finance	1. Ensure liquidity 2. Maximize profit 3. Assure corporate survival and growth 4. Eliminate expenses not contributing directly to profits 5. Minimize risks to the firm	1. Market only products that yield immediate profits 2. Select only most highly profitable products 3. Eliminate marginal products
General management	1. Maximize difference between revenue and cost 2. Maximize long-run profit 3. Ensure corporate survival and growth 4. Secure and increase profits over time	1. Market products with proven profitability 2. Balance highly profitable products with short lives against products that earn lower profits initially but exhibit excellent long-run profit potential 3. Provide for ease in managing and coordinating the firm's activities both internally and in the market place

be frustrating to production managers, who are charged with keeping labor costs and capital investment at a minimum. Multiple and custom products increase labor and equipment costs, and frequent changes in the product line may make it difficult to make fullest use of expensive equipment. Top management's task is to balance such conflicting interests so as to meet the objectives of the firm.

The objectives of the firm, while sometimes providing guidance in the product decision, often complicate the decision process. Consider the statements of corporate objectives in Figure 2.2, virtually all of which, if strictly interpreted, may run counter to one another when any given product is to be evaluated. For example, contrast objective 4, which allows no more than a year for new product development, with objective 5, which specifies "a sales volume among the top five companies." Can a company achieve a high sales volume if it limits itself to products which can be developed in less than one year?

Perhaps the overriding question in relating objectives to the product decision is whether the company actually knows what business it is in.

FIGURE 2.2

General corporate objectives (semiconductor manufacturer)

1. Remain an ethical manufacturer of semiconductor devices, providing customers with full value and establishing and maintaining a reputation for fair and honest business practices.
2. Provide a productive and satisfying work environment for employees, offering career opportunities for personal development and advancement.
3. Maximize return on investment, consistent with growth objectives, and operate to protect that investment. The Company has as its objective 15% profit before tax and 30% return on stockholders' equity and long-term debt in order to maximize long-term growth and profitability, remain a leader in the semiconductor industry in advanced technology, device development, and engineering.
4. Maintain a basic technological capability permitting the Company to develop, produce, and market a specific product within one year. Development is directed toward products which will have a significant market within 2 to 5 years.
5. Attain a sales volume among the top 5 companies in the semiconductor industry, participating with a broad line of products in approximately 75% of all markets, and competing for a minimum of 15% in each market.
6. Participate in industrial, military, and consumer markets. Although emphasis is on the military market, the percentage of industrial business will be increased. Consumer electronic and entertainment devices will be marketed.
7. Manufacture semiconductor devices in high quantity and at minimum cost consistent with customer quality and volume requirements. Continue to develop, produce, and market high-performance devices.
8. Maintain a standard-performance product line which can be produced and marketed at low cost and high volume. This product line will employ the technology developed for the high-performance products rather than depend upon new technology.
9. Develop a product line evolving from discrete components to solid-state circuits, subassemblies, and simple equipment including passive components. These products will include new-type solid-state devices as they begin to displace existing products.
10. Obtain more contract sales, particularly in areas where contract programs parallel company programs and product plans.
11. Consider domestic and foreign markets as one integrated world market, with interrelated technical, manufacturing, and marketing opportunities. The Company will exploit the advantages of foreign manufacturing and marketing.

Source: Melville C. Branch, *The Corporate Planning Process* (New York: American Management Association, 1962), p. 43.

That is, is a computer manufacturer in the business of selling electronic devices, computer programs, or data analysis systems and expertise? Is a particular hospital in the business of providing broad medical care for large numbers of people or in providing equipment and skills for any medical problem from organ transplants to unusual diseases?

Answering this question, and by extension, the decision to produce a new product, depends upon two factors: first, the nature of the firm's *primary task* and, second, its *distinctive competence*. The term *primary task* refers to that task which must be performed if the firm is to survive and thrive. The primary task is essentially a function of the firm's environment, the environment being broadly defined as the market and the cultural setting of the organization. A firm's *distinctive competence* is its particular set of skills which sets it apart from its competition. Thus, for a computer manufacturer, the primary task may be selling an average-quality line of computers, while its distinctive competence may lie in installing software systems. Clearly, if the firm incorrectly sees the reverse as true and uses it as a basis for determining whether a new computer should be added to its line, a poor decision may result. It should be apparent, too, that a formal statement of objectives may not necessarily be in agreement with an organization's true distinctive competence, or for that matter with its true primary task.

Origin of the product idea and selection from among alternatives

The product decision involves two major activities prior to final product design. The first is gathering ideas for alternative products, and the second is selecting from among the alternatives the product or products that are to be produced. We will consider these activities in order.

Before we consider where the product idea comes from, it is useful to define just what we mean by the term *product*. For our purposes, a product is the output from a productive system offered for sale (in the case of a business), or otherwise made available (in the case of a governmental or philanthropic organization), to some consumer. It should be noted that this is a production definition as opposed to a marketing definition. A marketing definition requires that the concept of a product include reference to such intangibles as satisfaction and symbolism in order to convey the fact that, for promotional purposes, a product must meet certain psychological demands for the consumer. Production, on the other hand, need only meet prescribed product specifications; it is not required to determine how the product is *perceived* in the marketplace.

Origin of the product idea. Product ideas may originate from any number of sources, some of which are not obvious. Marketing textbooks and journals frequently cite unusual examples of sources for new-product ideas to emphasize that businesses must be keenly attuned to all possible sources to ensure that the "golden idea" is not missed or passed over without adequate consideration. A meat packing company once got the idea of developing an onion soup from a suggestion of one of its executive's wives. An appliance manufacturer developed a foot warmer on the basis of a customer inquiry. A maker of pottery designed a new vase after seeing a similar one at a musesum exhibit. A producer of plastic products designed a film slide viewer after reading a list of needed inventions published by a bank.[1] While such examples constitute the exceptional rather than the more common sources of ideas for new products, they indicate that ideas are to be found almost anywhere and that aggressive firms cannot afford to discount an idea simply because it originates from an unusual source.

Nevertheless, one authoritative report of sources for new-product ideas indicates that the great majority of ideas are generated within the firm rather than by external sources. Table 2.1 was compiled after recording sources for new-product ideas in 71 major companies.

Choosing among alternative products. The idea-gathering process, if properly carried out, will often lead to more ideas than can be translated

---

[1] Thomas L. Berg and Abe Shuchman (eds.), *Product Strategy and Management* (New York: Holt, Rinehart & Winston, 1963), pp. 421–22.

TABLE 2.1

Sources of new-product ideas

Functional area	Percentage of ideas
Marketing	36.2
Research and development	29.7
Top management	14.7
New-product department	7.5
Management	4.1
Others	7.8

Source: Modified from "Management of New Products," Management Research Department, Booz, Allen, and Hamilton, Management Consultants, 1960, cited in Lewis N. Goslin, *The Product Planning System* (Homewood, Ill.: Richard D. Irwin, Inc., 1967), p. 3.

into producible products. Thus a screening procedure designed to eliminate those ideas which clearly are infeasible must be instituted. The screening procedure seeks to determine if the product is generally compatible with the company's objectives and resources. Regarding objectives, a product may be dropped if it is deficient in profit potential or in prospective growth or stability of sales, or if it is deleterious to the company image. In terms of resources, a product may be dropped if it exceeds the company's capital availability or is incompatible with the company's managerial and technical skills or physical facilities.

Of the several techniques available to aid in the screening process, perhaps the most commonly used are rating checksheets. In one such sheet, a number of important considerations are enumerated—for example, sales volume, patent protection, competition—and the product is categorized from "very good" to "very poor" for each of these considerations. The product selected will show a rating pattern that meets the company's standard, from favorable to unfavorable ratings. More refined rating devices apply numerical weights to the important considerations and quantify the "goodness" categories. An example of this type of checklist is illustrated in Table 2.2, where the object is to obtain a total score by which the product can be compared to other product possibilities or to a predetermined

TABLE 2.2

Product evaluation sheet

Performance feature	(A) Relative weight	(B) Rating					Factor score (A) × (B)
		Very good 40	Good 30	Fair 20	Poor 10	Very poor 0	
Sales	0.20	√					8
Competition (number and type)	0.05	√					2
Patent protection	0.05	√					2
Technical opportunity	0.10		√				3
Materials availability	0.10		√				3
Value added	0.10		√				3
Similarity to major business	0.20		√				6
Effect on present products	0.20				√		2
	1.00						29

cutoff score. For this list, the best score that could be obtained is 40 and the worst is 0. Note, however, that this approach attempts to quantify the unquantifiable and may create the illusion that a "very good" rating is, for example, four times as high as a "poor" rating.

If the product passes the screening procedure, more rigorous analysis of its cost and revenue characteristics is undertaken. Sometimes, this analysis consists of a comparison in which products are ranked according to an indexing formula such as the project value index:

$$PVI = \frac{CTS \times CCS \times AV \times P \times \sqrt{L}}{TPC}$$

where

PVI = Project value index
CTS = Chances for technical success on an arbitrary rating scale, say 0 to 10
CCS = Chances for commercial success on an arbitrary rating scale, say 0 to 10
AV = Annual volume (total sales of product in units)
P = Profit in dollars per unit, i.e., price minus cost
L = Life of product in years
TPC = Total project cost in dollars

Where a more detailed evaluation is deemed necessary, the tools of financial analysis—break-even charts and rate-of-return calculations—come into play. (These techniques are discussed in detail in the supplement to Chapter 3.) The major problem associated with these tools is that their value is limited to short-run evaluation of the product alternatives, since long-term developments in costs, the competition, and the economy make the numerical inputs inaccurate (in many cases) within a year. Furthermore, even in the short run, where cost and revenue are known with relative certainty, the techniques may not give clear-cut answers. Consider the break-even charts of the two proposed products shown in Figure 2.3. Both products have the same break-even volume; however, product 1 requires a greater cost outlay, but at the same time stands to generate a greater profit beyond the break-even point. Choosing between the two may present a real challenge for the manager in terms of his willingness to gamble.

In addition to financial analysis, which generally yields information as to how many units must be sold, marketing departments run studies of potential demand to determine how many units are likely to be sold, and marketing mix analyses, which attempt to determine how they are to be sold. According to one authority, only about half the ideas that reach the financial and detailed marketing analysis stage are adopted.[2] The striking mortality rate of new ideas from inception to commercialization, based on a sample of 51 companies, is shown in Figure 2.4. In Chapter 3 we will

---

[2] Edgar A. Pessemier, *New-Product Decisions: An Analytical Approach* (New York: McGraw-Hill, 1966).

FIGURE 2.3

Hypothetical break-even charts

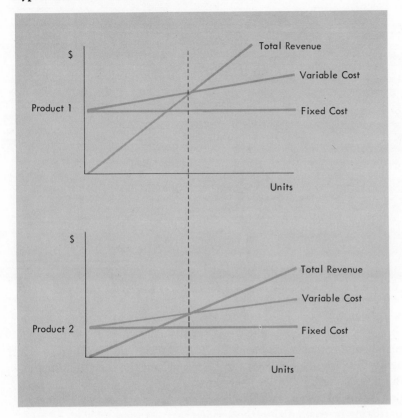

examine those surviving products with respect to the production manager's role in their production design.

Selecting the service product

Selecting the service product is usually a simpler as well as less costly process than selecting a manufactured product. This is so because the service product is generally labor-dominated and hence equipment and materials considerations play much smaller roles than they do in manufacturing. Services can generally be changed quite rapidly, either directly by modifying the nature of the service itself, or indirectly by sales promotions and pricing. Indeed, if we contrast a new service product idea with a new manufactured product idea in terms of a mortality curve such as that shown in Figure 2.4, we would find that the time needed for screening, business analysis, development, testing, and commercialization is generally greatly compressed for services, and hence more service product ideas can be investigated for a given investment of funds. Further evidence of service system flexibility in product selection appears in the ability of such systems to "change" the service product by the following actions:

FIGURE 2.4

Mortality of new-product ideas by stage of evolution (51 companies)

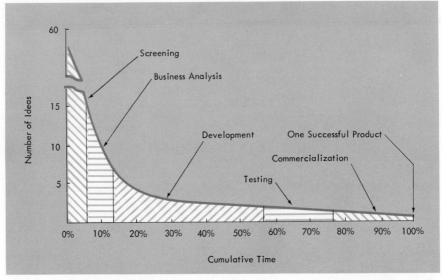

Source: David B. Uman, *New-Product Programs: Their Planning and Control* (New York: American Management Association, 1969), p. 18.

1. Increasing or decreasing capacity.
2. Reducing the distance between the customer and the service system.
3. Adding or eliminating "fringe" services.
4. Altering hours of service availability.
5. Standardizing or customizing the service.
6. Altering service procedures.
7. Obtaining or losing accreditation from outside agencies.
8. Changing the "atmosphere" of the service system.

In summary, selecting a new service product is usually a more subjective, but less costly undertaking than selecting a new manufactured product.

ORGANIZING FOR PRODUCTION

In the preceding section (on product selection) we presumed the existence of an ongoing organization with an operational production function. Now assume that the opposite situation holds; namely, that we have a product and must develop an organization to produce it. This problem poses the following questions:

1. What are the required activities of the production function?
2. What are the objectives of the production function?
3. What is the nature of the formal organization required to carry out the activities?

Required activities of the production function

These activities can best be understood in the context of our definition of operations management given in Chapter 1. Recall that operations management is concerned with "selecting, designing, operating, controlling, and updating productive systems." These activities can be further differentiated on the basis of the relative frequency of their occurrence, and selecting, designing, and updating activities in general occur far less frequently than operating and controlling activities. Hence we will refer to the former as "periodic" and to the latter as "continual." This distinction is useful because it provides an insight into the rationale for both the production literature and for the practitioners' giving "subsystem" status to some activities and

FIGURE 2.5

Organization of operations management activities

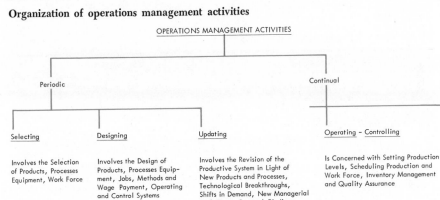

not to others. That is, periodic activities, while they may be performed according to a specific set of procedures, by their very nature do not present the daily time-pressure problems of information and action inherent in the continual activities. Partly for this reason, activities such as quality assurance, production planning, and output scheduling are generally viewed and constructed as "systems"[3] while such activities as product design, process selection, and job design are not. A summary of some of the major operations management activities following the periodic-continual dichotomy is presented in Figure 2.5. (The items under the "Operating-Controlling" heading represent the bases of Chapter 3 and Chapters 5 through 9.)

Objectives of the production function

In a general sense, the objectives of the production function are (1) to produce the desired product, (2) to achieve the desired rate, and (3) to

---

[3] "System" is used here to denote an ongoing series of interrelated activities or processes as distinct from one-shot or infrequent occurrences.

minimize the cost. However, for operational purposes we must be more specific, and classifying objectives is useful in this regard. The classification scheme we propose (though there are others) is one that separates objective into "output" and "cost" categories. The output category is further broken down into "volume" and "performance" categories, wherein volume refers to how much must be produced, inventoried, etc., and performance refers to the extent to which the system meets the standards set for quality, time, etc. Similarly, cost objectives are broken down into "explicit costs" and "implicit costs" categories, wherein explicit costs refers to those costs that are measured by standard cost accounting methods, such as costs of materials and wages, and implicit costs refers to those costs that cannot be measured by cost accounting methods, such as idle time and stockout costs. This classification is presented in Table 2.3.

TABLE 2.3

Classification of production function objectives

Output objectives		Cost objectives	
Volume objectives	*Performance objectives*	*Explicit costs*	*Implicit costs*
Production rate	Time schedules	Material input,	Stockouts
Inventory level	Quality	scrap, and rework	Grievances
Work force level	Efficiency of work force,	Direct and indirect	Late deliveries
	equipment, facilities	labor	Unused capacity
		Maintenance	Opportunity costs
			Equipment downtime

As in the case of the firm as a whole, these objectives are often in conflict, and to achieve a balance among them for many situations tests the mettle of any production manager. In this regard, the production literature habitually uses the term *optimal* to denote the end state desired from balancing these objectives, and this text maintains the tradition. Nevertheless, while useful in discussing production decisions, achievement of the optimal (i.e., the most desirable) solution is rarely possible, or even provable, for a variety of reasons, some of which follow.

1. Optimization requires that all possible alternatives be considered. Not only would this be a difficult task, the decision maker would likely not even be aware of many of them.

2. Optimization requires that the decision maker have all relevant data at his disposal. This is often a practical impossibility because of time, resources, and cost considerations.

3. Optimization is time dependent in that what constitutes an optimum at one point in time is not necessarily optimum at subsequent moments in time. Conditions change so rapidly in business organizations that it may be argued that for a decision to be truly optimal, the gathering and weighing of alternatives must be continued up to the moment of choice.

In the light of such limitations, most managers do not really optimize but, rather, attempt to achieve some satisfactory result. That is, they recognize, implicitly or explicitly, the imperfections and incompleteness of data and the complexity of the calculations required to achieve optimality. Hence they set themselves levels of achievement that, though not ideal, are feasible in terms of time and effort. This approach—setting feasible objectives (and pursuing them "within reason")—is commonly termed *satisficing*.

In summary, then, although we will be using *optimize* to describe the *goals* of various techniques used in production management, keep in mind that the person who employs such techniques is, more likely than not, *satisficing*.

Formal organization of the production function

Formal organization of the production function involves placing the aforementioned operations management activities into departments and assigning the authority and responsibility for their performance to a manager or supervisor. Not surprisingly, the most direct translation of a production activity to a functional department is evidenced in manufacturing organizations where such specific activities as quality control, production control, product design, and process selection are typically given departmental status. And though the locus of production activities is more difficult to determine when we consider nonmanufacturing installations, these activities are performed in most organizations; and common sense usually, though not always, is sufficient to "crack the code" of a given organization chart, allowing us to discern just where they are performed.

We have identified the location of "production" activities in four different types of organizations in Figure 2.6.[4] Aside from differences in terminology, the nonmanufacturing organizations depicted in Charts a, b, and d also differ from the manufacturing example in that certain production activities are scattered throughout the organization's structure. This does not mean that the activity is any less a production one, but only that it is deemed best performed under the aegis of a different department.

While these organization charts show (to varying degrees) where certain production management activities have been placed in these organizational structures, we would like to know how the decisions were made to place them there. Unfortunately, there are no hard and fast rules for assignment of activities that will hold for all situations; each organization is unique, and activity placement must take this fact into account. Still, certain criteria have proved useful in the assignment of production management, as well as other activities, and we will present some of them. Note that these criteria are not mutually exclusive, nor does one necessarily dominate the others in importance; like all criteria, judgment is important in using them.

Criteria for production activity assignment. Importance. The importance of a particular activity strongly influences its organizational placement. Quality assurance, for example, varies substantially from company

---

[4] For examples of operations management responsibilities in hospitals and universities, see Russell Morey, "Operations Management in Selected Nonmanufacturing Organizations," *Academy of Management Journal*, vol. 19, no. 1, March 1976, pp. 120–24.

FIGURE 2.6

Sample organization charts of four diverse firms

Chart (a): Airline

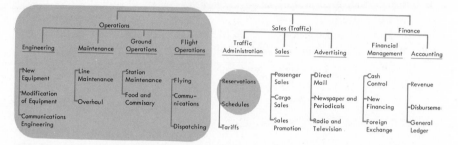
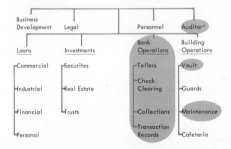

Chart (b): Commercial bank

Chart (c): Manufacturing firm

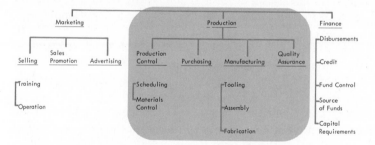

Chart (d): Department store

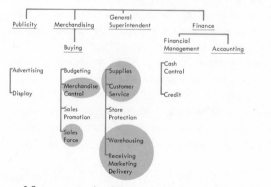

° Some aspects of auditing are equivalent to a quality assurance function.

to company. In most aerospace firms, where poor product performance can lead to heavy sanctions and loss of business, the quality assurance department would be placed above manufacturing departments to ensure that sufficient authority is provided to guarantee maximum product reliability. A toy company, on the other hand, may locate quality assurance at a very low level in the hierarchy since the consequences of poor product performance are generally much less serious.

Work flow. The assignment of activities by the criterion of work flow can be most easily visualized by reference to the accompanying diagram.

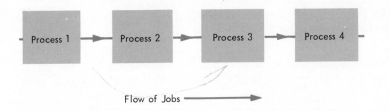

Suppose that process 1 and process 3 are similar and process 2 and process 4 also are similar. Assume, further, that we wish to divide the responsibility for the four processes between two managers. The traditional approach would be to have processes 1 and 3 report to one manager and processes 2 and 4 to the other. This arrangement, however, may lead to coordination problems since job priorities are more likely to be determined on the basis of process efficiencies rather than on completion of the job. For this reason, organization by work flow would lead to heterogeneous groupings, with one manager in charge of processes 1 and 2 and the other manager responsible for processes 3 and 4.

Usage. If a manager constantly requires the performance of an activity to accomplish his department's function, logic usually dictates that this activity be assigned to him. For example, the traffic function in a plant might be placed under the control of the manufacturing manager since his use of this service is continual and widespread, encompassing transport of materials to the plant, their flow through various processes, and their warehousing.

Customer. Organizations often allocate a complete "set" of production activities to one manager in order to satisfy the needs of a particular type of customer. For example, firms that have substantial dealings with military agencies and civilian organizations frequently find the requirements of the two groups in terms of specification, budgeting, quality, etc., so diverse that separate production (and sales) organizations become mandatory.

Power equalization. In some instances, activities are allocated specifically to maintain a system of checks and balances. The classic case is the rule of thumb that quality assurance be on the same organizational level as production control to assure that product quality will not be sacrificed for high production.

Managerial interest. Otherwise heterogeneous activities may be assigned to a particular manager if his interests and skills are such that he may direct them more effectively than if they were placed in otherwise more appropriate locations. For example, product design may be a minor activity in a company producing to customers' orders, such as a machine shop, and therefore this activity might be assigned to any manager who desires to undertake it.

ORGANIZATION STRUCTURE AND TECHNOLOGY

The relationship between the product selected and the organization structure can best be seen by considering the technology by which the product is produced. For a new organization, the choice of the product essentially determines the technology of production. In the established firm, the situation is reversed, and the product selected must match the technology that

FIGURE 2.7

Simplified version of Woodward's technology classification scheme

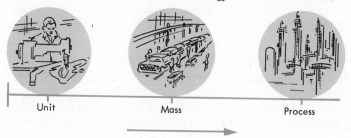

| Unit | Mass | Process |

Increasing Technological Complexity

already exists. In either situation, it has been shown that technology affects organization structure, and this interrelationship should be considered in designing the production organization.

The classic study relating technology and structure was performed by Joan Woodward. She used a sample of 100 companies operating in Great Britain. As shown in the simplified version of her classification (Figure 2.7), she found a direct correlation between increasing technological complexity and the absolute magnitude of such structural variables as the ratio of managers to total personnel, length of the chain of command, number of levels of management in the production departments, and size of the managerial group. In addition, she found that the most successful firms were closest to the mean in respective groups in such variables. For example, if the mean for mass production was high on a particular variable (say span of management), then mass production firms registering above or below this mean were less successful than those closer to the group's mean. This finding is especially intriguing since it implies that there might be an optimal organization structure for each type of technology.

Beyond Woodward's findings, which in general relate to technologies at one point in time, there is evidence to suggest that organizations subject to frequent *changes* in technology require different structures from those in which technological change is infrequent. The differences in structure seem to center on the extent of formal delineation of hierarchical relationships; organizations experiencing frequent technological changes require far more flexibility in structure.

This point was brought out in a study by Burns and Stalker,[5] who found, in a sample of British firms entering the turbulent electronics industry, that those that were effective in operating in their new environment were the ones that developed less rigid structures. Though they worked well in stable environments, rigid structures—which permit little variation in communication channels and authority relationships—responded too slowly to deal effectively with rapid technological change.

PRODUCTION POLICY AND CORPORATE STRATEGY[6]

Many students, as well as some corporate executives, tend to view the production function as removed from "the action" of strategic decisions made by the firm. In most successful companies, however, nothing could be further from the truth. Indeed, numerous firms have prospered because they used their production capabilities as a strategic weapon, while others have fallen by the wayside because they did not recognize the relationship between production decisions and corporate strategy. Writing in the *Harvard Business Review,* Wickham Skinner observes that "routine manufacturing decisions frequently come to limit the corporation's strategic options, binding it with facilities equipment, personnel, and basic controls and policies to a noncompetitive posture that may take years to turn around."[7] Skinner admonishes corporate executives to avoid thinking of manufacturing as the domain of technical specialists and consider instead how manufacturing (or production) policy can be made to fuse with the thrust of the firm in the market. He suggests that management, to do this, must recognize and deal with the abundance of tradeoffs that emerge in making a manufacturing decision. Some of the tradeoffs identified by Skinner are presented in Table 2.4.

As far as the product selection decision is concerned, each of the major decision areas given in the table affects, and is affected by, the product choice. In addition, four other factors of importance might be noted.

1. *Relationship between the product under consideration and the firm's existing production technology.* From a production standpoint, the product must be able to fit in with the current transformation process and produc-

[5] Tom Burns and G. M. Stalker, *The Management of Innovation* (London: Tavistock Publications, 1961).

[6] For purposes of this discussion, a *policy* is defined as a broad, general guide to action, and a *strategy* is defined as a particular alternative invoked in a specific situation. Thus a policy limits the range of potential strategies.

[7] Wickham Skinner, "Manufacturing—Missing Link in Corporate Strategy," *Harvard Business Review,* Vol. 47, No. 3 (May–June 1969), p. 136.

TABLE 2.4

Some important tradeoff decisions in manufacturing

Decision area	Decision	Alternatives
Plant and equipment	Span of process	Make or buy
	Plant size	One big plant or several smaller ones
	Plant location	Locate near markets or locate near materials
	Investment decisions	Invest mainly in buildings or equipment or inventories or research
	Choice of equipment	General-purpose or special-purpose equipment
	Kind of tooling	Temporary, minimum tooling or "production tooling"
Production planning and control	Frequency of inventory taking	Few or many breaks in production for buffer stocks
	Inventory size	High inventory or a lower inventory
	Degree of inventory control	Control in great detail or in lesser detail
	What to control	Controls designed to minimize machine downtime or labor cost or time in process, or to maximize output of particular products or material usage
	Quality control	High reliability and quality or low costs
	Use of standards	Formal or informal or none at all
Labor and staffing	Job specialization	Highly specialized or not highly specialized
	Supervision	Technically trained first-line supervisors or nontechnically trained supervisors
	Wage system	Many job grades or few job grades; incentive wages or hourly wages
	Supervision	Close supervision or loose supervision
	Industrial engineers	Many or few such men
Product design/engineering	Size of product line	Many customer specials or few specials or none at all
	Design stability	Frozen design or many engineering change orders
	Technological risk	Use of new processes unproved by competitors or follow-the-leader policy
	Engineering	Complete packaged design or design-as-you-go approach
	Use of manufacturing engineering	Few or many manufacturing engineers
Organization and management	Kind of organization	Functional or product focus or geographical or other
	Executive use of time	High involvement in investment or production planning or cost control or quality control or other activities
	Degree of risk assumed	Decisions based on much or little information
	Use of staff	Large or small staff group
	Executive style	Much or little involvement in detail; authoritarian or nondirective style; much or little contact with organization

Source: Wickham Skinner "Manufacturing—Missing Link in Corporate Strategy," *Harvard Business Review*, vol. 47, no. 3 (May–June 1969), p. 141.

tion expertise. Obviously, if a company currently produces products using an assembly line form of manufacture, it would be risky for it to adopt a product requiring much custom work at individual work stations. New skills would have to be learned, material handling patterns altered, inventory adjustments made, etc.

2. *Extent of protection from productivity competition.* As a strategic consideration, a firm would be unwise to select and develop a product which others could produce more efficiently. Victor Borge, the entertainer, tells how he and his associates decided to go into raising Cornish game hens for the U.S. market, whereupon they spent time and effort persuading the public of the culinary delights offered by the bird. They investigated how the hens could be raised domestically, and the stage was set for a profitable operation. At this point, however, poultry farmers and meat packing companies, recognizing a good thing when they saw it, entered the business and raised and marketed the hens at a much lower cost. Hence Borge was forced out of business, thereby finding out the hard way that he had embarked on production competition with firms whose distinctive competence was their production expertise, and who could quite easily take advantage of economies of scale.

Thus the lesson to be learned is that unless an organization has the productive skills to produce the product efficiently when the market for it grows (or has sufficient patent protection to act as a barrier to entry), it had better think twice about adopting that "golden idea."

3. *Reliability of supply.* A product may be eminently suited to existing production facilities and expertise, but some of its component parts may be obtainable from only one supplier. Thus, in such cases, a product decision is also a supplier decision, and management should carefully evaluate the reliability of the supplier regarding his ability to meet both deliveries and quality specifications.

A well-known example of supplier troubles was that encountered by Lockheed Aircraft. Lockheed's engine supplier for its Tri-Star airplane—Rolls-Royce—went into bankruptcy and was subsequently taken over by the British government. This placed Lockheed on the verge of bankruptcy and forced it to secure the controversial multimillion-dollar loan which had to be guaranteed by the U.S. government.

4. *Relationship between labor costs and the product selected.* One of the major problems facing U.S. industry is that the cost of labor is so high that it has a direct bearing on the product decision. Should the new product be subassembled abroad to take advantage of lower labor costs? Can it be produced in a part of the United States where rates are lower? Should an automated facility be developed to produce it? Will it be produced by union labor? These are important strategic issues that must be competently dealt with if the product venture is to succeed.

As to an approach for deciding upon a general production policy, Skinner suggests that a systematic procedure following the steps shown in Figure 2.8 would be useful. This approach, in essence, prescribes that manufacturing policy be determined by comparing the factors in the firm's environment with the firm's internal capabilities and goals. The emphasis is on identifying the features of the firm that set it apart from other firms—that is, its primary task and distinctive competence—and then selecting its manufacturing policy in light of these features.

FACILITY LOCATION

One of the major strategy decisions that must be made by any organization is where to locate its producing and storage facilities. For manufacturers, the problem is broadly categorized into factory location and warehouse location; within this categorization, we may be interested in locating the firm's first factory or warehouse or locating a new factory or warehouse relative to the locations of existing facilities. The general objective in choosing a location is to select that site or combination of sites that minimizes two classes of costs—regional costs and distribution costs. Regional costs are those associated with a given locale and include land, construction, manpower, and state and local expenses and regulations. Distribution costs are those directly related to the shipping of supplies and products to customers and other branches of the distribution network. Since the location of the initial factory is usually determined by the historical context of the firm, economic analysis of facility location has focused on the problem of adding warehouses or factories to the existing production-distribution system.

In service organizations, the facility location decision is also a major one, but as a rule, the choice of a locale is based upon nearness to the customer rather than on resource considerations. With the shift in the U.S. economy away from manufacturing and toward service, there is little question that opening of new service facilities has become far more common than opening new factories and warehouses. Indeed, there are few communities in which rapid population growth has not been paralleled by a concurrent rapid growth in public and private branch offices, franchises, and entertainment facilities.

Facility location in practice

While a number of mathematical and computer-based techniques[8] have been developed to solve facility location problems, the most common approach in practice appears to be simple ranking of alternative sites according to criteria that are developed by the firm making the decision. Typically, a site location committee first selects a geographic region, then a city or county, and finally a specific site. The evaluation of alternative regions, cities, and counties is commonly termed "macro analysis" and the evaluation of specific sites in the selected city or county is commonly termed "micro analysis." At the macro level, such factors as markets (size and growth trends), labor (rates, availability of skills), transportation (types, costs,

---

[8] Linear programming and Monte Carlo simulation are two quantitative techniques covered in this book that have been frequently applied to location studies.

FIGURE 2.8

The determination of manufacturing policy

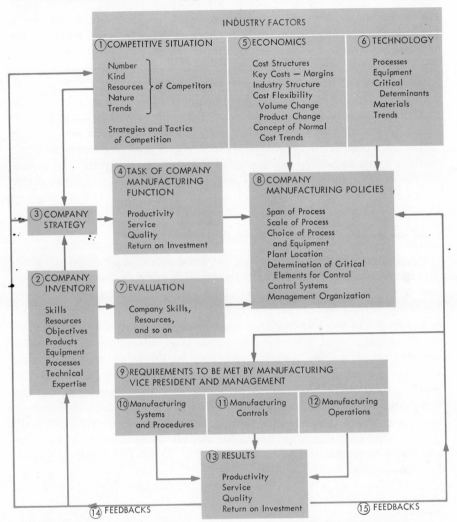

1. What the others are doing.
2. What we have got or can get to compete with.
3. How we can compete.
4. What we must accomplish in manufacturing in order to compete.
5. Economic constraints and opportunities common to the industry.
6. Constraints and opportunities common to the technology.
7. Our resources evaluated.
8. How we should set ourselves up to match resources, economics, and technology to meet the tasks required by our competitive strategy.

9. The implementation requirements of our manufacturing policies.
10. Basic systems in manufacturing (e.g., production planning, use of inventories, use of standards, and wage systems).
11. Controls of cost, quality, flows, inventory, and time.
12. Selection of operations or ingredients critical to success (e.g., labor skills, equipment utilization, and yields).
13. How we are performing.
14. Changes in what we have got, effects on competitive situation, and review of strategy.
15. Analysis and review of manufacturing operations and policies.

Source: Wickham Skinner "Manufacturing—Missing Link in Corporate Strategy," *Harvard Business Reveiw,* vol. 47, no. 3 (May–June 1969), p. 143.

schedules), and financial considerations (taxes, community inducements) are of dominant concern. At the micro level, engineering considerations (utilities, land configuration, etc.) become of major concern for factories, and traffic patterns, competitors' locations, and neighborhood attitudes become of major concern for service systems. Even after the location decision is made, it should be noted that most progressive firms—especially those in manufacturing and franchising—periodically re-evaluate their current locations to see whether a change to some other site would be profitable. In summary, it should be apparent after even this brief discussion that facilities location is a complicated problem, and though we present a simple heuristic method below to help in one aspect of the analysis, judgment and experience more often than not provide the ultimate bases upon which the choice is made.

Locating service facilities—A heuristic method

A common problem encountered by service providing organizations is deciding how many service outlets to establish within a geographical area, and where within that geographical area the service outlets are to be located. The problem is complicated by the fact that there are usually a large number of possible locations and several options in the absolute number of service centers that can be selected. Thus, attempting to find a good solution, much less an optimum one, can be extremely time-consuming, even for a relatively small problem. For example, there would be 243 possible solutions for a problem involving choosing among one, two, or three retail outlets to serve four geographically dispersed customer populations, even where there are only three possible locations for the outlets. To illustrate one approach to searching for feasible solutions to such problems, a heuristic method based on one described by Khumawala[9] will be applied to a sample problem.

Situation

Suppose that a medical consortium wishes to establish two clinics to provide medical care for people living in four communities in central Ohio. Assume that the sites under study are in the geographic center of each community and that the population within each community is evenly distributed within the community's boundaries. Further, assume that the potential use of the clinics by members of the various communities has been determined and weighting factors reflecting the relative importance of serving members of the population of each community have been developed. (This information is given in the first table below.) The objective of the problem can be stated as follows: Find the two clinics that can serve all communities at the lowest weighted-travel distance cost.

---

[9] Basheer M. Khumawala, "An Efficient Algorithm for Central Facilities Location," Paper No. 357, Krannert School of Industrial Administration, Purdue University, July, 1972.

TABLE 1

Distances, population, and relative weights

From community	To clinic A	B	C	D	Population of community	Relative weighting of population
1	0	11	8	12	10,000	1.1
2	11	0	10	7	8,000	1.4
3	8	10	0	9	20,000	0.7
4	9.5	7	9	0	12,000	1.0

Procedure

Step 1: Construct a weighted population-distance table from initial data table.

TABLE 2

Weighted population distances (distance × population × weighting factor) in thousands

From community	To clinic A	B	C	D
1	0	121	88	132
2	123.2	0	112	78.4
3	112	140	0	126
4	114	84	108	0

Step 2: Circle the smallest non-zero number in each row. Draw an arrow from that number to the zero in its row. This zero identifies the column (clinic) which can be eliminated at the lowest added cost of providing service to that clinic's community. Record the cost of eliminating that clinic. Draw a line through the column associated with the clinic with the lowest cost to indicate its elimination.

Community	Clinic A	B	C	D
1	0	121	(88)	132
2	123.2	0	112	(78.4)
3	(112)	140	0	126
4	114	(84)	108	0

Cost of eliminating clinic:

A	B	C	D
	78.4		

Step 3: Subtract the smallest circled number from itself and all remaining numbers in its row and construct a matrix reflecting this subtraction and the elimination of the clinic. If the specified number of clinics remaining open is now achieved, stop, otherwise repeat steps 2 and 3.

	Clinic		
Community	A	C	D
1	0	88	132
2	44.8	33.6	0
3	112	0	126
4	114	108	0

(subtractions made in row 2)

One more clinic must be eliminated, so we repeat steps 2 and 3. Step 2 (repeated):

	Clinic		
Community	A	C	D
1	0	(88)	132
2	44.8	(33.6)	0
3	(112)	0	126
4	114	(108)	0

Cost of eliminating clinic:

A	C	D
88	112	33.6
		108
88	112	141.6	Totals

Step 3 (repeated):

	Clinic	
Community	C	D
1	0	44
2	33.6	0
3	0	126
4	108	0

The problem is now solved: Clinic C serves communities 1 and 3; clinic D serves communities 2 and 4. The total cost of the solution (in population weighted distance) is $88 + 78.4$, or 166.4.

CONCLUSION

In this chapter we have dealt with two basic issues that must be considered at the birth of the productive system—the product and the production organization. While we have treated these factors for the most part as separate and distinct problems, their interrelationship, which is ultimately manifested via technology, should be kept in mind. We have also discussed the importance of the production function to corporate strategy; and many of the tradeoffs mentioned will be considered further throughout the book.

In the next chapter we will consider in detail the means by which the product is brought to fruition, and delve more deeply into the nature of technology. In later chapters we will examine the necessary adjustments to the organization structure as the productive system matures, and we will see the variety of ways in which the location chosen for the firm's facilities affects the performance of the productive systems contained within them.

PROPOSITIONS

Propositions contrasting services and manufacturing relative to the product decision and design of the production function

Product. A service firm tends to locate near its customers, whereas a manufacturing firm tends to be influenced in its location by the availability of labor, raw materials, power, and shipping facilities.

Technology of Transformation. Selecting the service product may be equivalent to selecting the physical process by which the service is created. (This is especially true in those services where the *process of transformation* is of vital concern to the customer, as in a hospital stay, an airline flight, or a shopping expedition.) In manufacturing, the customer is primarily concerned with the final product; there are usually a substantial number of different materials and processes that can be used to make a given end product.

Operating and control system. In a service system where the customer is directly involved in the transformation process and has prior knowledge of acceptable procedures, the operating and control system is essentially defined. In manufacturing, the customer is usually not concerned with the manner in which a product is produced, and the operating and control system is developed after the product is designed and ready for full scale production.

Workforce. In a service firm, the customer usually buys the skill of the processor (hairdresser, artist, mechanic, surgeon, dentist, consultant). Therefore, selecting the service is generally equivalent to describing the size and skill level of the workforce required to perform the service. In manufacturing, the workforce required is determined by technological choices relating to processes and work methods.

REVIEW AND DISCUSSION QUESTIONS

1. What is the role of the production function in making the product decision?
2. Give an example of a situation where a firm's distinctive competence was not matched to its primary task.
3. Provide or develop a statement of objectives for a church, dormitory, or other social group of which you are a member. What inconsistencies do you find? How are such inconsistencies resolved in practice?
4. What determines whether or not a decision is in fact "optimal"?
5. Distinguish between *continual* and *periodic* activities. What other ways are there to classify operations management activities?
6. What seems to be the relationship between organization structure and the type of environment (i.e., turbulent or stable) in which a firm operates?

7. Finding a suitable location for a productive facility entails balancing multiple objectives, some of which are highly subjective. What subjective factors would management have to consider before locating the following facilities in your community: (*a*) a nuclear power plant, (*b*) a paper mill, (*c*) a laboratory devoted to theoretical research?

8. "Production management is a nuts-and-bolts field which is really the realm of the technical specialist rather than the innovative manager." Comment.

9. "If the Slick Oil Company can make good deck shoes, which is not their main business, then they should be able to make good gasoline, which is their main business." Comment.

PROBLEMS

1. Using Table 2.3 as a guide, specify the output and the cost objectives of the following organizations:
    a.   A U.S. Forest Service regional office
    b.   A taxicab company in a large metropolitan area
    c.   A summer camp for children

2. For each of the organizations listed above,
    a.   Develop an organization chart.
    b.   Specify those positions which would be mainly productive in nature, that is, where production activities are performed.

3. The Tansik Luggage Company (T.L.C.) fabricates and assembles "soft sided" suitcases at a plant in Chicago but is contemplating shifting to a "twin plants" operation. The twin plants concept is a simple one: a firm fabricates the parts of its product in the United States and then ships them to assembly plants just across the border in Mexico. The assembled product is then shipped back to the U.S. plant (usually located near the border), where it is packed for shipping to wholesale and retail outlets. The primary advantage of a twin plants operation is the savings in labor cost in assembling the item. In Mexico the average hourly pay at a border plant is 40 cents, as opposed to about $2.75 in the United States. (The 1972–73 rate of 40 cents doubled to 80 cents by 1976, but devaluation and the floating peso reduced it again to about 40 cents.)

    If T.L.C. decides to embark on a twin plants strategy, it will close its facilities in Chicago and open a fabrication plant in Tucson, Arizona, and a "twin" assembly plant in Nogales, Sonora, Mexico. The production manager of the firm perceives the general flow of operations between the two facilities as shown in the diagram on the following page.

    Assignment: (*a*) Using Table 2.4 as a guide, develop a list of production decisions that must be made if the company embarks on the proposed twin plants operation. (*b*) For each decision, specify the nature of the tradeoff(s) that must be considered. (*c*) Indentify the factors beyond the control of T.L.C. that have a major bearing on the success of the endeavor.

Stamp sides of luggage and load in plastic bins in Tucson

↓

Ship by truck across the border

↓

Assemble suitcases and box them in Nogales

↓

Ship by truck back across the border

↓

Crate boxed suitcases in Tucson

↓

Load on railcars and ship to retailers

4. The manager of Kosher Mexican Food Company, Manuel Schwartz, is trying to decide which of two products should be developed by his firm. One of
these is *huevos rapidos* (instant eggs), which would be made by flash freezing and drying chicken eggs, and then mixed with a combination of chili
peppers specially grown for this purpose. The end result would be a Mexican
omelet for use by campers and harried housewives. The other product is a
chili bagel, which, according to a local delicatessen owner, "when topped
with smoked salmon and cream cheese will become a new taste sensation
that will displace both corned beef sandwiches and tamales as the standard
lunch of the Southwest."

Schwartz figures that the probability of being able to produce *huevos
rapidos* is 75 percent, the chances of it being a success in the market are 50–
50, and annual sales should be about 500,000 pounds for the next five years.
He figures he can sell the product at $0.75 a pound to retailers and that it
will cost $0.30 a pound. He estimates that the cost of developing the process
and the new chili will be about $20,000 and that modifications of existing
equipment to produce *huevos rapidos* at full-scale production levels will cost
about $2,000.

Schwartz estimates that the probability of producing a satisfactory chili
bagel, or "chigel" as the boys in R&D refer to it, is 95 percent. He figures
that the probability of its being a success in the market is 80 percent, with
annual sales being about 300,000 pounds for the next five years. Chigels
should cost about $0.50 a pound and sell for $0.85 a pound to retailers. The
cost of developing the chigel process is $2,000 and a high-speed bagel
press and special packaging line will have to be purchased at a total cost of
$60,000.

The work force required for either product is projected as six full-time
operators at $2 per hour.

Schwartz estimates his cost of capital as 10 percent.

Given the above information, choose between the products using the
project value index formula.

5. A drug store chain wants to locate two stores to serve four communities. Given the following population-weighted distance costs, which stores should be selected?

To community	From drug store			
	1	*2*	*3*	*4*
A	0	40	75	150
B	90	0	180	16
C	45	33	0	10
D	18	76	14	0

6. There is a simple way to solve Problem 5 for the special case of *one* store to be located to serve the four communities. Identify this method and solve the problem. Then solve using the heuristic method described in the chapter. Are the two answers identical? If not, explain why.

SELECTED BIBLIOGRAPHY

Berg, Thomas L., and Shuchman, Abe (eds.)   *Product Strategy and Management.* New York: Holt, Rinehart Winston, 1963.

Burns, Tom, and Stalker, G. M.   *The Management of Innovation.* London: Tavistock Publications, 1961.

Factory Report   "Picking the Right Plant Site," *Factory* (May 1976), pp. 61–62.

Flippo, Edwin B.   *Management: A Behavioral Approach.* Boston: Allyn & Bacon, 1968.

Francis, Richard L., and White, John A.   *Facility Layout and Location, An Analytical Approach,* Englewood Cliffs, N.J.: Prentice-Hall, 1974.

Goslin, Lewis N.   *The Product-Planning System.* Homewood, Ill.: Richard D. Irwin, Inc., 1967.

Johnson, Samuel C., and Jones, Conrad   "How to Organize for New Products," *Harvard Business Review,* vol. 35, no. 3 (May–June 1957), pp. 49–62.

Pessemier, Edgar A.   *New-Product Decisions: An Analytical Approach.* New York: McGraw-Hill, 1966.

Skinner, Wickham   "Manufacturing—Missing Link in Corporate Strategy," *Harvard Business Review,* vol. 47, no. 3 (May–June 1967), pp. 136–45.

Woodward, Joan   *Industrial Organization: Theory and Practice.* London: Oxford University Press, 1965.

Supplement to chapter two

Linear programming

LINEAR PROGRAMMING refers to several related mathematical techniques that are used to allocate limited resources among competing demands in an optimal way. Linear programming is the most popular of the approaches falling under the general heading of mathematical optimization techniques,[1] and, as will become apparent in subsequent chapters, it has been applied to a myriad of production management problems.[2] In this supplement we shall discuss the simplex method, which can be used to solve any type of linear programming problem, and the graphical, transportation, and assignment methods, which are useful in dealing with certain special cases. In addition to illustrating how linear programming methods lead to an opti-

---

[1] Dynamic programming and nonlinear programming are two other well known (but generally more complicated) forms of optimization techniques.

[2] See Table S.2.18 for a summary of uses.

mum solution for a given problem, we will discuss some of the valuable "free information" provided by the simplex method.

THE LINEAR PROGRAMMING MODEL

The linear programming problem entails an optimizing process in which nonnegative values for a set of decision variables $X_1, X_2 \ldots X_n$ are selected so as to maximize (or minimize) an objective function in the form

$$\text{Maximize (minimize) } Z = C_1X_1 + C_2X_2 + \ldots + C_nX_n$$

subject to resource constraints in the form

$$A_{11} X_1 + A_{12} X_2 + \ldots + A_{1n} X_n \leq B_1$$
$$A_{21} X_1 + A_{22} X_2 + \ldots + A_{2n} X_n \leq B_2$$

$$A_{m1} X_1 + A_{m2} X_2 + \ldots + A_{mn} X_n \leq B_m$$

where C_j, A_{ij}, and B_i are given constants.

Depending upon the problem, the constraints may also be stated with equal-to signs ($=$) or greater-than-or-equal-to signs ($\geq$).

For linear programming to be applicable, the following conditions must exist.

1. The objective function and each constraint equation must be linear. This excludes exponents and cross products in the problem statement and implies proportionality; for example, if it takes three men to produce one unit, it takes six men to produce two in the same time.
2. The constants must be known and assumed to be deterministic. In other words, the probability associated with the occurrence of any C_j, A_{ij}, and B_i value is presumed to be 1.0.
3. The decision variables must be divisible; that is, a feasible solution would permit half a unit of X_1, a quarter unit of X_2, etc., to be produced. (This obviously would eliminate such situations as scheduling air flights, since sending up half an airplane is not possible.)[3]

GRAPHICAL LINEAR PROGRAMMING

Though limited in application to problems involving two decision variables (or three variables for three-dimensional graphing), graphical linear programming provides a quick insight into the nature of linear programming and illustrates what takes place in the general simplex method described later.

We will describe the steps involved in the graphical method in the context of a sample problem, that of the Puck and Pawn Company, which

---

[3] In such situations the technique of integer programming, yielding only whole numbers in its solution, is often applied.

manufactures hockey sticks and chess sets. Each hockey stick yields an incremental profit of $2 and each chess set an incremental profit of $4. A hockey stick requires four hours of processing at machine center A and two hours at machine center B. A chess set requires six hours at machine center A, six hours at machine center B, and one hour at machine center C. Machine center A has a maximum of 120 hours of available capacity per day, machine center B has 72 hours, and machine center C has 10 hours.

If the company wishes to maximize profit, how many hockey sticks and chess sets should be produced per day?

1. Formulate the problem in mathematical terms. If H is the number of hockey sticks and C is the number of chess sets, the objective function may be stated as follows:

$$\text{Maximize } Z = \$2H + \$4C \text{ (profit)}$$

The maximization will be subject to the following constraints:

$$4H + 6C \leq 120 \text{ (machine center A)}$$
$$2H + 6C \leq 72 \text{ (machine center B)}$$
$$1C \leq 10 \text{ (machine center C)}$$
$$H, C \geq 0 \text{ (nonnegativity requirement)}$$

2. Plot constraint equations. The constraint equations are easily plotted by letting one variable equal zero and solving for the axis intercept of the other. (The inequality portions of the restrictions are disregarded for this step.) For the machine center A constraint equation, then, when $H = 0$, $C = 20$, and when $C = 0$, $H = 30$. For the machine center B constraint equation, when $H = 0$, $C = 12$, and when $C = 0$, $H = 36$. For the machine center C constraint equation, $C = 10$ for all values of H. These lines are graphed in Figure S.2.1.

3. Determine the area of feasibility. The direction of inequality signs in each constraint determines the area wherein a feasible solution will be found. In this case all inequalities are of the less-than-or-equal-to variety, which means that it would be impossible to produce any combination of products that would lie to the right of any constraint line on the graph. The region of feasible solutions is shaded on the graph and forms a convex polygon. A convex polygon exists when a line drawn between any two points in the polygon stays within the boundaries of that polygon. If this condition of convexity does not exist, the problem is either incorrectly set up or not amenable to linear programming.

4. Plot the objective function. The objective function may be plotted by assuming some arbitrary total profit figure and then solving for the axis coordinates, as was done for the constraint equations. Another term for the objective function, when used in this context, is the *iso-profit* or *equal contribution line*, because it shows all possible production combinations for any given profit figure. For example, from the light line closest to the origin on the graph we can determine all possible combinations of hockey sticks and chess sets that will yield $32 by picking a point on the line and reading the number of each product that can be made at that point. The combination yielding $32 at point A would be 10 hockey sticks and 3 chess sets. This can be verified by substituting $H = 10$ and $C = 3$ in the objective function:

$$\$2(10) + \$4(3) = \$20 + \$12 = \$32$$

5. Find the optimum point. It can be shown mathematically that the optimum combination of decision variables will always be found at an extreme point (corner point) of the convex polygon. In Figure S.2.1. there are four corner points (excluding the origin), and we can determine which one is the optimum by either of two approaches. The first approach is to find the values of the various corner solutions algebraically. This entails simultaneously solving the equations of various pairs of intersecting lines and substituting the quantities of the resultant variables in the objective function. For example, the calculations for the intersection of $2H + 6C = 72$ and $C = 10$ would be as follows.

Substituting $C = 10$ in $2H + 6C = 72$ gives $2H + 6(10) = 72$, $2H = 12$, or $H = 6$. Substituting $H = 6$ and $C = 10$ in the objective function, we get:

$$\begin{aligned} \text{Profit} &= \$2H + \$4C \\ &= \$2(6) + \$4(10) \\ &= \$12 + \$40 \\ &= \$52 \end{aligned}$$

A variation of this approach is to read the H and C quantities directly from the graph and substitute these quantities into the objective function,

FIGURE S.2.1

Graph of hockey stick and chess set problem

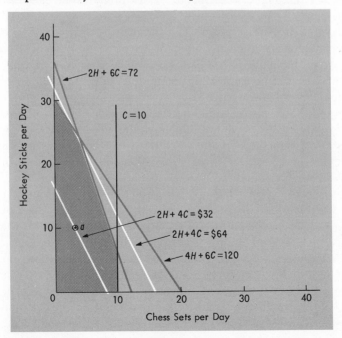

as shown in the previous calculation. The drawback in this approach is that in problems with a large number of constraint equations there will be many possible points to evaluate, and the procedure of testing each one mathematically is somewhat inefficient.

The second and generally preferred approach entails using the objective function or iso-profit line directly to find the optimum point. The procedure involves simply drawing a straight line *parallel* to any arbitrarily selected initial iso-profit line so that the iso-profit line is farthest from the origin of the graph. (In cost minimization problems, the objective would be to draw the line through the point closest to the origin.) In Figure S.2.1 the light line labeled $2H + $4C = $64 intersects the most extreme point. Note that the initial arbitrarily selected iso-profit line is necessary in order to display the slope[4] of the objective function for the particular problem. This is important since a different objective function (try profit = $3H + 3C$) might indicate that some other point is farthest from the origin. Given that $2H + $4C = $64 is optimum, the amount of each variable to produce can be read from the graph: 24 hockey sticks and 4 chess sets. No other combination of the products will yield a greater profit.

THE SIMPLEX METHOD

The simplex method[5] is an algebraic procedure that, through a series of repetitive operations, progressively approaches an optimum solution. Theoretically, the simplex method can solve a problem consisting of any number of variables and constraints, although for problems containing more than, say, four variables or four constraint equations, the actual calculations are best left to the computer. In this regard, however, it is well worth the effort to go through the simplex method manually a few times in order to fully understand and utilize the data provided by a computer.

Six-step solution procedure

There are a number of technical steps in the simplex method, and each one will be described in detail and summarized at the end of the section. We will use the hockey stick and chess set problem to demonstrate the procedure involved.

Step 1: Problem formulation. Recall that we had

$$\text{Maximize } Z = \$2H + \$4C \text{ (profit)}$$

subject to

$$4H + 6C \leq 120 \text{ (machine center A constraint)}$$
$$2H + 6C \leq 72 \text{ (machine center B constraint)}$$
$$1C \leq 10 \text{ (machine center C constraint)}$$
$$H, C \geq 0 \text{ (nonnegativity requirement)}$$

---

[4] The slope of the objective function is −2. If
  $p = $ profit,
  $p = \$2H + \$4C; \$2H = p - \$4C; H = p/2 - 2C.$ Thus the slope is −2.

[5] *Simplex* does not mean "simple"; it is a term used in *n*-space geometry.

Step 2: Set up initial tableau with slack variables in solution. To use the simplex method requires two major adjustments to the problem as stated: (*a*) the introduction of slack variables and (*b*) the establishment of a solution table or tableau.

Introduce slack variables. Each constraint equation is expanded to include a slack variable. A slack variable, which may be thought of as an idle resource in a practical sense, computationally represents the amount required to make one side of a constraint equation equal to the other—in other words, to convert the inequalities to equalities. For our problem, we need three slack variables: S_1 for the first constraint equation, S_2 for the second, and S_3 for the third.

The constraint equations appear as follows.

$$4H + 6C + 1S_1 = 120$$
$$2H + 6C + 1S_2 = 72$$
$$1C + 1S_3 = 10$$

So that all variables are represented in each equation, each slack variable not originally associated with a constraint equation is given a zero coefficient and added to that equation. Adjusting the system of equations in this way gives

$$4H + 6C + 1S_1 + 0S_2 + 0S_3 = 120$$
$$2H + 6C + 0S_1 + 1S_2 + 0S_3 = 72$$
$$0H + 1C + 0S_1 + 0S_2 + 1S_3 = 10$$

Note that the variable H, with a zero coefficient, is entered in the third equation to ensure that it also will be represented in all equations. Likewise, the objective function reflects the addition of slack variables, but since they yield no profit, their coefficient is $0:

$$Z = \$2H + \$4C + \$0S_1 + \$0S_2 + \$0S_3$$

Construct initial tableau (see Table S.2.1.). A tableau is a convenient way of setting up the problem for simplex computation. A tableau provides the following information.
1. The variables which are in the solution at that point.
2. The profit associated with the solution.
3. The variable (if any) that will add most to profit if brought into the solution.
4. The amount of reduction in the variables in the solution which results from introducing one unit of each variable. This amount is termed the *substitution rate.*
5. The worth of an additional unit (e.g., hour) of resource capacity. This is referred to as a *shadow price.*

The first four features will be discussed in reference to the first tableau; the last one will be considered later.

The top row of Table S.2.1 contains the C_j's, or the contribution to total profit associated with the production of one unit of each alternative product. This row is a direct restatement of the coefficients of the variables in the objective function, and therefore remains the same for all subsequent

TABLE S.2.1

Initial tableau of the hockey stick and chess set problem

C_j		$2	$4	$0	$0	$0	
	Solution mix	H	C	S_1	S_2	S_3	Quantity
$0	S_1	4	6	1	0	0	120
$0	S_2	2	6	0	1	0	72
$0	S_3	0	1	0	0	1	10←
	Z_j	$0	$0	$0	$0	$0	$0
	$C_j - Z_j$	$2	$4	$0	$0	$0	

tableaus. The first column, headed by C_j, merely lists, for convenience, the profit per unit of the variables included in the solution at any stage of the problem.

The variables chosen for the first tableau are listed under "solution mix." As can be seen, only slack variables are considered in the initial solution, and their profit coefficients are zero, which is indicated by the aforementioned C_j column.

The constraint variables are listed to the right of "solution mix," and under each one is the particular variable's coefficient in each constraint equation. That is, 4, 6, 1, 0, and 0 are the coefficients of the machine center A constraint; 2, 6, 0, 1, and 0 for machine center B; and 0, 1, 0, 0, and 1 for machine center C.

Substitution rates can be ascertained from the numbers as well. For example, consider 4, 2, and 0, listed under H in the third column. For every unit of product H introduced into the solution, four units of S_1, two units of S_2, and zero units of S_3 must be withdrawn from the solution in order to stay within the problem constraints.

The entries in the "quantity" column refer to how many units of each resource are available in each machine center. In the initial tableau, this is a restatement of the right-hand side of each constraint equation. With the exception of the value in the quantity column, the Z_j values in the second row from the bottom refer to the amount of *gross* profit that is given up by introducing one unit of that variable into the solution. The subscript *j* refers to the specific variable being considered. The Z_j value under the quantity column is the total profit for the solution. In the initial solution of a simplex problem, all values of Z_j will be zero because no real product is being produced (all machines are idle), and hence there is no gross profit to be lost if they are replaced.

The bottom row of the tableau contains the *net* profit per unit, obtained by introducing one unit of a given variable into the solution. This row is designated the $C_j - Z_j$ row. The procedure for calculating Z_j and each $C_j - Z_j$ is demonstrated in Table S.2.2.

The initial solution to the problem is read directly from Table S.2.1: the company will "produce" 120 units of S_1, 72 units of S_2, and 10 units of

TABLE S.2.2

Calculations of Z_j and $C_j - Z_j$

C_j	H	C_j	C	C_j	S_1	C_j	S_2	C_j	S_3	C_j	Quantity
$\$0 \times 4 =$	0	$\$0 \times 6 =$	0	$\$0 \times 1 =$	0	$\$0 \times 0 =$	0	$\$0 \times 0 =$	0	$\$0 \times$	120
	$+$		$+$		$+$		$+$		$+$		$+$
$\$0 \times 2 =$	0	$\$0 \times 6 =$	0	$\$0 \times 0 =$	0	$\$0 \times 1 =$	0	$\$0 \times 0 =$	0	$\$0 \times$	72
	$+$		$+$		$+$		$+$		$+$		$+$
$\$0 \times 0 =$	$\underline{0}$	$\$0 \times 1 =$	$\underline{0}$	$\$0 \times 0 =$	$\underline{0}$	$\$0 \times 0 =$	$\underline{0}$	$\$0 \times 1 =$	$\underline{0}$	$\$0 \times$	$\underline{10}$
$Z_H = \$0$		$Z_C = \$0$		$Z_{S_1} = \$0$		$Z_{S_2} = \$0$		$Z_{S_3} = \$0$		$Z_Q = \$0$	

$C_j - Z_j$ calculations:

$C_H - Z_H = \$2 - 0 = \$2$
$C_C - Z_C = \$4 - 0 = \$4$
$C_{S_1} - Z_{S_1} = \$0 - 0 = \$0$
$C_{S_2} - Z_{S_2} = \$0 - 0 = \$0$
$C_{S_3} - Z_{S_3} = \$0 - 0 = \$0$

S_3. The total profit from this solution is $0. Thus, no capacity has yet been allocated and no real product produced.

Step 3: Determine which variable to bring into solution. An improved solution is possible if there is a positive value in the $C_j - Z_j$ row. Recall that this row provides the net profit obtained by adding one unit of its associated column variable in the solution. In this example there are two positive values to choose from: $2, associated with H, and $4, associated with C. Since our objective is to maximize profit, the logical choice is to pick the value of the largest payoff to enter the solution, so variable C will be introduced. The column associated with this variable is termed the *optimum column* and is designated by the small arrow beneath column C in Table S.2.1. (It should be emphasized that only one variable at a time can be added in developing each improved solution.)

Step 4: Determine which variable to replace. Given that it is desirable to introduce C into the solution, the next question is to determine which variable it will replace. To make this determination, we divide each amount in the Quantity column by the amount in the comparable row of the C column and choose the variable associated with the smallest quotient as the one to be replaced:

For the S_1 row: $120/6 = 20$
For the S_2 row: $72/6 = 12$
For the S_3 row: $10/1 = 10$

Since the smallest quotient is 10, S_3 will be replaced, and its row is identified by the small arrow to the right of the tableau in Table S.2.1. This is the maximum amount of C that can be brought into the solution; that is, production of more than 10 units of C would exceed the available capacity of machine C. This can be verified mathematically by considering the constraint $C \leq 10$, and visually by examining the graphical representation of the problem in Figure S.2.1. The graph also shows that the 20 and 12 are the C intercepts of the other two constraints, and if $C \leq 10$ were removed, the amount of C introduced could be increased by 2 units.

TABLE S.2.3

Calculation of new row values for entering variable

$$
\begin{array}{c}
C \\
6 \\
6 \\
\end{array}
$$

S_3 0 ① 0   0   0   10 $0/1 = 0, 1/1 = 1, 0/1 = 0, 0/1 = 0, 1/1 = 1, 10/1 = 10$

$4

Step 5: Calculate new row values for entering variable. The introduction of C into the solution requires that the entire S_3 row be replaced. The values for C, the replacing row, are obtained by dividing each value presently in the S_3 row by the value in column C in the same row. This value is termed the *intersectional element* since it occurs at the intersection of a row and column. This intersectional relationship is abstracted from the rest of the tableau and the necessary divisions are shown in Table S.2.3.

Step 6: Revise remaining rows. The new third-row values (now associated with C) are 0, 1, 0, 0, 1, and 10, which in this case are identical to those of the old third row.

The introduction of a new variable into the problem will affect the values of the remaining variables, and a second set of calculations must be performed to update the tableau. Specifically, we want to determine the effect of introducing C on the S_1 and S_2 rows. These calculations can be carried out by using what is termed the *pivot method*, or by algebraic substitution. The pivot method is a more mechanical procedure, and is generally used in practice, while algebraic substitution is more useful in explaining the logic of the updating process. The procedure using the pivot method to arrive at new values for S_1 and S_2 is shown in Table S.2.4. (In essence, the method subtracts six times row 3 from both the S_1 and S_2 rows.)

Updating by algebraic substitution entails substituting the entire equation for the entering row into each of the remaining rows and solving for the revised values for each row's variable. The procedure, summarized in Table S.2.5, illustrates the fact that linear programming via the simplex method is essentially the solving of a number of simultaneous equations.

TABLE S.2.4

Pivot method

Old S_1 row	−	(Intersectional element of old S_1 row	× Corresponding element of new C row)	= Updated S_1 row	Old S_2 row	−	(Intersectional element of old S_2 row	× Corresponding element of new C row)	= Updated S_2 row
4	−	(6	× 0)	= 4	2	−	(6	× 0)	= 2
6	−	(6	× 1)	= 0	6	−	(6	× 1)	= 0
1	−	(6	× 0)	= 1	0	−	(6	× 0)	= 0
0	−	(6	× 0)	= 0	1	−	(6	× 0)	= 1
0	−	(6	× 1)	= −6	0	−	(6	× 1)	= −6
120	−	(6	× 10)	= 60	72	−	(6	× 10)	= 12

Algebraic substitution

To find new values for S_1,

1. Reconstruct old S_1 row as a constraint with slack variables added (from first tableau):

$$4H + 6C + 1S_1 + 0S_2 + 0S_3 = 120$$

2. Write entering row as a constraint with slack variables added (these are the values computed in Figure S.2.3):

$$0H + C + 0S_1 + 0S_2 + 1S_3 = 10$$

3. Rearrange entering row in terms of C, the entering variable:

$$C = 10 - S_3$$

4. Substitute $10 - S_3$ for C in the first equation (the old S_1 row) and solve for each variable coefficient:

$$4H + 6(10 - S_3) + 1S_1 = 120$$
$$4H + 60 - 6S_3 + 1S_1 = 120$$
$$4H + 1S_1 - 6S_3 = 120 - 60$$
$$4H + 1S_1 - 6S_3 = 60$$

or

$$4H + 0C + 1S_1 + 0S_2 - 6S_3 = 60$$

Isolating the variable coefficients yields the same values for the new S_1 row as did the pivot method: 4, 0, 1, 0, −6, 60.

The results of the computations carried out in steps 3 through 6, along with the calculations of Z_j and $C_j - Z_j$ are shown in the revised tableau, Table S.2.6. In mathematical programming terminology, we have completed one "iteration" of the problem.

In evaluating this solution we note two things: the profit is \$40, but, more important, further improvement is possible since there is a positive value in the $C_j - Z_j$ row.

Second iteration. The entering variable is H since it has largest $C_j - Z_j$ amount (2). The replaced variable is S_2 since it has the smallest quotient when the Quantity column values are divided by their comparable amounts in the H column:

$$S_1 = 60/4 = 15, S_2 = 12/2 = 6, S_3 = 10/0 = \infty$$

Values of entering (H) row are

$$2/2 = 1, 0/2 = 0, 0/2 = 0, 1/2 = 1/2, -6/2 = -3, 12/2 = 6$$

TABLE S.2.6

Second tableau of the hockey stick and chess set problem

C_j		\$2	\$4	\$0	\$0	\$0	
	Solution mix	H	C	S_1	S_2	S_3	Quantity
\$0	S_1	4	0	1	0	−6	60
\$0	S_2	2	0	0	1	−6	12 ←
\$4	C	0	1	0	0	1	10
	Z_j	\$0	\$4	\$0	\$0	\$ 4	\$40
	$C_j - Z_j$	\$2	\$0	\$0	\$0	\$−4	

↑

Updated S_1 row from Table S.2.7: 0, 0, 1, $-$ 2, 6, 36
Updated C row from Table S.2.7: 0, 1, 0, 0, 1, 10.
Using the result from Table S.2.7, we obtain the third tableau: Table S.2.8.

Examination of the third tableau indicates that further improvement is possible by introducing the maximum amount of S_3 that is technically feasible. As can be seen below the tableau, the maximum amount of S_3 that can be brought into the solution is 6 units because of the limited supply of S_1.

TABLE S.2.7

Updating S_1 and C rows

Old S_1 row	$-$	⎛Inter- sectional element of old ⎝S_1 row	$\times$	Corre- sponding element in new H row ⎞	New S_1 = row	Old C row	$-$	⎛Inter- sectional element of old ⎝C row	$\times$	Corre- sponding element of new H row ⎞	New C = row
4	$-$	(4	$\times$	1)	= 0	0	$-$	(0	$\times$	1)	= 0
0	$-$	(4	$\times$	0)	= 0	1	$-$	(0	$\times$	0)	= 1
1	$-$	(4	$\times$	0)	= 1	0	$-$	(0	$\times$	0)	= 0
0	$-$	(4	$\times$	$\frac{1}{2}$)	= -2	0	$-$	(0	$\times$	$\frac{1}{2}$)	= 0
-6	$-$	(4	$\times$	-3)	= 6	1	$-$	(0	$\times$	-3)	= 1
60	$-$	(4	$\times$	6)	= 36	10	$-$	(0	$\times$	6)	= 10

Third tableau of hockey stick and chess set problem

C_j		$2	$4	$0	$0	$0	
	Solution mix	H	C	S_1	S_2	S_3	Quantity
$0	S_1	0	0	1	-2	6	36 ←
$2	H	1	0	0	$\frac{1}{2}$	-3	6
$4	C	0	1	0	0	1	10
	Z_j	$2	$4	$0	$ 1	$-2	$52
	$C_j - Z_j$	$0	$0	$0	$-1	$ 2	
						↑	

$$36/6 = 6$$
$$6/-3 = -2 \text{ (negative)}^6$$
$$10/1 = 10$$

Replacing S_1 by S_3 and performing the updating operations yields the tableau shown in Table S.2.9. As can be seen from the $C_j - Z_j$ row of this tableau, no further improvement is possible, and an optimum solution ($H = 24$, $C = 4$) has been achieved in three iterations.

---

[6] Since there are three constraint equations, there must be three variables with non-negative values in the solution. Therefore a negative amount cannot be considered for introduction into the solution.

TABLE S.2.9

Fourth tableau of the hockey stick and chess set problem (optimum solution)

C_i		$2	$4	$0	$0	$0	
	Solution mix	H	C	S_1	S_2	S_3	Quantity
$0	S_3	0	0	$\frac{1}{6}$	$-\frac{1}{3}$	1	6
$2	H	1	0	$\frac{1}{2}$	$-\frac{1}{2}$	0	24
$4	C	0	1	$-\frac{1}{6}$	$\frac{1}{3}$	0	4
	Z_j	$2	$4	$ $\frac{1}{3}$	$ $\frac{1}{3}$	$0	$64
	$C_j - Z_j$	$0	$0	$-\frac{1}{3}$	$-\frac{1}{3}$	$0	

Summary of steps in the simplex method

1. Formulate problem in terms of an objective function and a set of constraints.
2. Set up initial tableau with slack variables in the solution mix and calculate the Z_j and $C_j - Z_j$ rows.
3. Determine which variable to bring into solution (largest $C_j - Z_j$ value).
4. Determine which variable to replace (smallest ratio of quantity column to its comparable value in the optimum column).
5. Calculate new row values for entering variable and insert into new tableau (row to be replaced plus intersectional element).
6. Update remaining rows and enter into new tableau; compute new Z_j and $C_j - Z_j$ rows (old row minus intersectional element of old row times corresponding element in new row). If no positive $C_j - Z_j$ value is found, solution is optimum. If there is a positive value of $C_j - Z_j$, repeat steps 3 to 6.

Minimization problems. An identical procedure is followed for solving minimization problems. Since the objective is to minimize rather than maximize, a negative $C_j - Z_j$ value indicates potential improvement; therefore the variable associated with the largest negative $C_j - Z_j$ value would be brought into solution first. Additional variables must be brought in to set up such problems, however, since minimization problems include greater-than-or-equal-to constraints, which must be treated differently from less-than-or-equal-to constraints, which typify maximization problems. (See section dealing with greater-than-or-equal-to and equal-to constraints in the simplex, below.)

Interpretation and summary of the simplex method

As mentioned in the description of the graphical solution to the sample problem, the optimum solution to linear programming problems is obtained by finding the extreme corner point. The simplex procedure always starts at the origin, searches for the most profitable direction to follow, and hops from point to point of intersecting lines (or planes in multidimensional space). The evaluation of a corner point takes one iteration, and when the furthermost point is reached (in the case of profit maximization problems as shown by the next point's decreasing profit), the solution is complete.

Consider the graph of the example problem shown in Figure S.2.2, where the simplex method began at point *a* (profit = $0). In the first iteration, 10 units of *C* were introduced at point *b* (profit = $40). In the second iteration, 6 units of *H* were introduced at point *c* (profit = $52). The third iteration left the problem at point *d* (profit = $64), which is optimum. Note that the solution procedure did not calculate profit for all corners of this problem. It did, however, *look ahead*—by virtue of the $C_j - Z_j$ calculations —to see if further improvement was possible by moving to another point (point *e*), but no improvement was indicated by such a change. These two characteristics—evaluating corner points and looking ahead for improvements—are the essential features of the simplex method.

Another feature that is also characteristic of the basic simplex method is that it does not necessarily converge on the optimum point by the shortest route around the feasible area. Reference to the graph will show that if the solution procedure had proceeded along the path $a \longrightarrow e \longrightarrow d$, an optimum would have been reached in two iterations rather than three.

The reason why this route was not followed was that the profit per chess set was higher than for a hockey stick, and therefore the simplex method indicated that *C*, rather than *H*, be introduced in the first iteration. This, in turn, set the pattern for subsequent iterations to points *c* and *d*. It should be noted that since the solution space forms a convex polygon (as previously defined), profit cannot increase, decrease, and then again increase. Thus, on the average, the number of intersections that must be examined is equal to half the total number plus one.

Shadow prices

As was mentioned in the discussion on constructing the initial tableau, a completed tableau also provides information as to the worth of an additional unit of resource capacity. This information is obtained from the $C_j - Z_j$ values associated with slack variables and is referred to variously as a *shadow price*, an *implicit cost*, or a *dual value*. In the final tableau of the simplex example, the shadow prices for S_1 were $1/3, or 33¢; $1/3 or 33¢ for S_2, and $0 for S_3. This means that management should be willing to pay up to 33 cents for an additional hour of capacity at machine center A (the constraint associated with S_1), 33 cents for an additional hour of capacity at machine center B, and nothing for additional capacity at machine center C. The validity and logic of this observation can be easily demonstrated graphically.

Recall the original formulation of the problem:

$$\text{Max } Z = \$2H + \$4C \text{ (profit)}$$

subject to

$$4H + 6C \le 120 \text{ (machine center A)}$$
$$2H + 6C \le 72 \text{ (machine center B)}$$
$$1C \le 10 \text{ (machine center C)}$$

FIGURE S.2.2

Graph of hockey stick and chess set problem showing successive corner evaluations

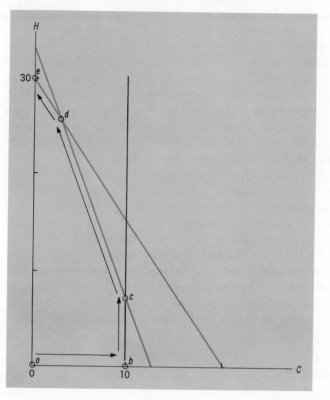

Suppose we wish to determine the value (shadow price) of an additional unit of capacity on machine A. This is equivalent to asking what is the change in total profit from a one-unit change in a constraint. Or, more simply, what is the ratio of Δ profit to Δ constraint? To make this determination, we graph the original constraints and calculate the total profit from that solution according to the graphical procedure described earlier. This solution corresponds to point *a* in Figure S.2.3. Next, the right-hand-side constraint of interest is increased by some arbitrary amount, chosen to facilitate graphical representation. Thus we add 12 units to the machine center A constraint equation:

$$4H + 6C = 120 + 12$$
$$4H + 6C = 132$$

Plotting this equation (intercept $H = 33$, $C = 22$) yields a new optimum at point *b*. Comparing solutions, we see that for the original constraint the optimum combination to produce is $24H$ and $4C$, and total profit is $64. With the increased capacity of 12 units, the optimal combination is $32H$

FIGURE S.2.3

Graph of hockey stick and chess set problem showing
shadow price determination

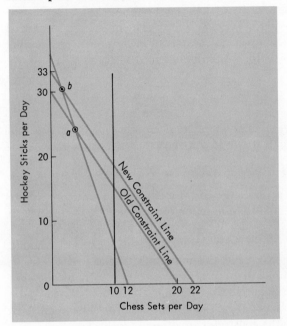

and $1C$, and the total profit increases to \$68. To find the value of *one* additional unit of capacity, we find

$$\frac{\Delta \text{ profit}}{\Delta \text{ constraint}} = \frac{\$68 - \$64}{132 - 120} = \frac{\$4}{12} = \$1/3 = \text{Shadow price } (S_1)$$

A similar analysis could be performed to prove that the value of an additional unit of capacity at machine center B is also 33 cents. By inspecting the graph, the reader may verify that an additional unit of capacity at machine center C is worth \$0.

Dealing with greater-than-or-equal-to and equal-to constraints in the simplex. Greater-than-or-equal-to constraints ($\geq$) and equal-to constraints ($=$) must be handled somewhat differently from the less-than-or-equal-to constraints ($\leq$) in setting up and solving simplex problems.

Recall that with $\leq$ constraints we added a slack variable to convert the inequality to an equality. For example, in converting the inequality $4H + 6C \leq 120$ to an equality, we added S_1, giving us $4H + 6C + S_1 = 120$. Now suppose that the sign was changed to a greater-than-or-equal-to sign yielding $4H + 6C \geq 120$. Initially, one would surmise that subtracting a slack variable would convert this to an equality and it would be written as $4H + 6C - 1S_1 = 120$. Unfortunately, this adjustment would lead to difficulties in the simplex method for the reason that the initial simplex solution starts with fictitious variables and hence a negative value ($-1S_1$) would be in the solution—a condition not permitted in linear programming. To over-come this problem, the simplex procedure requires that a different type of variable—an artificial variable—be added to each equation in which a slack variable is subtracted. An artificial variable may be thought of as represent-ing a fictitious product having a very high cost, which, though permitted in the initial solution to a simplex problem, would never appear in the final solution. Defining A as the artificial variable, the constraint given above would now appear as

$$4H + 6C - 1S_1 + 1A_1 = 120$$

And assuming that we were minimizing cost in the objective function rather than maximizing profit, it would appear as

$$\$2H + \$4C + \$0S_1 + \$MA_1$$

where $\$M$ is assumed to be a very large cost, for example, $1 million.[7] (Note also that S_1 is added to the objective function even though it is negative in the constraint equation.)

An artificial variable must also be included in constraints with equality signs. For example, if $4H + 6C = 120$, this must be changed to $4H + 6C + 1A_1 = 120$ to satisfy the simplex requirement that each constraint equation have a fictitious, nonnegative variable in the initial solution. It would be reflected in the objective function, again as $\$MA_1$, but would have no slack variable accompanying it in the constraint equation.

Procedurally, where such constraints exist, the simplex method starts with artificial variables in the initial solution but otherwise treats them the same as it would real or slack variables.

TRANSPORTATION METHOD

The transportation method is a simplified special case of the simplex method. It gets its name from its application to problems involving trans-porting products from several sources to several destinations.[8] The two common objectives of such problems are (1) minimize the cost of shipping n units to m destinations or (2) maximize the profit of shipping n units to m destinations. There are three general steps in solving transportation prob-lems, and we will discuss each one in the context of a simple example.

Suppose the Puck and Pawn Company has four factories supplying four warehouses and its management wants to determine the minimum-cost shipping schedule for its monthly output of chess sets. Factory supply, warehouse demands, and shipping costs per case of chess sets are as shown in Table S.2.10.

---

[7] When a $\geq$ or $=$ constraint is encountered in a maximization problem, an artificial variable is assumed to have a large negative profit coefficient in the *objective function* to assure that it would not appear in the final solution.

[8] For other applications, see Table S.2.18.

TABLE S.2.10

Data for chess set transportation problem

				Shipping costs per case (in $)			
Factory	*Supply*	*Warehouse*	*Demand*	*To*	*To*	*To*	*To*
				E	*F*	*G*	*H*
				From			
A........ 15		E.......... 10		A	25	35	36	60
B........ 6		F.......... 12		B	55	30	45	38
C........ 14		G.......... 15		C	40	50	26	65
D........ 11		H.......... 9		D	60	40	66	27

Step 1: Set up transportation matrix

The transportation matrix for this example appears in Table S.2.11, where supply availability at each factory is shown in the far right-hand column and the warehouse demands are shown in the bottom row. The unit shipping costs are shown in the small boxes within the cells. It is important at this step to make sure that the total supply availabilities and total demand requirements are equal. In this case they are both the same, 46 units, but quite often there is an excess supply or demand. In such situations, in order for the transportation method to work, a "dummy" warehouse or factory must be added. Procedurally, this entails the insertion of an extra row (for an additional factory) or an extra column (for an additional warehouse). The amount of supply or demand required by the dummy will be equal to the difference between the row and column totals.

For example, the problem below might be restated to indicate a total demand of 36 cases, and therefore a new column would be inserted with a demand of 10 cases to bring the total up to 46 cases. The cost figures in each cell of the dummy row would be set at zero, and therefore any units

TABLE S.2.11

Transportation matrix for chess set problem

To \ From	E	F	G	H	Factory Supply
A	25	35	36	60	15
B	55	30	45	38	6
C	40	50	26	65	14
D	60	40	66	27	11
Destination Requirements	10	12	15	9	46 / 46

"sent" there would not incur a transportation cost. Theoretically, this adjustment is equivalent to the simplex procedure of inserting a slack variable in a constraint inequality to convert it to an equation, and, as in the simplex, the cost of the dummy would be zero in the objective function.

Step 2: Make initial allocations

Initial allocation entails assigning numbers to cells in order to satisfy supply and demand constraints. There are several methods for carrying this out, and we shall describe two: the northwest-corner method and Vogel's approximation method (VAM).

Northwest-corner method of allocation. The northwest-corner method, as the name implies, begins allocation by starting at the northwest corner of the matrix and assigning as much as possible to cells in the first row.[9] The procedure is then repeated for the second row, third row, and so on, until all row and column requirements are met. Table S.2.12 shows a northwest-corner solution. (Cell *A-E* was assigned first, *A-F* second, *B-F* third, etc.)

Inspection of Table S.2.12 indicates some high-cost cells were assigned and some low-cost cells bypassed by using the northwest-corner method. Indeed, this is to be expected since this method ignores costs in favor of following an easily programmable allocation algorithm.[10]

VAM method of allocation. The VAM method, in contrast to the northwest corner method, uses the cost figures as additional information in making an initial allocation, and generally provides an optimum or near optimum initial solution.[11] The procedure in using VAM is as follows.

1. For each row and column, find and list the differences between the two lowest cost cells. (Include the costs associated with any dummy row or column in finding these differences.)
2. Choose the largest difference of a row or column.
3. Assign the maximum possible amount to the lowest cost cell in the selected row or column. By definition, this allocation will satisfy a row or column requirement.[12] If a tie exists in these different figures (or VAM numbers), allocate to the lowest cost cell in any of the tied rows or columns. If the lowest costs are also tied, allocate to one of them arbitrarily.

---

[9] It is important that as many units as possible be assigned to each cell in order to meet the requirements of having no more than $m + n - 1$ filled cells, where $m =$ number of rows and $n =$ number of columns. If more than this number is used, the problem will have excess routes and be difficult to optimize.

[10] For this reason the northwest-corner method is easy to computerize but is generally inefficient for manual calculation.

[11] It has been reported that VAM will yield an optimum solution about 80 percent of the time. (Those instances where it doesn't are typically encountered on examinations.)

[12] When a row *and* a column are satisfied by a single allocation, the problem is degenerate and adjustments must be made to the matrix to evaluate the solutions. These adjustments will be discussed later under "degeneracy."

4. Repeat 1 through 3, eliminating from consideration those rows or columns that have been satisfied, until all supply and demand requirements are met.

VAM will now be applied to the sample problem above, and Table S.2.13 shows the data. Note that rows and columns have been extended to show VAM numbers—that is, the difference between the two lowest cost cells in each row and column. The first allocation, to cell *A-E*, was made on the basis of the VAM number 15, shown in the first added row under column *E*. The VAM numbers were then recalculated, and the second allocation, to cell *C-G*, was made on the basis of VAM number 24 in the second added

TABLE S.2.12

Northwest corner assignment

To / From	E	F	G	H	Factory Supply
A	25 / 10	35 / 5	36	60	15
B	55	30 / 6	45	38	6
C	40	50 / 1	26 / 13	65	14
D	60	40	66 / 2	27 / 9	11
Destination Requirements	10	12	15	9	46 / 46

Total Cost = 10($25) + 5($35) + 6($30) + 1($50) + 13($26) + 2($66)
+ 9($27) = $1,368

column. The third allocation, to cell *D-H*, was made on the basis of VAM number 13 in the third added column. The fourth allocation, to cell *D-F*, was made on the basis of VAM number 26 in the fourth added column. The fifth allocation, to cell *B-F*, was made on the basis of VAM number 15 in the fifth added column. The sixth allocation, to *A-F*, was made on the basis of VAM number 1 in the sixth added column. The final allocation, to cell *A-G*, was made on the basis of inspection; there were no other cells available, and one unit was required to satisfy the remaining supply and demand requirements.

In comparing the two approaches—the northwest-corner method and VAM—we find that VAM yields a lower cost initial solution to the problem. The total cost for the VAM solution is $1,293, which is $75 less than the northwest-corner solution.

Logic of the VAM method. Each VAM number may be thought of as a penalty cost incurred from selecting some cell other than the lowest cost cell for allocation. For example, the VAM number 10 in the first added col-

TABLE S.2.13

VAM assignment of chess set problem

From \ To	E	F	G	H	Factory Supply	VAM Numbers Trial 1	2	3	4	5	6
A	25 / 10	35 / 4	36 / 1	60	15	10	1	1	1	1	(1)
B	55	30 / 6	45	38	6	8	8	8	15	(15)	--
C	40	50	26 / 14	65	14	14	(24)	--	--	--	--
D	60	40 / 2	66	27 / 9	11	13	13	(13)	(26)	--	--
Destination Requirements	10	12	15	9	46 / 46						
VAM Numbers Trial	(15)	5	10	11							
	--	5	10	11							
	--	5	9	11							
	--	5	9	--							
	--	--	--	--							

Total Cost = 10($25) + 4($35) + 1($36) + 6($30) + 14($26) + 2($40) + 9($27) = $1,293

umn may be interpreted as the penalty cost of selecting *A-F* rather than *A-E*. Likewise, VAM number 15 in the first added row represents the penalty cost of selecting *C-E* over *A-E*. The same logic may be applied to selecting the greatest difference (largest VAM number) from the entire matrix as the basis for allocation. That is, if the largest penalty cost is 15 for a column and 13 for a row, $2 is saved by allocating to the lowest cost cell in the column rather than the row.

VAM also may be used in maximization problems. In such cases the VAM numbers would represent the difference between the two highest profit cells in each row or column. The allocation would then be made to the highest profit cell within the row or column with the largest VAM number. Each VAM number may be thought of as profit forgone by not allocating to the highest profit cell.

Step 3: Develop optimum solution

To develop an optimum solution in a transportation problem entails evaluating each unused cell to determine whether a shift into it is advantageous from a total cost standpoint. If it is, the shift is made and the process is repeated. When all cells have been evaluated and appropriate shifts made, the problem is solved.

Stepping stone method of evaluation. One approach to making this evaluation is the stepping stone method. The term *stepping stone* appeared in early descriptions of the method in which unused cells were referred to as "water" and used cells as "stones"—from the analogy of walking on a path of stones half submerged in water. The method will now be applied to the northwest-corner solution to the sample problem, as shown in Table S.2.12.

Step a: Pick any empty cell.

Step b: Identify the closed path leading to the cell. A "closed path" consists of horizontal and vertical lines leading from an empty cell back to itself, turning 90 degrees at each occupied cell in the path.[13] Two closed paths are identified in Table S.2.14. Closed path *a* is required to evaluate empty cell *B-E;* closed path *b* is required to evaluate empty cell *A-H.*

TABLE S.2.14

Stepping stone method—identification of closed paths

From \ To	E	F	G	H	Factory Supply
A	25 10 *a*	35 5 *b*	36	60	15
B	55	30 6	45	38	6
C	40	50 1	26 13	65	14
D	60	40 2	66 9	27	11
Destination Requirements	10	11	15	9 46	46

Step c: Move one unit[14] *into the empty cell from a filled cell at a corner of the closed path and modify the remaining filled cells at the other corners of the closed path to reflect this move.* "Modifying" entails adding to and subtracting from filled cells in such a way that supply and demand constraints are not violated. This requires that one unit always be subtracted in a given row or column for each unit added to that row or column. Thus the following additions and subtractions would be required for path *a*.

Add one unit to *B-E* (the empty cell).

Subtract one unit from *B-F.*

---

[13] If assignments have been made correctly, the matrix will have only one closed path for each empty cell.

[14] More than one unit could be used to test the desirability of a shift. However, since the problem is linear, if it is desirable to shift one unit, it is desirable to shift more than one, and vice versa.

Add one unit to A-F.
Subtract one unit from A-E.

And, for the longer path b,

Add one unit to A-H (the empty cell).
Subtract one unit from D-H.
Add one unit to D-G.
Subtract one unit from C-G.
Add one unit to C-F.
Subtract one unit from A-F.

Step d: Determine desirability of the move. This is easily done by (a) summing the cost values of the cells to which a unit has been added, (b) summing the cost values of the cells from which a unit has been subtracted, and (c) taking the difference between the two sums to determine if there is a cost reduction. If the cost is reduced by making the move, as many units as possible should be shifted out of the evaluated filled cells into the empty cell. If the cost is increased, no move should be made and the empty cell should be crossed out or otherwise marked to show that it has been evaluated. (A large plus sign is typically used to denote a cell that has been evaluated and found undesirable in cost-minimizing problems. A large minus sign is used for this purpose in profit-maximizing problems.) For cell B-E, the pluses and minuses are as follows.

+			−	
$55	(B-E)		$30	(B-F)
35	(A-F)		25	(A-E)
$90			$55	

For cell A-H:

+			−	
$ 60	(A-H)		$27	(D-H)
66	(D-G)		26	(C-G)
50	(C-F)		35	(A-F)
$176			$88	

Thus in both cases it is apparent that no move into either of the empty cells should be made.

Step e: Repeat steps a–d until all empty cells have been evaluated. To illustrate the mechanics of carrying out a move, consider cell D-F and the closed path leading to it, which is a short one: C-F, C-G, and D-G. The pluses and minuses are

+			−	
$40	(D-F)		$ 50	(C-F)
26	(C-G)		66	(D-G)
$66			$116	

Since there is a savings of $50 per unit from shipping via D-F, as many units as possible should be moved into this cell. In this case, however, the maximum amount that can be shifted is one unit—because the maximum amount added to any cell may not exceed the quantity found in the lowest amount cell from which a subtraction is to be made. To do otherwise would violate the supply and demand constraints of the problem. Here we see that the limiting cell is *C-F* since it contains only one unit. The revised matrix, showing the effects of this move and the previous evaluations, is presented in Table S.2.15. Applying the stepping stone method to the remaining unfilled cells and making shifts where indicated[15] yields an optimum solution, which is the same solution as the initial VAM solution.

TABLE S.2.15

Revised transportation matrix

From \ To	E	F	G	H	Factory Supply
A	25 / 10	35 / 5	36	60 / +	15
B	55 / +	30 / 6	45	38	6
C	40	50 / +	26 / 14	65	14
D	60	40 / 1	66 / 1	27 / 9	11
Destination Requirements	10	11	15	9	46 / 46

Total Cost = 10($25) + 5($35) + 6($30) + 14($26) + 1($40)
+ 1($66) + 9($27) = $1,318

Degeneracy. Degeneracy exists in a transportation problem when the number of filled cells is less than the number of rows plus the number of columns minus one (i.e., $m + n - 1$). Degeneracy may be observed during the initial allocation when the first entry in a row or column satisfies *both* the row and column requirements. Degeneracy has no effect on real-world implications of the problems (i.e., a shipping schedule without degeneracy is no better than one with it), but it requires some adjustment in the matrix in order to evaluate the solution achieved. The form of this adjustment involves inserting some value in an empty cell in order that a closed path be developed to evaluate other empty cells. This value may be thought of as an infinitely small amount, having no direct bearing on the cost of the solution.

Procedurally, the value (often denoted by the Greek letter theta, θ) is used in exactly the same manner as a real number except that it may initially be placed in any empty cell, even though row and column require-

---

[15] Actually, only one more shift is required—to cell *A-G*.

ments have been met by real numbers. A degenerate transportation problem showing an optimum minimum cost allocation is presented in Table S.2.16, where we can see that if θ were not assigned to the matrix, it would be impossible to evaluate several cells (including the one where it is added). Once a θ has been inserted into the solution, it will remain there until it is removed by subtraction or until a final solution is reached.

While the choice of where to put a θ is arbitrary, it saves time if it is placed in such a location that it may be used to evaluate as many cells as possible without being shifted. In this regard, the reader should verify that θ is optimally allocated in Table S.2.16.

Alternate optimum solutions. When the evaluation of an empty cell yields the same cost as the existing allocation, an alternate optimum solution exists.[16] In such cases, management is given additional flexibility and is thereby able to invoke nontransportation cost factors in deciding on a final shipping schedule. (A large zero is commonly placed in an empty cell that has been identified as an alternate optimum route.)

TABLE S.2.16

Degenerate transportation problem with theta added

From \ To	W	X	Y	Factory Supply
T	8 / 3	6 / 8	4 / θ	11
U	9 /	8 /	0 / 9	9
V	5 / 3	3 /	10 / 3	3
Destination Requirements	6	8	9	23 / 23

$m + n - 1 = 5$ Filled Cells

Actual Allocation = 4 Filled Cells

ASSIGNMENT METHOD

The assignment method is described in detail in Chapter 7, so we will treat it only briefly here. This special form of linear programming is applied to situations where there are n supply sources and n demand uses (e.g., five jobs on five machines) and the objective is to minimize or maximize some measure of effectiveness. Assignment problems are quite similar to transportation problems, but the fact that each allocation in an assignment problem simultaneously satisfies a row and column requirement makes all such problems multidegenerate. The transportation problem specified in Table S.2.11 can be translated into an assignment problem if we specify that each factory must ship *all* of its supply to one and only one

---

[16] Assuming that all other cells are optimally assigned.

warehouse. This adjustment, of course, eliminates a major part of the problem, but on rare occasions where row and column requirements are identical, the assignment method can be employed to save computation time.

Table S.2.17 illustrates how the transportation problem would appear if it were cast as an assignment problem. Here the cell entries are the transportation costs, with those circled indicating the optimum assignments as determined by the simple algorithm described in Chapter 7. The fact that minimum cost values fall on a diagonal is coincidental. Note also that the structure of the assignment problem precludes having more than one assignment in a row or column.

TABLE S.2.17

Assignment matrix for modified transportation problem

From \ To	E	F	G	H
A	($25)	$35	$36	$60
B	$55	($30)	$45	$38
C	$40	$50	($26)	$65
D	$60	$40	$66	($27)

Typical operations management applications of linear programming

Table S.2.18 summarizes some typical production management applications of linear programming according to the particular technique by which the application is usually carried out. Because of space limitations, the table provides but a cursory statement of only a few of the many applications of linear programming to production management. (Other applications, along with detailed discussions of the applications listed, are presented in the Metzger and Naylor et al. references at the end of this supplement.)

Again, the simplex method can be applied to any of the situations presented in the table; however, it is generally more expedient to employ the transportation or the assignment method if the problem lends itself to these forms.

CONCLUSION

This supplement has dealt mainly with the mechanics of solution procedures for linear programming problems. In practice, however, formulating the objective function and constraints is the usual stumbling block in using linear programming methods, and certainly a supplement of equal length could be written on how to abstract data from a real-world situation and translate it into a form suitable for linear programming. In addition, there

TABLE S.2.18

Typical production management applications of linear programming*

*Simplex** -*

Aggregate production planning: Finding the minimum cost production schedule, including rate change costs, given constraints on size of work force and inventory levels

Product planning: Finding the optimum product mix where several products have different costs and resource requirements (e.g., finding the optimum blend of constituents for gasolines, paints, human diets, animal feeds)

Product routing: Finding the optimum routing for a product that must be processed sequentially through several machine centers, with each machine in a center having its own cost and output characteristics

Process control: Minimizing the amount of scrap material generated by cutting steel, leather, or fabric from a roll or sheet of stock material

Inventory control: Finding the optimum combination of products to stock in a warehouse or store

Transportation

Aggregate production planning: Finding the minimum cost production schedule, taking into account inventory carrying costs, overtime costs, and subcontracting costs

Distribution scheduling: Finding the optimum shipping schedule for distributing products between factories and warehouses or warehouses and retailers

Plant location studies: Finding the optimum location of a new plant by evaluating shipping costs between alternative locations and supply and demand sources

Materials handling: Finding the minimum cost routings of material handling devices (e.g., forklift trucks) between departments in a plant and of hauling materials from a supply yard to work sites by trucks, with each truck having different capacity and performance capabilities

Assignment

Scheduling: Minimum cost assignment of trucks to pickup points and ships to berths

Worker assignments: Minimum cost assignment of men to machines and to jobs

* The graphical method is not included since it may be applied in the same situations as simplex if the problem has fewer than three variables.

has been a great deal of development in variants of linear programming that overcome some of the inherent limitations of the simplex model. A particularly noteworthy innovation is *goal programming*, which is capable of solving linear programming type problems having multiple goals (e.g., profit, quality, and satisfaction). See the Lee and Moore bibliographical reference for an introduction to the methodology. Also of note is the remarkable development in linear programming computer programs that, in addition to solving large problems, provide a variety of collateral information for sensitivity analysis.[17] IBM's Mathematical Programming System and Honeywell's Linear Programming System are two such programs.

REVIEW AND DISCUSSION QUESTIONS

1. What structural requirements of a problem are needed in order to solve it by linear programming?
2. What type of information is provided in a solved simplex tableau?
3. What type of information is provided by shadow prices?
4. What are slack variables? Why are they necessary in the simplex method? When are they used in the transportation method?
5. It has been stated in this supplement that an optimum solution for a simplex problem always lies at a corner point. Under what conditions might an equally desirable solution be found anywhere along a constraint line?
6. What is a convex polygon? How is it identified?
7. How do you know if a transportation problem is degenerate? What must be done if a degenerate problem is to be tested for optimality?
8. What is the basic rationale of the VAM method? How does the relative magnitude of cost or profit values in a transportation problem affect the effectiveness of the VAM method?
9. Why is an assignment problem multidegenerate?

PROBLEMS

1. Product A yields a $2 profit per unit and product B yields a $1.50 profit per unit. The production constraints for the two units are as follows.

$$3A + 10B \le 1500$$
$$A + 2B \le 400$$
$$A \le 300$$

Find the optimum combination of products A and B using the graphical method.

---

[17] Sensitivity analysis refers to making changes in problem parameters (e.g., introducing different costs and different profits) and observing the effects of such changes on the optimal solution. This type of anlaysis is also termed *parametric programming* or *postoptimality analysis*.

2. Women's Lib Inc. makes two kinds of novelty hardhats—a Bella hat and a Gloria hat. A Bella hat costs $10 and a Gloria hat costs $12. To keep as many women employed as possible, it has been determined that at least 200 woman-hours per week be spent molding hats, 300 in painting hats, and 2,000 in packing hats. Both styles of hat require one hour each to mold; Bella hats take two hours to paint and Gloria hats take one hour to paint; and Bella hats take five hours to pack while Gloria hats take 12 hours. Find the minimum cost combination of hats per week using the graphical method.

3. Machismo Manufacturing makes a line of male toiletries, including Strength after-shave lotion and No Sweat deodorant. One bottle of Strength contributes $2 to profit and one can of No Sweat contributes $1.25. Each bottle of Strength uses 1 ounce of alcohol and 2 ounces of kumquat juice. Each can of No Sweat uses 1 ounce of "Essence of Repel," 1 ounce of Z-22 bacteria fighter, and 1 ounce of kumquat juice. The supply of each material available for the next batch of the end products is as follows: 70 ounces of alcohol, 100 ounces of Z-22, and 200 ounces of kumquat juice. There is an excess amount of Essence of Repel in inventory, so it has been decided that at least 40 ounces of this material must be used. Use the graphical method to find the optimum combination of the two products to be blended.

4. Logan Manufacturing wants to mix two fuels (A and B) for its trucks in order to minimize cost. It needs no less than 3,000 gallons in order to run its trucks during the next month. It has a maximum fuel storage capacity of 4,000 gallons. There are 2,000 gallons of fuel A and 4,000 gallons of fuel B available. The mixed fuel must have an octane rating of no less than 80.

   When mixing fuels, the amount of fuel obtained is just equal to the sum of the amounts put in. The octane rating is the weighted average of the individual octanes, weighted in proportion to the respective volumes.

   The following is known: Fuel A has an octane of 90 and costs 20¢ per gallon; Fuel B has an octane of 75 and costs $13\frac{1}{3}$¢ per gallon.
   a) Write out the equations expressing the above information.
   b) Solve the problem graphically, giving the amount of each fuel to be used. State any assumptions necessary to solve the problem.

5. A diet is being prepared for the University of Arizona dorms. The objective is to feed the students at the least possible cost, but the diet must have between 1,800 and 3,600 calories. No more than 1,400 calories can be starch and no less than 400 can be protein. The varied diet is to be made of two foods, A and B. Food A costs $0.75 per pound and contains 600 calories, 400 of which are protein and 200 starch. No more than 2 pounds of food A can be used per resident. Food B costs $0.15 per pound and contains 900 calories, of which 700 are starch, 100 are protein, and 100 are fat.
   a) Write out the equations representing the above information.
   b) Solve the problem graphically for the amounts of each food which should be used. (Note: This problem has a redundant constraint.)

6. Solve Problem 1 by using the simplex method.

7. The manager of the Novelty Division of Women's Lib Inc. must decide how many of each of two stuffed dolls—Tarzans and Janes—he should schedule for the coming month. Demand for both dolls is high; sales are limited only by his capacity to produce.

   The covers for both dolls are produced by the same cutting and sewing machine, which has a capacity of 4 dolls per minute (either model). Janes require longer to stuff than Tarzans; the stuffing line can complete 3 Janes or 5 Tarzans per minute. (Only one model type can be stuffed at a time, although the line can easily be switched to stuff the other type.) Tarzans are talking dolls, and voice boxes may be inserted at the rate of 3 per minute. Net profit is $2 per Tarzan and $1.50 per Jane.

a. At what production rate in dolls per minute should the manager schedule each of the two dolls to maximize profits?

b. What is the value (in dollar profit per eight-hour day) of this schedule?

c. The manager can work the voice box line overtime for a net cost of $2 per minute. Should he do it?

    (1) If yes, how much overtime should he schedule per eight-hour day (assuming no changes in other capacities)? How much would net profit per day increase?

    (2) If no, at what overtime cost rate would he be indifferent to expanding the voice box capacity? If overtime could be obtained for just under this rate, how much overtime should he schedule per eight-hour day (assuming no changes in other capacities)?

d. What should he be willing to pay for additional capacity on the stuffing line?

8. Women's Lib Inc. produces Repel perfume at its plants in Albuquerque and Chicago. Small vials of Repel sell for $0.40 apiece in the midwest and southwest (serviced by warehouses in Evanston, Ill., and Fort Worth respectively) and for $0.45 apiece in the Rocky Mountain area (which is served by a warehouse in Denver). Transportation costs per vial are as follows:

		Transportation cost to	
From	*Denver*	*Evanston*	*Fort Worth*
Albuquerque..........	$0.06	$0.08	$0.05
Chicago..............	0.10	0.03	0.10

Production and demand information is as follows:

Plant	*Monthly capacity*	*Unit production cost*	*Warehouse*	*Monthly demand*
A (lbuquerque).......	1,700	$0.33	D (enver)...........	800
C (hicago)..........	1,800	0.30	E (vanston)........	1,200
			F (ort Worth).......	1,000

a. What is the function to be optimized? (Write the equation in symbolic form.) For example, let x_{ij} be the number of vials shipped from the *i*th plant to the *j*th warehouse in 1 month. Define all other necessary variables in the same manner, using *A* and *C* for the plant subscripts and *D*, *E*, and *F* for the warehouses. Thus x_{AE} is the number of vials shipped from Albuquerque to Evanston.

b. Is this function to be maximized or minimized?

c. Write the equations that place all known restrictions upon values that can be assumed by the variables in the question you developed in (*a*) above.

d. Set up the transportation matrix that you would use to determine the optimum production-shipment schedule for vials. Find the optimum solution.

9. Maximize the following two transportation problems.

A.

From \ To	D	E	F	Supply
A	4	6	4	11
B	9	8	5	9
C	5	3	10	3
Demand	6	8	9	23 / 23

B.

From \ To	D	E	F	G	H	Supply
A	1	4	10	4	10	52
B	8	2	8	2	1	20
C	10	1	8	8	2	20
Demand	16	22	4	19	31	92 / 92

10. Minimize the following three transportation problems.

A.

To From	W	X	Y	Supply
A	8	15	3	15
B	5	10	9	7
C	6	12	10	6
Demand	12	8	8	28 / 28

B.

To From	D	E	F	Supply
A	4	6	2	100
B	8	7	10	70
C	6	1	4	80
Demand	40	90	120	250 / 250

C.

To From	E	F	G	H	Dummy	Supply
A	44	50	48	49	0	70
B	45	50	48	51	0	30
C	45	51	50	51	0	180
D	48	54	50	52	0	110
Demand	90	40	75	100	85	390 / 390

11. Use the graphical method to solve the following problem:

$$\text{Maximize } Z = 4x + 3y$$

subject to

$$2x + 3y \leq 6$$
$$2x + y \leq 4$$
$$-3x + 2y \leq 3$$

(Note that the problem requires graphing of a negative intercept.)

SELECTED BIBLIOGRAPHY

Lee, Sang M., and Moore, Laurence J.   *Introduction to Decision Science.* New York: Petrocelli/Charter, 1975.

Metzger, Robert W.   *Elementary Mathematical Programming.* New York: John Wiley & Sons, 1965.

Naylor, Thomas H., Byrne, Eugene T., and Vernon, John R.   *Introduction to Linear Programming: Methods and Cases.* San Francisco: Wadsworth Publishing Co., 1971.

Plane, Donald R., and Kochenberger, Gary A.   *Operations Research for Managerial Decisions.* Homewood, Ill.: Richard D. Irwin, Inc., 1972.

Thompson, Gerald L.   *Linear Programming.* New York: Macmillan, 1971.

Section two

Design of the
system

3

Product design
and process selection

T his chapter considers the related topics of product design and the selection of production processes. Product design draws heavily on inputs from the marketing function and several branches of engineering[1] (in the case of a physical product), as well as the production function. During the design phase the die is cast for the production system since it is here that the product is completely specified. If the design is poor from a production standpoint, it may entail costly adjustments to the production process in terms of equipment, material, and manpower. If the design is good, production costs may be low enough to substantially enhance a firm's profit and market position. The key role of good product design is rapidly becoming evident, and firms no longer can rely solely on special processes to gain a clear-cut advantage over competitors since other firms have access to the same technology. Firms preeminent in competitive markets tend to exploit details of design that shave pennies from production cost or develop product features that allow it to appeal to a wider market.

Process selection—choosing the methods by which raw material inputs are transformed into product outputs—likewise has its impact on the production system and on the firm's success. In manufacturing and process industries, the selection of capital equipment is a major economic decision which must weigh and balance the expected growth in demand, new developments in technology, and even psychosocial factors. In service industries and other labor-intensive industries where the main productive agents are people, the emphasis in process selection shifts to the study of procedures. A number of service systems, however, are often more reliant than manufacturing industries on the proper choice of equipment. Automatic car washes, airlines, and laundries are a few of the service industries almost totally dependent on the choice of the right equipment for survival.

In addition to the processes that are directly concerned with production (in both manufacturing and service industries), the selection of supporting processes may also affect the firm's viability. Of these supporting processes, perhaps the most ubiquitous is data processing, which ultimately requires the purchase or rental of a computer. Selecting a computer is almost always fraught with uneasiness, not only because the item is costly but because its selection and operation demand a set of skills different from those indigenous to most organizations. A successful firm generally knows what it can and cannot do with respect to its primary technology: a steel company knows how to fabricate steel, a finance company knows how to lend and invest funds, but only a computer manufacturer can be expected to know the ins and outs of this sophisticated product. Thus, although emphasis in this chapter will be on the selection of a process for direct production of an organization's product, it should be recognized that equipment employed in support activities, such as information handling, presents challenges in process selection, and in some cases warrants as much study.

---

[1] Branches of engineering typically represented in manufacturing product design (and process selection) are design engineering, plant engineering, manufacturing engineering, (tool engineering, and process engineering), industrial engineering, and metallurgical engineering.

PRODUCT DESIGN

From the production manager's point of view, the key output of the product design activity is the product's specifications. These specifications provide the basis for a host of decisions he must make, including the purchase of materials, selection of equipment, assignments of workers, and often even the size and layout of the productive facility.

Product specifications, while commonly thought of as blueprints or engineering drawings, may take a variety of other forms, ranging from highly precise quantitative statements to rather fluid guidelines. A sampling of specifications along a continuum ranging from the exact to the general is provided in Figure 3.1.

FIGURE 3.1

Specification continuum

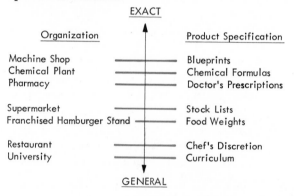

The product design process is depicted in flowchart form in Figure 3.2. At the outset, it should be understood that this is an idealized case, synthesized from a number of approaches to *product design.*[2] It should also be mentioned that product design and development rarely follow the discrete sequence suggested by the diagram. Typically, there are frequent loops to prior steps, and certain activities are often performed concurrently. Further, the extent to which these phases are formalized and specified varies from industry to industry. Generally, firms which require a good deal of research and tooling, or lean heavily on innovation to compete in the marketplace, adhere to a more formalized program than those that do not. These issues appear in the ensuing section, which discusses some of the activities listed in Figure 3.2.

Product selection

In the discussion of product selection in Chapter 2 it was noted that the product definition derived from the selection process varies in completeness

---

[2] Defined later in this chapter; see also Asimow, Uman, and Wallenstein bibliographical references.

FIGURE 3.2

Product design and development sequence

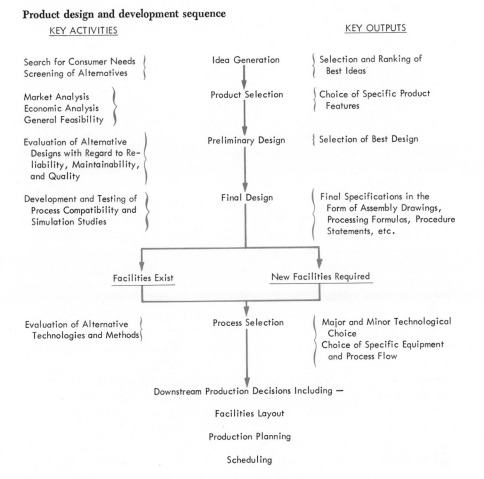

KEY ACTIVITIES

KEY OUTPUTS

Search for Consumer Needs
Screening of Alternatives

Idea Generation

Selection and Ranking of
Best Ideas

Market Analysis
Economic Analysis
General Feasibility

Product Selection

Choice of Specific Product
Features

Evaluation of Alternative
Designs with Regard to Reliability, Maintainability,
and Quality

Preliminary Design

Selection of Best Design

Development and Testing of
Process Compatibility and
Simulation Studies

Final Design

Final Specifications in the
Form of Assembly Drawings,
Processing Formulas, Procedure
Statements, etc.

Facilities Exist

New Facilities Required

Evaluation of Alternative
Technologies and Methods

Process Selection

Major and Minor Technological
Choice
Choice of Specific Equipment
and Process Flow

Downstream Production Decisions Including —

Facilities Layout

Production Planning

Scheduling

and is often intertwined with the product design decision. For a steel producer, for example, the decision to add a new alloy would constitute both the product decision and the product design. On the other hand, it is probably more typical for the product selection phase to yield just the "bare bones" of the final product. A refrigerator manufacturer may decide that it is profitable to branch out into home freezers, or a cigar manufacturer may decide to add a panatela to his line. In both instances, however, this decision would not require a detailed investigation of design factors at the selection phase since these companies presumably have mastered the general skills required to produce these products.

Preliminary design

Whether or not it is a separate phase in the sequence of design activities, preliminary design is usually devoted to developing several alternative designs that meet the conceptual features of the selected product. If the refrigerator manufacturer decides that he will produce freezers, questions of style, storage capacity, size of motor, etc., will likely be encountered here. During preliminary design it also is common to specify the key product attributes of reliability, maintainability, and service life.

Final design

During the final design phase, prototypes are developed and "bugs" are worked out of the design so that the product is sound from an engineering standpoint. Thus ultimate output of the final design includes the complete specification of the product, its components, and, in the case of a manufactured item, the assembly drawings, which provide the basis for its full-scale production. Again, the degree of design specificity varies according to the type of product being considered. To produce an automobile requires precise quantitative statements regarding the tensile strength of steel for the chassis, tolerances for the engine components, the composition and thickness of brake lining, and so on. In contrast, the final design of treatment given a hospital patient would be unspecified since the exact nature of medical care must of necessity be determined during the "production" (i.e., treatment) stage.

At this point, too, the effectiveness of alternative designs must be balanced with cost considerations, and—inevitably—compromises must be made. This is especially true in selecting the configuration and material for manufactured items. The complexity of this tradeoff can be seen when we consider that even such a relatively unsophisticated product as a home freezer has roughly 500 components, each of which could conceivably be subjected to an alternative cost analysis. Typical considerations that must enter the analysis are component *compatibility* and *simplification*.

"Compatibility" refers to the fitting together and proper articulation of parts during operation. Problems of compatibility arise not only with parts that must mesh, such as freezer door latches, but also with parts that must respond similarly to conditions of stress. Drawbridge components must of course fit together, but they must also have similar tensile strength so as to accommodate high winds and similar expansion coefficients so as to adjust equally to variations in heat and cold. "Simplification" refers to the exclusion of those features that raise production costs. Problems of simplification arise mainly in manufacturing, where such seemingly innocuous requirements as rounded edges or nonstandard hole sizes may create production bottlenecks and subsequent repair problems when the item is in use. Where the product is a service, simplification arises in regard to such things as form design (employment agencies) or customer routings (baggage pickup at an airline terminal).

In addition to the above activities, which are more or less universal, some organizations engage in rather formalized product testing programs and redesign activities during the final design stage. Product testing may take the form of test marketing in the case of consumer products or test firing of a weapons system in the case of the military. In both instances a good deal of planning would necessarily precede the tests. Product redesign generally takes place after the prototype has been tested, and may be major or minor in scope. If the redesign is major, the product may be recycled through the preliminary design phase; if the change is minor, the product will probably be carried through to production. It should be noted, however, that there are "minor changes *and* minor changes"; in some instances an apparently slight modification to some component may greatly alter the integrity of the entire product.

Computer-assisted design

One recent development in product design is the use of a man and a computer as a team in generating design concepts. This approach, termed *computer-assisted design* (CAD), enables design engineers to rough out a particular product configuration and receive immediate feedback on its specification, ability to meet operating constraints, and desirability relative to other configurations. Procedurally, the technique entails the engineer's drawing designs with a "light pen" on a computer-controlled cathode-ray screen and the computer's interpreting these drawings through a previously entered computer program. After the program is executed, the computer displays a simple drawing, which the engineer may then enlarge or view from any angle. If he wishes, the designer may directly modify the drawing by adding or deleting lines, changing statement parameters, or entering alternative statements. If the display is acceptable, he can direct the computer to produce a permanent copy of the drawing, using what is termed an image processer. After the design work is completed, the engineer may instruct the computer to produce control tapes for automatic drafting machines or machine tools.

CAD has been applied in design problems involving aircraft, automobiles, ships, transformers, and electronic circuitry. While at present the expense of both hardware and software generally limits CAD to large firms, it seems likely that CAD, after developmental costs have been absorbed and sharing large computers becomes less costly, will become feasible for many small companies as well.

Maintainability and reliability

"Maintainability" refers to the ability of the user to keep the product or system in operating condition with a reasonable amount of effort. This ability to maintain operation may entail the availability of some required service from the manufacturer or authorized repair facility, provision of a stock of replacement parts available to the user, and written maintenance and repair procedures. Good product design for maintainability usually implies ease of product disassembly and ease of access to areas within the product to facilitate routine service or replacement. Switches, valves, motors with brushes, oil fills, etc., should be located for ready access, with removable covers placed at convenient locations. The alternative to providing maintainability is to "overdesign"; that is, to use much better parts than normally are required for the function. This approach reduces the need for repair but raises production costs.

Maintainability considerations, to the consumer's chagrin, often come after the fact. Although good product planning dictates that maintainability be considered at the design stage, it is frequently built into subsequent models of the product in response to consumer complaints. Clearly, this procedure may also have an adverse effect on production because it may entail retooling, added inspection, and other changes to remedy maintainability faults.

"Reliability" may be defined as the probability, or degree of confidence, that a product will perform a specified number of times *under prescribed conditions*. For example, the reliability of an electrical relay may be defined as 0.9999 (i.e., one failure every 10,000 trials), but this may hold true only if it is operated with an input voltage of 24 volts DC, in an environmental temperature range of 0 to 80 degrees C., with humidity less than 90 percent, if its housing has never been opened, if it has been operated less than 1 million times, and if it is less than five years old.

When parts are interdependent, and especially when there is a large number of them, achieving a high degree of reliability for a product presents a real challenge. Consider the following notion from basic statistics. When the desired outcome of an operation depends on the specific occurrence of a series of statistically independent elements, the probability of success of the outcome is the product of the probabilities of the independent elements. Thus if two relays must operate in order for an action to occur, and if each relay has a probability (or reliability) of 90 percent, the probability of success is 0.90×0.90, or 81 percent.

Now consider this in the context of a much larger system with far more parts—say a manned space flight. Assume that 10 million "parts" are involved (control tower, launch vehicle, capsule, tracking stations, environmental support, human performance, etc.) and—for simplicity in this example—that the performance of each part is statistically independent. The average reliability, x, required for each of the 10 million parts for 90 percent success (a 90 percent chance that the astronauts will complete their mission and return) is that for which $x^{10,000,000} = 0.90$, or $x = 0.99999999$. This calculation is based on the assumption that each part is operated only *once*. Now suppose that, on the average, each part operates 100 times, so that the reliability of each part must be increased to 0.99999999996.

Because most components cannot be built to achieve such high reliability and because some parts may nevertheless be critical to the functioning of the system, a common design strategy is to build in *redundancy*. Such redundancy may take the form of duplicate components, such as additional fuel tanks and power units, or in the form of alternative methods, such as manual overrides for automatic control devices.

Figure 3.3 shows the reliability of the system for various numbers of component parts for a single operation. For multiple operation, reliability would be calculated as P^n, where P is the probability of a single operation

FIGURE 3.3

Reliability chart for a hypothetical missile system

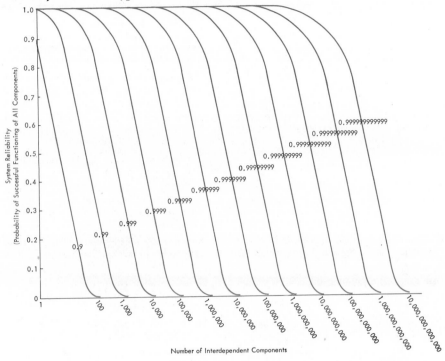

and *n* is the number of repetitions. (This assumes no change in part reliability due to repeated operation of the system.)

Despite the fact that some systems can be built to the statistically required reliability, many designers favor even higher reliability as a safety
margin. A traditional gibe at engineers, especially structural engineers, is
that they spend a great deal of time meticulously computing stress for
bridges to four decimal places and then, for safety purposes, multiply their
final specifications by a factor of four! (In fairness, however, it should be
mentioned that this practice is frequently required by law or construction
codes.)

Modular design

It is rare to find a firm that produces only a single type of product.
In the United States especially, competition is so keen and the market
so segmented that most manufacturers produce a variety of products. This
of course affects the product design function, and therefore it is not surprising that production management is interested in finding ways in which
combination products can be designed and produced with minimum cost.
An approach to this problem, which is receiving much interest, is *modular
design*. The essence of this approach is to develop a number of standard

TABLE 3.1

Advantages and disadvantages of standard subassemblies

Advantages	*Example*
Fewer types of standard designs must be inventoried in any one market.	Programming packages often contain several subroutines that can be combined to form a multitude of programs.
	Storage space for a few subroutines is much smaller than space for storing several complete programs.
Fewer types of standard parts provide tighter quality control and standard testing procedures.	Producing bigger quantities of the same circuit board means that standard testing procedures can be created.
	The costs of developing these procedures are spread over a greater number of boards.
Repair is simplified by ease of replacement.	Repairmen need carry only a few types of standard modules to quickly repair appliances.
Cannibalization (the use of parts from one application to repair a second) is simplified.	Standard modules removed from an unrepairable aircraft can be used to repair a radar van.
Additions to a product line can be simplified.	New-generation computers can be manufactured from standard subassemblies already designed and tested.
Adaptation to market segments is simplified.	Use of options can alter an automobile's market segment.

Disadvantages	*Example*
More parts than required are used.	Excess nuts and bolts in an assembly kit are thrown away.
Excess parts increase cost of transportation and handling.	Nuts and bolts which are not necessary are packaged and shipped at some cost.
Interconnection of modules may be difficult.	"Backboard wiring" of modules in a computer is time consuming and costly in terms of reliability.

Source: Timothy L. Shaftel, "How Modular Design Reduces Production Costs," *Arizona Review,* vol. 21, nos. 6–7 (June–July 1972), p. 4.

designs or modules consisting of various parts or subassemblies that can be used over a wide range of product designs. (Some sample applications are given in Table 3.1.) From an analytical standpoint, the "modular design problem" consists of finding how many of each part or subassembly are to be included in each module and how many of each module are to be used in each application. The objective is to find the product design that minimizes the costs of production, inventory, consumer disutility, repair, and maintenance.[3]

[3] For a discussion of the mathematical complexities and models used in finding the optimum size and number of modules, see David P. Rutenberg and Timothy L. Shaftel, "Product Design: Subassemblies for Multiple Markets," *Management Science,* vol. 18, no. 4 (December 1971), pp. B220–31, and Martin K. Starr, "Modular Production—A New Concept, *Harvard Business Review* (November–December 1965), pp. 131–42.

PROCESS SELECTION

Technological decisions in process selection

Process selection may be thought of as a series of decisions encompassing the theoretical feasibility of making the product, the general nature of the processing system, the specific equipment to be employed, and the specific routing through which the product must flow. These decisions—major technological choice, minor technological choice, specific component choice, and specific process flow choice—are summarized in Table 3.2.

Major technological choice. The basic issue is: Can the product be made—Does the technology exist for producing the product under consideration? This question has little to do with economic feasibility; it deals only with natural laws of science, and the question must be answered, even if only in probabilistic terms, before an organization can select a product. And it must be answered *conclusively* before it enters into production.

TABLE 3.2

Technological decisions in process selection

General-process decision	*Decision problem*	*Decision variables*	*Decision aids*
Major technological choice	Transformation potential	Product choice Laws of physics, chemistry, etc. State of scientific knowledge	Technical specialists
Minor technological choice	Selecting among alternative transformation processes	State of the art in equipment and techniques Environmental factors such as ecological and legal constraints Primary task of organization General financial and market strength	R&D reports Technical specialists Organizational objectives Long-run market forecasts Mathematical programs Simulation
Specific component choice	Selecting specific equipment	Existing facilities Cost of equipment alternatives Desired output level	Industry reports Investment analysis, including make-or-buy, break-even, and present-value methods Medium-range forecasts
Process flow choice	Selecting production routings	Existing layout Homogeneity of products Equipment characteristics	Product specifications Assembly charts Route sheets Flow process charts Equipment manuals Engineering handbooks

Because technological sophistication is increasing so rapidly, this issue is of more than academic interest. Indeed, the amount of current research underscores the importance of making this determination, and stories abound of the success of companies that made breakthroughs in technology amid cries that it couldn't be done. Still, it is often a long road from possibility to feasibility. Iron *can* be made into gold, water *can* be obtained from rock, and man *can* walk on Mars; but going into the *business* of doing these things would be less than profitable. Certainly, in the more exotic industries the production manager is pretty much dependent on technical specialists, and he must wait in the wings until the minor technological choice is made.

Minor technological choice. The complexity of minor technological choice can best be understood by considering the alternative processes for fabricating, joining, and finishing two pieces of metal. According to Table 3.3, there are 11 possible casting and molding processes, 8 cutting processes,

TABLE 3.3

Basic processes in manufacture of hardware

Casting and molding	Cutting	Forming	Assembly	Finishing
Sand casting	Turning	Forging	Soldering	Cleaning
Shell casting	Drilling	Extrusion	Brazing	Blasting
Investment casting	Milling	Punching	Welding	Deburring
Die casting	Shaping	Trimming	Mechanical	Painting
Permanent mold	Cutoff	Drawing	fastening	Plating
casting	Broaching	Rolling	Cementing	Heat
Powdered metal	Grinding	Forming	Press fitting	treatment
molding	Honing	Coining	Shrink fitting	Buffing
Compression molding		Swaging		Polishing
Transfer		Spinning		
Extrusion				
Injection molding				
Laminating				

Source: Donald F. Eary and Gerald E. Johnson, *Process Engineering for Manufacturing,* © 1962, Prentice-Hall, Inc. Reprinted by permission of the publisher.

10 forming processes, 7 assembly processes, and 8 finishing processes, or 44 processes in all. To evaluate all possible five-stage sequences would involve $(5) \times (11 \times 8 \times 10 \times 7 \times 8)$, or 246,400 decisions (assuming that the selection of a process in one stage does not eliminate a process in another)—clearly a large undertaking if we seek an optimum combination. In practice, of course, the assumption of no process dependence would be violated since some processes would not be performed on the same piece of metal—sand casting *and* forging, for example. Also, expert judgment, built upon technical training, substantially reduces the number of reasonable alternatives. Still, it can pose a tough problem, which can be more complex if the metals themselves become decision variables. Similar problems of choice arise in many manufacturing situations.

An example of where these processes are used in the manufacture of automobile engines, contrasted with the basic processes in the "manufacture" of a McDonald's-type hamburger, is given in Figure 3.4.

FIGURE 3.4

Automobile engine and fast food hamburger manufacturing stages and processes

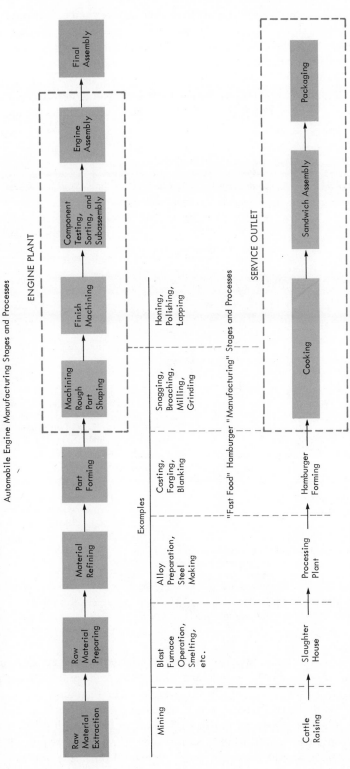

Automobile Engine Manufacturing Stages and Processes

ENGINE PLANT

| Raw Material Extraction | Raw Material Preparing | Material Refining | Part Forming | Machining Rough Part Shaping | Finish Machining | Component Testing, Sorting, and Subassembly | Engine Assembly | Final Assembly |

Examples

| Mining | Blast Furnace Operation, Smelting, etc. | Alloy Preparation, Steel Making | Casting, Forging, Blanking | Snagging, Broaching, Milling, Grinding | Honing, Polishing, Lapping |

"Fast Food" Hamburger "Manufacturing" Stages and Processes

SERVICE OUTLET

| Cattle Raising | Slaughter House | Processing Plant | Hamburger Forming | Cooking | Sandwich Assembly | Packaging |

Source of top part of figure: William J. Abernathy, *The Productivity Dilemma—Roadblocks to Innovation in the Automobile Industry*, in press.

While it is apparent that the minor technological choice decision requires technical specialists, it is also important that production, marketing, and general management provide guidance in the form of long-run market objectives and forecasts since these factors ultimately constrain the sophistication of the equipment selected. Indeed, the choice between an automated and a nonautomated factory or a specialized versus a generalized refinery is a policy issue that extends far beyond the realm of engineering feasibility.

TABLE 3.4

General versus special-purpose equipment choices

Decision variables	General-purpose equipment	Special-purpose equipment
Initial investment	Lower due to more suppliers and availability of used models	
Output rate		Higher due to less handling and rapid loading; not necessarily due to faster running speeds
Direct labor		Lower, but indirect may be higher
Flexibility	By definition they have a broader range of application	
Setup time	Less; problems are more predictable	
Maintenance	Less complex equipment requires less skill in repair; greater availability of parts	
Product quality		Greater consistency due to reduced relocation from one piece of equipment to another
Obsolescence	Less affected because of easier modification and easier use in other situations	
In-process inventory		Few breaks in production sequence and therefore less opportunity for inventory buildup
Amount of equipment required	Greater variety of operations can be performed on each piece of equipment, so redundant units are less likely to be required	
Operator skill requirements	Depends on equipment operation, monitoring, and setup	

Firms may have both general-purpose equipment and special-purpose equipment. For example, a machine shop would have lathes and drill presses (general-purpose) and could have transfer machines (special-purpose). A hospital would have a spectrophotometer to perform only one blood test at a time (general-purpose) and may have a multiphasic screening unit to perform multiple tests at the same time (special-purpose). An auto repair shop would have test gauges (general-purpose) and may have a diagnostic center (special-purpose). Some factors that enter into the choice between generalized and specialized equipment are summarized in Table 3.4.

One tool that is often employed to yield data of both a technical and an economic nature is computer simulation. This approach allows the process engineering personnel to test the functioning of different systems while simultaneously obtaining cost data that are useful to the other areas of the firm.[4]

TABLE 3.5

Make, buy, or lease decisions

Make or buy

Quantitative	*Qualitative*
Opportunity costs: May be defined as the monetary value sacrificed in rejecting an alternative. Facilities utilized in manufacturing a part or component are, in effect, sacrificed for any other use. The decision to make or buy often boils down to an attempt to optimize the utilization of facilities.	Product quality: Parts may be made in an attempt to control the overall quality of an end product even though it may be more economical to buy the parts.
Incremental costs: Only those costs that vary with the decision to make or buy are generally considered relevant. Other costs, sometimes called "wash costs," remain constant regardless of the decision and therefore need not be considered in the cost comparison.	Patents: Legal restrictions may prevent a company from making certain parts. Skills and materials: Required skills may be very technical or materials very rare, thereby precluding in-house manufacture of certain parts or components.
Idle facilities: Availability of idle facilities bears directly on the make or buy decision, particularly with regard to determining the incremental costs involved. If sufficient facilities are available, only variable costs— i.e., those costs that vary with volume—must be considered. Otherwise the cost of making the part or component should include any expenditures necessary to obtain the required facilities.	Long-term considerations: It may be more profitable in the short run, for example during slow periods, to utilize idle facilities by manufacturing more parts in house. However, this may result in poor relations with suppliers, or even in nonavailability of parts from outside sources during prosperous times when facilities could be used more profitably in other ways. Other factors: Factors of an intangible nature that may influence the make or buy decision are number of outside suppliers, flexibility, seasonal demands, and reliability of outside sources.

Leasing

Opportunity costs play a significant role in most decisions to lease equipment or other assets. If a company can earn a higher rate of return on its capital than that required by a leasing firm, it would probably be wise to lease and avoid tieing up capital equipment or assets. Some companies lease when it would seem to be more feasible, on purely economic grounds, to buy. However, this may be done to avoid the responsibilities of ownership, such as maintenance or obsolescence. This has been particularly true in decisions involving electronic data processing equipment, for which maintenance costs have been quite high and obsolescence quite rapid. Other companies lease to take advantage of what they consider a tax advantage, since rental costs may be deducted from taxable income as operating expense. As in make or buy decisions, however, the total incremental effect is important. Clearly, if the added cost in leasing is greater than the tax advantage, the savings are illusory.

---

[4] See "Supplement to Chapter 6—Simulation."

At this juncture the question of make, buy, or lease also arises. Table 3.5 summarizes some key factors to consider in making this decision.

Specific equipment choice

Once the form of processing has been decided, the next thing to consider is the make and model of the equipment to be selected. In some cases the "minor technological choice" may be predicated on the existence of a unit or system that is available through only one supplier, while in others a variety of models—both new and used—may be selected. In the latter instance especially, the tools of investment analysis come into play to evaluate such quantifiable factors as initial cost, operating cost per unit, and depreciation schedules. Beyond these considerations, management must also look at key subjective factors, including

1. Flexibility in handling product variation and meshing with other equipment,
2. Availability of replacement parts and special tooling (especially in the case of equipment manufactured abroad),
3. Supplier assistance in installation and debugging,
4. Special training of workers to use the equipment,
5. Normal maintenance and repairs, and
6. Safety of the equipment.

Automation.   One of the significant developments in the "specific equipment choice" area in recent years is *automation.* This term, while familiar to most people, still eludes a commonly agreed upon definition. Some authorities view automation as a totally new set of concepts that relate to the automatic operation of a production process; others view it as simply an evolutionary development in technology wherein machinery performs some or all of the process control function. The view of automation we prefer is, first, that it replaces human supervision of machines and productive processes by automatic supervision,[5] and second, that this substitution requires a closed loop or feedback control to enable the machine or process to control its performance at any moment by means of data supplied to the "automatic" control unit that supervises the operation.[6] By this conceptualization, automation is a new set of concepts (relating to control), and is also evolutionary in the sense that it is a logical and predictable step in the development of equipment and processes.

General categorizing of automation.   The following categorical breakdown helps summarize the general scope of automation in practice.

1. Raw materials automation. This encompasses applications in primary material processing industries where the end product is a material rather than a distinct article. Specific industries where this is found are agriculture, chemical processing, mining, and oil drilling.

2. Shaping and assembly automation. This covers applications in those

---

[5] Definition modified from David Foster, *Automation in Practice* (London: McGraw-Hill, 1968), p. 4.

[6] Definition modified from John Rose, *Automation: Its Anatomy and Physiology* (Edinburgh and London: Oliver and Boyd, 1967), p. 5.

industries which transform processed raw materials into a recognizable entity. The steel and automobile industries are major users of this type of automation.

3. Logistics and traffic automation. This covers applications in shipping and storing items, and includes automated ships, road traffic control, remote control of pipelines, and automatic warehouses.

4. Services automation. This includes the application of automatic systems to education, medicine, and the postal service.

5. Data processing automation. Unlike the above applications, this type of automation is concerned with inputs and outputs that are in the form of data rather than physical products. Obviously, data processing automation could be found as a supporting activity in industries that also use the other forms of automation in producing their physical products.

Automation in hot strip steel mills. The following excerpt provides a good overview of how a digital computer is used in controlling the total production process in this form of steel making.

More progress has been made with computer control in hot strip mills than in any of the other steelmaking processes. Although systems are not as numerous here as in the converting processes, they are gaining rapidly, and all new installations on order are true control computers for directly operating the process. Hot strip mills provide easier justification for sophisticated control because they are big, expensive, and critical to the entire process.

In recent typical applications, the computer performs several separate though interrelated functions. These are usually identified as primary data input, slab tracking, mill pacing, mill setup, temperature control, and production logging.

For primary data input the computer receives a rolling schedule prepared in machine language before the first slab on the schedule arrives at the furnace. Operators located at the furnace entry or discharge may interrupt to change the schedule. By means of the input schedule the identity of each slab entering the process is maintained in the computer until the slab has completely finished the hot strip process. Operators communicate to the computer information on which furnace a slab enters so that the computer has a record of slabs in each furnace.

Slab tracking begins after discharge from the furnace. Each slab is tracked through the mill by means of hot metal detectors located in zones in which only one slab may be present at any time. It is this slab tracking program that links the computer to the process in realtime. The program determines when necessary mill setup and temperature calculations must be made, maintains correlation between slab identity and rolling schedule, maintains identities for operating displays, and handles data logging.

Mill pacing is another function of a computer responsible for maximum mill utilization. The program sets the rate at which slabs are processed and maintains minimum separation between slabs so that they will just avoid collision at any point. This control is achieved by signaling the operation which discharges the slab from the furnace. To perform its task, the mill pacing program uses slab tracking data and the rolling schedule.

The mill setup function determines speed and roll openings for the entire hot strip mill and sends them to regulators at the appropriate time for each change in rolling schedule. The computer distributes drafting through the mill to establish required finish gauge at the head end.

Width control is also achieved by the setup function. Using incoming slab dimensions, the computer determines roll settings for the edgers and reduces the settings in a predetermined manner. Width gauges provide feedback for corrections and thereby compensate also for roll wear and other changing conditions.

Temperature control during finish rolling and coiling is critical because certain physical properties of the steel are influenced by temperature at these points. The computer's task, therefore, is to maintain temperature within specified limits at these points through the length of the steel coil. With the assistance of temperature sensing devices, the finish mill delivery speed and the roll openings in both finish and rough mills are modified so that the temperature will be correct when the steel arrives. When the head of the coil is in the coiler, the computer controls speedup rate and maximum speed to overcome temperature rundown. The computer controls runout table sprays and varies spray patterns according to rolling conditions and mill speeds.

The production logging function produces quality reports and production reports. It is synchronized with the slab tracking function so that the coil identity data and process readings are correlated with coil quality and production data. Therefore, in addition to regular reporting, the data may be used in a continual study of relationships between quality and process readings.[7]

Process flow choice

Although this is the last phase to be discussed, process flow considerations generally enter into the earlier specific component choice and minor

FIGURE 3.5

Plug assembly drawing

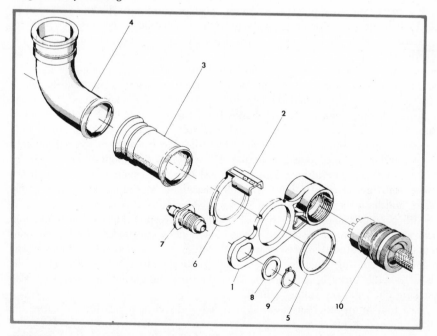

[7] Harry L. Cornish, Jr., and William L. Horton, *Computerized Process Control: A Management Decision* (New York: Hobbs, Dorman & Co., 1968), pp. 160–62.

FIGURE 3.6

Assembly chart for plug assembly

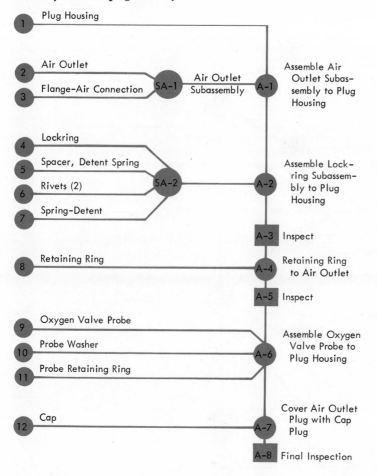

technological choice. Obviously, unless sufficient thought is given to the flow of the product through the factory, it is difficult to determine the type and number of machines required. One reason process flow is presented at this point is that, unlike the other choices, it recurs as output and product mix change. In job shops, for example, different products follow different routes through their manufacture, some even skipping entire operations for which equipment is available. In this type of production, therefore, the process flow can only be estimated at the time the equipment is selected, and thus presents a rather challenging problem in layout design (see Chapter 4).

Several production management tools are used in dealing with the process flow; the most common are assembly drawings, assembly charts, route sheets, and flow process charts. It should be noted that each of these charts is a useful diagnostic tool and therefore is employed for improving operations during the steady state of the productive system.

FIGURE 3.7

Assembly chart for a "Big Mac"-type hamburger

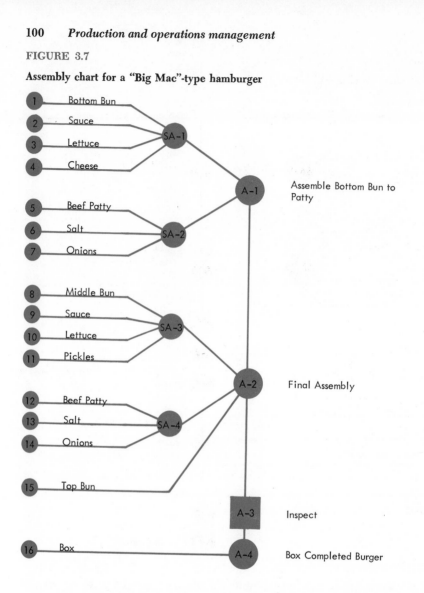

An *assembly drawing* such as Figure 3.5 is simply an "exploded" view of the product in terms of its component parts. An *assembly* or *Gozinto*[8] *chart* as Figures 3.6 and 3.7 utilizes the information presented in the assembly drawing, and defines (among other things) how parts go together, their order of assembly, and often the overall material flow pattern. An *operation and route sheet* (as in Figure 3.8), as its name implies, specifies operations and process routing for a particular part. It conveys such information as the type of equipment, tooling, and operations required to complete the item.

A *flow process chart* such as Figure 3.9 typically uses standard ASME

---

[8] A. Vazsonyi credits the development of this type of chart to the "celebrated Italian mathematician Zepartzat Gozinto." (See A. Vazsonyi, *Scientific Programming in Business and Industry*, New York: John Wiley, 1958, p. 429.)

FIGURE 3.8

Route sheet for plug assembly

Material Specs. _____			Part Name	Plug Housing		Part No.	TA 1274	
Purchased Stock Size _____			Usage	Plug Assembly		Date Issued _____		
Pcs. Per Pur. Size _____			Assy. No.	TA 1279		Date Sup'd. _____		
Weight _____			Sub. Assy. No. _____			Issued By _____		

Oper. No.	Operation Description	Dept.	Machine	Set Up Hr.	Rate Pc/Hr	Tools
20	Drill 1 hole .312 +.015 −.005	Drill	Mach 513 Deka 4	1.5	254	Drill Fixture L-76, Jig #10393
30	Deburr .312 +.015 −.005 Dia. Hole	Drill	Mach 510 Drill	.1	424	Multi-Tooth Burring Tool
40	Chamfer .900/.875, Bore .828/.875 dia. (2 Passes), Bore .7600/.7625 (1 Pass)	Lathe	Mach D109 Lathe	1.0	44	Ramet-1, TPG 221, Chamfer Tool
50	Tap Holes as designated - 1/4 Min. Full Thread	Tap	Mach 514 Drill Tap	2.0	180	Fixture #CR-353, Tap, 4 Flute Sp.
60	Bore Hole 1.133 to 1.138 Dia.	Lathe	H&H E107	3.0	158	L44 Turrett Fixture, Hartford
						Superspacer, pl. #45, Holder #L46,
						FDTW-100, Inser #21, Chk. Fixture
70	Deburr .005 to .010, Both Sides, Hand Feed To Hard Stop	Lathe	E162 Lathe	.5	176	Collet #CR179, 1327 RPM
80	Broach Keyway To Remove Thread Burrs	Drill	Mach. 507 Drill	.4	91	B87 Fixture, L59 Broach, Tap. . 875120 G-H6
90	Hone Thread I.D. .822/.828	Grind	Grinder		120	
95	Hone .7600/.7625	Grind	Grinder		120	

Source: Arizona Gear & Manufacturing Company.

(American Society of Mechanical Engineers) symbols to denote what happens to the product as it progresses through the productive facility. As a rule, the fewer the delays and storages in the process, the better the flow—although there are exceptions. For example, if there were no delays in processing for any product, it might signal that the system is not working to capacity since there is always free equipment and available personnel.

Production throughput strategies

Process throughput strategies interact with the aforementioned sequential decisions. These strategies are in essence volume or run-size alternatives in manufacturing systems and service alternatives in service systems.

Three of the categories in manufacturing—unit, batch, and mass—are identical to the technology headings used by Woodward, as discussed in the previous chapter. However, using the term *technology* in this manner overlooks—or at least does not convey—the broader application of the word to transformation processes in general. Hence it is employed in reference to the process decisions spelled out in Table 3.6.

With respect to the production throughput strategies, the manufacturing classification should be self-explanatory. Services, on the other hand, warrant clarification because they are distinguished on the basis of whether they are performed differently for each customer. Generally, provision of customized service tends to increase operating costs by requiring more personnel and by limiting the use of standardized procedures. The high-

FIGURE 3.9

Flow process chart of plug housing from plug assembly

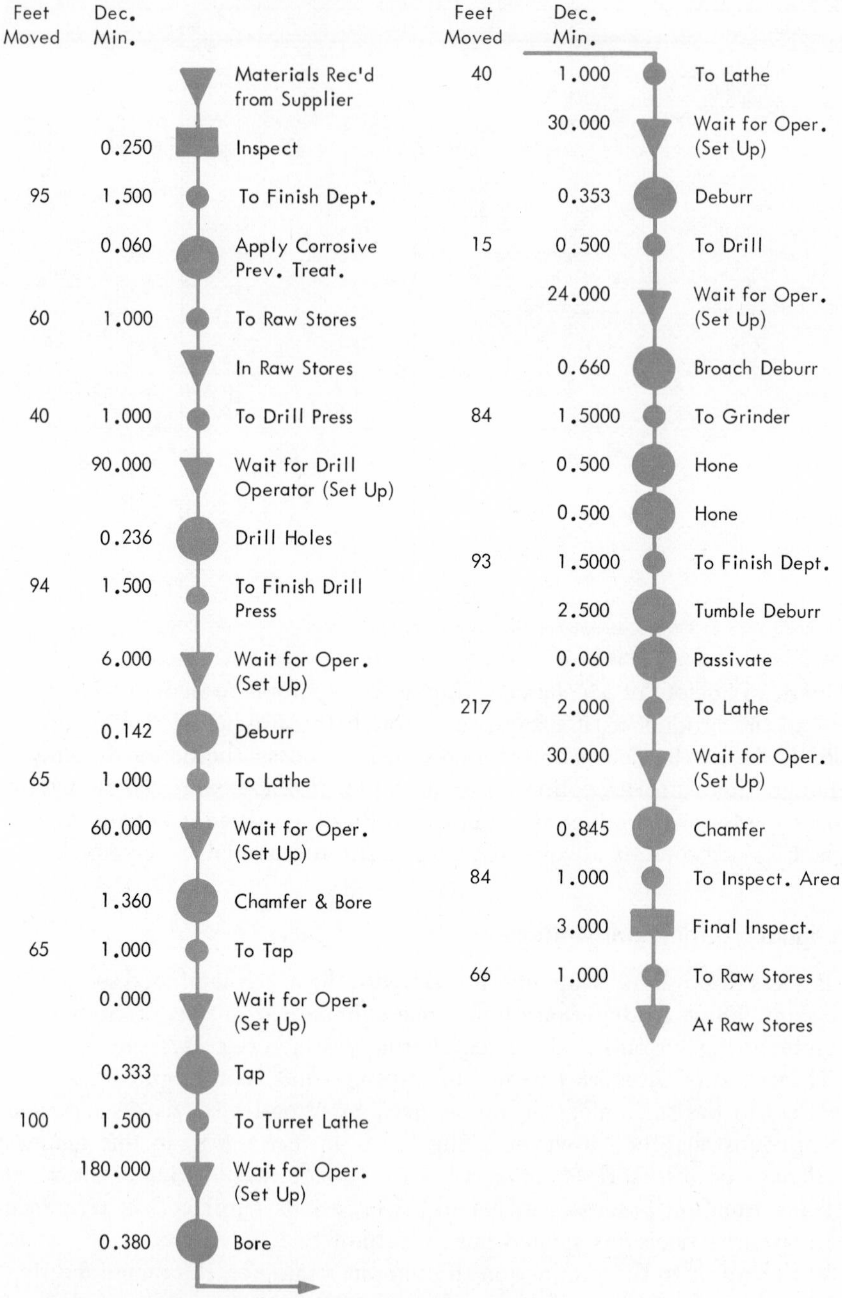

Feet Moved	Dec. Min.		Description	Feet Moved	Dec. Min.		Description
		▽	Materials Rec'd from Supplier	40	1.000	●	To Lathe
	0.250	■	Inspect		30.000	▽	Wait for Oper. (Set Up)
95	1.500	●	To Finish Dept.		0.353	●	Deburr
	0.060	●	Apply Corrosive Prev. Treat.	15	0.500	●	To Drill
60	1.000	●	To Raw Stores		24.000	▽	Wait for Oper. (Set Up)
		▽	In Raw Stores		0.660	●	Broach Deburr
40	1.000	●	To Drill Press	84	1.5000	●	To Grinder
	90.000	▽	Wait for Drill Operator (Set Up)		0.500	●	Hone
	0.236	●	Drill Holes		0.500	●	Hone
94	1.500	●	To Finish Drill Press	93	1.5000	●	To Finish Dept.
	6.000	▽	Wait for Oper. (Set Up)		2.500	●	Tumble Deburr
	0.142	●	Deburr		0.060	●	Passivate
65	1.000	●	To Lathe	217	2.000	●	To Lathe
	60.000	▽	Wait for Oper. (Set Up)		30.000	▽	Wait for Oper. (Set Up)
	1.360	●	Chamfer & Bore		0.845	●	Chamfer
65	1.000	●	To Tap	84	1.000	●	To Inspect. Area
	0.000	▽	Wait for Oper. (Set Up)		3.000	■	Final Inspect.
	0.333	●	Tap	66	1.000	●	To Raw Stores
100	1.500	●	To Turret Lathe			▽	At Raw Stores
	180.000	▽	Wait for Oper. (Set Up)				
	0.380	●	Bore				

Note: These production times were based on a run of 500 items.
Source: Arizona Gear & Manufacturing Company.

TABLE 3.6

Production throughput strategies

	Key feature	*Typical example*	*Typical labor-to-equipment ratio*
Manufacturing:			
Unit	One of a kind or produced one by one	Office buildings, special machine tools, orbiting satellites, ships	High
Batch	Finite number of items generally produced on order	Custom clothes, custom furniture	High
Mass	Indefinite or extremely large number of items of homogeneous nature	Automobiles, ball-point pens	Medium
Process	Continuous process-ing of primary materials	Chemicals, petroleum, lumber	Low
Services:			
Customized	High direct customer contact	Custom tailor, country store, doctor's office	
	Low direct customer contact	Wholesaler stocking customer's brand, insurance broker	
Standardized	High customer contact	Clothing store, supermarket, insurance office	
	Low direct customer contact	Wholesaler, clinical laboratory, mail order service	

direct- and low-direct-customer-contact categories underscore the fact that some service organizations do not deal directly with the ultimate consumer but utilize such intermediaries as retailers and service agents. As a rule, where direct consumer contact is not required, the need for such accouter-ments as advertising, customer relations departments, and attractive sales facilities is often substantially diminished. This in turn alters the nature of the service and, ultimately, the processes selected.

Process selection example

For an example of process selection, let us take a manufacturer of gas ranges in the mid-1960s who was looking for a major technological innova-tion so as to maintain his competitive position. He might have considered a self-cleaning oven or introduction of a microwave oven in some models of his ranges. To stay competitive, he would have had to include self-cleaning ovens. To gain an advantage, he should have investigated the possibility of introducing a microwave oven. (Analysis of the problems and potentialities of microwave ovens will be undertaken following the outline suggested in Table 3.2.)

Major technological choice. For a manufacturer of gas ranges, a microwave oven involves a whole new technology. (The heating and cooking properties of microwaves were noted and studied as an incidental part of radar development.) Microwave energy passes readily through glass and plastics and is reflected by metal surfaces. The energy turns to heat when it is absorbed by a material containing moisture, such as food products. The microwaves penetrate the food, and all parts are cooked at the same time. In a conventional oven, cooking works from the outside in.

Cooking with microwaves is feasible, and has been done on a commercial basis for several years in restaurants and industrial cafeterias. Although the gas-range manufacturer probably does not have the technical expertise in his organization, he can readily find people with the skills he needs in engineering schools, aerospace firms, or the military services.

Minor technological choice. The first design problem is the generation of the microwaves, and the most common method for this form of cooking is to use magnetron tubes operating at 2,400 megahertz. Although a manufacturer has developed a triode tube that operates at 900 megahertz, the magnetron tube has been in use longer and would seem to be a better choice. Magnetrons are expensive, and the manufacturer must also be aware that they generate great heat and therefore need a water cooling or air circulation system to control the temperature.

Microwaves, as a form of radio energy, come under the purview of the Federal Communications Commission, which would have to certify that the final oven design ensures against radiation leakage that might interfere with radio service. Also, because excess microwave radiation is known to be harmful to humans, causing cataracts and possibly damaging the nervous system, the Department of Health, Education, and Welfare is concerned with radiation from microwave ovens (as well as from color television sets). Thus the final design will also have to satisfy HEW's radiation leakage standards.

The microwave oven is also an electrical device, and as such should be tested by Underwriters' Laboratory—having first been designed to pass such tests. Because the inside of the oven is not warm—even when it is operating—users may not be aware that it is dangerous to place their hands inside when the oven is in operation. The manufacturer must therefore include fail-safe interlocks to eliminate accidents.

The technical and legal problems can be overcome, but there must be some indication that there is a potential market. In terms of the modern housewife's interest, the market for microwave ovens would seem to be expanding. Her most important "commodity" is her time, and because a microwave oven cuts the cooking time of all foods at least in half, this will give the homemaker more time for other things. Its speed in cooking frozen foods will also be a strong selling feature.

In evaluating microwave oven performance it was found that this technique does not "brown" foods, and thus Porterhouse steak, for example, does not have the charcoal broiled appearance we always associate with magazine pictures of the food. The manufacturer's test kitchen may therefore have to develop ways to brown food, along with recipes suited to this type of cooking. And because the properties of microwaves require that the cookware be ceramic or glass, the best way to ensure the use of proper cookware may be for the manufacturer to include a complete set with each oven sold.

Since our manufacturer has none of the equipment necessary to make a microwave oven, and to make any units would require setting up a very costly production facility, a test marketing program does not seem practical. The manufacturer will therefore have to rely on market surveys, or perhaps a market simulation.

In any case, there seems to be a long-term potential market, and competition is developing both domestically and from units imported from Japan. To realize some profits and to stay competitive, the gas-range manufacturer may have to add a microwave oven to his product line.

Specific component choice. The simplest way of adding a microwave unit to the product line would be to make it as a separate unit bearing the manufacturer's brand. However, a separate unit, such as a tabletop oven that looks like an *electric* appliance, would be out of place in the product line. A more suitable arrangement would be to install a microwave oven as part of a complete gas-range unit.

This approach can be further subdivided, and the most straightforward way would be to remove the gas oven and replace it with a microwave unit. A more expensive method would be to have a double oven, one gas and the other microwave. A third possibility would be a microwave unit combined with a gas unit in a single oven. The combination would not be difficult to implement, but excess heat from the gas portion could overheat the microwave electronics, which means that extra heat protection or cooling must be provided. The combination has the advantage that it will brown the outside of food and make it appear the way it does in the cookbooks.

The exact choice of a product model will depend on the results of the market studies and the problems involved in retooling the present production facilities to produce the various alternatives.

Whichever alternative is chosen, the manufacturer must decide how much of the work will be done in his own plant. With a high degree of certainty, we can say that he will not manufacture his own microwave tubes—this would be much too complex. There is, however, the choice of how much of the rest of the fabrication his plant will perform. It could perform all the chassis construction and assembly of all the electronic components if it appears this would be profitable and the plant can set up the production lines and train the personnel. It could buy all the units required as subassemblies and then perform the interconnection and installation operations. Another alternative might be to make an agreement with a

Japanese firm to import completed units to be used in the ranges, and also marketed under the plant's brand as tabletop ovens.

The final choice of the amount of assembly work to be done by the firm might depend on how soon the market is expected to develop and the potential volume. If the market were developing rapidly, it might wish to buy the units or subassemblies to avoid the long delays in starting up its own production. Likewise, if the market seems to lack potential, it might wish to avoid the expense of establishing its own production facilities. It is here that the tools of economic analysis, such as break-even charts and present-value analysis, come into play.

Process flow choice. The process flow choice entails dovetailing the production routing of the microwave oven into the existing production facility. The standard tools of process charts, route sheets, and assembly drawings would have to be developed by utilizing engineering handbooks and equipment manuals.

"McDonald's"—A Production Approach to Services

Process design for retail service has been revolutionized by the McDonald's Hamburger chain. In an insightful article, Theodore Levitt[9] suggests that an essential feature of McDonald's success is its treating the delivery of fast food as a manufacturing process rather than a service process. The value of this philosophy is that it overcomes many of the problems that are inherent in the concept of service itself. That is, service implies subordination or subjugation of the server to the served; manufacturing, on the other hand avoids this connotation because it focuses on things rather than people. Thus in manufacturing and in the case of McDonald's, "the orientation is toward the efficient production of results, not on the attendance on others." Levitt notes that besides McDonald's marketing and financing skills, the company carefully controls "the execution of each outlet's central function—the rapid delivery of a uniform, high quality mix of prepared foods in an environment of obvious cleanliness, order, and cheerful courtesy. The systematic substitution of equipment for people, combined with the carefully planned use and positioning of technology, enables McDonald's to attract and hold patronage in proportions no predecessor or imitator has managed to duplicate."[10] Levitt cites several aspects of McDonald's operations to illustrate these concepts:

> The McDonald's french fryer allows cooking of the optimum number of french fries at one time.
>
> A wide-mouthed scoop is used to pick up the precise amount of french fries for each order size. (The employee never touches the product.)

---

[9] Theodore Levitt, "Production-Line Approach to Service," *Harvard Business Review,* vol. 50, no. 5, September–October 1972, pp. 41–52.

[10] Ibid., p. 44.

Storage space is expressly designed for a predetermined mix of pre-packed and premeasured products. There is no space for any foods that were not designed into the system at the outset.

Cleanliness is pursued by providing ample trash cans in and outside each facility (and the larger outlets have motorized sweepers for the parking area).

Hamburgers are wrapped in color-coded paper and boxes.

"Through painstaking attention to total design and facilities planning, everything is built integrally into the (McDonald's) machine itself, into the technology of the system. The only choice available to the attendant is to operate it exactly as the designers intended."[11]

CONCLUSION

In this chapter we have attempted to organize product design and process selection in terms of the decisions that must be made in undertaking these activities. It should be emphasized that while means exist for improving product design[12] after full-scale production is under way, a systematic, before-the-fact analysis of production considerations (for example, simplification and compatibility) is generally far less costly. Undoubtedly, an ounce of prevention is worth a pound of cure. Likewise, to look beyond initial costs and process alternatives to questions of adaptability and obsolescence in process selection is obvious good sense. Unfortunately, such foresight is not found in a surprisingly large number of companies which end up prematurely scrapping equipment or, even worse, having to try to remain competitive while employing an obsolete technology.[13]

As for the degree of technical expertise required to make product design and process selection decisions, manufacturing and process industries require far more engineering and scientific personnel than do service industries. Service industries, by virtue of their simpler technologies, permit a larger say in these decisions by nonscientifically trained personnel. This assertion is substantiated when we observe the large number of business school graduates who assist in making these decisions as members of systems and procedures departments in financial institutions, hospitals, and food franchising operations.

---

[11] Ibid., p. 46.

[12] For example, *value analysis* programs (see Chapter 14, "Improving the Productive System").

[13] Great Britain has encountered this problem on a grand scale. Several of her industries, including petrochemicals, steel, and textiles, are confronted with the need to make huge investments in current technology just to remain competitive. Unfortunately, the lead time for re-tooling in such industries is two years or more. This means in all likelihood that new developments in production processes will be adopted in the interim by other nations, and Britain will still be at a competitive disadvantage even after her new technology begins operation.

PROPOSITIONS

Propositions contrasting service and manufacturing relative to product design and process selection

Product: Because the customer is involved in the creation of the service product, the specifications of the service cannot be completely determined prior to the start of the service. In manufacturing, the customer generally is not directly involved in the manufacturing process, and hence the product specifications are fixed prior to the initiation of production.

Technology of transformation: Because the customer is involved in the creation of the service product, the technology of transformation must be flexible enough to allow for a range of individual variation (even when the service provided is standardized in nature). In manufacturing, the production process creates inanimate objects with fixed design and raw material specifications, and therefore the technology of transformation need cope with relatively less variability.

Operating-control system: Because the technology of transformation must be more flexible in services than in manufacturing, the operating-control system for services generally must be able to respond more readily to variations than does that for manufacturing.

Workforce: In those service systems requiring direct contact with the customer, the service system workforce is an integral part of the product design. In manufacturing, the workforce executes the product design, but is not a part of it.

REVIEW AND DISCUSSION QUESTIONS

1. With reference to Figure 3.1, what form does the product specification take for the following organizations: a cattle ranch, a wine company, a book publisher, a railroad? Where would you place them on the exact–general continuum?

2. How does process selection in service industries such as banks, hotels, and restaurants differ from process selection in manufacturing? Does the nature of the product determine how "rational" this decision may be?

3. Describe some of the major and minor technological choice decision factors that might have entered into the United States' decision not to build a supersonic transport in 1970.

4. What is a "production throughput strategy"? Under which of these strategies would you find general-purpose equipment most likely to be employed? Special-purpose equipment? Explain.

5. Define the following terms: reliability, maintainability, component compatibility, component simplification, component redundancy.

6. How could a soup manufacturer's decision on the recipes to be used in different countries be cast as a modular design problem?

7. Automation is often thought of as a high-risk production strategy. What is the justification for this view?

8. What type of information is contained in an assembly chart, a route sheet, and a flow process chart?

9. What is CAD? How is it used in product design?

10. Explain how the producibility of the product acts as a help or hindrance to corporate strategy.

11. How do your experiences as a customer or employee at McDonald's compare with Levitt's view that "its modestly paid employees have a sense of pride and dignity"?

12. Levitt also states in his article that "Discretion is the enemy of order, standardization, and quality." Do you agree with this view?

PROBLEMS

1. Develop an assembly chart for a refillable ballpoint pen.

2. Develop a flow process chart for in-person student registration at a school with which you are familiar.

3. A plant manager is attempting to determine whether his firm should purchase a component part or make it at its own facilities. If it purchases the item, it will cost the company $1 per unit. The company can make the item on an assembly line at a variable cost of 25¢ per unit with a fixed cost of $2,000, or it can make it at individual stations at a variable cost of 50¢ per unit with a fixed cost of $1,000. Assuming that annual demand is expected to be 3,500 units, determine which alternative the plant manager should select.

SELECTED BIBLIOGRAPHY

Asimow, M.   *Introduction to Design.* Englewood Cliffs, N.J.: Prentice-Hall, 1966.

Branham, Richard   "The Case for Computerized Design," *Industrial Design* (March 1970), pp. 23–29.

Cornish, Harry L., Jr., and Horton, William L.   *Computerized Process Control: A Management Decision.* New York: Hobbs, Dorman & Co., 1968.

Foster, David   *Automation in Practice.* London: McGraw-Hill, 1968.

Levitt, Theodore   "Production-Line Approach to Service," *Harvard Business Review,* vol. 50, no. 5, September–October 1972, pp. 41–52.

———   "The Industrialization of Service," *Harvard Business Review,* vol. 54, no. 5, September–October 1976, pp. 63–74.

Uman, David B.   *New Product Programs: Their Planning and Control.* New York: American Management Association, 1969.

Vonalven, William H. (ed.)   *Reliability Engineering.* Englewood Cliffs, N.J.: Prentice-Hall, 1964.

Wallenstein, Gerd D.   *Concept and Practice of Product Planning.* New York: American Management Association, 1968.

Supplement to chapter three

Financial analysis

THE BASIC TOOLS of cost and investment analysis find usefulness in all aspects of the design and operation of a productive system. While we recognize the existence of a firm's multiple goals, such as growth, competitive position, safety of income, corporate perpetuity, and so on, in this supplement we concentrate on the economic objective of selecting among the least-cost or highest-profit alternatives. Some basic investment concepts, such as sunk costs, opportunity costs, and depreciation, are presented, as well as an introduction to cash flow budgeting. In addition, the more commonly used methods of ranking investment alternatives are treated in example form.

CONCEPTS AND DEFINITIONS

A few basic concepts drawn from the fields of economics, accounting, and finance are utilized in making investment decisions. Those included in the following discussions, while not difficult, are nonetheless essential for understanding the material in later sections.

Fixed costs. A fixed cost is any expense that remains constant regardless of the level of output. Although no cost is truly fixed, many types of expense are virtually fixed over a wide range of output. Examples of commonly incurred fixed costs are rent, property taxes, most types of depreciation, insurance payments, and salaries of top management.

Variable costs. Variable costs are expenses that fluctuate directly with changes in the level of output. Often, variable costs can be traced to each unit produced. For example, each additional unit of sheet steel produced by United States Steel requires a specific amount of material and labor. The incremental cost of this additional material and labor can be isolated and assigned to each unit of sheet steel produced. Many overhead expenses are also variable, inasmuch as utility bills, maintenance expense, etc., will vary with production level.

Figure S.3.1 illustrates the fixed and variable cost components of total cost. Note that total cost increases at the same rate as variable costs since fixed costs are constant.

Sunk costs. Sunk costs are expenses which have *no effect* on a decision and therefore should not be taken into account in considering investment alternatives. There are two types of sunk costs—past expenditures, which cannot be recovered or are unaffected by the decision, and costs that apply equally to all alternatives under consideration.

FIGURE S.3.1

Fixed and variable cost components of total cost

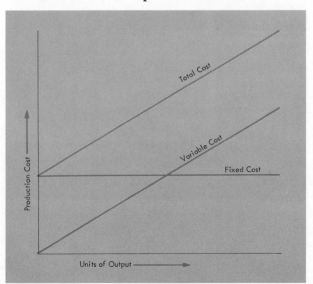

As an example of the first type, suppose an ice cream manufacturing firm occupies a rented building and is considering making sherbet in the same building. If the company enters sherbet production, its cost accountant will assign some of the rental expense to the sherbet operation. However, the building rent remains unchanged and therefore is not a relevant expense to be considered in making the decision. The rent is *sunk;* that is, it will continue to exist and will not change in amount regardless of the decision.

The second type of sunk cost is an expense that is common to all alternatives being considered, and therefore provides no basis for choice among them. All Seven-Eleven stores, a national chain of convenience grocery stores, are of uniform size and design. If the cost of building these stores is the same throughout a geographic area, construction costs are not an element to be considered by Seven-Eleven's management in choosing where to locate its stores in the area.

Opportunity cost. Opportunity cost is the benefit *foregone*, or advantage *lost*, which results from choosing one course of action over the *best known alternative* course of action. It is the *difference* between the best choice and any alternative. The opportunity cost of attending college is the highest salary the student could command if he chose to work instead. Alternatively, the opportunity cost of not attending college is the increased earning power he gives up in the long run by not holding a college degree. A person interested solely in maximizing his lifetime earnings would base his decision on attending college on which of the two opportunity costs was highest.

Let's examine a more specific example. Suppose a firm has $100,000 to invest and two alternatives of comparable risk present themselves, each requiring a $100,000 investment. Investment A will net $25,000; investment B will net $23,000. Investment A is clearly the better choice, with a $25,000 net return. If the decision is made to invest in B instead of A, the opportunity cost of B then is $2,000 which is the benefit foregone.

Investment possibilities cannot be put into proper perspective unless the opportunity costs are considered.

Risk and expected value. Risk is inherent in any investment, since the future can never be predicted with absolute certainty. It is a rare occurrence indeed when expected outcome and actual outcome coincide perfectly. To deal with this uncertainty, mathematical techniques for incorporating probability provide some assistance. Expected value, for example, is the expected outcome multiplied by the probability of its occurrence. Recall that, in the example above, the expected outcome of alternative A was $25,000 and B $23,000. Suppose the probability of A's actual outcome is 80 percent while B's probability is 90 percent. The expected values of the alternatives are determined as follows:

Expected outcome × Probability that actual outcome will be
the expected outcome = Expected value
Investment A: $25,000 × 0.80 = $20,000
Investment B: $23,000 × 0.90 = $20,700

Investment B is now seen to be the better choice, with a net advantage over A of $700. Risk is always present when dealing with the future and should be explicitly incorporated into the decision-making process where possible.

Economic life and obsolescence. When a firm invests in an income-producing asset, the productive life of the asset is estimated. For accounting purposes, the asset is depreciated over this period. It is assumed that the asset will perform its function during this time and then be considered obsolete or "worn out" and replacement will be required. This view of asset life rarely coincides with reality. Production techniques and technological improvements frequently render a machine obsolete long before its productive life has been exhausted.

Assume that a machine expected to have a productive life of 10 years is purchased. If at any time during the ensuing 10 years a new machine is developed that can perform the same task more efficiently or economically, the old machine has become obsolete. Whether it is "worn out" or not is irrelevant.

The economic life of a machine is the period over which it provides the best method for performing its task. When a superior method is developed. the machine has become obsolete. Thus the stated book value of a machine can be a meaningless figure.

Suppose a machine with an estimated 10-year life is purchased for $10,000 and will be depreciated by $1,000 per year to a zero salvage value. At the end of the fifth year the machine will be carried at $5,000. If a superior machine has become available, the $5,000 book value does not reflect the true value of the present machine. Technological obsolescence has reduced its value for prospective buyers, and also makes the use of such equipment costly by creating high opportunity costs.

Generally, economic lives are very short, and for machinery may not exceed more than five or six years on the average.

Depreciation. Depreciation is an accounting procedure used to periodically reduce the value of an asset on the company books. The value of any capital asset—buildings, machinery, etc.—decreases as its useful life is expended. *Amortization* is a term often used interchangeably with the term depreciation. Through convention, however, depreciation refers to the allocation of cost due to the physical or functional deterioration of *tangible* (physical) assets such as buildings or equipment, while amortization refers to the allocation of cost over the useful life period of *intangible* assets such as patents, leases, franchises, or goodwill.

Depreciation procedures may not reflect an asset's true value at any point in its life since obsolescence may at any time cause a large difference between true value and book value. Also, since depreciation rates significantly affect taxes, a firm may choose a particular method from the several alternatives with more consideration for its effect on taxes than its ability to make the book value of an asset reflect the true resale value.

Four commonly used methods of depreciation are described below. All methods, however, are computed by using three basic criteria:

1. Cost of the asset
2. Estimated life of the asset
3. Estimated salvage value

Straight-line method. Under this method, an asset's value is reduced in uniform annual amounts over its estimated useful life. The general formula is:

$$\text{Annual amount to be depreciated} = \frac{\text{Cost} - \text{Salvage value}}{\text{Estimated useful life}}$$

A machine costing $10,000, with an estimated salvage value of zero and an estimated life of 10 years, would be depreciated at the rate of $1,000 per year for each of the 10 years. If its estimated salvage value at the end of the 10 years is $1,000, the annual depreciation charge is:

$$\frac{\$10,000 - \$1,000}{10} = \$900$$

Sum-of-years'-digits (SYD) method. The purpose of the SYD method is to reduce the book value of an asset rapidly in early years and at a lower rate in the later years of its life. The procedure is best shown by the following example:

Cost of new asset......................... $17,000
Estimated useful life...................... 5 years
Estimated salvage value................... $ 2,000

First, determine the amount to be depreciated:

$$\text{Cost} - \text{Salvage value} = \$17,000 - \$2,000 = \$15,000$$

Second, total the number of years represented by *each year* in the asset's estimated useful life:

$$1 + 2 + 3 + 4 + 5 = 15$$

Third, depreciate the asset by $5/15$ after the first year, $4/15$ after the second year, and so on, down to $1/15$ in the last year. As a check on computation, the total of the fractions should equal one, and the annual depreciation charges should equal the total amount to be depreciated. The example is illustrated in the accompanying table.

Year	Yearly depreciation rate		Amount to be depreciated		Yearly depreciation charge	Stated value at end of year
1...............	5/15	×	$15,000	=	$ 5,000	$10,000
2...............	4/15	×	15,000	=	4,000	6,000
3...............	3/15	×	15,000	=	3,000	3,000
4...............	2/15	×	15,000	=	2,000	1,000
5...............	1/15	×	15,000	=	1,000	0
Total........	1				$15,000	

The accelerated depreciation during early years can be advantageous for two reasons. First, the effect of rapid technological obsolescence is reflected in the quickly falling book value; second, the rapid rate of depreciation provides early tax deductions, which may increase profits. In certain instances, however, the Internal Revenue Service does not allow the use of the SYD method.

Declining balance method.   This method also achieves an accelerated depreciation. The asset's value is decreased by reducing its book value by a constant percentage each year. The percentage rate used is often selected as the one that will just reduce book value to salvage value at the end of the asset's estimated life. In any case, the asset should never be reduced below estimated salvage value. Use of the declining balance method and allowable rates is controlled by Internal Revenue Service regulations. As a simplified illustration, the preceding example is used in the next table with an arbitrarily selected rate of 40 percent. Note that depreciation is based on full cost, *not* cost minus salvage value.

Year	Depreciation rate	Beginning book value	Depreciation charge	Accumulated depreciation	Ending book value
1...............	0.40	$17,000	$6,800	$ 6,800	$10,200
2...............	0.40	10,200	4,080	10,880	6,120
3...............	0.40	6,120	2,448	13,328	3,672
4...............	0.40	3,672	1,469	14,797	2,203
5...............		2,203	203	15,000	2,000

In the fifth year, reducing book value by 40 percent would have caused it to drop below salvage value. Consequently, the asset was depreciated by only $203, which decreased book value to salvage value.

A *double-declining balance* method uses as a percentage twice the straight-line rate. Thus a 10-year depreciable period would have a depreciation rate of $2 \times \frac{1}{10}$, or 0.20.

Depreciation-by-use method.   The purpose of this method is to depreciate capital investment in proportion to its use. It is applicable, for example, to a machine that performs the same operation many times. The life of the machine is not estimated in years but rather in terms of the total number of operations it may reasonably be expected to perform before wearing out. Suppose that a metal-stamping press has an estimated life of 1 million stamps and costs $100,000. The charge for depreciation per stamp is then $100,000/1,000,000, or $0.10. Assuming a zero salvage value, the depreciation charges are as shown on the next table.

Year	Total yearly stamps	Cost per stamp	Yearly depreciation charge	Accumulated depreciation	Ending book value
1...............	150,000	$0.10	$15,000	$ 15,000	$85,000
2...............	300,000	.10	30,000	45,000	55,000
3...............	200,000	.10	20,000	65,000	35,000
4...............	200,000	.10	20,000	85,000	15,000
5...............	100,000	.10	10,000	95,000	5,000
6...............	50,000	.10	5,000	100,000	0

This depreciation-by-use method is an attempt to gear depreciation charges to actual use and thereby coordinate expense charges with productive output more accurately. Also, since a machine's resale value is related to its remaining productive life, it is hoped that book value will approximate resale value. The danger, of course, is that technological improvements will render the machine obsolete, in which case book value will not reflect true value.

A WORD ABOUT TAXES

Tax rates for corporations occasionally change. The most recent tax schedule is 20 percent of the first $25,000 of income, 22 percent of the next $25,000 of income, and 48 percent of any income in excess of $50,000. For large corporations, then, the average rate will approach 48 percent. For this reason, all large firms employ specialists to deal with tax-associated problems. Avoidance of a tax yields a direct increase in profit. Tax avoidance, however, is not tax evasion. It is accomplished by choosing a form of organization and structuring investments in such a way as to minimize the firm's tax liability.

When choosing among investment proposals, tax considerations often prove to be the deciding factor since depreciation expenses directly affect taxable income and therefore profit. Consider the following example. Firms A and B both earn net incomes of $100,000 before depreciation expenses are considered. The depreciation expense for firm A is $50,000 while that for B is only $20,000. Since before-tax income in excess of $50,000 is subject to a 48 percent tax rate, profit for A will exceed the profit for B by $14,400. The calculations are shown in the following table.

		Firm A	Firm B
1.	Income before depreciation expenses and taxes	$100,000	$100,000
2.	Depreciation expense	50,000	20,000
3.	Income before taxes	$ 50,000	$ 80,000
4.	Taxes	10,500	24,900
5.	Net income	$ 39,500	$ 55,100
6.	Funds available for reinvestment [(5) + (2)]	$ 89,500	$ 75,100

The advantage of using accelerated depreciation methods is apparent. Large tax deductions for depreciation in early years provide an added source of funds for reinvestment. One qualification must be mentioned, however. Large deductions in early years necessitate small ones in later years. This could be disadvantageous if tax rates are expected to increase significantly in the future. Even in this case, though, the time value of money may offset the effects of any future tax rate increases.

In recent years, firms have been able to employ what is termed an *investment tax credit*. A tax credit allows a direct reduction in tax liability. Note that this is a deduction from taxes payable and not simply a reduction in taxable income.

Currently the tax credit authorizes 10 percent of the cost of new machinery and equipment to be deducted from the firm's tax liability. Thus, if a firm purchases new equipment for $100,000, it is permitted to reduce its tax payment by $10,000 in the year the purchase is made. The tax credit offers a high incentive for firms to invest, and it is a proven spur to the national economy. Though originally intended to be put into effect during periods of economic recession, it has been so effective that the Senate Finance Committee has voted to make the 10 percent tax credit permanent. The current bill expires in 1980.[1]

CASH MANAGEMENT AND BUDGETING

Companies, though otherwise financially sound, are frequently forced into bankruptcy because they lack the cash needed to carry on their normal business operations. In a stable company, this may occur due to a drop in sales revenue at a time when other sources of ready cash, such as loans or convertible assets, are lacking. In a company experiencing rapid growth, this situation typically arises for two reasons. The first is the delay between investment in new productive facilities and the receipt of revenue derived from sales—a transitional period when a firm's cash needs often are most acute. The second is the tieup of funds in inventories—transit stocks, safety stocks, in-process inventory, and so on. As demand for the product increases, the demand for inventory rises at an even more rapid rate to supply wholesale and retail warehouses and fill the marketing pipelines. This, coupled with the delays inherent in the production-distribution process, puts an overwhelming strain on the firm's cash resources. Clearly, cash budgeting to meet these and similar contingencies is a must. The ensuing discussion, using as an example a firm producing a seasonal product, considers how this is done.

A cash budgeting example

Outdoor Recreation Products, Inc. (ORP), manufactures fishing rods and reels and experiences peak sales during the spring and summer months. To prepare for the period of high sales, the firm must purchase the raw materials needed for production about five months prior to the selling season. Cash expenditures will be large during this period, while at the same time sales revenue will be very low. To project cash needs, a cash budget is formulated. This budget will project future cash needs on a month-by-month basis. With knowledge of its future cash needs, the firm may, if necessary, avoid liquidity problems by negotiating a bank loan well ahead of time.

The following data for ORP are given as a basis for formulating a cash budget. Highest production levels will be maintained from December

---

[1] "Panel Supports Tax Break of 10% Being Continued," *The Wall Street Journal* (May 24, 1976), p. 4.

TABLE S.3.1

Outdoor Recreation Products, Inc.

WORKSHEET

	November	December	January	February	March	April	May	June	July	August	September
Sales	$10,000	$10,000	$16,000	$ 50,000	$ 80,000	$100,000	$100,000	$ 80,000	$80,000	$ 30,000	$ 20,000
Collections											
1st month after sales		5,000	5,000	8,000	25,000	40,000	50,000	50,000	40,000	40,000	15,000
2nd month after sales			5,000	5,000	8,000	25,000	40,000	50,000	50,000	40,000	40,000
Total Collections		$ 5,000	$10,000	$ 13,000	$ 33,000	$ 65,000	$ 90,000	$100,000	$90,000	$ 80,000	$ 55,000
Purchases of raw materials	$25,000	$30,000	$35,000	$ 40,000	$ 35,000	$ 25,000	$ 10,000	$ 6,000	$ 4,000	$ 4,000	$ 4,000
Payments (1 month after purchases)		25,000	30,000	35,000	40,000	35,000	25,000	10,000	6,000	4,000	4,000

CASH BUDGET

	November	December	January	February	March	April	May	June	July	August	September
Revenues (collections)		$ 5,000	$10,000	$ 13,000	$ 33,000	$ 65,000	$ 90,000	$100,000	$90,000	$ 80,000	$ 55,000
Payments											
Purchases		$25,000	$30,000	$ 35,000	$ 40,000	$ 35,000	$ 25,000	$ 10,000	$ 6,000	$ 4,000	$ 4,000
Salaries		10,000	12,000	15,000	15,000	12,000	10,000	5,000	5,000	5,000	5,000
Rent and leases		2,000	2,000	2,000	2,000	2,000	2,000	2,000	2,000	2,000	2,000
Long-term debt retirement								30,000			
Income taxes						20,000					
Total Payments		$37,000	$44,000	$ 52,000	$ 57,000	$ 69,000	$ 37,000	$ 47,000	$13,000	$ 11,000	$ 11,000
Net cash increase (decrease) during month		($32,000)	($34,000)	($39,000)	($24,000)	($4,000)	$53,000	$53,000	$77,000	$69,000	$44,000
Beginning cash		10,000	(22,000)	(56,000)	(95,000)	(119,000)	(123,000)	(70,000)	(17,000)	60,000	129,000
Cumulative cash		(22,000)	(56,000)	(95,000)	(119,000)	(123,000)	(70,000)	(17,000)	60,000	129,000	173,000
Desired level of cash (safety level to ensure liquidity)		10,000	10,000	10,000	10,000	10,000	10,000	10,000	10,000	10,000	10,000
Excess cash (or additional financing required)*		($32,000)	($66,000)	($105,000)	($129,000)	($133,000)	($80,000)	($27,000)	$50,000	$119,000	$163,000

* Cumulative less desired.

through April, and highest sales levels will occur between March and July. The firm expects to pay its bills one month after incurring them, and to receive payments on sales as follows: 50 percent one month after sales are made and 50 percent two months after sales are made. Procedurally, a worksheet is first drawn up that accounts only for cash outflow due to the purchase of raw materials and for cash inflow resulting from sales. Then, with the worksheet as a basis, a cash budget that accounts for all causes of cash flow is developed. A cash budget for Outdoor Recreation Products is shown in Table S.3.1.

The cash budget for ORP shows why a business with a highly fluctuating cash level requires periodic external financing to carry on normal operations. The cash deficit is at a maximum in April, and the company will need to borrow at least $133,000 to maintain a safe cash level and ensure liquidity. Management is thus provided a tool with which to determine how much additional funds are necessary during any given month. Beginning in July, cash will exceed the level desired, and ORP can begin to repay the loan.

In general, sales require financing. The more cyclical a firm's sales, the greater the amount of financing that will be required. Outdoor Recreation could avoid financing only by holding very large cash reserves during the year in anticipation of the heavy need for cash during the months of high production. However, the opportunity cost of holding cash in such quantity is high. Therefore it may be in the firm's best interests to invest its excess cash in capital assets that yield higher rates of return and to borrow funds to finance production.

BREAK-EVEN ANALYSIS

Break-even analysis is used to determine the volume of sales (either in dollars or units of output) that must be achieved for the firm to break even; that is, to neither earn profits nor incur losses. The sales volume—in units or dollar amount—that gives this result is termed the *break-even point,* and calculation of the break-even point is quite simple. The accompanying formula is used to determine the break-even point in units of output.

$$\text{Break-even point in units} = \frac{\text{Total fixed costs}}{\text{Unit price} - \text{Variable cost per unit}}$$

Since variable costs are assumed to be the same for each unit of output, subtracting variable costs from price yields the amount of revenue each unit sold contributes toward the coverage of fixed costs. Fixed costs, of course, remain constant regardless of the level of output. The break-even point will be achieved when sales produce just enough revenue above variable costs to cover fixed costs.

Suppose a product is priced at $10 and the variable cost is $6 per unit. If total fixed costs are $1,000, the break-even point in units of output sold is

$$\text{Break-even point in units} = \frac{TFC}{P - VC} = \frac{\$1,000}{\$10 - \$6} = 250$$

The result is easily verified. Total costs = $1,000 fixed costs + $6 variable cost × 250 units = $1,000 + $1,500 = $2,500. Total revenue is $10 selling price × 250 units, or $2,500.

We can also look at the break-even point as the point where revenue equals variable costs plus fixed costs. If N is the number of units sold,

$$\text{Revenue} = \text{Variable costs} + \text{Fixed costs}$$
$$10N = 6N + 1{,}000$$
$$N = 250 \text{ units}$$

The analysis can be extended to allow for a profit goal. To the numerator in the formula, a desired level of profit is added to the fixed costs. The result gives the sales in units required to attain a given level of profit. Using the figures above, and assuming a profit goal of $3,000, the required sales in units is

Units required to yield a desired level of profit

$$= \frac{\text{Total fixed costs} + \text{Desired profit level}}{\text{Price} - \text{Variable costs}} \quad (1)$$

Units required to yield a $3,000 profit

$$= \frac{\$1{,}000 + \$3{,}000}{\$10 - \$6} = 1{,}000 \quad (2)$$

The sale of 1,000 units will yield a before-tax profit of $3,000.

FIGURE S.3.2

Relationships among costs, output, and profit (fixed costs = $1,000; variable costs = $6 per unit; selling price = $10 per unit)

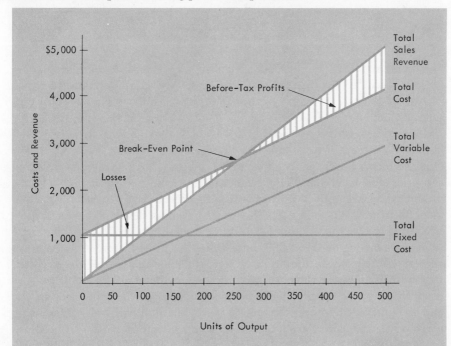

FIGURE S.3.3

Comparative relationship among costs, output, sales revenues, and profits when varying selling prices are used (fixed costs = $1,000; variable cost = $6 per unit; selling price A = $9 per unit; selling price B = $10 per unit)

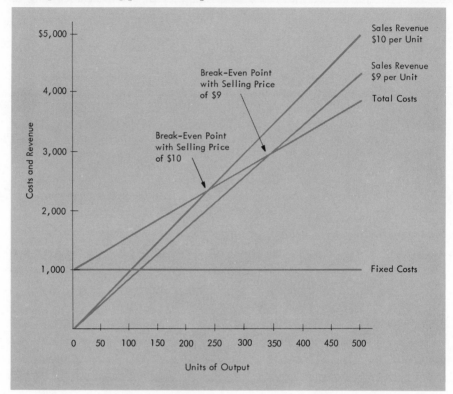

The relationships among costs, level of output, and revenue are shown graphically in Figure S.3.2. Reference to such a graph provides a quick picture of profits (or losses) as they may be expected to change with output.

It will now be shown how break-even analysis assists in pricing decisions. Suppose a firm produces a product with variable costs of $6 per unit and incurs fixed costs totaling $1,000. Because management is debating the price and can't decide whether to set a price of $9 or $10 for the product, the accounting department constructs a graph to assist management in making the decision. The same formulas developed earlier have been used to construct Figure S.3.3. Break even occurs at 250 units when the selling price is $10, and at 333 units when the price is $9. Which price is chosen will depend on the firm's estimated demand curve for the product. Beyond 250 units, any level of sales yields greater profits if a $10 price is used. But suppose the firm feels it can sell 250 units when the price is $10, and 450 units if the product is priced at $9. The firm will break even using a $10 price, and earn a profit using the $9 price. Alternatively, suppose 450 units can be sold at $10, and that sales will be 500 units if the price is $9.

In this case, notice that a larger profit can be earned if a $10 price is set, even though 50 additional units could be sold if the price were $9.

Once again, the price to be selected will depend on management's estimate of how much the market will absorb at each price. Break-even analysis does not indicate which price should be selected; rather, it aids management in making the decision by providing a picture of profits at various prices and levels of sales.

CHOOSING AMONG SPECIFIC INVESTMENT PROPOSALS

The capital investment decision has become highly rationalized, as evidenced by the variety of techniques available for its solution. In contradistinction to pricing or marketing decisions, the capital investment decision can usually be made with a higher degree of confidence because the variables affecting the decision are relatively well known and can be quantified with fair accuracy.

Investment decisions may be grouped into six general categories:

1. Purchase of new equipment and/or facilities
2. Replacement of existing equipment or facilities
3. Make-or-buy decisions
4. Lease-or-buy decisions
5. Temporary shutdown or plant abandonment decisions
6. Addition or elimination of a product or product line

Investment decisions are made with regard to the lowest acceptable rate of return on investment. As a starting point, the lowest acceptable rate of return may be considered to be the cost of investment capital needed to underwrite the expenditure. Certainly an investment will not be made if it does not return at least the cost of capital. Investments are generally ranked according to the return they yield in excess of their cost of capital. In this way a business with only limited investment funds can select investment alternatives that yield the highest *net* returns. (Net return is defined here as the earnings an investment yields after gross earnings have been reduced by the cost of the funds used to finance the investment.) In general, investments should not be made unless the return in funds exceeds the *marginal* cost of investment capital (marginal cost is defined as the incremental cost of each new acquisition of funds from outside sources).

A general view of the investment problem is presented graphically in Figure S.3.4. In constructing this graph, the assumption is made that the marginal cost of capital is a constant 8 percent up to $30 million, and increases rapidly thereafter. Given these alternatives, which should be selected? Clearly, since the alternative with the highest rate of return should be selected first, a firm which has $20 million to invest should select A, B, and C, in that order. If it has $30 million, it should select alternatives A through D. Since the remaining alternatives' cost of capital is in excess of net return, they should not be chosen. In this situation, $30 million is the maximum cutoff point for investments.

A major problem in choosing among alternatives is encountered when the expected lives of the investments differ. Comparison is easier and more accurate if the economic lives of the alternatives under consideration are the same. We will deal with this problem later, when we consider some specific proposals.

Several types of costs are used in capital investment decisions: (1) fixed costs, (2) variable costs, (3) opportunity costs, (4) sunk costs, and (5) avoidable costs. (The first four have been defined previously.)

FIGURE S.3.4

Priority among investment alternatives

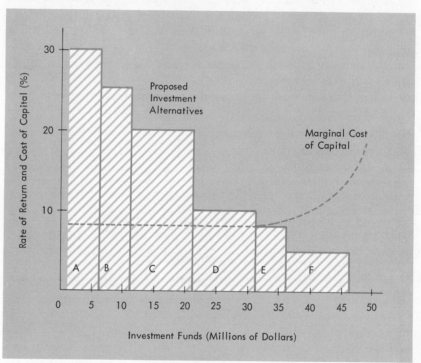

Avoidable costs include any expense that will *not* be incurred if an investment is made but that *must* be incurred if the investment is not made. Suppose a company owns a metal lathe that is not in working condition but is needed for the firm's operations. Since the lathe must be repaired or replaced, the repair costs are avoidable if a new lathe is purchased. Avoidable costs reduce the cost of a new investment because they will not be incurred if the investment is made. Avoidable costs are an example of how it is possible to "save" money by spending money.

INTEREST RATE EFFECTS

There are two basic ways to account for the effects of interest accumulation: one way is to compute the total amount created over the time period as the *compound value,* and the other way is to remove the interest rate effect over time by reducing all future sums to present-day dollars, or the *present value.*

Compound value

The compound value of a sum, say $10, is the value of the sum after it earns an annual rate of interest over a specified period. The sum earns interest during each period on the initial value *and* on the interest earned in the preceding periods. For example, the compound value of $10 earning 5 percent interest after three years is $11.58, and is derived as follows. The value of $10 after one year is $10 + ($10) (0.05) = $10.50, or $10 (1 + 0.05) = $10.50. Thus the value of a sum after any year is the beginning value times one plus the interest rate (i).

Year	Adding in interest rate $(1 + i)$	Value at beginning of year		Value at end of year
1.....................	$(1 + 0.05)$	$\times$ $10.000	=	$10.500
2.....................	$(1 + 0.05)$	$\times$ $10.500	=	$11.025
3.....................	$(1 + 0.05)$	$\times$ $11.025	=	$11.576 or $11.58

The process used to arrive at the $11.58 figure is generalized below, where V = value at the end of a specific year, P = principal, or value at the beginning of a specific year, i = the interest rate, and the subscript represents the length of the compounding period:

$$V_3 = P_3(1 + i) = P_1(1 + i)^3$$
$$= \$10.00 \ (1 + 0.05)^3$$
$$= \$10.00 \ (1.158)$$
$$= \$11.58$$

Thus the general formula for compound value is:

$$V_n = P_1(1 + i)^n$$

In practice, it is not necessary to compute compound values. Compound value tables are available that list the compound value for a number of years and various interest rates. Using Table S.3.2, we see that the value of $1 at 5 percent interest after three years is $1.158. Multiplying this figure by $10 gives $11.58, as computed previously. (Note: Tables S.3.2 through S.3.5 will be found as an appendix of this supplement.)

The compound value of an *annuity* is found in a similar manner. An *annuity* is the receipt of a constant sum each year for a specified number of years. Usually an annuity is received at the end of a period and does not earn interest during that period. Therefore, an annuity of $10 for three years would bring in $10 at the end of the first year (allowing the $10 to earn interest if invested for the remaining two years), $10 at the end of the second year (allowing the $10 to earn interest for the remaining one year), and $10 at the end of the third year (with no time to earn interest). If the annuity receipts were placed in a bank savings account at 5 percent interest, the total or compound value of the $10 at 5 percent for the three years would be:

Year	Receipt at end of year		Compound interest factor $(1 + i)^n$		Value at end of third year
1....................	$10.00	×	$(1 + 0.05)^2$	=	$11.02
2....................	10.00	×	$(1 + 0.05)^1$	=	10.50
3....................	10.00	×	$(1 + 0.05)^0$	=	10.00
					$31.52

The general formula for finding the compound value of an annuity is

$$S_n = R(1 + i)^{n-1} + R(1 + i)^{n-2} + \cdots + R(1 + i)^1 + R$$
$$= R[(1 + i)^{n-1} + (1 + i)^{n-2} + \cdots + (1 + i)^1 + 1]$$

where

S_n = Compound value of an annuity
R = Periodic receipts in dollars
n = Length of the annuity in years

Applying this formula to the above example, we get:

$$S_n = R[(1 + i)^2 + (1 + i) + 1]$$
$$= \$10[(1 + 0.05)^2 + (1 + 0.05) + 1]$$
$$= \$10 (3.152)$$
$$= \$31.52$$

Compound value tables for annuities also are available to simplify computation. Table S.3.3 lists the compound value factor of $1 for 5 percent after three years as 3.152. Multiplying this factor by $10 yields $31.52.

Present value

Compound values are used to determine the value of a sum after a specified period has elapsed. Present-value procedures accomplish just the reverse. They are used to determine the current value of a sum or stream of receipts expected to be received in the future. Most investment decision techniques utilize present-value concepts rather than compound values. Since decisions affecting the future are made in the present, it is better to convert future returns into their present value at the time the decision is being made. In this way, investment alternatives are placed in better perspective in terms of current dollars.

An example will make this more apparent. If a rich uncle offers to make you a gift of $100 today or $150 after 10 years, which should you choose? You must determine whether the $150 in 10 years will be worth more than the $100 now. Suppose that you base your decision on the rate of inflation in the economy and believe that inflation averages 5 percent per year. By deflating the $150, you can compare its relative purchasing power with $100 received today. Procedurally, this is accomplished by solving the compound formula for the present sum, P, where V is the future amount of $150 in 10 years at 5 percent. The compound value formula is

$$V = P(1 + i)^n$$

Dividing both sides by $(1 + i)^n$ gives:

$$P = \frac{V}{(1 + i)^n}$$
$$= \frac{\$150}{(1 + 0.05)^{10}}$$
$$= \$92.10$$

This shows that, at a 5 percent inflationary rate, $150 in 10 years will be worth $92.10 today. The rational choice, then, is to take the $100 now.

The use of tables is also standard practice in solving present-value problems. With reference to Table S.3.4, the present-value factor for $1 received 10 years hence is 0.614. Multiplication of this factor by $150 yields $92.10.

The present value of a future sum includes compounding at a specific interest rate, just as do compound value procedures. The difference lies in the fact that compounding takes place in reverse. The practice of reducing future sums or income streams to present values by using specified interest rates is often referred to as *discounting*. The discounted value of $150 after 10 years at 5 percent is $92.10. This is the same as *present value*, and the terms are generally interchangeable.

The present value of an annuity is the value of an annuity to be received over a future period expressed in terms of the present. The process of finding it is simply the reverse of finding the compound value of an annuity. Again, the purpose is to deal with values in the present rather than in the future. To find the value of an annuity of $100 for three years at 10 percent, find the factor in the present-value table which applies to 10 percent in *each* of the three years in which the amount is received and multiply each receipt by this factor. Then sum the resulting figures. Remember that annuities are usually received at the end of each period.

Year	Amount received at end of year		Present-value factor at 10%		Present value
1..........................	$100	×	0.909	=	$ 90.90
2..........................	100	×	0.826	=	82.60
3..........................	100	×	0.751	=	75.10
Total receipts..................	$300		Total P.V.	=	$248.60

The general formula used to derive the present value of an annuity is

$$A_n = R \left[\frac{1}{(1 + i)} + \frac{1}{(1 + i)^2} + \cdots + \frac{1}{n} \right]$$

where

A_n = Present value of an annuity of n years
R = Periodic receipts
n = Length of the annuity in years

Applying the formula to the above example gives

$$A_n = \$100 \left[\frac{1}{(1 + 0.10)} + \frac{1}{(1 + 0.10)^2} + \frac{1}{(1 + 0.10)^3} \right]$$
$$= \$100 \ (2.488)$$
$$= \$248.80$$

The $248.80 result differs from the answer obtained above because of rounding in the table of present-value factors. Tables for the present value of an annuity are also available. The present-value factor for an annuity of $1 for three years at 10 percent (from Table S.3.5) is 2.487. Since our sum is $100 rather than $1, we multiply this factor by $100 to arrive at $248.70. Again, the slight variance from the previous answers results from rounded figures in the table.

When the stream of future receipts is uneven, the present value of each annual receipt must be calculated. The present values of the receipts for all years are then summed to arrive at total present value. This process can sometimes be tedious, but it is unavoidable. Discounted at 10 percent, the total present value of $100 received in one year, $400 in two years, and $200 in five years would be as shown on the accompanying table.

Year	Annual receipt		Present-value factor at 10%		Present value
1....................	$100	×	0.909	=	$ 90.90
2....................	400	×	0.826	=	330.40
3....................	...		....		.....
4....................	...		....		.....
5....................	200	×	0.621	=	124.20
	$700				$545.50 = Total P.V.

METHODS OF RANKING INVESTMENTS

Payback period

The payback method ranks investments according to the time required for each investment to return earnings equal to the cost of the investment. The rationale underlying the use of payback is that the sooner investment capital can be recovered, the sooner it can be reinvested in new revenue-producing projects. Thus, supposedly, a firm will be able to get the most benefit from its available investment funds.

Consider two alternatives requiring a $1,000 investment each. The first will earn $200 per year for six years; the second will earn $300 per year for the first three years, and $100 per year for the next three years. The two alternatives are outlined in the accompanying table.

	Alternative A *Investment = $1,000*	*Alternative B* *Investment = $1,000*
Year	*Cash inflow*	*Cash inflow*
1........................	$ 200	$ 300
2........................	200	300
3........................	200	300
4........................	200	100
5........................	200	100
6........................	200	100
	$1,200	$1,200

If alternative *A* is selected, the initial investment of $1,000 will be recovered at the end of the fifth year. The income produced by *B* will total $1,000 after only four years. The selection of *B* will permit reinvestment of the full $1,000 in new revenue-producing projects one year sooner than *A*, and under this method, should be selected.

The payback method is declining in popularity as the sole measure in investment decisions. It is still frequently used, however, in conjunction with other methods to give an indication of the time commitment of funds. The major problems with payback are that it does not consider income beyond the payback period and it ignores the time value of money. Consider the investment alternatives shown in the next table.

	Investment A *Cost: $20,000*	*Investment B* *Cost: $20,000*	*Investment C* *Cost: $20,000*
Year	*Cash inflow*	*Cash inflow*	*Cash inflow*
1......................	$6,000	$4,000	$5,000
2......................	6,000	4,000	5,000
3......................	6,000	4,000	5,000
4......................	6,000	4,000	5,000
5......................	6,000	4,000	4,000
6......................	—	4,000	4,000
7......................	—	4,000	4,000
8......................	—	4,000	4,000
9......................	—	4,000	—
10......................	—	4,000	—
Payback period..........	3.33 years	5 years	4 years
Total receipts............	$30,000	$40,000	$36,000
Present value at 12%.....	$21,630	$22,600	$22,909

On the basis of payback, investment *A* represents the best alternative since it will return the original investment of $20,000 in only 3⅓ years. If, however, the firm discounts the cash flow of each investment by the cost of capital, in this case 12 percent, investment *C* is the most attractive of the three.[2] While investment *B* will return more in actual dollars than either

---

[2] This example ignores the availability of cash for reinvestment, which is obviously higher for alternative A. This problem is discussed again in this supplement under "Ranking investments with uneven lives," (page 133).

A or *C*, its present value is less than that for *C*. Total earnings do not afford the best basis for decision because, as with payback, the time value of money is ignored. The present value of the three income streams offers the best method of comparison because the alternatives can be compared in terms of their value at the same point in time.

Net present value

The net present-value method is commonly used in business. Under this method, decisions are based on the amount by which the present value of a projected income stream exceeds the cost of an investment. (Refer to the previous example.) The present values of the income streams, discounted at the cost of capital, exceed the cost of the investments by the amounts shown in the accompanying table.

	Investment A	Investment B	Investment C
Present value of total cash flows.......	$21,630	$22,600	$22,909
Cost of investment.................	20,000	20,000	20,000
Net present value.................	$ 1,630	$ 2,600	$ 2,909

Investment *C*, at $2,909, yields the highest net present value, and should be selected.

Now consider a case where the costs of investments differ. A firm is considering two alternative investments, the first costing $30,000 and the second $50,000. The expected yearly cash income streams are shown in the next table.

	Alternative A Cost: $30,000	Alternative B Cost: $50,000
Year	Cash inflow	Cash inflow
1...........................	$10,000	$15,000
2...........................	10,000	15,000
3...........................	10,000	15,000
4...........................	10,000	15,000
5...........................	10,000	15,000

To choose between alternatives *A* and *B*, find which alternative has the highest net present value. Assume an 8 percent cost of capital.

Alternative A:
3.993 (P.V. factor) × $10,000 = $39,930
Less cost of investment   = 30,000
Net present value   = $ 9,930

Alternative B:
3.993 (P.V. factor) × $15,000 = $59,895
Less cost of investment   = 50,000
Net present value   = $ 9,895

Investment A is the better alternative. Its net present value exceeds that of investment B by \$35 (\$9,930 − \$9,895 = \$35).

Internal rate of return

The internal rate of return may be defined as the interest rate that equates the present value of an income stream with the cost of an investment. There is no procedure or formula that may be used directly to compute the internal rate of return—it must be found by interpolation or iterative calculation.

Suppose we wish to find the internal rate of return for an investment costing \$12,000 that will yield a cash inflow of \$4,000 per year for four years. We see that the present value factor sought is

$$\frac{\$12,000}{\$4,000} = 3.000$$

and we seek the interest rate that will provide this factor over a four-year period. The interest rate must lie between 12 percent and 14 percent because 3.000 lies between 3.037 and 2.914 (in the fourth row of Table S.3.5). Linear interpolation between these values, according to the following equation

$$i = 12 + (14 - 12)\,\frac{(3.037 - 3.000)}{(3.037 - 2.914)}$$
$$= 12 + 0.602 = 12.602\%$$

gives a good approximation to the actual internal rate of return.[3]

When the income stream is discounted at 12.6 percent, the resulting present value closely approximates the cost of investment. Thus the internal rate of return for this investment is 12.6 percent. The cost of capital can be compared with the internal rate of return to determine the net rate of return on the investment. If, in this example, the cost of capital were 8 percent, the net rate of return on the investment would be 4.6 percent.

---

[3] Iterative calculation can be used to obtain i to any desired accuracy. The procedure seeks the value of i that satisfies the equation

$$\frac{4,000}{(1 + i)} + \frac{4,000}{(1 + i)^2} + \frac{4,000}{(1 + i)^3} + \frac{4,000}{(1 + i)^4} = 12,000$$

Dividing both sides by 4,000 and replacing $1/(1 + i)$ by j,

$$j + j^2 + j^3 + j^4 = 3.000$$

Because the sum of series

$$j + j^2 + j^3 + j^4 + \cdots + j^k$$

is equal to

$$\frac{j - j^{k+1}}{1 - j}$$

we obtain

$$\frac{j - j^5}{1 - j} = 3$$

or

$$j - j^5 = 3 - 3j$$

or

$$j^5 - 4j + 3 = 0$$

Taking i equal to \$.126 (from the interpolation), we use $j = 1/(1 + 0.126)$ as the first trial value. Observing the variation of $j^5 - 4j + 3$ with successive small variations of j quickly leads to a value accurate to several decimal places. (A few iterations with a hand calculator give $i = 0.1258985$.)

The net present-value and internal rate-of-return methods involve procedures that are essentially the same. They differ in that the net present-value method enables investment alternatives to be compared in terms of the dollar value in excess of cost whereas the internal rate-of-return method permits comparison of rates of return on alternative investments.

In most instances, each method will rank a series of alternatives in an identical manner. Sometimes, however, when investments are unequal amounts, the two methods will give different results. Such an instance is given below, where we assume a 7 percent cost of capital.

Year	Alternative A Cost: $55,000 Cash flows	Alternative B Cost: $75,000 Cash flows
1	$15,000	$20,000
2	15,000	20,000
3	15,000	20,000
4	15,000	20,000
5	15,000	20,000

Internal rates of return:
  Investment A:
    P.V. factor = $55,000/$15,000 = 3.667
    Internal rate of return = approximately 11.3% (interpolated in Table S.3.5)

  Investment B:

    P.V. factor = $75,000/$20,000 = 3.750
    Internal rate of return = approximately 10.4% (interpolated in Table S.3.5)

Net present values (cost of capital = 7%):

Investment A:		Investment B:	
4.100 × $15,000	= $61,500	4.100 × $20,000	= $82,000
Cost of investment =	55,000	Cost of investment =	75,000
Net present value =	$ 6,500	Net present value =	$ 7,000

The internal rate-of-return method would indicate that *A* should be chosen, while the net present-value method points to *B* as the best alternative. Because no clear answer can be given as to which investment should be made, the decision will depend heavily upon other factors, such as the relative risk of the two investments or the presence of other investment alternatives. As an example of the latter, suppose the firm had another alternative that would require a $20,000 investment. If the total net present value of alternative *A* and the $20,000 investment were greater than the net present value of *B*, *A* should be chosen.

Depreciation and cash flow

The examples have thus far referred to investment earnings as cash flows. The reason for this is that only the actual cash flow produced by an investment is relevant to the investment decision process. Earnings before depreciation and tax adjustments do not represent the actual benefits realized by a firm. Consequently, the expected income from an investment must be adjusted to represent only the realizable cash inflow before ranking can take place.

Assume that a machine costing $10,000 has an expected life of five years and is expected to produce gross earnings of $4,000 each year. With straight-line depreciation, no salvage value for the machine, and a 50 percent tax rate, the annual cash inflow in *each* of the five years will be

Gross earnings...............................	$4,000
Less: Depreciation expense...................	2,000
Income before taxes..........................	$2,000
Less: Taxes at 50%..........................	1,000
Net income....................................	$1,000
Plus: Depreciation expense...................	2,000
Cash inflow...................................	$3,000

In this example, with the straight-line method, the net present value of the investment, using a 10 percent cost of capital, is:

$$(3.791 \times \$3,000) - \$10,000 = \$1,373$$

Contrast this with the sum-of-years'-digits method of depreciation, which provides large cash flows in the early years of an investment's life. This will result in higher present values of income streams because the larger cash flows in the early years will not be affected by discounting as greatly as the smaller flows in later years. Under the SYD method, the cash flow for each year must be calculated separately since the flows will differ and therefore cannot be treated as an annuity. The results of applying the SYD method are summarized in the accompanying table.

Year	Present-value factor		Cash flow		Present value
1...............	0.909	×	$3,667	=	$ 3333.30
2...............	0.826	×	3,333	=	2753.06
3...............	0.751	×	3,000	=	2253.00
4...............	0.683	×	2,667	=	1821.56
5...............	0.621	×	2,333	=	1448.79
					$11,609.71 or $11,610

Also,

$$\text{Net present value} = \$11,610 - \$10,000 = \$1,610$$

Use of the SYD method in preference to the straight-line method increases net present value by $237 ($1,610 − $1,373 = $237).

Ranking investments with uneven lives

When proposed investments have the same life expectancy, comparison among them, using the preceding methods, will give a reasonable picture of their relative value. When lives are unequal, however, the net present-value and internal rate-of-return methods share a crucial shortcoming. In the example that used the payback method, notice that investment A has a life expectancy half that of B. When A is exhausted at the end of the fifth year, management would presumably reinvest the $20,000 cost. If this is done, the earnings on the new investment over the next five years must be compared with the earnings on B for years 6 through 10 if a true comparison between A and B is to be made. Suppose $20,000 is reinvested (after investment A expires) in investment A′, which has a life expectancy of five years. Since the reinvested $20,000 is the *same* $20,000 that were originally invested, over the 10-year period the investment funds used to finance A and A′ are equal to the investment in B, that is, $20,000.

The problem, then, concerns the rate of return on A′ over years 6 through 10. The earnings on A′ must be estimated before A can be compared with B. But how can this be done, when A′ does not even exist at the time of decision? The answer is that it cannot be done with specificity; yet some standard for comparison is needed for ranking to occur.

One approach is to assume that the second investment (A′ in this case) will return just the cost of capital. Another approach would be to use the internal rate-of-return method. If a firm operates with a 20 percent cutoff rate of return, it would be assumed that the new investment, A′, would earn the minimum acceptable rate of return, 20 percent. Which percentage to use depends on the historical rate of return on the firm's investments and its policy regarding cutoff rates of return. A third approach would be to assume new investments to be exact duplicates of the original in cost and cash inflow. In that case, unequal lives can be resolved by taking multiples of investments over an identical period (e.g., two investments in A at 5 years each compared to one in B for 10 years).

These approaches still do not provide a completely satisfactory method for dealing with investments having unequal lives. One immediately striking shortcoming is the assumption that machine A′, purchased five years hence, will be equivalent to machine A, purchased today. On the contrary, technological improvements can generally be expected to make A′ the better and more productive machine, and may provide a higher cash inflow. On the other hand, inflationary pressures may substantially increase the purchase price of A′.

No estimate dealing with investments unforeseen at the time of decision can be expected to reflect a high degree of accuracy. Still, the problem must be dealt with, and these approaches afford a reasonable basis for proceeding with ranking.

EXAMPLES OF INVESTMENT DECISIONS

An expansion decision

Problem. William J. Wilson Ceramic Products, Inc., leases plant facilities in which firebrick is manufactured. Because of rising demand, Wilson could increase sales by investing in new equipment to expand output. The selling price of $10 per brick will remain unchanged if output and sales increase. Based on engineering and cost estimates, the accounting department provides management with the following cost estimates based on an annual increased output of 100,000 bricks.

Cost of new equipment having an expected life of
   five years....................................... $500,000
Equipment installation cost.........................   20,000
Expected salvage value..............................   0
New operation's share of annual lease expense..........   10,000
Annual increase in utility expenses..................   40,000
Annual increase in labor costs.......................   160,000
Annual additional cost for raw materials..............   400,000

The sum-of-years'-digits method of depreciation will be used and taxes are paid at a rate of 40 percent. Mr. Wilson's policy is not to invest capital in projects earning less than a 20 percent rate of return. Should the proposed expansion be undertaken?

Solution. Compute cost of investment:

Acquisition cost of equipment.................... $500,000
Equipment installation costs.....................   20,000
Total cost of investment......................... $520,000

Determine yearly cash flows throughout the life of the investment:

The lease expense is a sunk cost. It will be incurred whether or not the investment is made, and is therefore irrelevant to the decision and should be disregarded. Annual production expenses to be considered are utility, labor, and raw materials. These total $600,000 per year.

Annual sales revenue is $10 × 100,000 units of output, or $1,000,000. Yearly income before depreciation and taxes is thus $1,000,000 gross revenue less $600,000 expenses, or $400,000.

Determine the depreciation charges to be deducted from the $400,000 each year using the SYD method (sum-of-years' digits $= 1 + 2 + 3 + 4 + 5 = 15$):

Year	Proportion of $500,000 to be depreciated				Depreciation charge
1............	5/15	×	$500,000	=	$166,667
2............	4/15	×	500,000	=	133,333
3............	3/15	×	500,000	=	100,000
4............	2/15	×	500,000	=	66,667
5............	1/15	×	500,000	=	33,333
Accumulated depreciation				=	$500,000

Find each year's cash flow when taxes are 40 percent. Cash flow for only the first year is illustrated:

Earnings before depreciation and taxes.........		$400,000
Deduct: Taxes at 40%....................	$160,000	
Add: Tax benefit of depreciation expense		
(0.4 × 166,667).....................	66,667	93,333
Cash flow (1st year).......................		$306,667

Determine present value of the cash flows:

Since Wilson demands at least a 20 percent rate of return on investments, multiply the cash flows by the 20 percent present-value factor for each year. The factor for each respective year must be used because the cash flows are not an annuity.

Year	Present-value factor		Cash flow		Present value
1....................	0.833	×	$306,667	=	$255,454
2....................	0.694	×	293,333	=	203,573
3....................	0.579	×	280,000	=	162,120
4....................	0.482	×	266,667	=	128,533
5....................	0.402	×	253,334	=	101,840
Total present value of cash flows (discounted at 20%)......................				=	$851,520

Find whether net present value is positive or negative:

Total present value of cash flows.................	$851,520
Total cost of investment.......................	520,000
Net present value............................	$331,520

Decision. Net present value is positive when returns are discounted at 20%. Wilson will earn an amount in excess of 20% on the investment. The proposed expansion should be undertaken.

A replacement decision

Problem. For five years Bennie's Brewery has been using a machine that attaches labels to bottles. The machine was purchased for $4,000 and is being depreciated over 10 years to a zero salvage value using straight-line depreciation. The machine can be sold now for $2,000. Bennie can buy a new labeling machine for $6,000 that will have a useful life of five years and cut labor costs by $1,200 annually. The old machine will require a major overhaul in the next few months. The cost of the overhaul is expected to be $300. If purchased, the new machine will be depreciated over five years to a $500 salvage value using the straight-line method. The company will invest in any project earning more than the 12% cost of capital. The tax rate is 40%. Should Bennie's Brewery invest in the new machine?

Solution. Determine the cost of investment:

Price of the new machine.................. $6,000
   Less: Sale of old machine.............. $2,000
       Avoidable overhaul costs.......... 300   2,300
Effective cost of investment............. $3,700

Determine the increase in cash flow resulting from investment in the new machine:

Yearly cost savings = $1,200.
Differential depreciation:
  Annual depreciation on old machine:

$$\frac{\text{Cost} - \text{Salvage}}{\text{Expected life}} = \frac{\$4,000 - \$0}{10} = \$400$$

Annual depreciation on new machine:

$$\frac{\text{Cost} - \text{Salvage}}{\text{Expected life}} = \frac{\$6,000 - \$500}{5} = \$1,100$$

Differential depreciation = $1,100 − $400 = $700
Yearly net increase in cash flow into the firm:

Cost savings....................................... $1,200
  Deduct: Taxes at 40%......................... $480
  Add: Advantage of increase in depreciation
    (0.4 × $700)............................ 280   200
Yearly increase in cash flow...................... $1,000

Determine total present value of the investment:

The five-year cash flow of $1,000 per year is an annuity.
Discounted at 12 percent, the cost of capital, the present value is

$$3.605 \times \$1,000 = \$3,605$$

The present value of the new machine, if sold at its salvage value of $500 at the end of the fifth year, is

$$0.567 \times \$500 = \$284$$

Total present value of the expected cash flows:

$$\$3,605 + \$284 = \$3,889$$

Determine whether net present value is positive:

Total present value..................... $3,889
Cost of investment..................... 3,700
Net present value..................... $ 189

Decision. Bennie's Brewery should make the purchase because the investment will return slightly more than the cost of capital.

Note: The importance of depreciation has been shown in this example. The present value of the yearly cash flow resulting from operations is *only*

$$\text{(Cost savings} - \text{Taxes)} \quad \text{(Present value factor)}$$
$$(\$1,200 - \$480) \qquad \times \qquad (3.605) \qquad = \$2,596$$

This figure is $1,104 less than the $3,700 cost of the investment. Only a very large depreciation advantage makes this investment worthwhile. The total present value of the advantage is $1,009:

$$\text{(Tax rate} \times \text{Differential depreciation)} \quad \text{(P.V. factor)}$$
$$(0.4 \times \$700) \qquad \times \qquad (3.605) \qquad = \$1,009$$

A make-or-buy decision

Problem. The Triple X Company manufactures and sells refrigerators. It makes some of the parts for the refrigerators and purchases others. The engineering department believes it might be possible to cut costs by manufacturing one of the parts currently being purchased for $8.25 each. The firm uses 100,000 of these parts each year, and the accounting department compiles the following list of costs based on engineering estimates.

Fixed costs will increase by $50,000.
Labor costs will increase by $125,000.
Factory overhead, currently running $500,000 per year, may be expected to increase 12 percent.
Raw materials used to make the part will cost $600,000.

Given the above estimates, should Triple X make the part or continue to buy it?

Solution. Find total cost incurred if the part were manufactured:

Additional fixed costs..................................... $ 50,000
Additional labor costs..................................... 125,000
Raw materials cost.. 600,000
Additional overhead costs = 0.12 × $500,000........... 60,000
    Total cost to manufacture...................... $835,000

Find cost per unit to manufacture:

$$\frac{\$835,000}{100,000} = \$8.35 \text{ per unit}$$

Decision. Triple X should continue to buy the part. Manufacturing costs exceed the present cost to purchase by $0.10 per unit.

A lease-or-buy decision

Problem. George Sprott is a small businessman who has need for a pickup truck in his everyday work. He is considering buying a truck for $3,000. If he buys the truck, he believes he will be able to sell it for $1,000 at the end of four years, so he will depreciate $2,000 of the truck's value on a straight-line basis. Sprott can borrow $3,000 from the bank and repay it in four equal annual installments at 6 percent interest. However, a friend advises him that he may be better off to lease a truck if he can get the same terms from the leasing company that he receives at the bank. Assuming that this is so, should Sprott buy or lease the truck? Taxes are 40 percent.

Solution. Find the cost to buy:

The bank loan is an installment loan at 6 percent interest, so the payments constitute a four-year annuity. Divide the amount of the loan by the present value factor for a four-year annuity at 6 percent interest to find the annual payment. Multiply the annual payments by four to find the total payment.

$$\frac{\$3,000}{3.465} = \$866 \text{ annual payment}$$

$$4 \times \$866 = \$3,464 \text{ total payment}$$

Next, find the present value of the cost of the loans:

(1) Year	(2) Yearly payment	(3) Interest at 6%	(4) Payment on principal	(5) Remaining balance	(6) Depreciation
1.........	$866	$180	$686	$2,314	$500
2.........	866	139	727	1,587	500
3.........	866	95	771	816	500
4.........	866	50	816	...	500

(7) Tax deductible expense (3) + (6)	(8) Tax saving 0.4 × (7)	(9) Cost of owning (2) − (8)	(10) Present-value factor	(11) Present value (9) × (10)
$680	272	$594	0.943	$ 560
639	256	610	0.890	543
595	238	628	0.840	527
550	220	646	0.792	497
	Total present value of payments...................			$2,127

Present value of salvage = 0.792 × $1,000 = $792
Present value of cost of loan = $2,127 − $792 = $1,335

Find the cost to lease:

(1) Year	(2) Lease payment	(3) Tax saving 0.4 × 866	(4) Lease cost after taxes (2) − (3)	(5) Present-value factor at 6%	(6) Present value (4) × (5)
1...........	$866	$346	$520	0.943	$490
2...........	866	346	520	0.890	463
3...........	866	346	520	0.840	437
4...........	866	346	520	0.792	411
	Total present value of lease payments (present value of				
	cost to lease)........................				$1,801

Compare present values of cost to buy and cost to lease:

Present value of cost to lease...................... $1,801
Present value of cost to buy....................... 1,335
Advantage of buying.............................. $ 466

Decision. Mr. Sprott should buy the truck.

Note: Again, the importance of depreciation may be noted. When Sprott purchases the truck, he gains the tax advantages to be had from depreciation. If the truck were leased, the lessor would depreciate the truck and gain advantage thereby. Sprott was also aided by being able to reduce the cost of buying by the present value of the salvage (or disposal) value of the truck.

In general, depreciation and salvage value reduce the cost of buying. However, if an asset is subject to rapid obsolescence, it may be less expensive to lease. This example should not be taken as a general demonstration of the virtues of buying rather than leasing. In many cases, leasing is less expensive than buying.

REVIEW AND DISCUSSION QUESTIONS

1. Break-even analysis is typically simplified by using constant-unit variable cost, revenue, and fixed cost. What would you expect realistic cost and revenues to be, and what would a break-even chart look like?

2. A supply of cash is necessary to operate any firm. Why is the need for cash especially high and critical in a rapidly growing firm?

3. If a firm is short of capital, what action might it take to conserve the capital it has and to obtain more?

4. Explain why the marginal cost for borrowing money increases. Why might the cost also be high for borrowing small amounts?

5. Are there any reasons for using present-value analysis rather than "future" value analysis?

6. Why might a decision maker like to see the payback analysis as well as the rate of return and the net present value?

7. Discuss why the comparison of alternative investment decisions is especially difficult when the investment choices have different life lengths.

8. Compare the advantages and disadvantages of each depreciation method.

PROBLEMS

1. Analysis of the market indicates with relative certainty that a minimum 10,000 units of a product could be sold at $4.20 per unit. However, if the price was reduced to $4 per unit, a minimum of 12,000 units could be sold.

Fixed costs   = $10,000
Fixed OH and G&A = $3,000
Direct labor   = $1.50/unit
Direct material   = $1.00/unit

a. Using break-even analysis, determine the break-even point.
b. Which of the two prices would you establish to maximize profits at the expected minimum sales levels?

2. The cost of producing between 1,500 units and 2,500 units of a product consists of $25,000 fixed cost and $10 per unit variable cost. With the selling price at $20 per unit, what is the break-even point? Suppose the price per unit was increased to $25. How does this affect the break-even point?

3. You are considering the purchase of a car and would like to decide whether to buy luxury car number one or luxury car number two. Each one comes in mauve, your favorite color, and has all the features you desire. Given a planning horizon of five years and the data below, decide between the vehicles by using present-value analysis.

	Car no. 1	*Car no. 2*
Initial cost......................	$7,000	$6,200
Operating expense (gas, oil, tires, insurance, repairs, etc.):		
1st year.......................	750	800
2nd year.......................	850	900
3rd year.......................	900	1,000
4th year.......................	950	1,100
5th year.......................	1,000	1,200
Salvage value at end of 5th year (trade-in allowance)............	2,000	1,800

Cost of money is considered as 10 percent.

4. A new machine has a cost of $24,000, an estimated economic life of eight years, and a salvage value of $4,000 at the end of the eight-year period. Assume that the annual operating costs will be $3,000 per year and that the going rate of interest is 10 percent.
    What is the present value of new expenditures for the machine?

5. Suppose a product is priced at $50 and the variable cost is $30 per unit. If the total fixed costs are $20,000, what is the break-even point in units of output sold?

6. What is the depreciation expense for the third year, using the sum-of-the-years'-digit method for the following cost (below) of a new machine?

Cost of machine...............................$35,000
Estimated life.....................................6 years
Estimated salvage value $5,000

7. Disregarding tax considerations, is it cheaper to buy or to lease a piece of equipment with the following costs for a five-year term?

	To buy	To lease
Purchase (or lease) cost...............	$50,000	$10,000/yr.
Annual operating cost..................	4,000/yr.	4,000/yr.
Maintenance cost......................	2,000/yr.	0
Salvage value at end of 5 years.........	$20,000	0

Interest value of money is 10 percent.

8. A new piece of office equipment must be purchased and the choice has been narrowed down to two styles, each capable of meeting the intended needs. With a 10-year horizon and an interest rate of 8 percent, which equipment should be purchased?

	Equipment A	Equipment B
Initial cost.......................................	$10,000	$7,000
Salvage value (10 years hence)....................	4,000	2,000
Estimated annual operation and maintenance cost...	1,000	1,500

9. The university is accepting bids for the hot dog and cold drink concession at the new stadium. The contract is for a five-year period, and it is your feeling that a bid of $40,000 will win the contract. A preliminary analysis indicates that annual operating costs will be $35,000 and average annual sales will be $50,000. The contract can be written off during the five years. Taxes are at the 40 percent rate, and your goal is to make a 20 percent return on your investment.

   a. Will you meet your goal if you use straight-line depreciation?

   b. Would you meet your goal using sum-of-the-years'-digits depreciation?

10. Because of the high demand for single-residence housing, Ackerman, Ballard, and Chessen decided to enter the construction business. As in any new business, they are faced with a variety of investment decisions. For example: Should they buy raw land and develop it themselves or should they purchase building lots in developed areas? Should they buy tools and equipment or should they lease them? Should they employ crews of their own or should they subcontract most of the work? In terms of price range, should they produce a large number of low-price homes or a small number of high-price homes?

   To analyze the first question, "Should ABC buy and develop raw land or should it buy lots with existing services?" Ackerman, after careful analysis of the city's growth direction, found a 40-acre parcel in a prime area that could be purchased for $115,000. However, roads would have to be put in and ditches dug for sewers, water, gas, and underground electric services. Also, the entire area would have to be graded and surveyed. This work would start immediately, at a cost of $100,000, to be paid at the rate of $25,000 at the end of each of the first four months (for a total of $100,000). The 40 acres would be divided into $\frac{1}{3}$-acre lots to provide a total of 120 lots. The first lots would be available for use or for sale in four months, and the expectations are that the entire area could be sold at a constant rate of 10 lots per month until all lots are sold ($120/10 = 12$ months).

Disregarding tax considerations and assuming that funds may be borrowed at a savings and loan institution at an 8 percent interest rate, what average price would ABC have to charge in order to obtain a present-value profit of $40,000? (Note: The present value of an annuity of $1 for 12 monthly increments at a simple 8 percent annual interest rate is $11.50.) The present value (on a monthly scale) of $1 based on a simple annual interest rate of 8 percent is

End of month	*Present value at 8 percent*
1	$0.9933
2	0.9868
3	0.9803
4	0.9740
5	0.9677
6	0.9615
7	0.9554
8	0.9493
9	0.9433
10	0.9375
11	0.9316
12	0.9259

11. ABC would like to build some homes on its lots and is now looking at ways to obtain needed equipment, such as mixers, a pickup truck, a flatbed truck, a compressor, a Payloader with a backhoe, mortar boxes, forms, scaffolding, and a variety of miscellaneous items. There are three ways to obtain this equipment: buy it new, buy it used, or lease it. Looking at only the Payloader under the alternatives of buy new or lease, which alternative should ABC select? (The Payloader has a life-span of 10 years; however, intentions are to sell it after five years to avoid the high cost of upkeep.) A bank loan has been set up for five years with equal annual loan payments. The cost of capital is 8 percent, and the tax rate is expected to be 40 percent.

Buy new

Purchase cost	$11,000
Maintenance and insurance	$ 500/year
Economic life	10 years
Salvage value after 5 years	$ 4,000
Depreciation method: double declining balance	

Lease

Lease cost on 5-year contract: $3,000/year
Operating costs are identical in either option.

Note: In double-declining balance the rate is double the straight-line schedule. To illustrate: for a 10-year life, straight-line depreciation is 10 percent and DDB is as follows:

Year	Rate of depreciation (double the 10%)		Beginning book value		Depreciation	Ending book value
1..........	0.20	×	$1,000	=	$200	$800
2..........	0.20	×	800	=	160	640
3..........	0.20	×	640	=	128	512
4..........	0.20	×	512	=	102	410

12. A parcel of land has been set aside by ABC to be the site of future construction. At the present time, ABC is interested in determining whether it should build $35,000 or $60,000 houses on the parcels as "speculative homes" (homes completed by a builder and available for sale to any buyer, as opposed to homes which are constructed at the request of a particular buyer). The $60,000 homes take longer to build, and sell at a lower rate, than the lower-price homes; however, each one yields a higher profit margin. For either type of house, the cost of capital is 8 percent.

Expenses incurred in building the $35,000 homes are as follows:

Cost of land................... $5,000 (immediate payment)
Time to complete home......... 3 months
Building cost of $20,000 incurred as
   1st month.............. 40%
   2nd month.............. 40%
   3rd month.............. 20%

A contingency allocation to cover the expected loss of 5 percent for material theft is included in the building cost. The average time required to sell a home is one month after completion. The entire amount of $35,000 is paid in cash either by the buyer or the new mortgage holder.

Expenses incurred for the $60,000 homes are as follows:

Cost of land................... $9,000 (immediate payment)
Time to complete home......... 5 months
Building cost of $30,000 incurred as
   1st month.............. 20%
   2nd month.............. 30%
   3rd month.............. 20%
   4th month.............. 20%
   5th month.............. 10%

The average time needed to sell the home is three months after completion, when the entire $60,000 is received in cash.

Assignment: Employ present-value analysis to help ABC make the decision as to which type of house it should build. (Use the monthly present-value figures provided in problem 10.)

13. ABC is planning to start one of each house discussed in the previous problem. At the completion of each house they will start another one of the same style, and so on. The land must be paid for at the start of the project, and when the home is sold the full selling price is to be paid to ABC by the buyer or the new mortgage holder.

Using the data from problem 12, construct a cash budget for ABC for the next 12 months. (In preparing the budget, disregard taxes and interest costs.) If all funds are borrowed, what amount of outside financing should ABC arrange for?

14. ABC's business has been going so well that the firm decides to diversify with a sideline business. Ballard, an experienced cabinet maker, has a great deal of know-how in making cabinets for kitchens and vanities for bathrooms. (Counter tops would be subcontracted because of the specialized equipment needed for molding and pressing.) The company is anticipating putting out a standard line of cabinets available in birch, walnut, mahogany, or oak veneer at no extra charge.

Three manufacturing methods are feasible for producing the cabinets. The first is largely manual, the second uses some semiautomated equipment, and the third is largely automatic. The equipment can be leased, so the fixed cost includes leasing or depreciation, overhead, and all other fixed burdens.

	Manual	*Semiautomatic*	*Mostly automated*
Annual fixed cost............	$15,000	$35,000	$80,000
Variable costs per complete kitchen			
Materials................	350	350	350
Direct labor..............	350	270	130
Crating and shipping........	120	110	100
Variable cost per unit........	$ 820	$ 730	$ 580

The wholesale price of these units will be $1,100 each. (The installed cost for the homeowner will be between $2,200 and $2,800.)

a. Construct a break-even chart for each of the three methods. If sales are expected to be 200 units per year, which manufacturing method should ABC choose?

b. ABC feels that if it sets a price of $1,000 per unit, it should be able to sell 350 units. Which production method should then be selected? How much profit will it realize?

15. In adding a new product line, a firm needs a new piece of machinery. An investigation of suitable equipment for the production process has narrowed the choice to the two machines listed below.

	Machine A	*Machine B*
Type of equipment..........	General purpose	Special purpose
Installed cost...............	$8,000	$13,000
Salvage value...............	800	3,000
Annual labor cost...........	6,000	3,600
Estimated life (years)........	10	5

Assume that at the end of five years a comparable replacement for machine B will be available. Using present-value analysis with a 10 percent interest rate, which machine would you choose?

SELECTED BIBLIOGRAPHY

Anthony, Robert N., and Welsch, Glenn A.   *Fundamentals of Management Accounting.* Homewood, Ill.: Richard D. Irwin, Inc., 1974.

Donaldson, Gordon   "Strategic Hurdle Rates for Capital Investment," *Harvard Business Review* (March–April 1972), pp. 50–58.

Grant, Eugene L., and Ireson, W. Grant   *Principles of Engineering Economy.* 5th ed. New York: Ronald Press, 1970.

Van Horne, James C.   *Financial Management and Policy.* 3d ed. Englewood Cliffs, N.J.: Prentice-Hall, 1974.

Welsch, Glenn A., and Anthony, Robert N.   *Fundamentals of Financial Accounting.* Homewood, Ill.: Richard D. Irwin, Inc., 1974.

Wert, James E., and Prather, Charles L.   *Financing Business Firms.* 5th ed. Homewood, Ill.: Richard D. Irwin, Inc., 1975.

APPENDIX: INTEREST TABLES

TABLE S.3.2

Compound sum of $1

Year	1%	2%	3%	4%	5%	6%	7%
1	1.010	1.020	1.030	1.040	1.050	1.060	1.070
2	1.020	1.040	1.061	1.082	1.102	1.124	1.145
3	1.030	1.061	1.093	1.125	1.158	1.191	1.225
4	1.041	1.082	1.126	1.170	1.216	1.262	1.311
5	1.051	1.104	1.159	1.217	1.276	1.338	1.403
6	1.062	1.126	1.194	1.265	1.340	1.419	1.501
7	1.072	1.149	1.230	1.316	1.407	1.504	1.606
8	1.083	1.172	1.267	1.369	1.477	1.594	1.718
9	1.094	1.195	1.305	1.423	1.551	1.689	1.838
10	1.105	1.219	1.344	1.480	1.629	1.791	1.967
11	1.116	1.243	1.384	1.539	1.710	1.898	2.105
12	1.127	1.268	1.426	1.601	1.796	2.012	2.252
13	1.138	1.294	1.469	1.665	1.886	2.133	2.410
14	1.149	1.319	1.513	1.732	1.980	2.261	2.579
15	1.161	1.346	1.558	1.801	2.079	2.397	2.759
16	1.173	1.373	1.605	1.873	2.183	2.540	2.952
17	1.184	1.400	1.653	1.948	2.292	2.693	3.159
18	1.196	1.428	1.702	2.026	2.407	2.854	3.380
19	1.208	1.457	1.754	2.107	2.527	3.026	3.617
20	1.220	1.486	1.806	2.191	2.653	3.207	3.870
25	1.282	1.641	2.094	2.666	3.386	4.292	5.427
30	1.348	1.811	2.427	3.243	4.322	5.743	7.612

Year	8%	9%	10%	12%	14%	15%	16%
1	1.080	1.090	1.100	1.120	1.140	1.150	1.160
2	1.166	1.188	1.210	1.254	1.300	1.322	1.346
3	1.260	1.295	1.331	1.405	1.482	1.521	1.561
4	1.360	1.412	1.464	1.574	1.689	1.749	1.811
5	1.469	1.539	1.611	1.762	1.925	2.011	2.100
6	1.587	1.677	1.772	1.974	2.195	2.313	2.436
7	1.714	1.828	1.949	2.211	2.502	2.660	2.826
8	1.851	1.993	2.144	2.476	2.853	3.059	3.278
9	1.999	2.172	2.358	2.773	3.252	3.518	3.803
10	2.159	2.367	2.594	3.106	3.707	4.046	4.411
11	2.332	2.580	2.853	3.479	4.226	4.652	5.117
12	2.518	2.813	3.138	3.896	4.818	5.350	5.936
13	2.720	3.066	3.452	4.363	5.492	6.153	6.886
14	2.937	3.342	3.797	4.887	6.261	7.076	7.988
15	3.172	3.642	4.177	5.474	7.138	8.137	9.266
16	3.426	3.970	4.595	6.130	8.137	9.358	10.748
17	3.700	4.328	5.054	6.866	9.276	10.761	12.468
18	3.996	4.717	5.560	7.690	10.575	12.375	14.463
19	4.316	5.142	6.116	8.613	12.056	14.232	16.777
20	4.661	5.604	6.728	9.646	13.743	16.367	19.461
25	6.848	8.623	10.835	17.000	26.462	32.919	40.874
30	10.063	13.268	17.449	29.960	50.950	66.212	85.850

TABLE S.3.2 (*continued*)

Year	18%	20%	24%	28%	32%	36%
1	1.180	1.200	1.240	1.280	1.320	1.360
2	1.392	1.440	1.538	1.638	1.742	1.850
3	1.643	1.728	1.907	2.067	2.300	2.515
4	1.939	2.074	2.364	2.684	3.036	3.421
5	2.288	2.488	2.932	3.436	4.007	4.653
6	2.700	2.986	3.635	4.398	5.290	6.328
7	3.185	3,583	4.508	5.629	6.983	8.605
8	3.759	4.300	5.590	7.206	9.217	11.703
9	4.435	5.160	6.931	9.223	12.166	15.917
10	5.234	6.192	8.594	11.806	16.060	21.647
11	6.176	7.430	10.657	15.112	21.199	29.439
12	7.288	8.916	13.215	19.343	27.983	40.037
13	8.599	10.699	16.386	24.759	36.937	54.451
14	10.147	12.839	20.319	31.691	48.757	74.053
15	11.974	15.407	25.196	40.565	64.359	100.712
16	14.129	18.488	31.243	51.923	84.954	136.97
17	16.672	22.186	38.741	66.461	112.14	186.28
18	19.673	26.623	48.039	85.071	148.02	253.34
19	23.214	31.948	59.568	108.89	195.39	344.54
20	27.393	38.338	73.864	139.38	257.92	468.57
25	62.669	95.396	216.542	478.90	1033.6	2180.1
30	143.371	237.376	634.820	1645.5	4142.1	10143.

Year	40%	50%	60%	70%	80%	90%
1	1.400	1.500	1.600	1.700	1.800	1.900
2	1.960	2.250	2.560	2.890	3.240	3.610
3	2.744	3.375	4.096	4.913	5.832	6.859
4	3.842	5.062	6.544	8.352	10.498	13.032
5	5.378	7.594	10.486	14.199	18.896	24.761
6	7.530	11.391	16.777	24.138	34.012	47.046
7	10.541	17.086	26.844	41.034	61.222	89.387
8	14.758	25.629	42.950	69.758	110.200	169.836
9	20.661	38.443	68.720	118.588	198.359	322.688
10	28.925	57.665	109.951	201.599	357.047	613.107
11	40.496	86.498	175.922	342.719	642.684	1164.902
12	56.694	129.746	281.475	582.622	1156.831	2213.314
13	79.372	194.619	450.360	990.457	2082.295	4205.297
14	111.120	291.929	720.576	1683.777	3748.131	7990.065
15	155.568	437.894	1152.921	2862.421	6746.636	15181.122
16	217.795	656.84	1844.7	4866.1	12144.	28844.0
17	304.914	985.26	2951.5	8272.4	21859.	54804.0
18	426.879	1477.9	4722.4	14063.0	39346.	104130.0
19	597.630	2216.8	7555.8	23907.0	70824.	197840.0
20	836.683	3325.3	12089.0	40642.0	127480.	375900.0
25	4499.880	25251.	126760.0	577060.0	2408900.	9307600.0
30	24201.432	191750.	1329200.	8193500.0	45517000.	230470000.0

TABLE S.3.3

Sum of an annuity of $1 for N years

Year	1%	2%	3%	4%	5%	6%
1	1.000	1.000	1.000	1.000	1.000	1.000
2	2.010	2.020	2.030	2.040	2.050	2.060
3	2.030	3.060	3.091	3.122	3.152	3.184
4	4.060	4.122	4.184	4.246	4.310	4.375
5	5.101	5.204	5.309	5.416	5.526	5.637
6	6.152	6.308	6.468	6.633	6.802	6.975
7	7.214	7.434	7.662	7.898	8.142	8.394
8	8.286	8.583	8.892	9.214	9.549	9.897
9	9.369	9.755	10.159	10.583	11.027	11.491
10	10.462	10.950	11.464	12.006	12.578	13.181
11	11.567	12.169	12.808	13.486	14.207	14.972
12	12.683	13.412	14.192	15.026	15.917	16.870
13	13.809	14.680	15.618	16.627	17.713	18.882
14	14.947	15.974	17.086	18.292	19.599	21.051
15	16.097	17.293	18.599	20.024	21.579	23.276
16	17.258	18.639	20.157	21.825	23.657	25.673
17	18.430	20.012	21.762	23.698	25.840	28.213
18	19.615	21.412	23.414	25.645	28.132	30.906
19	20.811	22.841	25.117	27.671	30.539	33.760
20	22.019	24.297	26.870	29.778	33.066	36.786
25	28.243	32.030	36.459	41.646	47.727	54.865
30	34.785	40.568	47.575	56.085	66.439	79.058

Year	7%	8%	9%	10%	12%	14%
1	1.000	1.000	1.000	1.000	1.000	1.000
2	2.070	2.080	2.090	2.100	2.120	2.140
3	3.215	3.246	3.278	3.310	3.374	3.440
4	4.440	4.506	4.573	4.641	4.770	4.921
5	5.751	5.867	5.985	6.105	6.353	6.610
6	7.153	7.336	7.523	7.716	8.115	8.536
7	8.654	8.923	9.200	9.487	10.089	10.730
8	10.260	10.637	11.028	11.436	12.300	13.233
9	11.978	12.488	13.021	13.579	14.776	16.085
10	13.816	14.487	15.193	15.937	17.549	19.337
11	15.784	16.645	17.560	18.531	20.655	23.044
12	17.888	18.977	20.141	21.384	24.133	27.271
13	20.141	21.495	22.953	24.523	28.029	32.089
14	22.550	24.215	26.019	27.975	32.393	37.581
15	25.129	27.152	29.361	31.772	37.280	43.842
16	27.888	30.324	33.003	35.950	42.753	50.980
17	30.840	33.750	36.974	40.545	48.884	59.118
18	33.999	37.450	41.301	45.599	55.750	68.394
19	37.379	41.446	46.018	51.159	63.440	78.969
20	40.995	45.762	51.160	57.275	72.052	91.025
25	63.249	73.106	84.701	98.347	133.334	181.871
30	94.461	113.283	136.308	164.494	241.333	356.787

TABLE S.3.3 (*continued*)

Year	16%	18%	20%	24%	28%	32%
1	1.000	1.000	1.000	1.000	1.000	1.000
2	2.160	2.180	2.200	2.240	2.280	2.320
3	3.506	3.572	3.640	3.778	3.918	4.062
4	5.066	5.215	5.368	5.684	6.016	6.362
5	6.877	7.154	7.442	8.048	8.700	9.398
6	8.977	9.442	9.930	10.980	12.136	13.406
7	11.414	12.142	12.916	14.615	16.534	18.696
8	14.240	15.327	16.499	19.123	22.163	25.678
9	17.518	19.086	20.799	24.712	29.369	34.895
10	21.321	23.521	25.959	31.643	38.592	47.062
11	25.733	28.755	32.150	40.238	50.399	63.122
12	30.850	34.931	39.580	50.985	65.510	84.320
13	36.786	42.219	48.497	64.110	84.853	112.303
14	43.672	50.818	59.196	80.496	109.612	149.240
15	51.660	60.965	72.035	100.815	141.303	197.997
16	60.925	72.939	87.442	126.011	181.87	262.36
17	71.673	87.068	105.931	157.253	233.79	347.31
18	84.141	103.740	128.117	195.994	300.25	459.45
19	98.603	123.414	154.740	244.033	385.32	607.47
20	115.380	146.628	186.688	303.601	494.21	802.86
25	249.214	342.603	471.981	898.092	1706.8	3226.8
30	530.312	790.948	1181.882	2640.916	5873.2	12941.0

Year	36%	40%	50%	60%	70%	80%
1	1.000	1.000	1.000	1.000	1.000	1.000
2	2.360	2.400	2.500	2.600	2.700	2.800
3	4.210	4.360	4.750	5.160	5.590	6.040
4	6.725	7.104	8.125	9.256	10.503	11.872
5	10.146	10.846	13.188	15.810	18.855	22.370
6	14.799	16.324	20.781	26.295	33.054	41.265
7	21.126	23.853	32.172	43.073	57.191	75.278
8	29.732	34.395	49.258	69.916	98.225	136.500
9	41.435	49.153	74.887	112.866	167.983	246.699
10	57.352	69.814	113.330	181.585	286.570	445.058
11	78.998	98.739	170.995	291.536	488.170	802.105
12	108.437	139.235	257.493	467.458	830.888	1444.788
13	148.475	195.929	387.239	748.933	1413.510	2601.619
14	202.926	275.300	581.859	1199.293	2403.968	4683.914
15	276.979	386.420	873.788	1919.869	4087.745	8432.045
16	377.69	541.99	1311.7	3072.8	6950.2	15179.0
17	514.66	759.78	1968.5	4917.5	11816.0	27323.0
18	700.94	1064.7	2953.8	7868.9	20089.0	49182.0
19	954.28	1491.6	4431.7	12591.0	34152.0	88528.0
20	1298.8	2089.2	6648.5	20147.0	58059.0	159350.0
25	6053.0	11247.0	50500.0	211270.0	824370.0	3011100.0
30	28172.0	60501.0	383500.0	2215400.0	11705000.0	56896000.0

TABLE S.3.4

Present value of $1

Year	1%	2%	3%	4%	5%	6%	7%	8%	9%	10%	12%	14%	15%
1	.990	.980	.971	.962	.952	.943	.935	.926	.917	.909	.893	.877	.870
2	.980	.961	.943	.925	.907	.890	.873	.857	.842	.826	.797	.769	.756
3	.971	.942	.915	.889	.864	.840	.816	.794	.772	.751	.712	.675	.658
4	.961	.924	.889	.855	.823	.792	.763	.735	.708	.683	.636	.592	.572
5	.951	.906	.863	.822	.784	.747	.713	.681	.650	.621	.567	.519	.497
6	.942	.888	.838	.790	.746	.705	.666	.630	.596	.564	.507	.456	.432
7	.933	.871	.813	.760	.711	.665	.623	.583	.547	.513	.452	.400	.376
8	.923	.853	.789	.731	.677	.627	.582	.540	.502	.467	.404	.351	.327
9	.914	.837	.766	.703	.645	.592	.544	.500	.460	.424	.361	.308	.284
10	.905	.820	.744	.676	.614	.558	.508	.463	.422	.386	.322	.270	.247
11	.896	.804	.722	.650	.585	.527	.475	.429	.388	.350	.287	.237	.215
12	.887	.788	.701	.625	.557	.497	.444	.397	.356	.319	.257	.208	.187
13	.879	.773	.681	.601	.530	.469	.415	.368	.326	.290	.229	.182	.163
14	.870	.758	.661	.577	.505	.442	.388	.340	.299	.263	.205	.160	.141
15	.861	.743	.642	.555	.481	.417	.362	.315	.275	.239	.183	.140	.123
16	.853	.728	.623	.534	.458	.394	.339	.292	.252	.218	.163	.123	.107
17	.844	.714	.605	.513	.436	.371	.317	.270	.231	.198	.146	.108	.093
18	.836	.700	.587	.494	.416	.350	.296	.250	.212	.180	.130	.095	.081
19	.828	.686	.570	.475	.396	.331	.276	.232	.194	.164	.116	.083	.070
20	.820	.673	.554	.456	.377	.312	.258	.215	.178	.149	.104	.073	.061
25	.780	.610	.478	.375	.295	.233	.184	.146	.116	.092	.059	.038	.030
30	.742	.552	.412	.308	.231	.174	.131	.099	.075	.057	.033	.020	.015

Year	16%	18%	20%	24%	28%	32%	36%	40%	50%	60%	70%	80%	90%
1	.862	.847	.833	.806	.781	.758	.735	.714	.667	.625	.588	.556	.526
2	.743	.718	.694	.650	.610	.574	.541	.510	.444	.391	.346	.309	.277
3	.641	.609	.579	.524	.477	.435	.398	.364	.296	.244	.204	.171	.146
4	.552	.516	.482	.423	.373	.329	.292	.260	.198	.153	.120	.095	.077
5	.476	.437	.402	.341	.291	.250	.215	.186	.132	.095	.070	.053	.040
6	.410	.370	.335	.275	.227	.189	.158	.133	.088	.060	.041	.029	.021
7	.354	.314	.279	.222	.178	.143	.116	.095	.059	.037	.024	.016	.011
8	.305	.266	.233	.179	.139	.108	.085	.068	.039	.023	.014	.009	.006
9	.263	.226	.194	.144	.108	.082	.063	.048	.026	.015	.008	.005	.003
10	.227	.191	.162	.116	.085	.062	.046	.035	.017	.009	.005	.003	.002
11	.195	.162	.135	.094	.066	.047	.034	.025	.012	.006	.003	.002	.001
12	.168	.137	.112	.076	.052	.036	.025	.018	.008	.004	.002	.001	.001
13	.145	.116	.093	.061	.040	.027	.018	.013	.005	.002	.001	.001	.000
14	.125	.099	.078	.049	.032	.021	.014	.009	.003	.001	.001	.000	.000
15	.108	.084	.065	.040	.025	.016	.010	.006	.002	.001	.000	.000	.000
16	.093	.071	.054	.032	.019	.012	.007	.005	.002	.001	.000	.000	
17	.080	.030	.045	.026	.015	.009	.005	.003	.001	.000	.000		
18	.089	.051	.038	.021	.012	.007	.004	.002	.001	.000	.000		
19	.030	.043	.031	.017	.009	.005	.003	.002	.000	.000			
20	.051	.037	.026	.014	.007	.004	.002	.001	.000	.000			
25	.024	.016	.010	.005	.002	.001	.000	.000					
30	.012	.007	.004	.002	.001	.000	.000						

TABLE S.3.5

Present value of an annuity of $1

Year	1%	2%	3%	4%	5%	6%	7%	8%	9%	10%
1	0.990	0.980	0.971	0.962	0.952	0.943	0.935	0.926	0.917	0.909
2	1.970	1.942	1.913	1.886	1.859	1.833	1.808	1.783	1.759	1.736
3	2.941	2.884	2.829	2.775	2.723	2.673	2.624	2.577	2.531	2.487
4	3.902	3.808	3.717	3.630	3.546	3.465	3.387	3.312	3.240	3.170
5	4.853	4.713	4.580	4.452	4.329	4.212	4.100	3.993	3.890	3.791
6	5.795	5.601	5.417	5.242	5.076	4.917	4.766	4.623	4.486	4.355
7	6.728	6.472	6.230	6.002	5.786	5.582	5.389	5.206	5.033	4.868
8	7.652	7.325	7.020	6.733	6.463	6.210	6.971	5.747	5.535	5.335
9	8.566	8.162	7.786	7.435	7.108	6.802	6.515	6.247	5.985	5.759
10	9.471	8.983	8.530	8.111	7.722	7.360	7.024	6.710	6.418	6.145
11	10.368	9.787	9.253	8.760	8.306	7.887	7.499	7.139	6.805	6.495
12	11.255	10.575	9.954	9.385	8.863	8.384	7.943	7.536	7.161	6.814
13	12.134	11.348	10.635	9.986	9.394	8.853	8.358	7.904	7.487	7.103
14	13.004	12.106	11.296	10.563	9.899	9.295	8.745	8.244	7.786	7.367
15	13.865	12.849	11.938	11.118	10.380	9.712	9.108	8.559	8.060	7.606
16	14.718	13.578	12.561	11.652	10.838	10.106	9.447	8.851	8.312	7.824
17	15.562	14.292	13.166	12.166	11.274	10.477	9.763	9.122	8.544	8.022
18	16.398	14.992	13.754	12.659	11.690	10.828	10.059	9.372	8.756	8.201
19	17.226	15.678	14.324	13.134	12.085	11.158	10.336	9.604	8.950	8.365
20	18.046	16.351	14.877	13.590	12.462	11.470	10.594	9.818	9.128	8.514
25	22.023	19.523	17.413	15.622	14.094	12.783	11.654	10.675	9.823	9.077
30	25.808	22.397	19.600	17.292	15.373	13.765	12.409	11.258	10.274	9.427

Year	12%	14%	16%	18%	20%	24%	28%	32%	36%
1	0.893	0.877	0.862	0.847	0.833	0.806	0.781	0.758	0.735
2	1.690	1.647	1.605	1.566	1.528	1.457	1.392	1.332	1.276
3	2.402	2.322	2.246	2.174	2.106	1.981	1.868	1.766	1.674
4	3.037	2.914	2.798	2.690	2.589	2.404	2.241	2.096	1.966
5	3.605	3.433	3.274	3.127	2.991	2.745	2.532	2.345	2.181
6	4.111	3.889	3.685	3.498	3.326	3.020	2.759	2.534	2.339
7	4.564	4.288	4.039	3.812	3.605	3.242	2.937	2.678	2.455
8	4.968	4.639	4.344	4.078	3.837	3.421	3.076	2.786	2.540
9	5.328	4.946	4.607	4.303	4.031	3.566	3.184	2.868	2.603
10	5.650	5.216	4.833	4.494	4.193	3.682	3.269	2.930	2.650
11	5.988	5.453	5.029	4.656	4.327	3.776	3.335	2.978	2.683
12	6.194	5.660	5.197	4.793	4.439	3.851	3.387	3.013	2.708
13	6.424	5.842	5.342	4.910	4.533	3.912	3.427	3.040	2.727
14	6.628	6.002	5.468	5.008	4.611	3.962	3.459	3.061	2.740
15	6.811	6.142	5.575	5.092	4.675	4.001	3.483	3.076	2.750
16	6.974	6.265	5.669	5.162	4.730	4.033	3.503	3.088	2.758
17	7.120	5.373	5.749	4.222	4.775	4.059	3.518	3.097	2.763
18	7.250	6.467	5.818	5.273	4.812	4.080	3.529	3.104	2.767
19	7.366	6.550	5.877	5.316	4.844	4.097	3.539	3.109	2.770
20	7.469	6.623	5.929	5.353	4.870	4.110	3.546	3.113	2.772
25	7.843	6.873	6.097	5.467	4.948	4.147	3.564	3.122	2.776
30	8.055	7.003	6.177	5.517	4.979	4.160	3.569	3.124	2.778

4

Layout of the physical system

E very productive physical facility encounters layout or relayout problems that must be solved if it is to operate at peak efficiency. This holds true for passive systems where no physical production is taking place, such as warehouses and department stores, as well as for manufacturing installations. In this chapter we will examine the layout problem in a variety of settings and will present some of the techniques and guidelines that are available to aid in layout design.

INPUTS TO THE LAYOUT DECISION

The layout decision problem may be defined as the determination of the optimal placement of the physical components within a productive system. The term *components* is used rather than, say, *machines* in order to emphasize the fact that such items as display racks, supply bins, light fixtures, and desks are often considered part of the layout decision. How one goes about solving this layout problem depends primarily upon the goals of the productive system, which, as pointed out in Chapter 2, are themselves often elusive and conflicting.

In general, we could postulate that the objective of the layout is to achieve a desired volume of output while holding the costs of inventories, work force, idle equipment, and overhead to acceptable levels. As we examine each basic layout type, we will find that while most of these elements are present in all layout decisions, their relative importance is far from uniform. For example, not all general hospitals are designed, or able, to provide identical service, even though they all have doctors, nurses, and beds. Also, a clinic differs from a sanitarium, and this difference is reflected in the flow pattern of patients, the size of different wards, the presence or absence of special-care units, etc.

A close second to "determination of goals" in importance to the layout decision is the estimation of the product demand. In this regard we are concerned with both the present and future levels of demand and the present and future mix of products. If we foresee a fairly stable market for our product in its present form, our layout strategy will be substantially different than if our product is subject to marked technological change, wide swings in the marketplace, or variation in product mix. This distinction, of course, ties in with our objectives since, in many industries, a company may choose among various strategies—for example, reliance upon a diversified product line, planning production solely for a specific class of consumers, and so on. The answer to the question posed in Chapter 2— What business is the company in?—should provide direction here.

Processing requirements provide the third major input to the layout decision, and they represent the key constraint on the type of layout to be selected. The data required for layout determination vary according to the product to be manufactured. In manufacturing installations where the product line is small and well defined (such as a household appliance plant), assembly charts are the primary inputs; in manufacturing systems characterized by a wide variety of products (such as a custom job shop),

155

the nature of the machinery specifications is of major interest. It is much more difficult to generalize about the amount and kind of process data required in nonmanufacturing installations because of the wide variety of transformation processes that fall under this heading. For example, substantial process data, such as process charts, flow diagrams, and equipment performance specifications, are required for a commercial laundry layout, whereas a department store layout planner would have little need for such information.

The fourth major type of input data required for the layout decision is the amount of space available in the building or site where the layout is to be located. Typically, the layout is constrained by the physical confines of a building, although there are of course exceptions. The layout decisions for factory loading docks, drive-in restaurants, and department store lawn-and-garden shops encompass both inside and outside space requirements. Highways, oil fields, and cemeteries, on the other hand, illustrate operations that take place completely outside any structure. Layouts for such operations, however, have obvious space limitations of their own, in the form of map coordinates rather than walls and ceilings.

MAKING THE LAYOUT DECISION

Once the inputs representing company objectives, customer demand, processing requirements, and space availability have been developed, the next step is to translate these factors into quantitative estimates of *desired capacity* and *available capacity.* "Desired capacity" refers to both the amount of production capability we would like to have to meet the immediate demands on the productive system and the production capability we would like to have to meet future demands over some extended period. "Available capacity" refers to either the productive capacity that could be obtained through relayout of the existing facility or to the capacity obtainable from laying out a brand new facility (within budgetary limitations).

Obtaining a quantitative estimate of capacity requires, first, selection of a suitable unit measure of capacity. Not all units are obvious, as will be seen from the typical units of measure for various productive systems in Table 4.1.

TABLE 4.1

Units of capacity measurement for selected productive systems

System	*Units*
Steel company	Tons per time period
Oil refinery	Barrels per time period
Aircraft company	Completed planes per time period
Textile company	Yards of cloth per time period
Restaurant	Seating capacity
Hospital	Number of beds
Machine shop	Machine hours
University	Students per year·
Department store	Sales revenue per square foot of floor space

With suitable units of measure established, the problem of determining the best level of capacity means comparing existing capacity with present and future capacity requirements. The result of this comparison—the actual capacity level chosen—will of necessity be a compromise between the design for maximum possible demand and the average expected demand over the life of the productive facility. This decision obviously becomes more difficult as uncertainty about future demand increases.

Intimately related to the question of capacity is the concept of adaptability. Ideally, the layout should be adaptive to a variety of environmental conditions, so that layout planning must account for new product lines as well as current and future demand variations for existing products. In addition, it should be able to respond to technological breakthroughs in processes and materials without incurring unduly high relayout costs. The following items are suggestive of the features that enhance adaptiveness for most formats.

a. Self-contained machines or work units
b. Special building construction (removable walls, high-stress floors, high ceilings, numerous power outlets)
c. Multiple path options in material handling devices, such as overhead conveyors
d. Earmarked areas for future expansion with predetermined flow routes

After these and similar details have been attended to, the next step in the layout procedure is to choose from the different layout formats. Since this decision rests on understanding the nature of these formats and the operational procedures involved in performing the layout, we will defer the discussion of selecting between alternative types to the latter part of this chapter.

BASIC LAYOUT FORMATS

The format by which departments and components within departments are arranged may be viewed either in terms of work flow or the function of the productive system. Looking first at work flow formats, we can specify three basic types: product layout, process layout, and fixed-position layout.

A *product layout* is one in which the components are arranged according to the progressive steps by which the product is made. Conceptually, the flow is an unbroken line from raw material input to finished goods. This type of layout is exemplified in automobile assembly, food processing, and furniture manufacture.

A *process layout* is one in which the processing components are grouped according to the general function they perform, without regard to any particular product. Custom job shops, department stores, and hospitals are generally arranged in this manner.

A *fixed-position layout* is one in which the product, by virtue of its bulk or weight, remains at one location. The equipment required for product manufacture is moved to the product, rather than vice versa. Sound stages on a movie lot, aircraft assembly shops, and shipyards typify this mode of layout.

With respect to the classification of layouts by productive system function, we can mention three common types: storage layout, marketing layout, and project layout.

Storage layout refers to the relative placement of the layout components in a warehouse or storeroom. It differs from other types of layout in that it is designed to fulfill an inventory function rather than to operate directly on the product or service being created.

Marketing layout refers to layouts whose components are arranged in such a fashion as to facilitate the sale of a product rather than its production. Retail stores, supermarkets, convention exhibits, and customer display rooms utilize this type of layout.

Project layout refers to the arrangement of components in "one shot" situations, such as those developed around building, dam, and highway construction sites. Although project layouts are identical in most respects to fixed-position layouts, the latter are characterized by a fixed facility that is designed to turn out more than one of a given product. A project layout, on the other hand, must be planned around the particular terrain where the work is being carried out, and in many cases is subject to shifts in location as the project progresses.

All these differences have significant ramifications in terms of economics. For example, investing in specialized, nonportable machines and building a facility to house them is generally warranted in fixed-position layout situations but is rarely feasible in a project layout undertaking.

It should be noted at this point that many layouts are designed with more than one function in mind, and therefore functional combinations are common. For example, a supermarket, though primarily arranged on the basis of marketing criteria, displays more than one line of brand items on its shelves and therefore is partly a storage layout. In addition, combinations of work flow and functional arrangements are quite common. Storing wine in a cellar represents not only layout by function (storage) but layout by work flow (perhaps product layout).

QUANTITATIVE LAYOUT ANALYSIS

Of the several formats discussed, process formats, along with assembly line balancing (a special case of product layout), have been most heavily subjected to analysis, with the result that a number of quantitative techniques have been developed to aid in their solution. These formats have received wide attention not only because of their extensive employment in productive systems but also because they present challenging theoretical problems in combinatorial mathematics. We shall consider several of these techniques in depth shortly. Much less quantitative analysis has appeared in the operations management literature on the other formats, and therefore we will emphasize guidelines (rather than techniques) in dealing with them.

Process layout

The most common approach in developing a process layout is to arrange departments consisting of like components so as to optimize their relative placement. In many installations, optimal placement often means that the *material handling* costs for the total layout are minimized by placing departments that have large amounts of interdepartment traffic adjacent to one another. For example, in a steel mill producing custom items, this rationale might dictate the placement of finishing machines (such as high-tolerance turret lathes) next to rough machining facilities since many items follow this sequence of manufacture. In many situations, however, the concept of material handling cost must be broadened to include the cost of the individuals who carry the material. In the steel mill, for instance, it might be desirable to have the tool crib area near the skilled machinists in order to minimize the time they are away from their machines. In a large insurance office, it might be desirable to have files on the insured persons close to the underwriter's desk.

The general approach to process layout, and some of the unique problems it poses, can be illustrated by the following example. Suppose that we want to arrange the eight departments of a toy factory in order to minimize the interdepartmental material handling cost. Initially, let us make the simplifying assumption that all departments have the same amount of space, say 40 feet by 40 feet, and that the building is 80 feet wide and 160 feet long (and thus compatible with the former dimensions). The first thing we would want to know is the nature of the flow between departments and the way the material is transported. If the company has an-

TABLE 4.2

Interdepartmental flow

	Flow between Departments (Number of Moves)							Department	Activity
	1	2	3	4	5	6	7	8		
1		175	50	0	30	200	20	25	1	Shipping and Receiving
2			0	100	75	90	80	90	2	Plastic Molding and Stamping
3				17	88	125	99	180	3	Metal Forming
4					20	5	0	25	4	Sewing Department
5						0	180	187	5	Small Toy Assembly
6							374	103	6	Large Toy Assembly
7								7	7	Painting
8									8	Mechanism Assembly

FIGURE 4.1

Building dimensions and departments

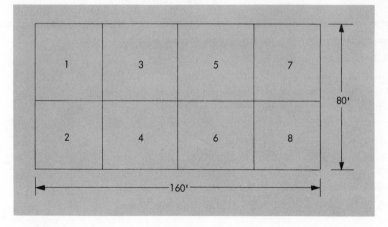

other factory that makes similar products, information about flow patterns might be abstracted from the records. On the other hand, if this is a new-product line, such information would have to come from routing sheets (see Chapter 3) or from estimates by knowledgeable personnel such as process or industrial engineers. Of course these data, regardless of their source, will have to be modified to reflect the nature of future orders over the projected life at the proposed layout.

Let us assume, further, that the information is available, and we find that all material is transported in a standard-size crate by forklift truck, one crate to a truck (which constitutes one "load"). Now suppose that transportation costs are $1 to move a load between adjacent departments and $1 extra for each department in between. The expected loads between departments for the first year of operation are tabulated in Table 4.2; the available plant space is depicted in Figure 4.1.

Given this information, our first step is to illustrate the nature of the

FIGURE 4.2

Interdepartmental flow graph with number of annual movements

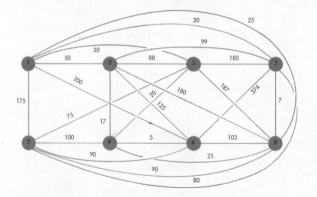

TABLE 4.3

Cost matrix—first solution

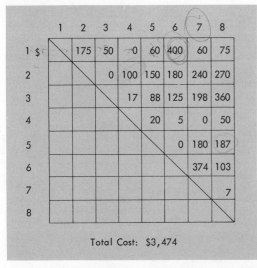

	1	2	3	4	5	6	7	8
1 $		175	50	0	60	400	60	75
2			0	100	150	180	240	270
3				17	88	125	198	360
4					20	5	0	50
5						0	180	187
6							374	103
7								7
8								

Total Cost: $3,474

interdepartmental flow by a schematic model, such as that in Figure 4.2. This provides the basic layout pattern, which we will try to improve.

The second step is to determine the cost of this layout by multiplying the material handling cost by the number of loads moved between each department. Table 4.3 presents this information, which is derived as follows. The annual material handling cost between departments 1 and 2 is $175 ($1 × 175 moves), $60 between departments 1 and 5 ($2 × 30 moves), $60 between departments 1 and 7 ($3 × 20 moves), etc.

Step three entails a search for departmental changes that will reduce costs. Looking at the graph and the cost matrix, it would appear desirable to place departments 1 and 6 closer together since their high move-distance costs can be substantially reduced by making them adjacent to each other. However, creation of this adjacency requires the shifting of several other

FIGURE 4.3

Revised interdepartmental flow graph (only interdepartmental flow having effect on cost is depicted)

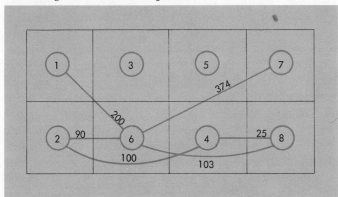

departments, thereby affecting their move-distance costs and the total cost of the second solution. Figure 4.3 shows the revised layout resulting from the relocation of department 6 and an adjacent department (department 4 is arbitrarily selected for this purpose). The revised cost matrix for the exchange, with the cost changes circled, is given in Table 4.4—where the total cost is $262 *greater* than in the initial solution. Clearly, the fact that the distance between departments 6 and 7 was doubled accounts for the major part of the cost increase. This points out the fact that, even in a small problem, it is rarely easy to make the correct "obvious move" on the basis of casual inspection.

TABLE 4.4

Cost matrix—second solution

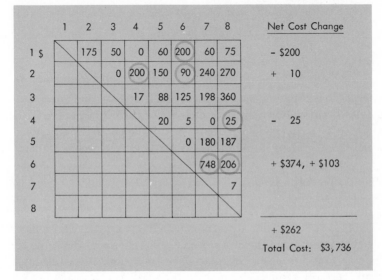

	1	2	3	4	5	6	7	8	Net Cost Change
1 $		175	50	0	60	200	60	75	− $200
2			0	200	150	90	240	270	+ 10
3				17	88	125	198	360	
4					20	5	0	25	− 25
5						0	180	187	
6							748	206	+ $374, + $103
7								7	
8									

+ $262

Total Cost: $3,736

Thus far we have shown only one exchange among a large number of potential exchanges; in fact, for an eight-department problem there are 8! (or 40,320) possible arrangements. Therefore, the procedure we have employed would have only a remote possibility of achieving an optimum combination in a "reasonable" number of tries. Nor does our problem stop here.

Suppose that we *do* arrive at a good cut-and-try solution solely on the basis of material handling cost, such as that shown in Figure 4.4 (whose total cost is $3,244). We would note, first of all, that our shipping and receiving department is near the center of the factory—an arrangement that probably would not be acceptable. Note also that the sewing department is next to the paint department, introducing the hazard that lint, thread, and cloth particles might drift onto painted items. Further, small toy assembly and large toy assembly are located at opposite ends of the plant, which would increase travel time for assemblers, who very likely would be needed in both departments at various times of the day, as well as the travel time of supervisors, who might otherwise supervise both departments simultaneously.

Other basic assumptions of this example also could be challenged:

1. Equality of department size. This would be an exception rather than the rule in most installations. Even if the same amount of area is allocated to various departments, L or U shapes may be more suitable than squares or rectangles.

2. No restriction on location of equipment. Forming and stamping equipment, for example, might have to be placed in special rooms on high-stress floors.

FIGURE 4.4

A feasible layout

Small Toy Assembly	Mechanism Assembly	Shipping & Receiving	Large Toy Assembly
5	8	1	6
Metal Forming	Plastic Molding & Stamping	Sewing	Painting
3	2	4	7

3. Unlimited access to departmental areas. In practice, there may be only one or two entrances for material handling purposes, so that actual travel distances might differ significantly from the simple assumption of distances as a function of adjacency.

4. Material handling method. It is quite likely that a variety of material handling methods would be used. Small loads of material might be moved by hand trucks rather than forklifts, or in some instances by belt or roller conveyor. Any of these alternatives would affect interdepartmental move costs.

Systematic Layout Planning. In certain types of layout problems, numerical flow of items between departments is either impractical to obtain or really does not reveal the qualitative factors that may be crucial to the placement decision. In these situations, the technique known as Systematic Layout Planning (SLP)[1] is commonly used. The technique requires the creation of a relationship chart showing the degree of importance of having each department located adjacent to every other department. From this

---

[1] See the Muther and Wheeler bibliographical reference.

FIGURE 4.5

Systematic Layout Planning for a floor of a department store.

A. Relationship Chart (Based upon Tables B and C)

From	2	3	4	5	Area (Sq. Ft.)
1. Credit Dept.	I / 6	U / —	A / 1,6	U / —	100
2. Toy Dept.		U / —	I / 1	A / 1,6	400
3. Wine Dept.			A / 2,3	E / 1	300
4. Camera Dept.				X / 1	100
5. Candy Dept.					100

Letter	← Closeness Rating
Number	← Reason for Rating

B.

Code	Reason*
1	Type of customer
2	Ease of supervision
3	Common personnel
4	Contact necessary
5	Share same space
6	Psychology

*Others may be used.

C.

Value	Closeness	Line Code*	Color Code†
A	Absolutely necessary	═══	Red
E	Especially important	══	Orange
I	Important	──	Green
O	Ordinary closeness OK		Blue
U	Unimportant		None
X	Undesirable	ＡＡＡ	Brown

* Used for example purposes only.
† Used in practice.

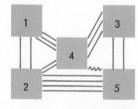

Initial Relationship Diagram (Based upon Tables A and C)

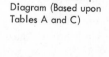

Initial Layout Based upon Relationship Diagram (Ignoring Space and Building Constraints)

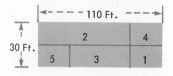

Final Layout Adjusted by Square Footage and Building Size

chart is developed an activity relationship diagram similar to an interdepartmental flow graph used for illustrating material handling between departments. The activity relationship diagram is then adjusted by trial and error until a satisficing adjacency pattern is obtained. This pattern, in turn, is modified department-by-department to meet building space limitations. Figure 4.5 illustrates the technique as applied to a simple five-department problem involving the laying out of a floor of a department store.

It should be apparent at this point that making a good process layout entails the simultaneous solution of mathematical, economic, and technological problems—any one of which may be highly complex in its own right. To come to grips with this problem, researchers work with computer-based models that, in a general sense, follow the approach in our simple example. In addition, however, they provide for more sophisticated measurements of flow and permit adjustments for a variety of constraints, such as building construction features (for example, stairwells and elevators) and fixed departmental locations. These models also have the capability of dealing with the relayout problem, which is often far more demanding than the initial layout case we have discussed.[2] The characteristics of these computerized approaches are summarized in Table 4.5.

The best choice among the three methods depends on the particular objectives and characteristics of the layout problem under study; therefore, to provide guidelines for specific situations would be a massive undertaking. However, certain features of these techniques should be understood prior to application:

1. ALDEP and CORELAP, as defined by their developers, employ preference ratings that have the advantage of being inclusive in terms of the features that are important in department location. On the other hand, the scoring techniques used in these methods require the quantification of subjective preferences, which is inherently risky. Both approaches employ the "Muther scale" as used in SLP (see Muther bibliographical reference [1955]), which assumes, for instance, that the weights of 4 ("absolutely essential to be located near department") and 3 ("essential to be located near department") maintain their relative numeric position in any situation. Clearly, this is a tenuous assumption.

CRAFT avoids this problem by using cost per unit distance between department centroids as its criterion. However, this approach depends upon the assumption that cost per unit distance is the appropriate measure and that department centroids are the approximate material pickup and delivery points. Both of these assumptions are open to question.

2. CRAFT requires that the user provide a feasible initial layout. The program then modifies this layout by exchanging departments two or three at a time until no further reduction in total material handling cost is possible. A second initial layout might then be developed and the program run again. This interactive process is repeated until a satisfactory layout is obtained.

---

[2] We will consider various aspects of this problem in Chapter 14, "Areas and Techniques for Improvement."

TABLE 4.5

Summary of three computerized layout techniques*

Required inputs	Problem size handled	Outputs	Measure of effectiveness	Distinguishing features
ALDEP: (Automated Layout Design Program)†				
1. Size and number of each department to be located in the building	1. 63 departments	1. Layout matrix with departments and aisles drawn by plotter (58 layouts were plotted for sample 11-department problem, each entailing 1.03 minutes on IBM 7090 computer)	1. Maximum preference score (for all layouts generated)	1. Program can layout a multistory building up to 3 floors
2. Description of building dimensions, which must include areas assigned to specific building features (aisles, stairwells, etc.). These data are fed into program in form of a matrix		2. Preference score for each layout		2. Departmental exchanges may be made randomly or according to criteria
3. Preference table giving relative department location preferences, denoted by letters A, B, C, V, F, X, which range from "absolutely essential" (A) to "undesirable" (F). Letters are then converted to a numerical scale; i.e., $A = 4, B = 2$, etc.				3. Departments are exchanged 2 at a time
				4. Authors favor using the program in concert with a layout planner who, at various stages, inserts departments into intermediate layouts
4. Control cards to activate subroutines, such as "number of layouts to be tried"				5. Best suited for relayout problems

CORELAP (Computerized Relationship Layout Planning)‡

Inputs	Outputs	Objective	Characteristics
1. Relationship chart similar to preference chart used in ALDEP	1. Numerical layout matrix printout	1. Maximum total closeness rating (for all layouts tested)	1. Not confined to any particular building shape
2. Building width-length ratio	2. Can use digital plotter, such as CALCOMP plotter (27-department problem solved in 2.46 minutes on IBM 7090 computer)		2. Yields near optimum solutions according to authors
3. Departmental area restrictions			3. Requires little computer time
4. Size of area modules to be manipulated to form each department			
5. Number of modules per department			

CRAFT (Computerized Relative Allocation of Facilities Technique) §

Inputs	Outputs	Objective	Characteristics
1. Initial block layout	1. Block layout, shaped to conform to building dimensions	1. Minimum total material handling cost	1. Final solution is function of initial layout
2. Load matrix (tabulation of loads, e.g., materials, which flow between all combinations of departments)	2. Cost of each solution leading up to final solution (22-department problem solved in 0.62 minutes on IBM 7090 computer)		2. Later versions exchange departments 3 at a time rather than 2 at a time, as in ALDEP and CORELAP
3. Material handling cost matrix (handling costs between departments)			3. Distances computed between department centroids
			4. Limited to single-story building
			5. Departments can be fixed in location

* An expanded comparison of these techniques is presented in Richard L. Francis and John A. White, *Facility Layout and Location* (Englewood Cliffs, N.J.: Prentice-Hall, 1974), pp. 95–141.

† Jarrold M. Seehof and Wayne O. Evans, "Automated Layout Design Programs," *Journal of Industrial Engineering,* vol. 18, no. 12 (December 1967), pp. 690–95.

‡ Robert S. Lee and James M. Moore, "CORELAP—Computerized Relationship Layout Planning," *Journal of Industrial Engineering,* vol. 18, no. 3 (March 1967), pp. 195–200.

§ Elwood S. Buffa, Gordon C. Armour, and Thomas E. Vollmann, "Allocating Facilities with CRAFT," *Harvard Business Review* (March–April 1964), pp. 136–50.

ALDEP either generates a series of random layouts within the program and selects the one with the best preference score or generates one random layout and makes pairwise departmental exchanges until no further improvement can be made in the preference score.

CORELAP simply generates a predetermined number of random layouts and selects the one with the best "total closeness rating" (preference score).

3. The outputs from each program must be "hand smoothed" to make an acceptable layout. For instance, the best layout developed by the computer program may show departments that have very long and narrow sides or more than four sides—characteristics that might be undesirable in practice.

4. ALDEP, CORELAP, and CRAFT are heuristic programs; that is, they do not investigate every possible departmental arrangement, nor do they necessarily yield optimal solutions. Therefore, regardless of which technique is selected, the chances of a good layout are greatly enhanced by generating a large number of possible layouts.

In summary, process layout presents substantial problems in terms of the potential number of alternative arrangements and in the selection and utilization of layout criteria. Computerized techniques, while they have obvious advantages over "hand" methods of developing alternative layouts, are based on rather severe assumptions that must be carefully evaluated before they can be employed in a specific situation. For these reasons it is difficult to overemphasize the importance of selecting the appropriate measure of effectiveness in dealing with process layout problems.

Product layout—assembly lines

The distinguishing characteristic between product layout and process layout is the pattern of work flow. In process layout, the pattern can be highly variable. Product layout, on the other hand, is highly predictable because it is a function of the manufacturing stages of the product itself. For this reason the relative location of departments within a product-oriented system, and the positioning of components within a product-oriented department, present less of a challenge than in process layouts. Nevertheless, the layout planner is confronted with a challenging problem in a special case of product layout—the assembly line. The objective of such a layout is to achieve a smooth flow of product assembly with minimum idle time on the part of workers who man the line. Essentially, this is a question of workload equalization, and thus the term *assembly line balancing* is used to denote the problem area.

Assembly line balancing. In most instances the initial layout of the assembly line is based on the output required from the line. Once the line has been established, however, the assembly line balancing problem is to a large degree a scheduling problem. These two opposing starting points—a given desired output versus a given established line—may be expressed as the following formulation of the assembly line balancing problem:

Find (*a*) the minimum number of work stations for a given cycle time.

or

Find (*b*) the minimum cycle time for a given number of work stations.
(A "work station" is a specified location for performance of a given
amount of work usually, but not always, manned by one operator, and
"cycle time" is the elapsed time between units coming off the line.)

If we are dealing with (*a*), our problem is a layout problem since we
must determine the number of work stations required to achieve the specified cycle time. If we are dealing with (*b*), we have a scheduling problem
since we know the number of work stations and therefore the essential
nature of the layout. In practice, however, those who design assembly line
systems rarely make this layout-scheduling distinction because the solution
procedures—that is, line balancing methods—treat (*a*) and (*b*) together
once the type and length of the assembly line are specified.

To illustrate the nature of the assembly line balancing problem and

TABLE 4.6

Assembly steps and times for model J wagon

Task	Performance time (in seconds)	Description	Tasks that must precede
A......	45	Position rear axle support and hand fasten 4 screws to nuts	—
B......	11	Insert rear axle	A
C......	9	Tighten rear axle support screws to nuts	A, B
D......	50	Position front axle assembly and hand fasten with 4 screws to nuts	—
E......	15	Tighten front axle assembly screws	D
F......	12	Position rear wheel #1 and fasten hub cap	A, B, C
G......	12	Position rear wheel #2 and fasten hub cap	A, B, C
H......	12	Position front wheel #1 and fasten hub cap	D, E
I......	12	Position front wheel #2 and fasten hub cap	D, E
J......	8	Position wagon handle shaft on front axle assembly and hand fasten bolt and nut	A, B, C, D, E, F, G, H, I
K......	9	Tighten bolt and nut	J

Cycle time determination:
Demand per day (*D*): 500 wagons
Productive time per day (*P*): 420 minutes
Total time for all tasks (*T*): 195 seconds

Cycle time (*C*) in seconds $= \dfrac{60P}{D} = \dfrac{60 \times 420}{500} = \dfrac{25,200}{500} = 50.4$ seconds

Theoretical minimum number of work stations (N) $= \dfrac{DT}{60P} = \dfrac{500 \times 195}{25,200} = \dfrac{97,500}{25,200} = 3.87$

methods for its solution, we will again employ the example of the toy factory. This time, however, our focus will be on the large toy assembly department, in which we consider how a toy wagon might be assembled on a belt conveyor line.[3] To perform the analysis, we would require a list of the assembly tasks that go into making each unit, their operation time, and their sequence restrictions. In addition, we would need an estimate of the desired cycle time. This information, which is generally based on assembly chart data (see Chapter 3) and a demand forecast, is presented in Table 4.6. To visualize the sequence relationships more easily, refer to the precedence graph in Figure 4.6.

Before we proceed to balance the line, we can make the following observations about the range of cycle times we might use. At one extreme, the

FIGURE 4.6

Precedence graph for model J wagon

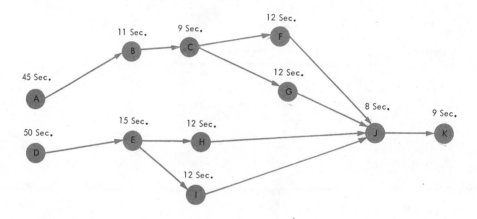

50 seconds associated with task D is the shortest cycle time we could employ if we do not split this task among two or more workers. At the other extreme, the longest cycle time (assuming no penalty for extra tool handling and operator movements) would be the sum of all of the assembly task times: 195 seconds. This would be the figure when one operator does the entire assembly. Finally, if this problem had no sequential restrictions, there would be 11! (or 39,916,800) possible task performance arrangements. However, the sequence requirements in this situation would substantially reduce the number of possible arrangements.

Referring to Table 4.6, we note that the cycle time required to meet the hypothesized demand of 500 units per day is 50.4 seconds. Thus our objective is to find the minimum *actual* number of work stations required to meet this cycle time. ("Actual" is emphasized because—although we have calculated the *theoretical* minimum number of stations in Table 4.6—we

---

[3] As any father of small children will attest, bicycles, tricycles, and wagons are rarely assembled at the factory. This example is selected as much from wishful thinking as for simplicity in conveying line balancing concepts.

will not be able to balance exactly to this number since we are designing for an integral number of stations.) Further, the precedence constraints and the problem of trying to combine whole elements within each work station may necessitate more work stations than the theoretical minimum. Given a cycle time, the first step in balancing the line is to decide upon a rule by which tasks may be allocated to the different work stations. In this example we have selected two simple rules:

1. First allocate those tasks that have the largest number of following tasks.
2. First allocate those tasks that have the longest operation time.

To make the first balance, we will use rule 1 and break ties with rule 2. The reverse procedure will be followed for the second balance.

Utilizing rule 1, we initially array the tasks in the following order:

Task	Number of following tasks
A.	6
B or D.	5
C or E.	4
F, G, H, or I.	2
J.	1
K.	0

Tasks are then assigned in sequence to stations, subject to precedence restrictions (that is, a task cannot be selected until all prior tasks in the sequence have been assigned) and to cycle time constraints (task time must be less than the remaining unassigned station time). The balance achieved and station idle time are shown in Table 4.7.

TABLE 4.7

Balance made according to largest number of following tasks

	Task	Task time (in seconds)	Remaining unassigned time (in seconds)	Feasible remaining tasks	Task with most followers	Task with longest operation time
Station 1	A	45	5.4 idle	none		
Station 2	D	50	0.4 idle	none		
Station 3	B	11	39.4	C, E	C, E	E
	E	15	24.4	C, H, I	C	
	C	9	15.4	F, G, H, I	F, G, H, I	F, G, H, I
	F*	12	3.4 idle	none		
Station 4	G	12	38.4	H, I	H, I	H, I
	H*	12	26.4	I		
	I	12	14.4	J		
	J	8	6.4 idle	none		
Station 5	K	9	41.4 idle	none		

* Denotes task arbitrarily selected where there is a tie between longest operation times.

TABLE 4.8

Balance made according to longest-operation time rule

	Task	Task time (in seconds)	Remaining unassigned time (in seconds)	Feasible remaining tasks	Task with longest time	Task with most followers
Station 1	D	50	0.4 idle	none		
Station 2	A	45	5.4 idle	none		
Station 3	E	15	35.4	B, H, I	H, I	H, I
	H*	12	23.4	B, I	I	
	I	12	11.4	B		
	B	11	0.4 idle	none		
Station 4	C	9	41.4	F, G	F, G	F, G
	F*	12	29.4	G		
	G	12	17.4	J		
	J	8	9.4	K		
	K	9	0.4 idle	none		

* Denotes task arbitrarily selected where there is a tie between the number of following tasks.

Utilizing rule 2, our initial array of tasks would be: D, A, E, (F, G, H, or I), B, (C or K), J. Station assignments and idle time are shown in Table 4.8.

Analyzing the two balances achieved, we see that rule 1, supplemented with rule 2, resulted in a given station balance with a total of 57 seconds of idle time. Rule 2, supplemented with rule 1, yielded a four-station balance with a total idle time of 6.6 seconds, and clearly is preferable in this case. The obvious question at this point is: Would we expect similar results in other line balancing problems? About all we can say is "It depends."

It depends mainly on the number of tasks being considered and their order strength (that is, the extent of precedence constraints), which, unfortunately, interact to such an extent that it is impossible to provide general guidelines. Moreover, other useful heuristic rules apply task-weighting techniques and may perform as well or better than our rule 2.[4] In practice, probably the best strategy is to try several different rules if the problem is relatively small, say fewer than 30 tasks. For larger problems, computerized techniques employing more elaborate weighting procedures[5] or mathematical programming approaches[6] would be warranted.[7]

Our previous example developed the best balance for a specific cycle time. Management, however, is also extremely interested in the sensitivity of the line to changes in production rate and number of work stations. By varying the cycle time length and the size of the work force, we can derive an "efficiency" relationship between the line idle time and line productive

[4] Commonly employed heuristic rules are given in Ignall and Buxey *et al.* bibliographical references.

[5] See Helgeson-Birnie and Mastor bibliographical references.

[6] See Buffa-Taubert and Moore bibliographical references.

[7] A discussion of the extent of use of formal, published assembly line balancing techniques is presented in R. B. Chase, "Survey of Paced Assembly Lines," *Industrial Engineering*, vol. 6, no. 2 (February, 1974), pp. 14–18.

time. This entails generating a number of balances over a range of cycle times and quantitatively solving for measures of efficiency. Once these calculations are made, a graph is constructed from which the efficiency of any cycle time–work force combination may be determined.

Using the wagon line, we might investigate combinations from 50 seconds (1.2 units per minute) to, say, 70 seconds (0.86 units per minute). Our measure of efficiency may be obtained as follows.

$$\text{Efficiency } (E) = \frac{\sum_{i=1}^{11} t_i}{nc}$$

where

t_i = Time per task, i = 1,2,3, . . . 11
n = Actual number of work stations
c = Selected cycle time

Thus, for the balance achieved by rule 1,

$$E = \frac{195}{(5)(50.4)} = 0.77, \text{ or } 77\%$$

And for rule 2:

$$E = \frac{195}{(4)(50.4)} = 0.97, \text{ or } 97\%$$

These efficiencies, along with others obtained from different balances, are plotted in Figure 4.7.

It is apparent, in evaluating this graph, that it would be inefficient to use five work stations unless the bottleneck operation, *D*, is reduced below 50 seconds. Likewise, it would be inefficient to use four stations when 65 seconds (or more) is an acceptable cycle time. In addition, although 100 percent efficiency is possible in this example—when $c = 65$ and $n = 3$— with only a slight loss in efficiency a substantial increase in output may be made by adding one man and balancing the line at 50 seconds.

Factors other than those represented on the graph also affect the ultimate line balance choice. Labor considerations, such as keeping the work force intact, may dictate that the line be run at an output level that will result in substantial idle time. If only enough parts and subassemblies are available for 420 wagons per day, this volume is too large for a three-station balance, but an alternate choice of running the line at higher speeds for less than a full day may cause inventory and coordination problems. Considerations such as these abound in practice. Indeed, an argument can be made that these problems are of such significance that top management should acquire more than a casual understanding of line balancing concepts *before* a line technology is selected.[8]

---

[8] See Richard B. Chase, "Strategic Considerations in Assembly Line Selection," *California Management Review*, vol. 18, no. 1, Fall 1975, pp. 17–23.

FIGURE 4.7

Efficiency graph of selected *n-c* combinations

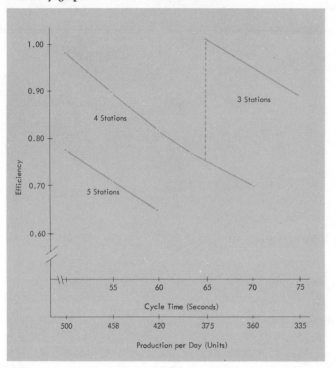

Other balancing considerations. Time is only one of several criteria by which jobs may be assigned to work stations. A partial list of other criteria, which might be used separately or in conjunction with time, are given below. Procedurally, these criteria would be admitted to the "feasible remaining task" list in the same fashion as if they were precedence or time criteria.

1. Operator wage rates: Since it is common practice to pay operators according to their highest skilled tasks, costs may be kept down by having premium tasks performed at one station.
2. Equipment location: Tasks requiring the same tools or machines may be assigned to a special equipment work station.
3. Parts space: Tasks would be allocated so that bulky parts would not be used excessively at any one work station.
4. Parts similarity: Tasks requiring the same parts might be grouped together so as to minimize the number of storage locations along the line.
5. Social-psychological factors:[9] To achieve a sense of completion by the operator, tasks may be combined into meaningful wholes. Tasks may also be grouped so as to facilitate two people working together.

---

[9] These factors are of crucial importance in practice and are dealt with at length in Chapter 10, "Job Design."

6. Task characteristics: Dirty tasks, such as painting, oiling, or greasing, may be located in the same area, while incompatible tasks, such as painting and sanding, should be separated.

Finally, we have assumed that the task times used in balancing are deterministic; however, since assembly lines are operated by people rather than by machines, this assumption is far from warranted in practice. Indeed, we would expect to find variations in the time required by a worker to perform the same task, rather than a constant time repeatedly achieved. Further, the magnitude of this variance differs from operator to operator, and even for the same operator on different days.[10]

Computerized line balancing. Companies engaged in assembly methods commonly employ a computer for line balancing. While it appears that most of these firms develop their own computer programs, commercial

FIGURE 4.8

Sample computer output

```
ENTER ØPTIØN NUMBER?3

ENTER TARGET EFFICIENCY?.85


TØTAL EFFICIENCY   =   82 %
STANDARD DEVIATIØN=      0.0153
TARGET CYCLE TIME =    0.347
MINIM. CYCLE TIME =    0.343
NØ. ØF STATIØNS =   19

TØTAL EFFICIENCY   =   80 %
STANDARD DEVIATIØN=      0.0175
TARGET CYCLE TIME =    0.368
MINIM. CYCLE TIME =    0.368
NØ. ØF STATIØNS =   18

TØTAL EFFICIENCY   =   75 %
STANDARD DEVIATIØN=      0.0214
TARGET CYCLE TIME =    0.417
MINIM. CYCLE TIME =    0.415
NØ. ØF STATIØNS =   17
```

Source: General Electric Company, *Assembly-Line Configuration, ASYBL$ User's Guide* (1975), p. 28.

package programs are also widely applied. One of these is General Electric's *Assembly-Line Configuration* (*ASYBL$*), which uses the "ranked positional weight" rule in selecting tasks for work stations. Specifically, this rule states that tasks are assigned according to their positional weights, where a positional weight is the time for a given task plus the task times of all those which follow it. Thus, the task with the highest positional weight would be assigned to the first work station (subject to time, precedence, and zoning constraints). As is typical with such software, the user has several options in terms of how the problem is to be solved. Figure 4.8

[10] See Brennecke and the Kottas–Lau bibliographical references for methods of dealing with this problem.

illustrates a portion of program output when a target level of efficiency is used as a basis for deriving and comparing different balances for a 35-task assembly line. (The program can handle up to 450 tasks.) Note the trade-offs that take place as the number of work stations changes. In this case, the larger number of work stations allows for a better balance and therefore a higher efficiency.

Fixed-position layout

Fixed-position layout is characterized by a relatively low number of production units in comparison with process and product layout formats. In developing a fixed-position layout, we may visualize the product as the hub of a wheel with materials and equipment arranged concentrically around the production point in their order of use and movement difficulty. Thus in shipbuilding, for example, rivets that are used throughout construction would be placed close to or in the hull; heavy engine parts, which must travel to the hull only once, would be placed at a more distant location; and cranes would be set up close to the hull because of their constant use.

In fixed-position layout, a high degree of task ordering is common, and to the extent that this precedence determines production stages, a fixed-position layout might be developed by arranging materials according to their technological priority. This procedure would be expected in making a layout for a large machine tool, such as a stamping machine, where manufacture follows a rigid sequence; assembly is performed from the ground up, with parts being added to the base in almost a building-block fashion. As far as quantitative layout techniques are concerned, there is little in the literature devoted to fixed-position formats, even though they have been utilized for thousands of years. This lack of research effort probably stems from their low-volume characteristics and the high degree of technological ordering found in fixed-position products.

Marketing layout

The broad objective of marketing layout is to maximize the net profit per square foot of display space. Operationally, this goal is often translated into such criteria as "minimize handling cost" or "maximize product exposure." Although appealing in their simplicity, employing these and similar criteria in layout planning "results in stores that look like warehouses and require shoppers to approach the task like order pickers or display case stockers." Such criteria are "retailer- rather than customer-oriented."[11] The suggestion also has been made that product groupings be based upon the shopper's view of related items, as opposed to the physical characteristics of the products or shelf-space and servicing requirements.[12] The prevalence of this grouping-by-association philosophy is seen in the

---

[11] Montrose S. Sommers and Jerome B. Kernan, "A Behavioral Approach to Planning, Layout and Display," *Journal of Retailing* (Winter 1965/66), pp. 21–27.

[12] Ibid.

recent trend of adding boutiques in department stores and gourmet sections in supermarkets.

In addition to product grouping, aisle characteristics are of particular interest in marketing layout. Aside from determining the number of aisles to be provided, decisions must be made as to the width of the aisles, since this is a direct function of expected or desired traffic. To enhance the shopper's view of merchandise as she proceeds down a main aisle, secondary and tertiary aisles may be set at an angle.

Consider the two layouts depicted in Figure 4.9.

The rectangular layout would probably require less expensive fixtures and contain more display space, and if storage considerations are important to the store management, this would be the more desirable choice. On the other hand, the angular layout provides the shopper with a much clearer

FIGURE 4.9

Sample marketing layouts

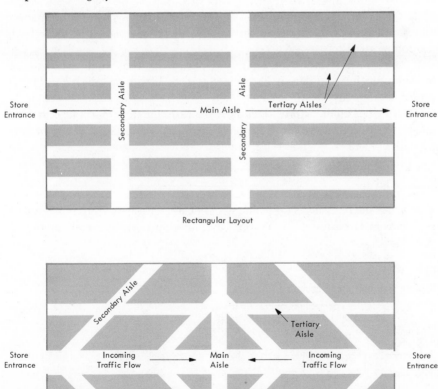

Rectangular Layout

Angular Layout

Key:

▨ Merchandise Counters

Abstracted from Ronald E. Gist, *Retailing Concepts and Decisions* (New York: John Wiley & Sons, 1968), p. 238.

view of the merchandise and, other things being equal, presents a more desirable selling environment.

There are other layouts, of course; some are blends of these two patterns, while others are "custom" types, consisting of circular or free-form components, which might be more appropriate than either of the two basic layout types. Suffice it to say that making the layout choice is not simply a matter of choosing between display space and ease of inspection. Pricing policies, store location, store image, product line considerations, and a myriad of other factors enter into the decision.

As might be gathered from the foregoing, the influence of behavioral factors makes the development of hard-and-fast rules for marketing layout a questionable pursuit. Nevertheless, a few guidelines have been derived from marketing research that are worthy of mention:

1. People in supermarkets tend to follow a perimeter pattern in their shopping behavior, and therefore placing high-profit items along the walls of a store will enhance their probability of purchase.

2. "Sale" merchandise placed at the end of an aisle in supermarkets almost always sells better than the same "sale" items placed in the interior portion of an aisle.

3. Credit and other nonselling departments that require customers to wait for the completion of their services should be placed either on upper floors or in "dead" areas.

4. In department stores, locations nearest the store entrances and adjacent to open front-window displays are most valuable in terms of sales potential.

Storage layout

Storage layout, especially in warehouses, presents some interesting problems in criteria determination. Obtaining an optimal layout involves a

FIGURE 4.10

Sample warehouse configurations

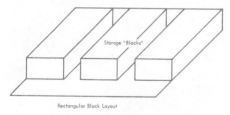

Rectangular Block Layout

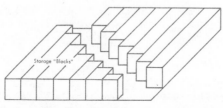

Diagonal Gangway Layout

multidimensional tradeoff in the sense that the height and depth of storage areas, variety of items in storage, physical access requirements, building occupation costs, and horizontal distance transportation costs must be considered jointly. One approach to the problem, developed by Berry, employs geometrically based equations that quantify these factors (and other variables, such as desired gangway width and pallet dimensions) in arriving at an optimum solution for a specified layout configuration.[13] (Sample configurations are shown in Figure 4.10). Though Berry's formulas are complex, they appear to be quite valuable, especially for examining movement costs, storage costs, and warehouse volume requirements as a function of alternate layouts and varying numbers of stock lines.

Some of the more interesting conclusions that Berry obtained from his layout equations are as follows.

1. The warehouse layout that gives maximum utilization of space is different from one that minimizes handling distances.

2. If the number of gangways is less than optimum, the higher the cost of a building in comparison to the movement cost of the goods within it, the longer the gangway length. If there is more than the optimum number of gangways, as the building-cost ratio rises, the shorter will be the gangway length.

3. If provision is to be made for future expansion of a warehouse, it is necessary to know not only whether the volume stored will increase but also whether the rate of throughput and number of stock lines will change.

4. When rectangular shelving blocks are used, the optimum layout plan will be approximately square only when the optimum number of gangways is used. The more the number of gangways differs from the optimum, the more the optimum layout will differ from a square.

5. If stock locations are allocated to specific stock lines, it is likely that an asymmetrical layout will produce lower total costs.

6. A diagonal gangway layout will give lower total costs than an optimum rectangular block layout when the number of stock lines is small. It may also give lower total costs when the cost of volume or the area cost is low in comparison to handling-distance cost.

Project layout

As in assembly line balancing, project layout is a blend of the physical placement of components and activity scheduling. In project layout, however, the amount of space required is affected to a much greater degree by the "tightness" of delivery schedules. Indeed, where space for material placement is extremely limited (as in the case of constructing a large building in a congested business district), the scheduling problem *is* the layout problem. In situations where adequate space is available for storage, the materials scheduling problem is diminished, allowing management to realize project economies by careful material and equipment placement.

In construction projects, one of the first duties of the project superintend-

---

[13] J. R. Berry, "Elements of Warehouse Layout," *International Journal of Production Research,* vol. 7, no. 1 (1968), pp. 105–21.

ent is to prepare a scale drawing of the project site, denoting the area available for offices, warehouses, materials storage, equipment, earth, construction forms, and reinforcing steel. In practice, unfortunately, the measures of effectiveness, and hence the criteria by which the scale drawing is rendered, are somewhat subjective. This point is illustrated by the following guidelines, drawn from the literature on construction layout.

1.   Keep the amount of material rehandling down by delivering materials close to the point of use.

2.   Materials that are similar in use should be stored close together.

3.   Locate the general office near the main entrance so that business visitors will not have to travel around construction areas.

4.   Locate the warehouse near the entrance to facilitate delivery and control of materials.

In certain situations more objective criteria may be specified, and the layout might then be amenable to quantitative analysis. For instance, if material handling cost is significant and the construction site permits more or less straight-line material movement, the CRAFT process layout technique might be advantageously employed.

CONCLUSION

Although we have tended to deal with the plant layout problem in isolation, the reader should be aware that the selected physical layout has great impact not only on the things that one can see, such as product flow and worker placement, but on the less obvious elements of organization structure and communication flow. The operational effect of these unseen factors is to broaden the criteria by which the layout is derived.

In process formats, for example, the layout planner could relate the organization structure to the layout procedure by altering the definition of a department from "a place where a particular transformation takes place" to "a group of activities supervised by a given manager." Although the effect of this redefinition might be to create some strange bedfellows in terms of the combined technologies, substantial benefits might be derived from the standpoint of administration.

Much has been written about the relative advantages of product and process layouts. Generally, the evaluation centers on a tradeoff between expected volume and desired machine utilization. Where demand is high for a homogeneous product line, the decision tends toward product layout since redundant equipment can be justified. On the other hand, where a wide variety of items is produced, fewer machines of a given type are required and process layout is generally preferred. Other factors, however, must also be considered in the decision: need for flexibility, supervision requirements, labor force composition, and available plant space.[14] For these and other reasons, most factory installations are blends of the two types of flow formats, and management often makes it a point to continually

---

[14] For more complete discussions of these factors, see the Buffa-Taubert and Moore bibliographical references.

evaluate the desirability of changing the flow formats. (In the case of functional layout formats, comparison is not particularly relevant; by definition, each is intended for a different purpose.)

In conclusion, the development of layout techniques has been extensive in the past decade. What remains is for the computerized methods to see greater use. This will require greater awareness on the part of management as to what the techniques are and what they can do, and will require that specialists in the techniques create and disseminate applications-oriented programs.

PROPOSITIONS

Propositions contrasting services and manufacturing relative to layout of the physical system

Product: In services, the nature of the service generally dictates the layout (process, product, or fixed position). In manufacturing, the nature of the product is unaffected by the plant layout, and the format is usually dictated by the desired rate of output.

Technology of transformation: Because the technology of transformation for services generally must be more flexible than for manufacturing, service systems are more likely to use general purpose equipment and process layout formats than are manufacturing systems (even where both systems are characterized by high volume).

Operating-control system: Because of the intangible nature of most services, the bases for measuring the effectiveness of a service system layout will generally be more subjective than those for a manufacturing system.

Workforce: In service systems, the layout decision generally specifies the placement of the workforce. In manufacturing, the layout decision is generally limited to specifying the location of processes and equipment.

REVIEW AND DISCUSSION QUESTIONS

1. What are the major inputs to the layout decision?
2. What is the general approach to making the layout decision?
3. Sketch a schematic relating the basic layout formats.
4. What is meant by the statement that process formats and assembly line balancing "present challenging theoretical problems in combinatorial mathematics"? In general, how do the methods described in this chapter attempt to meet this challenge?
5. Contrast the measures of effectiveness used in assembly line balancing problems and process layout problems.

6. What do you see as the key differences between ALDEP, CORELAP, and CRAFT?

7. Why is it that efficiency graphs (such as that shown in Figure 4.6) appear as sawtooth graphs? What is the nature of the tradeoff they depict?

8. Under what conditions is the scheduling problem equivalent to the layout problem?

9. Give some examples of marketing layout problems you have encountered as a customer.

10. If you get a chance, ask a construction foreman how he decides on the placement of components at a construction site.

11. What advice would you give a supermarket manager about where he should locate a slow-moving item?

12. What are the major differences between the minimum material flow approach and the SLP approach to process layout?

PROBLEMS

1. Suppose you are requested by the administrator of a planned 200-bed general hospital to develop an "efficient" layout for the new facility.
   a. What questions would you ask him in undertaking the project?
   b. Outline your plan of action in developing such a layout.

2. See if you can develop a departmental arrangement for the toy factory example in this chapter whose material handling costs would be less than $3,282.

3. The Trauma Toy Company has decided to manufacture a new plastic novelty whose production is broken into six steps, as follows.

Task	Performance time in seconds	Tasks that must precede
A	20	—
B	30	A
C	15	A
D	15	A
E	10	A, B, C
F	30	A, B, C, D, E
	120	

An output of 5,000 items per week is required. Trauma will work a seven-hour day, five days per week. Can its new line be balanced in four stations? If it cannot, why not? If it can, what will the stations consist of?

4. The Aristocratic University of Goniffland, a newly chartered university, was created for the purpose of providing higher education for the aristocracy of the kingdom, the sons and daughters of resident foreign dignitaries, and other loyal and influential subjects.

   The regent of the university (the king) has allocated a rectangular (40 by 80 feet) portion of the first floor of the south wing of the Imperial Palace for the purpose of constructing lecture halls, laboratories, etc. The interior layout was designed by T. Kratpc Fhlzet, A.I.A., and is one of the first examples of flexible layout by means of modular partitions in Goniffland. The basic module is 10 feet square, and the tentative design is shown in Figure 4.11.

Unlike most American universities, Aristocratic has only six categories of students. The members of each category are assigned the same classes and schedules during their years at the university. Each class meets for 50 minutes each day and the students are required to proceed directly to their next class. The schedule for the current semester is indicated in Figure 4.12.

FIGURE 4.11

Architect's layout for The Aristocratic University of Goniffland

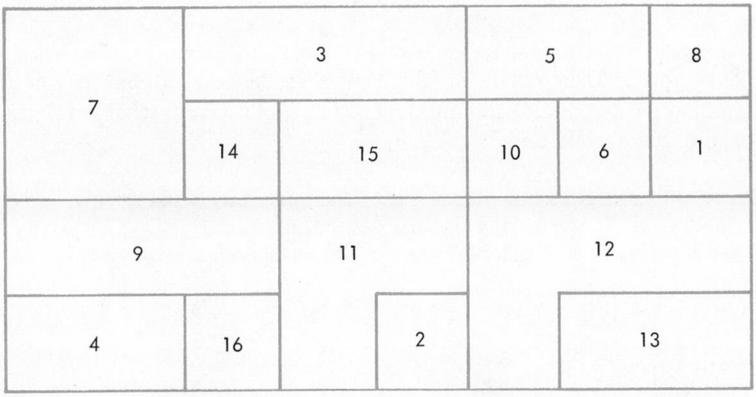

Number	Activity	Number	Activity
1...........	Entrance	9...........	Accounting
2...........	Physics	10...........	Electrical engineering
3...........	Basketweaving*	11...........	Psychology
4...........	Calculus	12...........	Sex education
5...........	Arithmetic	13...........	Humanities
6...........	Finance	14...........	Art
7...........	Production management	15...........	Philosophy
8...........	Economics	16...........	Exit

* Location must remain fixed due to its proximity to the fountain for soaking the weaving material.

The architect is interested in gaining the favor of the king and has contracted for you to verify his layout and suggest improvements. He has asked you to:

a. Prepare a flow matrix for the class sequence similar to the load summary shown in Table 4.2.
b. Determine the cost of the existing layout in terms of walking. (Since the architect wishes to gain favor with the king, he values each foot walked by the male children of the king as equivalent to two feet walked by the female children of the king and to four feet walked by all others.)
c. Create a better layout, keeping room areas the same and fitting into a 40 by 80-foot rectangular space. Note: the entrance and exit must remain in the same position.

FIGURE 4.12
The Aristocratic University of Goniffland's semester schedule

Category	Number of students	Class meeting time										
		8	9	10	11	12	1	2	3	4	5	6
		Classroom										
1. King's male children..	8	15	4	7	11	6	10	12	13	2	9	8
2. King's female children.............	4	3	14	5								
3. Merchants' children.............	32	5	9	6	8	11	7					
4. Nobles' children......	25	12	3	13	7	4						
5. Children of idle rich...	42	7	12	14	13	3						
6. Children of foreign officials.............	17	2	7	4	10	15	6	14				

5. Given the following data on the task precedence relationships for an assembled product and assuming the tasks cannot be split, what is the theoretical minimum cycle time?

Task	Performance time in minutes	Tasks that must precede
A....................	3	—
B....................	6	A
C....................	7	A
D....................	5	A
E....................	2	A
F....................	4	A, C, B
G....................	5	A, C
H....................	5	A, B, C, D, E, F, G

  a. Determine the minimum number of work stations needed to achieve this cycle time using the "longest operation time" rule.
  b. Determine the minimum number of stations needed to meet a cycle time of 10 minutes according to the "largest number of following tasks" rule.
  c. Compute the efficiency of the balances achieved.

6. Develop your own heuristic balancing rule and apply it to the data in problem 5.

7. Sketch the floor plan and identify the location of major items of furniture and appliances at your residence.
  a. Specify the bases for placing the components in their present positions.
  b. Develop a hypothetical layout that would optimize your utilization of facilities. Be sure to specify the measure of effectiveness you will use in your analysis.

8. Ward Healer, a physician and architect, would like your help in developing a layout for a new outpatient clinic to be built in Off-tackle, Ohio. Based upon analysis of another recently built clinic, he obtains the following data for (1) number of trips made by patients between departments on a typical day (shown above diagonal line), and (2), the closeness ratings (defined

Interdepartmental Flow and Closeness Ratings

Departments	2	3	4	5	6	Area Requirement (Sq. Ft.)
1 Reception	2 / A	5 / O	200 / E	0 / U	10 / O	100
2 X-Ray		10 / E	300 / I	0 / U	8 / O	100
3 Surgery			100 / I	0 / I	4 / A	200
4 Examining Rooms (5)				0 / U	15 / I	500
5 Lab					3 / O	100
6 Nurses' Station						100

in Figure 4.5c) between departments as specified by the new clinic's physicians (below diagonal). The new building will be 60 feet by 20 feet.

a. Develop an interdepartmental flow graph which minimizes patient travel.

b. Develop a "good" relationship diagram using Systematic Layout Planning.

c. Choose either of the layouts obtained in a or b and sketch the departments to scale within the building.

d. Will this layout be satisfactory to the nursing staff? Explain.

SELECTED BIBLIOGRAPHY

Brennecke, Donald "Two Parameter Assembly Line Balancing Models," in *Models and Analysis for Production Management,* ed. Michael P. Hottenstein, pp. 215–35. Scranton, Pa.: International Textbook Co., 1968.

Buffa, E. S., Armour, G. C., and Vollmann, T. E. "Allocating Facilities with CRAFT," *Harvard Business Review* (March–April 1964), pp. 136–58.

———— **and Taubert, William H.** *Production Inventory Systems: Planning and Control,* pp. 303–66. Rev. ed. Homewood, Ill.: Richard D. Irwin, Inc., 1972.

Buxey, G. M., Slack, N. P., and Wild, R. "Production Flow System Design— A Review." *AIIE Transactions,* vol. 5, no. 1 (March 1973), pp. 37–48.

Chase, R. B. "Survey of Paced Assembly Lines." *Industrial Engineering,* vol. 6, no. 2 (February 1974), pp. 14–18.

———— "Strategic Considerations in Assembly-Line Selection." *California Management Review,* vol. 18, no. 1 (Fall 1975), pp. 17–23.

Francis, R. L., and White, J. A. *Facility Layout and Location: An Analytical Approach.* Prentice-Hall, Inc.; Englewood Cliffs, N.J., 1974.

Helgeson, W. B., and Birnie, D. P. "Assembly Line Balancing Using the Ranked Positional Weight Technique," *Journal of Industrial Engineering,* vol. 12, no. 6 (November–December 1961), pp. 394–98.

Ignall, Edward J. "A Review of Assembly Line Balancing," *Journal of Industrial Engineering,* vol. 16, no. 4 (July–August 1965), pp. 244–54.

Kottas, J. F., and Lau, H. "A Cost-Oriented Approach to Stochastic Line Balancing." *AIIE Transactions,* vol. 5, no. 2 (June 1973), pp. 164–71.

Lee, Robert S., and Moore, James M. "CORELAP—Computerized Relationship Layout Planning," *Journal of Industrial Engineering*, vol. 18, no. 3 (March 1967), pp. 195–200.

Mastor, Anthony A. "An Experimental Investigation and Comparative Evaluation of Production Line Balancing Techniques," *Management Science*, vol. 16, no. 11 (July 1970), pp. 728–46.

Moore, James M. *Plant Layout and Design.* New York: Macmillan, 1962.

Muther, Richard *Practical Plant Layout.* New York: McGraw-Hill, 1955.

Muther, Richard, and Wheeler, John D. "Simplified Systematic Layout Planning," *Factory*, vol. 120, nos. 8, 9, 10 (August, September, October 1962), pp. 68–77, 111–19, 101–13.

Seehof, Jarrold M., and Evans, Wayne O. "Automated Layout Design Program," *Journal of Industrial Engineering*, vol. 18, no. 12 (December 1967), pp. 690–95.

Wild, Ray *Mass Production Management.* London: John Wiley, 1972.

5

Design of the quality control system

The Prime Minister was not told that his food was scrutinized for poison; but officials were unable to hide the fact that his cigars were examined, for the simple reason that whenever he received this sort of gift he did not see it for days, sometimes weeks. On one occasion, when he was running out of Havana cigars, an admirer sent him a supply of ten thousand. 'But where are they?' he fumed. 'Who's whisked them away? It doesn't seem too much to ask that I should be allowed to enjoy my own cigars . . .' So he was told that Victor Rothschild, whose grandfather [the famous financier] had entertained him as a youth, was vetting them for explosives or other lethal substances. In order to satisfy Churchill's impatience Lord Rothschild decided to rely on statistical techniques, testing one in every ten, or some such number. Apparently this fascinated Churchill, who liked to speculate on the gamble, comparing it romantically to Russian roulette.*

Quality control was one of the first fields to be approached scientifically by business organizations. The procedures used by quality control specialists have evolved apace with the evolution of production processes and statistics so that now "Q.C." is perhaps the most highly refined support area of general manufacturing. Indeed, a glance at a recent quality control journal should readily indicate the depth and breadth of the procedures by which contemporary quality control is performed. From a management perspective, quality control can be viewed as consisting of two classes of decisions: strategic decisions and tactical decisions. Strategic decisions are those that must be made at the highest (or corporate) level of the organization and, in effect, determine the influence of quality control in the long-run operation of the firm. These decisions are:

1. Organizational role of the quality control function
2. Quality of product design

The tactical decisions relate to the means by which quality control is conducted on a day-by-day basis and include:

1. Degree of conformance to product design specifications
2. Acceptance sampling procedures
3. Process control procedures
4. Location and frequency of inspection activities
5. Personnel considerations

In this chapter, we will initially discuss quality control by developing the seven strategic and tactical decisions listed above. Then we will consider the role of quality in several service industries, and conclude with some examples of commercial quality control computer programs for acceptance sampling and process control.

ROLE OF THE QUALITY CONTROL FUNCTION

Prior to the early 1900s, quality control was loosely organized in business enterprises. Generally, the inspection function was performed by a worker

---

* Virginia Cowles, *Rothschilds: Family of Fortune* (N.Y.: Alfred A. Knopf. 1973 c), p. 221–222.

who reported to the line foreman, who, in addition, was responsible for detecting errors and correcting the manufacturing process. As organizations grew in size and inspection became more technical, there was a tendency to group inspectors together and make them responsible to an inspection foreman or chief inspector, who reported to the manufacturing manager. Not until the 1920s was the importance of quality in all areas of organization performance firmly realized and quality responsibility consolidated

FIGURE 5.1

Organizational structures that emphasize the quality responsibility

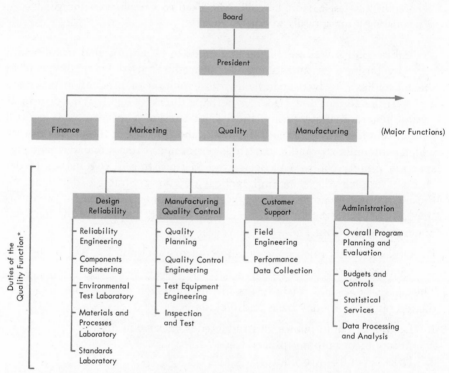

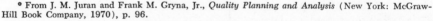

* From J. M. Juran and Frank M. Gryna, Jr., *Quality Planning and Analysis* (New York: McGraw-Hill Book Company, 1970), p. 96.

as a separate function, often on the same level as the manufacturing manager. The most recent trend, strongly evidenced in large manufacturing companies, is to place quality responsibility on a par with other major corporate functions. Such an organizational structure placement is shown in Figure 5.1, along with some duties of the quality function.

The pervasiveness of quality control inputs throughout one company's product development cycle can be seen in Figure 5.2. The QA in the center stands for "quality assurance," a program for "prevention, detection and correction of product defects that would cause customer dissatisfaction."[1]

---

[1] P. J. Ernster, "Quality Assurance Assures Customer Satisfaction," *Quality Progress*, no. 1 (January 1970), pp. 21–24.

At the left of Figure 5.2, outside the main figure, the generation of a product idea is symbolized, perhaps originating in the market research department. Design engineers, management, and other personnel discuss this idea in relation to its manufacturability and marketability as a finished product. If the anticipated selling price and manufacturing costs are reasonable, the proposal is presented to the appropriate level of management for approval. A functional design is made without any regard for the appearance of the product (called a "breadboard"). Interest is solely in designing a product to operate as intended. Once this breadboard design is accepted, a prototype is made of the complete product, incorporating the breadboard design and styling for appearance. Designs are released and necessary materials ordered. Several products are made, and the process is

FIGURE 5.2

Quality inputs from product inception through use analysis

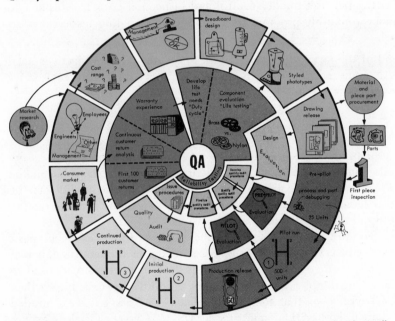

Adapted from P. J. Ernster, "Quality Assurance Assures Customer Satisfaction," *Quality Progress*, no. 1 (January 1970), p. 24. Reprinted by permission of the American Society for Quality Control, Inc.

viewed closely for improvements in design or in production methods and equipment. This small product run is frequently performed by the design and development staff. When results of the pilot run are satisfactory, the product is released to the production staff. Production commences and in due course the product is delivered to the customer.

Quality decisions occurred throughout the above sequence—in parts evaluation, reliability testing, design evaluation, inspections, and analysis of customers' use of the product. The cycle may be partially repeated if feedback from the customers indicates a need for changes in the product.

Objectives of a quality control system

Any system, if it is to be of value, must have objectives. In the case of quality control, objectives may typically be directed toward reducing the scrap rate, reducing the number of returns from customers, maintaining the desired degree of conformance to product design, increasing the average level of outgoing product quality, decreasing the amount of defective raw materials from vendors, etc.

Quality control objectives should be set down in specific terms and for a prescribed period. The following might be the quality control goals of a firm for the coming year.

1. Reduce the number of customer complaints to 3 percent.
2. Reduce the number of customer returns to 2 percent.
3. Reduce the maximum rework level to 5 percent.
4. Lower the per unit quality control and inspection costs by 10 percent.
5. Conduct a monthly program for training and updating inspection personnel.

At the end of the year, success or failure in meeting these objectives must be seriously analyzed. The objectives may be either extended or revised for the following year.

QUALITY OF PRODUCT DESIGN

Quality of product design refers to the product's inherent worth as defined by its component cost, its manufacturing cost, and its value in the eyes of the consumer. In some sense, a product's design quality can be measured by comparing it to competing products in terms of three quality concepts—grade, fitness for use, and consistency.

Grade. To most persons, quality implies such attributes as smoothness; purity of color or texture, taste, or odor; closeness of fit; small number of flaws; reliability; range of operation; etc. In this sense, quality is used to imply grade. One might say that the quality of a Rolls-Royce is higher than that of a Chevrolet, or that the quality of a New York–cut steak graded USDA Prime is higher than one graded USDA Choice. Grade classifies characteristics into groupings: grades 1, 2, 3, 4, etc., or A, B, C, D, or USDA Prime, Choice, Good, Fancy, or Commercial.

The confusing part of grading is that universal standards do not always exist and the grading system may be made by someone other than the ultimate user—perhaps the producer, wholesaler, retailer, or an association. Therefore grade A might seem to imply that it is the producer's top grade, whereas he also has AA, AAA, and perhaps AAAA. In liquors, for example, one might be happy buying the "3 Star" grade—until he discovers the "5 Star," or finds that the top quality (with limited distribution) is actually "7 Star" grade.

Fitness for use. This quality concept refers to the degree to which a product satisfies the user. The user's satisfaction generally depends on three factors: the grade itself, the consistency of quality within that grade, and, for a functioning item, its reliability and maintainability. To elaborate on the last factor, a product should function for some specified time under specified conditions, and repair service and replacement parts should be available (unless, of course, the product is not expected to undergo repair, as in the case of "throwaway" items like nonrefillable lighters or inexpensive radios).

Consistency. Products or services are designed, and the output of this design stage is a set of specifications for each component of the product. How well the finished product meets the design specifications is called the "quality of conformance" and will be discussed in more detail later. What often is more important to the customer, however, is the consistency of succeeding units of the product relative to certain key criteria.

Consider two automobile service agencies, one that usually does high-quality service but occasionally botches a job, and a second agency that consistently does mediocre work. The customer may care little about either agency's quality design or conformance level; the decision he is faced with is trading off the probability of excellent versus bad service by one agency and the high likelihood of an average job by the other.

Or consider the plight of a student attempting to ascertain what material is covered in a particular college course. Should he refer to the catalog for a course description, hoping that the "quality of conformance" is high; that is, that the course actually conforms to the description? Should he try to find out if a new course description has been developed? Or should he try to find out from other sources if the course has been consistently taught in the same fashion, regardless of the description? In many cases, consistency may be more important than quality of conformance. Obviously, in the ideal situation the course is consistently taught in conformance to an accurate description, or, conversely, the description conforms consistently to the course as taught.

QUALITY OF CONFORMANCE

Quality of conformance quite simply refers to the degree to which a product meets its design specifications. As previously mentioned, the output of the design stage is a set of specifications for each component of the product. Specifications generally contain a specific measurement, and also an acceptable range or tolerance: the diameter of a steel shaft may be specified as 1.000 inch $\pm$ 0.005. To produce this shaft, the decision must be made as to how well the machinery process should meet the specifications as designed; that is, what the quality of conformance should be. If a very expensive machining process is chosen, perhaps it may be able to produce virtually all shafts to 1 inch $\pm$ 0.003. It would then be producing to a high degree of conformance, but also to a higher quality than originally designed. The amount of reject work would decrease—but at the added cost of a more expensive production process. Conversely, if the process output is in the other direction—that is, an inexpensive process that produces output rang-

FIGURE 5.3

Degree of conformance to design specifications

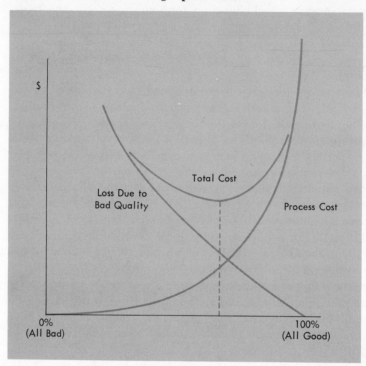

ing far outside the 1 inch ± 0.005—then the production process would cost less but the costs due to rejects, customer complaints, product failures, etc., would increase. Figure 5.3 shows this relationship of process cost and costs due to the product's not meeting the specifications related to the degree of conformance. Optimal conformance is found where total cost is at the minimum.

Quality of conformance greatly affects product assembly. If all parts of a certain type conform to specifications, the operator may select any at random. If conformance is poor and parts vary outside specifications, "fitting" is required; that is, individual parts must be selected to fit together. For example, if steel shafts with poor conformance are to be used with bearings, the operator will have to search for larger bearings to fit the larger shafts and smaller bearings for the undersize shafts. While this practice often is used for better fit, problems may be experienced by the user at some future time if he must replace the shaft. Overconformance, on the other hand, while perhaps contributing to a "better" product, is usually more costly to produce.

ACCEPTANCE SAMPLING PROCEDURES

Acceptance sampling is performed to determine what percentage of products conform to specifications. These products may be items received from another company and evaluated by the receiving department or they may be components that have passed through a processing step and are evaluated by company personnel either in production or later in the warehousing function. Acceptance sampling is based upon the statistical concept that a random sample of appropriate size will have within it a proportional representation of all items in the parent population. One estimates product quality through sampling in order to determine whether or not complete (100%) inspection should be part of the manufacturing process. (The economics of this decision are discussed in the section entitled "costs to justify inspection.") There are two general ways of describing the degree of conformance to design quality in acceptance sampling (and process control). One measures attributes and the other measures variables.

The differentiation between attributes and variables may be described as follows. Two clear-cut types of observations are possible: an item of production or service may be recognized as *either good or bad,* or it may be measured to determine *how much it varies* from other units or from the design specifications. The first type is usually termed *sampling by attributes.* Examples of this are testing lamp bulbs to determine whether they light or not; checking the buttons on a shirt in a laundry (if all are present, the shirt is passed on for pressing; if not, it goes to sewing); testing a stereo tape player (if the frequency response falls within a specified range, the unit is passed, if not, it is set aside for repair). The use of attributes in acceptance sampling is usually based on the binomial statistical distribution. In process control, attributes of a product or service are used to determine a proportion which, in turn, may be used to construct a control chart.

The second type, measuring the *amount* of deviation of an observation, is called *sampling by variables.* Rather than accept the shirt if all buttons are present or reject it if one or more are missing, the interest may be in the actual number of buttons missing. The stereo examination might include the plotting of a frequency-amplitude response curve to obtain the actual output characteristics, rather than just an accept-reject decision. Actual measurement of the particular variable has considerable usefulness if analysis and control of the productive process is of interest. Variables sampling is based on the normal statistical distribution.

n = # units in Sample

c = # units accepted that are defective before lot rejected

Design of a Single Sampling Plan

Acceptance sampling is executed through the development and operation of a sampling plan. In this section, we will illustrate the planning procedures for a single sampling plan—that is, a plan in which the quality of conformance is decided upon the evaluation of one sample. (Other plans may be developed using two or more samples on which to base the accept-reject decision.)

A single sampling plan is defined by n and c, where n is the number of units in the sample, and c is the acceptance number. The size of n may vary from one up to all of the items in the lot (usually denoted as N) from which it is drawn. The acceptance number c denotes the maximum number of defective items that can be found in the sample before the lot is rejected.

FIGURE 5.4

Tradeoffs and decisions in sampling plan development

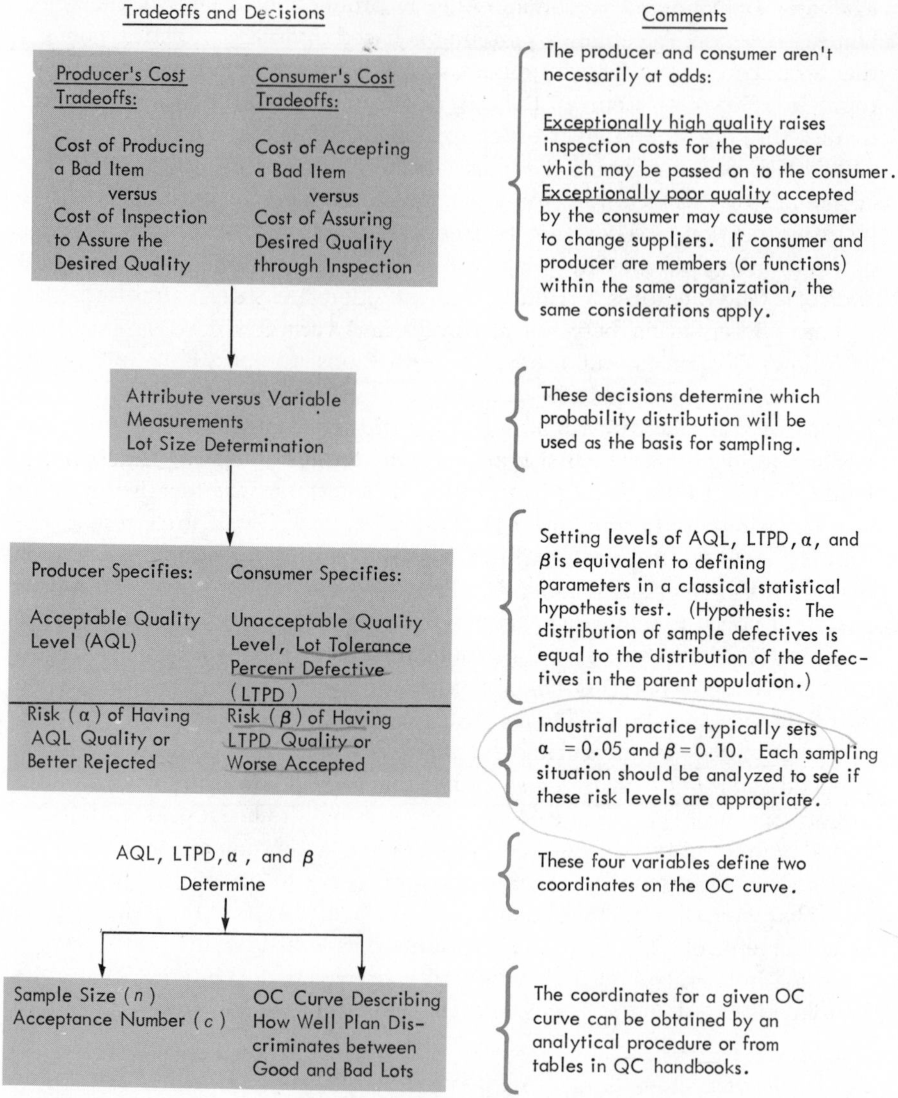

Tradeoffs and Decisions | Comments

Producer's Cost Tradeoffs: | Consumer's Cost Tradeoffs:

Cost of Producing a Bad Item versus Cost of Inspection to Assure the Desired Quality | Cost of Accepting a Bad Item versus Cost of Assuring Desired Quality through Inspection

The producer and consumer aren't necessarily at odds:

Exceptionally high quality raises inspection costs for the producer which may be passed on to the consumer. Exceptionally poor quality accepted by the consumer may cause consumer to change suppliers. If consumer and producer are members (or functions) within the same organization, the same considerations apply.

Attribute versus Variable Measurements Lot Size Determination

These decisions determine which probability distribution will be used as the basis for sampling.

Producer Specifies: | Consumer Specifies:

Acceptable Quality Level (AQL) | Unacceptable Quality Level, Lot Tolerance Percent Defective (LTPD)

Risk (α) of Having AQL Quality or Better Rejected | Risk (β) of Having LTPD Quality or Worse Accepted

Setting levels of AQL, LTPD, α, and β is equivalent to defining parameters in a classical statistical hypothesis test. (Hypothesis: The distribution of sample defectives is equal to the distribution of the defectives in the parent population.)

Industrial practice typically sets $\alpha = 0.05$ and $\beta = 0.10$. Each sampling situation should be analyzed to see if these risk levels are appropriate.

AQL, LTPD, α, and β Determine

These four variables define two coordinates on the OC curve.

Sample Size (n) Acceptance Number (c) | OC Curve Describing How Well Plan Discriminates between Good and Bad Lots

The coordinates for a given OC curve can be obtained by an analytical procedure or from tables in QC handbooks.

Values for n and c are determined by the interaction of four factors that quantify the objectives of the producer of the product and the consumer of the product. The objective of the producer is to assure that the sampling plan has a low probability of rejecting good lots. Lots are defined as "good" if they contain no more than a specified level of defectives, termed the acceptable quality level (AQL). The objective of the consumer is to assure that the sampling plan has a low probability of accepting bad lots. Lots are defined as "bad" if the percentage of defectives is greater than a specified amount, termed lot tolerance percent defective (LTPD). The probability associated with rejecting a good lot is denoted by the Greek letter alpha (α) and is termed the *producer's risk*. The probability associated with accepting a bad lot is denoted by the letter beta (β) and is termed the *consumer's risk*. The selection of particular values for AQL, α, LTPD, and β is an economic decision based upon a cost tradeoff. The nature of this tradeoff and subsequent decisions in sampling plan development are summarized in Figure 5.4.

The following example using an excerpt from a standard acceptance sampling table illustrates how these four parameters—AQL, α, LTPD, and β—are used in developing a sampling plan.

Situation. The Old C.B. Company of Shaky-town manufactures citizens'-band radios. These units use the speakers made by a subsidiary in Chi-town. The subsidiary producing the speakers works to an acceptable quality level (AQL) of 2% defectives and is willing to run a 5% risk (α) of having lots of this level or fewer defectives, rejected. Old C.B. considers lots of 8% or more defectives (LTPD) to be unacceptable, and wants to assure that they will accept such poor quality lots no more than 10% of the time (β). A convoy has just delivered a lot of size N. What values of n and c should be selected to determine the quality of this lot?

TABLE 5.1

Excerpt from a sampling plan table for
$\alpha = 0.05$, $\beta = 0.10$

(1) c	(2) $LTPD \div AQL$	(3) $(n) \cdot (AQL)$
0	44.890	0.052
1	10.946	0.355
2	6.509	0.818
3	4.890	1.366
4	4.057	1.970
5	3.549	2.613
6	3.206	3.286
7	2.957	3.981
8	2.768	4.695
9	2.618	5.426

Solution. The parameters of the problem are as follows: AQL = 0.02, $\alpha = 0.05$, LTPD = 0.08, and $\beta = 0.10$. We can use Table 5.1 to find c and then n.

First divide LTPD by AQL ($0.08 \div 0.02 = 4$).

Then find the ratio in column 2 that is equal to or just greater than that amount, i.e., 4. This value is 4.057, which is associated with $c = 4$.

Finally, find the value in column 3 that is in the same row as $c = 4$, and divide that quantity by AQL to obtain n ($1.970 \div 0.02 = 98.5$).

The appropriate sampling plan is: $c = 4$, $n = 99$.

Interpretation. While the sampling plan meets our requirements for the extreme values of good and bad quality, we can't readily determine how well the plan discriminates between good and bad lots at intermediate values. For this reason, sampling plans are generally displayed graphically through the use of operating characteristic (OC) curves. These curves (which are unique for each combination of n and c) simply illustrate the probability of accepting lots with varying percent defectives. The procedure we have followed in developing the plan, in fact, specifies two points on an OC curve. Curves for common values of n and c can be computed using the binomial distribution. They are also available in handbooks, or can be derived by standard computer routines. (See "quality control computer programs" at the end of this chapter.) The OC curve for the example plan is shown in Figure 5.5.[2]

FIGURE 5.5

Operating characteristic curve for AQL = 0.02, α = 0.05, LTPD = 0.08, β = 0.10

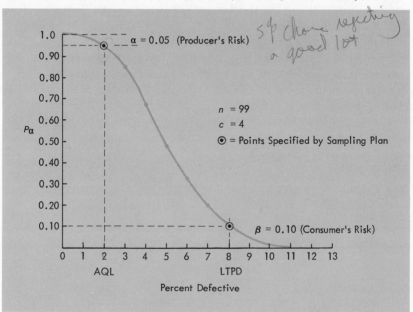

Percent Defective

Average outgoing quality. When the same sampling plan is used repeatedly, the average outgoing quality (AOQ) of the product or service can be calculated if any lot that fails to pass the sampling plan is completely inspected. AOQ generally applies to the producer, however, since the consumer may simply reject the lot and send it back, rather than perform a complete inspection of all items in bad lots.

If defective items are removed but not replaced (thereby reducing the lot size), the average quality is

---

[2] Figure 5.5 was computed using cumulative probability curves of the Poisson distribution (which can be used to approximate the binomial distribution). These curves enable the determination of the probability of occurrence of c or fewer defects in a sample of n items from a large lot size in which the fraction defective is p. See H. F. Dodge and H. G. Romig, *Sampling Inspection Tables—Single and Double Sampling* (2d ed.: New York; John Wiley & Sons, 1959). p. 35.

$$AOQ = \frac{P_a p (N - n)}{N - pn - p(1 - P_a)(N - n)}$$

where P_a is the probability of acceptance, p is the fraction defective, N is the lot size, and n is the sample size.

If defective items are replaced with good ones (thereby returning the lot to its original size, N),

$$AOQ = \frac{P_a p (N - n)}{N}$$

Costs to justify inspection. Total inspection is justified when the cost of a loss incurred by not inspecting is greater than the cost of inspection. For example, suppose a faulty item results in a $10 loss. If the average percentage of defective items in a lot is 3, the expected cost due to faulty items is 0.03 × $10, or $0.30 each. Therefore, if the cost of inspecting each item is less than $0.30, the economic decision is to perform 100 percent inspection.

FIGURE 5.6

Ideal discriminating sampling plan

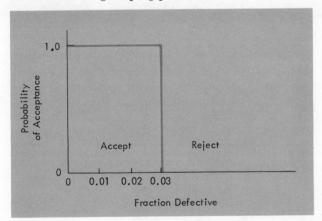

Not all defective items will be removed, however, since inspectors will pass some bad items and reject some good ones.[3]

In theory, one searches for an OC curve that discriminates perfectly between good and bad lots, as defined by the ratio of cost of inspection to cost of defects. In our example, this would be a plan that accepts lots of $\leqq 3$ percent and rejects lots of > 3 percent, based on the ratio of $0.30 to $10. (This yields the curve shown in Figure 5.6.) In practice, however, such a plan is possible only with complete inspection of all parts (and consequently is not a sampling plan). As an alternative, a sampling plan may be selected that has an OC curve that is steep in the region of 0.03 and

---

[3] Sometimes inspectors are tested by being subjected to inspection of test lots with a known number of defectives. At Federal Reserve banks, for example, unfit and counterfeit bills are inserted into incoming bundles of bills from commercial banks as a means of appraising the performance of bill counters.

FIGURE 5.7

Effect of increasing the sample size from n_1 to n_2 with the same c

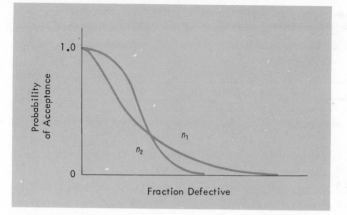

is derived by varying n and c. Increasing the sample size n will steepen the curve for any given c, as in Figure 5.7. By keeping n the same and decreasing c, the OC curve also becomes steeper, moving closer to the origin, as in Figure 5.8.

In selecting any sampling plan, the cost of sampling must be weighed against the losses that would be incurred if no sampling were performed. A sampling plan is then computed or selected from a source of plans, by choosing the sample size n and the allowable rejects c that most closely fit the specific needs.[4]

FIGURE 5.8

Effect of increasing c from c_1 to c_4 with the same sample size n

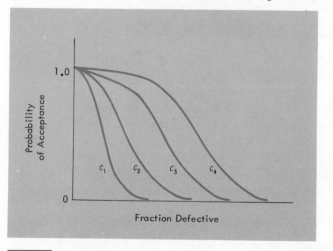

    [4] See, for example, H. F. Dodge and H. G. Romig, *Sampling Inspection Tables— Single and Double Sampling* (2d ed.; New York; John Wiley & Sons, 1959).

Sequential sampling plans

Rather than selecting a sample from a lot and inspecting all items in the sample to make the accept-reject decision, a sequence of smaller samples may be used. The advantage of such a sequence is that fewer items need be inspected for the same degree of accuracy. Such series of samples are termed *sequential sampling plans.* The limit in sequential sampling plans is the plan that inspects items one at a time. In a sequential sampling plan, the results are accumulated and a decision is made to (1) reject the lot, (2) accept the lot, or (3) inspect another item.

Wald, who instituted one of the well-known sequential plans, estimated that this sequential plan could reduce the average sample size by about one-half, as compared to a single sampling plan.[5] His plan entailed a decision each time an item was inspected, and required three inputs—the producer's risk (α), the consumer's risk (β), and a "sequential probability ratio." This ratio is a method of keeping score, and is also the probability of getting a particular sample result if the material is of p_2' quality compared to the probability of getting the result if the material were p_1' quality. In practice, it is not necessary to compute this ratio. Instead, a chart or form may be constructed from sampling limits. Then each inspection result is plotted until the lot is accepted or rejected.

The limit lines of a sequential plan are defined by

$$X_1 = sn + h_2$$

and

$$X_2 = sn - h_1$$

where

$$h_1 = \frac{\log\left(\frac{1-\alpha}{\beta}\right)}{\log\left[\frac{p_2'(1-p_1')}{p_1'(1-p_2')}\right]}$$

$$h_2 = \frac{\log\left(\frac{1-\beta}{\alpha}\right)}{\log\left[\frac{p_2'(1-p_1')}{p_1'(1-p_2')}\right]}$$

$$s = \frac{\log\left(\frac{1-p_1'}{1-p_2'}\right)}{\log\left[\frac{p_2'(1-p_1')}{p_1'(1-p_2')}\right]}$$

Tables are available so that it is not necessary to compute the values of h_1, h_2, and s through the formulas (see Appendix, page 225). The following example illustrates the method of constructing a sequential sampling plan.

---

[5] A. Wald, *Sequential Analysis* (New York: John Wiley & Sons, 1947).

Assume that the producer's risk α is 5 percent at the point where p_1' is 0.01; that is, the producer wants a 95 percent probability of accepting as good any lots of items that are 1 percent or less defective. Further, assume that β is 10 percent and p_2' is 0.06; that is, the consumer wants only a 10 percent chance of accepting any lots that are 6 percent or more defective.

Using the appendix to this chapter, the appropriate values can be read off at $p_1' = 0.01$ and $p_2' = 0.06$. Corresponding values are $h_2 = 1.5678$, $h_1 = 1.2211$, and $s = 0.02811$.

Since the control chart is linear, to draw the chart requires the definition of two points for each line. One convenient point is the vertical axis where $n = 0$; that is, where no items have yet been sampled.

At $n = 0$,

$$X_1 = sn + h_2$$
$$= 0 + 1.5678$$
$$= 1.5678$$
$$X_2 = sn - h_1$$
$$= 0 - 1.2211$$
$$= -1.2211$$

A second point is chosen at another convenient location, say where $n = 100$. Then, at $n = 100$,

$$X_1 = sn + h_2$$
$$= (0.02811)(100) + 1.5678$$
$$= 2.811 + 1.5678$$
$$= 4.3788$$
$$X_2 = sn - h_1$$
$$= (0.02811)(100) - 1.2211$$
$$= 2.811 - 1.2211$$
$$= 1.5899$$

These are plotted on Figure 5.9 and the points are connected to form the boundaries for the plan. Both the accept and reject regions lie above the horizontal axis, so that for this example no acceptance of a lot is possible until at least 44 units have been inspected.

If one prefers, a table can be made showing the decisions rather than referring to the graph. Table 5.2 was derived from Figure 5.9.

TABLE 5.2

Accept or reject decisions over a range of defects and numbers sampled

Range of n	Reject when number of defectives found is:	Range of n	Accept when number of defectives found is:
2–15	2	0–43	No decision possible. Continue sampling.
16–51	3		
52–86	4	44–80	0
87–121	5	81–114	1
		115–150	2

FIGURE 5.9

Sequential sampling plan with $\alpha = 5$ percent at $p_1' = 0.01$ *and* $\beta = 10$ percent at $p_2' = 0.06$

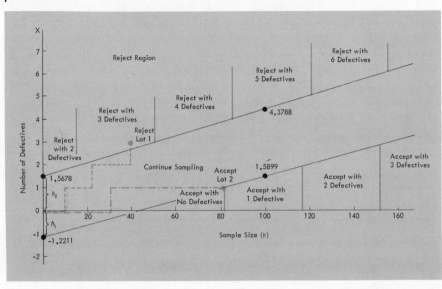

The following example is based on Figure 5.9 and/or Table 5.2. Two lots, 1 and 2, are inspected on an item-by-item basis, resulting in the following action (these examples are plotted in Figure 5.9).

Lot 1: Items 1–10   OK   Lot 2: Items 1–30   OK
                  11   Defective   31   Defective
               12–23   OK   32–81   OK
                  24   Defective   Action: Accept lot 2
               25–40   OK
                  41   Defective
        Action: Reject lot 1

PROCESS CONTROL PROCEDURES

Process control is concerned with monitoring quality *while the product or service is being produced.* Typical objectives of process control plans are: (1) to provide timely information on whether currently produced items are meeting design specifications; and (2) to detect shifts in the process which signal that future products may not meet specifications. The actual control phase of process control occurs when corrective action is taken such as a worn part replaced, a machine overhauled, or a new supplier found. Process control concepts, especially statistically based control charts, have seen wide use outside the factory. The following example, in fact, illustrates how a control chart for attributes (called a "*p*-chart") is developed and used in the context of employee performance monitoring.

Process control using attribute measurements

Suppose one wants to establish some control device for keypunch operators with which he could monitor their performance over time. After the key punching has been verified, suppose further that he randomly selects 200 cards out of each punched box and notes the number of errors made. By dividing the number of errors by 200, he may then derive the fraction of errors in the sample. If he does not as yet have a measure of performance of his keypunch operators, he can use the samples collected from all of his operators to construct a control chart. He can then plot the fraction on his chart to gain an indication of the quality of each keypunch operator. If he has initially collected, say, 30 samples (as listed in Table 5.3), he may use this as a basis for constructing the control chart.

TABLE 5.3

Number of keypunch errors for samples of size $n = 200$

Sample number	Number of errors	Fraction defective (number errors /200)	Sample number	Number of errors	Fraction defective (number errors/200)
1	4	0.02	16	17	0.085
2	8	0.04	17	9	0.045
3	12	0.06	18	13	0.065
4	10	0.05	19	12	0.06
5	14	0.07	20	14	0.07
6	9	0.045	21	14	0.07
7	11	0.055	22	12	0.06
8	13	0.065	23	21	0.105
9	14	0.07	24	13	0.065
10	8	0.04	25	12	0.06
11	10	0.05	26	13	0.065
12	11	0.055	27	12	0.06
13	7	0.035	28	7	0.035
14	11	0.055	29	14	0.07
15	12	0.06	30	11	0.055

The overall fraction defective ($\bar{p}$), standard deviation (s_p), and upper and lower control limits are calculated as follows:

$$\bar{p} = \frac{\text{Total number of defects from all samples}}{\text{Number of samples} \times \text{Sample size}}$$

$$\bar{p} = \frac{348}{30 \times 200} = 0.058$$

$$s_p = \sqrt{\frac{\bar{p}(1 - \bar{p})}{n}}$$

$$s_p = \sqrt{\frac{0.054636}{200}} = 0.0165$$

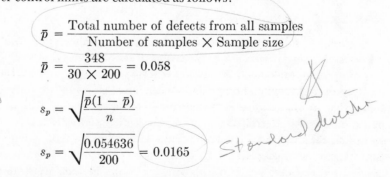

Standard deviation

The most common confidence limits are 99.0 and 99.7 percent, or where the chance of an occurrence is one in 100 and 3 in 1,000 respectively. From a two-tailed normal distribution table, 99 percent of the area under the curve is included in the mean plus-or-minus 2.58 standard deviations, and 99.7 percent includes the mean plus-or-minus 3.0 standard deviations.

For a confidence of 99 percent, limits are placed at $\bar{p} \pm 2.58 s_p$. Thus

$$UCL = \bar{p} + 2.58 s_p = 0.10057$$
$$LCL = \bar{p} - 2.58 s_p = 0.01543$$

The control limits and individual sample results are plotted in Figure 5.10. Performance of the keypunch operators can now be observed over time, and, by identifying the source of the sample, the output of individual operators vis-à-vis the group average can be compared. Note, for instance, that sample 23 is outside the control limits, suggesting an investigation as to the cause.

FIGURE 5.10

Control chart of keypunch operators (sample size $n = 200$; firm's own $\bar{p}$, LCL, and UCL calculated from 30 samples; industry $\bar{p}$, LCL, and UCL plotted from known industrywide operator performance)

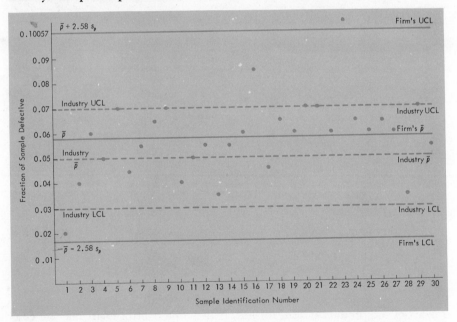

Suppose, as additional information, that the industry average for keypunch operators classified as "good" is 5 percent errors ± 2 percent (with 99 percent confidence). These limits can also be placed on the graph to give an additional measure of control. (The limits are plotted as 3 and 7 percent.) Such a control chart, if occasionally updated for $\bar{p}$ and s_p, will give a running measure of performance and progress over time.

Process control using variable measurements

The development of process control techniques (and acceptance sampling plans) using variables parallels the development procedures using attributes. The statistical manipulations in using variables are somewhat more involved, however, and are beyond the scope of this discussion. Worthy of mention, though, is a valuable type of control chart that is particularly useful in variable measurement situations. Termed a *dynamic control chart*, it is highly appropriate when there is a predictable trend in process output over time. Frequently, when equipment has been set up and operation begun, tool wear or other changes in the system cause measure-

FIGURE 5.11

Dynamic control chart for process control

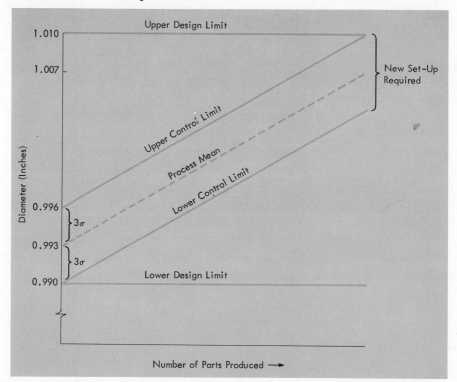

ments of the product output to shift. A dynamic control chart may be constructed to determine the initial setup position to assure that the process is performing as expected. In addition, the chart will indicate when the process should be temporarily halted for machine readjustment.

Either of two charts is useful: (*a*) an $\bar{X}$ chart, on which the means of small samples (perhaps four or five items) are plotted, or (*b*) a chart for sequential sampling, such as for measuring every 10th or 20th item. The sequential plan is easiest because only one unit at a time is plotted and no computations are involved.

Consider the following example. Suppose a particular part to be manufactured has the specified diameter of 1.000 ± 0.010 inch, and the output from the particular machine to be used can be represented by a normal distribution with $\sigma = 0.001$ inch. Suppose further that 3σ is established as the control limits; that is, 99.73 percent of the parts produced will fall within design specifications. The problem, then, is to develop a control chart for sequential unit sampling (parts get larger as production continues).

The procedure is as follows. Since the lower design limit allows a diameter as small as 0.990 inch (1.000 − 0.010), 0.003 (3σ) is simply added to 0.990 to arrive at the initial machine setup of 0.993 inch. The first parts produced should then vary from 0.990 to 0.996 inch. Subsequent parts would be expected to fall within the band, as illustrated in Figure 5.11. If they do not fall in this band, the equipment may be examined for possible slippage or wear of bearings or other parts, depending on how the output shifts.

Dynamic control charts of this type find their greatest use for long product runs which require periodic resetting of tools.

LOCATION AND FREQUENCY OF INSPECTION ACTIVITIES

Location of Inspection Activities

Inspection is required for both acceptance sampling and process control. The decision of where in the production process such inspections must be performed depends on the cost of inspecting at any given location versus the cost of allowing a defective product to continue throughout the production cycle. Performing a cost analysis on each potential inspection location is a significant undertaking for many firms, and mathematical techniques and computer programs to solve the problem are still being developed. Baker[6] suggests that the problem of locating inspection stations can be alleviated by starting with the end product and charting (using an engineering process flow chart) each characteristic in the product that requires inspection. "Then decide at what point in the manufacturing cycle that particular characteristic could first be inspected."[7] (Rules of thumb are: "Do each inspection as early in the manufacturing cycle as possible," and "Perform each inspection only once.") This information is noted on the flow chart for each characteristic. "Then work backwards through the manufacturing cycle doing the same thing at each point along the way. At completion, a clear pattern of inspection points will be defined. Finally each potential inspection point is evaluated to decide whether it is economical to move it to a later point in the process."[8] (Specific sampling plans and process control procedures are then determined for the selected inspection points.) An example of a process chart showing the final location of inspection points in the manufacture of recording cassettes is illustrated in Figure 5.12.

---

[6] Eugene M. Baker, "Why Plan Your Inspection?" *Quality Progress*, July, 1975, pp. 22–27.

[7] Ibid, p. 23.

[8] Ibid, p. 24.

FIGURE 5.12

Location and type of inspection points for recording cassette manufacture

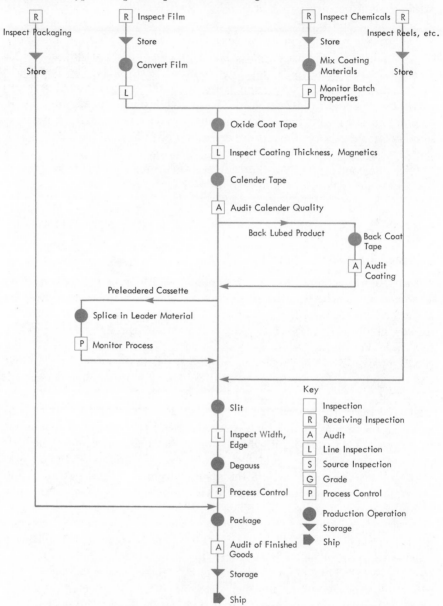

Source: Eugene M. Baker, "Why Plan Your Inspection?" *Quality Progress*, July, 1975, p. 23.

Frequency of Inspection Activities

Once the decision has been made as to which inspection is to be done, the next problem is to determine how often it is to be done. Again, a trade-off is involved between the cost of inspection and the cost of defective products and work caused by not detecting defective components. A systematic way of determining the frequency of inspection in manufacturing is through the use of Economic Inspection Interval (EII) tables developed by Meske.[9] To use these tables four factors of the particular manufacturing situation are required:

1. The delay interval—the time in minutes between initiation of an inspection and the termination of the loss it discovered. (Contributing to this interval are the time to get authorization to stop the process, to prepare a reject tag, to adjust a machine, etc.).
2. The reliability interval—the average time in hours between process failures for a given job.
3. Manufacturing loss—the cost per hour of defects to the company as reflected in rework, sorting, scrap, wasted labor and machine time, etc.
4. Inspection cost—the cost per hour of the inspection act.

The following example problem illustrates how EIIs are used.

Situation. A three-shift operation evaluated over a five-week period encompassed a total running time of 555 hours. During this period, 10 rejections occurred, and the average reliability interval was therefore 55.5 hours. The delay interval was 15 minutes, and the manufacturing loss was $44 per hour. The inspection cost was $14 per hour, and the inspection time was 2 minutes. The inspection cost per unit is $14 ÷ 30 inspections per hour, or $0.47.

Solution. The appropriate EII table is shown in Table 5.4. It has a delay interval of 15 minutes, and a reliability interval of 60 hours (which is sufficiently close to the desired 55.5 hours to be applicable).

We can derive the economic inspection frequency as follows:

1. Locate the figure for manufacturing loss that is closest to $44. This is $45.
2. Locate the figure for inspection cost that is closest to $0.47.
3. The two values at the intersection of these two costs indicate the EII (41 minutes) and the number of inspections per shift (12).

Interpretation. This analysis indicates that every 41 minutes one unit should be inspected. In an 8 hour shift, therefore, approximately 12 inspections should be made. For the entire 555-hour run, inspection costs are: 555 hours × 60 minutes/hour ÷ 41 minutes = 812 inspections × $0.47 per inspection = $381.64.

A defective unit may be produced at the beginning of the 41-minute interval (just after the last inspection) or at the end (just prior to inspection). On the average, therefore, the defect will occur 20.5 minutes after an inspection. Adding to this the 15 minutes required to respond to the defect gives a cost per defect of 35.5 minutes ÷ 60 minutes/hour × $44 per hour, or $26.03 × 10 = $260.30. The total of inspection costs and manufacturing losses is therefore $381.64 + $260.30 = $641.94.

In this analysis, however, one must bear in mind that the per unit inspection cost may not be accurate since it assumes a per unit cost derived

⁹ See "A Management Standard for Economic Inspection," *Quality*, January, 1976, pp. 28–30.

TABLE 5.4

The intervals between inspections and the number of inspections per 8 hour shift for cases in which a defect is produced on the average of every 60 hours and the time for manufacturing to respond is 15 minutes.

Inspection Cost	Manufacturing loss (dollars per hour)												
	5	7	9	12	15	20	26	35	45	60	78	100	134
$0.15	73/7	61/8	53/9	45/11	40/12	33/15	29/17	24/20	20/24	17/28	14/34	12/40	10/48
0.19	83/6	69/7	60/8	51/9	45/11	38/13	33/15	28/17	24/20	20/24	17/28	14/34	12/40
0.24	95/5	79/6	69/7	59/8	52/9	44/11	38/13	32/15	27/18	23/21	19/25	16/30	14/34
0.30	107/4	89/5	78/6	66/7	59/8	50/10	43/11	36/13	31/15	26/18	22/22	19/25	16/30
0.38	121/4	101/5	88/5	76/6	67/7	57/8	49/10	42/11	36/13	30/16	26/18	22/22	18/27
0.48	137/4	114/4	100/5	86/6	76/6	65/7	56/9	47/10	41/12	35/14	30/16	26/18	21/23
0.60	154/3	129/4	113/4	97/5	86/6	73/7	63/8	54/9	47/10	40/12	34/14	29/17	24/20
0.76	174/3	146/3	128/4	110/4	97/5	83/6	72/7	61/8	53/9	45/11	39/12	34/14	28/17
0.95	195/2	164/3	144/3	123/4	110/4	94/5	82/6	69/7	60/8	51/9	44/11	38/13	32/15

Source: "A Management Standard for Economic Inspection," *Quality*, January, 1976, p. 29.

by dividing the cost per hour by the inspection rate. The inspector may be a fixed cost, or there may be travel time involved such that to inspect just one unit every 41 minutes may be much higher than $0.47. If this is the case, the per unit inspection cost more than likely could be obtained or estimated and this figure used for computation instead.

The EII tables are a new development in quality control and generalizing about their effectiveness is premature. Nevertheless, a number of companies have reported substantial savings from them and they no doubt will receive wide attention in the future.

PERSONNEL CONSIDERATIONS

Management, job design, and wage payment present special problems in quality control. First, quality control is often a staff department in large organizations, and therefore the quality control manager's authority is limited to advising the production area in matters of quality. Even if the quality control manager is in a line position, as is shown in Figure 5.1, his role should be one of accomodation with the production area to assure that the Q.C. function does not impede the production process. This need for accomodation, however, may conflict with quality requirements and the inherent adversary relationship between quality control and various production departments may evolve into hostility. Thus, the quality control manager must have human relations skills as well as technical competence if his department is to maximize its contribution to organizational goals.

Second, inspection work, which comprises the major portion of quality control activities, is often both demanding and monotonous. Therefore, finding ways of making inspection jobs more attractive is a continuing job design problem. Third, finding the appropriate basis for wage payment for inspection tasks is a difficult problem. Incentive plans basing inspectors' pay on the number of defects discovered may result in wide variations in their income and/or rejecting items which are marginally good. To include the "good" items rejected as an added factor makes for a complicated pay scheme. Hourly pay plans, on the other hand, tend to reduce vigilance by removing the direct monetary reward for finding poor quality items. In practice, plans combining incentives with hourly pay are employed to cope with these problems. (See Chapters 10 and 11 for a more extensive discussion of the general topics of job design and wage payment.)

QUALITY CONTROL FACTORS IN SERVICE INDUSTRIES

As stated previously, to develop a quality control program five points must be specifically stated: (1) What is to be inspected? (2) Where it is to be inspected? (3) How is the inspection to be performed? (4) What are the units of measurement? and (5) What are the criteria for acceptance or rejection?

When an area has not previously been subjected to statistical quality control, cost factors are frequently difficult to compute and inadequate to

TABLE 5.5

Some essential features of a hospital quality control system

Points of inspection	Examples of what to look for	Consequences of deviations	Possible method of inspection
Lab tests	Accuracy in reading	Inaccurate diagnosis, possibly serious consequences	Chief lab technician samples completed tests. Automatic equipment checked for reasonable readings and tests on known samples
Pharmacy	Expiration dates of medications; accuracy in requests	Ranging from minor to fatal	Complete recheck. Pharmacist fills prescriptions, checks, and packages; questions MD on large dosages
Housekeeping	Cleanliness	Dirty areas increase likelihood of infection	Supervisor checks against standards
Operating rooms	Sterile conditions; correct equipment, surgical procedures, scrubbing, attire	Lawsuits, malpractice, possible death or injury, loss of image	Armband verifies correct patient for surgery; verify chart and sugical procedure; sponge and instrument count
Admissions	Verify information with patient; forms all filled in	Usually minor inconveniences, or later questions	If computerized, verified by techniques such as format of insurance numbers, age of children versus age and marital status of patient
Billing	Insurance claims filed, late billings, accuracy in amount	Lost money or late receipts	Compare patients' stay with billing date and insurance filing
Nursing service	Up-to-date charts, medication on time, correct medication, temperature and pulse readings on time, progress reports	Discomfort, delayed patient recovery, degrading to image	Supervisor checks work; incident reports reviewed daily
Laundry	Cleanliness, on-time schedule	Degrades image, possible contamination	Supervisor inspects linen
Food service	Quality of precooked food, method of preparation, meals on time and satisfactory	Patient satisfaction, hospital's image	Dietician inspects all food; prepackaged frozen food sampled for diet constraints and quality; patient complaints observed
Outpatient	Available facilities, degree of usage	Crowding or underutilization	Perhaps emergency room department may review

TABLE 5.5 (*continued*)

Points of inspection	Examples of what to look for	Consequences of deviations	Possible method of inspection
Central supply	Stocking of linens, surgical instruments, syringes; sterility of supplies	Delays, infection from unsterilized items	Tapestrip indicating sterilization performed. Indicator to determine if packages opened or leaking; packages dated
Medical staff	Competence, accuracy in diagnosis, acceptable surgery or service	Lawsuits, malpractice suits, hospital image, patient death or injury	Adequate observation by specialists before hospital privileges granted. Analysis of procedures reviewed on all difficult cases. Tissue committee reviews all charts for pathology reports

use as a sole basis for justifying the inspection procedure. Poor quality may have such a variety of impacts on the organization that it is useful, as a first step, to create a list stating the consequences of poor quality in various operational areas. In the table for a typical hospital, for example, the major effect of poor quality in the laundry may be the degradation of the hospital's image—a minor offense. Poor quality of the medical staff, however, may result in the death of patients and lawsuits, as well as injury to the hospital's image. In either case, a table of this type, which broadly states the consequences of bad quality, is useful in establishing a priority hierarchy and indicates which areas should be dealt with first when planning an overall quality control program.

Health care

Nearly all quality control procedures may be used in the health care industry, where one often hears such comments as "Traditional scientific methods do not apply when a human life is at stake" or "No price can be placed on human life." Statements like these have no rhyme or reason. Indeed, the fact that this industry *does* deal with human life makes it all the more important to use the best available techniques to determine and assure acceptable quality levels. Table 5.5 lists some essential features of a hospital quality control system.

Banking

Banks, at the present time, do not use a significant amount of statistical quality control. Generally, various ratios or account compositions are compared to some established norm. This norm may be determined by legal regulation or by an individual bank's policy.

Although formal statistical sampling plans are not generally used in banks, sampling is periodically performed on savings and checking ac-

TABLE 5.6

Some essential features of a bank quality control system

Points of inspection	Examples of what to look for	Consequences of deviations	Possible method of inspection
Loan ratio	Too low or too high	Loss of profit, inadequate funds	Complete tabulation, compared to standard
Equity base	Small or large	Committed to lower-yield, less risky use of funds; high equity permits greater risk	Routine reports
Liquidity ratio	Ratio of short term to total	High-ratio loss of potential profit; Low-ratio inability to meet withdrawals or make new loans	Tabulation compared to norm
Loan portfolio	Collateral backing, degree of risk, term length	Possible defaults	Internal audits, also audits by Federal Reserve and state for some banks
Margin	Adequate reserves	Violation of regulation	Routine observation
Savings accounts	Accuracy	Not serious to bank but creates unhappy customers, loss of prestige and business	Sampling of accounts
Checking accounts	Accuracy, overdrawn accounts	As above, plus possible losses on overdrafts if honored	Routine sampling plus flagged accounts
Savings to total deposits	Ratio	High ratio results in higher interest costs	Occasional observation
Teller operations	Shortages, overages, neatness, manners	Loss of prestige	Daily tally sheets, general subjective observation

counts. The quality of a loan portfolio, however, is observed primarily by examining the larger loans, usually those over 1 percent or 0.1 percent of the total loan portfolio. A bank's status and operation in some areas is periodically spotchecked by an internal audit team, but these examinations are not statistically based. Certain bank functions, such as investment portfolios and maintenance of liquidity ratios, are not handled at branch offices. The home office retains the responsibility for unit banks in branch banking. Correct liquidity ratios are maintained by the home office by periodically issuing general guidelines to the branches, such as "No personal notes over

90 days," "No commercial loans," or "Improvement loans only to customers' owner-occupied residences." Table 5.6 lists some essential features of a bank quality control system.

Insurance companies

A large part of an insurance company's operations involve record processing and accounting, and statistical quality control can be readily applied to the many similar accounts. Standardized forms can be examined; repeated errors may indicate the probability of improper or vague wording.

TABLE 5.7

Some essential features of an insurance company quality control system

Points of inspection	Examples of what to look for	Consequences of deviations	Possible method of inspection
Mailroom	Correct routing	Loss of time and/or item	Inspection and tabulation of errors
Processing of subscriber applications	Legibility, correct spelling, reasonableness of data	Expensive reprocessing. Policies awarded to unqualified or at wrong premium rates	Examination by supervisor; use of sampling and control charts for error trends
Premium-due billing	Accuracy in amount, assurance that customer is actually billed	Loss of customer goodwill. Unintentional policy lapsing	Sampling by supervisor
Receipt of premium payments	Unreasonable amounts, invalid codes, improper data	Financial losses, lapsed policies, loss of customers	Inspection by supervisor
Claims	Policy number and code validity. Accuracy in claim	Customer complaints, loss of company image, poor service, increased correspondence with customer, financial loss to company	Random sampling by supervisor; 100 percent inspection of large claims

Billing, premium payments, and claims are easily sampled to determine accuracy. However, systematic sampling, rather than random sampling, is easier to use. For example, if the degree of confidence from a sampling plan stipulates that 10 percent of the accounts should be sampled, a "system" can be used—one that inspects each account ending in zero, for example. Some of the essential features of a quality control system are shown in Table 5.7.

COMPUTER PROGRAMS FOR QUALITY CONTROL

The advent of computers has added a new dimension in relieving most of the tedious calculations formerly required to install and maintain a quality control system. A wide variety of computer programs is available in both batch processing and by time sharing via a remote terminal. All computer manufacturers and many computer service companies make computer programs available to customers. The following examples illustrate just a few of the many programs available from one of these companies:[10]

Program	Description
ML105$	Determines sampling plan to fit combinations of AOQL, lot size, etc., and randomly determines which parts to sample according to Mil-Std-105D.
TABF1$ 414F1$	Performs analysis of samples with variability unknown, standard deviation method according to Mil-Std-414.
HISTO$	Produces sample statistics and plots a histogram with variable scaling.
MLBIN$	Evaluates multiple level sampling plans where user inspects a number of parts from a large lot and accepts, rejects, or resamples based on the number of defectives found (binomial distribution).
RANDM$	Randomly selects parts for inspection for a specified lot and sample size. Eliminates inspector bias in determining which items to inspect.
OCBIN$	Plots the operating characteristic curve or probability of acceptance as a function of the number of defectives (binomial distribution). User supplies the sample size and number of defectives required to reject the lot.
PCHRT$	Provides a control chart on the reject rate. The program determines the upper and lower control limits and plots a control chart for the data provided.
CONLM$	Determines confidence limits and sample statistics on a process average.
TOLLM$	Calculates natural tolerance limits for 90 percent confidence that 95 percent of units are satisfactory. Particularly useful in analyzing early production rate.
MLREG$	Assists in determining the relationship among a number of variables by curve fitting and an index of determination.
TRIWY$	Analyzes the effects of varying three factors. For example, is there an effect of the shift, production line, and product model on the reject rate? Provides an analysis of variance table.
MTBFM$3	Evaluates a multiple life testing plan when user specifies test length, and acceptance, rejection, or resample based on the number of failures. Program plots an OC curve based on the mean time between failures.
TSBIN$	Analyzes results of several samples for significant differences between reject rates; e.g., if samples of supplies received from two vendors contain a different number of rejects, is there a difference between vendors?

---

[10] TIME/WARE Corp., 688 Main Street, Redwood City, CA 94063. Appreciation is extended for permission to reproduce portions of its *Quality Control Package-User's Manual.*

FIGURE 5.13

Computer terminal output of the program MLBIN$

<u>RUN</u>

MULBIN   06:59   03/26/70

INPUT THE NUMBER OF LEVELS IN YOUR SAMPLING PLAN.   EG 2
? <u>2</u>

INPUT THE SIZE OF THE FIRST SAMPLE, THE NUMBER OF REJECTS
WHICH WILL CAUSE RESAMPLING, AND THE NUMBER OF REJECTS
WHICH WILL CAUSE REJECTION OF THE LOT
? <u>15,2,3</u>

INPUT THE SIZE OF THE LAST LOT AND THE TOTAL NUMBER OF
REJECTS WHICH WILL CAUSE REJECTION OF THE LOT   EG 20,5
? <u>10,3</u>

```
LOT                PERCENT CHANCE OF ACCEPTING THE LOT
  %              10    20    30    40    50    60    70    80    90   100
DEF.      %      !....!....!....!....!....!....!....!....!....!....!
0        100   -                                                    *
2.5       98.4-                                                   *
5         91   -                                              *
7.5       78.7-                                         *
10        64.2-                                   *
12.5      50   -                            *
15        37.5-                        *
17.5      27.2-                  *
20        19.2-              *
22.5      13.2-           *
25         6.9-       *
27.5       5.9-      *
30         3.6-    *
32.5       2.4- *
35         1.5- *
37.5       0.9-*
40         0.5-*
42.5       0.3-*
45         0.2-*
47.5       0.1-*
```


THE A.O.Q.L. OVER THE SPECIFIED RANGE IS 6.42

DO YOU WANT TO SEE THE A.O.Q. AND THE AVE. # SAMPLED? <u>YES</u>

% DEF.	A.O.Q.	AVE. # SAMPLED
0	0	10
2.5	2.38	13.51
5	4.07	15.88
7.5	4.79	16.98
10	4.75	17.14
12.5	4.28	16.72
15	3.65	16.01
17.5	3	15.2
20	2.41	14.38
22.5	1.91	13.62
25	1.49	12.94
27.5	1.14	12.35
30	0.87	11.85
32.5	0.65	11.44
35	0.48	11.1
37.5	0.34	10.82
40	0.24	10.61
42.5	0.17	10.44
45	0.11	10.31
47.5	0.08	10.22
50	0.05	10.15
52.5	0.03	10.1
55	0	10.06

To illustrate the ease in using these programs, two examples will be given, one producing an operating characteristic curve (OC) and the second plotting a control chart.

1. *Sampling by attributes with a double sampling plan.* A shipment has just been received and a decision must be made to accept or reject the lot.

FIGURE 5.14

Computer terminal output of the program UCHRT$

RUN

UCHRT$ 19:48   06/04/70

```
ENTER THE NUMBER OF SAMPLES?   20
INPUT, ONE SAMPLE AT A TIME, THE NUMBER OF DEFECTS
AND THE NUMBER OF UNITS INSPECTED
SAMPLE #  1 ?   20,10
SAMPLE #  2 ?   18,10
SAMPLE #  3 ?   16,10
SAMPLE #  4 ?   30,10
SAMPLE #  5 ?   35,10
SAMPLE #  6 ?   18,10
SAMPLE #  7 ?   26,10
SAMPLE #  8 ?   14,10
SAMPLE #  9 ?   40,10
SAMPLE #10 ?    8,10
SAMPLE #11 ?    7,10
SAMPLE #12 ?   26,10
SAMPLE #13 ?   22,10
SAMPLE #14 ?   20,10
SAMPLE #15 ?   35,10
SAMPLE #16 ?   18,10
SAMPLE #17 ?   16,10
SAMPLE #18 ?    8,10
SAMPLE #19 ?   15,10
SAMPLE #20 ?   16,10
```

```
                          U CHART

        0.685009              2.3425              4
VAL.    :....:....:....:....:....:....:....:....:....:
2       :                 *:                 :
1.8     :              *   :                 :
1.6     :          *       :                 :
3       :                  :             *   :
3.5     :                  :                 :*
1.8     :              *   :                 :
2.6     :                  :        *        :
1.4     :          *       :                 :
4       :                  :                 :        *
0.8     : *                :                 :
0.7     :*                 :                 :
2.6     :                  :        *        :
2.2     :                  :   *             :
2       :                 *:                 :
3.5     :                  :                 :*
1.8     :              *   :                 :
1.6     :          *       :                 :
0.8     : *                :                 :
1.5     :        *         :                 :
1.6     :          *       :                 :
```

The inspected items are declared either good or bad. A double sampling plan is considered as follows.

Take a sample size of 15. If none or one is bad, accept the lot. If three or more are bad, reject the lot. If two are bad, take a second sample.

Then, with a second sample size of 10, accept the lot only if all 10 units are good; otherwise reject it.

The problem is to plot the operating characteristic curve and determine the average quality level. Figure 5.13 shows the terminal/man interaction. The underlined portions are those input by the man. All other parts are computer printout.

2. *Control chart for the number of defects.*[11]   A number of characteristics are to be inspected in each unit of output, with each defect carrying

---

[11] A u chart is a control chart where $u = \dfrac{c}{k}$; c is the total number of defects in any sample and k is the number of inspection units in the sample.

equal weight. A control chart is to be instituted that will display the results from examining a daily random sample of 10 parts to determine if the process is in control (i.e., within acceptable limits).

Data on the number of defects for the past 20 days are:

Day	Number of defects	Number in sample	Day	Number of defects	Number in sample
1................	20	10	11................	7	10
2................	18	10	12................	26	10
3................	16	10	13................	22	10
4................	30	10	14................	20	10
5................	35	10	15................	35	10
6................	18	10	16................	18	10
7................	26	10	17................	16	10
8................	14	10	18................	8	10
9................	40	10	19................	15	10
10................	8	10	20................	16	10

Figure 5.14 shows the computer output. As in the previous example, the underlined portions are those input by the terminal operator.

Control limits for the chart are set at 3 sigma, implying that 99.7 percent of the data should fall within these limits. Since three units out of 20 are outside limits, the process would be suspected to be out of control (since the average number outside should be three out of 1,000). Three other units of data fall just inside the lower limit. With this wide scatter at both the lower and upper limit, the process would be examined for some cause of the wide variance. A machine, for example, would be suspected of worn gears, bearings, or loosening of parts.

CONCLUSION

Quality decisions permeate most organizations, influencing company image, product selection, manufacturing processes, and customer relations. A large part of this chapter has been devoted to this pervasive influence, as well as to showing the structure of various Q.C. systems in manufacturing and nonmanufacturing environments. We see the future development of quality control as focusing on refining the total framework of quality control systems and extending their application to all types of organizations, as opposed to developing new statistical concepts. As mentioned in the introduction, the statistical aspects of the topic are quite well developed, and now it remains for industry to translate theory into practice.

The "ideal" quality of a firm's output may be defined as the point of maximum difference between production cost and the value to the customer; hence in general the output of a firm should seldom be perfect quality since the increase in product value to the customer rarely compensates for the expense of perfection. In all cases, in deciding on a quality control program a balanced view must be taken of the objectives of the firm, the environment in which it operates, and the relevant costs.

PROPOSITIONS

Propositions contrasting services and manufacturing relative to the design of the quality control system

Product: Because of the inherent subjectivity in defining quality of design for a service, quality of conformance will be more difficult to specify and measure for services than for manufacturing.

Technology of transformation: Because of the difficulty in specifying quality of conformance in service systems, the measuring devices used in services will be based on attributes (quantity, time, satisfaction) rather than variables (dimensions, strength, weight), which are commonly used in manufacturing.

Operating-control system: Because the way in which a service is created is an integral part of that service, the quality control system in services is often an integral part of the service product. In manufacturing, the quality control system is distinct from the product that it helps to create.

Workforce: Because the quality control system is often an integral part of the service product, the jobs of the service system workforce must include quality control duties. In manufacturing, quality control is typically a separated function, carried out by specialists.

REVIEW AND DISCUSSION QUESTIONS

1. Discuss some of the difficulties encountered in trying to define quality. State some ways in which a definition may be possible.
2. Ideally, what is the optimal quality level that should be sought by a firm?
3. What is your response to the often-heard comment that one should strive to achieve the highest quality possible?
4. Why should the general level of product quality be set by corporate-level management rather than by a lower level?
5. What responsibilities does a firm have to its customers to guarantee the quality of its products?
6. Should a company be legally responsible for its output of defective products (for example, a pacemaker implant, a steering mechanism in an automobile, children's toys)?
7. Discuss the flow of events described in the overall quality assurance program depicted in Figure 5.2.
8. How might you determine at what organizational level the manager of quality control should be placed?
9. In order to have a quality control system, what basic quantities must be specified?
10. Suppose, as assistant administrator of a hospital, you were asked to propose a quality control plan for next year and one for five years hence. What might these plans look like?
11. Briefly summarize how sampling by attributes differs from sampling by variables.

12. What is the meaning of producer's risk and consumer's risk?

13. When is the cost for inspection justified, or when is it not worthwhile to institute an inspection procedure?

14. How might quality control procedures be used in the following types of services? Airline, auto dealership, physician's office, drug store, and department store.

PROBLEMS

1. The state and local police departments are trying to analyze crime rate areas so that they can shift their patrols from areas with decreasing crime rates to areas that are increasing. The city and county have been geographically segmented into areas containing 5,000 residences. The police recognize that all crimes and offenses are not reported; people either "do not want to become involved," consider the offenses too small to report, are too embarrassed to make a police report, or do not take the time—among other reasons. Every month, because of this, the police are contacting by phone a random sample of 1,000 of the 5,000 residences for data on crime (the respondents are guaranteed anonymity). The data collected for the past 12 months for one area are as follows.

Month	Crime incidence	Sample size	Crime rate
January...	7	1,000	0.007
February...	9	"	0.009
March...	7	"	0.007
April...	7	"	0.007
May...	7	"	0.007
June...	9	"	0.009
July...	7	"	0.007
August...	10	"	0.010
September...	8	"	0.008
October...	11	"	0.011
November...	10	"	0.010
December...	8	"	0.008

Construct a p chart for 95 percent confidence (1.96σ) and plot each of the months. If the next three months show crime incidences in this area as

   January = 10 (out of 1,000 sampled)
   February = 12   "   "   "
   March = 11,   "   "   "

what comments can you make regarding the crime rate?

2. Some of the citizens complained to city councilmen that there should be equal protection under the law against the occurrence of crimes. The citizens' arguments stated that this "equal protection" should be interpreted as indicating that high crime areas should have more police protection than low crime areas. Therefore police patrols and other methods for preventing crime (such as street lighting or "cleaning up" abandoned areas and buildings) should be used proportionately to crime occurrence.

In a fashion similar to problem 1, the city has been broken down into 20 geographical areas, each containing 5,000 residences. The 1,000 sampled from each area showed the following incidence of crime during the past month.

Area	Number of crimes	Sample size	Crime rate
1....................	7	1,000	0.007
2....................	3	"	0.003
3....................	9	"	0.009
4....................	8	"	0.008
5....................	7	"	0.007
6....................	12	"	0.012
7....................	6	"	0.006
8....................	9	"	0.009
9....................	6	"	0.006
10....................	3	"	0.003
11....................	9	"	0.009
12....................	7	"	0.007
13....................	6	"	0.006
14....................	8	"	0.008
15....................	6	"	0.006
16....................	12	"	0.012
17....................	4	"	0.004
18....................	9	"	0.009
19....................	6	"	0.006
20....................	13	"	0.013
	150		

Suggest a reallocation of crime protection effort, if indicated, based upon a p chart analysis. In order that you may be reasonably certain in your recommendation, select a 95 percent confidence level (i.e., 1.96σ).

3. A process has been set up to make bearings for a line of washing machine motors. In order to fit correctly, the inside diameter of the bearings must be 0.7000 inch plus-or-minus 0.0050 inch. The machinery has a natural variation in output of $\sigma = 0.0005$ inch (normally distributed) and the diameter of the bearings get smaller as the tool wears.

   a. Construct a dynamic control chart for accepting 99 percent of the output (2.58σ) for the longest period of time before the tool must be replaced.

   b. If the process mean shifts 0.001 inch for every 100 bearings made, how many may be made before the process must be stopped for a tool change?

4. Pistons for diesel engines produced in one part of a locomotive works are used later in the assembly area. One hundred percent inspection is performed, and an inspector can check pistons for quality at an average rate of one every three minutes. In the process of inspecting, the inspector removes and discards all bad pistons. The total cost for the inspector, including fringe benefits, burden, and salary, is $8 per hour. The production output of pistons is 95 percent good; if a bad piston is installed in an engine, it requires a mechanic one hour to replace, whose overall cost is $9.50 per hour. Is this inspection justified? What is the net savings or loss from performing the inspection?

5. To ease the control function, a manufacturer would like to make a control chart for the number of mounting bracket hole discrepancies (off center, out of round, burred, or not drilled) in the power supply chassis of an 18 inch TV set. Fifteen samples of size 100 have been taken and the discrepancies are as follows.

Sample number	Number of errors	Fraction defective (errors/100)	Sample number	Number of errors	Fraction defective (errors/100)
1.........	3	0.03	9.........	3	0.03
2.........	14	0.14	10.........	1	0.01
3.........	8	0.08	11.........	3	0.03
4.........	2	0.02	12.........	8	0.08
5.........	6	0.06	13.........	4	0.04
6.........	7	0.07	14.........	6	0.06
7.........	2	0.02	15.........	2	0.02
8.........	9	0.09			

    a. Construct a control chart for 99 percent confidence (2.58σ).

    b. How might you explain that sample 2 is outside the limits?

    c. If the next three samples have 9, 10, and 11 defectives respectively, what action would you take?

6. A machinist, temporarily in charge of manufacturing a simple part, is attempting to determine whether the process is in control. Taking a quick look at the control chart given to him by the quality control department, he sees that the upper control limit has been set at 0.062 and the central line at 2 percent defective. Seeking no further information, he takes a sample of 25 parts from the output and determines that the sample contains two defectives. Should he stop the process?

7. The Old C.B. Company has decided to tighten up its acceptance sampling plan described on page 197. The company is satisfied with its risk levels and AQL but believes that poor quality should be defined as 6 percent defective rather than 8 percent.

    a. What will be the acceptance sampling plan if this change is made?

    b. Indicate the approximate shape of the new OC curve that would be associated with the new plan.

8. Using Figure 5.12 as a guide, flow chart the location of inspection points from receipt to sales (or equivalent) of the following items:

    a. produce in a supermarket

    b. a pre-induction military physical examination

    c. the work required in your operations management class

9. The Old C.B. Company is planning its inspection procedures for its new line of "Good Buddy" brand citizens'-band radios. Management is particularly concerned with how often they should conduct inspection of the output of their final assembly line. Based upon their experience with similar radios, they have developed the following estimates:

    Manufacturing loss—$15 per hour

    Inspection cost—$0.30 per unit

    Time to inspect and correct an error in the assembly process—15 minutes

Old C.B. runs two eight-hour shifts, five days a week, and has observed that errors in assembly occur on average every 60 hours.

    a. Based upon this information, what inspection frequency do you recommend?

    b. What is the expected cost per week of your recommended plan?

10. Testing one of the new line-of-sight ground-to-ground missiles entails the actual firing and destruction of the missile. Thus it is desirable to test as few units as possible in order to accept or reject a lot. A sequential sampling plan offers the advantages of a small test number.

    a. Design a sequential sampling plan such that the missile manufacturer has a 95 percent probability of accepting any lots with 0.05 percent defectives and the consumer (the army) has a 90 percent assurance that it will not accept any lots that have more than 3 percent defective (i.e., $\alpha = .05$, $\beta = 0.10$, $p_1 = 0.005$, $p_2 = 0.03$).

    b. What minimum number of units must be tested in order to accept the lot? Suppose one defective missile was found; how large a sample must be tested?

SELECTED BIBLIOGRAPHY

"A Management Standard for Economic Inspection," *Quality* (January 1976), pp. 28–30.

Baker, E. M.   "Why Plan Your Inspection?" *Quality Progress* (July 1975), pp. 22–27.

Benich, J. J., and Enrick, N. L.   "Inspectors Get Worse Before They Get Better," *Quality Progress* (January 1975), pp. 23–24.

Duncan, Acheson J.   *Quality Control and Industrial Statistics.* 4th ed. Homewood, Ill. Richard D. Irwin, Inc., 1974.

APPENDIX: CHARACTERISTICS OF SEQUENTIAL TESTS OF BINOMIAL DISTRIBUTION

CHARACTERISTIC QUANTITIES OF SEQUENTIAL TESTS OF THE BINOMIAL DISTRIBUTION
COMPUTED FOR VARIOUS COMBINATIONS OF p_1', p_2', $\alpha = 0.05$, AND $\beta = 0.10$*

p_1'	p_2'	h_2	h_1	s	$\bar{n}_0$	$\bar{n}_1$	$\bar{n}_{p_1'}$	$\bar{n}_s$	$\bar{n}_{p_2'}$
0.005	0.01	4.1398	3.2245	0.007216	447	5	1,289	1,863	1,222
	0.02	2.0624	1.6064	0.01084	149	3	244	309	185
	0.03	1.5906	1.2389	0.01400	89	2	122	143	82
	0.04	1.3664	1.0643	0.01693	63	2	79	87	49
	0.05	1.2305	0.9585	0.01970	49	2	58	61	33
	0.06	1.1371	0.8857	0.02237	40	2	45	46	25
	0.07	1.0679	0.8318	0.02496	34	2	37	36	19
0.010	0.03	2.5829	2.0118	0.01824	111	3	216	290	181
	0.04	2.0397	1.5887	0.02172	74	3	120	153	92
	0.05	1.7510	1.3639	0.02499	55	2	81	98	58
	0.06	1.5678	1.2211	0.02811	44	2	60	70	40
	0.07	1.4391	1.1209	0.03113	37	2	47	53	30
	0.08	1.3426	1.0458	0.03406	31	2	38	43	24
0.015	0.03	4.0796	3.1776	0.02166	147	5	423	612	402
	0.04	2.8716	2.2367	0.02554	88	3	188	258	163
	0.05	2.3307	1.8153	0.02917	63	3	113	149	92
	0.06	2.0169	1.5710	0.03263	49	3	79	100	61
	0.07	1.8089	1.4089	0.03596	40	2	60	74	44
0.02	0.03	6.9527	5.4154	0.02467	220	8	1,027	1,565	1,073
	0.04	4.0495	3.1541	0.02889	110	5	314	455	300
	0.05	3.0509	2.3763	0.03282	73	4	164	228	146
	0.06	2.5348	1.9743	0.03655	55	3	106	142	89
	0.07	2.2146	1.7250	0.04012	43	3	76	99	61
	0.08	1.9941	1.5532	0.04359	36	3	58	74	45
	0.09	1.8315	1.4265	0.04696	31	2	47	58	35
	0.10	1.7056	1.3285	0.05025	27	2	39	47	28

Abridged with permission from Table 2.23 of Statistical Research Group, Columbia University, *Sequential Analysis of Statistical Data: Applications* (New York: Columbia University Press, 1945), pp. 2.39–2.42.

6

Design of the production planning system

Production planning is concerned with developing a specific course of action for the production system over an extended time. In general terms, this entails forecasting the demand for the firm's product line and selecting that combination of human and material resources that can produce the necessary output to meet that demand in the most efficient manner. In more specific terms, the production planning *problem* is to find that production rate that satisfies output requirements and minimizes the attendant costs of work force fluctuation and inventories.

Production planning is often termed *aggregate scheduling* to differentiate it from the day-to-day (or disaggregate) scheduling by which the production plan is carried out. *Aggregate* planning or scheduling refers to planning in general terms—considering product groups, special promotions, trends in work force availability, changes in resource suppliers, etc. The objective of aggregate planning is to effectively allocate system capacity—men, materials, and equipment—over some time horizon. An aggregate plan is made operational through a *master schedule* that identifies exact items and production dates. From the master schedule a daily schedule is generated, giving specific job orders and releases. (These operations are considered in Chapter 7.)

In this chapter we will first look at the necessary information inputs to a production planning system and the strategies available for attacking the production planning problem. Then we will consider some of the models that are available to forecast demand and to derive a production plan. We will then turn to the problem of implementation of the production plan, and conclude with several suggestions for developing an effective planning system.

INFORMATION GATHERING

At the outset, the distinction between data and information should be made clear. *Data* can be defined as the raw statistics or observed characteristics about some occurrence. Until some analysis is made, data by themselves tell us little about the situation. The output of data analysis is *information* that is usable in decision making. For example, a tabulation of sales figures for the past year is raw data. However, analysis of trends, seasonal components, and a measure of variability—this is the information that is useful in forecasting.

To gather relevant data, the characteristics of the market must be defined—whether it is relatively stable or volatile, together with the state of the economy. Is there any direct or inverse correlation with, say, the gross national product, or the labor market—its current wage rates, labor quality, estimates of turnover rates, and union status and strength? And, as for the activities necessary to make the product or service, are the funds, equipment, and raw materials available? Inputs to the production planning system are shown in Figure 6.1.

Sources for these data vary widely. Many publications are sponsored by state and local governments, by private sources such as banks and utility

FIGURE 6.1

Required inputs to the production planning system

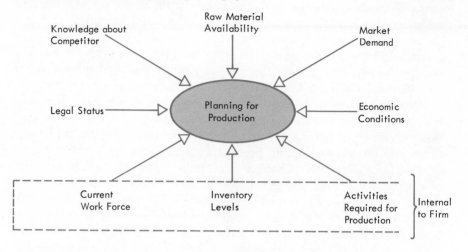

companies, by nonprofit promotional organizations sponsored by local businessmen, and by some commercial specialty sources. Some of the economic indicators of the Department of Commerce can be useful for general market effects. *Thomas's Register of Manufacturers* is a valuable source for suppliers of parts and equipment. The firm's own sources, such as inventory and payroll records, must be tapped, and obviously its sales personnel are valuable for supplying sales estimates and potential customer attitudes. The essential point to consider is that the production plan proposes the making of a product or service, which is directed toward a specific market, by employing labor and other resources that have an economic cost, the sum of which will result in an economic gain for the firm. Therefore the production planner must be supplied with the needed data and information, which must be appropriate, reliable, and timely.

INFORMATION INTERPRETATION

Assuming that meaningful data have been obtained from varied sources concerning product demand, costs, and related activities, we must then look to forecasting methods, production strategies, and aggregate planning for production. In this chapter, production planning is confined to aggregate planning, wherein only gross amounts are determined: total work force, total demand, the entire inventory, and total facilities requirements. Chapter 7 will cover scheduling, which encompasses the "disaggregate" planning phase.

PRODUCTION PLANNING STRATEGIES

Two roles can be adopted in planning for production. The first role is passive; that is, the firm simply responds to and tries to satisfy product demand. The second role is active; that is, the firm attempts to influence or manipulate demand.

Passive response to demand

There are many situations in which a firm would remain "passive," taking demand as given without making any attempt to change demand. A newly formed company with low capitalization may not have the funds or the personnel to do much more than, perhaps, modify price. Or a rapidly growing company in a new product line may be faced with such a large demand that its essential problems are to produce as much as it can and, at the same time, obtain needed financing for expansion. A third situation is that in which firms engage in relatively "pure" competition in the economic sense; that is, the product is relatively homogeneous, each firm's output is small in relation to the total market so that each firm obtains only a reasonable profit, and each firm is operating near its optimum rate.

In the passive role, the firm attempts to satisfy demand by changing the size and combination of the variables, which are work force size, inventory levels, production rate, subcontracting, and product mix.

The terms *pure* and *mixed strategy* are sometimes employed to indicate how the variables are used. A "pure strategy" implies that the productive output is varied by changing only one of the variables above while holding all others constant. As demand varies, for example, the work force can be increased or decreased in direct relation to demand. This strategy is particularly suitable with labor-intensive products. Another pure strategy is to vary the production rate while holding all other variables constant, and the effect on the work force is to cause underutilization (idle time) or overutilization (overtime).

The remaining pure strategies are used to satisfy demand through drawing inventories down during high demand and building inventories up during low demand. Subcontracting can be used to satisfy any demand over some minimum level, or to meet peak demands. For example, the production facility can maintain a constant production rate by producing for its low demands and then satisfy any demands over this amount by subcontracting. Variation in product mix offers an opportunity to maintain stability in the other variables. Frequently product requirements are somewhat out of phase—while the demand for some products is high, the demand for others may be low. Therefore, shifting resources among products as demand fluctuates makes some smoothing possible. This is one of the leading arguments for product diversification.

A "mixed strategy" is one that modifies two or more variables at a time. For example, a low product demand may be satisfied by simultaneously reducing both the work force and the production rate. A more detailed example will be given in this chapter in the section on graphical production planning techniques.

Active influence on demand

Thus far the firm has been treated as if it were passive, but most enterprises, in the most common situations, can take an active role both in influencing their environment and in adapting themselves to the environment. For example, the firm can influence demand, or select a contracyclical product mix, or create order backlogs.

During periods of low demand, increased sales can be generated through price cuts, managerial pressure on the sales force, and various incentives and campaigns. Automobile price cuts at the end of the model year help to keep demand up. Vacation resorts use reduced off-season rates to attract customers (sometimes customers other than vacationers—conventioneers, for example).

By selecting contracyclical products, some stability in the productive facilities is possible. Although demand for air conditioners can be brought up during winter months through price cuts and other promotion gimmicks, a better alternative may be to produce home heating units during this off season.

The order backlog is ideal for maintaining production stability. Its success, of course, lies in the customers' willingness to accept the backlog time. In some cases a customer may be unwilling to wait for the product, and in other cases he might decline to accept delivery prior to his contracted delivery date if the backlog time turns out to be less than expected. The ability of marketing personnel to select and persuade customers to accept delivery within a wider time range is important. The customer also may be influenced by incentives such as discounts and an early or late penalty clause.[1]

FORECASTING TECHNIQUES

In order to establish a production plan that stipulates the requirements for production, the first necessity is to have a demand forecast on which to base the plan. Then, given a forecast, plans may be made for manpower and material needs, production rates, and inventory levels.

Two approaches can be used to develop a forecast. These are a statistical approach that involves quantitative analysis, and a subjective or judgmental approach that is based on estimates and opinions. The statistical approach is founded on the assumption that past history is indicative of future expectations and uses past data to project an estimated demand. The judgmental approach is developed through such means as customer surveys, salesmen's estimates, correlation with economic or consumer trends, technological advances, and consensus. In practice, the two methods are used jointly. A forecast can be developed statistically and then modified by the expected influence of factors that will cause historical trends to deviate. Or, conversely, a forecast can be developed without regard to company history

---

[1] For further discussion of the points brought out in this section, see Jay R. Galbraith, "Solving Production Smoothing Problems," *Management Science*, vol. 15, no. 1 (August 1969), pp. 665–73.

and then compared to the statistical analysis for confirmation or the need to explain significant differences.

The most common and relatively easy methods for developing a forecast from past data are the simple moving average, weighted moving average, exponential smoothing, and regression analysis. These methods are easily used by a clerk with a desk calculator. Whether more involved and costly forecasting techniques employing complex curve fitting, time series analysis, or Monte Carlo simulation (see supplement to Chapter 6 for a discussion of this methodology) are justified depends on such factors as market size, potential profit, and available personnel to perform the analysis. In this text only the first group is discussed.

Components of demand

In most cases the observed demand for products or services can be broken down into six components: average demand for the period, a trend, seasonal influence, cyclical elements, random variation, and autocorrelation. Figure 6.2 illustrates a demand over a four-year period showing the average, trend, seasonal components, and randomness around the smoothed demand curve.

Cyclical factors are more difficult to determine since the time span may be unknown or the cause of the cycle may not be considered. Cyclical influence on demand may be due to such occurrences as political elections, war, economic conditions, or sociological pressures.

Random deviations are caused by natural chance variation. When all known causes for demand are removed from the total demand (average, trend, seasonal, cyclical, and autocorrelative), what remains is the unexplained portion of demand. If one is unable to attribute the cause of this

FIGURE 6.2

Historical product demand consisting of a growth trend and seasonal demand

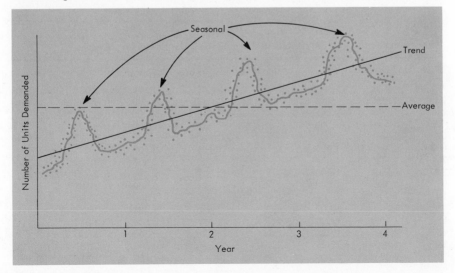

demand to specific sources, it is attributed to natural chance randomness.

Autocorrelation denotes the persistence of occurrence—the value expected at any point in time is highly correlated with its own past values. In queuing theory, the length of a waiting line is highly autocorrelated. That is, if a line is relatively long at one point in time, then shortly after that time one would expect the line still to be long.

When the demand is random, the demand from one week to another may vary widely. Where high autocorrelation exists, the demand will not be expected to change very much from one week to the next.

Simple moving average

When demand for a product does not have a rapid growth or seasonal characteristics, a moving average can be useful in removing the random fluctuations for forecasting. Although moving averages are frequently "centered," it is more convenient to use past data to predict the following period directly. To illustrate, a centered five-month average of January, February, March, April, and May gives an average centered on March. However, all five months of data must already exist. If our objective is to forecast for June, we must project our moving average—by some means—from March to June. However, if the average is not centered but is at the forward end, we can forecast more easily, though perhaps we will lose some accuracy. Thus if we want to forecast June with a five-month moving average, we can take the average of January, February, March, April, and May. When June passes, the forecast for July would be the average of February, March, April, May, and June. This is the way in which Table 6.1 and Figure 6.3 were computed.

Although it is important to try to select the best period to use for the moving average, there are several conflicting effects of different period lengths: the longer the moving average period, the greater the effect of

TABLE 6.1

Forecast demand based on a three- and a nine-week simple moving average

Week	Demand	3 week	9 week	Week	Demand	3 week	9 week
1.......	800			16......	1,700	2,000	1,800
2.......	1,400			17......	1,800	1,833	1,811
3.......	1,000	1,067		18......	2,200	1,900	1,911
4.......	1,500	1,300		19......	1,900	1,967	1,933
5.......	1,500	1,333		20......	2,400	2,167	2,011
6.......	1,300	1,433		21......	2,400	2,233	2,111
7.......	1,800	1,533		22......	2,600	2,467	2,144
8.......	1,700	1,600		23......	2,000	2,333	2,111
9.......	1,300	1,600	1,367	24......	2,500	2,367	2,167
10......	1,700	1,567	1,467	25......	2,600	2,367	2,267
11......	1,700	1,567	1,500	26......	2,200	2,433	2,311
12......	1,500	1,633	1,556	27......	2,200	2,333	2,311
13......	2,300	1,833	1,644	28......	2,500	2,300	2,378
14......	2,300	2,033	1,733	29......	2,400	2,367	2,378
15......	2,000	2,200	1,811	30......	2,100	2,333	2,344

FIGURE 6.3

Moving average of three- and nine-week periods versus actual demand

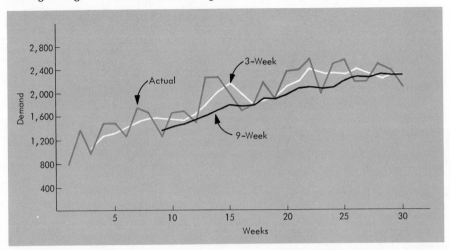

smoothing any random variation—which may be desirable. However, if there is a trend in the data—either increasing the demand or decreasing it—the moving average has the adverse characteristic of lagging the trend. Therefore, while a shorter time span produces more oscillation, there is a closer "following" of the trend. Conversely, a longer time span gives a smoother response but lags the trend.

Figure 6.3, a plot of the data in Table 6.1, illustrates the effects of various lengths of the period of a moving average. We see that the growth trend levels off at about the 23rd week. The three-week moving average responds better in following this change than the nine week, although overall the nine-week average is smoother.

The main disadvantage in calculating a moving average is that all individual elements must be carried as data since a new forecast period involves adding new data and dropping the earliest data in the moving average string. For a three- or six-period moving average, this is not too severe; however, for a long period, such as the 200-day moving average of the New York Stock Exchange, there is a costly amount of data to carry along.

Weighted moving average

Whereas the simple moving average gave equal effects to each component of the moving average data base, a weighted moving average allows any weights to be placed on each element, providing, of course, that the sum of all weights equals one. For example, a department store may find that, from a four-week data source (28 days), the closest forecasts are made by using 40 percent of the sales experience for the same day in the four previous weeks and the remaining 60 percent as the average of the remaining 24 days. Mathematically, this could be stated as:

$$F_t = 0.40 \frac{(F_{t-7} + F_{t-14} + F_{t-21} + F_{t-28})}{4}$$

$$+ 0.60 \frac{\left(\sum_{t=1}^{6} F_t + \sum_{t=8}^{13} F_t + \sum_{t=15}^{20} F_t + \sum_{t=22}^{27} F_t \right)}{24}$$

A simpler example can be used for easier calculation. Suppose that in a four-month period the best forecast is derived by using 40 percent of the actual sales for the most recent month, 30 percent of two months ago, 20 percent of three months ago, and 10 percent of four months ago. If actual sales experience was as follows,

Month 1	Month 2	Month 3	Month 4	Month 5
100	90	105	95	?

the forecast for month 5 would be:

$$F_5 = 0.40(95) + 0.30(105) + 0.20(90) + 0.10(100)$$
$$= 38 + 31.5 + 18 + 10$$
$$= 97.5$$

Suppose sales for month 5 actually turned out to be 110; then the forecast for month 6 would be:

$$F_6 = 0.40(110) + 0.30(95) + 0.20(105) + 0.10(90)$$
$$= 44 + 28.5 + 21 + 9$$
$$= 102.5$$

The weighted moving average has a definite advantage in being able to vary the effects of past data, but it also has the disadvantage of "remembering" the total history for the time period.

Exponential smoothing

In the previous methods of forecasting (simple moving average, weighted moving average) the major drawback is the need to continually carry a large amount of historical data. (This is also true for regression analysis techniques, which will be covered in the next section.) As a new piece of data is added in these methods, the oldest unit is dropped and the new forecast is calculated. In many applications (perhaps in most) the most recent occurrences are more indicative of the future than those in the more distant past. If this premise is valid—that the importance of data diminishes as the past becomes more distant—then exponential smoothing may be the most logical and easiest method to use.

In using the exponential smoothing method, only three pieces of data are needed to forecast the future: the most recent forecast, the actual demand that occurred for that forecasted period, and a smoothing constant (α). This smoothing constant determines the level of smoothing and the speed of reaction to differences between forecasts and actual occurrences. The value for the constant is arbitrary, and is determined both by the nature of the product and the feeling by managers of the firm as to what constitutes a good response rate. For example, if a firm produced a standard item with relatively stable demand, the reaction rate to differences between actual and forecasted demand would tend to be small—perhaps just a few percentage points. However, if the firm were experiencing growth, it would be desirable to have a higher reaction rate in order to give greater importance to recent growth experience. The more rapid the growth, the higher the reaction rate should be.

The equation for a single exponential smoothing forecast is simply

$$F_t = F_{t-1} + \alpha(A_{t-1} - F_{t-1})$$

where

F_t is the exponentially smoothed forecast for period t
F_{t-1} is the exponentially smoothed forecast made for the prior period
A_{t-1} is the actual demand in the prior period
α is the desired response rate, or smoothing constant

This equation states that the new forecast is equal to the old forecast plus an adjustment proportional to the difference between the previous forecast and the actual experience.[2]

To demonstrate the method, assume that the long-run demand for the product under study is relatively stable and a smoothing constant (α) of 0.05 is considered appropriate. If the exponential method were used as a continuing policy, a forecast would have been made for last month.[3] Assume that last month's forecast (F_{t-1}) was 1,050 units. If 1,000 actually were demanded, rather than 1,050, the forecast for this month would be

$$\begin{aligned}
F_t &= F_{t-1} + \alpha(A_{t-1} - F_{t-1}) \\
&= 1050 + 0.05(1000 - 1050) \\
&= 1050 + 0.05(-50) \\
&= 1047.5 \text{ units}
\end{aligned}$$

Since the smoothing coefficient is small, the reaction of the new forecast to an "error" of 50 units is to decrease this next month's forecast by only 2½ units.

That this method is in fact an exponentially smoothed weighting may be shown by viewing several periods in the past with the equation expanded:

$$\begin{aligned}
F_t &= F_{t-1} + \alpha(A_{t-1} - F_{t-1}) \\
F_{t-1} &= F_{t-2} + \alpha(A_{t-2} - F_{t-2}) \\
F_{t-2} &= F_{t-3} + \alpha(A_{t-3} - F_{t-3})
\end{aligned}$$

When expanded to t periods, the general model becomes

$$F_t = \alpha[A_{t-1} + (1-\alpha)A_{t-2} + (1-\alpha)^2 A_{t-3} + (1-\alpha)^3 A_{t-4} + \cdots + (1-\alpha)^{t-1}A_0] + (1-\alpha)^t F_0$$

As can be seen, the equation applies exponential weighting since each increment in the past is decreased by $(1 - \alpha)$, or

---

[2] Some writers on the topic prefer to call F_t a smoothed average.

[3] When exponential smoothing is first introduced, the initial forecast or starting point may be obtained by using a simple estimate, or an average of preceding periods.

Weighing at α = 0.05

Most recent weighting $= \alpha(1 - \alpha)^0$........ 0.0500
Data 1 time period older $= \alpha(1 - \alpha)^1$........ 0.0475
Data 2 time periods older $= \alpha(1 - \alpha)^2$........ 0.0451
Data 3 time periods older $= \alpha(1 - \alpha)^3$........ 0.0429

As in all of the forecasting methods presented in this chapter, single exponential smoothing has the same shortcoming of lagging changes in demand. Figure 6.4 shows a hypothetical demand curve for a product. On an increase, the forecast lags the actual demand, and when a change in direction occurs, the forecast "overshoots." To help in closer tracking of actual demand during periods involving trends, double or triple exponential smoothing may help. Exponential smoothing methods may also be used in the presence of seasonal or cyclical demands. These refinements on exponential smoothing may be found in one of the reference sources.[4]

Linear regression analysis

Although computationally more difficult than the moving average methods, linear regression analysis is a very useful forecasting technique if past data appear to fall about a straight line. However, an estimate of how good the line "fits" the data is computed as part of the procedure.

Linear regression "regresses" one variable on another variable. For example, we know that consumption is a function of income. If we let Y represent consumption (the dependent variable) and x represent income (the independent variable), the linear model becomes

$$Y = a + bx$$

where

y or Y = consumption
a = the y intercept
b = the slope of the line
x = income

The uppercase Y is used to denote consumption as computed by the equation and the lowercase y is consumption as directly observed in the data.

The accepted method to determine which line is the best fit is the "least squares" method. This technique seeks to minimize the sum of the squares of the distance between each unit of data and its corresponding point on the assumed line. Figure 6.5 shows five data points defining consumption levels (y) for specific income levels (x). If we draw a straight line through the general area of the points, we can show the difference between consumption at the data point (y) and the corresponding point (Y) on the

---

[4] See, for example, Robert Goodell Brown, *Smoothing, Forecasting and Prediction of Discrete Time Series* (Englewood Cliffs, N.J.: Prentice-Hall, 1963).

FIGURE 6.4

Exponential forecasts versus actual demands for units of a product over time showing the forecast lag

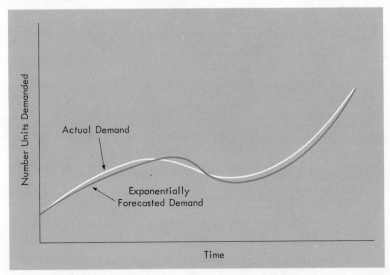

line. The sum of the squares of the differences between the plotted data points and the line points is

$$(y_1 - Y_1)^2 + (y_2 - Y_2)^2 + (y_3 - Y_3)^2 + (y_4 - Y_4)^2 + (y_5 - Y_5)^2$$

The best line to use is the one that minimizes this total.

We will not delve into the derivation of the equations but will simply state them. The equation for a straight line is $Y = a + bx$, and the problem is to determine the values for a and b. Mathematically, they are

$$a = \bar{y} - b\bar{x}$$
$$b = \frac{\Sigma xy - n\bar{x}\bar{y}}{\Sigma x^2 - n\bar{x}^2}$$

where

$a = $ the y intercept

$b = $ the slope of the line

$\bar{y} = $ the average of all y's

$\bar{x} = $ the average of all x's

$x = $ the x value at each data point

$y = $ the y value at each data point

$n = $ the number of data points

$Y = $ the value of the dependent variable computed with the regression equation

The standard error of estimate, or how well the line fits the data, is

$$S_{yx} = \sqrt{\frac{\sum_{i=1}^{n} (y_i - Y_i)^2}{n}}$$

FIGURE 6.5

Fitting a least squares regression line to data of consumption as a function of income

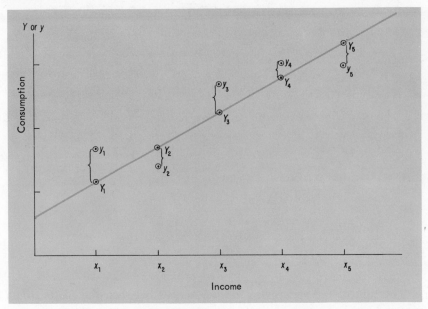

This is the same expression as that for the standard deviation of an arithmetic mean. To illustrate the procedure for determining a regression line, a sample problem will be presented.

Example. The history of housing starts within a particular community for the years 1960 to 1972 is shown in Figure 6.6. The coordinates of each data point are listed in the first two columns of Table 6.2.

FIGURE 6.6

Annual number of housing starts

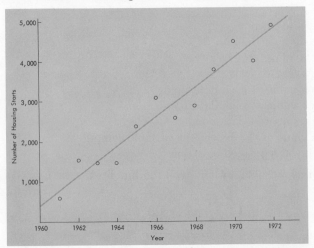

TABLE 6.2 [2nd] [PGM] 1 [SBR] [Cu]
Least squares analysis for the number of annual housing starts

[X=T for X]
[2nd Σ for Y]

Housing starts	Year				For computation of error (from equation $Y = a + bx$)
y	x	xy	x^2	y^2	Y
1 400	'60	24,000	3,600	160,000	430 [2nd] [op] [14]
2 600	'61	36,600	3,721	360,000	791
3 1550	'62	96,100	3,844	2,402,500	1152
4 1500	'63	94,500	3,969	2,250,000	1513
5 1500	'64	96,000	4,096	2,250,000	1874
6 2400	'65	156,000	4,225	5,760,000	2235
7 3100	'66	204,600	4,356	9,610,000	2596
8 2600	'67	174,200	4,489	6,760,000	2957
9 2900	'68	197,200	4,624	8,410,000	3318
10 3800	'69	262,200	4,761	14,440,000	3679
11 4500	'70	315,000	4,900	20,250,000	4040
12 4000	'71	284,000	5,041	16,000,000	4401
13 4900	'72	352,800	5,184	24,010,000	4762
33,750	858	2,293,200	56,810	112,662,500	

$$\bar{x} = \frac{\Sigma x}{n} = \frac{858}{13} = 66 \quad X=T$$

$$\bar{y} = \frac{\Sigma y}{n} = \frac{33,750}{13} = 2596.15 \quad [2nd] \quad \bar{x}$$

$$b = \frac{\Sigma xy - n\bar{x}\bar{y}}{\Sigma x^2 - n\bar{x}^2} = \frac{2,293,200 - 13(66)(2596.15)}{56,810 - 13(66)^2} = 361 \quad [2nd] \text{ op } 12 \; [x=T]$$

$$a = \bar{y} - b\bar{x} = 2,596.15 - (361)(66) = -21,230 \quad [2nd] \text{ op } 12$$

Therefore
$$Y = a + bx$$
$$Y = -21,230 + 361x$$

[2nd op 13 = Correlation Coefficient]
[$r^2 = 2nd$ op, 13, x^2]

To determine the least squares regression line we must first compute the slope b. Procedurally, the easiest way to do this is in tabular form, and the complete calculations are shown in Table 6.2. (The last column has nothing to do with developing the line equation but is there for convenience in calculating the standard error, S_{yx}.) The final equation for the least squares line is shown as $Y = -21,230 + 361x$. In order to draw this line on Figure 6.6 we can pick two values of x, solve for Y at these points, and draw a straight line. Two convenient points are the extremes of the data, where $x = 60$ and $x = 72$. Solving the equation for Y (above) at these two values of x gives $Y = 430$ (at $x = 60$) and $Y = 4,762$ (at $x = 72$).

The standard error of estimate is computed from the first and last columns of Table 6.2. From the equation

$$S_{yx} = \sqrt{\frac{\sum_{i=1}^{n} (y_i - Y_i)^2}{n}}$$

we can compute S_{yx} as

$$S_{yx} = \sqrt{\frac{(400 - 430)^2 + (600 - 791)^2 + (1,550 - 1,152)^2 \ldots (4,900 - 4,762)^2}{13}}$$

$$S_{yx} = 319.8$$

To forecast the number of housing starts for 1973, then, from the final straight line equation

$$Y = -21{,}230 + 361(x)$$
$$Y_{73} = -21{,}230 + 361(73) = 5{,}123$$

Therefore the expected number of housing starts for 1973 is 5,123, with a standard error estimate of 319.8[5]

This regression analysis is the least squares method, containing one dependent and one independent variable and fitting a straight line to the data. There is also curvilinear regression analysis—fitting, as implied, a curve rather than a straight line to explain the data. Another forecasting method is multiple regression analysis, in which a number of variables are considered, together with the effects of each on the item of interest. For example, in the home furnishings field the effects of the number of marriages, disposable income, housing starts, and trend can be expressed in a multiple regression equation,[6] as

$$S = B + B_m(M) + B_h(H) + B_i(I) + B_t(T)$$

where

S = Gross sales for year
B = Base sales, a starting point from which other factors have influence
M = Marriages during the year
H = Housing starts during the year
I = Annual disposable personal income
T = Time trend (first year = 1, second = 2, third = 3, etc.)

B_m, B_h, B_i, and B_t represent the influence on expected sales due to the number of marriages and housing starts, income, and trend.

Forecasting by multiple regression is very appropriate when a number of factors influence a variable of interest—in this case sales. Its difficulty lies with the data gathering, and particularly with the mathematical computation. Fortunately, standard programs for multiple regression analysis are available for most computers, relieving the need for tedious manual calculation.

FORECAST ERRORS

Demand for a product is generated through the interaction of a number of factors. Because this interaction is too complex to describe accurately in

---

[5] An equation for the standard error which is often easier to compute is:

$$S_{yx} = \sqrt{\frac{\Sigma y^2 - a\Sigma y - b\Sigma xy}{n}}.$$

Using data from Table 6.2,

$$S_{yx} = \sqrt{\frac{112{,}662{,}500 - (-21{,}230)(33{,}750) - 361(2{,}293{,}200)}{13}} = 391.82.$$

[6] G. C. Parker and Edelberto L. Segura, "How to Get a Better Forecast," *Harvard Business Review*, vol. 49, no. 2 (March–April 1971), pp. 99–109.

a model, all forecasts will certainly contain some error. In discussing the forecast errors, it is convenient to distinguish between *sources of error* and the *measurement of error*.

Sources of error

When we talk about statistical errors, such as in regression analysis, we are referring to the deviations of our observations from our regression line. It is common to attach a confidence band (i.e., statistical control limits as described in Chapter 5), to the regression line to reduce the unexplained error. However, when we then use this regression line as a forecasting device by projecting it into the future, the error may not be correctly defined by the projected confidence band. This is so simply because the confidence interval is based on past data; it may or may not hold for projected data points and therefore cannot be used with the same confidence. Experience has shown that the actual errors tend to be greater than those predicted from forecast models.

Errors can be classified as *bias* or *random*. Bias errors occur when a consistent "mistake" is made. Sources of bias are: failure to include the right variables; using the wrong relationships among variables; employing the wrong trendline; shift of seasonal demand from its historic calendar occurrence; and the existence of some undetected secular trend.

Random errors can be defined as those that cannot be explained by the forecast model employed. There is a bit of irony in this statement, though, since, if one desires to minimize the error in explaining past data, he can use a sophisticated model such as a Fourier series with a large number of terms. While this can reduce the forecasting model's error on the data to almost zero, it may do no better in forecasting future demand than a simpler model with a higher error.

Measurement of error

Several of the common terms used to describe the degree of error are: standard error, mean squared error (or variance), and mean absolute deviation. In addition, "tracking signals" may be used to indicate the existence of any positive or negative bias in the forecast.

Standard error was defined in the linear regression section of this chapter. Since the standard error is the square root of a function, it is often more convenient to use the function itself. This is called the mean squared error, or variance.

The mean absolute deviation (MAD) was in vogue in the past but subsequently was ignored in favor of standard deviation and standard error measures. In recent years MAD has made a comeback because of its simplicity and usefulness in obtaining tracking signals (discussed below).

The mean absolute deviation (MAD) is computed using the differences between the actual demand and the forecasted demand without regard to sign. Since it is the mean (or average) deviation the sum of the absolute deviations is divided by the number of data points, or stated in equation form,

$$\text{MAD} = \frac{\sum_{t=1}^{n} |A_t - F_t|}{n}$$

where

t = period number
A = actual demand for the period
F = forecasted demand for the period
n = total number of periods
$\|$ is a symbol used to indicate the absolute value disregarding positive and negative signs

When the errors that occur in the forecast are normally distributed (the usual case), the mean absolute deviation relates to the standard deviation as,

1 standard deviation

$$= \sqrt{\frac{\pi}{2}} \times \text{MAD where } \pi = 3.1416, \text{ or approximately } 1.25 \times \text{MAD}$$

or conversely,

$$1 \text{ MAD} = 0.8 \text{ standard deviation}$$

The standard deviation is the larger unit of measure. If the MAD of a set of points was found to be 60 units, then the standard deviation would be 75 units. And, in the usual statistical manner, if control limits were set at plus or minus 3 standard deviations (or $\pm$ 3.75 MADs) then 99.7 percent of the points would fall within these limits.

A *tracking signal* is a measurement that indicates whether the forecast average is keeping pace with any genuine upward or downward changes

TABLE 6.3

Computing the mean absolute deviation (MAD), the running sum of forecast errors (RSFE), and the tracking signal from forecasted and actual data.

Month	Forecast	Actual	Actual deviation	Running sum of forecast errors (RSFE)	Absolute deviation
1......	1,000	950	−50	−50	50
2......	1,000	1,070	+70	+20	70
3......	1,000	1,100	+100	+120	100
4......	1,000	960	−40	+80	40
5......	1,000	1,090	+90	+170	90
6......	1,000	1,050	+50	+220	50

Total absolute deviation = 400
Mean absolute deviation (MAD) = 400 ÷ 6 = 66.7

$$\text{Tracking signal} = \frac{\text{RSFE}}{\text{MAD}} = \frac{220}{66.7} = 3.3 \text{ MADs}$$

in demand (as opposed to random changes). The tracking signal is calculated using the arithmetic sum of forecast deviations divided by the mean absolute deviation. Table 6.3 illustrates the procedure for computing MAD and the tracking signal for a six-month period wherein the forecast had been set at a constant 1,000 and the actual demands that occurred are as shown. In this example, the forecast, on the average, was off by 66.7 units and the tracking signal was equal to 3.3 mean absolute deviations.

Acceptable limits for the tracking signal depend on the size of the demand being forecasted (high volume or high revenue items should be monitored ferquently) and the amount of personnel time available (lower acceptable limits cause more forecasts to be out of limits and therefore require more time to investigate). Table 6.4 shows the area within the control limits for a range of zero to four MADs.

The sum of the actual forecast errors in a perfect forecasting model would be expected to be zero; that is, the random errors that result in over-

TABLE 6.4

The percentages of points included within the control limits for a range of 0 to 4 MADs.

Control limits		
Number of MADS	Related number of standard deviations	Percentage of points lying within control limits
±1	0.798	57.048
±2	1.596	88.946
±3	2.394	98.334
±4	3.192	99.856

estimates should be offset by errors that are underestimates. The tracking signal would then also be zero, indicating an unbiased model, neither leading nor lagging the actual demands.

Often, MAD is used to forecast errors. It might then be desirable to make the MAD more sensitive to recent data. A useful technique to do this is to compute an exponentially smoothed MAD as a forecast for the next period's error range. The procedure is similar to single exponential smoothing previously covered in this chapter. The value of the MAD forecast is to provide a range of error; in the case of inventory control, this is useful in setting safe stock levels.

$$\text{MAD}_t = \alpha \, |A_{t-1} - F_{t-1}| + (1 - \alpha) \, \text{MAD}_{t-1}$$

where

MAD_t = the forecasted MAD for the tth period
α = smoothing constant (normally in the range of 0.05 to 0.15)
A_{t-1} = actual demand in the period $t - 1$
F_{t-1} = demand forecasted for period $t - 1$

Adapting to forecast errors

A common criticism of statistical forecasting is that it uses a variety of techniques to fit some type of line to *past data*. Decision makers, however, must make decisions concerning *future performance*. Nevertheless, in spite of the inaccuracies in statistical forecasting, there is still much value in the procedure. For example, the pattern of seasonal variations is likely to persist, and any upward or downward trend will likely continue unless some specific event occurs to change it. Further, when statistical forecasts are properly made, they are accompanied by some estimate of forecast error as an indicator of the expected range in forecast variation. Hence, there are checks and balances in statistical forecasting that keep forecast errors under control.

Another challenging question relating to forecast errors is whether more time should be spent to develop more accurate forecasts, or whether better operating techniques within the firm should be developed to allow more rapid response to changes in forecasts. A quicker response to changes in forecasts implies working more efficiently with poorer forecasts (rather than trying to develop better forecasts). Many productive systems now utilize computer operating routines that make more rapid adjustment possible, thereby lessening the seriousness of forecast errors.

Developing a workable forecasting system[7]

The marketing department and the production department each have a responsibility in forecasting. Since most large firms maintain several thousand or more items in inventory, it is rather unlikely that the marketing department will forecast the demand for each item. However, because of their knowledge of external events such as economic conditions, competitors' prices, and consumer trends, the marketing department can and should make good sales forecasts for

1. Product groups.
2. Promotion items.
3. New products.
4. Individual items expected to be unusually sensitive to external factors.

Production and inventory control personnel, however, can make the routine individual item forecasts better than anyone else. This is because they possess all the past data on each item, and, since most items are usually produced for inventory stock, an averaging of the past sales data is usually the best indicator. (Exponential smoothing is the most common forecasting technique in this case.)

PRODUCTION PLANNING TECHNIQUES

The objective of production planning on an aggregate basis is to determine the size of inventories, the total work force, and total production (in

---

[7] For more detailed coverage, see Oliver W. Wight, *Production and Inventory in the Computer Age*. (Boston: Cahners Books, 1974), pp. 164–66.

common units such as machine hours, gallons, or tons of product). The most commonly used method still involves charting techniques. However, considerable effort is being devoted to the development of mathematical and heuristic approaches to aid the production planner in carrying out this difficult chore.

Graphical and charting approaches

Given the forecast for the planning period, the production planner constructs a chart of the cumulative product requirements. To meet this cumulative need, he tries alternate strategies by varying the work force size, production rate, and inventory level. His criterion for judging the best plan is minimization of costs. These costs can be listed as follows:

Costs due to inventory variation:
Carrying costs (storage, obsolescence, deterioration, pilferage, interest, etc.)
Costs due to production rate variation:
Undertime (workers having excess idle time)
Overtime (premiums for overtime work or second- and third-shift operation)
Costs due to variation in the size of the work force:
Increase in size (hiring and training costs)
Decrease in size (severance pay, unemployment insurance costs, friction with worker groups, unions, or community in general)

Rather than vary his production output, he could produce at a reasonably level rate and subcontract or purchase enough products from competitors or other contractors to meet peak demands. Subcontracting cost is the added premium paid for outside manufacture over in-house production costs.

Example of production scheduling.   For brevity, we will use a six-month scheduling horizon. In practice, a 12-month schedule would normally be more appropriate because the 12-month plan will display the full range of demand fluctuation for the year. Assume that we have been supplied with a monthly demand forecast, the current inventory stock level of 400 units, the safety stock policy of requiring one-fourth of the month's forecast, and the number of working days available each month. These data are used to compute the production requirements and are shown entered in Table 6.5. Line 4 was computed as one-fourth of the month's forecast. Line 5 is the required number of units for the month. For January, however, the beginning inventory of 400 units is subtracted from the total demand for January: Demand + Safety stock − Beginning inventory = January requirements (1,800 + 450 − 400 = 1,850). For planning purposes, the actual demand is presumed to be the same as the forecasted demand. In the case of perfect forecasts, the safety stock would be unused and therefore be the beginning inventory for the following month. Therefore the February requirement is Demand forecast (1,500) + Safety stock (375) − Beginning inventory (450) = 1,425. The entries for the remaining months are computed

TABLE 6.5

Aggregate production scheduling requirements

	January	February	March	April	May	June
Line 1: Beginning inventory.....	400	450	375	275	225	275
Line 2: Forecasted demand......	1,800	1,500	1,100	900	1,100	1,700
Line 3: Cumulative demand.....	1,800	3,300	4,400	5,300	6,400	8,100
Line 4: Safety stock...........	450	375	275	225	275	425
Line 5: Production requirements (Line 2 + Line 4 − Line 1)...............	1,850	1,425	1,000	850	1,150	1,850
Line 6: Cumulative production required...............	1,850	3,275	4,275	5,125	6,275	8,125
Line 7: Working days..........	22	19	21	21	22	20
Line 8: Cumulative working days.................	22	41	62	83	105	125

similarly. Shortages are backordered and satisfied from next month's production.

The procedure now is to try a variety of production plans that will satisfy demand. Each proposed plan will differ in cost because of the effects of variation in production rates, inventory levels, work force size, and subcontracting.

Suppose that the additional information relating to costs is as follows:

Manufacturing cost = $100 per unit
Storage costs (obsolescence, opportunity costs, etc.) = 1.5 percent of manufacturing cost per month ($1.50/unit/ mo)

Standard pay rate = $4 per hour
Overtime rate = 150 percent or $6 per hour
Marginal cost of stockout = $5 per unit per month
Marginal cost of subcontracting = $2 per unit (subcontracting cost of $102 less manufacturing cost of $100)
Hiring and training cost = $200 per man
Layoff costs = $250 per man
Man-hours required per unit = 5

Since the best production plan will result from a series of tries using alternate strategies, we will not seek the optimum but will illustrate the method by using just three possible production plans, shown in Table 6.6.

The strategy for Plan 1 is to produce to exact production requirements by varying the work force size on regular hours. The strategy for Plan 2 is to maintain a constant work force level based on a six-month average [(8,125 units × 5 hours each) ÷ (125 days × 8 hours per day) = 41 men]. Inventory is allowed to accumulate with shortages filled from the next month's production. Plan 3 is based on the strategy of holding the work force constant for a total six-month period at the level to meet the low April demand [(850 units × 6 months × 5 hours per unit) ÷ (125 days × 8 hours per day) = 25 men] and subcontracting any monthly difference between requirements and production.

Each of these plans is tabulated and a comparison is made in Table 6.7. We can see that making use of subcontracting resulted in the lowest cost (Plan 3). Figures 6.7 and 6.8 (pages 250–51) depict the effects of the three plans. These graphs illustrate the expected results both on a daily rate and on the total production requirement.

There are obviously many other feasible plans, some of which would require overtime, or a combination of work force change with overtime and some subcontracting. The optimum plan results from a thorough search of a variety of alternatives.

Mathematical techniques

In the previous section on planning to satisfy product demands over a time horizon, the method used to arrive at a low-cost plan was one of trial and error. Mathematical approaches to the optimal solution to this problem are presently nonexistent for the general case. Several mathematical methods for specialized conditions are available, however, and two of them will be discussed: production planning by the transportation method of linear programming and the linear decision rule.

Production planning by linear programming. Bowman introduced the idea of structuring the product demand and the available means to satisfy this demand into a transportation-type matrix.[8] Demands for the product by periods were established as the destinations, and the varied means to obtain the product were construed to be the sources of supply. In the context of the previous example, the months January through June are the destinations, and the product sources are the work force under regular working hours, overtime hours, subcontracting, and the amount of inventory on hand at the start.

To illustrate how the method works, we will develop an example similar to the previous one, using the production requirements stated in Table 6.5, line 5. Assume that the situation is one of a constant work force with overtime and subcontracting permitted. If demands for each period must be satisfied either through in-house production or subcontracting (no shortages allowed), the linear programming matrix can be easily constructed. The solution to the linear model will yield the optimal plan stating the source of items produced (workers on regular time or overtime or subcontracting) and the monthly production/purchasing schedule.

Consider the following data for this problem. Carrying and storage costs = $1.50 per unit per month. Therefore a unit produced in period 1 and not used until period 2 has an additional cost of $1.50; holding it until period 3 would add $3; until period 4, $4.50; etc.

---

[8] E. H. Bowman, "Production Planning by the Transportation Method of Linear Programming," *Journal of the Operations Research Society* (February 1956). Also see the supplement to Chapter 2 for a discussion of the mechanics of the transportation method.

TABLE 6.6

Three possible production plans

Plan 1

	(1)	*(2)* Production hours required *(1)* × *5*	*(3)* Hours per month per man *(days × 8)*
Month	*Production required*		
January	1,850	9,250	176
February	1,425	7,125	152
March	1,000	5,000	168
April	850	4,250	168
May	1,150	5,750	176
June	1,850	9,250	160

Plan 2*

	(1)	*(2)* Production hours available *(days × 8 × 41 men)*	*(3)* Units produced *(2)* ÷ *5*
Month	*Cumulative production requirement*		
January	1,850	7,216	1,443
February	3,275	6,232	1,247
March	4,275	6,888	1,378
April	5,125	6,888	1,378
May	6,275	7,216	1,443
June	8,125	6,560	1,312

Plan 3†

	(1)	*(2)* Production hours available *(days × 8 × 25)*	*(3)* Units produced *(2)* ÷ *5*
Month	*Production requirement*		
January	1,850	4,400	880
February	1,425	3,800	760
March	1,000	4,200	840
April	850	4,200	840
May	1,150	4,400	880
June	1,850	4,000	800
	8,125		5,000

* Notes for Plan 2:

Column 1, taken from Table 6.5, line 6.

Column 2, the total of 8 hours per day for 41 men over the number of working days in each month given by Table 6.5, line 7.

Column 3, the number of production hours available divided by 5 hours' production time for each unit.

Columns 5–8, as a policy decision in this example to maintain control of the level of stockout protection, shortage costs and inventory costs are based on the planned production requirement, which includes forecast and safety stock. Actually, as far as customer demand is concerned, no shortage occurs until the safety stock is depleted.

† Notes for Plan 3:

Column 2, number of days in each month from Table 6.5, line 7.

Column 3, each unit requires 5 hours' production time.

(4) Men required (2) ÷ (3)	(5) Men hired	(6) Hiring cost (5) × $200	(7) Men laid off	(8) Layoff cost (7) × $250
53				
47	0	0	6	1,500
30	0	0	17	4,250
25	0	0	5	1,250
33	8	1,600	0	0
58	25	5,000	0	0
		$6,600		$7,000

(4) Cumulative production	(5) Units short (1) − (4)	(6) Shortage cost (5) × $5	(7) Units excess (4) − (1)	(8) Inventory cost (7) × $1.50
1,443	407	$2,035		
2,690	585	2,925		
4,068	207	1,035		
5,446			321	$ 482
6,889			614	921
8,201			76	114
		$5,995		$1,517

(4) Units subcontracted (1) − (3)	(5) Subcontracting cost (4) × $2
970	$1,940
665	1,330
160	320
10	20
270	540
1,050	2,100
3,125	$6,250

TABLE 6.7

Comparison of the three plans

Strategy	Plan 1 *Exact production; vary work force*	Plan 2 *Constant work force; vary inventory and stockout*	Plan 3 *Constant low work force; subcontract*
Hiring cost...........	$ 6,600	0	0
Layoff cost...........	7,000	0	0
Excess inventory cost..	0	$1,517	0
Shortage cost........	0	5,995	0
Subcontracting cost...	0	0	$6,250
Total Cost	$13,600	$7,512	$6,250

Material cost for in-house production = $40 per unit.

Regular time pay rate = $4 per hour. Since each unit required five hours for processing, the labor under regular time = $20 per unit.

Overtime pay rate = $6 per hour. This becomes $30 per unit labor cost (5 hours × $6).

Subcontracting cost = $72 per unit, which includes the outside labor and materials.

Overtime capacity = 25 percent over the regular time capacity.

An unlimited supply of products is obtainable by subcontract.

FIGURE 6.7

Daily production rates for the three production plans

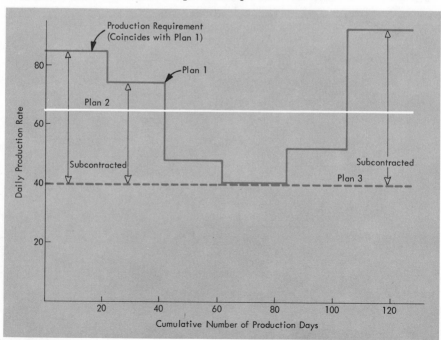

FIGURE 6.8

Three plans for satisfying a production requirement over the number of production days available

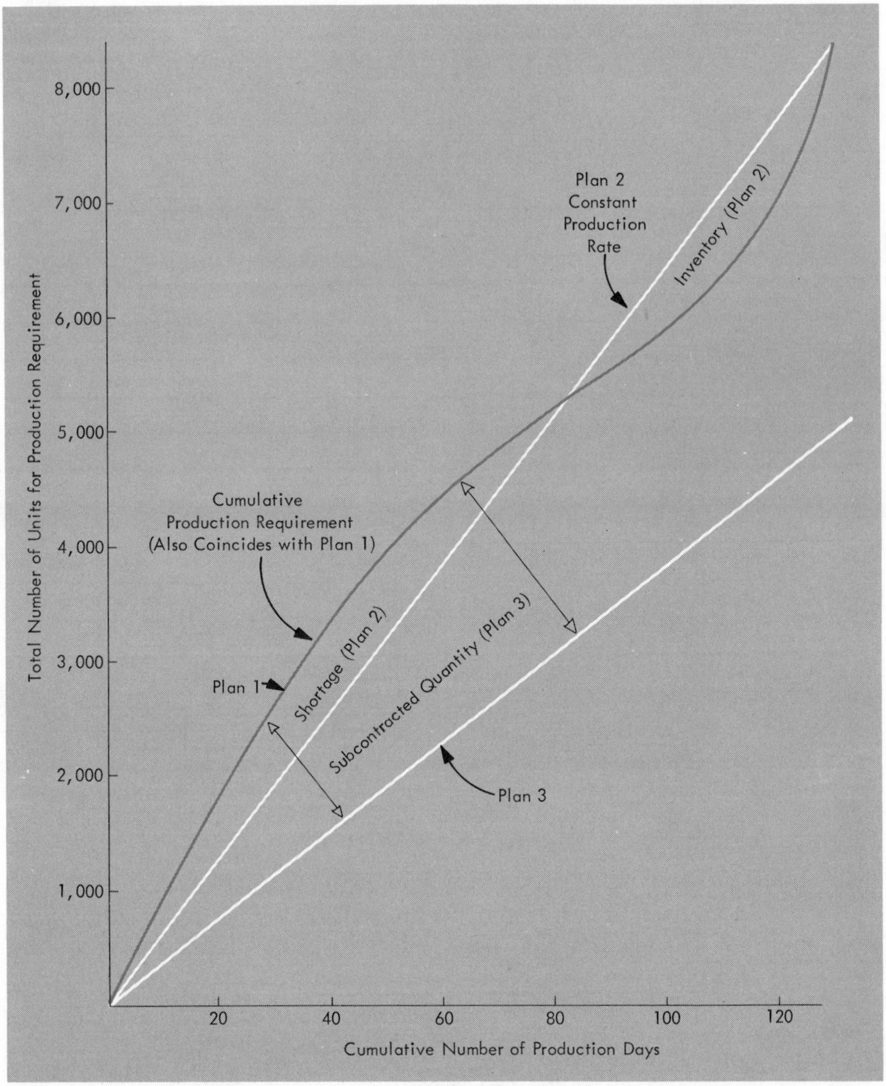

Beginning inventory = 400 units.

There is a constant work force of 30 men.

Figure 6.9 displays the additional costs incurred during the planning horizon of six months. The reasoning for each cost entry and the resulting equations is described below (conventional subscript notation is used: the first subscript refers to the row and the second subscript refers to the column).

FIGURE 6.9

Production planning by the transportation method of linear programming

	(1) January	(2) February	(3) March	(4) April	(5) May	(6) June	(7) Unused Capacity	Total Amount Available from Source
Beginning Inventory	[0] 400	[1.50]	[3]	[4.50]	[6]	[7.50]	[9]	400
Jan – Regular Time	[60] 1,056	[61.50]	[63]	[64.50]	[66]	[67.50]	[20]	1,056
– Overtime	[70] 264	[71.50]	[73]	[74.50]	[76]	[77.50]	[0]	264
– Subcontracted	[72] 130						[0] 9,870	10,000
Feb – Regular Time		[60] 912	[61.50]	[63]	[64.50]	[66]	[20]	912
– Overtime		[70] 228	[71.50]	[73]	[74.50]	[76]	[0]	228
– Subcontracted		[72] 285					[0] 9,715	10,000
Mar – Regular Time			[60] 1,000	[61.50]	[63]	[64.50] 8	[20]	1,008
– Overtime			[70]	[71.50]	[73]	[74.50]	[0] 251	251
– Subcontracted			[72]				[0] 10,000	10,000
Apr – Regular Time				[60] 850	[61.50] 94	[63] 64	[20]	1,008
– Overtime				[70]	[71.50]	[73]	[0] 251	251
– Subcontracted				[72]			[0] 10,000	10,000
May – Regular Time					[60] 1,056	[61.50]	[20]	1,056
– Overtime					[70] 264	[71.50]	[0]	264
– Subcontracted					[72]		[0] 10,000	10,000
Jun – Regular Time						[60] 960	[20]	960
– Overtime						[70] 240	[0]	240
– Subcontracted						[72] 314	[0] 9,686	10,000
Requirement	1,850	1,425	1,000	850	1,150	1,850	59,773	67,898

Beginning inventory. No carrying cost, if used in the first period, and $1.50 added for each month it remains unused. If carried into a subsequent six-month planning period, the cost is 6 months × $1.50 = $9.00. Therefore

$$x_{11} + x_{12} + x_{13} + x_{14} + x_{15} + x_{16} + x_{17} = 400$$

and

$$0(x_{11}) + 1.50(x_{12}) + 3(x_{13}) + 4.50(x_{14}) + 6(x_{15}) + 7.50(x_{16}) + 9(x_{17}) = \text{Cost}$$

Regular time. For January, the number of units producible under regular time with 30 men is 1,056 (30 men × 8 hours/day × 22 days ÷ 5 hours per unit). Costs, if used in January, are $60 ($20 labor + $40 materials); if carried over to February, $61.50 ($60 + carrying cost of $1.50); March, $63; etc. Because work force is constant, unused regular time will cost only the basic $20 for idle labor.

$$x_{21} + x_{22} + x_{23} + x_{24} + x_{25} + x_{26} + x_{27} = 1056$$
$$60x_{21} + 61.50x_{22} + 63x_{23} + 64.50x_{24} + 66x_{25} + 67.50x_{26} + 20x_{27} = \text{Cost}$$

Overtime. Allowance is one-fourth the regular time. Computation is similar to regular time except there is an additional 50 percent premium cost for labor. For January, allowed overtime is one-fourth the regular time, or $\frac{1}{4}(1056) = 264$.

Subcontracting. Costs are \$72 plus carrying cost if purchased and not used until later periods. To ease the working of the matrix, rather than use an unlimited amount available under subcontracting, an arbitrary amount is selected which exceeds the total demand for the planning period. If no units are subcontracted, the cost for subcontracting is zero. Then

$$x_{41} + x_{42} + x_{43} + x_{44} + x_{45} + x_{46} + x_{47} = 10,000$$

and

$$72x_{41} + 73.50x_{42} + 75x_{43} + 76.50x_{44} + 78x_{45} + 79.50x_{46} + 0x_{47} = \text{Cost}$$

Subsequent months are computed similarly, and Figure 6.9 is the complete linear programming matrix for the six-month planning horizon. Since no stockouts were allowed, production in any month to satisfy a preceding month's demand is not a feasible alternative. This is shown in the matrix by the colored assignments. Subcontracting units for future periods are also colored as unreasonable alternatives for this particular problem. Since subcontracting costs remain constant, there is no reason, for example, to subcontract in January for delivery in March or April. The best decision is to wait until the month occurs and then subcontract for what is needed. However, if there were cost changes, such as a discount for future delivery on a subcontract, then all periods would be included.

The optimal solution is shown by the values in the matrix. Demand for February, for example, is satisfied by producing 912 units during regular time, 228 units in overtime, and 285 subcontracted units. Two other solutions result in the same cost, and these are represented by a shift around either of the dashed paths in the center of the matrix. The linear programming supplement explains the technique for making the shift.

Linear decision rule. The linear decision rule was developed in the early 1950s by Holt, Modigliani, Muth, and Simon of the Carnegie Institute of Technology.[9] This method's objective is the derivation of linear equations or "decision rules" that can be used to specify the optimum production rate and work force level over some prescribed production planning horizon. In a well-known study, the developers applied the method to a paint company, for which they devised a month-by-month production plan for a one-year period. The objective of their study was to minimize the expected value of total cost (C_T) where

$$C_T = \text{Regular payroll costs} + \text{Hiring and layoff costs}$$
$$+ \text{Overtime costs} + \text{Inventory costs}$$

They argued that each of these cost categories may be approximated by a separate quadratic cost curve (as depicted in Figure 6.10).[10] Then, based on this presumption, they differentiated the equation and solved for the values

---

[9] Charles C. Holt, Franco Modigliani, John F. Muth, and Herbert A. Simon, *Planning Production, Inventories, and Work Force* (Englewood Cliffs, N.J.: Prentice-Hall, 1960).

[10] A quadratic curve is one that is defined by an equation of the second order (i.e., includes one or more squared terms).

FIGURE 6.10

Quadratic cost assumptions (represented by the light lines) in the linear decision rule

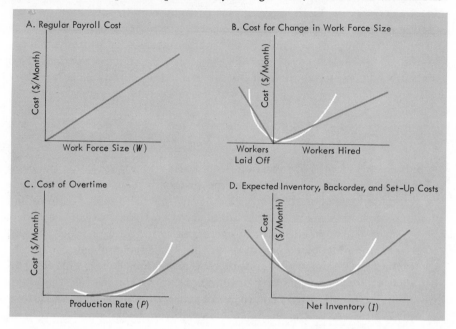

at the minimum point. Although the procedure, and especially the proof of the method, is somewhat involved, the result is two equations that, when real data is substituted for the variables, specify work force level and production rate.

It is interesting to look at the form of the two equations (from the paint factory study) developed from their detailed analysis of related costs:

$$P_t = \begin{Bmatrix} +0.463\ O_t \\ +0.234\ O_{t+1} \\ +0.111\ O_{t+2} \\ +0.046\ O_{t+3} \\ +0.013\ O_{t+4} \\ -0.002\ O_{t+5} \\ -0.008\ O_{t+6} \\ -0.010\ O_{t+7} \\ -0.009\ O_{t+8} \\ -0.008\ O_{t+9} \\ -0.007\ O_{t+10} \\ -0.005\ O_{t+11} \end{Bmatrix} + 0.993\ W_{t-1} + 153. - 0.464\ I_{t-1}$$

$$W_t = 0.743\ W_{t-1} + 2.09 - 0.010\ I_{t-1} + \begin{Bmatrix} +0.0101\ O_t \\ +0.0088\ O_{t+1} \\ +0.0071\ O_{t+2} \\ +0.0054\ O_{t+3} \\ +0.0042\ O_{t+4} \\ +0.0031\ O_{t+5} \\ +0.0023\ O_{t+6} \\ +0.0016\ O_{t+7} \\ +0.0012\ O_{t+8} \\ +0.0009\ O_{t+9} \\ +0.0006\ O_{t+10} \\ +0.0005\ O_{t+11} \end{Bmatrix}$$

where

P_t is the number of units of product that should be produced during
  the forthcoming month, t;

W_{t-1} is the number of employees in the work force at the beginning of
  the month (end of the previous month);

I_{t-1} is the number of units of inventory minus the number of units on
  backorder at the beginning of the month;

W_t is the number of employees that will be required for the current
  month, t (the number of employees that should be hired is therefore
  $W_t - W_{t-1}$);

O_t is a forecast of number of units of product that will be ordered for
  shipment during the current month, t;

O_{t+1} is the same for the next month, $t + 1$, etc.

One might be tempted to challenge the equations because the numeric
quantities are so specific. In the work force equation, for example, the work
force level for next month (W_t) is a function of the work force last month
(W_{t-1}), last month's inventory level (I_{t-1}), the forecast requirements for
the next 12 months $(O_t$ to $O_{t+11})$, *plus* 2.09. To add 2.09 workers to this
equation seems too precise, but it must be remembered that this is an optimal solution using the costs the authors developed. There is one bothersome
point, however. Notice that in the production equation the coefficients of
the future orders for products are negative beyond O_{t+5}. This states that the
need for products during that period has a depressing effect on next month's
production schedule. The authors explain this phenomenon by stating that
evidently the optimal method to prepare for future orders is first to build
up work force slowly, then increase production rate gradually.

To illustrate the simplicity in using the equations, suppose that we are
given the data in Table 6.8 and must decide on the work force and production rate for next month. In this case we are at the end of December with
a 12-month forecast ahead of us. In using the method, we are planning the
production level and work force needs for January.

Using the same equations as the authors used,

$$P_t = (\text{forecast effect}) + 0.993W_{t-1} + 153 - 0.464I_{t-1}$$

From Table 6.8,

$$P_t = 203.05 + 0.993(40) + 153 - 0.464(160) = 321.53$$

$$W_t = 0.743W_{t-1} + 2.09 - 0.01(I_{t-1}) + (\text{forecast effect})$$
$$= 0.743(40) + 2.09 - 0.01(160) + 12.489$$
$$= 42.70$$

Therefore our January production schedule is 322 units and our work force
is 43, which means we would have to hire three men.

There are three major drawbacks of the linear decision rule. First, there
is a severe limitation because application is restricted to quadratic cost relationships. Second, the difficulty involved in obtaining the cost information from the firm's operations may be prohibitively tedious. Third, since

TABLE 6.8

Data for linear decision rule equations

	(1)	(2) Production equation Coefficient	(3) Production equation Forecast effect $(1) \times (2)$	(4) Work force equation Coefficient	(5) Work force equation Forecast effect $(1) \times (4)$
Month	*Forecast*				
January..........	240	0.463	111.12	0.0101	2.424
February.........	250	0.234	58.50	0.0088	2.200
March...........	270	0.111	29.97	0.0071	1.917
April............	290	0.046	13.34	0.0054	1.566
May.............	310	0.013	4.03	0.0042	1.302
June............	320	−0.002	−0.64	0.0031	0.992
July............	330	−0.008	−2.64	0.0023	0.759
August..........	300	−0.010	−3.00	0.0016	0.480
September........	280	−0.009	−2.52	0.0012	0.336
October..........	270	−0.008	−2.16	0.0009	0.243
November........	250	−0.007	−1.75	0.0006	0.150
December........	240	−0.005	−1.20	0.0005	0.120
			203.05		12.489

Beginning inventory (I_{t-1}) = 160 units
Present work force size (W_{t-1}) = 40 men

there are no limitations placed on the variables, it may be possible to generate negative production and work force schedules. (A negative demand would indicate a shipment from the customer to the factory.) The persistence of this technique in the literature is due to its continued use in research as a benchmark against which other planning techniques can be compared.

Heuristic techniques. Heuristics originally was a branch of logic whose purpose was to investigate the methods of discovery and invention. More recently, "heuristic rules" have taken the meaning of useful guides to action. Such heuristics have sometimes been called rules of thumb, although not all such rules are good nor necessarily logical. To illustrate, a good decision rule would be: To avoid getting wet while walking in the rain, carry an umbrella. Another good rule would be: A way to increase one's salary within an organization is to work hard to advance in the corporate hierarchy. A bad rule would be: To live a long life, one should take up drinking, smoking, and auto racing. A heuristic rule need not be logical to be a good rule. If someone continually won at horse racing or in a lottery by applying a formula using his wife's weight times his age divided by the number of their children, it would be obligatory to say that in the historical chain of events his illogical heuristic rule performed well for him.

Management coefficients theory. In the real world, most decisions are made by heuristic rules, and a number of research studies have been undertaken to define the effective heuristic rules used by decision makers. One of the more widely reported efforts along this line is the management coefficients theory, developed by Bowman, in which a manager's past performance is used to devise formal decision rules for production planning.

Use of managements' own performance to establish guidelines for future decisions stems from their sensitivity or "feel" for situations. A manager may make a decision that he may not be able to fully explain—a result of numerous small occurrences, something he subconsciously derived, or an educated guess. The major difficulty, Bowman relates, is that a manager may delay reacting to a situation, and when he does, he may overreact. This, then, while producing a good decision on the average, introduces a significant and costly variance in his decisions. Since most cost relationships are relatively shallow and dish shaped, a deviation from the optimum does not increase cost rapidly. This deviation from the optimum may be peculiar to a manager (his own bias), but this bias is easily tolerable. His variance about the bias is the real culprit, and it is this that the management coefficients rule seeks to minimize.

The procedure to develop a rule based on managements' own performance involves a multiple regression analysis of management's past behavior in similar decisions. The regression analysis then provides the value of the coefficients for each variable in the equation as determined by past decisions. This equation is then used to indicate the future decision—still possessing bias but minimizing variance. The specific assumptions of Bowman's theory are summarized as follows.[11]

1. Experienced managers are quite aware of and sensitive to the criteria of a system.
2. Experienced managers are aware of the system variables that influence these criteria.
3. Managers, in their present position through a process of natural screening, make decisions (that is, implicitly operate decision rules) with a sense and intuition that relate the variables to these criteria imperfectly *—but they are more erratic than biased.*
4. Most cost or criteria surfaces, as a function of the decision variables, are shallow and dish shaped at the bottom (top), and even with bias in the manager's behavior, it is the far-out examples (variances) of behavior that are really expensive or damaging.
5. If managers' behavior had paralleled the decision rules with their average or mean coefficients, their experience would have been better according to the (their) criteria.

Search rules. As previously stated, Bowman's method used managements' performance for determining coefficients in production planning. An alternative approach is to search the realm of feasible solutions to find the value of the coefficients for least cost. Three of these search procedures, with brief descriptions, are:

1. Jones's parametric production planning. This model assumes quadratic costs for backorders, inventory, work force changes, and overtime costs, and utilizes a heuristic grid search technique to find the coefficients.[12]

2. Taubert's search decision rule. Using this approach permits the use of

[11] Edward H. Bowman, "Consistency and Optimality in Managerial Decision Making," *Management Science,* vol. 4 (January 1963), pp. 100–103.

[12] Curtis H. Jones, "Parametric Production Planning," *Management Science* (July 1967), pp. 843–66.

either quadratic or other types of cost structures for backorders, inventory, work force changes, and overtime costs; a heuristic search method is used to find the least cost coefficients.[13]

3. Vergin's scheduling by simulation. This approach develops a production plan through simulation and a search procedure. Linear, quadratic, and step costs are used.[14]

TABLE 6.9

A comparison of three approaches to production planning

Approach	Basic assumptions of the model	Criticisms
HMMS linear decision rule	Cost functions are quadratic. (These are used for mathematical convenience and are basic to the method).	May be a source of serious error. For example, in hiring and firing, quadratic assumptions defeat the notion of economies of scale.
Bowman's management coefficient's model	Managers are basically good decision makers. Statistical regression analysis develops more consistent decisions by eliminating "erratic" managerial behavior.	The specific manager being modeled may not, in fact, be a good decision maker. The model applies to a specific manager or group. Personnel changes invalidate the model, requiring that a new one be created. Statistical regression analysis is an arbitrary form to explain managerial behavior and may be erroneous.
Linear programming models	Cost functions are linear. Demand and supply forecasts are deterministic.	Ignores the added expense of small lots and the economies of scale for large lots. Ignores the effects of forecasting errors, although period-by-period scheduling allows some error correction through updating with actual, rather than forecasted, data as they occur.

For a more thorough discussion of these approaches along with the Deziel and Eilon (DE) rule, and the production switching model, see Samuel Eilon, "Five Approaches to Aggregate Production Planning," *AIIE Transactions*, vol. 7, no. 2, June 1975, pp. 118–131.

For further information regarding these search procedures, the reader should consult the original sources.

Table 6.9 compares three approaches to production planning presented

---

[13] William H. Taubert, "A Search Decision Rule for the Aggregate Scheduling Problem," *Management Science* (February 1968), pp. B343–59.

[14] Robert C. Vergin, "Production Planning under Seasonal Demand," *Journal of Industrial Engineering* (May 1966), pp. 260–66.

in this chapter: production planning by linear programming, with the linear decision rule, and by the management coefficients heuristic model.

IMPLEMENTATION

The Master Schedule

The master production schedule comes next in the sequence of events to produce a product or service. It is preceded by a demand forecast and a production plan. The production plan created a feasible schedule (usually by product group) while considering such factors as capacity constraints, normal work shifts, holidays, and vacation periods. The master schedule then breaks the production plan into greater detail and provides the means to keep a valid schedule by updating it with actual orders as they occur (rather than as they were forecasted), and actual production output (rather than that which had been previously planned). The updated master schedule then becomes an input to detailed scheduling, which specifies when a job should be started, where it is to be performed, and what materials, equipment, and manpower are required. In computerized systems, the master schedule is the input to the Materials Requirements Planning System (MRP), which is discussed in Chapter 9.

In many aspects a fine line is drawn between what might be called production planning and what may be classified as production scheduling. *Time* is the most useful index to separate planning and scheduling. In most industrial operations scheduling is done on a daily, weekly, or monthly basis. When the time horizon extends beyond a month for determining production rates and inventory levels, and especially when changes in the work force size are involved, this may more appropriately be called planning. When the time horizon shortens to a daily or hourly basis, the activity sometimes is referred to as dispatching, or having to decide specifically where production or service is to be performed, when, and by whom. Therefore, in a time sequence, planning becomes scheduling and scheduling becomes dispatching. There is also expediting, which follows dispatching and is a followup either to assure completion on time of high-priority orders or to chase down orders behind schedule. This text will include dispatching within the meaning of scheduling (the topic of the next chapter).

Unless the environment assumed in the production plan is realistic, it might not be possible to implement the results of the plan. For example, this chapter has presented various models to determine production rates and work force levels. The specific assumptions in these models are that hiring or laying off workers is possible, but this is not always so. The labor pool may be limited or worker skills specialized, or union contracts may contain special restrictions dealing with hiring or layoffs. Further, goodwill and the corporate image are frequently reflected in the stability of the work force. This combination of factors may mean that establishing costs for hiring or layoff for use in the models is a questionable guess, while the best decision may be to maintain a constant work force.

GUIDELINES FOR DEVELOPING AN EFFECTIVE PLANNING SYSTEM

1. Obtain an estimate of future sales—a year's demand on a monthly basis is common to most industries. Establish the desired level of safety stocks.
2. Develop meaningful and accurate costs for the relevant variables: costs involved in carrying inventory (storage, insurance, obsolescence, pilferage, breakage, deterioration, opportunity cost, etc.); costs of hiring, training, and layoff (severance pay, unemployment insurance, internal procedural costs to terminate an employee); costs for regular hourly rate and overtime rates (overtime rates must consider the supervision required, appropriate allocation of burden, and other costs resulting from overtime operation); backorder costs (loss of customer, loss of goodwill, additional paper work, and shipping costs).
3. Analyze the future sales estimates for seasonality, trends, and cyclical factors. Use a mathematical forecasting technique if appropriate.
4. Plan the overall production schedule for the entire period (usually a year). Either by a trial-and-error method, a mathematical method, or simulation, select a plan that provides an acceptable cost.
5. Review the results of the plan to assure that the strategies are feasible and implementable.

CONCLUSION

The problem of production planning is not an easy one by any means. The conditions for planning are filled with assumptions and uncertainties from start to finish. Questions arise about the source and method of forecasts, about the realism of cost assumptions for inventory, shortages, and work force level changes; and about the firm's ability to implement the plan once it is developed. The manager needs insight and courage to come up with a plan that he will stand behind.

It is interesting to note that in spite of the fact that forecasting techniques such as those discussed in this chapter have been around for many years, many firms do not use them in their planning. All too often they rely on salesmen's estimates or managerial opinions, without developing a meaningful relationship with historical performance. Good forecasting alone would improve the profit performance of many firms.

The most-used planning technique is the graphical trial-and-error approach. Mathematical techniques still have shortcomings because of limitations in the model size and in the solution procedure. Simulation methods appear to hold the greatest promise, simply because a variety of alternative decision rules can be explored once the simulation program is operational. Also, the assumptions of the simulation model may be specified with more freedom, which will help minimize the difficulties encountered in implementation. At the present time, simulation costs are usually high since applications are individually tailored to the firm's needs, but costs should decrease as more generally usable models become available.

PROPOSITIONS

Propositions contrasting services and manufacturing systems relative to the design of production planning systems

Product: The primary consideration in forecasting demand for a service product is the size of the customer population that is, or will be, in the vicinity of the service system. In manufacturing, the location of customers relative to the production system commonly has little influence on the demand forecast.

Technology of Transformation: In services, change in system capacity to adjust for changes in demand affects the specification of the service product. In manufacturing, a change in system capacity has little bearing on the specifications of the end product.

Operating-control system: In services, production smoothing is carried out by such means as appointment schedules since the customer must be in the system. In manufacturing, production smoothing may be carried out by such means as altering inventory levels or workforce size and creating backorders.

Workforce: Because of the inherent variability in the service product, there is generally only a loose relationship between the size of the direct workforce and the output of the service system. In manufacturing, there is generally a close (often linear) relationship between the size of the direct workforce and output of the manufacturing system.

REVIEW AND DISCUSSION QUESTIONS

1. What basic feature distinguishes information from data?
2. What strategies are used by the following businesses to influence demand? Supermarkets, airlines, hospitals, banks, and cereal manufacturers.
3. From the choice of simple moving average, weighted moving average, exponential smoothing, and regression analysis, which forecasting technique would you consider the most accurate? Why?
4. What is the main disadvantage of daily forecasting using regression analysis?
5. Give some heuristic rules that might apply to: Investing in the stock market, selecting a family dentist, buying a used car, deciding how to dress for the day, and choosing from several employment opportunities.
6. What is the "production planning problem?" What major decisions must be made to solve it?
7. Contrast linear programming with the linear decision rule in terms of the basic approach and basic assumptions of each.

8. Discuss the basic differences between the mean absolute deviation (MAD) and the standard deviation.

9. What implications do the existence of forecast errors have for the search for ultra-sophisticated statistical forecasting models?

PROBLEMS

1. Sunrise Baking Company markets doughnuts through a chain of food stores and has been experiencing over- and underproduction because of forecasting errors. The following data are their demands in dozens of doughnuts for the past four weeks. The bakery is closed Saturday, so Friday's production must satisfy both Saturday and Sunday demand.

	4 weeks ago	3 weeks ago	2 weeks ago	Last week
Monday.........	2,200	2,400	2,300	2,400
Tuesday.........	2,000	2,100	2,200	2,200
Wednesday......	2,300	2,400	2,300	2,500
Thursday........	1,800	1,900	1,800	2,000
Friday..........	1,900	1,800	2,100	2,000
Saturday ⎫ Sunday ⎭	2,800	2,700	3,000	2,900

Make a forecast for this week on the following basis:
   a. Daily, using simple four-week moving average.
   b. Daily, using a weighted average of 0.40, 0.30, 0.20, and 0.10 for the past four weeks.
   c. By least squares regression for Wednesday, Thursday, and Friday.

2. In planning its purchases of ingredients, Sunrise Baking Company makes a weekly forecast for each product. Its bread production had been forecast for last week at 22,000 loaves; however, only 21,000 loaves were actually demanded.
   a. Using exponential smoothing with $\alpha = 0.10$, what would Sunrise's forecast be for this week?
   b. Supposing this week's demand actually turns out to be 22,500, what would the new forecast be for the following week?

3. With the present popularity of ecology, the Ponce de Leon Purified Water Company has found that demand for its spring water dispensers has been growing. It appears that its present water sources will not be sufficient, and it would like to have some idea of its future needs in order to advise Tiny Peachfork, its divining rod specialist, how many new springs he must find. De Leon's demands for spring water for last year were as follows.

Month	Demand	Month	Demand
January.............	4,200 gal.	July................	5,300 gal.
February............	4,300 "	August..............	4,900 "
March...............	4,000 "	September..........	5,400 "
April................	4,400 "	October............	5,700 "
May.................	5,000 "	November..........	6,300 "
June................	4,700 "	December...........	6,000 "

a. Using least squares regression analysis, what would you estimate demand to be for December of next year? Construct a graph showing the two-year period.

b. To be reasonably confident of having adequate water, de Leon decides to use three standard errors of estimate for safety. What water supply should it plan on having on hand?

4. The historical demand for a product is: January, 80; February, 100; March, 60; April, 80; and May, 90.

a. Using a simple four-month moving average, what is the forecast for June? If June experienced a demand of 100, what would your forecast be for July?

b. Using single exponential smoothing with $\alpha = 0.20$, if the forecast for January had been 70, compute what the exponentially smoothed forecast would have been for the remaining months through June.

c. Using least squares regression analysis, compute a forecast for June, July, and August.

d. Using a weighted moving average with weights of 0.30, 0.25, 0.20, 0.15, and 0.10, what is June's forecast?

5. Precision Portable Fuel Company manufactures a line of small gasoline-operated electric generators for use as temporary power sources, primarily by vacationers. The cost for producing a generator during regular work hours is $50 each; the cost for production during overtime is $75 each. Units that are produced in one time period but carried forward to satisfy future demand cost $5 per time period held. The inventory on hand at the beginning of the planning period is 50 units.

The following matrix-type table contains the available production capacity and the demands for each period.

Sales Periods

Production Periods (Sources)		1	2	3	4	Inventory	Unused Capacity	Total Capacity
Beginning Inventory								50
I	Regular Time							700
	Overtime							350
II	Regular Time							700
	Overtime							250
III	Regular Time							700
	Overtime							250
IV	Regular Time							700
	Overtime							250
Total Requirements		800	800	800	800	500	250	3,950

a. Indicate the appropriate costs on the matrix.

b. Develop a feasible production plan.

6. While the text treated production planning for a single product by using the transportation method of linear programming, multiple products may be planned in a similar way. The following problem considers three perishable products.

The same productive equipment is used to produce products K, L, and M. The objective is to meet the demands for the three products at minimum cost by resorting to overtime. The demand forecast for the next four months, in required hours, is as follows.

Product	April	May	June	July
K..................	600	800	800	1,200
L..................	700	600	900	1,100
M..................	500	700	700	850

Because the product deteriorates rapidly, there is a high loss in quality, and consequently a high carryover cost into subsequent periods. Each hour's production carried into future months costs $3 per productive hour of K, $4 for L, and $5 for M.

Production can take place either during regular working hours or during overtime. Regular time is paid at $4 when working on product K, $5 for L, and $6 for M. Overtime premium is 50 percent and is limited to half the number of regular-time hours.

The available production capacity for regular time and overtime is

	April	May	June	July
Regular time.........	1,500	1,300	1,800	1,700
Overtime............	750	650	900	850

a. Set the problem up in matrix form and show appropriate costs.
b. Show a feasible solution.

7. Milford Television and Electronics, a small color-TV manufacturer, must come up with a production plan for the next 12 months. Since Milford is a small concern located in a quiet Midwestern city, the owner/president feels that he has an employment obligation to the citizenry. Although he feels free to change the employment level at the start of each year, he feels there should be no further changes. Additionally, all employees should put in full work weeks, even if this is not the lowest cost alternative. The forecast for the next 12 months is as follows.

Month	Forecast demand	Month	Forecast demand
January...............	600	July...................	200
February.............	800	August................	200
March...............	900	September.............	300
April................	600	October...............	700
May.................	400	November.............	800
June.................	300	December.............	900

Manufacturing cost is $200 per set, equally divided between materials and labor. Inventory storage costs are $5 per month. A shortage of sets results in lost sales and is estimated to cost an overall $20 per unit short.

The inventory on hand at the beginning of the planning period is 200 units. Ten man-hours are required per TV set. The work day is eight hours.

Develop an aggregate production schedule for the year using a constant work force. For simplicity, assume 22 working days each month except July, when the plant closes down for three weeks' vacation (leaving seven working days).

8. National Appliance Service, Inc., would like an evaluation of their forecasting model. Customer demand for appliance repair is sometimes stable for several weeks and then may change (perhaps due to such causes as weather changes or vacation periods when people stay home to allow the repairman to conduct the service).

   Forecasts for the past eight weeks along with the actual demands which occurred during those weeks were as follows:

	Number of service calls	
Week	*Forecasted*	*Actual*
1.....................	140	137
2.....................	140	133
3.....................	140	150
4.....................	140	160
5.....................	140	180
6.....................	150	170
7.....................	150	185
8(most recent week)....	150	205

   a. Compute the mean absolute deviation (MAD) of the forecast errors.
   b. Using the running sum of forecast errors (RSFE) compute the tracking signal.
   c. Based on the results of *a* and *b*, comment on the forecast model used.

9. Develop a production schedule to produce the exact production requirements by varying the work force size for the following problem. Use the example in the chapter shown on Tables 6.5 through 6.7 as a guide (Plan 1).

   The monthly forecast for product X for January, February, and March are 1,000, 1,500, and 1,200 respectively. Safety stock policy recommends that one half of the forecast for that month be defined as safety stock. There are 22 working days in January, 19 in February, and 21 in March. Beginning inventory is 500 units.

   Following are additional data: Manufacturing cost is $200 per unit, storage costs are $3 per unit per month, standard pay rate is $6 per hour, overtime rate is $9 per hour, cost of stockout is $10 per unit per month, marginal cost of subcontracting is $10 per unit, hiring and training cost is $200 per man, layoff costs are $300 per man, and production man hours required per unit is 10.

SELECTED BIBLIOGRAPHY

Anthony, Robert N. *Planning and Control Systems: A Framework for Analysis.* Boston: Harvard University Press, 1965.

Bowman, E. H.   "Production Planning by the Transportation Method of Linear Programming," *Journal of the Operations Research Society* (February 1956).

Brown, Robert G.   *Smoothing, Forecasting, and Prediction of Discrete Time Series.* Englewood Cliffs, N.J.: Prentice-Hall, 1963.

————   *Statistical Forecasting for Inventory Control.* New York: McGraw-Hill, 1959.

Buffa, Elwood S., and Taubert, William H.   *Production-Inventory Systems: Planning and Control.* Rev. ed. Homewood, Ill.: Richard D. Irwin, Inc., 1972.

Eilon, Samuel   *Elements of Production Planning and Control.* New York: Macmillan, 1962.

————   "Five Approaches to Aggregate Production Planning," *AIIE Transactions.* (June 1975).

Greene, James H.   *Production and Inventory Control: Systems and Decisions.* Rev. ed. Homewood, Ill.: Richard D. Irwin, 1974.

Holt, Charles C., Modigliani, Franco, and Simon, Herbert A.   "A Linear Decision Rule for Production and Employment Scheduling," *Management Science* (October 1955).

————, **Modigliani, Franco, Muth, John F., and Simon, Herbert A.**   *Planning Production, Inventories, and Work Force.* Englewood Cliffs, N.J.: Prentice-Hall, 1960.

Magee, J. F., and Boodman, D. M.   *Production-Planning and Inventory Control.* 2nd ed. New York: McGraw-Hill, 1967.

Niland, Powell   *Production Planning, Scheduling, and Inventory Control.* New York: Macmillan, 1970.

Parker, G. C., and Segura, Edelberto L.   "How to Get a Better Forecast," *Harvard Business Review,* vol. 49, no. 2 (March–April 1971), pp. 99–109.

Wight, Oliver W.   *Production and Inventory Management in the Computer Age,* Boston, Mass.: Cahners Books, 1974.

Supplement to chapter six

Simulation

. . . THE TROUBLE BEGAN while the astronauts were on the far side of the moon, out of communication with earth, during the 13th revolution, the one that was supposed to have culminated in the lunar landing. The lunar module with Astronauts Duke and Young had separated from the command and service module carrying Astronaut Mattingly. At 2:36 (EST) Commander Mattingly was supposed to have fired the SPS engine to push his spacecraft out of its elliptical orbit into a nearly circular orbit around the moon where he would stay during the next three days, while his fellow astronauts explored the moon.

Landing "Waved Off"

As the two spacecraft came around the edge of the moon into communication with earth, however, they reported that Commander Mattingly had run into trouble with the controls that position the SPS engine for firing and thus hadn't fired the engine.

As the result the lunar module was "waved off" from its planned lunar landing. The main reason was that if it turned out the SPS engine was inoperable, the lunar module, with its rocket engines still unused, could return to the command and service module. The lunar module rockets could then be used to return the spacecraft to earth.

Ground controllers, at that time, calculated that they had about 10 hours to discover the cause of the trouble and decide whether to go ahead and attempt the lunar landing or whether to use the lunar module engines for a return to earth. After that time, the lunar module's orbital path would have taken it too far from the planned landing site for a moon landing without undue maneuvering resulting in excessive fuel use.

. . . The hasty simulations of what would happen to the spacecraft if the engine fired while it was rapidly wiggling left and right showed it would "present no structural hazard to the spacecraft," Apollo controllers said. Thus, on their 15th revolution about the moon, the lunar module astronauts were told to go ahead and make the landing on the next revolution, a little less than six hours later than planned. . . .[1]

This excerpt from a news release serves to introduce the topic of simulation in a rather dramatic context. Nevertheless, the procedures followed by ground control in tracing the possible effects of a malfunctioning spacecraft engine in many respects mirror the simulation procedures employed by earthbound production managers in dealing with problems in their operations. Indeed, in both instances simulation is used to provide insight into the behavior of a dynamic system in order to make predictions about how that system will respond to changing conditions. In this supplement we will describe how simulation models generate such predictions about dynamic systems in general and illustrate how they are constructed.

Our plan of presentation is as follows. First we will define simulation and comment briefly on where it is used. Then we will present a simple problem as a vehicle to relate the mechanics of the widely used Monte Carlo method of simulation, and we will consider general simulation methodology and computerization. Next we will discuss some large-scale simulation models used to study "total systems." We will conclude the supplement with a discussion of the pros and cons of simulation as it relates to experimentation on the real system and to mathematical models in general.

---

[1] Jerry Bishop, *The Wall Street Journal*, April 21, 1972.

NATURE OF SIMULATION

The term *simulation* has various meanings, depending upon the area where it is being applied.[2] In business situations, however, it generally refers to using a digital computer to perform experiments on a model of a real system. Such experiments may be undertaken before the real system is operational so as to aid in its design, or to see how the system might react to changes in its operating rules, or to evaluate the system's response to changes in its structure. Simulation is particularly appropriate to situations where the size and/or complexity of the problem makes the use of optimizing techniques difficult or impossible. Thus job shops, which are characterized as complex queuing problems, have been studied extensively via simulation, as have certain types of inventory, layout, and maintenance problems (to name but a few).

In addition, simulation is useful in training managers and workers in how the real system operates, in demonstrating the effects of changes in system variables, in real-time control (as in the moon landing), and in developing new theories about mathematical or organizational relationships. A list of the areas in which simulation methods are currently used is given in Table S.6.1.

It is commonly suggested by simulation teachers that the best way to learn about simulation is to simulate. Therefore we will turn to a simple simulation problem and develop the topic as we go along.

A simulation example: Al's fish market

Al, the owner of a small fish market, wishes to evaluate his daily ordering policy for codfish. His current rule is *order the amount demanded the previous day,* but he thinks another rule should be considered as well. Al purchases codfish at $0.20 a pound and sells it for $0.60 a pound. The fish are ordered at the end of each day and are received the following morning. Any fish not sold during the day are thrown away.

From past experience Al has determined that his demand for codfish has ranged between 30 and 80 pounds per day. He has also kept a record of the relative frequency with which each amount has been demanded and has tabulated this information as follows.

Demand per day	Relative frequency
30–40 pounds	1/10
40–50	3/10
50–60	2/10
60–70	3/10
70–80	1/10

---

[2] Webster's defines "to simulate" as "to assume or have the mere appearance of without reality." The following activities represent other types of simulation: dry-run testing of a chemical plant, wind-tunnel testing of a scale model airplane, and business gaming, wherein participants compete in managing hypothetical firms.

TABLE S.6.1

Current application of simulation methods

Air traffic control queuing
Aircraft maintenance scheduling
Airport design
Ambulance location and dispatching
Assembly line scheduling
Bank teller scheduling
Bus (city) scheduling
Circuit design
Clerical processing system design
Communication system design
  Computer time sharing
  Telephone traffic routing
  Message system
  Mobile communications
Computer memory-fabrication test-
  facility design
Consumer behavior prediction
  Brand selection
  Promotion decisions
  Advertising allocation
  Court system resource allocation
Distribution system design
  Warehouse location
  Mail (post office)
  Soft drink bottling
  Bank courier
  Intrahospital material flow
Enterprise models
  Steel production
  Hospital
  Shipping line
  Railroad operations
  School district
Equipment scheduling
  Aircraft
Facility layout
  Pharmaceutical center
Financial forecasting
  Insurance
  Schools
  Computer leasing
Insurance manpower hiring decisions
Grain terminal operation
Harbor design

Industry models
  Textiles
  Petroleum (financial aspects)
Information system design
Intergroup communication (sociological studies)
Inventory reorder rule design
  Aerospace
  Manufacturing
  Military logistics
  Hospitals
Job shop scheduling
  Aircraft parts
  Metals forming
  Work-in-process control
  Shipyard
Library operations design
Maintenance scheduling
  Airlines
  Glass furnaces
  Steel furnaces
  Computer field service
National manpower adjustment system
Natural resource (mine) scheduling
  Iron ore
  Strip mining
Parking facility design
Numerically controlled production facility design
Personnel scheduling
  Inspection department
  Spacecraft trips
Petrochemical process design
  Solvent recovery
Police response system design
Political voting prediction
Rail freight car dispatching
Railroad traffic scheduling
Steel mill scheduling
Taxi dispatching
Traffic light timing
Truck dispatching and loading
University financial and operational forecasting
Urban traffic system design
Water resources development

Source: James R. Emshoff and Roger L. Sisson, *Design and Use of Computer Simulation Models* (New York: Macmillan, 1972), p. 264.

After some deliberation, Al settles on the following ordering rule, which he would like to compare with his current rule: *Each day order the amount of fish that was demanded in the past* (that is, the expected value based on past daily demands) which in this case is

$$(35 \times 1/10) + (45 \times 3/10) + (55 \times 2/10) + (65 \times 3/10) \times (75 \times 1/10)$$
$$= 55 \text{ pounds}$$

Analysis. We will designate Al's current ordering rule as rule 1 and the alternative rule as rule 2. These rules can be stated mathematically, as follows.

$$\text{Rule 1:} \quad Q_n = D_{n-1}$$
$$\text{Rule 2:} \quad Q_n = 55$$

where

$$Q_n = \text{Amount ordered on day } n$$
$$D_{n-1} = \text{Amount demanded the previous day}$$

These ordering rules can be compared in terms of Al's daily profits, which can be stated as follows.

$$P_n = (S_n \times p) - (Q_n \times c)$$

where

$$P_n = \text{Profit on day } n$$
$$S_n = \text{Amount sold on day } n$$
$$p = \text{Selling price per pound}$$
$$Q_n = \text{Amount ordered on day } n \text{ (as defined above)}$$
$$c = \text{Cost per pound}$$

To prepare the problem of simulation at this point requires that we develop some method of generating demand each day in order to compare the two decision rules. One way this could be done is to treat demand generation as a game of roulette,[3] wherein the roulette wheel would be partitioned in such a way that the slots into which a roulette ball might fall would be associated with specific levels of demand. For example, if the wheel has 100 slots, we might apportion them so that 10 of them represent a demand for 35 pounds, 30 of them represent a demand for 45 pounds, 20 of them represent a demand for 55 pounds, and so forth. Proceeding this way, and using the relative frequencies listed previously, would permit each turn of the wheel to simulate one day of demand for Al's fish.

While a roulette wheel has a certain appeal, a more efficient way of generating demand is to use a probability distribution and a random number table. This approach entails converting the relative frequency values to probabilities. Then specific numbers are attached to each probability value to reflect the proportion of numbers from 00 to 99 that corresponds to each probability entry.[4] For example, 00 to 09 represent 10 percent of the numbers from 00 to 99, 10 to 39 represent 30 percent of the numbers, 40 to 59 represent 20 percent of the numbers, and so on. The probabilities

---

[3] The term *Monte Carlo*, taken from the name of the famous European gambling casino, is applied to simulation problems in which a chance process is used to generate occurrences in the system.

[4] A *cumulative* probability distribution is sometimes developed to help assure that each random number is associated with only one level of demand. It is our experience, however, that this step, as well as graphing such a distribution, is not necessary in understanding or performing a simulation.

TABLE S.6.2

Demand per day	Relative frequency	Probability	Random number interval
35......................	1/10	0.10	00–09
45......................	3/10	0.30	10–39
55......................	2/10	0.20	40–59
65......................	3/10	0.30	60–89
75......................	1/10	0.10	90–99

and their associated random numbers (arranged in intervals) are given in Table S.6.2.

With this information and a random number table (Table S.6.3), we are ready to carry out a hand simulation to determine the relative desirability of ordering rules 1 and 2. If the initial demand for day zero is arbitrarily set at the average demand level of 55 pounds and a 20-day period is selected as the run length, each rule would be tested as follows.

1. Draw a random number from Table S.6.3 (The starting point on the table is immaterial but a consistent, unvaried pattern should be followed in drawing random numbers. Taking the first two digits in each entry in row 1, then row 2, row 3, etc., would be satisfactory in this regard.)
2. Find the random number interval associated with the random number.
3. Read the daily demand (D_n) corresponding to the random number interval.
4. Calculate the amount sold (S_n). If $D_n \geqslant Q_n$, then $S_n = Q_n$; if $D_n < Q_n$, $S_n = D_n$.
5. Calculate daily profit [$P_n = (S_n \times p) - (Q_n \times c)$].
6. Repeat steps 1 to 5 until 20 days have been simulated.

TABLE S.6.3

Uniformly distributed random numbers

06433	80674	24520	18222	10610	05794	37515	48619	02866
39208	47829	72648	37414	75755	01717	29899	78817	03500
89884	59051	67533	08123	17730	95862	08034	19473	03071
61512	32155	51906	61662	64130	16688	37275	51262	11569
99653	47635	12506	88535	36553	23757	34209	55803	96275
95913	11045	13772	76638	48423	25018	99041	77529	81360
55804	44004	13122	44115	01691	50541	00147	77685	58788
35334	82410	91601	40617	72876	33967	73830	15405	96554
59729	88646	76487	11622	96297	24160	09903	14041	22917
57383	89317	63677	70119	94739	25875	38829	68377	43918
30574	06039	07967	32422	76791	39725	53711	93385	13421
81307	13314	83580	79974	45929	85113	72208	09858	52104
02410	96385	79007	54039	21410	86980	91772	93307	34116
18969	87444	52233	62319	08598	09066	95288	04794	01534
87803	80514	66800	62297	80198	19347	73234	86265	49096
68397	10538	15438	62311	72844	60203	46412	05943	79232
28520	54247	58729	10854	99058	18260	38765	90038	94200
44285	09452	15867	70418	57012	72122	36634	97283	95943
80299	22510	33517	23309	57040	29285	07870	21913	72958
84842	05748	90894	61658	15001	94055	36308	41161	37341

TABLE S.6.4

Hand simulation of Al's fish market

Day	RN	D_n	Rule 1			Rule 2		
			Q_n	S_n	P_n	Q_n	S_n	P_n
0.............	..	55	..	...	...	..	...	...
1............	06	35	55	35	$ 10	55	35	$ 10
2.............	39	45	35	35	14	"	45	16
3.............	89	65	45	45	18	"	55	22
4............	61	65	65	65	26	"	55	22
5............	99	75	65	65	26	"	55	22
6............	95	75	75	75	30	"	55	22
7............	55	55	75	55	18	"	55	22
8............	35	45	55	45	16	"	45	18
9............	57	55	45	45	18	"	55	22
10............	59	55	55	55	22	"	55	22
11............	30	45	55	45	16	"	45	16
12............	81	65	45	45	18	"	55	22
13............	02	35	65	35	8	"	35	26
14............	18	45	35	35	14	"	45	16
15............	87	65	45	45	18	"	55	22
16............	68	65	65	65	26	"	55	22
17............	28	45	65	45	14	"	45	16
18............	44	55	45	45	18	"	55	22
19............	80	65	55	55	22	"	55	22
20............	84	65	65	65	26	"	55	22
Total.....		1,120	1,110	1,000	$378	1,100	1,010	$404
Daily average.		56	55.5	50.00	$ 18.90	55	50.5	$ 20.20

The results of this procedure, along with the random numbers (*RN*) used, are summarized in Table S.6.4. We will compare these results with those achieved by a computer simulation of the problem later in the supplement.

SIMULATION METHODOLOGY

Figure S.6.1 is a flowchart of the major phases in carrying out a simulation study. To the right of the chart are listed the key factors or decisions that pertain to each phase. In this section we will develop each of these phases with particular reference to the key factors.

Problem definition

Problem definition for purposes of simulation differs little from problem definition for any other tool of analysis. Essentially, it entails the specification of objectives and the identification of the relevant controllable and uncontrollable variables of the system to be studied. The variables of course affect the performance of the system and determine the extent to which the objectives are achieved. The objective of a fish market owner was given as maximizing the profit on sales of codfish. The relevant controllable variable (i.e., under the control of the decision maker) was taken as the

FIGURE S.6.1

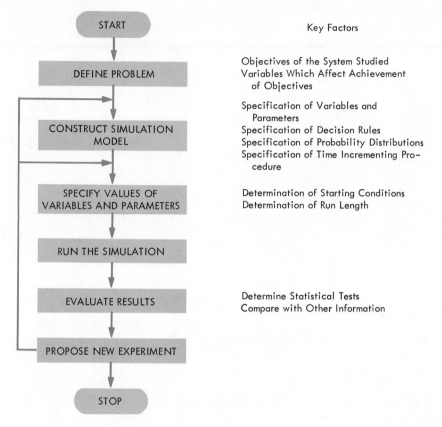

ordering rule; the relevant uncontrollable variables were taken as the daily demand levels for codfish and the amount of codfish sold. Other objectives could have been to maximize profit from the sale of all fish or to maximize profit from the sale of herring. Other variables, such as the number of display cases and the use of customer priority rules, could have been identified, and it could be argued that demand could be controlled in part by charging a higher or lower price.

Construct simulation model

A *model* is a representation of a real system. A *simulation model* of a real system is a model in which the system's elements are represented by arithmetic, analogic, or logical processes that can be executed, either manually or by computer, to predict the dynamic properties of the real system.[5] This ability to deal with dynamic systems is one of the features that distinguishes

---

[5] A simulation can also represent a model of a system as well as the system itself. One might, for example, construct a cost model of an inventory system and, because of intractable analytical problems, estimate the properties of the model by simulation.

these models from other models used in problem solving. In the fish market problem, an inventory formula, along with appropriate cost data, could have been used to determine the optimum ordering rule, but a simulation run would still be necessary to determine the effects of this rule on a day-to-day basis. Similarly, problems solved through the use of techniques such as queuing theory or linear programming yield only a course of action to follow. It remains for simulation (or the actual operation of the system) to gauge the performance of the solution achieved.

Another feature that distinguishes simulation from these other techniques is the fact that a simulation model must be custom built for each problem situation. (A linear programming model, in contrast, can be used in a variety of situations with only a restatement of the values for the objective function and constraint equations.) The unique nature of simulation models, in turn, means that the procedures discussed below for building and executing a model represent a synthesis of various approaches to simulation and are guidelines rather than rigid rules (such as those developed from rigorous mathematical deduction).

Specification of variables and parameters. The first step in the construction of a simulation model entails determining which properties of the real system are to be allowed to vary and which ones are to remain constant throughout the simulation run. Those allowed to change are termed *variables* and those held constant are termed *parameters*. In the fish market example, the variables were the amount of fish ordered, the amount demanded, and the amount sold; the parameters were the cost of the fish and the selling price of the fish. In most simulations the focus is on the status of the variables at different points in time, such as the number of pounds of fish demanded and sold each day.

The determination of which variables from the real system are to be included in the model, as well as how many, depends upon the purpose of the simulation as defined by the problem statement. As a general rule, it is desirable to keep the number of variables as low as possible, at least during the initial development of the model. This obviously simplifies the writing and debugging of the computer program and facilitates the validation of the model in trial runs. Once the program is tested, additional variables can be added to improve the representation of the system modeled.

Specification of decision rules. Decision or operating rules are sets of conditions under which the behavior of the simulation model is observed. These rules are either directly or indirectly the focus of most simulation studies. In our example we compared decision rules (in two separate simulations), and thus they were the focus of the analysis. In other situations the focus of the study may be to determine what goes on in the system as currently designed, but even here the way in which the system works is dependent upon the existing decision rules. For example, we may wish to examine the time it takes to process a claim in an insurance office after the introduction of a computerized information system. However, even though the focus of attention is on computer processing time and the manner of routing a claimant's form to and from the computer, the fact that the particular asssumptions about the operation must be formalized into decision rules is inescapable.

In many simulations, decision rules are in fact priority rules (for example, which customer to serve first, which job to process first), and in certain situations they can be quite involved in that they take into account a large number of variables in the system. For example, an inventory ordering rule could be stated in such a way that the amount to order would depend upon the amount in inventory, the amount previously ordered but not received, the amount backordered, and the desired safety stock.

Specification of probability distributions.   Two categories of distributions can be used for simulation: empirical frequency distributions and mathematical frequency distributions. In the fish market example we used

FIGURE S.6.2

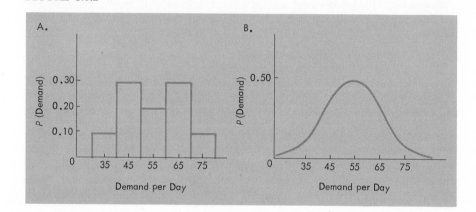

an empirical distribution—one derived from observing the relative frequency of various demands for fish. In other words, it is a custom-built demand distribution that is relevant only to our particular problem. It might have happened, however, that the demand for fish closely approximated some known distribution, such as the normal, Poisson, or gamma. If this were the case, data collection and input to the simulation would be greatly simplified.

To illustrate the procedure in using a known distribution, let us suppose that, instead of using the empirical demand distribution for fish (shown in histogram form in Figure S.6.2A), it was decided that demand could be described by a normal distribution having a mean of 55 and a standard deviation of 10 (Figure S.6.2B).[6] Under this assumption, the generation of daily demand would employ a table of randomly distributed *normal* num-

---

[6] In practice, standard "goodness-of-fit" statistical tests, such as chi square, are used to determine how well a particular, known distribution approximates the empirical frequency distribution. It is rather clear in this case, however, that the normal distribution would be a very poor approximation of the empirical distribution and therefore should not be used.

TABLE S.6.5

Randomly distributed normal numbers

1.23481	.56176	-.23812
1.54221	1.49673	.18124
.19126	1.22318	-1.35882
-.54929	1.00826	-1.45402
1.14463	-2.75470	-.28185
-.63248	1.11241	1.16515
-.29988	-.55806	-.28278
-.32855	-.49094	1.64410
.35331	-.04187	.32468
.72576	-.98726	.34506
.04406	-.26990	.20790
-1.66161	.52304	.70681
.02629	.24826	.16760
1.18250	-1.19941	-.17022
-.87214	1.08497	2.24938
-.23153	.04496	-.95339
-.04776	-.00926	-.96893
-.31052	-.94171	.36915
-.93166	.82752	

bers (or deviates) in conjunction with the statistical formula $D_n = \bar{x} + Z_n\sigma$ (terms defined below), derived from the Z transform used to enter a standard normal table.[7] The specific steps are as follows:

1. Draw a five- or six-digit figure from Table S.6.5. The entries in this table are randomly developed deviate values that pertain to a normal distribution having a mean of zero and a standard deviation of one. The term *deviate* refers to the number of standard deviations some value is from the mean, and in this case represents the number of standard deviations that any day's demand will be from the mean demand. In the above formula for D_n, it would be the value for Z on day n. If we are simulating day 1 and using the first entry in Table S.6.5, then $Z_1 = 1.23481$. A negative deviate value means simply that the particular level of demand to be found by using it will be less than the mean, not that demand will be a negative value.

2. Substitute the value for Z_1, along with the predetermined values for $\bar{x}$ and σ, into the formula

$$D_n = \bar{x} + Z_n\sigma$$

where

---

[7] The basic formula is $Z = \dfrac{x - \mu}{\sigma}$, which, when restated in terms of x, appears as $x = \mu + Z\sigma$. We then substituted D_n for x, and $\bar{x}$ for μ in order to relate the method more directly to the sample problem.

D_n = Demand on day n

$\bar{x}$ = Mean demand (55 in this example)

σ = Estimated standard deviation (10 in this example)

Z_n = Number of standard deviations from the mean

Thus $D_n = 55 + (1.23481)(10)$.

3. Solve for D_n:

$$D_n = 55 + 12.3481$$
$$D_n = 67.3481$$

4. Repeat steps 1 to 3, using different normal deviates from the table, until the desired number of days have been simulated.

Specification of time-incrementing procedure. In a simulation model, time can be advanced by one of two methods: (1) fixed-time increments or (2) variable time increments. Under both methods, the concept of a simulated clock is important. In the fixed-time increment method, uniform clock time increments (e.g., minutes, hours, days) are specified and the simulation proceeds by fixed intervals from one time period to the next. At each point in "clock time" the system is scanned to determine if any events are to occur. If they are, the events are simulated and time is advanced; if they are not, time is still advanced by one unit. This was the method employed in the fish market example, where one day was the time increment and time would have been advanced even if an event (an order) had not taken place.

In the variable time increment method, clock time is advanced by the amount required to initiate the next event. This approach would be appropriate in the fish market example if orders were placed when the inventory of fish reached a certain level, rather than being placed at the end of each day.

As for which method is most appropriate, experience suggests that the fixed-time increment is desirable when events of interest occur with regularity or when the number of events is large, with several commonly occurring in the same time period. The variable time increment method is generally desirable in opposite situations, and since it is usually more efficient computationally, it is frequently employed where computer running time is a major concern.[8]

Specify values of variables and parameters

Determination of starting conditions. A variable, by definition, will take on different values as the simulation progresses; but some decision must be made at the outset as to the initial values of each one. In our example, since the amount ordered was dependent upon previous orders, we assumed an average value of 55 for demand on day zero. After day zero, the generation of random numbers determined the values for demand in each successive day. An alternative approach would be to start on day 1 and assume no

---

[8] It "ignores" time intervals where nothing happens, and therefore is desirable for simulations covering an extended time period.

previous demand. For rule 1, however, this would mean that no orders would be placed, since the amount ordered under this rule would be equal to the previous day's demand.

The values for parameters in the example were $0.60/pound for the price of the fish and $0.20/pound for the cost of the fish. As mentioned earlier, the value of a parameter does not change during the course of a simulation, but it may be changed as different alternatives are studied in other simulations.

The determination of starting conditions for variables is a major tactical decision in simulation. As McMillan and Gonzales note, "the problem is that the output of the model will be biased by the set of initial values until the model has warmed up or, more precisely, has obtained a steady state where that term is taken to mean an arbitrarily close approximation to the system's equilibrium state."[9]

To cope with this problem, researchers have followed various approaches, such as (1) discarding data generated during the early parts of the run, (2) selecting starting conditions that reduce the duration of the warmup period, or (3) selecting starting conditions that eliminate bias.[10] To employ any of these alternatives, however, implies that the analyst has some idea of the range of output data he is looking for; so in one sense he is biasing the results by invoking them. On the other hand, one of the unique features of simulation is that it allows judgment to enter into the design and analysis of the simulation; so if the analyst has some information that bears on the problem, it is not necessarily wrong to include it.

Determination of run length. The length of the simulation run depends upon the purpose of the simulation. Perhaps the most common approach is to continue the simulation until it has achieved an equilibrium condition. In the context of the fish market example, this would mean that simulated demands correspond to their historical relative frequencies. Another approach is to run the simulation for a set period, such as a month, a year, or a decade, and see if the conditions at the end of the period appear reasonable. A third approach is to set run length so that a sufficiently large sample is gathered for purposes of statistical hypothesis testing. This alternative is considered further under "Evaluate Results" (below).

Evaluate results

Determine statistical tests. The types of conclusions that can be drawn from a simulation depend, of course, on the degree to which the model reflects the real system, but they also depend upon the design of the simulation in a statistical sense. Indeed, many researchers view simulation as a form of hypothesis testing with each simulation run providing one or more pieces of sample data that are amenable to formal analysis through inferential statistical methods. For example, we might wish to test the

---

[9] Claude McMillan and Richard Gonzalez, *Systems Analysis: A Computer Approach to Decision Models* (Homewood, Ill.: Richard D. Irwin, Inc., 1968), p. 496.

[10] Ibid., p. 497.

hypothesis that the average amount of fish sold per day is 55 pounds, assuming a normal distribution of demand and a standard deviation 10 pounds. In order to accept this hypothesis (or, more correctly, fail to reject it) at a particular level of statistical confidence, we would have to run the simulation for a sufficient number of days to satisfy the sample size requirements for the particular statistical test we might employ.[11] Following this approach might well alter both the length of the simulation study and the implications of the results.

In a similar vein, statistical methods could be employed to find the best alternative in a group of several competing alternatives, although in this situation some rather sophisticated mathematical search routines are required.[12]

Compare with other information. In most situations the analyst has other information at his disposal with which he can compare his simulation results. Typical sources of such information are past operating data from the real system, operating data from the performance of similar systems, and his own intuitive understanding of the real system's operation. Admittedly, however, the information obtained from these sources is unlikely to be sufficient for validation of the conclusions derived from the simulation, and thus the only true test of a simulation is how well the real system performs after the results of the study have been implemented: The proof of the pudding is in the eating.

Propose new experiment

Under this heading fall changes in most of the previously mentioned factors of a simulation model, including parameters, variables, decision rules, starting conditions, and run length.

As for parameters, we might be interested in replicating the simulation under, say, several different costs or prices of a product to see if the original simulation result would be applicable if these factors take on new values in the real system.

Trying different decision rules would obviously be in order if the initial rules led to poor results or if these runs yielded new insights into the problem. (The procedure of using the same stream of random numbers, as was done in comparing rules 1 and 2 in the fish market example, is a good general approach in that it sharpens the differences among alternatives and permits shorter runs.) Changing the starting conditions is certainly desirable if the model is sensitive to them or if the first simulation runs were relatively short. In some instances, using the average values obtained from previous runs may be more representative of the real system's starting conditions, and therefore they would be a desirable input to an experiment in which decision rules or parameter values are being manipulated.

---

[11] Some of the statistical procedures commonly used in evaluating simulation results are analysis of variance, regression analysis, and *t* tests.

[12] See S. W. Schmidt and R. E. Taylor, *Simulation and Analysis of Industrial Systems* (Homewood, Ill.: Richard D. Irwin, Inc., 1970), pp. 517–76.

Finally, whether trying different run lengths constitutes a new experiment rather than a replication of a previous experiment depends upon the types of events that occur in the system operation over time. It might happen, for example, that the system has more than one stable level of operation and that reaching the second level is time dependent. Thus while the first series of runs of, say, 100 periods show stable conditions, doubling the length of the series may provide new and distinctly different, but equally stable, conditions. In this case, then, running the simulation over 200 time periods could be thought of as a new experiment.

Computerization

While the use of a computer is often the only feasible way of performing a simulation study, it brings with it a whole new set of factors about which decisions must be made. Although it is beyond the scope of this book to go into detail about the technical aspects of computer programming, some of these factors bear directly on simulation and therefore should be described. These factors are

1. Computer language selection
2. Flowcharting
3. Computer coding and translation
4. Data generation
5. Output reports
6. Validation

Computer language selection. Computer languages can be divided into general-purpose and special-purpose types. General-purpose languages are FORTRAN, COBOL, PL/1, and BASIC. They have the advantage of being applicable to a wide variety of needs. SIMSCRIPT, GPSS, and GASP are commonly used special-purpose simulation languages that are especially suitable for queuing and scheduling problems since they require less programming time for these types of problems than the general-purpose languages. In addition, they have special output formats and error-checking mechanisms that add to their desirability.

Flowcharting. Flowcharting a simulation program is usually more difficult than flowcharting other kinds of programs since it requires the analyst to visualize how the system responds under dynamic conditions. Indeed, few analysts are brave enough to attempt to code a problem without a flowchart, even if they can develop highly complex static programs without this step.

Coding. Coding refers to translating the flowchart into a computer language. If the programmer is using FORTRAN or some other general-purpose language, the mechanics of writing a computer code are the same as for any mathematical or engineering problem.

Data generation. A considerable amount of theoretical study has been applied to the generation of random numbers in digital computers. The problem is that random number tables use too much space when entered in a computer's memory and that storing them on tape requires too much time. While at first glance random number generation may not appear to be a major endeavor, the fact is that no one method can simultaneously meet the needs for any and all simulations. In particular, such criteria as reproducibility of a previous stream of random numbers, a large quantity of random numbers, true randomness, and computational efficiency cannot be met by any one of the existing methods. For most purposes, though, the built-in random number generators at most computer facilities are adequate. However, if an individual is planning to execute a fairly long simulation program, he must have some knowledge of random number generation in order to decide which approach is most desirable for his particular purpose.

Output reports. General-purpose languages permit the analyst to specify any type of output report (or data) he wishes, providing he is willing to pay the price in programming effort. Special-purpose languages, notably GPSS and SIMSCRIPT, have standard routines that can be activated by one or two program statements to print out such data as means, variances, and standard deviations. Regardless of language, however, our experience has been that too much data from a simulation can be as dysfunctional to problem solving as too little, since both situations tend to obscure important, truly meaningful information about the system under study.

Validation. In this context, validation refers to testing the computer program to ensure that the simulation is correct. Specifically, it is a check to see whether the computer code is a valid translation of the flowchart model and whether the simulation model adequately represents the real system. Errors may arise in the program from mistakes in the coding or from mistakes in logic. Mistakes in coding are usually rapidly spotted since the program will most likely not be executed by the computer. Mistakes in logic, however, present more of a challenge. In these cases the program runs, but it fails to yield correct results.

To deal with this problem, the analyst has three alternatives: (1) have the program print out each calculation and verify these calculations by hand, (2) simulate present conditions and compare the results with the existing system, or (3) pick some point in the simulation run and compare its output to the answer obtained from solving a relevant mathematical model of the situation at that point. While the first two approaches have obvious drawbacks, they are more likely to be employed than the third, since if one had a "relevant" mathematical model in mind, he would probably be able to solve the problem without the aid of simulation.

COMPUTERIZATION OF THE FISH MARKET EXAMPLE

This problem's flowchart, computer program, and comparative output reports for rules 1 and 2 (based upon 2,000 days) are reproduced in Figures S.6.3 through S.6.6.

FIGURE S.6.3

Simulation flowchart for fish market problem

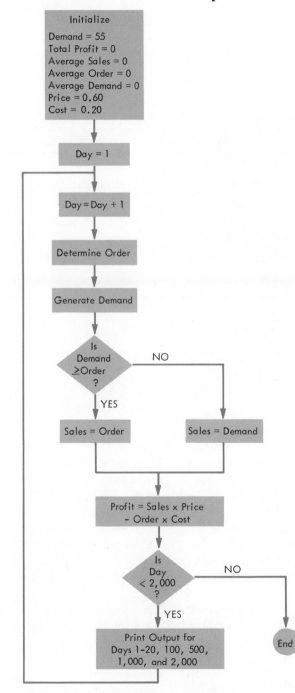

FIGURE S.6.4

FORTRAN program for simulation of Al's fish market

```
100 PROGRAM FISHMKT (INPUT,OUTPUT)
250 DEMAND=55
260 TPROFIT=0.
265 ADD=0.
270 AOO=0.
275 ASS=0.
300 DO 100 I=1,2000
400 IDAY=I
450 ORDER=55
500 X=RANF(0)*100.
600 IF (X.GE.0.AND.X.LT.10) DEMAND=35
700 IF (X.GE.10.AND.X.LT.40) DEMAND=45
800 IF (X.GE.40.AND.X.LT.60) DEMAND=55
900 IF (X.GE.60.AND.X.LT.90) DEMAND =65
1000 IF (X.GE.90.AND.X.LT.100) DEMAND=75
1050 SALES=DEMAND
1100 IF (DEMAND.GT.ORDER) SALES = ORDER
1200 COST=.20
1300 PRICE =.60
1400 PROFIT=SALES*PRICE-ORDER*COST
1500 TPROFIT=TPROFIT+PROFIT
1550 DAY=IDAY
1560 ADD=ADD+DEMAND
1565 AD=ADD/DAY
1570 AOO=AOO+ORDER
1575 AO=AOO/DAY
1580 ASS=ASS+SALES
1585 AS=ASS/DAY
1600 AVPROF=TPROFIT/DAY
1700 IF(IDAY.GE.1.AND.IDAY.LE.20.OR.IDAY.EQ.100.OR.IDAY.EQ.500)GO TO 99
1800 IF(IDAY.EQ.1000.OR.IDAY.EQ.2000) GO TO 99
1850 GO TO 100
1900 99   PRINT 999,IDAY,DEMAND,AD,ORDER,AO,SALES,AS,PROFIT,AVPROF
2000 999   FORMAT (I5,8F8.2)
2100 100. CONTINUE
2150 PRINT 37,ADD,AOO,ASS,TPROFIT
2175 37 FORMAT(F15.2)
2200 STOP
2300 END
```

Comparing the results of this program (written in FORTRAN IV) with the results of the hand simulation, we observe that rule 2 outperformed rule 1 in both cases. For the hand simulation covering 20 days, daily profit for rule 1 ($Q_n = D_{n-1}$) was $18.90 and the average daily profit for rule 2 ($Q_n = 55$) was $20.20. For the computer simulation, average daily profit for rule 1 was $18.05, compared to $19.02 for rule 2. As we can see from the results of the 2,000-day run, the expected profits were overstated in the hand simulation, suggesting that 20 days is too short a time for reliable results.

Looking at the totals for the computer simulation, it is interesting to note that rule 2 yielded $1,944 greater profit than rule 1, yet the amount of fish ordered was 330 pounds *less* under rule 2. This finding would tend to make rule 2 even more attractive if the problem were enriched to include such factors as inventory holding costs and the opportunity cost of funds. Similarly, we note that rule 2 resulted in 3,130 more orders being filled (compared to rule 1), which would enhance the desirability of rule 2 if a stockout penalty were to be included in the problem.

FIGURE S.6.5

Simulation of fish market—rule 1 output

```
READY.
450 ORDER=DEMAND
RUN.
PROGRAM TRANSFERRED TO COMPILER
```

Day	Demand	Cumulative Average Demand	Order for Day	Cumulative Average Order	Sales for Day	Cumulative Average Sales	Profit for Day	Cumulative Average Profit
1	35.00	35.00	55.00	55.00	35.00	35.00	10.00	10.00
2	45.00	40.00	35.00	45.00	35.00	35.00	14.00	12.00
3	75.00	51.67	45.00	45.00	45.00	38.33	18.00	14.00
4	45.00	50.00	75.00	52.50	45.00	40.00	12.00	13.50
5	65.00	53.00	45.00	51.00	45.00	41.00	18.00	14.40
6	65.00	55.00	65.00	53.33	65.00	45.00	26.00	16.33
7	65.00	56.43	65.00	55.00	65.00	47.86	26.00	17.71
8	55.00	56.25	65.00	56.25	55.00	48.75	20.00	18.00
9	75.00	58.33	55.00	56.11	55.00	49.44	22.00	18.44
10	55.00	58.00	75.00	58.00	55.00	50.00	18.00	18.40
11	55.00	57.73	55.00	57.73	55.00	50.45	22.00	18.73
12	65.00	58.33	55.00	57.50	55.00	50.83	22.00	19.00
13	45.00	57.31	65.00	58.08	45.00	50.38	14.00	18.62
14	65.00	57.86	45.00	57.14	45.00	50.00	18.00	18.57
15	45.00	57.00	65.00	57.67	45.00	49.67	14.00	18.27
16	45.00	56.25	45.00	56.88	45.00	49.38	18.00	18.25
17	45.00	55.59	45.00	56.18	45.00	49.12	18.00	18.24
18	65.00	56.11	45.00	55.56	45.00	48.89	18.00	18.22
19	65.00	56.58	65.00	56.05	65.00	49.74	26.00	18.63
20	35.00	55.50	65.00	56.50	35.00	49.00	8.00	18.10
100	65.00	55.30	35.00	55.20	35.00	48.20	14.00	17.88
500	75.00	55.24	75.00	55.20	75.00	48.40	30.00	18.00
1000	45.00	55.22	45.00	55.23	45.00	48.52	18.00	18.07
2000	65.00	55.17	35.00	55.16	35.00	48.46	14.00	18.05

Total demand	110340.00
Total order	110330.00
Total sales	96930.00
Total profit	36092.00

LARGE SCALE SIMULATION

Since the early 1960s a considerable amount of effort has been devoted to the development of models that attempt to simulate the effect of managerial decisions on the firm as a whole. This interest derives from the recognition that the firm is a system wherein a decision made by one of its component subsystems has an effect on other subsystems and on the firm as a whole. Clearly, decisions made by, say, the production function regarding inventory levels, worker allocation, and order sequencing can be expected to have ramifications for purchasing, sales, and finance functions. Likewise, decisions made by these functional areas are ultimately felt by the production area. This interactive effect of decision making, coupled with the ever changing nature of organizations, makes it difficult, if not impossible, to predict the effects on many managerial decisions by means other than simulation.

In this section we will look at two general approaches to carrying out large-scale simulations, or, as they are often termed, *total systems simulations*. We will label these general approaches special-purpose simulation models and modular simulation models.

FIGURE S.6.6

Simulation of fish market—rule 2 output

```
450 ORDER=55
RUN.
PROGRAM TRANSFERRED TO COMPILER
```

Day	Demand	Cumulative Average Demand	Order for day	Cumulative Average Order	Sales for Day	Cumulative Average Sales	Profit for Day	Cumulative Average Profit
1	35.00	35.00	55.00	55.00	35.00	35.00	10.00	10.00
2	45.00	40.00	55.00	55.00	45.00	40.00	16.00	13.00
3	75.00	51.67	55.00	55.00	55.00	45.00	22.00	16.00
4	45.00	50.00	55.00	55.00	45.00	45.00	16.00	16.00
5	65.00	53.00	55.00	55.00	55.00	47.00	22.00	17.20
6	65.00	55.00	55.00	55.00	55.00	48.33	22.00	18.00
7	65.00	56.43	55.00	55.00	55.00	49.29	22.00	18.57
8	55.00	56.25	55.00	55.00	55.00	50.00	22.00	19.00
9	75.00	58.33	55.00	55.00	55.00	50.56	22.00	19.33
10	55.00	58.00	55.00	55.00	55.00	51.00	22.00	19.60
11	55.00	57.73	55.00	55.00	55.00	51.36	22.00	19.82
12	65.00	58.33	55.00	55.00	55.00	51.67	22.00	20.00
13	45.00	57.31	55.00	55.00	45.00	51.15	16.00	19.69
14	65.00	57.86	55.00	55.00	55.00	51.43	22.00	19.86
15	45.00	57.00	55.00	55.00	45.00	51.00	16.00	19.60
16	45.00	56.25	55.00	55.00	45.00	50.63	16.00	19.38
17	45.00	55.59	55.00	55.00	45.00	50.29	16.00	19.18
18	65.00	56.11	55.00	55.00	55.00	50.56	22.00	19.33
19	65.00	56.58	55.00	55.00	55.00	50.79	22.00	19.47
20	35.00	55.50	55.00	55.00	35.00	50.00	10.00	19.00
100	65.00	55.30	55.00	55.00	55.00	50.00	22.00	19.00
500	75.00	55.24	55.00	55.00	55.00	50.02	22.00	19.01
1000	45.00	55.22	55.00	55.00	45.00	50.05	16.00	19.03
2000	65.00	55.17	55.00	55.00	55.00	50.03	22.00	19.02

```
Total demand   110340.00
Total ordered  110000.00
Total sales    100060.00
Total profit    38036.00
```

Special-purpose simulation models

A special-purpose simulation model is one in which a program is written "from the ground up" to describe the specific structure and operation of a total system. Under this heading fall such large-scale models as the Mark I model, developed by the Systems Development Corporation, which shows the effect of various decision rules on an imaginary firm making four products; the Bonini model, developed by Professor Charles P. Bonini of Stanford, which also deals with a hypothetical firm but predicates decision rules on behavioral concepts; and Industrial Dynamics, developed by Professor Jay Forrester of M.I.T., which employs a special computer language in simulating the information feedback properties of any system. Of these approaches, we will describe only the last one in detail since the other two are basically vehicles for research on organizational operations rather than production management tools.

Industrial dynamics. The term *industrial dynamics* was coined by Forrester to designate "a way of studying the behavior of industrial systems to show how policies, decisions, structure, and delays are interrelated to influence growth and stability."[13]

---

[13] Jay W. Forrester, *Industrial Dynamics* (Cambridge, Mass.: M.I.T. Press, 1958), p. 7.

This approach views the industrial organization as an information feedback system, which Forrester defines as existing "whenever the environment leads to a decision that results in action which affects the environment." Such systems, in turn, owe their behavior to what he terms *structure, delay,* and *amplification.* "Structure" refers to how the parts of the system are related; "delay" refers to the time lag between getting information and taking action; and "amplification" refers to the heightened effect on system operations arising from the decision-making activity itself. At various locations within such systems are decision points where corrective action is taken to increase or decrease the rate of flow of the elements through the system (such regulated elements are production rates, sales order rates, personnel hiring, and information flows). Each time an adjustment is made in some element of the system, it is reflected by a change in the quantity or "level" of that element. Within any given system, we may identify order levels, personnel levels, inventory levels, money levels, etc. To see how these three concepts—information feedback, flow rates, and element levels—are incorporated into an industrial dynamics model, we will summarize a case study titled "The Precision Company," where the approach was applied.

The Precision Company is a job shop supplier of high-quality machined parts.[14] Its customers are primarily contractors in defense industries, and it obtains the bulk of its business through competitive bidding. The company employs 100 people and has an annual sales volume of $3 million. The purpose of the industrial dynamics study of the firm was to identify the causes of extreme fluctuations in the work load, which necessitated continual adjustment in the employment level.

The first step of the study entailed interviewing key members of the firm to obtain data for developing a verbal model of its current operations. Specific questions were asked pertaining to the manner of handling flows of materials and information, the time delays involved, etc. No thought was given to organization charts or written procedures; rather, the intent was to obtain a true picture of the inner workings of the firm. On the basis of these interviews, the structure depicting interactions between the company and the customer was derived (see Figure S.6.7). The critical element of this structure is *delivery delay,* which is defined as the interval between receiving an order and delivery of the finished product. It was discovered that this factor was common to all five information feedback loops (shown in the diagrams as dashed lines *A, B, C, D,* and *E*).

Feedback loop A involves the interactions among delivery delay, managerial efforts for generating bids, bid generation, order rate, and backlog. A decrease in backlog would cause a decrease in delivery delay and a greater emphasis on new bids, which in turn cause an increase in order rate. Loop B relates the customer's willingness to place bids based on the company's ability to deliver on time; supposedly, the longer the delay, the less willing are customers to place orders. Loop C involves the delivery delay, employment level, production rate, and the hiring and firing policy.

[14] "Industrial Dynamics Case: The Precision Company, Part I" (Cambridge, Mass.: M.I.T. Press, 1964).

As the delivery delay increases, more employees are hired, trained, and placed in the work force; as production increases, delivery delay is reduced. Loop D is the same as C but includes the backlog of orders (as production goes up, orders are filled, thus reducing the backlog, which in turn reduces delivery delay). Loop E displays the interrelationship between delivery delay, productivity, and production. An increase in delivery delay increases the usage of overtime in the plant, which increases the weekly production rate of each worker. This, in turn, ultimately leads to a decrease in delivery delay.

FIGURE S.6.7

Basic structure and information flows of the Precision Company

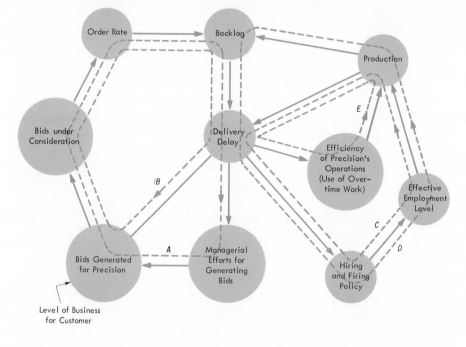

Once the basic structure was determined, equations were developed to describe the interrelationship within the feedback loops. These equations, written in a specially developed computer language termed DYNAMO, are of two types—one defining the rate of adjustment and one defining the levels of quantities after adjustment. Two rate equations, for example, were required to define delivery delay in loop C, where delivery delay is equal to the backlog of orders divided by the average production finishing rate. In symbolic terms, the equations are

$$DD.K = \frac{BL.K}{APFR.K}$$

$$APFR.K = APFR.J + (DT)(1/DAPFR)(PFR.JK - APFR)$$

where

$DD.K$ = Delivery delay in period K
$BL.K$ = Backlog in period K
$APFR.K$ = Average production finishing rate in period K
$APFR.J$ = Average production finishing rate in previous period J
DT = Delta time (the time increments in the model)
$DAPFR$ = Delay in average production finishing rate
$1/DAPFR$ = A smoothing constant
$PFR.JK$ = Production finishing rate over the time period JK

Finally, experiments were run on the completed simulation model to determine the system's response to changes in such factors as backlog, management effort in bidding, and the bids generated for Precision. The results of a simulation that tested the effect of a 20 percent step increase in delivery delay are shown in Figure S.6.8. Such graphs provide the major output of any industrial dynamics simulation, and the state of the system is judged by the amount of oscillation generated by introducing various input changes. Figure S.6.8, for instance, shows substantial oscillation from introducing a change in delivery delay. The effect of such oscillation was inefficient work load distribution, resulting in excessive adjustments in the size of the work force.

To summarize the findings of the study: it became apparent to management that delivery delay was in fact the basis of organizational planning and adjustment. The results of the simulation indicated rather clearly, however, that this was an inappropriate foundation for operating decisions, and structural changes were made in the model to see if a better basis for decision making could be found. Of these changes, treating order rate as the interrelating factor yielded the best results, although further trial-and-error manipulation of the model was subsequently undertaken.

Comment on industrial dynamics. While the case presented above is highly condensed, it provides clues to both the advantages and disadvantages of the industrial dynamics methodology. Certainly, describing a system in terms of information flows can yield real insights into how the system functions, and therefore as a training or pedagogical device it can be of real value.[15] On the other hand, industrial dynamics models are generally complex and expensive to build. The development of the equations is tricky, and great care must be taken to accurately define rates and levels along the appropriate time dimensions. Of even greater importance, though, is the type of results provided by industrial dynamics simulations: the presumption is that much oscillation in the variables is bad and that little or none is good. However true this may be in general, the only way to be sure for a given situation is to consider the cost of such oscillations or evaluate them according to some concrete measure of effectiveness.

---

[15] In fact, Forrester has even examined future world-population growth and food production through the industrial dynamics methodology. See Jay W. Forrester, *World Dynamics* (Cambridge, Mass.: Wright-Allen Press, 1971), for some dire predictions about life in the 21st century.

FIGURE S.6.8

Behavior of the model in response to a 20 percent step input for increased delay in completing bids

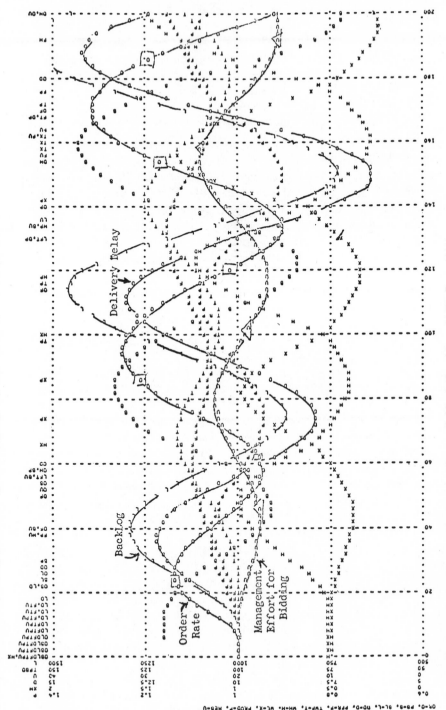

Source: "Industrial Dynamics Case: The Precision Company" (Cambridge, Mass.: M.I.T. Press, 1964).

Unfortunately, industrial dynamics has no provision within the model structure to directly relate measure of effectiveness to decision rules of the system, and therefore evaluations of system performance must be made outside the simulation model by attaching costs or payoffs to the results of each run. Although this can be done, it is an inefficient and expensive process.

In summary, while industrial dynamics has received a great deal of attention in schools of business administration, its drawbacks—as noted above—seem to be so severe that it will remain an analytical tool of the academic researcher rather than as an aid in the daily decision making of the production manager.[16]

Modular simulation models

A modular simulation model is essentially an aggregation of distinct "canned programs" that are called into play to analyze a particular problem.[17] Thus it differs from other simulation approaches in that the model is assembled from existing programs rather than developed anew for each situation. Operationally, the linkage between the component programs is obtained through a general program that is stored in a time-shared computer. To develop a simulation model using this approach to analyze a given problem requires that the user has entered the logic and data peculiar to his operations in the general program and that he specify the type of output he wishes from the canned programs he has selected. Prior to the simulation run, the user generates from the computer a forecast of the factors that affect the system he is studying. Typically, these factors are sales or output demands, and are forecasted by a technique such as exponential smoothing applied to his data. The user then initiates the simulation by programming "what if?" questions: What if production increases by 10 percent? What if a new process is added? The simulation run provides answers to these questions in the form of statistical data or financial reports, or both.

Two examples, drawn from an article by Boulden, provide an insight into how modular modeling, or the "instant modeling approach" (as he calls it), is applied to specific situations.

Steel manufacture. The model is used to simulate steel production operations in order to determine raw material requirements needed to meet sales forecasts and to estimate unit costs at various levels of production. (See Figure S.6.9.)

The modeling system consists of five major process models and two finished product models, all of which are linked so that the output of one becomes the input to another. Each process model is composed of several submodels with provision for simulating any level of operation for each facility, using nonlinear cost

---

[16] Indeed, a visit by one of the authors of this book to the Sprague Electric Company in North Adams, Massachusetts, which provided the initial proving ground for industrial dynamics, revealed that this firm no longer uses the approach in its operations.

[17] The particular modular modeling approach described here was developed by James B. Boulden, president of On-Line Decisions, Inc., Berkeley, California.

General structure of a modular simulation model

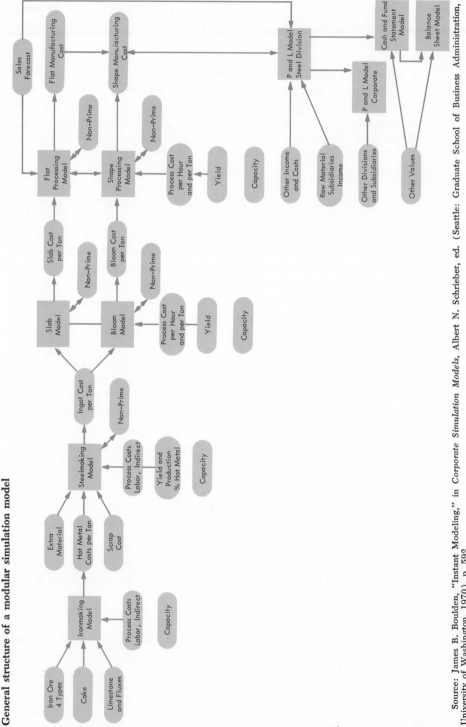

Source: James B. Boulden, "Instant Modeling," in *Corporate Simulation Models*, Albert N. Schrieber, ed. (Seattle: Graduate School of Business Administration, University of Washington, 1970), p. 592.

functions. The modeling system can be run backward from sales to materials in-put, or forward from input to output. Financial information is consolidated into corporate statements. Output includes key production figures including facility utilization and scrap estimates with various time, dollar, and volume estimates. The time spent in developing the model was less than three months. The cost was less than that required to compute one iteration by hand calculator. Cost estimates by the model have proved to be accurate within 1/2 of 1 percent.

Cement manufacture. The model is used for simulating production and stor-age costs for more than 100 facilities and has the ability to vary production schedules and modes of transportation to obtain improved profit.

A massive data base is required, including inventory, production, transporta-tion, and sales data for each plant and facility. These data are used in deciding whether to produce or buy cement, and at what plant, for shipment to which location. Plant operations are consolidated into corporate profit and loss state-ments.

Three man-months were required to develop the model and carry it through the debugging stage.[18]

Comment on modular simulation models.   Modular simulation—as de-scribed here—is sold as a service by consulting firms and hence full informa-tion about its operation is proprietary.[19] Nevertheless, it appears to us that modular simulation has a number of advantages over the other approaches to large-scale simulation. First of all, the initial development of a model is far cheaper for the using company than building its own large Monte Carlo models or industrial dynamics models. Modular models require little origi-nal programming since only the logic of a particular company's operation and its actual data must be coded. Second, they are run on *time sharing*, which means that the user is charged only for the running time on his com-puter terminal and his use of a central processing unit. Third, they are ex-tremely flexible in that modules may be added or deleted as desired. For example, linear programming packages, inventory programs, and the like may be introduced into the general program with little or no modification. Thus the simulation may become as robust as desired, with relatively little additional programming and minimum loss of comprehension on the part of the user. This latter point is especially important since it helps to bring line personnel into the modeling process. Finally, this approach is eminently appealing on logical grounds—Why write a simulation from scratch when usable programs are already developed?

As far as disadvantages of this approach are concerned, there is the operational problem of linking existing models on time sharing to the real-time data stored in in-house computers. In addition, there is some inherent inefficiency in combining modules since each is a general-purpose program and has more capability than is likely to be required for any problem seg-

---

[18] James B. Boulden, "Instant Modeling," in *Corporate Simulation Models*, Albert N. Schrieber, ed. (Seattle: Graduate School of Business Administration, University of Washington, 1970), pp. 578–99.

[19] Certain simulation languages, such as GPSS and CSS/360, use what might be loosely termed *canned subroutines* and therefore may be thought of as modular ap-proaches as well.

ment. This extra capability, which is provided by each module, means the total simulation run time is likely to be longer than if the program were built from scratch. Beyond these minor limitations, it is hard to find fault with the idea of modular modeling, although, as its use spreads, industrial experience and impartial research may bring more problems to light.

CONCLUSION

Table S.6.6 summarizes the advantages of simulation relative to using the real system for experimentation and relative to using mathematical models for problem solving.

The drawbacks of simulation do not lend themselves to tabulation, but they can be summarized as follows. First, simulation models are time consuming to build and require a certain amount of computer experience and expertise on the part of the user. Thus they are often not a practical means

TABLE S.6.6

Simulation is desirable when experimentation on the real system	*Simulation is desirable when a mathematical model*
1. would disrupt ongoing activities	1. is not available to handle the problem
2. would be too costly to undertake	2. is too complex or arduous to solve
3. requires many observations over an extended period of time	3. is beyond the capability of available personnel
4. does not permit exact replication of events	4. is not rich enough to provide information on all factors of interest
5. does not permit control over key variables	

for solving many of the problems faced by the production manager. Second, simulation is subject to the same limitations as mathematical models—the impossibility of quantifying certain key variables, the difficulty of casting complex problems in equation form, etc. And yet, by virtue of the fact that simulations can be made to run under any type of assumption, such flaws can easily be overlooked. Finally, simulation is in its infancy in terms of its theoretical development. There are very few principles of simulation to guide the user in making decisions on what to include in the model, the length and number of simulation runs, or the general effects that changes in inputs will have on simulation outputs. Thus, at present, simulation must be classified as an art rather than a science.

REVIEW AND DISCUSSION QUESTIONS

1. How do custom built simulation models differ from mathematical models? What are the major advantages of simulation as a problem-solving tool?

2. What are the general steps in developing and running a simulation model? How do you evaluate the output of such a model?

3. What methods are used to increment time in a simulation model? Explain how they work.

4. What are the pros and cons of starting a simulation with the system empty? With the system in equilibrium?

5. Distinguish between industrial dynamics and modular simulation models. What are the advantages and disadvantages of each?

6. Distinguish between "known mathematical distributions" and "empirical distributions." What information is needed to simulate using a known mathematical distribution?

7. What is the importance of run length in simulation? Is a run of 100 observations twice as valid as a run of 50? Explain.

8. This supplement is really just a review for you, since you have been simulating for a long time. Consider for example, the parlor game of "Monopoly." What are the variables and parameters of the game? How are random numbers generated? What are some sample decision rules? When is the warm-up period over? If you were to simulate the game on a computer, what are the relevant factors in determining how valid your results would be in subsequent play? Would the results change if each player (real or simulated) started play with twice as much in his bank account as the rules specify?

PROBLEMS

1. The purpose of this classroom simulation exercise is twofold: (1) to provide further exposure to the concepts of simulation mentioned in the supplement and (2) to focus attention on the problems of decision rule formulation in a dynamic business environment.

    Situation. Fish Forwarders supplies fresh shrimp to a variety of customers in the New Orleans area. It places orders for cases of shrimp from fleet representatives at the beginning of each week to meet a demand from its customers at the middle of the week. The shrimp are subsequently delivered to Fish Forwarders and then, at the end of the week, to its customers.

    Both the supply of shrimp and the demand for shrimp are uncertain. The supply may vary as much as ±10 percent from the amount ordered, and, by contract, Fish Forwarders must purchase this supply. The probability associated with this variation is: −10 percent, 30 percent of the time; 0 percent, 50 percent of the time; and +10 percent, 20 percent of the time. The weekly demand for shrimp is normally distributed with a mean of 800 cases and a standard deviation of 100 cases.

    A case of shrimp costs Fish Forwarders $30 and it sells it for $50. Any shrimp not sold at the end of the week are sold to a cat food company at $4 per case. Fish Forwarders may, if it chooses, order the shrimp "flash-frozen" by the supplier at dockside, but this raises the cost of a case by $4, and hence costs Fish Forwarders $34 per case. Flash freezing enables Fish Forwarders to maintain an inventory of shrimp, but it costs $2 per case per week to store the shrimp at a local icehouse. The customers are indifferent to whether they get regular or flash-frozen shrimp. Fish Forwarders figures that its shortage cost is equal to its markup; that is, each case demanded but not available costs the company $50 − $30 or $20.

Procedure for play. The game requires that each week a decision be made as to how many cases to order of regular shrimp and flash-frozen shrimp. The number ordered may be any amount.

The steps in playing the game are as follows.

a. Decide on the order amount of regular shrimp and/or flash-frozen shrimp and enter the figures in column 3 of the worksheet (see Table S.6.7). Assume that there is no opening inventory of flash-frozen shrimp.

b. Determine the amount that arrives and enter it at *Orders Received*. This will be accomplished by the referee's drawing a random number from a uniform random number table (such as that in Table S.6.3) and finding its associated level of variation from following random number intervals: 00 to 29 = −10 percent, 30 to 79 = zero percent, and 80 to 99 = +10 percent. If the random number is, say, 13, the amount of variation will be −10 percent. Thus if you decided to order 1,000 regular cases of shrimp and 100 flash-frozen cases, the amount you would actually receive would be 1,000 − 0.10(1,000), or 900 regular cases, and 100 − 0.10(100), or 90 flash-frozen cases. (Note that the amount of variation is the same for both regular and flash-frozen shrimp.) These amounts are then entered in column 4.

c. Add the amount of flash-frozen shrimp in inventory (if any) to the quantity of regular and flash-frozen shrimp just received and enter this amount in column 5. This would be 990, using the figures provided above.

d. Determine the demand for shrimp. This will be accomplished by the referee's drawing a random normal deviate value from Table S.6.5, which he enters into the equation at the top of column 6. Thus if the deviate value is −1.76, demand for the week will be 800 + 100(−1.76) or 624.

e. Determine the amount sold. This will be the lesser of the amount demanded (column 6) and the amount available (column 5). Thus if a player has received 990 and demand is 624, the quantity entered will be 624 (with 990 − 624, or 366 left over).

f. Determine the excess. The amount of excess is simply that quantity remaining after demand for a given week is filled. Always assume that regular shrimp are sold before the flash-frozen. Thus, if we use the 366 figure obtained above, the excess would include all the original 90 cases of flash-frozen shrimp.

g. Determine shortages. This is simply the amount of unsatisfied demand each period, and it occurs only when demand is greater than sales. (Since all customers use the shrimp within the week in which they are delivered, backorders are not relevant.) The amount of shortages (in cases of shrimp) is entered in column 9.

Profit determination. Table S.6.8 is provided for determining the profit achieved at the end of play. The values to be entered in the table are obtained by summing the relevant columns of Table S.6.7 and making the calculations.

Assignment. Simulate operations for a total of 10 weeks. It is suggested that a 10-minute break be taken at the end of week 5 and the players attempt to evaluate how they may improve their performance. They might

TABLE S.6.7

Simulation worksheet

(1) Week	(2) Flash Frozen Inventory	(3) Orders Placed Regular	(3) Orders Placed Flash Frozen	(4) Orders Received Regular	(4) Orders Received Flash Frozen	(5) Available (Regular and Flash Frozen)	(6) Demand (800 + 100Z)	(7) Sales (Minimum of Demand or Available)	(8) Excess Regular	(8) Excess Flash	(9) Shortages
1											
2											
3											
4											
5											
6											
7		MARDI GRAS									
8											
9											
10											
Totals											

*Flash Frozen Only

TABLE S.6.8

Profit from Fish Forwarders' operations

Revenue from sales
    ($50 × Col. 7) $_____
Revenue from salvage
    ($4 × Col. 8 reg.) $_____
    Total revenue $_____
Cost of regular purchases ($30 × Col. 4 reg.) $_____
Cost of flash-frozen purchases
    ($34 × Col. 4 flash) $_____
Cost of holding flash-frozen shrimp
    ($2 × Col. 8 flash) $_____
Cost of shortages ($20 × Col. 9) $_____
    Total cost $_____
        Profit $══════════════

also wish to plan an ordering strategy for the week of Mardi Gras, when no shrimp will be supplied.

2. Ebb and Flow are workers on a two-station assembly line. The distribution of activity time at their stations is as follows.

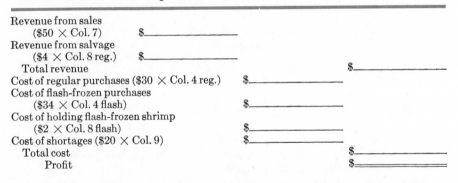

Time (seconds)	Time frequency for Ebb (operation 1)	Time frequency for Flow (operation 2)
10	4	4
20	6	5
30	10	6
40	20	7
50	40	10
60	11	8
70	5	6
80	4	4

   a. Assign random numbers to the two frequency distributions in such a
       way that you may simulate operation of the line.
   b. Simulate operation of the line for eight items. Use the random numbers
       given below.

Operation 1		Operation 2	
25	14	36	97
16	01	76	41
82	96	55	13
03	44	25	34

   c. Assuming Flow must wait until Ebb completes the first item before
       starting work, will he have to wait to process any of the other eight
       items? Explain your answer, based upon your simulation.
3. Use a fair coin to simulate Aquilano's theory of betting strategy that a coin
   "remembers" its previous flips, and will in fact tend to balance out the
   number of heads and tails in a sample of 20 flips.
4. The Slick Oil Transport Company has pipelines from several producing companies. It holds oil in a storage field (in oil storage tanks) until the oil is
   needed. It ships, through its output lines, to a large refinery.
       Because of legal limitations on the producing firms, either 40,000 or 60,-
   000 gallons of oil are being shipped to Slick; there is equal probability of
   either. The refinery uses the oil with the following probability distribution.
   The company has 100,000 gallons storage capacity.

Use per day	Probability
25,001–35,000 gal.........	0.1
35,001–45,000............	0.2
45,001–55,000............	0.3
55,001–65,000............	0.4

   a. What is the expected number of gallons used per day? (Assume that
       within any use range—for instance, 25,001 to 35,000—the use averages
       to the middle—i.e. 30,000 gallons.)
   b. Construct a frequency distribution and random number scheme that
       could be used in a simulation of Slick's activities.
   c. Simulate these activities (receiving and shipping oil) for 20 days.
   d. Does your simulation indicate that Slick should build more storage
       capacity? If so, what additional capacity should be constructed? If not,
       can you say anything about the operation?
5. This simulation problem deals with customer activity in a cafeteria. Assume
   that the sections of the cafeteria are divided as follows: entrance, tray and
   silver section, salad section, dessert section, main hot line, and cashier. The
   probabilities that any individual will proceed from one section to another
   are stated below.
   a. Using the Monte Carlo method, simulate the path followed by 10 in-
       dividuals (one at a time) from each one's entrance into the cafeteria
       until he gets to the cashier. Note that a person may backtrack; that is,
       he may go from one section to another and return.

b. From your simulation, what is the probability of somebody's getting two desserts? Assume that entering the dessert section always leads to a purchase.

Going from	To	Probability
Entrance	Tray and silver section	0.80
Entrance	Dessert section	0.10
Entrance	Salad section	0.05
Entrance	Main hot line	0.05
Entrance	Cashier	0.0
Tray and silver section	Dessert section	0.25
Tray and silver section	Salad section	0.25
Tray and silver section	Main hot line	0.50
Tray and silver section	Cashier	0.0
Salad section	Tray and silver section	0.10
Salad section	Dessert section	0.25
Salad section	Main hot line	0.30
Salad section	Cashier	0.35
Main hot line	Tray and silver section	0.02
Main hot line	Dessert section	0.08
Main hot line	Salad section	0.40
Main hot line	Cashier	0.50
Dessert section	Tray and silver section	0.05
Dessert section	Salad section	0.15
Dessert section	Main hot line	0.25
Dessert section	Cashier	0.55

SELECTED BIBLIOGRAPHY

Berry, W. L., and D. C. Whybark   *Computer Augmented Cases in Operations and Logistics Management.* Cincinnati, Ohio: South-Western Publishing Co., 1972.

Carlson, J. G., and Misshauk, M. J.   *Introduction to Gaming: Management Decision Simulations.* New York: John Wiley & Sons, 1972.

Conway, R. W.   "Some Tactical Problems in Digital Simulations," *Management Science,* vol. 10, no. 1 (1963), pp. 47–61.

Forrester, Jay W.   *Industrial Dynamics.* New York: John Wiley and Sons, 1961.

Harris, Roy D., and Maggard, Michael J.   *Computer Models in Operations Management: A Computer-Augmented System.* New York: Harper & Row, 1972.

McMillan, C., and Gonzalez, R. F.   *Systems Analysis: A Computer Approach to Decision Models.* 3d ed. Homewood, Ill.: Richard D. Irwin, Inc., 1973.

Meier, R. C., Newell, W. T., and Pazer, H. L.   *Simulation in Business and Economics.* Englewood Cliffs, N.J.: Prentice-Hall, 1969.

Naylor, T. H., Balintfy, J. L., Burdick, D. S., and Chu, K.   *Computer Simulation Techniques.* New York: John Wiley & Sons, 1968.

Schrieber, Albert N. (ed.)   *Corporate Simulation Models.* Seattle: Graduate School of Business Administration, University of Washington, 1970.

Wyman, F. P.   *Simulation Modeling: A Guide to Using Simscript.* New York: John Wiley & Sons, 1970.

7

Design of the scheduling system

A schedule is a timetable for performing activities, utilizing resources, or allocating facilities. The process of scheduling can be thought of as the implementation phase of production planning and as a continual activity in the life of a productive system. The purpose of scheduling is to *disaggregate* the general production plan into time-phased weekly, daily, or hourly activities. In other words, to specify in precise terms the planned work load on the productive system in the very short run.

In designing a scheduling system, provision must be made for efficient performance of the following functions:

1. Allocating orders, equipment, and personnel to work centers or other specified locations. Essentially, this is a decision based on a comparison of required capacity with available capacity.
2. Determining the sequence of order performance; that is, establishing job priorities.
3. Initiating performance of the scheduled work. This is commonly termed the *dispatching of orders.*
4. Reviewing the status of orders as they progress through the system. This is often referred to as *followup.*
5. Expediting late and critical orders.
6. Revising the schedule in light of changes in order status.

Relating these factors on the basis of information flow provides the structure for the generalized scheduling system depicted in Figure 7.1.

Scheduling systems cannot be designed without an appreciation of the productive system under which they are found. With this in mind, the remainder of the chapter will be devoted to describing the general scheduling problems confronted in a variety of organizations, following the categories developed for the production throughput strategies discussed in Chapter 3. Note, however, that certain scheduling techniques are useful in several of these situations and that many productive systems employ blends of two or more throughput strategies.

We have seen (Chapter 3) that the production throughput strategies are as follows.

Manufacturing:
 Unit—one of a kind or produced one by one
 Batch—finite number of items produced to order
 Mass—indefinite or extremely large number of items of homogeneous nature
 Process—continuous processing of primary materials

Services:
 Customized services
 Standardized services

UNIT SCHEDULING

Unit scheduling may be divided into *project scheduling* and *job shop scheduling* situations.

FIGURE 7.1

Generalized scheduling system

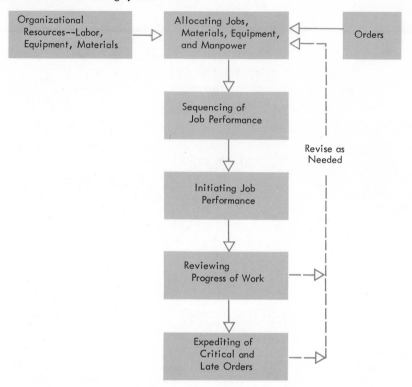

Project scheduling situations

A project is a series of related jobs that are usually directed toward some major output and require an extensive period of time to perform. Typical project scheduling situations are found in aerospace engineering, shipbuilding, large construction operations, and heavy equipment production. For most projects, the primary scheduling task is coordinating resources—men, material, equipment—to assure that they are where they are needed when they are needed. Further, since such projects as highways, dams, pipelines, and building construction are at the mercy of the elements, controlling the schedule progress may be doubly difficult.

In recent years, unit scheduling situations have been subjected to networking techniques such as CPM (critical path method) and PERT (program evaluation and review technique) especially in construction and aerospace operations. (Since these concepts are fully developed in the supplement to Chapter 12, we will not go into them here.) The simple work flow chart, applied to highway construction (Figure 7.2), is similar in concept to these approaches and is at least as widely used as the more sophisticated networking techniques.

Perhaps the most pervasive scheduling device, in construction as well as

.FIGURE 7.2

Basic highway construction flow chart

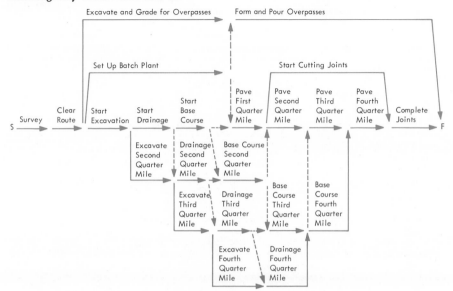

Source: James J. O'Brien, *CPM in the Construction Industry* (New York: McGraw-Hill Book Company, 1969), p. 449.

in other scheduling situations, is the bar chart or Gantt chart developed by H. L. Gantt in 1917. This technique is interesting for historical reasons since it is one of the first recorded attempts to relate activity to time. Figure 7.3 illustrates a typical Gantt type chart applied to construction.

A scheduling device that is commonly used for defense projects is the milestone chart. A "milestone" represents an important event in the completion of a project, and milestones can be further distinguished by relative importance, for example, "major milestones," "footstones," and "inchstones." Milestone charts are typically used in conjunction with reports provided by individual managers who oversee the various milestone activities. The overall progress of a milestone-scheduled project is monitored by reference to a chart similar to that depicted in Figure 7.4.

Job shop scheduling situations

A job shop scheduling situation exists when a productive facility handles a variety of orders and treats an incoming order as a "mini project." That is, production routing is developed separately for each order, separate records are kept for each job, and the progress of each job through the system is closely monitored. This is not to say that products would not travel through such systems in batches with other products; indeed, in many instances individual orders are combined with others as they progress through the various transformation stages. However, because these are special orders with different completion schedules, and with different material and service

FIGURE 7.3

Building bar graph

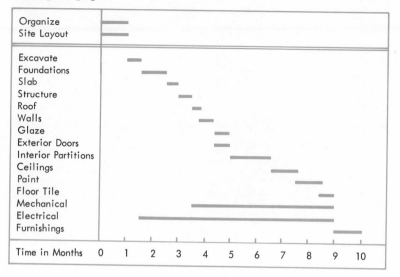

| | Time in Months | 0 | 1 | 2 | 3 | 4 | 5 | 6 | 7 | 8 | 9 | 10 |

Source: James J. O'Brien, *CPM in the Construction Industry* (New York: McGraw-Hill Book Company, 1965), p. 3.

FIGURE 7.4

Milestone chart

Event No.	Milestones	1965	1966	1967
		O N D	J F M A M J J A S O N D	J F M
12	Maintenance Equipment Fabrication Completed			
13	Training of Operating Personnel Completed			
14	Installation and Checkout Equipment Fabrication Completed			
15	Missile Erection Equipment Fabrication Completed			
16	Missile Transportation Vehicle Fabrication Completed			
18	Missile Fabrication Completed			
19	Emplacement Equipment Fabrication Completed			
20	Preliminary Checkout of Installation and Checkout Equipment Completed			
21	Ground Equipment Fabrication Completed			
30	Site Construction Completed			
33	Missile Installation Completed			
35	First Operational Unit Completed			

LEGEND:
  Action Completed on Schedule (Completed Action)
  Action Not Completed on Schedule (Actual Slippage)
  Anticipated Delayed Accomplishment of Future Action (Anticipated Slippage)
  Scheduled (or Rescheduled) Action

Source: J. N. Holtz, "Analysis of Major Scheduling Techniques in the Defense Systems Environment," in *Systems, Organizations, Analysis, Management: A Book of Readings*, D. I. Cleland and W. R. King, eds. (New York: McGraw-Hill Book Co., 1969), p. 330.

inputs required along the way, it is unlikely that they will take identical routes through the system at identical times.

The job shop scheduling problem has received a great deal of attention in the production literature, although the focus of the vast majority of studies is theoretical rather than applied. Areas of particular interest are as follows.

1. Manner in which jobs arrive
2. Number and variety of machines in the shop
3. Number of men in the shop
4. Flow pattern of jobs through the shop
5. Rules by which jobs are allocated to machines
6. Criteria by which the schedule will be evaluated.

1. *Job arrival patterns.* Jobs can arrive at the scheduler's desk either in a batch (not to be confused with batch *scheduling*) or over a time interval according to some statistical distribution. In the former case, such an arrival pattern is termed *static*, while the latter is termed *dynamic*. Static arrival does not mean that orders are placed by customers at the same moment, only that they are subject to being scheduled at one time. Such a situation is found where a production control clerk makes out a schedule, say, once a week and does not dispatch any jobs until he has all the previous week's incoming orders before him. In the dynamic arrival case, jobs are dispatched as they arrive and the overall schedule is updated to reflect their effect on the production facility.

2. *Number and variety of machines in the shop.* The number of machines in the shop obviously affects the scheduling process. If there is but one machine, as in the case of a computer, the scheduling problem is greatly simplified. On the other hand, as the number and variety of machines increase, the more complex the scheduling problem is likely to become if more than one machine operation is to be performed on each job.

3. *Number of men in the shop.* A key distinguishing feature in job shops is the number of men available for work in comparison to the number of machines. If there are more men than machines, or an equal number of men and machines, the shop is referred to as a *machine-limited system*. If there are more machines than men, it is referred to as a *labor-limited system*. The machine-limited system has received far and away a greater amount of study, although recent investigations suggest that labor-limited systems are more pervasive in practice. In studying labor-limited systems, the primary areas of concern are the utilization of the man on several machines and determination of the best way to allocate men to machines.

4. *Flow patterns of jobs through the shop.* The pattern of flow through the shop ranges from what is termed a *flow shop*, wherein all the jobs follow the same path from one machine to the next, to a *randomly routed job shop*, where there is no similar pattern of movement from one machine to the next. Both these extremes are rare in reality: most shops fall somewhere in between. The extent to which a shop is a flow shop or a randomly routed

FIGURE 7.5

Simple job-shop networks

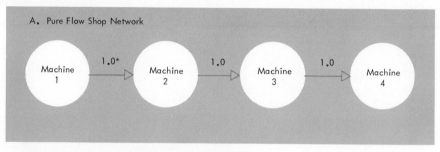

A. Pure Flow Shop Network

° Probability of a job's going from machine *i* to machine *j*.

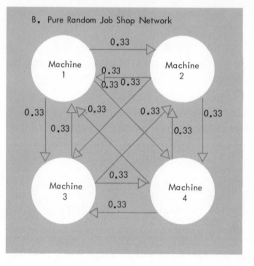

B. Pure Random Job Shop Network

job shop can be determined by noting the statistical probability of a job's moving from one machine to the next. For example, Figure 7.5A is a "pure" flow shop since the probability of movement from any machine to another machine is 1. On the other hand Figure 7.5B is sometimes referred to as a "pure" random job shop since the transitional flow probabilities are all the same, in this case 0.33.

Obviously, an infinite number of intermediate probabilities are available between the two extreme cases, even for a simple four-machine shop. One interesting and fairly common mixture of the two is the *hybrid job shop,* depicted in Figure 7.6. In this case the movement between departments follows that of a flow shop in that it is unidirectional, but the probability of movement from any machine in department A to any other machine either in department A or in B is equiprobable as in a random job shop. Thus if a job is on machine 1, it has a 33 percent probability of going to any other machine for further processing, while if a job has progressed to

FIGURE 7.6

Hybrid job-shop network

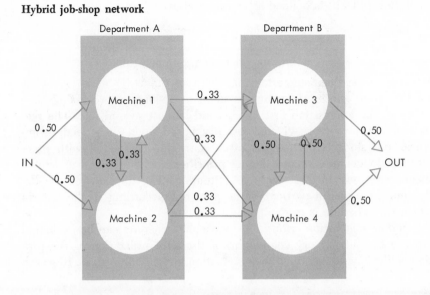

machine 3, it has a 50 percent probability of going to machine 4 and a 50 percent probability of leaving the system (OUT).

5. *Priority rules for allocating jobs to machines.* A priority rule is simply a rule for selecting which job is started first on some machine or work center. Examples of simple priority rules are selection of jobs on first-come-first-served, shortest processing time, and earliest due date bases.

Examples of more complex rules are "slack time per remaining operations" (where "slack" is defined as the amount of time remaining before the job must be started if it is to be completed on time), "the shortest operating time to total work time" (i.e., assign the job that has the smallest weighted ratio of processing time to work remaining), and COVERT (delay cost over processing time).

What rules are commonly used in industry? According to Richard Conway[1] the following rules are widely employed when job lateness is of concern.

1. Assign highest priority to jobs with the earliest due dates.
2. Assign highest priority to the job with the least slack, where "slack" is defined as the time remaining until due date, after deducting the remaining time.
3. Assign highest priority to the job with the earliest due date at that machine. Allowable shop time is divided equally among the operations of the job to obtain the due date for each operation listed in the job route.

---

[1] Richard W. Conway, "Priority Dispatching Rules and Job Lateness in a Job Shop," *Journal of Industrial Engineering*, vol. 16, no. 4 (July–August 1965).

4. Assign highest priority to the job that has the least slack per remaining operation. "Slack" is defined as in rule 2 above.[2] I.e.,

$$\text{Priority} \quad \frac{\left(\begin{array}{l}\text{Time remaining}\\\text{before due date}\end{array}\right) - \left(\begin{array}{l}\text{Remaining machine}\\\text{involvement time}\end{array}\right)}{\text{Number of remaining operations}}$$

However, it has been suggested that many of the assignment rules used in practice come closer to being classified as a longest processing time rule; that is, the longest job first, the second longest second, etc. The reason is that many jobs are given a priority based upon their relative importance, and since importance is often positively correlated with processing time, longer jobs receive higher priorities.

No one rule will be best for every situation. The ultimate choice depends upon how well a particular rule performs according to the criteria by which the schedule is evaluated.

6. Schedule evaluation criteria. A particular schedule can be evaluated in terms of the satisfactory completion of the jobs, utilization of the productive facilities, and meeting the organization's overall objectives. Research

Job	Due date	Processing time in days	Job slack (Due date − processing time)
A.....	4 days hence	3	1
B.....	9 days hence	6	3
C.....	5 days hence	5	0
D.....	9 days hence	7	2

on scheduling has for the most part concentrated on the satisfactory completion of the jobs, utilizing what are termed *local criteria*. In particular, a great deal of study has been given to the relative merits of the various priority rules in meeting such evaluation criteria as minimizing mean job flow time and mean job lateness (both defined below) for some fixed number of jobs that progress through one or more machines.

We will now consider these criteria with respect to a simple scheduling problem involving four jobs that must be processed on one machine. In scheduling terminology, this class of problems is referred to as an "*n* job —one-machine problem," or simply *n*/1 ($n = 4$). The theoretical difficulty of this type of problem increases as more machines are considered, rather than by the number of jobs that must be processed; therefore the only restriction on *n* is that it be a specified, finite number.

Job operation times are listed below. Priority rules are: (*a*) Assign jobs according to their minimum slack time, where slack is the amount of time remaining before the job must be started if it is to be completed on

---

[2] New, based upon his experience, states that rule 4 is "by far the most frequently used rule in implemented systems." (See C. Colin New, "Job Shop Scheduling: Who Needs a Computer to Sequence Jobs?" *Production and Inventory Management,* 4th Quarter, 1975, p. 39.)

TABLE 7.1

Job	Flow time	Time until due date	Lateness (flow time − time available)
Minimum slack rule*			
A.........................	8	4	4
B.........................	21	9	12
C.........................	5	5	0
D.........................	15	9	6
Total.....................	49		22
Shortest processing time rule†			
A.........................	3	4	0‡
B.........................	14	9	5
C.........................	8	5	3
D.........................	21	9	12
Total.....................	46		20

* Mean flow time: 49/4 = 12¼ days; mean lateness: 22/4 = 5½ days.
† Mean flow time: 46/4 = 11½ days; mean lateness: 20/4 = 5 days.
‡ Job is finished 1 day early.

time, and (*b*) Assign jobs according to shortest processing time. Evaluation criteria are: (*a*) Minimum mean flow time, where flow time is the time the job spends in the shop, and (*b*) Minimum mean lateness, where lateness is the difference between the time remaining before the job's due date and its flow time.

By the minimum slack priority rule, the jobs would be performed in the following order: C, A, D, B. The effect of these rules, in terms of the evaluation criteria, is shown in Table 7.1. The flow times listed were developed with the aid of the scheduling graphs shown in Figure 7.7.

Returning to the schedule results, note that the shortest processing time rule gave better results, not only for flow time criteria but for lateness criteria as well. Is this luck? Not really, for it can be shown mathematically that the shortest processing time rule yields not only a shorter flow time

FIGURE 7.7

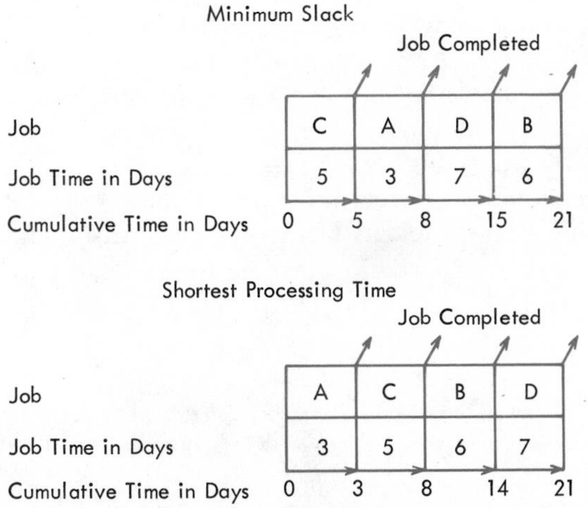

Minimum Slack

Job Completed

Job	C	A	D	B
Job Time in Days	5	3	7	6

Cumulative Time in Days   0   5   8   15   21

Shortest Processing Time

Job Completed

Job	A	C	B	D
Job Time in Days	3	5	6	7

Cumulative Time in Days   0   3   8   14   21

schedule and lateness time schedule than the minimum slack rule but also an optimum solution in terms of both these criteria. Moreover, the shortest processing time rule yields an optimum solution for the $n/1$ case in terms of such other evaluation criteria as mean waiting time and mean completion time. In fact, so powerful is this simple rule that it has been termed "the most important concept in the entire subject of sequencing."[3]

The next step up in the complexity level of job shop types is the $n/2$ flow shop case, where two or more jobs must be processed on two machines in a common sequence. As in the $n/1$ case, there is an approach that leads to an optimum solution according to certain criteria. This approach, termed Johnson's method (after its developer), consists of the following steps.

1. List the operation time for each job on both machines.
2. Select the shortest operation time.
3. If the shortest time is for the first machine, do the job first; if it is for the second machine, do the job last.
4. Repeat steps 2 and 3 for each remaining job until the schedule is complete.

This procedure can be seen in scheduling four jobs through two machines:

Step 1: List operation times.

Job	Operation time on machine 1	Operation time on machine 2
A	3	2
B	6	8
C	5	6
D	7	4

Steps 2 and 3: Select shortest operation time and assign. Job A is shortest on Machine 2, and is assigned first and performed last.

Step 4: Repeat steps 2 and 3. Job D is second shortest on Machine 2, and is assigned second and performed second last. Job C is third shortest on Machine 1, and is assigned third and performed first. Job B is fourth shortest on Machine 1, and is assigned fourth and performed second.

In summary, the solution sequence is C→B→D→A and the flow time is 25 days, which is a minimum. Also minimized are total idle time and mean idle time. The final schedule appears in Figure 7.8.

Johnson's method has been extended to yield an optimal solution for the $n/3$ case. When flow shop scheduling problems larger than $n/3$ arise (and they generally do), analytical solution procedures leading to optimality are not available. The reason for this is that even though the jobs may arrive in static fashion at the first machine, the scheduling problem becomes dynamic

---

[3] See R. W. Conway, William L. Maxwell, and Louis W. Miller, *Theory of Scheduling* (Reading, Mass.: Addison-Wesley, 1967), for definitions of these terms; quotation on p. 26.

FIGURE 7.8

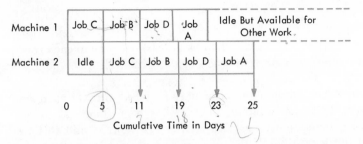

and series of waiting lines start to form in front of machines downstream.

The queuing theory supplement to this chapter discusses approaches to deal with scheduling problems that fall under the "dynamic arrivals" heading. However, in both the static and dynamic cases, Monte Carlo simulation is often the only way of determining the relative merits of different priority rules in real-world situations.

The assignment method

This technique, a special case of the transportation method of linear programming, can be used in job shop scheduling to allocate men to jobs, jobs to machines, etc. Like the Johnson method, the technique is "quick and dirty," and can be applied to problems which have the following characteristics.[4]

1. There are n "things" to be distributed to n "destinations."
2. Each "thing" must be assigned to one and only one "destination."
3. Only one criterion can be utilized—minimum cost, maximum profit, minimum completion time.

TABLE 7.2

| Job | *Machine* | | | | |
	A	*B*	*C*	*D*	*E*
I.............	$5	$6	$4	$8	$3
II.............	6	4	9	8	5
III.............	4	3	2	5	4
IV.............	7	2	4	5	3
V.............	3	6	4	5	5

For example, suppose that a scheduler has five jobs that can be performed on any of five machines ($n = 5$) and that the cost of completing each job-machine combination is shown in Table 7.2. The scheduler would like to devise a minimum cost assignment. (There are 5!, or 120, possible

---

[4] For more "quick and dirty" techniques, see R. D. Woolsey and H. S. Swanson, *Operations Research for Immediate Application, A Quick & Dirty Manual* (New York: Harper & Row, 1975).

assignments.) This problem may be solved by the assignment method, which consists of the following steps.

1. Subtract the smallest number in each *row* from itself and all other numbers in that row. (There will then be at least one zero in each row).
2. Subtract the smallest number in each *column* from all other numbers in that column.
3. Determine if the *minimum* number of lines required to cover each zero is equal to n. If so, an optimum solution has been found, since job-machine assignments must be made at the zero entries and this test proves that this is possible. If the minimum number of lines required is *less* than n, go to step 4.
4. Draw the least possible number of lines through all the zeros (these may be the same lines used in step 3). Subtract the smallest number not covered by lines from itself and all other uncovered numbers and add it to the number at each intersection of lines. Repeat step 3.

For the problem above, the steps listed in Table 7.3 would be followed.

TABLE 7.3

Step 1: Row reduction—the smallest number is subtracted from each row.

Machine

Job	A	B	C	D	E
I..	2	3	1	5	0
II..	2	0	5	4	1
III..	2	1	0	3	2
IV..	5	0	2	3	1
V..	0	3	1	2	2

Step 2: Column reduction—the smallest number is subtracted from each column.

Machine

Job	A	B	C	D	E
I..	2	3	1	3	0
II..	2	0	5	2	1
III..	2	1	0	1	2
IV..	5	0	2	1	1
V..	0	3	1	0	2

Step 3: Apply line test—the number of lines to cover all zeros is 4; since 5 are required, go to step 4.

Machine

Job	A	B	C	D	E
I..	2	3	1	3	0
II..	2	0	5	2	1
III..	2	1	0	1	2
IV..	5	0	2	1	1
V..	0	3	1	0	2

Step 4: Subtract smallest uncovered number and add to intersection of lines—using lines drawn in step 3, smallest uncovered number is 1.

Machine

Job	A	B	C	D	E
I..	1	3	0	2	0
II..	1	0	4	1	1
III..	2	2	0	1	3
IV..	4	0	1	0	1
V..	0	4	1	0	3

Optimum solution—by "line test."

Machine

Job	A	B	C	D	E
I..	1	3	0	2	0
II..	1	0	4	1	1
III..	2	2	0	1	3
IV..	4	0	1	0	1
V..	0	4	1	0	3

Optimum assignments and their costs.

Job I to Machine E.............	$3
Job II to Machine B.............	$4
Job III to Machine C.............	$2
Job IV to Machine D.............	$5
Job V to Machine A.............	$3
Total cost....................	$17

Note that even though there are two zeros in three rows and three columns, the solution shown in Table 7.3 is the only one possible for this problem since Job III must be assigned to Machine C to meet the "assign to zero" requirement. Other problems may have more than one optimum solution, depending, of course, on the costs involved.

The nonmathematical rationale of the assignment method is one of minimizing opportunity costs.[5] For example, if we decided to assign Job I to Machine A instead of to Machine E, we would be sacrificing the opportunity to save $2 ($5 − $3). Now this is just a one-to-one comparison, and the assignment algorithm in effect performs such comparisons for the entire set of alternative assignments by means of row and column reduction, as described in steps 1 and 2. It makes similar comparisons in step 4. Obviously, if assignments are made to zero cells, no opportunity cost, with respect to the entire matrix, is incurred.

Monitoring job performance (the schedule chart). The Gantt chart (mentioned earlier) appears in various forms, and several of these are used for monitoring order progress in job shops. An example of a schedule chart, along with conventional Gantt chart symbols, is illustrated in Figure 7.9.

In this example, Job A is behind schedule by about four hours, Job B is ahead of schedule, and Job C has been completed, after a delayed start for equipment maintenance.

Computerized job shop scheduling (general shop scheduler program)

A number of computer firms have developed job shop scheduling programs, and many of these programs have been used with a good deal of success in industry. One such program package is the General Shop Scheduler, GJSCH$ developed by the General Electric Company and available on time sharing. The essential features of this program, from the user's point of view, can be described as follows.[6]

The purpose of GJSCH$ is to produce feasible schedules for work activities in situations where a job is moved from work center to work center during its production process. It may be used for direct scheduling of the shop; as a "first cut" picture of shop load, to be later refined by other (perhaps manual) techniques; or as a tool for developing job promise dates. It is generally applicable to shops that are characterized by (1) one-of-

---

[5] The underlying rationale of the procedure of adding and subtracting the smallest cell values is as follows: Additional zeros are entered into the matrix by subtracting an amount equal to one of the cells from all cells. Negative numbers, which are not permissible, will occur in the matrix. In order to get rid of the negative numbers, an amount equal to the maximum negative number must be added to each element of the row or column in which it occurs. This results in adding this amount twice to any cell that lies at the intersection of a row and a column that were both changed. The net result is that the lined rows and columns revert to their original amounts, and the intersections increase by the amount subtracted from the uncovered cells. (The reader may wish to prove this to himself by solving the example without using lines.)

[6] Much of this section is drawn from General Electric Company's *User's Guide to General Shop Scheduler GJSCH$* (1970).

FIGURE 7.9

Schedule (or Gantt) chart

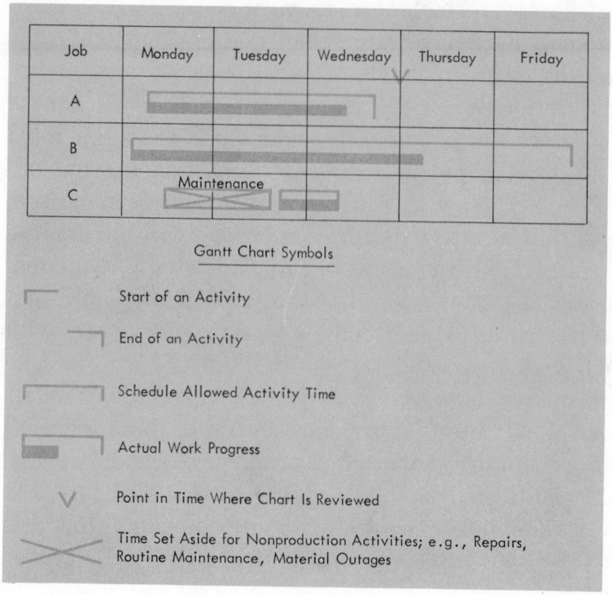

Job	Monday	Tuesday	Wednesday	Thursday	Friday
A					
B					
C					

Gantt Chart Symbols

Start of an Activity

End of an Activity

Schedule Allowed Activity Time

Actual Work Progress

Point in Time Where Chart Is Reviewed

Time Set Aside for Nonproduction Activities; e.g., Repairs, Routine Maintenance, Material Outages

a-kind jobs that are processed through several operations in a variety of work centers, (2) little or no production of items for stock, (3) a high incidence of "specials" work, and (4) infrequent repeat orders for items previously produced. Thus typical applications would be in custom machine shops, maintenance activities, tool and die shops, and foundries.

The program can handle any number of jobs in up to 75 work centers (that is, $n \times 75$ job shop problems). It can schedule "forward" (from today's date forward) or can be "backed off" from the due date. It permits modification of all aspects of work center capacity, and a separate definition of setup time per job. In addition, it permits the inclusion of transit times for a given job between work centers.

The program requires two input files: a machine center file and a job file. The machine center file contains two subfiles. The first describes the on-site machines in terms of their capacity in machine hours; the second describes farm-out centers (i.e., work done outside the shop, usually by subcontractors). Farm-out capacity is expressed in days (and tenths of days), whereas on-site machine capacity is expressed in hours (and tenths of hours). The job file contains a description in hours of the work to be scheduled on each required process. As mentioned above, the program permits inclusion of setup time but will not execute files containing intermixed setup/no setup job data.

To operate the program, the user must respond to a series of questions concerning shop capacity, such as the number of days in the week to be scheduled, whether he wishes to change a specific day's capacity for all machines or a specific machine, etc. Following these questions (ten in all), the user is interrogated as to the type of scheduling and reporting to be performed. He will be asked the name of the job file to be scheduled, whether it contains setup data and transit times, and what type of schedule he prefers.

The user has the choice of a regular schedule or infinite load schedules. A "regular" schedule is prepared within the constraints of the machine center file and responses to the previous questions. "Infinite load" schedules are of two types: one schedules job operations one day apart; the other also schedules jobs one day apart, but the difference between this schedule and machine center capacity is noted. Depending upon the options selected, the user will be asked to respond to as many as eight questions on schedule preparation.

Finally, two reports are generated by GJSCH$. The first is a "job schedule report," detailing the schedule assignments by day, hours, machine center name, and so forth. The second is a "machine center load report," reflecting unassigned time by work center and by day. These reports are shown in Figure 7.10, which should be examined with the following points in mind:

Operations numbers are developed by the program and are reflected in the column immediately following *JOB #*.

Operations that will not meet the job due date are flagged with #.

The numbers of remaining hours necessary to complete an operation (on a given day) are reflected in the *REM HRS* column.

Report titles identify the type of schedule (for example, Forward Loading, Due-Date Loading).

Invalid due dates are not handled on the due date schedule; note job HI.

In evaluating this fairly representative programming package we can see that it is easy to use and flexible (the developers indicate that priorities of jobs can be adjusted by physically moving the position of job data within the job file). On the other hand, there are some disconcerting features about this and similar programs. The user does not really know how the schedule is being generated within the computer, and he does not know how good the schedule is. That is, while the program provides a feasible schedule, it may be a far cry from an optimal one. Nevertheless, such packages generally provide better overall scheduling than can be done by hand methods, and certainly are a boon to firms that cannot afford to develop their own computerized scheduling system.[7]

---

[7] It should be mentioned that when innovations such as computerized scheduling are introduced, a good deal of care should be taken to assure that operating personnel are "sold" on the system. In looking at computer scheduling applications in a variety of facilities, we have observed several cases of a former scheduling system's operating in parallel with its more sophisticated replacement. The reason for this, in general, is that the new system was not adequately explained to department managers and foremen, and hence they had little faith in its reliability.

FIGURE 7.10

Job shop scheduler reports

JOB SCHEDULE REPORT

(NOTE: ITEMS WITH A "#" IN FAR-RIGHT COLUMN WILL NOT MEET DUE DATE)

AVAIL CAP. SCH. - FORWARD LOADING
STD. TRANSIT TIME

JOB#	OP	MACH W.C.	REM HRS	SCH HRS	SCH.DAY	DUE DATE	#
ABCD	1	AB01	0.	6.0	324	406	
ABCD	2	AB02	5.2	8.0	325	406	
ABCD	2	AB02	0.	5.2	326	406	
ABCD	3	AB03	0.	7.8	327	406	
ABCD	4	AB01	6.2	10.0	328	406	
ABCD	4	AB01	0.	6.2	329	406	
HI	1	AB01	4.0	4.0	324	301	#
HI	1	AB01	0.	4.0	325	301	#
HI	2	AB02	5.2	2.8	326	301	#
HI	2	AB02	0.	5.2	327	301	#
HI	3	AB06	0.	7.5	328	301	#
HI	4	AB02	0.	4.0	329	301	#
A17	1	AB01	10.0	6.0	325	411	
A17	1	AB01	0.	10.0	326	411	
XX47	2	AB02	8.4	2.8	327	416	
XX47	2	AB02	0.4	8.0	328	416	
XX47	2	AB02	0.	0.4	329	416	
XX47	3	AB03	1.4	8.0	331	416	
XX47	3	AB03	0.	1.4	401	416	

MACHINE CENTER LOAD REPORT

MACHINE/WORK CENTER LOAD REPORT
REGULAR LOAD
WITH PREV. CAP.

(MACHINES OR WORK CENTERS)

DATE	AB01	AB02	AB03	AB04	AB05	AB06
324	0.	8.0	8.0	8.0	8.0	8.0
325	0.	0.	8.0	8.0	8.0	8.0
326	0.	0.	8.0	8.0	8.0	8.0
327	10.0	0.	0.2	8.0	8.0	8.0
328	0.	0.	8.0	8.0	3.0	0.5
329	3.8	3.6	8.0	8.0	5.0	8.0
330	0.	0.	0.	0.	0.	0.
331	10.0	8.0	0.	8.0	5.0	8.0
401	10.0	8.0	6.6	8.0	8.0	8.0
402	10.0	8.0	8.0	8.0	8.0	8.0
403	10.0	8.0	8.0	8.0	8.0	8.0
404	10.0	8.0	8.0	8.0	8.0	8.0
405	0.	8.0	0.	0.	0.	0.
406	0.	0.	0.	0.	0.	0.
407	10.0	8.0	8.0	8.0	8.0	8.0
408	10.0	8.0	8.0	8.0	8.0	8.0
409	10.0	8.0	8.0	8.0	8.0	8.0
410	10.0	8.0	8.0	8.0	8.0	8.0

Source: General Electric Company, *General Shop Scheduler, GJSCH$ User's Guide* (1970), pp. 11–12.

BATCH SCHEDULING

Batch production is the manufacture of a finite number of identical items, either to meet a specific order or to satisfy continuous demand. When manufacture of the batch is completed, the productive system is available for the production of other products.

Eilon lists three types of batch production:[8]

1. A batch produced only once.
2. A batch produced repeatedly at irregular intervals, when the need arises.
3. A batch produced periodically at known intervals, to satisfy continuous demand.

The first type of batch production presents scheduling problems very similar to the unit scheduling job shop case; the major difference is that producing a batch of items obviously ties up certain equipment longer than if just one of the items is produced (but at the same time it provides for a smaller unit cost since setup costs may be allocated over a number of items). Other differences that affect the scheduling systems are the possibilities for lot splitting in batch production (that is, producing some items now and some later, as a function of other orders in the system) and the option of filling partial orders in batch production (that is, shipping part of a lot before all items are completed, as a convenience to the customer).

The other two types of batch production are commonly associated with productive systems that manufacture their own items for stock, where orders are either received directly from a stock point or wholesaler, or—as is most often the case—are specified by the production plan weeks or months ahead of consumption. Batch production under these conditions presents managers with a certain amount of flexibility in deciding upon a "good" schedule because it relieves them of the pressures of meeting customers' due dates. On the other hand, it adds some complexity to production scheduling because batch size decisions, as well as sequencing decisions, must be made, and these decisions are interrelated: the size of the batch[9] determines the length of the production run, which in turn affects the production schedule and batch sizes of other products.

Batch scheduling by the runout method

The "runout time" method can be used to determine production runs for a group of items that share the same production facilities. Runout time is that period of time for which previously scheduled production, plus inventory on hand, will satisfy demands for an item. The basic objective of this method is to balance the utilization of production capacity—for example, machine hours—so that the runout time for all items is the same.

---

[8] Samuel Eilon, *Elements of Production Planning and Control* (New York: Macmillan, 1962), p. 12.

[9] The economic batch (or lot) size often can be developed in the same manner as the economic order quantity, which is discussed in the next chapter as part of inventory theory.

TABLE 7.4

Runout time calculations

Item	(1.1) Inventory on hand (units)	(1.2) Production time (machine hours per unit)	(1.3) Forecasted usage (units)	(1.4) Inventory on hand (in machine hours) (1.1) × (1.2)	(1.5) Forecasted weekly usage (in machine hours) (1.2) × (1.3)
A........	125	0.2	60	25.00	12.00
B........	250	0.08	85	20.00	6.80
C........	75	0.5	30	37.50	15.00
D........	300	0.09	96	27.00	8.64
E........	239	0.15	78	35.85	11.70
F........	98	0.7	42	68.60	29.40
Aggregate totals.............................				213.95	83.54

$$\text{Aggregate runout time} = \frac{\begin{array}{c}\text{Aggregate}\\\text{inv. on hand}\\(\text{mach. hrs.})\\(\text{col. 1.4})\end{array} + \begin{array}{c}\text{Available}\\\text{machine}\\\text{hours}\end{array} - \begin{array}{c}\text{Aggregate}\\\text{forecasted}\\\text{weekly}\\\text{usage}\\(\text{col. 1.5})\end{array}}{\begin{array}{c}\text{Aggregate forecasted}\\\text{weekly usage (col. 1.5)}\end{array}} = \frac{213.95 + 96.5 - 83.54}{83.54}$$

$$= 2.72 \text{ weeks}$$

Production efforts are thereby balanced across the group of items rather than concentrated on a few items (while other items are neglected).

This procedure is illustrated in Tables 7.4 and 7.5 for six items, where 96.5 machine hours are available to be scheduled during a week. The aggregate runout time (2.72 weeks) is then used in column 2.1 of Table 7.5 to determine the inventories needed at the end of the week if each item is to have a runout time of 2.72 weeks. Column 2.3 shows units that must be scheduled for production in order to meet these inventory requirements.

Runout time method with lot sizes. In many situations, lot sizes are established to achieve an optimum balance between machine setup costs and inventory holding costs, while in other situations they may be dictated solely by such physical limitations as machine capacity.

The runout time method can be applied in scheduling production in both

TABLE 7.5

Schedule required to achieve desired runout time

Item	(2.1) Desired ending inventory (1.3) × 2.72	(2.2) Total items required (1.3) + (2.1)	(2.3) Scheduled (units) (2.2) − (1.1)	(2.4) Production (mach. hrs.) (2.3) × (1.2)
A.............	163	223	98	19.6
B.............	231	316	66	5.3
C.............	82	112	37	18.5
D.............	261	357	57	5.0
E.............	212	290	51	7.7
F.............	114	156	58	40.6

TABLE 7.6

Scheduling lot sizes

Item	Units	Predetermined lot size Machine hours (per unit)	Machine hours (extended)
A................	90	0.2	18.0
B................	150	0.08	12.0
C................	70	0.5	35.0
D................	160	0.09	14.4
E................	100	0.15	15.0
F................	70	0.7	49.0

TABLE 7.7

Runout time determination for items with established lot sizes

Item	(4.1) Inventory on hand or in production	(4.2) Forecasted weekly usage	(4.3) Runout time (weeks) (4.1)/(4.2)
A.............	125	60	2.08
B.............	250	85	2.94
C............	75	30	2.5
D............	300	96	3.12
E............	239	78	3.06
F............	98	42	2.33

situations. For instance, consider the example in the previous section but assume that lot sizes have been established as in Table 7.6.

The objective is to determine the runout time for each item (that time for which previously scheduled production plus inventory on hand will satisfy demands for an item) and then to schedule production in the prescribed lots, starting with the item having the shortest runout time, until the 96.5 machine hours have been scheduled. These runout times are determined in Table 7.7 by dividing the number of items in inventory and in production by forecasted weekly usage.

The 96.5 machine hours would be assigned to items A, F, and C—in that order—since these items have the lowest runout times. Notice that the total machine hours required to produce these three items in their respective lot sizes are 102 (from Table 7.6). Since only 96.5 machine hours are to be scheduled for the period, the difference of 5.5 hours for item C would be scheduled during the following period.

MASS PRODUCTION SCHEDULING

Though mass production is often thought of as synonymous with automobile production, it appears in other forms as well—in the manufacture of electronic components such as resistors (which are made on automatic equipment), in the forming and assembly of appliances and watches, and in the cutting and sewing of clothing, to name but a few. One way of viewing mass production is to think of it as the extreme case of batch production, where one production order becomes the focus of the production facility for an extended period of time. Special-purpose equipment, highly specialized tools, and straight-line production are typical in mass production.

It could be argued, however, that *pure* mass production is a rarity, since even high-volume operations permit variation in the item manufactured. Thus, while a General Motors plant fabricates and assembles Chevrolets, each car may have some special feature making it different from preceding or succeeding cars on the line. Hence the requirement of product homogeneity in the definition of mass production must be loosely interpreted.

The approach used in scheduling mass production operations depends greatly on the technology by which the product is transformed. If the work is mainly manual and utilizes a production line, as in the assembly stages of telephone manufacture, the scheduling problem becomes one of determining the operator task time required to achieve the desired output rate and then evenly distributing these tasks among the production workers. In such situations, the assembly line balancing techniques discussed in Chapter 4 would be appropriate.

Beyond the balancing problem posed in many mass production operations is the problem of coordinating the flow of materials both to and from the point of transformation, whether that transformation is performed on one large machine, in stages in different departments, or on an assembly line. What management wants to avoid is excessive inventory buildup of raw materials at the initial processing point, in-process inventory at various stages in the process, and finished goods inventory at the end of the process. At the same time, management also wants to assure that raw materials, subassemblies, and finished goods are always available to assure a smooth flow of production and to meet customer demand. Achieving this balance requires the development of subschedules relating to the ordering of raw materials, the completion time for subassemblies, and the removal of finished products to storage areas. In the case of large products that are expensive to store, the production schedules have to be dovetailed with transportation schedules for outside shipping agencies such as railroads and ships.

Line of balance

A widely used technique for mass production scheduling is line of balance (LOB),[10] which utilizes the "management by exception" concept. It attempts to identify lagging elements in the production process early enough to avoid delay in delivery of the end item. LOB, developed by the Navy Special Projects Office, is comprised of four elements:

1. A cumulative delivery schedule, termed *the objective*
2. A production plan

---

[10] LOB is also frequently employed in batch scheduling situations.

3. A progress chart
4. Comparison of program progress to the objective—the line of balance that relates progress to the objective

The elements are normally applied in the order listed, but the most vital component is the production plan. The production plan shows, in tree form, the planned sequencing of raw materials, parts, fabrication stages, subassemblies and assemblies, along with pertinent lead time information. This "assembly tree," a network plan, is similar in form to a PERT chart (see Chapter 12 supplement).

The remaining phases of a LOB are represented in the objective chart and the progress chart. Examples of these charts—and a production plan—are shown in Figure 7.11. Planned delivery schedules are plotted on the objective chart as the *objective delivery schedule*. As time progresses, the actual delivery schedule is plotted on the same chart as shown in Figure 7.11. Actual versus planned production rates can be compared by observing the differences in the slopes of the lines, while differences between the actual and the scheduled delivery of subassemblies are represented by the vertical differences between the two lines.

FIGURE 7.11

Line of balance (LOB) charts

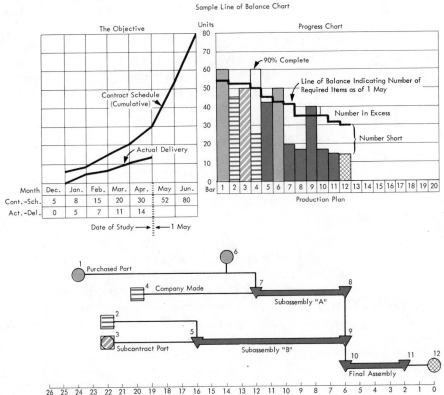

Working Days Prior to Shipment –22 Work Days per Month

The same ordinate (vertical axis) is used on the progress chart as was used for the objective chart. The abscissa scale (horizontal axis) corresponds to the control points shown in the production plan. The colors (or design) in the status or quantity bars in the progress chart correspond to the colors (or design) in the nodes of the production plan. These bars show the quantities of materials, parts, and subassemblies available at the control points at a given time. The *line of balance* (as shown in the example for May (relates the objective, the production plan, and the program progress. This line is the basis for comparing the program progress to the objective, and it depicts the quantities that must be available at each control point if program progress is to remain in line with the objective. It should be apparent that there are more components than end items in most products, and the line of balance will drop as production proceeds. (The procedure for constructing the line of balance is rather involved, and therefore the interested reader is referred to the O'Brien reference in the bibliography, which treats the methodology in detail.)

By studying the objective chart and the progress chart, in conjunction with the production plan, it is possible to identify those elements that are lagging and causing production to fall behind schedule. The element that is lagging in the example is subassembly A (control point 7). By referring to the production plan, it is evident that subassembly A depends on parts 1, 6, and 4. The progress chart shows that parts 1 and 6 are well ahead of schedule whereas part 4 is well behind schedule, but the scheduled units are 90 percent complete. (The bar for part 4 on the progress chart is commonly referred to as a *ghost bar*. The uncolored portion of the bar indicates that an appreciable quantity has been nearly completed, in addition to those units already completed at this point. It would seem that if additional efforts are expended on part 4, it should be possible to bring subassembly A into line with production plans rather rapidly.)

It has been suggested that LOB is a dated technique in light of some of the newer computerized production planning methods. William Fischer, however, points out that LOB still has utility, especially for small firms, prime contractors, and non-manufacturing operations.[11]

PROCESS SCHEDULING

Separating scheduling from aggregate production planning is extremely difficult in process industries since the desired product output combinations and sequences are generally determined during the planning phase. In an oil refinery, for example, an optimum schedule can be derived for the quantity and mix of various fuels, taking into account the productive capacity, storage costs, and profit by use of the linear programming simplex algorithm. The scheduling problem then becomes one of controlling the refining process from the distillation of crude oil through blending and

---

[11] William A. Fischer, "Line of Balance: Obsolete after MRP?", *Production & Inventory Management,* 4th Quarter, 1975, pp. 63–77.

storage. Typical scheduling problems of priorities, sequencing, and evaluation criteria are essentially answered before the fact.

Some interesting problems in process scheduling are encountered in utilities such as electrical plants. A unique feature of these operations is that the product output cannot be stored, yet it must always be available to meet a continuous though varying demand.

A particular power plant might experience a weekly demand pattern as shown in Figure 7.12. The task is to schedule the generators to minimize the operating costs of startup, level, and shutdown operations entailed in meeting these demand variations. The typical basis for such determinations is the incremental cost at various output levels coupled with the incremental costs of changing operating levels. These cost comparisons are ideally suited to computerization. In fact, a number of installations employ computers to monitor the system-loading conditions, to determine the most economical allocation of generation among units, and to send control impulses to each of the units.

FIGURE 7.12

Weekly demand pattern for a power plant

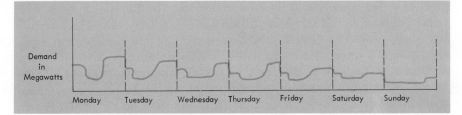

Underground mining also presents some interesting scheduling problems since operations have to be carried out in cycles along a changing workface. For example, drilling, blasting, loading, roof bracing, and movement of machines are carried out one after another; however, since the time of each mining operation will vary according to the nature of the deposit, these operations occur not at fixed times but at random intervals. Fortunately, given enough observations of cycle time variations, it is possible to derive statistical distributions that can become inputs to a queuing theory analysis or a simulation analysis. The findings from such analyses can then be used to derive a schedule for efficient allocation of personnel and machinery at the work area and to determine the timing and sequencing of transportation equipment.

SCHEDULING CUSTOMIZED SERVICES

In terms of scheduling techniques, most custom service systems use very primitive methods that range from appointment lists to "take a number" systems to determine service priorities. In small service operations such simple procedures suffice; however, for large custom service operations, such as hospitals and branch banking (which may have several stages), greater effort must go into designing scheduling systems. Banks have made conscious efforts to improve their customer scheduling through the provision of more tellers, drive-in windows, and extended business hours, although their scheduling rules (first-come, first-served) remain unchanged. Hospitals, on the other hand, present a far more difficult area for efficient scheduling. We will now turn to three aspects of hospital operations that have significant scheduling problems—admissions, surgery, and nursing.

Hospital admissions scheduling

Milsum, Turban, and Vertinsky[12] have developed a schematic representation of three admission systems, which they relate to an input-output model consisting of three decision points or "filters." At the top of Figure 7.13 we see this input-output model and beneath it, three selected admission (and referral) systems which are found in different parts of the world.

In North America (System A), physicians are granted hospital privileges and make a tentative decision as to which hospital each patient will be sent. This decision is subject to approval by hospital administrators and is monitored by a hospital utilization committee. In Europe, System B is typical of countries in which health care is centralized. Here the referring physician is usually a general practitioner, and full-time specialists at available hospitals screen incoming patients. Also in Europe, System C, first instituted in Rotterdam, utilizes a city-wide Central Admissions Bureau (CAB), which directs patients of referring physicians to any one of several hospitals according to bed availability. (The authors note that the system has several advantages over the other two.)

Four major decision variables come into play in analyzing different scheduling policies. These are cited in Table 7.8 along with the quantitative techniques and measures of system effectiveness that have been applied to the problem.

Surgery scheduling

Three researchers[13] used simulation to evaluate five strategies for improving the utilization of operating rooms, recovery rooms, and medical personnel. These strategies (justified on the grounds that operating and recovery times are fairly predictable) were as follows:

1. Random input to surgery. This was the strategy currently being followed by the hospital being studied.

---

[12] Modified from J. Milsum, E. Turban, and I. Vertinsky, "Hospital Admissions Systems: Their Evaluation and Management," *Management Science*, vol. 19, no. 6, February, 1973, pp. 656–58.

[13] N. Kwak, P. Kuzdrall, and H. Schmitz, "The GPSS Simulation of Scheduling Policies for Surgical Patients," *Management Science*, Vol. 22, No. 9, May, 1976, pp. 972–981.

FIGURE 7.13

Schematic representation of selected admission systems.

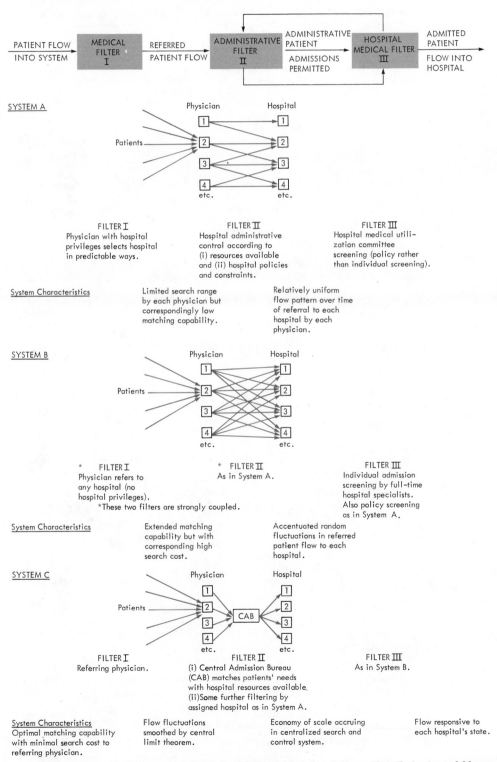

Source: J. Milsum, E. Turban, and I. Vertinsky, "Hospital Admissions Systems: Their Evaluation and Management," *Management Science*, vol. 19, no. 6, February, 1973, p. 649.

TABLE 7.8

Decision variables and techniques used in studies of hospital admissions schedules

Decision variables	Decision making policies	Evaluation technique	Sample measures of effectiveness
Number of patients be scheduled daily	Schedule a constant number every day	Queuing Simulation	1. Level of occupancy 2. Overflow (overload) 3. Stabilization in bed occupancy 4. Variation in daily admission
	Schedule a variable number each day as a function of bed occupancy		
Feasible admission date for each applicant	Analysis of each applicant Number of patients with same health needs should be assigned to a starting date	Linear programming	Deviation from ideal starting date vs. turning a patient away
Scheduling of operations in operating rooms	1. First came, first served 2. Longest cases first 3. Shortest cases first	Simulation	1. Utilization of facilities 2. Average no. of patients waiting 3. Delayed cases 4. Average overtime per day
Scheduling of a standby emergency hospital	Every nth day, or k_1 consecutive days on with k_2 consecutive days off	Simulation	Stabilization of bed occupancy

Source: Modified from J. Milsum, E. Turban, and I. Vertinsky, Hospital Admissions Systems: Their Evaluation and Management, *Management Science*, vol. 19, no. 6, February, 1973, pp. 656–658.

2. Preemptive priority according to need for patient's use of recovery room (without regard to length of surgery).
3. Inverted lineup. Patients requiring the longest surgery are served first. (Long surgery typically requires a stay in the recovery room.) Those not requiring the use of the recovery room are operated on last, with their surgery priority determined by longest surgery first.
4. Longest surgery first, but no priority assigned to those not needing recovery rooms.
5. Special categories of patients first according to rule 3. (That is, patients who require major surgery of long duration and recovery room facilities are scheduled first.)

The main findings of the study were that strategies 2 through 5 provided improvements in utilization rates for both surgery and recovery facilities. On average, Strategies 2 through 5 yield schedules requiring 2.4 hours per day less time in staffing recovery than the current strategy. This comes about because patients arrive later in recovery rooms. Following rule 4 would require one less registered nurse and one less operating room tech-

TABLE 7.9

General problems in nurse scheduling

Problem	*Possible solution*
Accuracy of patient load forecast	Forecast frequently and rebudget monthly. Closely monitor seasonal demands, communicable diseases, and current occupancy.
Forecasting nurse availability	Develop work standards for nurses for each level of possible demand (requires systematic data collection and analysis).
Complexity and time to rebudget	Use available computer programs.
Flexibility in scheduling	Use variable staffing: Set regular staff levels slightly above minimum and absorb variation with broad-skilled float nurses, part-time nurses, and overtime.

nician. The authors point out that the savings in salaries would be greater than the cost of scheduling.

Nurse scheduling

Abernathy, Bayloff, and Hershey state, "The key element of effective nurse staffing is a well-conceived procedure for achieving an overall balance between the size of the nursing staff and the expected patient demand."[14] Their procedure, termed "aggregate budgeting," is predicated on a variety of interrelated activities and has a primary output, a short-term schedule. A number of severe practical problems confront hospitals in deriving an effective yet low-cost aggregate budget. These difficulties along with possible remedies are listed in Table 7.9.

Though most hospitals still use cut-and-try methods in schedule development, management scientists have applied optimizing techniques to the problem with some success. For example, a linear programming model has been developed[15] that, assuming a known, short-run (that is, 3–4 days) demand for nursing care, develops a staffing pattern that:

1. Specifies the number of nurses of each skill class to be assigned among the wards and nursing shifts.
2. Satisfies total nursing personnel capacity constraints.
3. Allows for limited substitution of tasks among nurses.
4. Minimizes the cost of nursing care shortage for the scheduling period.

SCHEDULING STANDARDIZED SERVICES

Standardized service scheduling, as opposed to customized service scheduling, is facilities-oriented rather than customer-oriented. The transporta-

[14] W. Abernathy, N. Bayloff, & J. Hershey, "The Nurse Staffing Problem: Issues and Prospects," *Sloan Management Review*, vol. 13, no. 1, Fall, 1971.

[15] D. Warner and J. Prawda, "A Mathematical Programming Model for Scheduling Nursing Personnel in a Hospital," *Management Science*, vol. 19, no. 4, December, 1972, pp. 411–422.

tion industry is a case in point. Its arrival and departure schedules—theoretically at least—are rigorously adhered to and generally there is little flexibility to meet any one customer's need. Similar schedule inflexibility is found in providing food service to members of institutions, such as prisons, military bases, and college dormitories, and in the operation of governmental services, such as mail delivery, street improvements, and trash removal.

As our final examples of service system scheduling, we will consider two very diverse transportation problems, both of which are of vital concern to the public. These are school bus scheduling and airline scheduling.

School bus scheduling

The general objectives of bus scheduling are to minimize the number of routes, keep mileage at a minimum, have no overloaded buses, and keep route travel time at or below some acceptable level. Angel *et al.* have developed a two-stage approach to solve this problem.[16] The first stage consists of collecting data about students (grade, address, and school) and making the assignment of students to pick-up points. Then, utilizing a map, distances between stops and bus travel time between them is obtained. A mathematical programming algorithm is then applied to find the shortest path in time between any pair of bus stops. Also the number and capacities of the buses, maximum route time in minutes, loading time per student, and allowance for extra time at each stop are obtained. The second stage consists of the actual scheduling, which in essence entails the use of mathematical programming to combine pairs of stops in such a way as to minimize time and distance traveled. The schedule output identifies the number of students, arrival time of the bus, and the time to load the bus, for each stop. It also contains summary data about the route on such factors as route time, loading time, driving speed, total students, total stops, and miles driven.

Airline scheduling

One of the most complex standardized service situations is encountered in the airline branch of the transportation industry. Airline scheduling is essentially a list of single-leg flights to which specific aircraft are ultimately routed.[17] Since airplane flight times, refueling times, maintenance times, etc., are variable, scheduled departure and arrival times will not always be met unless the allowed times are appreciably longer than the average time taken for these activities. Hence the maxim, "The tighter a schedule, the worse its inherent performance."

The scheduling problem encountered by airlines extends beyond the

[16] R. Angel, W. Caudle, R. Noonan, and A. Whinston, "Computer Assisted School Bus Scheduling," *Management Science*, vol. 18, no. 6, February 1973.

[17] Airline scheduling is often confused with airline routing. The distinction is that *scheduling* refers to determining between which places and at what times flights are to be provided while *routing* refers to assigning available planes to those scheduled services in an optimal manner.

equipment itself. Crew scheduling for instance, presents a sizable problem: Pilots' salaries are quite high, and thus it behooves management to make full use of their flying skills each month. Likewise, it is desirable to keep stewardesses working on as many flights as their contracts allow and to avoid "deadheading" and paying for in-transit lodging for airline personnel in general.

In terms of the specific techniques of scheduling, a number of airlines are using computerized Monte Carlo simulation models as a basis for their equipment, manpower, and maintenance schedules. These models have the capability of simultaneously handling such relevant factors as aircraft capacity and availability, maintenance requirements, customer demand, cost per flight, and crew availability, and simulating them in "real time" to arrive at a scheduling decision.[18] By way of example, suppose that a particular plane is in transit, and is grounded for minor repairs. The scheduling system would take note of this and determine, via simulation, whether another plane should be dispatched to continue the flight. Entering into this decision (and the simulation) would be the disposition of the original crew (Should it be part of the continuation flight or should it be rerouted?), the effect on other flights of removal of the backup plane, and, of course, the expected time to complete repairs.

Scheduling of airplane landings and takeoffs has also been simulated, and CRT display units are used by flight controllers to evaluate alternative approach paths, runways, and circling patterns in light of existing air traffic and weather conditions. The sophistication of these systems is such that it is possible to obtain a progressive graphic display of simulated alternative airplane locations in the air and on the ground.[19]

CONCLUSION

The objective of this chapter has been to provide some insight into the nature of scheduling and the diversity of systems where it is performed. To date, the most studied area in the scheduling literature is the job shop. This topic has occupied researchers because of the mathematical problems it poses and because the conclusions drawn from its analysis help provide insight into analogous scheduling situations. Now, however, scheduling research, augmented by the computer, has been undertaken in virtually every type of productive system. In manufacturing, its focus has shifted to integrating the short-run scheduling problem with long-term capacity planning in the context of materials requirements planning (see Chapter 9). In services, it has tended to focus on areas of major public concerns—health care, fuel production, and transportation. It seems now that the major constraints in application of scheduling research lie in making the schedul-

---

[18] An information system is said to operate in "real time" when it has the ability to collect data on events as they occur, to process that data immediately, and to use the new information to influence succeeding events.

[19] Julian Reitman, *Computer Simulation Applications* (New York: John Wiley, 1971), pp. 367–401.

ing systems understandable to those who must use them and making them sufficiently flexible to cope with "the trivial, mundane daily events which conspire to destroy well made plans."[20]

PROPOSITIONS

Propositions contrasting services and manufacturing systems relative to design of the scheduling systems

Product: Because the customer is involved in the creation of the service, the production schedule has a direct effect on him and thus becomes an intrinsic part of the service. In manufacturing the production schedule is distinct from the product it helps to create.

Technology of transformation: In services, the production schedule specifies the timing of an exchange process between the consumer and producer at the point of product consumption. In manufacturing the production schedule specifies only the required operations leading up to the exchange process.

Operating-control system: Because the customer is involved in the creation of the service product, production starting time and total processing time have a direct bearing on the value of the service product. In manufacturing, the customer's primary concern is with completion time.

Workforce: Because there is only a loose relationship between size of the service direct workforce and output, an "optimum" workforce schedule will be difficult, if not impossible, to derive for service systems. In manufacturing, which is characterized by a close relationship between output and workforce size, a provably optimum schedule can often be derived.

REVIEW AND DISCUSSION QUESTIONS

1. Distingiush between a job shop, a flow shop, and a hybrid job shop.
2. What is meant by a schedule evaluation criterion?
3. What is the key operational difference between scheduling standardized services and scheduling customized services?
4. It has been suggested that many of our country's pressing social problems are essentially scheduling problems. Defend this assertion by using some examples.
5. What scheduling rules are commonly used in industry? What is a longest-processing-time rule? Why might it be employed?
6. What is the difference between sequencing and dispatching? Between airline routing and airline scheduling?

---

[20] From a speech by Joseph Orlicky, Manufacturing Industry Education Manager, IBM.

7. Draw a schematic diagram relating the production throughput strategies to the various scheduling techniques described in this chapter.

8. What information is conveyed by the line of balance? How do the three LOB charts interrelate?

9. In the United States we make certain assumptions about the customer service priority rules used in banks, restaurants, and retail stores. If you have the opportunity, ask a foreigner what rules are used in his country. To what factors might you attribute the differences, if any?

10. What are some specific advantages of the System C hospital admission structure from the point of view of scheduling? What are some disadvantages of the system from the point of view of the patient? The physician?

11. A patient in a hospital encounters several schedules besides the ones noted in the chapter. What are these other schedules? Suggest how they might conflict with one another, for a given patient.

PROBLEMS

1. Joe's Auto Seat Cover and Paint Shop is bidding on a contract to do all the custom work for Smiling Ed's used car dealership. One of the main requirements in obtaining this contract is rapid delivery time, since Ed—for reasons we shall not go into here—wants the cars facelifted and back on his lot in a hurry. Ed has told Joe that if he can refit and repaint five cars which he, Ed, has just received (from an unnamed source) in 24 hours or less, the contract will be his. Below is the time (in hours) required in the refitting shop and the paint shop for each of the five cars. Assuming that cars go through the refitting operations before they are repainted, can Joe meet the time requirements and get the contract?

Car	Refitting time	Repainting time
A....................	6 hours	3 hours
B....................	0	4
C....................	5	2
D....................	8	6
E....................	2	1

2. Joe has three cars that must be overhauled by his ace mechanic, Jane. Given the following data about the cars, use Conway's "Rule 4" (least slack per remaining operation) to determine Jane's scheduling priority for each.

Car	Customer pick-up time (hours hence)	Remaining overhaul time (hours)	Remaining operations
A..........	10	4	Painting
B..........	17	5	Wheel alignment, painting
C..........	15	1	Chrome plating, painting, seat repair

3. Joe has branched out into overhauling motorcycles for the local police department. He picks up several cycles at the station and returns each one immediately after completion. The chief of police, however, has been concerned of late with what seems to him to be overlong waiting periods in getting his cycles repaired at Joe's shop. (This is particularly vexing because there has been a wave of auto thefts in the area, and he wants all of his motorcycle officers out on patrol.) In view of his concern, the chief decides to confront Joe and show him that the *average* time his cycles spend in the shop is too long, even though Joe's actual overhaul times are the same as were estimated. Using the last batch of cycles worked on as a case in point, the chief is sure that Joe spent 10 days more on the average than he had to. Given that Joe took an average of 19.8 days per cycle, is the chief correct in his assertion? The overhaul time data for the sample batch of cycles are: A, 8 days; B, 9 days; C, 3 days; D, 2 days; and E, 4 days.

4. Joe has the opportunity to do a big repair job for a local motorcycle club, "The Cretins." (Their cycles were accidentally run over by a garbage truck.) The compensation for the job is good, but it is very important that the total repair time for the five cycles to be fixed be less than 40 hours. (The leader of the club has stated that he would be very distressed if the cycles were not available for a planned "rumble.") Joe knows from experience that repairs of this type often entail several trips between processes for a given cycle, so estimates of time are difficult to provide. Still, Joe has historical data about the probability that a job will start in each process, processing time in each process, and transitional probabilities between each pair of processes. (The data are tabulated below.)

Process	Probability of job starting in process	Processing time probability (hours)			Probability of going from process to other processes or completion (out)			
		1	*2*	*3*	*Frame*	*Engine work*	*Painting*	*Out*
Frame repair	0.5	0.2	0.4	0.4	—	0.4	0.4	0.2
Engine work	0.3	0.6	0.1	0.3	0.3	—	0.4	0.3
Painting	0.2	0.3	0.3	0.4	0.1	0.1	—	0.8

Given this information, use simulation to determine the repair times for each cycle and display your results on a Gantt chart. (Assume that up to five cycles can be worked on at a time in each process.) Based upon your simulation, what do you recommend Joe do next?

5. For a variety of reasons, Joe finds himself in charge of what might be referred to as a "captive machine shop" in a government-operated establishment. The machine shop fabricates and paints metal products, including license plates, road signs, window screens, and door frames, and Joe's major responsibility is to balance the utilization of the equipment across all four products in such a way that demand for each product is satisfied. Given the following data, how might Joe schedule the four products in order to achieve this objective for the next week? What would his schedule look like?

Item	Inventory	Production time per unit	Forecasted weekly usage
Window screens....	200	0.1 hour	100
Door frames.......	100	0.06	50
Road signs........	70	0.3	60
License plates.....	150	0.7	125

Available machine hours = 90/week.

6. Joe has achieved a position of some power in the institution in which he currently resides and works. In fact, things have gone so well that he has decided to divide the day-to-day operations of his business activities among four trusted subordinates: Big Louie, Dirty Dave, Baby Face Nick, and Tricky Dick. The question is how he should do this in order to take advantage of his associates' unique skills and to minimize the costs from running all areas for the next year. The following matrix summarizes the costs that arise under each possible combination of men and areas.

	Area			
	1	*2*	*3*	*4*
Big Louie..............	$1,400	$1,800	$ 700	$1,000
Dirty Dave............	600	2,200	1,500	1,300
Baby Face Nick........	800	1,100	1,200	500
Tricky Dick...........	1,000	1,800	2,100	1,500

7. With reference to problem 5, suppose that Joe has established the following production lot sizes for each product: window screens, 70; door frames, 30; road signs, 35; and license plates, 50.
   a. What would be the runout time in weeks for each product?
   b. How would machine hours be assigned to each item?

8. You and a friend must flow-chart and write six computer programs to be turned in to your data-processing instructor by the end of the semester. You have stalled until the last week of the semester so you can make one continuous run at the six jobs. All of a sudden, your instructor announces that the programs will be due in 40 hours from now, and that all must be turned in to get a passing grade. Given the following processing times, will you and your teammate meet the 40 hour processing time? In what order will you perform the jobs?

Job	Flow-chart time (hours)	Program writing time (hours)
1................	9	1
2................	8	3
3................	5	4
4................	7	11
5................	6	8
6................	2	9

SELECTED BIBLIOGRAPHY

Baker, K. R.   *Introduction to Sequencing and Scheduling.* New York: John Wiley & Sons, 1974.

Buffa, E. S.　*Operations Management: The Management of Productive Systems.* New York: Wiley/Hamilton, 1976.

Conway, R. W., Maxwell, William L., and Miller, Louis W.　*Theory of Scheduling.* Reading, Mass.: Addison-Wesley, 1967.

Day, James E., and Hottenstein, Michael P.　"Review of Sequencing Research," *Naval Research Logistics Quarterly,* vol. 27, no. 1 (March 1970), pp. 11–39.

Eilon, Samuel　*Elements of Production Planning and Control.* New York: Macmillan, 1962.

Johnson, S. M.　"Optimal Two Stage and Three Stage Production Schedules with Setup Times Included," *Naval Logistics Quarterly,* vol. 1, no. 1 (March 1954), pp. 61–68.

Magee, J. F., and Boodman, D. M.　*Production Planning and Inventory Control.* 2d ed. New York: McGraw-Hill, 1967.

Niland, Powell　*Production Planning, Scheduling, and Inventory Control.* New York: Macmillan, 1971.

O'Brien, James J.　*Scheduling Handbook.* New York: McGraw-Hill, 1969.

Woolsey, R. D., and Swanson, H. S.　*Operations Research for Immediate Application, A Quick and Dirty Manual.* New York: Harper & Row, 1975.

Supplement to chapter seven

Waiting line theory

WAITING LINE or queuing theory was originated in the early 1900s by the Danish mathematician A. K. Erlang, who employed it to study problems of telephone traffic. Since that time, and especially since the end of World War II, waiting line theory has had extensive application in industry and has become a standard tool of operations management.

Though a number of formulas for solving waiting line problems will be provided, the emphasis of this supplement is on the structure and solution of waiting line situations rather than on the mathematical aspects of the topic. The reason for this approach is twofold. First, the mathematics underlying waiting line theory is fairly sophisticated, even for the simpler models, and defies summarization in a form useful to the beginning student. Second, and more importantly, the key problem in waiting line theory is determining whether a particular situation is in fact amenable to a queuing approach. This type of insight rests upon comprehending the "big picture," which is most readily imparted by presenting the range of queuing structures.

THE WAITING LINE PROBLEM

A waiting line situation arises whenever arrivals at a service facility desire similar services. Such situations, of course, exist in virtually every productive system and are a fact of life in even the most prosaic human activities.

Central to the waiting line problem is a tradeoff decision—that is, comparing the extra cost of providing more rapid service (more traffic lanes, additional checkout stands, etc.) with the inherent costs of waiting (lost customers, larger waiting rooms, longer waiting lines, etc.). In some instances this cost tradeoff decision is straightforward. For example, if we find that the total time our employees spend in line waiting to use a copying machine would otherwise be spent in productive activity, we could compare the cost of adding an additional machine to the value of employee time saved. The decision could then be reduced to dollar terms and the choice easily made.

On the other hand, suppose that our waiting line problem centers upon the demand of patients for beds in a hospital. We can compute the cost of additional beds by summing the costs for building construction, additional equipment required, and increased maintenance. But what is on the other side of the scale? Here we are confronted with the problem of trying to place a dollar figure on a patient's need of a hospital bed and finding none available. While we can arrive at an estimate of lost hospital income, what about the human cost arising from this lack of adequate hospital care?

Consider another waiting line that forms every fall—the registration line in college. If we desire to speed the registration process by adding more service lines, the college will incur additional costs in paying more clerks and student assistants. To be weighed against this additional cost to the college is the time saved by the students—a commodity that defies economic quantification. Some may state that the cost of a student's standing in line is a negligible factor in the university budget, although the student will be reluctant to agree that his time has no value.

In summary, these two examples show that the mere existence of a tradeoff does not guarantee that it can be adequately quantified or that it will be explicitly considered in decision making. Of course, such considerations extend far beyond waiting line problems.

WAITING LINE CHARACTERISTICS

Figure S.7.1 depicts a conceptual framework for viewing the various characteristics of waiting line problems. A detailed examination of these characteristics, under the major framework headings, is given in Figure

FIGURE S.7.1

Framework for viewing waiting line situations

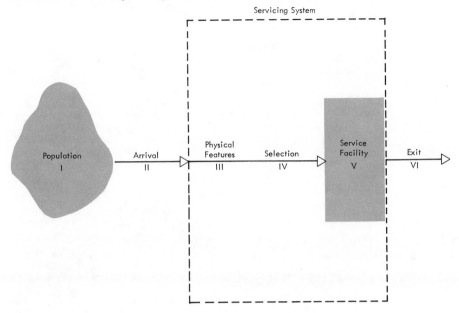

S.7.2. The ensuing discussion is devoted to elaboration upon each of these items.

I. Population source

The source of arrivals at a service system may be a *finite* or an *infinite* population. A factory has a finite number of machines that may require repair—that is, become *arrivals* to the repair facility or repair crew. A physician has a finite number of regular patients. In practical terms, an infinite population, in contrast, is one that is large in *comparison* to the service system. Thus, for a barbershop, 200 customers may be treated as an infinite population, but at least several hundred thousand vehicles would be required to constitute an infinite population for the California freeway system

II. Arrival characteristics

Pattern. The arrivals at a system are far more *controllable* than is generally recognized. Barbers may decrease their Saturday arrival rate (and supposedly shift it to other days of the week) by charging an extra 50 cents for adult haircuts and/or charging adult prices for children's haircuts. Department stores run sales during the off-season or "one-day-only" sales in part for purposes of control. Airlines offer "excursion" and off-season rates for similar reasons. The simplest of all arrival-control devices is the posting of business hours.

FIGURE S.7.2

Characteristics of waiting line problems

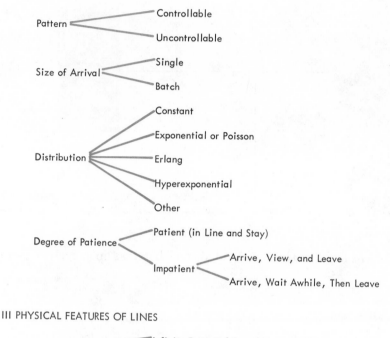

Some service demands are clearly *uncontrollable*, such as emergency medical demands on a city's hospital facilities. However, even in these situations the arrivals at emergency rooms in specific hospitals are controllable to some extent by, say, keeping ambulance drivers informed of each hospital's status.

Size of arrival units. A *single arrival* may be thought of as one unit when a unit is defined as the smallest number handled. A single arrival on the floor of the New York Stock Exchange is 100 shares of stock; a single arrival at an egg processing plant might be a dozen eggs or a flat of two and a half dozen.

A *batch arrival* is some multiple of the unit, as a block of 1,000 shares

FIGURE S.7.2 (*continued*)

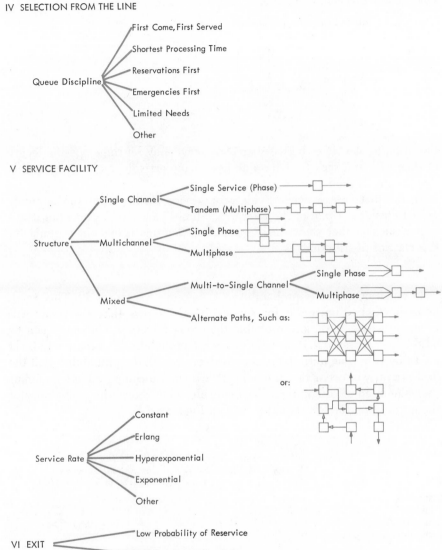

IV SELECTION FROM THE LINE

Queue Discipline
- First Come, First Served
- Shortest Processing Time
- Reservations First
- Emergencies First
- Limited Needs
- Other

V SERVICE FACILITY

Structure
- Single Channel
  - Single Service (Phase)
  - Tandem (Multiphase)
- Multichannel
  - Single Phase
  - Multiphase
- Mixed
  - Multi-to-Single Channel
    - Single Phase
    - Multiphase
  - Alternate Paths, Such as:

  or:

Service Rate
- Constant
- Erlang
- Hyperexponential
- Exponential
- Other

VI EXIT
- Low Probability of Reservice
- Return to Source Population

on the NYSE, a case of eggs at the processing plant, or a party of five at a restaurant.

Distribution of arrivals. A *constant* arrival distribution is periodic, with exactly the same time period between successive arrivals (see Figure S.7.3). In productive systems, about the only arrivals that truly approach a constant interarrival period are those that are subject to machine control.

Two views can be taken of any arrival process. Either we can look at the time between successive arrivals to gain some insight into the probabili-

FIGURE S.7.3

Constant arrival pattern with time interval $= t$ and variance $= 0$

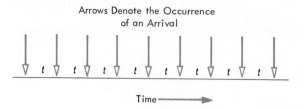

Arrows Denote the Occurrence
of an Arrival

Time ⟶

ties of particular times between arrivals or we may set some specific length of time (T) and seek to determine how many arrivals might occur within that length of time (see Figure S.7.4).

In the first case, when arrivals at a service facility occur on a purely random fashion, a plot of the interarrival times yields an *exponential* distribution such as that shown in Figure S.7.5. The mathematical formula for this class of distributions is

$$f(t) = \lambda e^{-\lambda t} \tag{1}$$

In equation (1), the probability $f(t)$ is often written as P_t. This equation, shown in Figure 7.5 for single arrivals, shows that short intervals between arrivals are more probable than long intervals. The curve can be used in two ways: first, it directly shows the probability that there will be at least t units of time until the next arrival, or second, the probability that the next arrival will occur in a time of t or less can be computed as one minus the value read off the curve. The following table shows the probability of the next arrival for several values of t in Figure S.7.5.

t	Probability that the next arrival will occur in t minutes or more. (Read directly from Figure S7.5) f(t)	Probability that the next arrival will occur in t minutes or less [1 − f(t)]
0 minutes	1.0	1 − 1.0 = 0
1 minute	0.35	1 − 0.35 = 0.65
2 minutes	0.15	1 − 0.15 = 0.85
4 minutes	0	1 − 0 = 1.0

FIGURE S.7.4

Variable arrival pattern

T

t_1 t_2 t_3 t_4 t_5 t_6

Time ⟶

FIGURE S.7.5

Exponential distribution of $\lambda e^{-\lambda t}$ where $\lambda = 1$

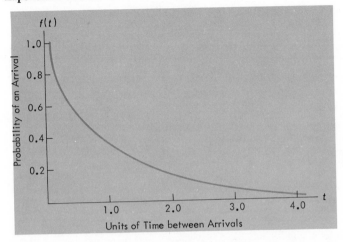

In the second case, where one is interested in the number of arrivals during some time period T, the distribution appears as in Figure S.7.6 and is obtained by finding the probability of n arrivals during T. If the arrival process is random, the distribution is the *Poisson*, and formula 2 applies.

$$P_T(n) = \frac{(\lambda T)^n e^{-\lambda T}}{n!} \tag{2}$$

Equation (2) shows the probability of exactly n arrivals in time T. For example, if the arrival rate of units into a system is 3 per minute ($\lambda = 3$) and we want to find the probability that exactly 5 units will arrive within a 1 minute period ($n = 5, T = 1$), we have,

FIGURE S.7.6

Poisson distribution for $\lambda T = 4$.

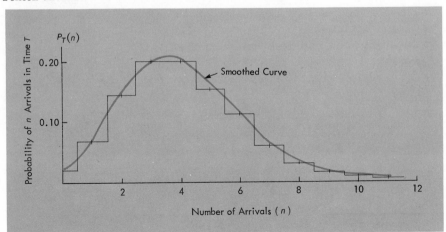

$$P_{1,\,5} = \frac{(3 \times 1)^5 e^{-3 \times 1}}{5!} = \frac{3^5 e^{-3}}{120} = 2.275 e^{-3} = 0.114$$

That is, there is an 11.4% chance that there will be 5 arrivals in any one minute interval.

Although often shown as a smoothed curve, as in Figure S.7.5, the Poisson distribution is a discrete distribution (the curve becomes smoother as n becomes larger). The distribution is discrete because n refers, in our example, to the number of arrivals in a system, and this must be an integer (for example, there cannot be 1.5 arrivals).

The term *Erlang* applies to a class of density functions that are useful in representing a variety of interarrival time distributions. The generic function for any Erlang distribution is

$$f(t) = \frac{K\lambda (K\lambda t)^{K-1} e^{-K\lambda t}}{(K-1)!} \qquad (3)$$

All such distributions have a mean of $1/\lambda$ and a variance of $1/K\lambda^2$. In this formula K is any positive integer and is used to distinguish one Erlang distribution from another; that is, if $K = 1$ we would be referring to a first-order Erlang distribution, if $K = 2$, to a second-order Erlang distribution, and so forth.

Depending on which value of K is selected, a distribution may be shaped to approximate the actual observed data. Examining the extremes of this equation, we note that when $K = 1$, the time to observe one arrival reduces to $\lambda e^{-\lambda t}$, which is in fact the exponential distribution. When K becomes very large, the variance becomes zero, which means that the time between arrivals becomes constant. Figure S.7.7 shows several Erlang distributions with $\lambda = 1$.

The exponential distribution has a mean of $1/\lambda$ and a variance of $1/\lambda^2$, and the Poisson distribution has both a mean and a variance that are equal to λ. Frequently, empirically observed distributions have the same mean as the simple exponential or Poisson distributions but exhibit greater variability. When this occurs, the prefix *hyper* is used to denote them. A *hyperexponential* variance has the form j/λ^2 and a *hyperpoisson* variance is $j\lambda$, where j is greater than 1. When $j = 1$, the variances become the simple exponential or Poisson distribution variances.

A frequent application of the hyperexponential distribution occurs in a service facility that has several channels with differing exponential service rates. The hyperexponential distribution that results is the weighted average of the service distribution of each channel and the probability that an arrival will be assigned to that channel (see the Saaty bibliographical reference).

Other distributions. Most real-life arrival distributions differ from the mathematical equations stated above. The degree to which they vary will obviously be reflected in the accuracy of results when these mathematical distributions are used to approximate the real-world occurrence. When

FIGURE S.7.7

Erlang distributions with $\lambda = 1$

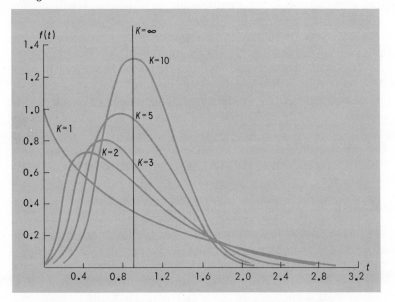

this difference is substantial, or when higher precision is desired, the technique of simulation is the logical alternative.

Degree of patience. A *patient* arrival is one who waits as long as necessary until the service facility is ready to serve him. (Even if an arrival grumbles and behaves *impatiently*, the fact that he waits is sufficient to label him as a patient arrival for purposes of waiting line theory.)

There are two classes of *impatient* arrivals. The first class arrives, surveys both the service facility and the length of the line, and then decides to leave. The second class arrives, views the situation and joins the waiting line, and then, after some period of time, departs. The behavior of the first type is termed *balking* and the second is termed *reneging*.

III. Physical features of lines

Length. In a practical sense, an infinite line is very long in terms of the capacity of the service system. Examples of *infinite potential length* are a line of vehicles backed up for miles at a bridge crossing or customers waiting to purchase tickets at a theater who must form a line around the block.

Such systems as gas stations, loading docks, and parking lots have *limited line capacity* due to legal restrictions or physical space characteristics. This complicates the waiting line problem not only in terms of service system utilization and waiting time computations but in terms of the shape of the actual arrival distribution as well. The arrival who is denied entry into the line because of lack of space may rejoin the population for a later try, or he may seek service elsewhere. Either action makes an obvious difference in the finite population case.

Number of lines. A *single line* or single file is, of course, one line only. The term *multiple lines* refers either to the single lines that form in front of two or more servers or to single lines that converge at some central redistribution point. The disadvantage of multiple lines in a busy facility is that arrivals often will shift lines if several previous services have been of short duration or if those customers currently in other lines appear to require a short service time. Although the overall characteristics of the facility and the expected waiting time of a customer remain the same, the variability within customers' waiting time will increase if customers are not equally skilled in the art of switching lines. When this inequality exists, the effect is the same as if special priorities are given to a particular class of customer.

IV. Selection from the waiting line

Queue discipline. A queue discipline is a priority rule, or set of rules, for determining the order of service to customers in a waiting line. As pointed out with respect to scheduling in Chapter 7, the rules selected can have a dramatic effect on the system's overall performance. In waiting line situations, the number of customers in line, the average waiting time, the range of variability in waiting time, and the efficiency of the service facility are just a few examples of factors that are affected by the choice of priority rules.

By way of illustration, if the major objective of the service facility is to maximize the number of jobs processed, it may be shown mathematically[1] that the best priority rule to use is the *shortest processing time* (SPT). This rule states that after the processing time required by all jobs in line is listed, the job requiring the shortest time will be selected next. The list is continually updated for each new arrival. However, the problem with this rule is that some jobs will never be processed since the customers who require long service will be bypassed by new arrivals. This may result either in customers' withdrawing from the line to go elsewhere or perhaps the incurring of a penalty cost by the system for processing delays.

Probably the most common priority rule is *first-come first-served* (FCFS). This rule states that the customers in line are served solely on the basis of their chronological arrival; no other characteristics has any bearing on the selection process. This is popularly accepted as the "fairest" rule, but in practice it discriminates against the arrival requiring a short service time. A common example occurs in the supermarket, where the shopper with a single item must either wait a long time or rely on the largesse of those ahead of him who may have shopping baskets full of groceries (express lines are mentioned below under "line structuring rules").

Reservations first, emergencies first, highest-profit customer first, largest orders first, best customers first, longest waiting time in line, and *soonest*

---

[1] See Chapter 7.

promised date are other examples of priority rules. As was pointed out in Chapter 7, each rule has attractive features as well as shortcomings.

Line structuring rules. "Single transactions only" (as in a bank) or "limited needs" (such as a quick checkout in a market) are directives that are similar to priority rules, though in reality they are methodologies for structuring the line itself. Such lines are formed of a specific class of customers with similar characteristics. Within each line, however, priority rules still apply (as before) to the method of selecting the next customer to be served. A classic case of line structuring is the fast checkout line for customers with six items or less in a busy supermarket. Interestingly enough, the advantage of such a separate line is mainly psychological, since the same service could be achieved by permitting people who buy six items or less to go to the head of the line.

V. Service facility

Structure. The physical flow of items to be serviced may go through a single line, multiple lines, or some mixture of the two. The choice of format depends partly on the volume of customers served and partly on the restrictions imposed by sequential requirements as to the order in which service must be performed.

Single channel, single phase. This is the simplest type of waiting line structure, and straightforward formulas are available to solve the problem for standard distribution patterns of arrival and service. When the distributions are nonstandard, the problem is easily solved by computer simulation. A typical example of a single-channel, single-phase situation is the one-man barbershop.

Single channel, tandem service. A carwash is an illustration of this multiphase case, for a series of services—vacuuming, wetting, washing, rinsing, drying, window cleaning, and parking—is performed in a fairly uniform sequence. A critical factor in the single-channel case with service in series is the amount of buildup of items allowed in front of each service, which in turn constitutes separate waiting lines.

Because of the inherent variability in service times, the optimal situation in terms of maximizing the utilization of the service station is to allow the building of an infinite waiting line in front of each station. The worst situation is that in which no line is permitted and only one customer at a time is allowed. When no sublines are allowed to build up in front of each station, as in a car wash, the utilization of the overall service facility is governed by the probability that a long service time will be required by any one of the servers in the system. This problem is common in most product-oriented systems. In process-oriented systems, such as job shops, the processing of orders in lots—rather than singly—permits maximum utilization of the server by allowing the inventory of available items to absorb the variation in performance time.

Multichannel, single phase. Tellers' windows in a bank and checkout counters in a supermarket exemplify this type of structure. The difficulty with this format is that the uneven service time given each customer will result in unequal speed or flow among the lines. This, in turn, results in some customers' being served before others who arrived earlier, as well as in some degree of line shifting. Varying this structure to assure the servicing of arrivals in chronological order would entail the forming of a single line, from which, as a server becomes available, the next customer in the queue is assigned to that server.

The major problem of this structure is that it requires rigid control of the line to maintain order and to direct customers to available servers. In some instances, assigning numbers to customers in order of their arrival helps alleviate this problem.

Multichannel, multiphase. This case is similar to the one above, except that two or more services are performed in sequence. The admission of patients in a hospital follows this pattern because a specific sequence of steps is usually followed: initial contact at the admissions desk, filling out forms, making identification tags, obtaining a room assignment, escorting the patient to the room, etc. Since several servers are usually available for this procedure, more than one patient at a time may be processed.

Mixed. Under this general heading we may consider two subcategories: (a) *multi-to-single-channel structures* and (b) *alternate path structures*. Under (a) we find either lines that merge into one for single-phase service, as at a bridge crossing where two lanes merge into one, or lines that merge into one for multiple phase service, such as subassembly lines feeding into a main line. Under (b) we encounter two structures that differ in directional flow requirements. The first is similar to the multiple channel–multiple phase case, except that (1) there may be switching from one channel to the next after the first service has been rendered and (2) the number of channels and phases may vary—again—after performance of the first service.

The second structure has no flow restrictions, and customers arriving at this facility may obtain whatever services are required and in any sequence. This is the job shop format, and here we encounter a very complex scheduling problem. To date there are no known methods for obtaining an optimal solution for such problems. Most progress has been through computer simulation that uses a variety of configurations and priority rules (see supplement to Chapter 6).

Service rate. The rationale underlying these distributions is similar to the descriptions under the heading "distribution of arrivals." A *constant* service time rule states that each service takes exactly the same time. As in constant arrivals, this characteristic is generally limited to machine-controlled operations. Analogous to their use in arrival rates, the *Erlang* and *hyperexponential* distributions are used to represent service times when they appear to be better approximations of the observed rate than is a simpler distribution.

A frequently used illustration of the *Erlang* distribution employs a single-channel, tandem-service situation. However, the conditions that must be met for the Erlang approximation are so severe as to make practical application rare. The distribution applies only when each service in the series is exponentially distributed with the same mean and no time delay is allowed between them. An example will illustrate the restrictions in one application. Suppose that, in rebuilding machines, one repairman has a sequence of five operations to perform. If his service time for *each* operation is exponentially distributed, with *each* having the same average completion time, the Erlang equations may be used to solve the problem (with K equal to the number of services, or five in this example). Such conditions, however, are seldom found in practice.

The *exponential* distribution is frequently used to approximate the actual service distribution. This practice, however, often leads to incorrect results in that very few service situations are closely represented by the exponential function, since the service facility must be capable of performing services of very short duration relative to the average time of service. Telephone usage (the original subject of queuing theory) is one of the few systems that embodies this feature, and therefore it is well approximated by the exponential. This is so because telephone usage may range from a few seconds —where the user picks up the receiver and replaces it, having changed his mind about making the call, or where the user dialed the first number wrong and starts over again—to a conversation of an hour or more.

Even in telephony, however, this distribution has its peculiarities. For example, it has been shown that there is a noticeable variation between the actual service time and the exponential approximation between 20 and 30 seconds. This happens in the case of a caller who, having dialed a number, waits for an answer to determine whether the call is to the correct destination and whether the party he is calling is available. Another deviation from the exponential approximation occurs with toll calls when a minimum charge is made for a specific number of minutes. If the caller is charged for three minutes' usage, there is an observed tendency on the part of the caller to approach that minimum rather than complete his call in one or two minutes.

Most other types of services also have some "practical" minimum time. A clerk in a checkout line may have a three-minute average service time but a one-minute minimum time. This is particularly true where another checkout aisle provides quick service. Likewise in a barbershop: while the average service time of a barber may be 20 minutes, he rarely cuts hair or gives a shave in less than 10 or more than 45 minutes.

Hence these and similar types of services that have strong time dependency are poorly characterized by the exponential curve. Unfortunately, data collectors on a given problem frequently group their data in increments so that, when they are plotted as a histogram, the exponential approximation seems valid. If smaller time increments were taken, however, the inapplicability of the distribution would be obvious at the lower time values.

VI. Exit

Once a customer is served, two exit fates are possible: (1) he can *return to the source population* and immediately become a competing candidate for service again or (2) he may enter a category with a *low probability of reservice*. The first case can be illustrated by a machine which has been routinely repaired and returned to duty but may break down again; the second can be illustrated by a machine that has been overhauled or modified and has a low probability of reservice over the near future. In a lighter vein, we might refer to (1) as the "recurring common cold case" and to (2) as the "appendectomy only once case."

It should be apparent that when the population source is finite, any change in the service performed on customers who return to the population will modify the arrival rate at the service facility. This, of course, will alter the characteristics of the waiting line under study and necessitate reanalysis of the problem.

SAMPLE PROBLEMS

Model 1

Western National Bank is considering opening a drive-in window for customer service. Management estimates that customers will arrive for service at the rate of 15 per hour. The teller whom it is considering to staff the window can service customers at the rate of one every three minutes.

Assuming Poisson arrivals and exponential service, find
1. Utilization of the teller
2. Average number in the waiting line
3. Average number in the system
4. Average waiting time in line
5. Average waiting time in the system

Solution (using model 1 equations from Table S.7.3).
1. The average utilization of the teller is

$$\rho = \frac{\lambda}{\mu} = \frac{15}{20} = 75 \text{ percent}$$

2. The average number in the waiting line is

$$\bar{n}_l = \frac{\lambda^2}{\mu(\mu - \lambda)} = \frac{(15)^2}{20(20 - 15)} = 2.25 \text{ customers}$$

3. The average number in the system is

$$\bar{n}_s = \frac{\lambda}{\mu - \lambda} = \frac{15}{20 - 15} = 3 \text{ customers}$$

4. Average waiting time in line is

$$\bar{t}_l = \frac{\lambda}{\mu(\mu - \lambda)} = \frac{15}{20(20 - 15)} = 0.15 \text{ hour or 9 minutes}$$

5. Average waiting time in the system is

$$\bar{t}_s = \frac{1}{\mu - \lambda} = \frac{1}{20 - 15} = 0.2 \text{ hour or 12 minutes}$$

Because of limited space availability and a desire to provide an acceptable level of service, the bank manager would like to assure, with 95 per-

TABLE S.7.1

Properties of some specific waiting line models

Model	Layout	Service phase	Source population	Arrival pattern	Queue discipline	Service pattern	Permissible queue length	Typical example
(1)	Single channel	Single	Infinite	Poisson	FCFS	Exponential	Unlimited	Drive-in teller at bank, one-lane toll bridge
(2)	Single channel	Single	Infinite	Poisson	FCFS	Constant	Unlimited	Automatic car wash, roller coaster rides in amusement park
(3)	Single channel	Single	Infinite	Poisson	FCFS	Exponential	Limited	Ice cream stand, cashier in a restaurant
(4)	Single channel	Single	Infinite	Poisson	FCFS	Any distribution	Unlimited	Empirically derived distribution of flight time for a transcontinental flight
(5)	Single channel	Single	Infinite	Poisson	FCFS	Erlang	Unlimited	One-man barbershop
(6)	Multiple channel	Single	Infinite	Poisson	FCFS	Exponential	Unlimited	Parts counter in auto agency, two-lane toll bridge
(7)	Single channel	Single	Finite	Poisson	FCFS	Exponential	Unlimited	Machine breakdown and repair in a factory

TABLE S.7.2

Notation for queuing formulas (infinite)

σ = Standard deviation

λ = Arrival rate

μ = Service rate

$\dfrac{1}{\mu}$ = Average service time

$\dfrac{1}{\lambda}$ = Average time between arrivals

ρ = Potential utilization of the service facility (defined as λ/μ)

$\bar{n}_l$ = Average number waiting in line

$\bar{n}_s$ = Average number in system (including any being served)

$\bar{t}_l$ = Average time waiting in line

$\bar{t}_s$ = Average total time in system (including time to be served)

K = Kth distribution in the Erlang family of curves

n = Number of units in the system

M = Number of identical service channels

Q = Maximum queue length (sum of waiting space and service space)

P_n = Probability of exactly n units in system

P_w = Probability of waiting in line

Finite queuing notation (based on Peck and Hazelwood tables)

D = Probability that an arrival must wait in line

F = Efficiency factor, a measure of the effect of having to wait in line

H = Average number of units being serviced

J = Population source less those in queuing system $(N - n)$

L = Average number of units in line

M = Number of service channels

n = Average number of units in queuing system (including the one being served)

N = Number of units in population source

P_n = Probability of exactly n units in queuing system

T = Average time to perform the service

U = Average time between customer service requirements

W = Average waiting time in line

X = Service factor, or proportion of service time required

TABLE S.7.3
Equations for models in Table S.7.1 (see Table S.7.2 for explanation of notation)

Model 1

$$\bar{n}_l = \frac{\lambda^2}{\mu(\mu-\lambda)} \qquad \bar{t}_l = \frac{\lambda}{\mu(\mu-\lambda)} \qquad P_n = \left(1 - \frac{\lambda}{\mu}\right)\left(\frac{\lambda}{\mu}\right)^n$$

$$\bar{n}_s = \frac{\lambda}{\mu-\lambda} \qquad \bar{t}_s = \frac{1}{\mu-\lambda} \qquad \rho = \frac{\lambda}{\mu}$$

Model 2

$$\bar{n}_l = \frac{\lambda^2}{2\mu(\mu-\lambda)} \qquad \bar{t}_l = \frac{\lambda}{2\mu(\mu-\lambda)}$$

$$\bar{n}_s = \bar{n}_l + \frac{\lambda}{\mu} \qquad \bar{t}_s = \bar{t}_l + \frac{1}{\mu}$$

Model 3

$$\bar{n}_l = \left(\frac{\lambda}{\mu}\right)^2 \left[\frac{1 - Q\left(\frac{\lambda}{\mu}\right)^{Q-1} + (Q-1)\left(\frac{\lambda}{\mu}\right)^Q}{\left(1-\frac{\lambda}{\mu}\right)\left(1-\left(\frac{\lambda}{\mu}\right)^Q\right)}\right]$$

$$\bar{n}_s = \bar{n}_l + \frac{\lambda}{\mu}\left[\frac{1 - (Q+1)\left(\frac{\lambda}{\mu}\right)^Q + Q\left(\frac{\lambda}{\mu}\right)^{Q+1}}{\left(1-\frac{\lambda}{\mu}\right)\left(1-\left(\frac{\lambda}{\mu}\right)^{Q+1}\right)}\right] \qquad P_n = \left[\frac{1-\frac{\lambda}{\mu}}{1-\left(\frac{\lambda}{\mu}\right)^{Q+1}}\right]\left(\frac{\lambda}{\mu}\right)^n$$

Model 4

$$\bar{n}_l = \frac{\left(\frac{\lambda}{\mu}\right)^2 + \lambda^2\sigma^2}{2\left(1-\frac{\lambda}{\mu}\right)} \qquad \bar{t}_l = \frac{\frac{\lambda}{\mu^2} + \lambda\sigma^2}{2\left(1-\frac{\lambda}{\mu}\right)}$$

$$\bar{n}_s = \bar{n}_l + \frac{\lambda}{\mu} \qquad \bar{t}_s = \bar{t}_l + \frac{1}{\mu}$$

Model 5

$$\bar{n}_l = \frac{K+1}{2K} \cdot \frac{\lambda^2}{\mu(\mu-\lambda)} \qquad \bar{t}_l = \frac{K+1}{2K} \cdot \frac{\lambda}{\mu(\mu-\lambda)}$$

$$\bar{n}_s = \bar{n}_l + \frac{\lambda}{\mu} \qquad \bar{t}_s = \bar{t}_l + \frac{1}{\mu}$$

Model 6

$$\bar{n}_l = \frac{\lambda\mu\left(\frac{\lambda}{\mu}\right)^M}{(M-1)!(M\mu-\lambda)^2}P_0 \qquad \bar{t}_l = \frac{P_0\left(\frac{\lambda}{\mu}\right)^M}{\mu M M!\left(1 - \frac{\lambda}{\mu M}\right)^2}$$

$$\bar{n}_s = \bar{n}_l + \frac{\lambda}{\mu} \qquad \bar{t}_s = \bar{t}_l + \frac{1}{\mu}$$

$$P_0 = \frac{1}{\sum\limits_{n=0}^{M-1}\frac{\left(\frac{\lambda}{\mu}\right)^n}{n!} + \frac{\left(\frac{\lambda}{\mu}\right)^M}{M!\left(1-\frac{\lambda}{\mu M}\right)}} \qquad P_w = \left(\frac{\lambda}{\mu}\right)^M \frac{P_0}{M!\left(1 - \frac{\lambda}{\mu M}\right)}$$

Model 7

This is a finite queuing situation that is most easily solved by using finite queuing tables. These tables, in turn, require the manipulation of specific terms (see Table S.7.2 for notation).

$$X = \frac{T}{T+U} \qquad H = FNX \qquad L = N(1-F)$$

$$P_n = \frac{N!}{(N-n)!}X^n P_0 \qquad J = NF(1-X)$$

$$W = \frac{L(T+U)}{N-L} = \frac{LT}{H} \qquad F = \frac{T+U}{T+U+W}$$

$$n = L + H$$

cent confidence, that not more than three cars will be in the system at any one time. What is the present level of service for the three-car limit? What level of utilization of the teller must be attained and what must be the service rate of the teller to assure the 95 percent level of service?

Solution. The present level of service for three cars or less is the probability that there are 0, 1, 2, or 3 cars in the system.

From Model 1, Table S.7.3:

$$P_n = \left(1 - \frac{\lambda}{\mu}\right)\left(\frac{\lambda}{\mu}\right)^n$$

at $n = 0$ $P_0 = (1 - {}^{15}\!/_{20})({}^{15}\!/_{20})^0 = 0.250$

at $n = 1$ $P_1 = (\frac{1}{4})$ $({}^{15}\!/_{20})^1 = 0.188$

at $n = 2$ $P_2 = (\frac{1}{4})$ $({}^{15}\!/_{20})^2 = 0.141$

at $n = 3$ $P_3 = (\frac{1}{4})$ $({}^{15}\!/_{20})^3 = \underline{0.106}$

                                       0.685 or 68.5 percent

The probability of having more than three cars in the system is 1.0 minus the probability of three cars or less ($1.0 - 0.685 = 31.5$ percent).

For a 95 percent service level to three cars or less, this states that $P_0 + P_1 + P_2 + P_3 = 95$ percent.

$$0.95 = \left(1 - \frac{\lambda}{\mu}\right)\left(\frac{\lambda}{\mu}\right)^0 + \left(1 - \frac{\lambda}{\mu}\right)\left(\frac{\lambda}{\mu}\right)^1 + \left(1 - \frac{\lambda}{\mu}\right)\left(\frac{\lambda}{\mu}\right)^2 + \left(1 - \left(\frac{\lambda}{\mu}\right)\right)\left(\frac{\lambda}{\mu}\right)^3$$

$$0.95 = \left(1 - \frac{\lambda}{\mu}\right)\left[1 + \frac{\lambda}{\mu} + \left(\frac{\lambda}{\mu}\right)^2 + \left(\frac{\lambda}{\mu}\right)^3\right]$$

We can solve this by trial and error for values of $\frac{\lambda}{\mu}$. If $\frac{\lambda}{\mu} = 0.50$:

$$0.95 \overset{?}{=} 0.5(1 + 0.5 + 0.25 + 0.125)$$
$$0.95 \neq 0.9375$$

With $\frac{\lambda}{\mu} = 0.45$,

$$0.95 \overset{?}{=} (1 - 0.45)(1 + 0.45 + 0.203 + 0.091)$$
$$0.95 \neq 0.96$$

With $\frac{\lambda}{\mu} = 0.47$,

$$0.95 \overset{?}{=} (1 - 0.47)(1 + 0.47 + 0.221 + 0.104) = 0.95135$$
$$0.95 \approx 0.95135$$

Therefore, with the utilization ($\rho = \frac{\lambda}{\mu}$) of 47 percent, the probability of three cars or less in the system is 95 percent.

To find the rate of service required to attain this 95 percent service level, we simply solve the equation $\lambda/\mu = 0.47$, where $\lambda =$ number of arrivals per hour. This gives $\mu = 32$ per hour.

That is, the teller must serve approximately 32 people per hour—a 60 percent increase over the original 20 per hour capability—for 95 percent confidence that not more than three cars will be in the system. Perhaps service may be speeded up by modifying the method of service, adding another teller, or limiting the number or types of transactions available at the drive-in window. It should also be noted that, with the condition of 95 percent confidence that three or fewer cars will be in the system, the teller will be idle 53 percent of the time.

Model 2

The Robot Company franchises combination gas and carwash stations throughout the United States. Robot follows a policy of giving a free carwash for a fill-up of gasoline or, for a wash alone, charging $0.50. Past experience shows that the number of customers that have carwashes following fill-ups is about the same as for a wash alone. The average profit on a gasoline fill-up is about $0.70 and the cost of the carwash to Robot is $0.10. Robot stays open 14 hours per day.

Robot has three power units and drive assemblies, and a franchisee must determine which unit he prefers. Unit I can wash cars at the rate of one every five minutes and is leased for $12 per day. Unit II, a larger unit, can wash cars at the rate of one every four minutes but costs $16 per day. Unit III is the largest unit available, costing $22 per day, and can wash a car in three minutes.

The franchisee estimates that customers will not wait more than an average five minutes in line for a carwash. A longer time will cause Robot to lose the gasoline sales as well as the carwash sale.

If the estimate of customer arrivals resulting in washes at the franchisee's proposed location is 10 per hour, which wash unit should be selected?

Solution. Using Unit I, calculate the average waiting time of customers in the wash line (μ for Unit I $= 12$ per hour). From the Model 2 equations (Table S.7.3),

$$\bar{t}_l = \frac{\lambda}{2\mu(\mu - \lambda)} = \frac{10}{2(12)(12 - 10)} = 0.208 \text{ hour or } 12.5 \text{ minutes}$$

For Unit II at 15 per hour,

$$\bar{t}_l = \frac{10}{2(15)(15 - 10)} = 0.067 \text{ hour or } 4 \text{ minutes}$$

If waiting time is the only criterion, Unit II should be purchased. However, before we make the final decision we must look at the profit differential between both units.

The installation of Unit I would result in some customers balking and reneging because of the 12.5-minute wait. And although this greatly complicates the mathematical analysis, we can gain some estimate of lost sales with Unit I by inserting $t = 5$ minutes or $\frac{1}{12}$ hour (the average length of time customers will wait) and solving for λ. This would be the effective arrival rate of customers:

$$\bar{t}_l = \frac{\lambda}{2\mu(\mu - \lambda)}$$

$$\lambda = \frac{2\bar{t}_l\mu^2}{1 + 2\bar{t}_l\mu}$$

$$\lambda = \frac{2(\frac{1}{12})(12)^2}{1 + 2(\frac{1}{12})(12)} = 8 \text{ per hour}$$

Therefore, since the original estimate of λ was 10 per hour, an estimated two customers per hour will be lost. Lost profit of 2 customers per hour $\times$ 14 hours $\times$ $\frac{1}{2}$ ($0.70 fill-up profit + $0.40 wash profit) = $15.40 per day.

Since the additional cost of Unit II over Unit I is only $4 per day, the loss of $15.40 profit obviously warrants the installation of Unit II.

The original constraint of a five-minute maximum wait is satisfied by Unit II. Therefore Unit III is not considered unless the arrival rate is expected to increase in the future.

Model 3

A drive-through ice cream stand has space for a four-car line, including the car being served (the stand is on a main thoroughfare and the line cannot extend onto the street). The average arrival rate of potential customers is 40 cars per hour and the service rate in filling the ice cream orders is 50 cars per hour. Average profit on the ice cream purchased per car is $0.50. Additional driveway space is available from the owner of the lot next door at a leased rate of $5 per day. The stand is open 14 hours per day.

Assuming Poisson arrivals and exponential service, should space be rented in the adjacent lot? If so, how many spaces?

Solution. This is a limited queue-length problem and the Model 3 formulas are applicable. The easiest approach to solving this problem is to assume an increasing number of auto spaces and compare the additional profit generated by each space. Additional spaces will be rented until the profit becomes less than the $5 cost of rental.

Ice cream will be served to customers at the rate of 50 cars per hour any time there are cars in the system. To find the amount of time there are customers, we can solve for the probability of zero in the system and subtract this from 1. This will give us the percent of time ice cream is served.

From Model 3, Table S.7.3:

$$P_n = \left[\frac{1 - \frac{\lambda}{\mu}}{1 - \left(\frac{\lambda}{\mu}\right)^{Q+1}} \right] \left(\frac{\lambda}{\mu}\right)^n$$

For the probability of zero cars in the system, with four spaces on the premises ($Q = 4$):

$$P_0 = \left[\frac{1 - \frac{\lambda}{\mu}}{1 - \left(\frac{\lambda}{\mu}\right)^{Q+1}} \right] \left(\frac{\lambda}{\mu}\right)^0 = \left[\frac{1 - \frac{40}{50}}{1 - \left(\frac{40}{50}\right)^5} \right] 1 = \frac{0.2}{1 - 0.328} = 0.298$$

And ice cream is being served $1 - 0.298 = 0.702$, or 70.2 percent of the time.

When one space is rented $(Q = 4 + 1 = 5)$,

$$P_0 = \left[\frac{0.2}{1 - \left(\frac{40}{50}\right)^6} \right] = 0.271$$

Service is then being carried out $(1 - 0.271) = 0.729$, or 72.9 percent of the time, or an increase of 2.8 percent $(72.9 - 70.2)$. In profit, this is worth

0.028 (50 cars per hour $\times$ 14 hours per day $\times$ $0.50 per car) = $9.80

When a second space is rented $(Q = 4 + 2 = 6)$,

$$P_0 = \left[\frac{0.2}{1 - \left(\frac{40}{50}\right)^7} \right] = 0.253$$

and the facility is busy $1 - 0.253 = 0.747$, or 74.7 percent of the time.

Thus the additional space increases the utilization of the stand by 1.8 percent $(74.7\% - 72.9\%)$ and increases profit by $6.30 $(0.018)(50 \times 14 \times$0.50). Since this amount is greater than the $5 rental charge, the space should be rented.

A third rented space, with $Q = 4 + 3 = 7$, gives

$$P_0 = \left[\frac{0.2}{1 - \left(\frac{40}{50}\right)^8} \right] = 0.241$$

and $1 - 0.241 = 0.759$.

Increased service is 1.2 percent $(75.9\% - 74.7\%)$ and added profit is $(50 \times 0.012 \times 14 \times $0.50) or $4.20. The third space should not be rented since it would incur an $0.80 loss ($5 - $4.20).

The optimal solution, then, is to rent just two spaces. The profit will be $261.45 per day $(0.747)(50 \times 14 \times $0.50)—quite reasonable for a good location.

We can also obtain some other useful information about the ice cream stand. The average number of cars in the system, both in line and being served, when two rented spaces are added, is

$$\bar{n}_s = \frac{\lambda}{\mu} \left[\frac{1 - (Q + 1)\left(\frac{\lambda}{\mu}\right)^Q + Q\left(\frac{\lambda}{\mu}\right)^{Q+1}}{\left(1 - \frac{\lambda}{\mu}\right)\left(1 - \left(\frac{\lambda}{\mu}\right)^{Q+1}\right)} \right]$$

$$\bar{n}_s = \frac{40}{50} \left[\frac{1 - (6 + 1)\left(\frac{40}{50}\right)^6 + 6\left(\frac{40}{50}\right)^7}{\left(1 - \frac{40}{50}\right)\left[1 - \left(\frac{40}{50}\right)^7\right]} \right]$$

$$\bar{n}_s = 2.15 \text{ cars}$$

It is interesting to note that if an unlimited waiting line were possible, the increase in the efficiency (working time) of the ice cream stand would be increased by only 5.3 percent (the efficiency for an infinite line is just $\rho = \lambda/\mu = \frac{4}{5} = 0.80$, or 80%). The average number of cars in the system, on the other hand, would almost double since $\dfrac{\lambda}{\mu - \lambda} = 4$ for the infinite case, as opposed to 2.15, as found above for a maximum of six cars.

Model 4

The C. J. Ballard Company is entering its second year in building residential homes. In transferring to this city, you, as an individual, are considering contracting with Ballard to build a home, but first you would like some idea of the completion time in order to plan the sale of your old home and time the cross-country move to this new home.

From your discussions you found that Ballard completed 10 homes last year. To speed the building time span, Ballard uses one basic floor plan so that it can prepour the concrete floor slabs on selected lots. This saves not only the time of excavating, form building, laying the service lines (plumbing, electrical conduit, and air conditioning return ducts), and pouring concrete but also the time necessary for concrete curing. Ballard has only a small crew of workmen and therefore builds only one house at a time, carrying it to completion before starting the next one.

Once a customer has picked the lot and signed the contract, Ballard is able to build a house from its various style plans in about a month. Actual figures for completion time per home last year were 30, 32, 29, 34, 27, 29, 29, 33, 30, and 31 calendar days.

Although Ballard built just 10 homes last year, it has the capability of building 12 homes per year ($\mu = 12$). Further investigation shows that of the various people who discuss home building with Ballard, nine actually contract with the firm. These contracts appear to be randomly distributed (Poisson) through the year ($\lambda = 9$).

Estimate the completion time of your home if you should sign a contract.

Solution. Without any justification for assuming a common frequency distribution curve for the building time (such as exponential, normal, or Erlang), we can use the equation from basic statistics to estimate the mean and variance of service times.

$$\bar{X} = \frac{\sum\limits_{i=1}^{N} X_i}{N} \tag{1}$$

where
$\bar{X}$ = the average time
X = the actual time data point
i = the identification of each time element
N = the number of time elements

$$\sigma^2 = \frac{\sum\limits_{i=1}^{N}(X_i - \bar{X})^2}{N} \tag{2}$$

$\sigma^2 =$ variance of the distribution

Using the data given in the problem and equation 1 (above), we get:

$$\bar{X} = \frac{30 + 32 + 29 + 34 + 27 + 29 + 29 + 33 + 30 + 31}{10} = 30.4 \text{ days}$$

From Equation 2, we get:

$$\sigma^2 = \frac{\begin{aligned}(30 - 30.4)^2 + (32 - 30.4)^2 + (29 - 30.4)^2 + (34 - 30.4)^2 \\ + (27 - 30.4)^2 + (29 - 30.4)^2 + (29 - 30.4)^2 + (33 - 30.4)^2 \\ + (30 - 30.4)^2 + (31 - 30.4)^2\end{aligned}}{10}$$

$$\sigma^2 = \frac{0.16 + 2.56 + 1.96 + 12.96 + 11.6 + 1.96 + 1.96 + 6.76 + 0.16 + 0.36}{10}$$

$$\sigma^2 = \frac{40.44}{10} = 4.044 \text{ days, or } 0.01105 \text{ year}$$

From Table S.7.3, Model 4, we see that

$$\bar{l}_s = \frac{\dfrac{\lambda}{\mu^2} + \lambda\sigma^2}{2\left(1 - \dfrac{\lambda}{\mu}\right)} + \frac{1}{\mu}$$

$$\bar{l}_s = \frac{\dfrac{9}{(12)^2} + 9(0.01105)}{2\left(1 - \dfrac{9}{12}\right)} + \frac{1}{12}$$

$$\bar{l}_s = 0.3239 + 0.0833 = 0.4072 \text{ year, or } 148 \text{ days}$$

Under the assumption of the problem—that is, that homes are built in the order of their contract signing (first come, first served)—you will have to wait 148 days, or almost five months, for your home to be built. (This example shows that "logical guesses" in queuing problems are often wide of the mark. Intuitively, one might have estimated the time from contract signing to completion to be about two months.)

Ballard's average number of active contracts (homes waiting to be started plus any being built) is

$$\bar{n}_s = \frac{\left(\dfrac{\lambda}{\mu}\right)^2 + \lambda^2\sigma^2}{2\left(1 - \dfrac{\lambda}{\mu}\right)} + \frac{\lambda}{\mu}$$

$$\bar{n}_s = \frac{2\left(\dfrac{9}{12}\right)^2 + (9)^2(0.01105)}{2\left(1 - \dfrac{9}{12}\right)} + \frac{9}{12}$$

$$\bar{n}_s = 2.914 + 0.75$$
$$\bar{n}_s = 3.664 \text{ contracts}$$

Model 5

The barber at the one-man Speedway Barbershop averages 15 minutes per haircut. Customers arrive at the shop in Poisson fashion with a mean arrival rate of two per hour. Suppose you want a haircut and you have an appointment with your tax accountant 30 minutes after you arrive at the shop.

Assuming that it is a three-minute walk to your appointment location from the shop and that haircutting time is Erlang distributed with $K = 3$, would you expect to be on time to meet your accountant?

Solution. Given that $\lambda = 2$ arrivals per hour and $\mu = 4$ haircuts per hour, the problem is simply to determine the expected time in the system, $\bar{t}_s$. Using the $\bar{t}_s$ formula from Table S.7.3, Model 5, we have

$$\bar{t}_s = \frac{K+1}{2K} \cdot \frac{\lambda}{\mu(\mu - \lambda)} + \frac{1}{\mu}$$

Substituting

$$\bar{t}_s = \frac{3+1}{2(3)} \cdot \frac{2}{4(4-2)} + \frac{1}{4}$$

we get

$$\bar{t}_s = \frac{1}{6} + \frac{1}{4} = \frac{5}{12} \text{ of an hour, or 25 minutes}$$

Thus you should make your appointment (if you don't dawdle along the way).

Model 6

In the service department of the Glenn-Mark Auto Agency, mechanics requiring parts for auto repair or service present their request forms at the parts department counter. The parts clerk fills a mechanic's request while he waits. Mechanics arrive in a random (Poisson) fashion at the rate of 40 per hour and a clerk can fill requests at the rate of 20 per hour (exponential). If the cost for a parts clerk is $2 per hour and the cost for a mechanic is $4.50 per hour, determine the optimum number of clerks to staff the counter. (Because of the high arrival rate, an infinite source may be assumed.)

Solution. First, assume that three clerks will be utilized because only one or two clerks would create long lines (since $\lambda = 40$ and $\mu = 20$). From Table S.7.3, Model 6

$$P_0 = \frac{1}{\sum\limits_{n=0}^{M-1} \frac{\left(\frac{\lambda}{\mu}\right)^n}{n!} + \frac{\left(\frac{\lambda}{\mu}\right)^M}{M!\left(1 - \frac{\lambda}{\mu M}\right)}}$$

with $M = 3$.

$$P_0 = \cfrac{1}{\displaystyle\sum_{n=0}^{2} \cfrac{\left(\frac{40}{20}\right)^n}{n!} + \cfrac{\left(\frac{40}{20}\right)^3}{3!\left(1 - \frac{40}{20(3)}\right)}}$$

$$P_0 = \cfrac{1}{\cfrac{(2)^0}{0!} + \cfrac{(2)^1}{1!} + \cfrac{(2)^2}{2!} + \cfrac{(2)^3}{3!\left(1 - \frac{2}{3}\right)}} = \cfrac{1}{1 + 2 + 2 + 4} = 0.111$$

The average number in line is

$$\bar{n}_l = \frac{\lambda\mu\left(\frac{\lambda}{\mu}\right)^M}{(M - 1)!(M\mu - \lambda)^2} P_0$$

$$\bar{n}_l = \frac{40(20)\left(\frac{40}{20}\right)^3}{(3 - 1)![3(20) - 40]^2} (0.111) = \frac{800(8)}{2(60 - 40)^2} (0.111)$$

$$\bar{n}_l = \frac{6400}{800} (0.111) = 0.888 \text{ mechanic}$$

At this point we see that we have an average of 0.888 mechanic waiting all day. For an eight-hour day at $4.50 per hour, this is a loss of mechanic's time worth 0.888 mechanic $\times$ $4.50 per hour $\times$ 8 hours = $31.97.

Our next step is to recalculate the waiting time if we add another parts clerk. We will then compare the added cost of the additional employee with the time saved by the mechanics. Using our P_0 equation, when $M = 4$:

$$P_0 = \cfrac{1}{\displaystyle\sum_{n=0}^{3} \cfrac{(2)^n}{n!} + \cfrac{(2)^4}{4!\left(1 - \frac{4}{2(4)}\right)}}$$

$$P_0 = \cfrac{1}{\cfrac{(2)^0}{0!} + \cfrac{(2)^1}{1!} + \cfrac{(2)^2}{2!} + \cfrac{(2)^3}{3!} + \cfrac{16}{24\left(1 - \frac{1}{2}\right)}}$$

$$P_0 = \cfrac{1}{1 + 2 + 2 + \frac{8}{6} + \frac{8}{6}} = 0.130$$

$$\bar{n}_l = \frac{40(20)(2)^4}{(4 - 1)![4(20) - 40]^2} (0.130)$$

$$\bar{n}_l = \frac{800(16)}{6(80 - 40)^2} (0.130)$$

$$\bar{n}_l = 1.333 \times 0.130 = 0.173 \text{ mechanic in line}$$

0.173 $\times$ $4.50 $\times$ 8 hours = $6.23 cost of mechanic's waiting in line

Value of mechanics' time saved is $31.97 − $6.23 = $25.74

Cost of additional parts clerk is 8 hr $\times$ $2/hr   =   16.00

Cost reduction by adding 4th clerk $ 9.74

This problem could be expanded to consider the addition of runners to deliver parts to mechanics, so that the problem would be to determine the optimal number of runners. This, however, would have to include the added cost of lost time due to errors in parts receipts. For example, a mechanic would recognize a wrong part at the counter and obtain immediate correction whereas the parts runner quite likely would not.

Model 7

Studies of a bank of four weaving machines at the Loose Knit textile mill have shown that, on average, each machine needs adjusting every hour and that the current service man averages $7\frac{1}{2}$ minutes per adjustment.

Problem. Assuming Poisson arrivals, exponential service, and a machine idle time cost of $40 per hour, determine if a second service man (who also averages $7\frac{1}{2}$ minutes per adjustment) should be hired at a rate of $7 per hour.

Solution. This is a finite queuing problem that can be solved by using finite queuing tables. The approach in this problem is to compare the costs due to machine downtime (either waiting in line or being serviced) and the cost of one repairman, to the cost of machine downtime and two repairmen. We do this by finding the average number of machines that are in the service system and multiply this number by the downtime cost per hour. To this we add the repairmen's cost.

Before we proceed we will first define some terms:

N = the number of machines in the population
M = the number of repairmen
T = the time required to service a machine
U = the average time a machine runs before requiring service
X = the service factor, or proportion of service time required for each machine ($X = T/(T + U)$
L = the average number of machines waiting in line to be serviced
H = the average number of machines being serviced

The values that will be determined from the finite tables are:

D, the probability that a machine needing service will have to wait
F, the efficiency factor, which is a measure of the effect of having to wait in line to be serviced

The tables are arranged according to three variables: N, population size; X, service factor; and M, the number of service channels (repairmen in this problem). To look up a value, first find the table for the correct N size, then search the first column for the appropriate X, and finally find the line for M. D and F are then read off. (In addition to these values, other characteristics about a finite queuing system can be found by using the finite formulas.)

To solve the problem above, consider Case I with one repairman, and Case II with two repairmen.

Case I: one repairman. From the problem statement,

$$N = 4$$
$$M = 1$$
$$T = 7\tfrac{1}{2} \text{ minutes}$$
$$U = 60 \text{ minutes}$$
$$X = \frac{T}{T + U} = \frac{7.5}{7.5 + 60} = 0.111$$

From Table S.7.5, the correct table for $N = 4$, F is interpolated as being approximately 0.957 at $X = 0.111$ and $M = 1$.

The number of machines waiting in line to be serviced is L, where

$$L = N(1 - F) = 4(1 - 0.957) = 0.172 \text{ machines}$$

The number of machines being serviced is H, where

$$H = FNX = 0.957(4)(0.111) = 0.425 \text{ machines}$$

Table S.7.4 shows the cost resulting from the machine unproductive time and the cost of the repairman.

Case II: two repairmen.

From Table S.7.4, at $X = 0.111$ and $M = 2$, $F = 0.998$

The number of machines waiting in line, L, is

$$L = N(1 - F) = 4(1 - 0.998) = 0.008 \text{ machines}$$

The number of machines being serviced, H, is

$$H = FNX = 0.998(4)(0.111) = 0.443 \text{ machines}$$

The costs for the machines being idle and for the two repairmen are shown in Table S.7.4. The final column of Table S.7.4 indicates that retaining just one repairman is the best choice. The hourly costs with one repairman are \$30.88 versus hourly costs of \$32.04 with two repairmen.

TABLE S.7.4

A comparison of downtime costs for service and repair of a population of four machines.

Number of repairmen	Number of machines down (H + L)	Cost per hour for machines down (H + L) × $40/hour	Cost of repairmen $7/hour each	Total cost per hour
1	0.597	$23.88	$ 7.00	$30.88
2	0.451	18.04	14.00	32.04

TABLE S.7.5

Finite queuing tables

POPULATION   4

X	M	D	F
.015	1	.045	.999
.022	1	.066	.998
.030	1	.090	.997
.034	1	.102	.996
.038	1	.114	.995
.042	1	.126	.994
.046	1	.137	.993
.048	1	.143	.992
.052	1	.155	.991
.054	1	.161	.990
.058	1	.173	.989
.060	1	.179	.988
.062	1	.184	.987
.064	1	.190	.986
.066	1	.196	.985
.070	2	.014	.999
	1	.208	.984
.075	2	.016	.999
	1	.222	.981
.080	2	.018	.999
	1	.237	.978
.085	2	.021	.999
	1	.251	.975
.090	2	.023	.999
	1	.265	.972
.095	2	.026	.999
	1	.280	.969
.100	2	.028	.999
	1	.294	.965
.105	2	.031	.998
	1	.308	.962
.110	2	.034	.998
	1	.321	.958
.115	2	.037	.998
	1	.335	.954
.120	2	.041	.997
	1	.349	.950
.125	2	.044	.997
	1	.362	.945
.130	2	.047	.997
	1	.376	.941
.135	2	.051	.996
	1	.389	.936
.140	2	.055	.996
	1	.402	.931
.145	2	.058	.995
	1	.415	.926
.150	2	.062	.995
	1	.428	.921
.155	2	.066	.994
	1	.441	.916
.160	2	.071	.994
	1	.454	.910
.165	2	.075	.993
	1	.466	.904
.170	2	.079	.993

X	M	D	F
	1	.479	.899
.180	2	.088	.991
	1	.503	.887
.190	2	.098	.990
	1	.526	.874
.200	3	.008	.999
	2	.108	.988
.200	1	.549	.862
.210	3	.009	.999
	2	.118	.986
	1	.572	.849
.220	3	.011	.999
	2	.129	.984
	1	.593	.835
.230	3	.012	.999
	2	.140	.982
	1	.614	.822
.240	3	.014	.999
	2	.151	.980
	1	.634	.808
.250	3	.016	.999
	2	.163	.977
	1	.654	.794
.260	3	.018	.998
	2	.175	.975
	1	.673	.780
.270	3	.020	.998
	2	.187	.972
	1	.691	.766
.280	3	.022	.998
	2	.200	.968
	1	.708	.752
.290	3	.024	.998
	2	.213	.965
	1	.725	.738
.300	3	.027	.997
	2	.226	.962
	1	.741	.724
.310	3	.030	.997
	2	.240	.958
	1	.756	.710
.320	3	.033	.997
	2	.254	.954
	1	.771	.696
.330	3	.036	.996
	2	.268	.950
	1	.785	.683
.340	3	.039	.996
	2	.282	.945
	1	.798	.670
.360	3	.047	.994
	2	.312	.936
	1	.823	.644
.380	3	.055	.993
	2	.342	.926
	1	.846	.619

X	M	D	F
.400	3	.064	.992
	2	.372	.915
	1	.866	.595
.420	3	.074	.990
	2	.403	.903
	1	.884	.572
.440	3	.085	.986
	2	.435	.891
	1	.900	.551
.460	3	.097	.985
	2	.466	.878
	1	.914	.530
.480	3	.111	.983
	2	.498	.864
.480	1	.926	.511
.500	3	.125	.980
	2	.529	.850
	1	.937	.492
.520	3	.141	.976
	2	.561	.835
	1	.947	.475
.540	3	.157	.972
	2	.592	.820
	1	.956	.459
.560	3	.176	.968
	2	.623	.805
	1	.963	.443
.580	3	.195	.964
	2	.653	.789
	1	.969	.429
.600	3	.216	.959
	2	.682	.774
	1	.975	.415
.650	3	.275	.944
	2	.752	.734
	1	.985	.384
.700	3	.343	.926
	2	.816	.695
	1	.991	.357
.750	3	.422	.905
	2	.871	.657
	1	.996	.333
.800	3	.512	.880
	2	.917	.621
	1	.998	.312
.850	3	.614	.852
	2	.954	.587
	1	.999	.294
.900	3	.729	.821
	2	.979	.555
.950	3	.857	.786
	2	.995	.526

From L. G. Peck and R. N. Hazelwood, *Finite Queueing Tables* (New York: John Wiley & Sons, 1958), pp. 3–4.

TABLE S.7.5 (*continued*)

POPULATION 5

X	M	D	F
.012	1	.048	.999
.019	1	.076	.998
.025	1	.100	.997
.030	1	.120	.996
.034	1	.135	.995
.036	1	.143	.994
.040	1	.159	.993
.042	1	.167	.992
.044	1	.175	.991
.046	1	.183	.990
.050	1	.198	.989
.052	1	.206	.988
.054	1	.214	.987
.056	2	.018	.999
	1	.222	.985
.058	2	.019	.999
	1	.229	.984
.060	2	.020	.999
	1	.237	.983
.062	2	.022	.999
	1	.245	.982
.064	2	.023	.999
	1	.253	.981
.066	2	.024	.999
	1	.260	.979
.068	2	.026	.999
	1	.268	.978
.070	2	.027	.999
	1	.275	.977
.075	2	.031	.999
	1	.294	.973
.080	2	.035	.998
	1	.313	.969
.085	2	.040	.998
	1	.332	.965
.090	2	.044	.998
	1	.350	.960
.095	2	.049	.997
	1	.368	.955
.100	2	.054	.997
	1	.386	.950
.105	2	.059	.997
	1	.404	.945
.110	2	.065	.996
	1	.421	.939
.115	2	.071	.995
	1	.439	.933
.120	2	.076	.995
	1	.456	.927
.125	2	.082	.994
	1	.473	.920
.130	2	.089	.993
	1	.489	.914
.135	2	.095	.993
	1	.505	.907
.140	2	.102	.992
.145	1	.521	.900
	3	.011	.999
	2	.109	.991
.150	1	.537	.892
	3	.012	.999
	2	.115	.990
	1	.553	.885
.155	3	.013	.999
	2	.123	.989
	1	.568	.877
.160	3	.015	.999
	2	.130	.988
.165	1	.582	.869
	3	.016	.999
	2	.137	.987
	1	.597	.861
.170	3	.017	.999
	2	.145	.985
	1	.611	.853
.180	3	.021	.999
	2	.161	.983
	1	.638	.836
.190	3	.024	.998
	2	.177	.980
	1	.665	.819
.200	3	.028	.998
.200	2	.194	.976
	1	.689	.801
.210	3	.032	.998
	2	.211	.973
	1	.713	.783
.220	3	.036	.997
	2	.229	.969
.230	1	.735	.765
	3	.041	.997
	2	.247	.965
	1	.756	.747
.240	3	.046	.996
	2	.265	.960
	1	.775	.730
.250	3	.052	.995
	2	.284	.955
	1	.794	.712
.260	3	.058	.994
	2	.303	.950
	1	.811	.695
.270	3	.064	.994
	2	.323	.944
	1	.827	.677
.280	3	.071	.993
	2	.342	.938
	1	.842	.661
.290	4	.007	.999
	3	.079	.992
	2	.362	.932
	1	.856	.644
.300	4	.008	.999
	3	.086	.990
	2	.382	.926
	1	.869	.628
.310	4	.009	.999
	3	.094	.989
	2	.402	.919
	1	.881	.613
.320	4	.010	.999
	3	.103	.988
	2	.422	.912
	1	.892	.597
.330	4	.012	.999
	3	.112	.986
	2	.442	.904
	1	.902	.583
.340	4	.013	.999
	3	.121	.985
	2	.462	.896
	1	.911	.569
.360	4	.017	.998
	3	.141	.981
	2	.501	.880
	1	.927	.542
.380	4	.021	.998
	3	.163	.976
	2	.540	.863
	1	.941	.516
.400	4	.026	.997
	3	.186	.972
	2	.579	.845
	1	.952	.493
.420	4	.031	.997
	3	.211	.966
	2	.616	.826
	1	.961	.471
.440	4	.037	.996
	3	.238	.960
	2	.652	.807
	1	.969	.451
.460	4	.045	.995
	3	.266	.953
	2	.686	.787
	1	.975	.432
.480	4	.053	.994
	3	.296	.945
	2	.719	.767
	1	.980	.415
.500	4	.063	.992
	3	.327	.936
	2	.750	.748
	1	.985	.399
.520	4	.073	.991
	3	.359	.927
	2	.779	.728
	1	.988	.384
.540	4	.085	.989
	3	.392	.917
	2	.806	.708
	1	.991	.370
.560	4	.098	.986
	3	.426	.906
	2	.831	.689
	1	.993	.357
.580	4	.113	.984
	3	.461	.895
	2	.854	.670
	1	.994	.345
.600	4	.130	.981
	3	.497	.883
	2	.875	.652
	1	.996	.333
.650	4	.179	.972
	3	.588	.850
	2	.918	.608
	1	.998	.308
.700	4	.240	.960
	3	.678	.815
	2	.950	.568
	1	.999	.286
.750	4	.316	.944
	3	.763	.777
	2	.972	.532
.800	4	.410	.924
	3	.841	.739
	2	.987	.500
.850	4	.522	.900
	3	.907	.702
	2	.995	.470
.900	4	.656	.871
	3	.957	.666
	2	.998	.444
.950	4	.815	.838
	3	.989	.631

REVIEW AND DISCUSSION QUESTIONS

1. What is the waiting line problem? What are some of its basic structures, and what assumptions are necessary to solve the simple models?
2. What factors or elements must be present for a waiting line problem to exist?
3. When may the population source of customers for a service facility be considered infinite? Can a source of 1,000 be considered infinite (in a practical sense) for a barbershop, telephone exchange, country store, mail order house, voice teacher?
4. What are the advantages of assuming a finite population source rather than an infinite one?
5. Can the exponential distribution be used to approximate the service times for
   a. Buying a ticket at the theater?
   b. Getting a haircut?
   c. Going through the checkout counter in a small grocery store?
   d. Going through a highway toll booth?
   e. Answering questions at an information counter?
6. How would you propose to speed up service at
   a. An automobile repair shop?
   b. A gas station?
   c. A university's registration?
   d. A restaurant?
7. Define, in a practical sense, what is meant by an exponential service time.

PROBLEMS

1. A group of high school students is considering running a carwash special on a particular Saturday. They estimate that customers will arrive for service at the rate of seven per hour and figure that they can service customers at the rate of one every six minutes. The students operate as a team on one car at a time.
   Assuming Poisson arrivals and exponential service time, find
   a. Utilization of the student wash team.
   b. The average number of cars in line.
   c. The average time a car waits before it is washed.
   d. The total time it takes to go through the system (i.e., waiting in line plus wash time).
2. The Better Food for Everyone (BFFE) Automat Company supplies vended food to a large university. Since, out of anger and frustration, students kick the machines at every opportunity, management has a constant repair problem. The machines break down at an average of three per hour, and the breakdowns are distributed in a Poisson manner. Downtime costs the company $25/hour/machine, and each maintenance worker gets $4 per hour. One worker can service machines at an average rate of five per hour, dis-

tributed exponentially; two workers, working together, can service seven per hour, distributed exponentially; and a team of three workers can do eight per hour, distributed exponentially.

What is the optimum maintenance crew size for servicing the machines?

3. Irving Impresario, the manager of the Frenetic Flick movie theater, has some questions about the efficiency of his operation. Since he knows of your quantitative abilities, he asks you for your assistance. Further, since he knows you are independently wealthy and therefore indifferent to money, he promises to reward you with a date with your favorite actress, Carla Curvy, if you can help him.

Irving gives you the following data. The theater has a single ticket booth and a cashier who is capable of maintaining a mean service rate of 300 customers per hour—distributed according to an exponential distribution. Arrivals are assumed to be Poisson distributed with a mean arrival rate of 200 per hour.

To help Irving (and to get the date), determine the following.
a. The average number of people waiting in line to purchase tickets.
b. The average number of people purchasing and waiting for tickets.
c. The probability of having a waiting line.
d. The average time the arrival waits in line to get to the ticket window.
e. The average time an arrival spends in the system.

4. Big Jack's drive-through hamburger service is planning to build another stand at a new location and must decide how much land to lease to optimize returns. Leased space for cars will cost $1,000 per year per space. Big Jack is aware of the highly competitive nature of the quick-food service industry and knows that if his drive-in is full, customers will go elsewhere. The location under consideration has a potential customer arrival rate of 30 per hour (Poisson). Customers' orders are filled at the rate of 40 per hour (exponential) since Big Jack prepares food ahead of time. The average profit on each arrival is $0.60 and the stand is open from noon to midnight every day. How many spaces for cars should be leased?

5. A cafeteria serving line has a coffee urn from which customers serve themselves. Arrivals at the urn follow a Poisson distribution at the rate of three per minute. In serving themselves, customers take about 15 seconds, exponentially distributed.
a. How many customers would you expect to see on the average at the coffee urn?
b. How long would you expect it to take to get a cup of coffee?
c. What percentage of time is the urn being utilized?
d. What is the probability that there would be three or more people in the cafeteria?

If the cafeteria installs an automatic vendor that dispenses a cup of coffee at a constant time of 15 seconds, how does this change your answers to a and b?

6. An engineering firm retains a technical specialist to assist five design engineers working on a project. The help that the specialist gives the engineers ranges widely in terms of time consumption. Some answers he has available in memory, others require computation, and still others require significant search time. On the average each request for assistance takes the specialist one hour.

The engineers require help from the specialist on the average of once each day. Since each assistance takes about an hour, each engineer can work for seven hours, on the average, without assistance. One further point: engineers needing help do not interrupt the specialist when he is already involved with another problem, but rather wait until he is finished.

Treat this as a finite queuing problem and answer the following questions:

a. How many engineers, on the average, are waiting for the technical specialist for help?

b. What is the average time that an engineer has to wait for the specialist to get to him?

c. What is the probability that an engineer will have to wait in line for the technical specialist?

7. A graphics reproduction firm has four units of equipment that are automatic, but occasionally become inoperative because of the need for supplies, maintenance, or repair. Each unit requires service roughly twice each hour, or more precisely, each unit of equipment will run an average of 30 minutes before needing service. Service times vary widely, ranging from a simple service (such as hitting a restart switch or repositioning paper) to more involved equipment disassembly. The average service time, however, is 5 minutes.

Equipment downtime results in a loss of $20 per hour. The one attendant that is employed is paid $3 per hour.

Using finite queuing analysis, answer the following questions:

a. What is the average number of units in line?

b. What is the average number of units still in operation?

c. What is the average number of units being serviced?

d. The firm is considering adding another attendant at the same $3 rate. Should they do it?

SELECTED BIBLIOGRAPHY

Beckmann, Petr   *Introduction to Elementary Queueing Theory and Telephone Traffic.* Boulder, Colo.: Golden Press, 1968.

Cooper, Robert B.   *Introduction to Queueing Theory.* New York: Macmillan, 1972.

Gross, Donald, and Harris, Carl M.   *Fundamentals of Queuing Theory.* New York: John Wiley & Sons, 1974.

Morse, Phillip M.   *Queues, Inventories, and Maintenance.* New York: John Wiley & Sons, 1958.

Panico, J. A.   *Queueing Theory.* Englewood Cliffs, N.J.: Prentice-Hall, 1969.

Saaty, T. L.   *Elements of Queueing Theory.* New York: McGraw-Hill, 1961.

Thierauf, R. J., and Klekamp, R. C.   *An Introduction to Quantitative Methods for Decision Making.* New York: Holt, Rinehart, and Winston, Inc., 1974.

Wagner, Harvey   *Principles of Operations Research,* 2d ed. Englewood Cliffs, N.J.: Prentice-Hall, 1975.

8

Design of inventory systems for independent demand: Classical models and practice

The topic of inventory control is vast and important and warrants fairly extensive coverage, even in an introductory book on production management. In light of this, we have allocated two chapters to its discussion. In this chapter we will introduce the basic inventory concepts and mathematical models essential to designing an inventory system based on independent demand. We will then describe the Inventory Management Program and Control Technique (IMPACT), which is one of the commercially available programs designed for an independent demand environment. In Chapter 9, we will present the topic of Materials Requirements Planning, which is based on dependent demand. (In that chapter, we will also discuss two commercial computer programs designed for manufacturing firms operating in a dependent-demand environment.)

INDEPENDENT VERSUS DEPENDENT DEMAND

The distinction between dependent and independent demand is a critical one in dealing with current-day inventory problems. From our discussions in Chapter 6, the reader no doubt has recognized the importance in general production planning of being able to predict demand. Where demand is known and certain, highly efficient production is possible and practicable; where it is not, compensating mechanisms—varying the work force, subcontracting, etc.—must be brought into play to cope with uncertainty. An analogous situation exists for inventory control procedures. If the demand for an end item is known, then the demand for component items is also known, and securing the right quantities at the right times of these components is, conceptually at least, a straightforward mechanical process. By way of example, if an auto company knows that it will sell 2,000 cars next month, it knows that it must have in stock or on order 10,000 wheels (including the spares). In this situation, we would say that the number of wheels required is derived from the number of cars to be sold and that demand for wheels is *dependent* on sales of the end item (cars). In contrast, when demand for a product or component is unpredictable, then inventory ordering procedures must be modified to account for this uncertainty by trading off the cost of holding extra inventory with the cost of more frequent ordering and safety stock. Situations such as these commonly arise in job shops and various service systems (for example, hospital supplies, retailing, book publishing), and are characterized as *independent* demand environments. The remainder of this chapter is concerned with what may be termed "classical" inventory systems and models that are appropriate for independent demand situations. The reader should note, however, that some of the models are used to solve manufacturing inventory problems, which may also be analyzed using the dependent material requirements planning method covered in Chapter 9. Citing examples in manufacturing seems warranted in any event because of the historical development of inventory theory in factory settings and because of the widespread contemporary use of independent demand concepts in these systems.

ROLE OF INVENTORY

The term "inventory" refers to the stock of any item used in the operation of an organization. In its complete scope, inventory would include inputs such as human, financial, energy, equipment, and raw materials; outputs such as parts, components, and finished goods, and interim stages of the process such as partially finished goods or work in process. The choice of which items to include in inventory depends on the organization. A manufacturing operation can have an inventory of personnel, machines, and working capital, as well as raw materials and finished goods. An airline can have an inventory of seats, a farm an inventory of uncut wheat, and an engineering firm an inventory of talent.

Two key questions determine whether an item can be classified as inventory:

1. "Can the item be *specifically identified* as different from all other items?" Thus to be different the item must be changed in some manner by the process. This may be a change in physical form or shape (casting a steel housing or milling wheat), a change in the physical or chemical characteristics (hardening the steel housing or enriching the flour), or a change in appearance (painting the housing or bleaching the flour).

2. "Can the item be stored?" *Storability* refers to the ability to be placed into storage for some period of time. "Temporary storage" refers to the brief storage of items in the production area waiting for the next phase. "Permanent storage" generally implies that the item will be physically moved into a storage area and a record kept showing data such as the number of units on hand and date of placement in inventory. Items are withdrawn from permanent inventory either to be used in the productive process or to satisfy an outside demand.

Product inventory versus service inventory

Writers have often wrestled with a definition to distinguish between a "product" and a "service." Most commonly, the differentiation tends to be made along the lines of stating that a product offers a service to the consumer (though the service may be deferred to a later time), while a service is being consumed at the same rate that it is being produced. A major difference between a product and a service is that *a service is not storable.* Thus, for an automobile tune-up service, while specific phases of the service sequence are identifiable (spark plugs changed, points adjusted, carburetor cleaned, etc.) a tune-up, as such, must be performed on the vehicle and cannot, itself, be stored as inventory. The closest one can come to stocking a service is to prepackage the required components to be used in the service; for example, a package containing a set of spark plugs, a set of points, and a condenser. Therefore, it seems reasonable to define manufacturing inventory in terms of *product output,* and service inventory in terms of service *capacity.* If we accept this distinction, we can then expand the definitions as follows:

In manufacturing, inventory generally refers to *inanimate physical entities that contribute to or become part of a firm's product output,* and is typically classified as:

Raw materials.

Finished products.

Component parts.

Supplies.

Work in process.

In services, inventory refers to the *productive components necessary to administer the service* and may be classified as:

Physical space.

Number of channels or work places.

Service personnel.

Productive equipment.

Parts.

Supplies.

Thus, a beauty salon would list as inventory the number of chairs for operators to work on customers, the number of hair dryers and other appliances used, the stock of supplies, the number of operators, and the number of seats in the waiting room. Wholesalers and retailers would have an inventory of items for sale and the personnel and service capabilities to dispense these items. A repair facility would have an inventory of spare parts and supplies along with the service personnel and available space to perform the repair service. A hospital would have an inventory of rooms, patients' beds, medical supplies, housekeeping supplies, food supplies, medical and nursing staff, and food service, housekeeping, and maintenance personnel.

The objective of inventory analysis in manufacturing is to specify (1) when items should be ordered and (2) how large the order should be. In services, the objective of inventory analysis is to specify (1) which units of productive capacity should be available to perform the service, and (2) how many units are to be available in each time period in order to provide some specified level of service. Determining the particular units, the "When?" and "How many?" decisions in inventory are complicated by the varied purposes of inventory and the variety of costs involved.

PURPOSES OF INVENTORY

A stock of inventory is kept to satisfy the following needs.

1. *To maintain independence of operations.* If a supply of needed materials is kept at a work center and if the work produced by that center is not immediately needed anywhere else, there is some flexibility in operating that center. Since there are costs for making each new production setup, this independence in operating the center allows management to consider

economic production lot sizes. Within the production system, partially completed units are called *work in process.*

An example of completely dependent operations is an assembly line that is fed raw materials to correspond with the line speed and has no work-in-process inventory other than what each worker is working on. The unit in process passes from one person to the next.

2. *To meet variation in product demand.* If the demand for the product is known precisely, it is feasible (though not necessarily economical) to produce the product to meet the demand exactly. In the usual case, however, demand is not completely known and a *safety* or *buffer stock* must therefore be maintained to absorb variation. Increases in demand because of promotional campaigns or seasonal demands can be planned for. Such *seasonal inventory* allows a more gradual build up of stock in anticipation of this higher demand and permits a more stable employment level with lower capital investment.

3. *To allow flexibility in production scheduling.* The maintenance of higher levels of finished goods inventory relieves the pressure on the production system to get the goods out. This gives longer lead times, which allow not only production planning for smoother flow but permit lower-cost operation through more economical lot size production. High setup costs, for example, favor the production of a larger number of units once the setup has been made.

4. *To provide a safeguard for variation in raw material delivery time.* When material is ordered from a vendor, delays can occur for a variety of reasons: the normal variation in shipping time, which occasionally will be great; a shortage of materials at the vendor's plant, causing him to backlog orders; an unexpected strike at the vendor's plant or at one of the shipping companies; a lost order; or incorrect or defective material. Depending on the severity of the consequences of material shortage, a safety stock level is determined. If the materials or supplies are crucial to the operation of the production system, a high level of stock will be maintained.

5. *To take advantage of economic purchase order size.* Obviously, there is a procedural cost for placing an order for goods, and the larger the size of each order, the fewer the number of orders that need be written. The placement of a larger order is also favored by the nonlinearity of shipping costs; that is, the larger the shipment, the lower the per unit cost.

INVENTORY COSTS

In making any decision that will affect inventory size, the following costs must be considered.

Holding (or carrying) costs. This is a broad category that includes the costs for storage facilities, handling, insurance, pilferage, breakage, obsolescence, depreciation, taxes, and the opportunity cost of capital. Obviously, high holding costs tend to favor low inventory levels and frequent replenishment.

Production change (or setup) costs. To make each different product involves obtaining the necessary materials, arranging specific equipment set-ups, filling out the required papers, appropriately charging time and materials, and moving out the previous stock of material. In addition, other costs may be involved in hiring, training, or layoff of workers, and in idle time or overtime.

If there were no costs or loss of time in changing from the production of one product to another, many small lots of products would be produced. This would reduce inventory levels, with a resulting savings in cost. However, changeover costs usually exist.

Since these costs are frequently difficult to identify within the inventory models that determine the size of lots for production, they are summarized under the catch-all heading of "setup" costs.

Ordering costs. These costs refer to the managerial and clerical costs entailed in preparing the purchase or production order. Common terminology subdivides these into two categories: (1) *header cost*, which is the cost of identifying and issuing an order to a single vendor, and (2) *line cost*, which is the cost for computing each separate item order from the same vendor. Thus ordering three items from a vendor entails one header cost and three line costs.

Shortage costs. When the stock of an item is depleted, an order for that item must either wait until the stock is replenished, or be canceled. There is a tradeoff between carrying stock to satisfy demand and the costs resulting from stockout. This balance is sometimes difficult to obtain since it may not be possible to place a value on lost profits, lost customers, or lateness penalties. Frequently, the amount of the shortage cost is little more than a guess.

The determination of quantities purchased from other vendors or the size of lots submitted to the firm's productive facilities involves a search for the minimum total cost resulting from the combined effects of three individual costs: holding costs, production or ordering costs, and shortage costs. This determination, obtained by using mathematical models, is traditionally conceded to be the essence of inventory theory. This chapter will introduce several specific models to assist in searching for this minimum-cost combination.

INVENTORY SYSTEMS

An inventory system provides the organizational structure and the operating policies for maintaining and controlling goods to be inventoried. The inclusion of one or more inventory models within this system enables the determination of ordering and stocking rules. The system is responsible for ordering and receipt of goods: timing the order placement and keeping track of what has been ordered, how much, and from whom. Further, the system must provide followup to enable the answering of such questions as: Has the vendor received the order? Has it been shipped? Are the times correct? Are the procedures established for reordering or returning undesirable merchandise?

Classifying models by fixed quantity or fixed time period

There are two general approaches to inventory systems, which in turn are commonly denoted by the models they employ. These systems, or models, are (1) the *fixed-order quantity* system and (2) the *fixed-order period* system (also referred to variously as the *periodic* system, the *periodic review* system, and the *fixed-order interval* system).

The basic distinction between fixed-order quantity models and fixed-order period models is that the former is "event-triggered" while the latter is "time-triggered." That is, a fixed-order quantity model initiates an order when the "event" of reaching a specified reorder level occurs. This event may take place at any time, depending upon the demand for the items considered. In contrast, the fixed-order period model is limited to placing orders at the end of a predetermined time period; hence the passage of time alone "triggers" the model. This important distinction, along with its resultant effect on the order quantity, Q, is summarized in Table 8.1.

TABLE 8.1

Model	Occurrence of order	Order size, Q
Fixed quantity (event-triggered)	When number of units remaining reaches established reorder point	Constant
Fixed period (time-triggered)	At the end of a specified time period	Variable

Figure 8.1 depicts what occurs when each of the two models is put into use and becomes an operating system. As we can see, the fixed-order quantity system focuses on order quantities and reorder points. Procedurally, each time a unit is taken out of stock the withdrawal is logged and the amount remaining in inventory is immediately compared to the reorder point. If it has dropped to this point, an order for Q items is placed. If it has not, the system remains in an idle state until the next withdrawal.

In the periodic review system, a decision to place an order is made after the stock has been counted or "reviewed." Whether an order is actually placed depends upon the inventory status at that time. If inventory is below a certain amount (termed the *replenishment level*), an order is placed for that quantity of items that is the difference between the replenishment level and the number of units on hand at the time. If inventory has not dropped below that level, no order is placed.

An interesting feature of this system is that no physical count of items is made after an item is withdrawn—the tallying of inventory occurs only at the time designated for review. As shown in the diagram, this characteristic of periodic systems results in two separate and independent loops: one for placing orders and another for issuing stock. The result of this independence is that inventory protection against stockout must be provided not

FIGURE 8.1

Comparison of fixed-order quantity and fixed-order period reordering inventory systems

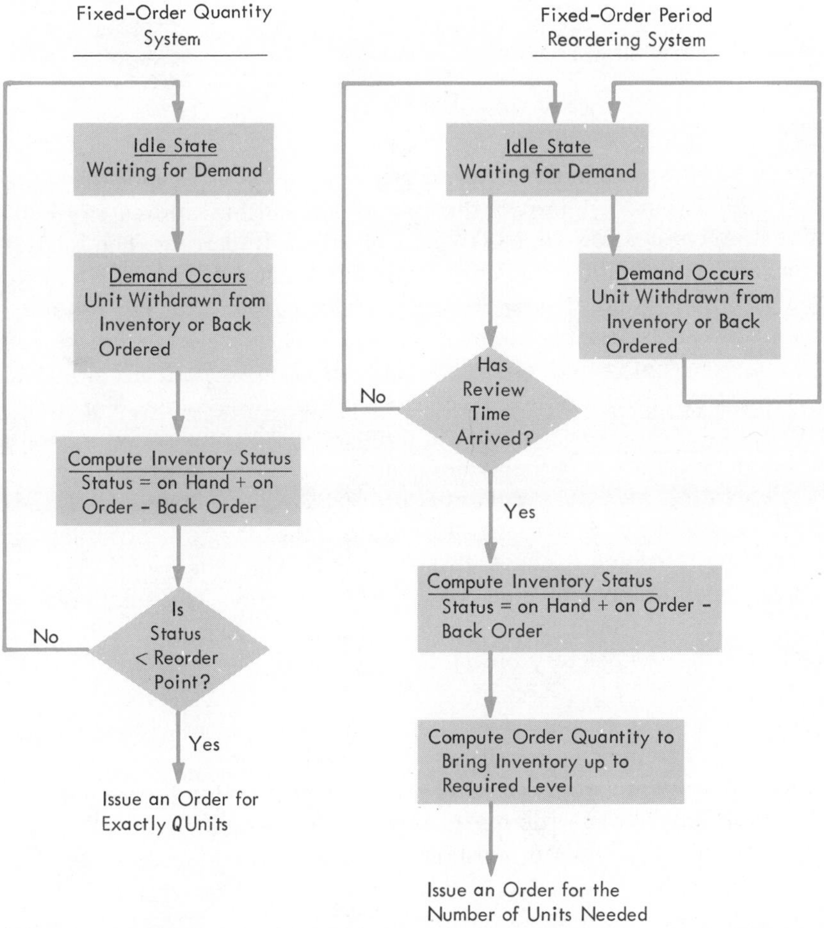

Fixed-Order Quantity System

Fixed-Order Period Reordering System

Idle State
Waiting for Demand

Demand Occurs
Unit Withdrawn from
Inventory or Back
Ordered

Compute Inventory Status
Status = on Hand + on
Order – Back Order

Is
Status
< Reorder
Point?

No

Yes

Issue an Order for
Exactly Q Units

Idle State
Waiting for Demand

Demand Occurs
Unit Withdrawn from
Inventory or Back
Ordered

Has
Review
Time
Arrived?

No

Yes

Compute Inventory Status
Status = on Hand + on Order –
Back Order

Compute Order Quantity to
Bring Inventory up to
Required Level

Issue an Order for the
Number of Units Needed

only for the time between the issuance of a replenishment order and the receipt of the new stock (that is, the lead time) but for the entire period between reviews as well. Thus, in comparing the two systems, the periodic review system will generally require a larger amount of inventory than the fixed-order quantity system. (More will be said about this point later.)

BASIC MODEL TYPES

The inventory models that will be covered in this chapter are broadly organized according to whether the demand is deterministic (known) or probabilistic (uncertain). Within each of these classes, fixed quantity (economic order) and fixed period (periodic) models are then presented.

The first models to be described under conditions of deterministic or known demand are the simple economic order or fixed-quantity models, the fixed-quantity model with usage, and the fixed-order quantity model with backorders allowed. This will be followed by the probabilistic models, which consist of the fixed-order quantity model and the fixed-period model. A price-break model and a single-period model will then be presented. The last model technique to be presented is the determination of order quantities through marginal analysis.

Deterministic models (conditions of certainty)

The simplest models in this category occur when all aspects of the situation are known with certainty. If the annual demand for a product is 1,000 units, it is precisely 1,000—not 1,000 plus or minus 10 percent. The same is true for setup costs and holding costs. Although the assumption of complete certainty is rarely valid, it provides a good starting point for our coverage of inventory models. In addition, there are times when the errors introduced by assuming certainty are less costly than collection of perfectly accurate data or construction of a more complicated probabilistic model. For example, when unit cost or carrying costs are low, a simple model that assumes conditions of certainty is probably adequate.

Fixed-quantity models (economic order quantity models). Fixed-quantity models attempt to determine the specific point, R, at which an order will be placed and the size of that order, Q. The order point, R, is always a specified number of units actually in inventory. The solution to a fixed-order quantity model may stipulate something like this: When the number of units of inventory on hand drops to 36, place an order for 57 more units.

Figure 8.2 and the ensuing derivation of the optimal order quantity are based on the following characteristics of the model:

Demand for the product is constant and uniform through the period,

Lead time (time from ordering to receipt) is constant,

Price per unit of product is constant,

FIGURE 8.2

Basic fixed-order quantity model

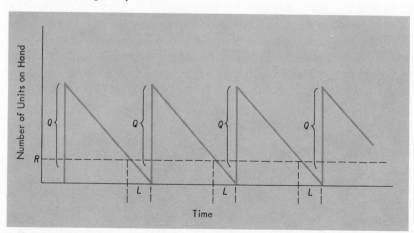

Inventory holding cost is based on average inventory,

Ordering or setup costs are constant, and

All demands for the product will be satisfied (no backorders are allowed).

The "sawtooth effect" relating Q and R in Figure 8.2 shows that when inventory drops to point R, a reorder is placed. This order is received at the end of time period L, which doesn't vary in this model.

In constructing any inventory model, the first step is to develop a functional relationship between the variables of interest and the measure of effectiveness. In this case, since we are concerned with cost, the following equation would pertain.

$$TC \doteq DC + \frac{D}{Q}S + \frac{Q}{2}H$$

where

TC = Total annual cost

D = Annual demand

C = Purchase cost per unit

Q = Quantity to be ordered (the optimum amount is termed the *economic order quantity*—EOQ—or Q_{opt})

S = Cost of placing an order or making a production setup

H = Annual holding and storage cost per unit of average inventory

R = Reorder point

L = Lead time

On the right-hand side of the equation, DC is the annual purchase cost for the units, $(D/Q)S$ is the annual ordering cost (the actual number of orders placed, D/Q, times the cost of each order, S), and $(Q/2)H$ is the annual holding cost (the average inventory, $Q/2$, times the cost per unit for holding and storage, H). These cost relationships are shown graphically in Figure 8.3.

The second step in model development is to find that order quantity, Q, for which total cost is a minimum. In the basic model, this may be done by simple algebra if we recognize that DC is not a decision variable and hence not a factor in the ordering decision. Then—with reference to Figure 8.3—total cost is minimum at the point where the cost of ordering is equal to the cost of carrying, or

$$\frac{DS}{Q} = \frac{Q}{2}H$$

which in turn is solved as follows:

$$DS = \frac{Q^2H}{2}$$

$$2DS = Q^2H$$

$$Q^2 = \frac{2DS}{H}$$

$$Q_{opt} = \sqrt{\frac{2DS}{H}}$$

FIGURE 8.3

Annual product costs, based on size of the order

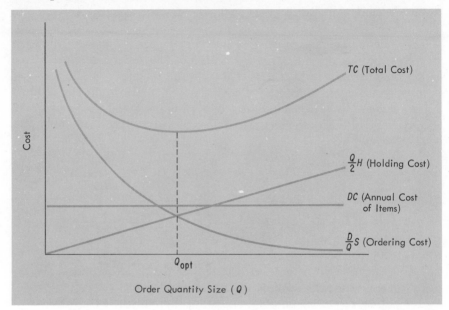

When more complex cost equations are involved, this simple algebraic approach will not suffice and differential calculus must be employed. The appropriate calculus procedure involves taking the derivative of total cost with respect to Q. For the basic model considered here, the calculations would be as follows.

$$TC = DC + \frac{D}{Q}S + \frac{Q}{2}H$$

$$\frac{dTC}{dQ} = 0 + \left(\frac{-DS}{Q^2}\right) + \frac{H}{2} = 0$$

$$Q_{opt} = \sqrt{\frac{2DS}{H}}$$

Since this simple model assumes constant demand and lead time, no safety stock is necessary, and the reorder point, R, *is simply* $R = \bar{d}L$ where

$$\bar{d} = \text{Average daily demand [constant] and}$$
$$L = \text{Lead time in days [constant].}$$

Example 8.1. Find the economic order quantity and the reorder point, given the following data:

$$\text{Annual demand } (D) = 1{,}000 \text{ units}$$
$$\text{Average daily demand } (\bar{d}) = 1{,}000/365$$
$$\text{Ordering cost } (S) = \$5 \text{ per order}$$
$$\text{Holding cost } (H) = \$1.25 \text{ per unit per year}$$
$$\text{Lead time } (L) = 5 \text{ days}$$
$$\text{Cost per unit } (C) = \$12.50$$

The optimum order quantity is

$$Q_{\text{opt}} = \sqrt{\frac{2DS}{H}} = \sqrt{\frac{2(1,000)5}{1.25}} = \sqrt{8,000} = 89.4 \text{ units}$$

The reorder point is

$$R = \bar{d}L = \frac{1,000}{365}(5) = 13.7 \text{ units}$$

Rounding to the nearest unit, the inventory policy is as follows: When the number of units in inventory drops to 14, place an order for 89 more.

The total annual cost will be

$$TC = DC + \frac{D}{Q}S + \frac{Q}{2}H$$

$$= 1,000(12.50) + \frac{1,000}{89}(5) + \frac{89}{2}(1.25)$$

$$= 12,500 + 56.18 + 55.63$$

$$= \$12,611.81.$$

The ordering cost and the holding cost ($56.18 and $55.63) are not equal because of rounding to an even number of units for Q. (Note that in this example the purchase cost of the units was not required to determine the order quantity and the reorder point.)

Simple fixed-order quantity model with usage. Example 8.1 assumed that the quantity ordered would be received in one lot, but frequently this is not the case. In many situations, in fact, production of an inventory item and usage of that item take place simultaneously. This is particularly true where one part of a production system acts as a supplier to another part. For example, while aluminum extrusions are being made to fill an order for aluminum windows, the extrusions are cut and assembled before the entire extrusion order is completed.

The production with usage inventory model is only slightly different from the preceding model. If we let d denote a constant demand rate for some item going into production and p the production rate of that process which uses the item, we may develop the following total cost equation.[1]

$$TC = DC + \frac{D}{Q}S + \frac{(p - d)QH}{2p}$$

Again differentiating with respect to Q and setting the equation equal to zero, we obtain

$$Q_{\text{opt}} = \sqrt{\frac{2DS}{H} \cdot \frac{p}{(p - d)}}$$

This model is shown in Figure 8.4; but even here we can see that the number of units on hand will always be less than the order quantity, Q.

Example 8.2. Product X is a standard item in a firm's inventory. Final assembly of the product is performed on an assembly line which is in operation every day. One of the components of product X (call it com-

---

[1] Obviously, the production rate must exceed the rate of usage; otherwise Q would be infinite, resulting in continual production.

FIGURE 8.4

Fixed-order quantity model with usage during production time

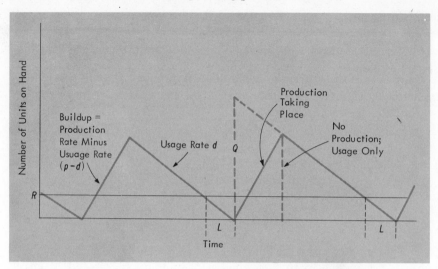

ponent X_1) is produced in another department. This department, when it produces X_1, does so at the rate of 100 units per day. The assembly line uses component X_1 at the rate of 40 units per day.

Given the following data, what is the optimal lot size for production of component X_1?

$$
\begin{aligned}
\text{Daily usage rate } (d) &= 40 \text{ units} \\
\text{Annual demand } (D) &= 10,000 \ (40 \text{ units} \times 250 \text{ working days}) \\
\text{Daily production } (p) &= 100 \text{ units} \\
\text{Cost for production setup } (S) &= \$50 \\
\text{Annual holding cost } (H) &= \$0.50 \\
\text{Cost of component } X_1 \ (C) &= \$7 \\
\text{Lead time } (L) &= 7 \text{ days}
\end{aligned}
$$

$$
Q_{\text{opt}} = \sqrt{\frac{2DS}{H} \cdot \frac{p}{p-d}} = \sqrt{\frac{2(10,000)50}{0.50} \cdot \frac{100}{100-40}} = \sqrt{3,333,333}
$$
$$
= 1,826 \text{ units}
$$
$$
R = Ld = 7(40) = 280 \text{ units}
$$

This states that an order for 1,826 units of component X_1 should be placed when the stock drops to 280 units.

At 100 units per day, this run will take 18.26 days and will provide a 45.65-day supply for the assembly line (1,826/40). Theoretically, the department will be occupied with other work for the 27.39 days when component X_1 is not being produced.

Simple fixed-order quantity model with backorders allowed. The first model presented in this chapter assumed that all demands would be met (shortages were not allowed). This was done indirectly, by assuming that the cost of running out of stock was infinite. Certainly there are cases where meeting all demands is just not worth the cost of carrying the necessary stock, and the most economical decision is to allow shortages. These shortages are filled as soon as the new order is received. Figure 8.5 illustrates this simple model with shortages allowed.

M = Replenishment level (in this case the maximum inventory level at the beginning of each order period)

Q = Economic order quantity

t_1 = Time when inventory surplus exists

t_2 = Time when inventory shortage exists

H = Annual holding cost per unit

π = Annual shortage cost per unit

S = Setup or ordering cost

D = Annual demand

The geometry of this model allows us to specify the following relationships. The average inventory cost during time t_1 is

$$\frac{M}{2} H t_1$$

The average shortage cost during time t_2 is

$$\frac{Q - M}{2} \pi t_2$$

The total cost for the time interval $t_1 + t_2$, wherein one order quantity is ordered and consumed, is

$$\frac{MHt_1}{2} + \frac{Q - M}{2} \pi t_2 + S$$

On an annual basis there are D/Q such periods. Thus, multiplying the above equation by D/Q gives the total annual cost:

$$\frac{D}{Q}\left(\frac{M}{2} Ht_1 + \frac{Q - M}{2} \pi t_2 + S\right)$$

FIGURE 8.5

Fixed-order quantity with shortages

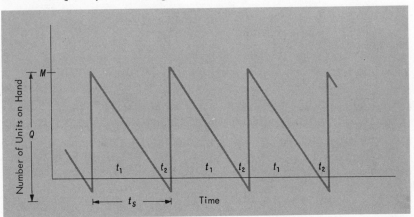

By the geometry of similar triangles,

$$\frac{t_1}{t_s} = \frac{M}{Q} \quad \text{or} \quad t_1 = \frac{M}{Q} t_s$$

$$\frac{t_2}{t_s} = \frac{Q - M}{Q} \quad \text{or} \quad t_2 = \frac{(Q - M)}{Q} t_s$$

Substituting for t_1 and t_2 in the above equation gives

$$\frac{D}{Q}\left(\frac{M^2 H t_s}{2Q} + \frac{(Q - M)^2 \pi t_s}{2Q} + S\right)$$

The time t_s is equal to Q/D, the reciprocal of the number of orders per year. Substituting for t_s gives the total annual cost as

$$TC = \frac{M^2 H}{2Q} + \frac{(Q - M)^2 \pi}{2Q} + \frac{SD}{Q}$$

By partial differentiation with respect to Q and M, we obtain

$$Q_{\text{opt}} = \sqrt{\frac{2DS}{H}} \sqrt{\frac{H + \pi}{\pi}}$$

$$M = \sqrt{\frac{2DS}{H}} \sqrt{\frac{\pi}{H + \pi}}$$

These equations give the optimal order size and the maximum inventory level (M) for each period. To find the period or cycle time (T), the time between orders, we can substitute D/T for Q in the equation and obtain

$$T = \sqrt{\frac{2S}{DH}} \sqrt{\frac{H + \pi}{\pi}}$$

Example 8.3. A manufacturer is faced with a constant and known demand for his product at the rate of 10,000 per year. The cost to set up for production is $150 and the annual cost to carry the item in inventory is $2 each. If the manufacturer runs out of stock, there is an annual shortage cost of $5 per unit. This shortage will be filled as soon as the new lot is produced. The problem is to determine the optimal order quantity.

$$D = 10{,}000$$
$$S = 150$$
$$H = 2$$
$$\pi = 5$$

$$Q_{\text{opt}} = \sqrt{\frac{2DS}{H}} \sqrt{\frac{H + \pi}{\pi}} = \sqrt{\frac{2(10{,}000)150}{2}} \sqrt{\frac{2 + 5}{5}}$$
$$= (1{,}224.8)(1.18) = \underline{1{,}445.3 \text{ units}}$$

The maximum number of units that will be on hand is

$$M = \sqrt{\frac{2DS}{H}} \sqrt{\frac{\pi}{H + \pi}} = 1{,}224.8(0.845) = 1{,}035 \text{ units}$$

The number of units by which he will be short at the end of each run is then

$$M - Q = 1,035 - 1,445.3 = -410 \text{ units}$$

The optimum time between placing orders is

$$T = \sqrt{\frac{2S}{DH}} \sqrt{\frac{H + \pi}{\pi}} = \sqrt{\frac{2(150)}{10,000(2)}} \sqrt{\frac{2 + 5}{5}} = 0.145 \text{ year}$$

An order for 1,445 units would be placed every 0.145 year, or about every 7½ weeks.

Fixed-period models (periodic models). As was mentioned previously, fixed-period models generate order quantities that vary from period to period, depending on the usage rates. From an operational standpoint, there are many situations where it is more desirable to count inventory and place an order for restocking on a repetitive time basis rather than place orders every time stock drops to the reorder point. Specifically, this procedure facilitates planning, since employees can know—for example—that every two weeks all the stock on hand from distributor X must be counted. In addition, it reduces the cost of ordering and shipping since items from the same vendor can be ordered and shipped together.

However, as was also mentioned previously, periodic systems generally require a higher level of safety stock than is required under a fixed-order quantity system. This is so because the EOQ formulas in the latter system assume continual monitoring, with an order immediately placed when the reorder point is reached. In contrast, the standard periodic models assume that inventory is recorded only at the time specified. Therefore, during the entire time between reviews, safety stock must be provided to protect against stockouts during the review period itself, as well as during the lead time from order placement to order receipt.

We will now develop a fixed-period model under certainty. Looking first at the sawtooth graph in Figure 8.6, we see that demand and lead time are again constant, but also that some new terms have been added. Consider first the *q*s. These refer to the amounts ordered after each stock review and represent the difference between the replenishment inventory level and the amount of inventory currently on hand and on order. Because demand is constant in this case, *q* is the same for each order. *L* indicates the lead time needed between the time *q* is ordered and the time it arrives. *M* stands for the replenishment level, and the only time inventory would reach this level would be if the demand during the lead time were zero.

Now consider the term *T*, which refers to the review period or cycle time. As the graph shows, this time period runs from the time one order is placed to the time of the next order placement. In theory, stock counting occurs instantaneously at time t_i. In practice, it could begin at any point during this period, but it must be completed by time period t_{i+1}. Thus the first review runs from t_1 to t_2, the second from t_2 to t_3, and so forth. This rather clearly indicates a feature of a fixed-period model; namely, that the amount of inventory ordered must be sufficient to cover the review period *plus* the lead time.

FIGURE 8.6

Fixed-period inventory model under conditions of constant demand and constant
lead time

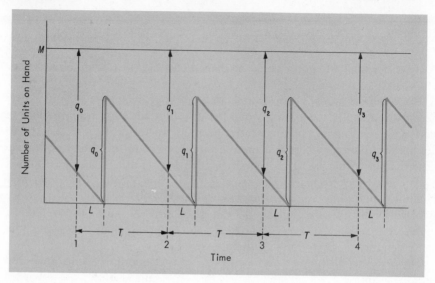

Turning now to the development of total cost equations, we may start
with the one derived for the basic fixed-order quantity model:

$$TC = DC + \frac{DS}{Q} + \frac{QH}{2}$$

where

TC = Total annual cost
D = Annual demand
C = Purchase cost per unit
Q = Quantity to be ordered
S = Cost for placing an order or making a production setup
H = Annual holding and storage cost per unit of average inventory
T = Cycle time in fraction of a year

There are two possible variables in this period model: T and Q. Frequently, because of ordering a number of units from the same vendor or
for convenience in the operating schedule, time period T may be fixed at
some constant time. In that case, the objective would be to find a way to
determine the optimal order size. If T can be set at any time length, our
objective is to find the review period that minimizes the cost involved.
To find the optimal T (as a fraction of a year), we can proceed as follows:
There are D/Q cycles per year; therefore the value of T can be equated to
the reciprocal of this amount, or Q/D. This relationship, $T = Q/D$, can then
be restated as $Q = DT$, which allows us to substitute DT for Q in the total
cost equation:

$$TC = DC + \frac{DS}{DT} + \frac{DTH}{2}$$

Differentiating with respect to T and solving gives

$$T_{opt} = \sqrt{\frac{2S}{DH}}$$

This equation yields the same order quantity as $Q = \sqrt{2DS/H}$, where Q/D is substituted for T.

Example 8.4. The annual demand for product alpha is 1,500 units. The cost to make a production setup is \$100 and annual holding costs are \$5 per unit. Determine the optimal time for review.

$$T_{opt} = \sqrt{\frac{2S}{DH}} = \sqrt{\frac{2(100)}{1,500(5)}} = \sqrt{\frac{200}{7,500}} = \sqrt{0.0267} = 0.163 \text{ year}$$

or about every two months (59.5 days). The optimum quantity to produce is

$$Q_{opt} = DT_{opt} = 1,500(0.163) = 245 \text{ units}$$

The inventory policy for this product is: Every 60 days order 245 units.

Probabilistic inventory models (conditions of uncertainty)

The previous models assumed that demand was constant and known. In the majority of cases, though, demand is not constant but varies from day to day. Safety stock must therefore be maintained to provide some level of protection against stockouts. This degree of protection is usually based on one of two criteria; that is, set safety stock (1) at the point that provides some level of customer service (for example, a management policy that 95 percent of the demands will be met directly from stock on hand), or (2) at the point that minimizes the cost of shortages and the cost of carrying added inventory.

The first criterion requires that we know something about the cost of running out of stock. Usually we do not know this cost exactly, but, since inventory costs are generally fairly shallow and dish-shaped curves, some error in cost estimate is tolerable. (To find out how this error affects the decision, we can try several different estimates. This will give us a range showing the sensitivity of cost.)

In this section we will examine two models that consider variation in demand. The first is a probabilistic fixed-order quantity model, which we will develop mathematically. The second is a probabilistic fixed-period model, which we will describe in words.

Fixed-order quantity model. The danger of stockout in this model occurs only during the lead time; that is, between the time an order is placed and the time it is received. As shown in Figure 8.7, an order is placed when the inventory level drops to the reorder point, R. During this lead time (L), a range of demands is possible. This range is determined either from

FIGURE 8.7

Fixed-order quantity model with variation in demand and constant lead time

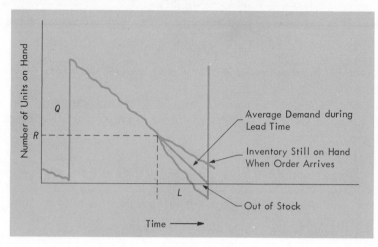

an analysis of past demand data or from an estimate (if past data are not available). This model does not have a safety stock, and the average maximum inventory is Q. There will be, however, a high probability of stock shortages. A buffer or safety stock for protection can be added, as shown in Figure 8.8. The size of the safety stock is such that when the maximum demand we want to satisfy occurs, the safety stock level is brought down to zero.

The objective in determining safety stock is to establish some desired level of meeting demands for the product. A term frequently used in this

FIGURE 8.8

Fixed-order quantity model with variation in demand, a constant lead time, and a safety stock

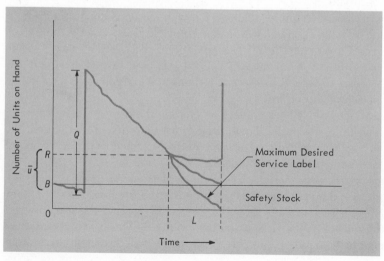

determination is *service level,* which can be interpreted in either of two ways: (1) as the ratio of the number of units supplied to the number of units demanded or (2) as the ratio of the number of customers receiving the product to the number of customers demanding the product. To illustrate both interpretations, suppose that, out of 10 customers, nine demand 100 units each and the tenth demands 500 units. If the nine demands of 100 units are filled and the tenth is unfilled, the service level under (1) is 900/1400, or 64.3 percent, and is 9/10, or 90 percent, under (2). Thus, in a practical sense, the main difference is whether one is interested in satisfying units of demand or satisfying a number of customers who place varying size orders. In the discussion and example that follow, the second definition will be used—in which service level refers to the percentage of satisfied customers.

When safety stock is added to meet a specified service level, the average maximum inventory level is increased by the average unused safety stock. The reorder point (R) is equal to the average usage during lead time $(\bar{u})$ plus the safety stock (B): $R = \bar{u} + B$. The average usage or demand $(\bar{u})$ during the lead time (L) is $\bar{u} = \bar{d}L$. And the required level of safety stock for a specified degree of protection against stockout during the lead time period is $B = a\sigma_u$.

> u = A random variable, equal to the usage during lead time
> $\bar{u}$ = Average usage during lead time
> $\bar{d}$ = Average daily demand
> R = Reorder point in units
> L = Lead time in days
> B = Buffer or safety stock in units
> σ_u = Standard deviation of usage during lead time
> a = Number of standard deviations needed for a specified confidence level
> σ_d = Standard deviation of daily demand

To illustrate, suppose that demand for a product is normally distributed and that the objective is to have a 95 percent probability of satisfying every customer during the lead time. From a cumulative probability table, 95 percent corresponds to 1.645 standard deviations. Therefore the appropriate reorder point is $R = \bar{d}L + 1.645\sigma_u$.

The optimum reorder quantity for this model is of the same form as that for the fixed-quantity model with continuous demand. In this case, however, demand (D) is the average demand $(\bar{D})$.

$$Q_{\text{opt}} = \sqrt{\frac{2\bar{D}S}{H}}$$

Example 8.5. The daily demand for a product is normally distributed with a mean of 60 and a standard deviation of 7. Further, the source of supply is reliable and maintains a constant lead time of six days. If the cost of placing the order is $10 and annual holding costs are $0.50 per unit, find the order quantity and reorder point to satisfy 95 percent of the customers who place orders during the reorder period. There are no stockout costs, and unfilled orders are filled as soon as the order arrives. Assume sales occur over the entire year.

$$\bar{d} = 60$$
$$\sigma_d = 7$$
$$\bar{D} = 60(365)$$
$$S = \$10$$
$$H = \$0.50$$
$$L = 6$$

The optimal order quantity is

$$Q_{opt} = \sqrt{\frac{2\bar{D}S}{H}} = \sqrt{\frac{2(60)365(10)}{0.50}} = \sqrt{876,000} = 936$$

The reorder point for 95 percent confidence is $R = \bar{d}L + 1.645\sigma_u$.

The standard deviation of usage during the total lead time of six days depends on the variance of the individual days. Since each day's demand is independent,[2]

$$\sigma_u = \sqrt{\sum_{i=1}^{L} \sigma_{di}^2}$$

$$\sigma_u = \sqrt{6(7)^2} = \sqrt{294} = 17.2$$

The mean usage during lead time is $\bar{d}L = 60$ per day $\times$ 6 days $= 360$. Therefore

$$R = \bar{d}L + 1.645\sigma_u$$
$$= 60(6) + 1.645(17.2) = 360 + 28.3$$
$$= 388.3 \text{ units}$$

The safety stock (B) is 28.3 units since $B = 1.645\sigma_u$.

To summarize the policy derived in this example, an order quantity for 936 units is placed every time the number of units remaining in inventory drops to 388 units. (This includes a safety stock of 28 units.)

Fixed-period model. The fixed-period model under uncertainty differs from the model under certainty through the provision of a safety or buffer stock. Figure 8.9 illustrates this situation, where not only demand varies but lead time as well. This problem is a bit more involved than our intentions, so the interested reader should consult the references for detailed treatment.

There are two different approaches to treating the problem, depending on the kind of variation involved. When the demand and lead time can be approximated with known continuous distributions, the solution can be derived mathematically by using a joint probability distribution. When the variation is discrete (the more common case), the easiest way to solve the problem is to build tables showing the range of outcomes.

In this fixed-period model, if the frequency for inventory review can be

---

[2] From basic statistics, the standard deviation of a sum of independent random variables is equal to the square root of the sum of the variances.

FIGURE 8.9

Fixed-period inventory model with variation in demand and lead time

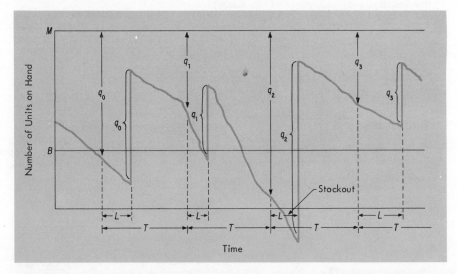

set at any time period, the problem is to determine T (the optimal time between inventory reviews) and M (a replenishment level used to determine order quantity). Lowercase q is used to indicate that order size changes from period to period. If T is already established,

$$q = M - I$$

and

$$M = B + \bar{d}(T + \bar{L}),$$

where

q = Quantity to be ordered
M = Replenishment level in units
I = Number of units of inventory on hand
B = Buffer or safety stock in units
$\bar{d}$ = Average daily demand
T = Review period
$\bar{L}$ = Average lead time

The difficulties encountered in this problem are in determining the safety stock (B) and treating the interaction of T and M. Obviously, if the review period or lead time increases, the replenishment level must also increase. This interaction requires that the problem be solved through several iterations, until it converges on the optimal values.

Special-purpose models

The fixed-quantity and the fixed-period models presented thus far differed in their assumptions but had two characteristics in common: (1) the cost

FIGURE 8.10

Curves for three separate order quantity models in a three-price break situation (solid line depicts feasible range of purchases)

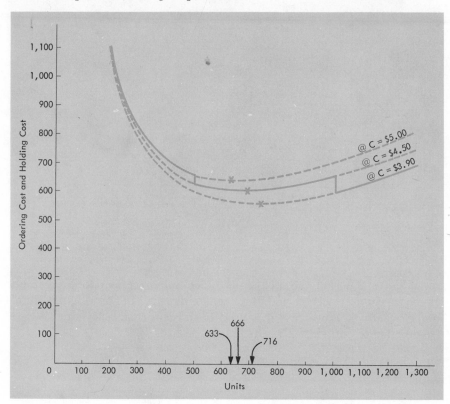

of units remained constant for any order size and (2) the reordering process was continuous; that is, the items were ordered and stocked with the expectation that the need would continue. This section presents two new models: the first illustrates the effect on order quantity when unit price changes with order size; the second is a single-period model (sometimes called a *static model*) in which ordering and stocking require a cost trade-off each time.

Price-break models. Generally the selling price or cost of an item varies with the order size. This is a discrete or step change rather than a per unit change. For example, wood screws may cost 2 cents each for 1 to 99 screws, $1.60 per 100, and $13.50 per 1,000. In order to determine the optimal quantity of any item to order, the procedure involves simply solving for the economic order quantity for each price and at the point of price change. However, not all of the economic order quantities determined by the formula will be feasible. In the wood screw example, the EOQ formula might tell us that the optimal decision at the price of 1.6 cents is to order 75 screws. This would be impossible, however, since 75 screws would cost 2 cents each.

The total cost for each feasible economic order quantity and price-break quantity is tabulated, and the Q that leads to the minimum cost is the optimal order size.

If holding cost is based on a percentage of unit price, it may not be necessary to compute economic order quantities at each price. Procedurally, the largest order quantity (lowest unit price) is solved first; if the resulting Q is valid, that is the answer. If not, the next largest order quantity (second lowest price) is derived. If that is feasible, the cost of this Q is compared to the cost of using the order quantity at the price break above, and the lowest cost determines the optimal Q.

Looking at Figure 8.10, we see that order quantities are solved from right to left, or from the lowest unit price to the highest, until a valid Q is obtained. Then the order quantity at each price break above this Q is used to find which order quantity has the least cost—the computed Q or the Q at one of the price breaks.

Example 8.6. Consider the following case, where

D = 10,000 units (annual demand)
S = \$20 to place each order
H = 20% of cost (annual carrying cost, storage, interest, obsolescence, etc.)
C = Cost per unit (according to the order size: orders of 0 to 499 units, \$5.00 per unit; 500 to 999, \$4.50 per unit; and 1,000 and up, \$3.90 per unit)

The appropriate equations from the basic fixed quantity case are

$$TC = DC + \frac{D}{Q}S + \frac{Q}{2}H$$

and

$$Q = \sqrt{\frac{2DS}{H}}$$

Solving for the economic order size at each price, we obtain

$@C$ = \$5.00, Q = 633
$@C$ = \$4.50, Q = 666
$@C$ = \$3.90, Q = 716

In Figure 8.10, which displays the cost relationship and order quantity range, note that most of the order quantity-cost relationships lie outside the feasible range and that only a single, continuous range results. This should be readily apparent, since, for example, the first order quantity specifies buying 633 units at \$5 per unit. However, if 633 units are ordered, the price is \$4.50—not \$5. The same holds true for the third order quantity, which specifies an order of 716 units at \$3.90 each. This \$3.90 price is not available on orders of less than 1,000 units.

Table 8.2 itemizes the total costs at the economic order quantities and at the price breaks. The optimal order quantity is shown to be 1,000 units.

TABLE 8.2

Relevant costs in a three-price-break model

	Price break 500	Q = 633 where C = $5	Q = 666 where C = $4.50	Q = 716 where C = $3.90	Price break 1,000
Holding cost $\left(\frac{Q}{2}H\right)$......	$\frac{500}{2}(0.20)4.50$ = $225		$\frac{666}{2}(0.20)4.50$ = $299.70		$\frac{1,000}{2}(0.20)3.90$ = $390
Ordering cost $\left(\frac{D}{Q}S\right)$......	$\frac{10,000(20)}{500}$ = $400	Not feasible	$\frac{10,000(20)}{666}$ = $300	Not feasible	$\frac{10,000(20)}{1,000}$ = $200
Holding and ordering cost..	$625		$600		$590
Item cost (DC)..	10,000($4.50)		10,000($4.50)		10,000($3.90)
Total cost......	$45,625		$45,599.70		$39,590

Single-period models. The term *single period* derives from the fact that the time horizon for inventory decision making covers only one demand period wherein a single procurement is made. These types of models are applicable when (1) there is a high level of demand for an item at relatively infrequent intervals or (2) where there is uncertain demand for a short-lived item at relatively frequent intervals. The first situation is typified by promotional and fad items ordered by retail stores; the second by highly perishable items (fresh fish, flowers) and high-obsolescence items (newspapers, other periodicals).

To show how to solve a single-period problem, we will again resort to an example.

Example 8.7. Suppose we are faced with the problem of deciding how many units of a perishable product we should order for the upcoming sales period. Unsold units have no salvage value, so the objective is to order the number of units that maximizes profit for the period. The selling price of the item is $60 and its cost is $40. The range of possible demands and their associated probabilities are presented in the first two columns of Table 8.3.

To begin, we would like to obtain a profit figure for each possible order quantity. That is, for an order size of 70 we would like to know the profit if demand were equal to 70, 80, 90, 100, 110, and 120. We would then make similar calculations for stocking 80 units, 90 units, and so forth. The expected number of items to be sold would then be tabulated, as in the fifth column of Table 8.3, which shows (for example) that if we wish to know the number of units that would be sold if we placed an order for $Q = 100$ units, we can expect all of the first 70 to be sold, 9 of the next 10 to be sold, $7\frac{1}{2}$ of the next 10, and $5\frac{1}{2}$ of the last 10—for a total of 92.

Profit is then computed from the relationship

Profit = Revenue − Cost
= Number sold × Selling price − Order quantity × Cost

$@Q = 70$, Profit $= 70(\$60) - 70(\$40) = \$1,400$
$@Q = 80$, Profit $= 79(\$60) - 80(\$40) = \$1,540$, etc.

TABLE 8.3

Single-order model to determine optimal order quantity

(D) Range of possible demands	(p) Probability of this demand	(P) Probability of selling this unit is		(Q) If quantity ordered is set at	Expected number to be sold is therefore		Expected revenue is price ($60) × number sold	Cost for units is $40 × Q	Expected profit is revenue minus cost
70	0.10	70 or less:	1.00	70	70(1.00)	= 70	$4,200	$2,800	$1,400
80	0.15	71–80:	0.90	80	70 + 10(0.90)	= 79	4,740	3,200	1,540
90	0.20	81–90:	0.75	90	79 + 10(0.75)	= 86.5	5,190	3,600	1,590
100	0.25	91–100:	0.55	100	86.5 + 10(0.55)	= 92	5,520	4,000	1,520
110	0.20	101–110:	0.30	110	92 + 10(0.30)	= 95	5,700	4,400	1,300
120	0.10	111–120:	0.10	120	95 + 10(0.10)	= 96	5,760	4,800	960
		120 or more	0	120+	96 + (0)	= 96			

From Table 8.3, we see that maximum profit occurs when the quantity ordered (Q) is 90 units, resulting in a profit of $1,590. If unsold items had some salvage value, this would simply be added into revenue to increase the resulting profit in each case.

INVENTORY CONTROL THROUGH MARGINAL ANALYSIS

A different way of solving certain types of inventory problems is through the classic economic approach of marginal analysis. The optimal stocking decision, using marginal analysis, occurs at the point where the benefits derived from carrying the next unit are less than the costs for that unit. Of course the selection of the specific benefits and costs depends on the problem; for example, we may be looking at costs of holding versus shortage costs, or (as we will develop further) marginal profit versus marginal loss.

In the situation where stocked items are sold, the optimal decision— using marginal analysis—is to stock that quantity where the profit from the sale or use of the last unit is equal to or greater than the losses if the last unit remains unsold. In symbolic terms, this is the condition where $MP \geqq$ ML, where

MP = Profit resulting from the Nth unit if it is sold

ML = Loss resulting from the Nth unit if it is not sold

Marginal analysis is also valid when we are dealing with probabilities of occurrence. In these situations we are looking at expected profits and expected losses. By introducing probabilities, the marginal profit-marginal loss equation becomes

$$P_1(MP) \geq P_2(ML)$$

where P_1 is the probability of the unit's being sold and P_2 is the probability of the unit's not being sold.[3] Since one or other must occur (the unit is sold or is not sold), $P_1 + P_2$ must equal one, and we can state P_2 (in terms of P_1) as $P_2 = 1 - P_1$.

Our marginal profit-marginal loss equation then becomes

$$P_1(MP) \geq (1 - P_1)ML$$

We can drop the subscript while retaining P as the probability of selling a unit and $1 - P$ as the probability of not selling it. Then, solving for P, we obtain

$$P \geq \frac{ML}{MP + ML}$$

This equation states that we should continue to increase the size of the inventory so long as the probability of selling the last unit added is equal to or greater than the ratio $ML/(MP + ML)$.

Salvage value. Salvage value, or any other benefits derived from unsold goods, can easily be included in the problem. This simply reduces the marginal loss, as demonstrated in the following example.

---

[3] P is actually a cumulative probability since the sale of the Nth unit depends not only on exactly N being demanded but also on the demand for any number greater than N.

TABLE 8.4

Number of units demanded	(p) Probability of this demand	(P) Probability of selling this unit is	
35...............	0.10	35 or less:	1.00
36...............	0.15	36th:	0.90
37...............	0.25	37th:	0.75
38...............	0.25	38th:	0.50
39...............	0.15	39th:	0.25
40...............	0.10	40th:	0.10
41...............	0	41 or more:	0

Example 8.8. A product is priced to sell at $100 per unit and its cost is constant at $70 per unit. Each unsold unit has a salvage value of $30. Demand is expected to range between 35 and 40 units for the period: 35 units definitely can be sold and no units over 40 will be sold. The demand probabilities and the associated cumulative probability distribution (P) for this situation are shown in Table 8.4.

The marginal profit if a unit is sold is the selling price less the cost, or $MP = \$100 - \$70 = \$30$.

The marginal loss incurred if the unit is not sold is the cost of the unit less the salvage value, or $ML = \$70 - \$30 = \$40$.

The optimal number to stock for the period is

$$P \geq \frac{ML}{MP + ML} = \frac{40}{30 + 40} = 0.57$$

According to the cumulative probability table above, the probability of selling the unit must be equal to or greater than 0.57; therefore 37 units should be stocked. The probability of selling the 37th unit is 0.75. The net benefit from stocking the 37th unit is the expected marginal profit minus the expected marginal loss.

$$\begin{aligned} \text{Net} &= P(MP) - (1 - P)(ML) \\ &= 0.75(\$100 - \$70) - (1 - 0.75)(\$70 - \$30) \\ &= \$22.50 - \$10.00 = \$12.50 \end{aligned}$$

For the sake of illustration, Table 8.5 shows all possible decisions. From the last column, we can confirm that the optimum decision is 37 units.

Carryover costs. These costs—obsolescence, depreciation, handling— can be included as part of the marginal loss in determining the optimum stocking point. Since the carryover cost will occur if the unit is not sold, the expected carryover cost is $(1 - P)CC$, as shown in the following example.

Example 8.9. Assume that inventory restocking is a continual process from period to period. The selling price is still $100 per unit and unit cost is $70. If the unit is not sold, it is held over until the next period, but there is a $15 cost per unit for handling and storage. Demand is the same as previously.

TABLE 8.5

Marginal inventory analysis for units having salvage value

(N) Units of demand	(p) Probability of demand	(P) Probability of selling Nth unit	(MP) Expected marginal profit of Nth unit P(100 − 70)	(ML) Expected marginal loss of Nth unit (1 − P)(70 − 30)	(Net) (MP) − (ML)
35.......	0.10	1.00	$30	0	$30.00
36.......	0.15	0.90	27	$ 4	23.00
37.......	0.25	0.75	22.50	10	12.50
38.......	0.25	0.50	15	20	(5.00)
39.......	0.15	0.25	7.50	30	(22.50)
40.......	0.10	0.10	3	36	(33.00)
41.......	0	0			(40.00)

Note: Expected marginal profit is the selling price of $100 less the unit cost of $70 times the probability the unit will be sold.

Expected marginal loss is the unit cost of $70 less the salvage value of $30 times the probability the unit will not be sold.

The marginal profit if a unit is sold is $MP = \$100 - \$70 = \$30$.
The marginal loss if a unit is not sold is the carryover cost: $ML = \$15$.
The optimal number to stock, then, is

$$P \geq \frac{ML}{MP + ML} = \frac{\$15}{\$30 + \$15} = 0.33$$

From the cumulative table of demand (Table 8.6), the probability of selling the 38th unit is 0.50 and the 39th unit is 0.25. Therefore 38 units should be stocked. The net benefit from stocking the 38th unit is the expected marginal profit less the expected marginal loss, or

$$
\begin{aligned}
\text{Net} &= P(MP) - (1 - P)(ML) \\
&= 0.50(\$100 - \$70) - (1 - 0.50)(\$15) \\
&= \$15 - \$7.50 = \$7.50
\end{aligned}
$$

Table 8.7 shows the resulting marginal profits, losses, and net benefits for the full range of units stocked.

As an aside, it should be pointed out that the example used in the previous section (page 392) on single-period models could have been solved by

TABLE 8.6

Number of units demanded	(p) Probability of this demand	(P) Probability of selling this unit is	
35.............	0.10	35th or less:	1.00
36.............	0.15	36th:	0.90
37.............	0.25	37th:	0.75
38.............	0.25	38th:	0.50
39.............	0.15	39th:	0.25
40.............	0.10	40th:	0.10
		41st or more:	0

TABLE 8.7

Marginal inventory analysis for units with carryover costs

(N) units of demand	(p) Probability of demand	(P) Probability of selling the Nth unit	(MP) Expected marginal profit of Nth unit P(100 − 70)	(ML) Expected marginal loss due to carrying cost (1 − P)15	(Net) (MP) − (ML)
35......	0.10	1.00	$30	$ 0	$30
36......	0.15	0.90	27	1.50	25.50
37......	0.25	0.75	22.50	3.75	18.75
38......	0.25	0.50	15	7.50	7.50
39......	0.15	0.25	7.50	11.25	(3.75)
40......	0.10	0.10	3	13.50	(10.50)
41......	0	0	0	15.00	(15.00)

Note: The expected marginal profit is the selling price less the cost times the probability that the unit will be sold.

The expected marginal loss is the carryover cost times the probability that the unit will not be sold.

using marginal analysis. In that problem, the selling price was $60 and cost was $40 per unit. Since there was no salvage or other cost,

$$MP = (\$60 - \$40) = \$20$$
$$ML = \$40$$
$$P \geq \frac{M_L}{MP + ML} = \frac{\$40}{\$20 + \$40} = 0.67$$

Table 8.8 restates the probabilities of demand for that single-period problem, and also lists a cumulative probability column. According to this table, the probability at 90 is 0.75 and at 100 it is 0.55. With the restriction that $P \geq 0.67$, the optimum order size is 90, which agrees with our previous decision.

TABLE 8.8

Demand probabilities from Table 8.3

(N) Demand	(p) Probability of demand	(P) Probability of selling the Nth unit
70.................	0.10	1.00
80.................	0.15	0.90
90.................	0.20	0.75
100................	0.25	0.55
110................	0.20	0.30
120................	0.10	0.10
130................	0	0

ABC-TYPE INVENTORY PLANNING

Any inventory system must specify when an order is to be placed for an item and how many units to order. In most situations involving inventory control, there are too many items involved for it to be practical to model

and give thorough treatment to each item. To get around this problem, the ABC classification scheme divides inventory items into three groupings: high dollar volume (A), moderate dollar volume (B), and low dollar volume (C). This dollar volume is a measure of the importance of an item; that is, an item low in cost but high in volume is usually more important than a high-cost item with low volume.

ABC classification

If the annual usage of items in inventory is listed according to dollar volume, observation of the list will generally show that a small number of items accounts for a large dollar volume and that a large number of items accounts for a small dollar volume. Table 8.9 illustrates the relationship.

TABLE 8.9

Annual usage of inventory by value

Item number	Annual dollar usage	Percent of total value
22...................	95,000	40.8
68...................	75,000	32.1
27...................	25,000	10.7
03...................	15,000	6.4
82...................	13,000	5.6
54...................	7,500	3.2
36...................	1,500	0.6
19...................	800	0.3
23...................	425	0.2
41...................	225	0.1
	233,450	100.0

The ABC approach divides this list into three groupings by item value, wherein A items consist of roughly the top 15 percent of the items, B items the next 35 percent, and C items the last 50 percent. From observation, it appears that the list in Table 9.1 may be meaningfully regrouped with A including 20 percent (two of the 10), B including 30 percent, and C including 50 percent. These points show clear delineations between sections. The result of this segmentation is shown in Table 8.10 and is plotted in Figure 8.11.

The purpose of classifying items into groups is to establish the appropriate degree of control over each item. On a periodic basis, for example, class

TABLE 8.10

ABC grouping of inventory items

Classification	Item number	Annual dollar usage	Percent of total
A..............	22, 68	170,000	72.9
B..............	27, 03, 82	53,000	22.7
C..............	54, 36, 19, 23, 41	10,450	4.4
		233,450	100.0

FIGURE 8.11

ABC inventory classification (inventory value for each group versus the group's portion of the total list)

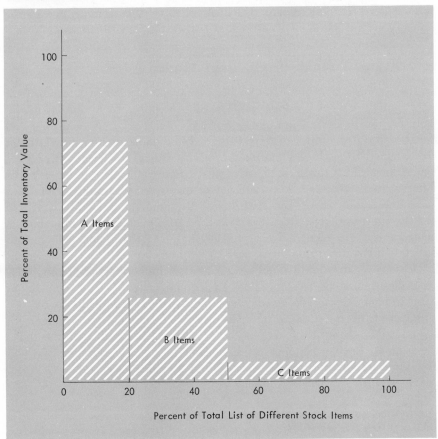

A items may be more closely controlled with weekly ordering, B items may be ordered biweekly, and C items may be ordered monthly or bimonthly. Note that the unit cost of items is not related to their classification. An A item may have a high dollar volume through a combination of either low cost and high usage or high cost and low usage. Similarly, C items may have a low dollar volume either because of low demand or low cost. In an automobile service station, gasoline would be an A item with daily tabulation; tires, batteries, oil, grease, and transmission fluid may be B items; and C items would consist of valve stems, windshield wiper blades, radiator caps, hoses, fan belts, oil and gas additives, car wax, etc. C items may be ordered every two or three months, or even be allowed to run out before reordering since the penalty for stockout is not serious.

In general, the total inventory cost will usually be reduced and the level of service improved when a greater portion of time is spent on the items that represent the highest investment.

Sometimes, an item may be critical to a system if its absence creates a sizable loss. In this case, regardless of the item's classification, sufficiently large stocks should be kept on hand to prevent runout. One way to assure closer control is to designate this item an A or a B, forcing it into the category even if its dollar volume does not warrant such inclusion.

DEPARTMENT STORE INVENTORY POLICY

The common term used to identify an inventory item in a department store is *SKU*, or stock-keeping unit. The SKU identifies each item, its manufacturer, and its cost. The number of SKUs becomes large even for small departments. For example, if towels carried in a domestic items department are obtained from three manufacturers in three quality levels, three sizes (hand towel, face towel, and bath towel), and four colors, there are 108 different items ($3 \times 3 \times 3 \times 4$). Even if towels are sold only in sets of a hand towel, face towel, and bath towel, the number of SKUs needed to identify the towel sets is $3 \times 3 \times 1 \times 4$, or 36. Depending on the store, a housewares department may carry 3,000 to 4,000 SKUs, and a linen and domestic items department may carry 5,000 to 6,000.

Obviously, such large numbers mean that individual economic order quantities cannot be calculated for each item by hand. How, then, does a department keep tab on its stock and place orders for replenishment? We will answer this question in the context of two examples, one dealing with a housewares department and the other with a linen and domestic items department, since each operates somewhat differently. But first we will give some background on the operation of a typical department in a department store.

Operations of a department

Individual departments in a department store are generally autonomous units and are accountable for profit or loss. The staff consists of a buyer, who is also head of the department, an assistant buyer, a secretary, clerks, and stock personnel. Items are separated into categories, generally as staple items and fashion or promotional items. Staple items are standard stock items and have a fairly predictable demand pattern. Promotional and fashion items are special-purpose items. Such items and their promotion method are never precisely repeated, and usually they are not regular stock.

The buyer's efforts are concentrated primarily on the second category, fashion and promotion items. He (or she) searches for special purchase opportunities from vendors, including product line closeouts. The objective with promotional and fashion items is to clear out the stock by the end of the season or by the final day of the promotional campaign. Determining what the selling price should be and what demand to expect is to a large extent based on the experience and market sensitivity of the buyer. If the demand is underestimated, the shortage may embarrass the department by creating unhappy customers, or, more costly merchandise must be substituted. Too large a purchase or too high a selling price will leave unsold items at the end of the promotion. The problem, then, is how to clear out the stock. Extending its length defeats the idea of a promotion, indicating that perhaps the item has become standard stock.

To estimate demand for promotion and fashion items, advertising history results are useful, and the attempt is made to correlate the number of units sold at particular prices with their promotional advertising. Although promotions at different points of time are rarely identical, some indications can nevertheless be derived by comparing a planned promotion with previous ones.

More than half of the buyer's time is spent in finding new products, closing out old items, searching for factory specials, preparing advertising, and determining promotional strategies. The remaining time is devoted to overseeing the operation of the department.

Housewares department. A wide variety of ways is available to operate this type of department. Generally, housewares are divided into staple and promotional items, as previously described. Within these major divisions, further classifications are used, such as cookware and tableware. Also, items are frequently classified by price, as $5 items, $4, $3, etc.

The housewares department usually purchases from a distributor rather than directly from a vendor. The use of a distributor who handles products from many vendors has the advantage of fewer orders and faster shipping time (shorter lead time). Further, the distributor's sales personnel may visit the housewares department weekly and count all the items he supplies to this department. Then, in line with the replenishment level that has been established by the buyer, the distributor's salesman will place orders for the buyer. This saves the department time in counting inventory and placing orders. The typical lead time for receipt of stock from a housewares distributor is two or three days. The safety stock, therefore, is quite low, and the buyer establishes the replenishment level so as to supply only enough items for the two- to three-day lead time, plus expected demand during the period until the distributor's sales personnel's next visit.

It is interesting to note that a formal method of estimating stockout and establishing safety stock levels is usually not followed, because the number of items is too great. Instead, the total value of items in the department is monitored. Thus, replenishment levels are set by dollar allocation.

Through planning, each department has an established monthly value for inventory. By tabulating inventory balance, monthly sales, and items on order, an "open-to-buy" figure is determined ("open-to-buy" is the yet unspent portion of the budget). This dollar amount is the sum available to the buyer for the following month. Figure 8.12 is the form used by one department store to compute the open-to-buy position; and as the form indicates, it is the policy of this store to value inventory at retail price rather than at cost. When an increase in demand is expected (Christmas, Mother's Day, etc.), the allocation of funds to the department is increased, resulting in a larger open-to-buy position. Then the replenishment levels are raised

FIGURE 8.12

An open-to-buy order form for a department store

OPEN TO BUY POSITION AT RETAIL DATE__________

DEPT. ________

RETAIL STOCK ON HAND AT RETAIL AND INFLUX	$
ON ORDER AT RETAIL PLUS MKT. REQUISITION	$
PLUS INTERIM ORDERS PLACED SINCE SURVEY	$
TOTAL STOCK PLUS OUTSTANDING AT RETAIL	$

Month	ACTUAL SALES LAST YEAR Amount	PLANNED SALES THIS YEAR Amount
	$	$
	$	$
	$	$
	$	$
	$	$
	$	$
TOTAL SALES	$	$
Markdowns		
Ending Inventory		

TOTAL DEDUCTIONS	$
OPEN TO BUY	$
OVER-BOUGHT	$

SPENT LAST YEAR: REQUISITION AT RETAIL				SPEND THIS YEAR: REQUISITION AT RETAIL			
Month	Regular Interim	Spec. Ord. Interim	Market	Month	Regular Interim	Spec. Ord. Interim	Market

in line with the class of goods responding to the demand increase, thereby creating a higher stock of goods on hand.

In practice, the open-to-buy funds are largely spent during the first days of the month. However, the buyer tries to reserve some of the funds for special purchases or to restock fast-moving items. (Promotional items in housewares are controlled individually [or by class] by the buyer.)

Linen and domestic items department. The buyer's responsibilities here are similar to those of the housewares buyer in that concentration is on special purchases or factory closeouts, advertising, and promotion. A major difference, though, is that purchases are made directly from vendors rather than from distributors. Lead times are therefore much greater—a month or two rather than a day or two. Total demand during lead time may vary widely, and a larger safety stock must be carried to guard against shortages.

Ordering from vendors also places the burden of counting stock on hand and the actual ordering process directly on the department. Because several thousand items are involved, the stock may be segmented so that each item is counted every four to six weeks. An order then may be computed from the replenishment level formula on page 389, which provides for expected sales over the lead time and review period plus some level of safety stock (perhaps half a month's sales). Here again, the replenishment levels are greatly influenced by the department's total inventory value and the resulting open-to-buy position.

To determine lost sales in any department in a department store is more difficult than initially appears, since at least four basic patterns may be followed by customers. (1) They may enter the department, not see the item and leave, but return later. (2) they may not see the item and leave to purchase it elsewhere. (3) they may inquire and be advised that the item is out of stock and leave. Or (4) they may inquire and place a special order for the out of stock item. If the item is out of stock, a customer inquiry does not necessarily mean a sale was lost—only that a sale *may* have been lost, since they may have been "just looking." A good deal of the time that an item is out of stock is due to the lag between the sale of the last item and the time someone in the department becomes aware of it. In many cases items may be out of stock for days without the buyer's knowledge.

There are usually no formal rules for establishing some degree of stock-out protection or for measuring stockouts in a department store. Attempts to find the extent of shortages generally take the form of a "lost sales sheet," on which a sales clerk lists inquiries by customers for items that are out of stock. A prescribed ABC-type breakdown of items also is unusual. Buyers pay close attention to high dollar-volume sales, but a systematic classification and reorder procedure is not followed in the average store.

MAINTAINING AUTO REPLACEMENT PARTS INVENTORY

A firm in the automobile service business purchases the bulk of its parts supplies from a small number of distributors. Franchised new car dealers purchase the great bulk of their supplies from the automobile manufacturer. A dealer's demand for auto parts originates primarily from the general public and other departments of the agency, such as the service department or body shop. The problem, in this case, is to determine the order quantities for the several thousand items carried.

A franchised automobile agency of medium size may carry a parts inventory valued in the area of $200,000. Because of the nature of this industry, alternate uses of funds are plentiful and therefore opportunity costs are high. For example, dealers may lease cars, carry their own contracts, stock a larger new car inventory, or open sidelines such as tire shops, trailers, or recreational vehicles—all with potentially high returns. This creates pressure to try to carry a low inventory level of parts and supplies while still meeting an acceptable service level.

While many dealers still perform their inventory ordering by hand, there is a definite trend in the industry to using a computer for parts ordering. For both manual and computerized systems, an ABC-type classification works well. Expensive and high turnover supplies are counted and ordered frequently; low-cost items are ordered in large quantities at infrequent intervals. A common drawback of frequent order placement is the extensive amount of time needed to physically put the items on the shelves and log them in. (However, this restocking procedure does not greatly add to an auto agency's cost since parts department personnel generally do this during lulls or "slow" periods.)

A great variety of computerized systems is currently in use. One program gives a choice of using either a simple weighted average or exponential smoothing to forecast the next period's demand. In a monthly reordering system, for example, the items to be ordered are counted and the number on hand is entered into the computer. By subtracting the number on hand from the previous month's inventory and adding the orders received during the month, the usage rate is determined. The computer program stores the usage rate for, say, four previous months. Then, with the application of a set of weighting factors, a forecast is made in the same manner as described in Chapter 6. This works as follows. Suppose usage of a part during January, February, March, and April was 17, 19, 11, and 23 respectively and the set of corresponding weights was 0.10, 0.20, 0.30 and 0.40. Thus the forecast for May is $0.10(17) + 0.20(19) + 0.30(11) + 0.40(23)$, or 18 units. If the order policy including safety stock is based on a two-month demand, 36 units will be ordered, less whatever is on hand at the time of order placement. The simple two-month rule allows for forecasted usage during the lead time plus the review period, with the balance providing the safety stock.

The computer output provides a useful reference file since it identifies the item, lists the cost, states the order size, and gives the number of units on hand. The output itself constitutes the purchase order and is sent to the distributor or factory supply house. The simplicity in this is attractive since, once the forecast weighting is selected, all that must be done is to input the number of units of each item on hand. Thus, negligible computation is involved and very little preparation is needed to send the order out.

SAVINGS AND LOAN INSTITUTIONS INVENTORY FOR CONSTRUCTION LOANS

A large part of the funds of a savings and loan institution is invested in mortgages and construction loans. *Mortgage* loans are single-sum loans, effective on the transfer of existing property. *Construction* loans are made to contractors to cover their expenses incurred during the construction process. The latter are usually made in segments, and a loan terminates when the construction project is completed. At the start of a project a contractor's financial needs are small, but as the project nears completion the contractor has a sizable investment and consequently a greater need for funds. The ideal timing of the sequence of loans to a contractor to support a project would be such that it corresponds with the contractor's investment in that project. A contractor who is building individual residential homes, for example, might draw five equal cash sums on each home from a prearranged bank loan, totaling to the agreed upon loan. Large construction projects, such as commercial buildings or shopping centers, may draw cash in 20 to 30 unequal sums, as needed.

The problem for the loan institution is to predict the cash flow. The inventory in this case is cash, and the exogenous demand on this cash inventory is the cash draw on approved mortgages and construction loans. Whereas inventory shortages and averages are vague in department stores, they are specific and obvious in financial institutions. If the demand for mortgage and construction cash exceeds the inventory set aside by the loan institution, funds must be immediately obtained elsewhere to avoid violation of operating statutes. There is a strong desire, therefore, not to run short of funds. Conversely, excess cash inventory results in lost income to the institution because it has not invested this unused portion in interest-bearing loans or securities.[4]

Consider the following construction loan example of an institution that, for illustration, is restricted solely to single-unit residential construction. In planning for a housing development, a contractor approaches the institution and obtains a construction loan on each home in his proposed development. A condition of the loan contract is that the contractor may draw cash from the total loan in five equal installments. (The size of draws may vary, but for most home construction loans five draws is common.) In theory, the construction loan is awarded to the contractor in increments rather than as a lump sum. The idea, as previously mentioned, is that as construction of the home progresses it increases in value, and therefore provides increased collateral for the mortgage. Further, the contractor's need for funds increases as his investment in the home increases. Thus on a $30,000 construction loan arrangement, a contractor may go to the institution and make five withdrawals of $6,000 each against this loan (less the interest charges). Thus if the contractor takes five months to complete this home and his investment in labor, materials, and equipment increases linearly, he would draw $6,000 against the loan in each of the five months of construction. When the home is sold, the buyer (or new mortgage holder) pays off the construction loan.

The difficulties for the loan institution in forecasting draws on construction loans arise because there are many contractors who have many homes under development. Progress and investment on the construction are *not* linear and contractors do not draw sums of money against the loans at the *same* time intervals. Also, a contractor frequently skips a draw, completing the home—for—example—after having taken only 60 or 80 percent of his available loan. He then may draw the last two increments simultaneously. This variation in the timing of draws, combined with the operating differences among contractors, makes the calculation of cash needs difficult.

This situation, however, lends itself to solution by computer simulation.

---

[4] The amount of lost revenue due to excess cash inventory can be significant. For a $2 million construction loan operation (a relatively small operation), a 5 percent excess in cash amounts to a surplus of $100,000, which if invested at 6 percent represents an annual loss of $6,000. Losses are actually larger than this since errors between forecasted and actual cash draws by contractors leave more in the order of 15 percent excess cash in inventory.

As is discussed in the supplement to Chapter 6, the procedure is to design a model of the real system and then simulate the behavior of that system over time. The model, in this case, consists of the approved loans, the contractors who are likely to draw against the loans, and the cash inventory. The simulation procedure requires that the history of each contractor and his draws be analyzed, and then a probability forecast is made for each contractor's likelihood of making specific cash draws. Then, based on these sets of probabilities, the model is run a number of times on the computer in simulation of the planning period, and this gives a range of possible cash inventory needs. Confidence intervals are computed and printed out to allow the loan officer to select an inventory level with the degree of risk to suit his judgment.

For example, the simulation of cash draws by contractors in one simulation had a mean expected cash flow of $2 million. However, 90 percent of the loans ranged from $1.75 to $2.3 million, and 95 percent were included in the range $1.6 to $2.5 million.[5] In light of this, if the loan officer planned that $2.3 million in cash would be drawn during the month, there would be a 5 percent chance that more than $2.3 million would be drawn. By computing various confidence intervals, the loan officer has a good estimate of the range of cash demands and can plan on alternative ways to meet them.

INVENTORY MANAGEMENT PROGRAM AND CONTROL TECHNIQUES (IMPACT)

IBM's Inventory Management Program and Control Techniques software system (IMPACT) was designed for firms whose main concern is the distribution phase of a production/distribution system.[6] Wholesalers, for example, are prime users. In these applications the basic decisions of order size, order points, etc., become of paramount importance since they are an essential, rather than a peripheral, feature of the firm's mission as a supplier. In this section the theoretical bases of the IMPACT system will be presented, along with discussion on various aspects of the computer program itself.

IMPACT is based on independent demand and therefore uses traditional or classical inventory analysis. The reason for this is obvious after a moment's thought. In order for a *dependent* demand to exist, there must be a demand for a more complex item that is composed of parts or supplies, or that in some other way creates a demand for items because of its own demand. For cases such as wholesalers, retailers, or suppliers of basic materials, each item is separate, and most items ordered are in their own right and not because of the simultaneous order for some other item. (Ob-

---

[5] K. G. Brown and J. C. Heckman, "The Prediction of Construction Loan Cash Flow" (College of Business and Public Administration, University of Arizona, June 1971).

[6] This section is based on the following IBM publications: *Inventory Control*, 520–14491; *Introduction to IBM Wholesale IMPACT*, E20–0278–0; *Basic Principles of Wholesale IMPACT*, E20–8105–1; *Wholesale IMPACT—Advanced Principles and Implementations Manual*, E20–0174–0.

viously, however, there is the desire to consolidate orders where possible to save handling and shipping charges.)

Functions and objectives of IMPACT

The goal of IMPACT is to provide operating rules to minimize cost. In order to do this, the following functions must be performed.

1. Forecast future demand
2. Determine the safety stock required for a specified level of service
3. Determine the order quantity and time for reorder
4. Consider the effects of freight rates and quantity discounts
5. Estimate the expected results of the inventory plan

The IMPACT system does all this in two phases: a startup phase and an operating phase. The startup phase (Figure 8.13) consists of the initializing and estimating segment, which sets up the system and is brought into play whenever conditions or objectives change. The basic functions in this phase are:

1. Select the forecasting model and ordering strategy
2. Calculate starting values for factors used in forecasting and ordering
3. Estimate the results

FIGURE 8.13

IMPACT startup: Initializing and estimating

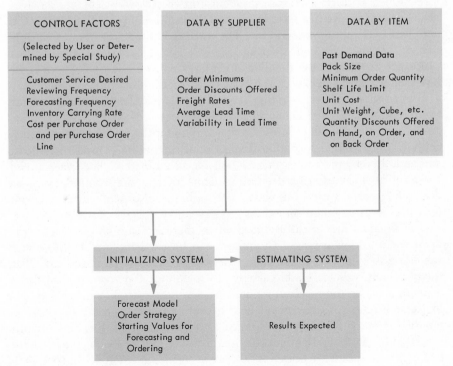

CONTROL FACTORS	DATA BY SUPPLIER	DATA BY ITEM
(Selected by User or Determined by Special Study)		Past Demand Data Pack Size
Customer Service Desired Reviewing Frequency Forecasting Frequency Inventory Carrying Rate Cost per Purchase Order and per Purchase Order Line	Order Minimums Order Discounts Offered Freight Rates Average Lead Time Variability in Lead Time	Minimum Order Quantity Shelf Life Limit Unit Cost Unit Weight, Cube, etc. Quantity Discounts Offered On Hand, on Order, and on Back Order

INITIALIZING SYSTEM → ESTIMATING SYSTEM

Forecast Model
Order Strategy
Starting Values for
Forecasting and
Ordering

Results Expected

On a day-to-day basis, the operating system does the following.

1. Decides when and how much to order
2. Makes new forecasts of demand and forecast error
3. Keeps records of issues, receipts, inventory status, etc.
4. Collects data to measure performance of the system

Figure 8.14 shows the workflow of the IBM IMPACT system. In this diagram, the solid black line indicates that transactions are entered. They may occur at any time.

The solid color line indicates functions that are performed every review period. If a periodic plan is used, items are reviewed each week, biweekly, or monthly. In a reorder point system, the inventory status is reviewed after each transaction to see if the stock on hand has dropped to the reorder point, justifying placement of a new order.

The dashed color line indicates that new forecasts are made. Typically, demand forecasts are made for periods of one, two, or four weeks.

The dashed black line shows initialization or reinitialization. This occurs when the program is started and whenever the conditions or objectives are changed.

The flows in the figure are typical, although differences may appear in individual applications because of various program options.

To operate the system, the users provide their own program routines, which are to be used in combination with the IMPACT program. They write their own programs for record keeping, updating the master file, forecasting, performance measurement, order followup (preparing purchase orders, status listings, etc.), and linkages between their programs and IMPACT library functions. (The IMPACT library programs for initializing, estimating, and ordering.)

To get an idea of the detailed operations carried out by IMPACT, we have summarized (below) the way it treats forecasting and ordering.

Forecasting.   The forecasting models used in IMPACT are horizontal, trend, and seasonal (or cyclical) models.

The *horizontal* model represents demand about the average value, which contains only random variation. Exponential smoothing is used to forecast demand, thereby placing more emphasis on recent history. The *trend* model looks for an increasing or decreasing demand over time. Trends may be determined in a variety of ways, although the IMPACT program itself uses double exponential smoothing.

The *seasonal* model can be used when there is some known reason for upswings and downswings. The model can be used for prediction only if the cause is identifiable or if it is repetitive over time. IBM suggests that the peaks and valleys should vary by at least 30 to 50 percent to justify the expense of using the seasonal model. Seasonal items are handled by applying a multiplier to each period of the year. For example, if the average monthly demand for the year is taken as a base value of one, each month is related to that base. If August demand is twice that of the average month, its index would be 2. If March is 60 percent of the average, its index is 0.6.

FIGURE 8.14

Workflow and functions performed in a typical IMPACT system

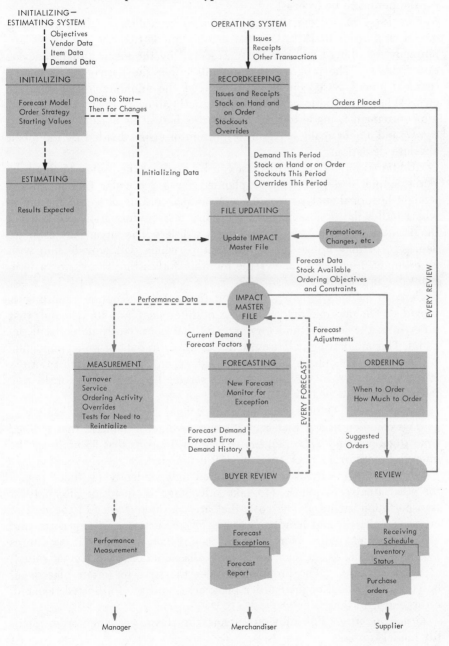

A seasonal forecast is then derived by forecasting average demand by exponential smoothing and multiplying the resultant value by the index value for the period to be forecast.

Forecast error. Deviations are expected regardless of the forecasting model employed. In IMPACT, the assumption is that the deviations are normally distributed and can be represented by the mean absolute deviation (MAD).[7] The program recommends either the horizontal, trend, or seasonal model, based on its calculation of the minimum mean absolute error. When errors in forecasts are consistently above or below the forecast, a measurement is made to help correct this bias. This is called a *tracking signal,* and algebraically is equal to the sum of errors divided by the mean absolute deviation.

Additional inputs to the forecast can be made at the option of the user. For example, if a promotion is planned for a particular time period, a straight historical analysis would be incomplete in this case, and the buyer who handles the promotion must therefore insert information about when the promotion is to start and how long it will last. The buyer may estimate demands, or may utilize a program feature which will provide him with an estimate. Figure 8.15 shows the monthly forecasting results for a ballpoint pen promotion.

Forecast monitoring. To guard against errors, exception reporting is provided. The program detects significant differences both for demands that differ from the forecast and for forecasts that consistently differ from demand. This monitoring will usually detect errors in data or in keypunching.

Ordering. This phase determines what, when, and how much to order. It is accomplished by establishing some service level and then considering the appropriate inventory costs.

Service level. The IMPACT program defines service level the same way as does common usage; that is, as the percentage of demand that is filled from stock on hand. A 98 percent service level means that 98 units can be offered directly from stock for each 100 demanded.

Order strategy. Items may be ordered independently (without regard for other items) or jointly (to take advantage of quantity discounts or transportation savings). The costs that are considered are (1) the cost of ordering (clerical and handling costs), (2) inventory carrying costs, and (3) opportunity costs (for example, savings or avoidable expenditures available but not taken, such as quantity discounts or lower freight rates).

When to order. The program decides the time for order placement, based on individual or joint order placement, and the forecasted demand, error, and lead time.

Order quantity. For individual items, the classic economic order quantity model is used:

$$Q = \sqrt{\frac{2DS}{H}}$$

---

[7] As stated in Chapter 6, MAD is the average of the differences between the forecast sales and the actual sales, disregarding the plus or minus signs.

FIGURE 8.15

Example of forecasting an item with machine computation of promotion estimates

α = 0.1
Tracking Signal Limits = ±6

Item #4364
Description: Bargain Ball Point Pens

Period	Demand	Forecast (Made Previous Period)	Error	MAD	Error SUM	Tracking Signal	This Period Promotional Effect	Error from old Promotional Forecast	New Promotion Index	Promotion Forecast MAD	Next Month Forecast (Index)
Initial Values				(329)	(-125)				(900)	(500)	(2750)
June	3285	2750	+535	350	+410	+1.17					2804
July	3047	2804	+243	339	+653	+1.93					2828 (+900)
*Aug.	3873	2828 (+900)	**	**	**	**	+1045	+145	915	(464)	2828 (***)
Sept.	2661	2828 (***)	-167	322	+486	+1.51					2811
Oct.	2806	2811	-5	290	+481	+1.66					2810
Nov.	2514	2810	-296	291	+185	+.64					2780
Dec.	2909	2780	+129	275	+314	+1.10					2793 (+915)
*Jan.	3889	2793 (+915)	**	**	**	**	+1096	+181	933	(436)	2793 (***)
Feb.	2873	2793 (***)	+80	255	+391	+1.55					2801
Mar.	2659	2801	-142	244	+252	+1.03					2787
Apr.	3133	2787	+346	254	+598	+2.35					2822
May	2729	2822	-93	238	+505	+2.12					2813

* Promotion month.
** Not calculated; use value for former period.
*** Use same forecast and MAD as for previous month but exclude promotional corrections.

where

Q = Economic order quantity
D = Annual demand
S = Cost for handling and processing an order
H = Inventory carrying costs, such as insurance, taxes, depreciation, etc.

If discounts are available for larger-quantity purchases, the program computes the additional feasible order quantities and selects the lowest cost.

When several items are ordered at the same time (termed a *joint ordering strategy*), the total must meet some quantity range (such as a carload lot) while at the same time satisfying individual item service level requirements. This is accomplished by an "allocation" subroutine that adjusts the total order up or down, based on individual economic order quantities and desired service levels.

Overrides in order placement are always allowed. This may be purely a management decision, for whatever purpose, or may be aimed to correct such things as erroneous data.

Two outputs of the IMPACT program are the status report and the suggested order quantities, which are shown in Figures 8.16 and 8.17 with the report descriptions. This report may be further modified, or if it is satisfactory, a purchase order is directly written to the particular vendor.

Results from using the IMPACT system

Among the results claimed by users of IMPACT are:

1. Reduced inventory costs because
    a. Either inventory size has been reduced with no loss in service to customers or service levels have increased with no additional inventory stocking
    b. Buyers can spend more time in problem areas or in developing new strategies since they have been relieved of routine purchasing decisions
2. Improved management control because
    a. The specified rules and objectives are consistent
    b. Rules and objectives can be easily revised
    c. Effective measures of system effectiveness are available
    d. Service is more stable
    e. There is a smoother work load for personnel
    f. Awareness of inventory concepts brought out by this program brings improvement in other areas
    g. The process of data gathering needed to set up the program points out unprofitable product lines and abnormally slow-moving items
    h. The costs output from the program are valuable for profit analysis and planning

FIGURE 8.16

Sample of merchandise status report (for description of column headings see Figure 8.17)

MERCHANDISE STATUS REPORT

DATE 12 13 _____

ADV. X	S.S.	COST	C/D	RECEIPTS	CODE	DESCRIPTION	PACK & SIZE	4 WEEKS SALES	LAST WKS. SALES	INV. ON HAND	ON ORDER	CALC. ORDER	TIE	WEIGHT	ORDER	CODE	C/D CODE	PO GROUP CODE	D/A	R/O/I/R
(1)	(2)	(3)	(4)	(5)	(6)	(7)	(8)	(9)	(10)	(11)	(12)	(13)	(14)	(15)	(16)	(17)	(18)	(19)	(20)	(21)
	356	356			3750	PURINA DOG CHOW	12 2 LB	116	26	54	72 S	32	08	32.		3750	7	6262	4	5
	626	626		20	3752	PURINA DOG CHOW	10 5 LB	352	89	111	192 S	224	16	51.		3752	3	6262	4	5
	548	548			3754	PURINA DOG CHOW	5 10 LB	228	57	30	133 S	136	04	51.		3754	9	6262	4	5
	490	490			3756	PURINA DOG CHOW	2 25 LB	579	160	156	297 S	280	04	53.		3756	4	6262	4	5
	455	455			3757	PURINA DOG CHOW	1 50 LB	56*	12	55	20 S	21	03	51.		3757	2	6262	4	5
	365	365			3930	PURINA CAT CHOW	12 22 OZ	141	36	64	88 S	40		18.		3930	5	6262	4	5
	890	890	8		3932	PURINA CAT CHOW	12 4 LB	42	10	77	40 S	㉘	05	52.		3932	1	6262	4	5
	604	604			5335	RAL CORN CHEX	24 13 OZ	105	42	23	51 S	45	05	22.		5335	5	6262	4	5
	515	515			5337	RAL WHEAT CHEX	24 12 OZ	144	51	80	64 S	70	07	23.		5337	1	6262	4	5
	602	602			5339	RAL RICE CHEX	24 9 OZ	137	49	41	57 S	63	07	14.		5339	7	6262	4	5
	483	483			5341	INSTANT RALSTON	18 18 OZ	112	33	44	41 S	78	06	24.		5341	3	6262	4	5
	276	276			6099	RY KRISP	12 8 1/20Z	30	13	24	9 S	16		8.		6099	6	6262	4	5

㉒ THIS ORDER TO VENDOR 6262 INCLUDES 1005 SELLING UNITS AND THEY TOTAL TO 41657 POUNDS.   ㉔ TO ARRIVE 12 20 63

㉕ 4061   ㉖ 125   ㉓ 41657   ㉗ 12

FIGURE 8.17

Merchandise status report (heading descriptions used in Figure 8.16)

Column Headings	Description
(1) ADV.X	X in this column if item is on newspaper advertisement
(2) S.S.	Cost in dollars and cents to member retailer
(3) COST	Cost of item in dollars and cents
(4) C/D	Cash discount: 1 = 1 percent, A = 1-1/2 percent, 2 = 2 percent, B = 2-1/2 percent, etc. An & means that the item is on hand but not yet listed for sale
(5) RECEIPTS	Receipts (in units) during this past week
(6) CODE	Item card number
(7) DESCRIPTION	Item description
(8) PACK AND SIZE	Number of cans, jars, etc., in shipping unit, and size of the cans, jars, etc.
(9) 4 WEEKS SALES	Number of units sold during past four weeks
(10) LAST WKS. SALES	Sales this past week
(11) INV. ON HAND	Inventory on hand
(12) ON ORDER	Units currently on order
(13) CALC. ORDER	Suggested order quantity
(14) TIE	Vendor pack, cases in a layer on a pallet, cases in a pallet, etc. (Order quantities should always be in multiples of this number)

Column Headings	Description
(15) WEIGHT	Shipping weight per unit in pounds
(16) ORDER	Quantity to be ordered this reviewing cycle. This is written in by the merchandiser if he chooses to alter the suggested order quantity under heading no. 13.
(17) CODE	Item code number (repeated for convenience in key-punching purchase order cards if the actual amount ordered deviates from suggested order)
(18) CD	Check digit for item code number
(19) P.O. GROUP CODE	Purchase order group code, used to group items shipped and invoiced together
(20) DAY	The day in the cycle when item is reviewed
(21) MDSER	Identifying number of merchandiser who reviews this item
(22)	Total number of units to be ordered from this vendor
(23)	Extended pounds, dollars, etc., of suggested order
(24)	Specified delivery date for this suggested order
(25)	Dollar value of current inventory for this vendor
(26)	Dollar value of receipts this past week for this vendor
(27)	Number of items carried under this vendor number
(28)	An S in CALC. ORDER field indicates that item is being handled by system. Any item without the S is a new item, a discontinue-when-out item, etc., and must be controlled by the merchandiser.

i. A framework is created that can be expanded to include potentially valuable applications, such as automatic generation and placement of orders with the vendor and provision of forecasts and other information directly to the retailer

CONCLUSION

To reiterate the focus of this chapter, demand for inventory items falls into two main classes: independent demand, for the most part referring to the external demand for a firm's end product, and dependent demand, usually referring—within the firm—to the demand for items created because of the demand for more complex items of which they are a part. Most industries, however, have items in both classes. In manufacturing, for example, independent demand is common for finished products, service and repair parts, and operating supplies; and dependent demand is common for those parts and materials needed to produce the end product. In wholesale and retail sales, most demand is independent since each item is an end item with no assembly or fabrication taking place, although there are some supply type items for which the demand may be imputed from customer orders. That is, demand for wrapping paper and boxes for a wholesaler is a function of the size and number of shipments, demand for bagging material in the produce area of a market is derived from the volume of produce sold, and the demand for plastic trays and plastic wrap in the meat department is related to the volume of meat sold.

For independent demand, the subject of this chapter, analysis for inventory control is based on statistics. Several fixed-quantity and fixed-period models were described. Two special purpose models—price break and single period models—were also presented. Inventory control through marginal analysis was discussed as a means of handling probabilistic inventory problems, and ABC analysis was offered as a means for distinguishing among item categories for purposes of general inventory analysis and control.

The brief descriptions of inventory procedures in a department store, an auto parts shop, and a savings and loan institution were intended to illustrate some of the simpler ways in which non-manufacturing firms carry out their inventory control function. Finally, the IMPACT program was presented as one example of the many useful computer programs that enable managers to deal effectively with complex independent demand situations.

PROPOSITIONS

Propositions contrasting services and manufacturing systems relative to design of inventory systems

Product: Because a service is an operation or activity performed on a customer, a service, per se, cannot be stored as inventory. In manufacturing, the entire product may be kept in inventory.

Technology of transformation: In service systems a unit of inventory is commonly defined in terms of space or capacity that is rented to the customer, or to the product that the customer obtains in the service facility. In manufacturing, a unit of inventory is completely defined in terms of a component or end item, which the customer generally keeps.

Operating-control system: In a service system, an inventory of service capacity is allocated to a customer during the time scheduled for the service. Unutilized capacity is lost. In manufacturing, excess or idle capacity can be used to produce products stored in inventory for future use.

Workforce: In services, the direct workforce is often considered part of the service system inventory. In manufacturing, the direct workforce is viewed as being separate from the product that it produces.

REVIEW AND DISCUSSION QUESTIONS

1. What are the various purposes of inventory.
2. Distinguish between in-process inventory, safety stock inventory, and seasonal inventory.
3. Discuss the nature of the costs that affect inventory size.
4. Under what conditions would one elect to use a fixed-order quantity model, as opposed to a fixed-period model? What are the disadvantages of using a periodic ordering system?
5. The two main categories for inventory models are deterministic and probabilistic models. What are the distinguishing differences of these categories?
6. Discuss the general procedure for determining the order quantity when price breaks are involved. Would there be any differences in the procedure if holding cost were a fixed percentage of price rather than a constant amount?
7. What two basic questions must be answered by an inventory control decision rule?
8. Discuss the assumptions that are inherent in production setup cost, ordering cost, and carrying costs. How valid are they?
9. "The nice thing about inventory models is that you can pull one off the shelf and apply it so long as your cost estimates are accurate." Comment.
10. What type of inventory system do you use in the following situations?
    a. Supplying your kitchen with fresh food
    b. Obtaining a daily newspaper
    c. Buying gasoline for your car
    To which of the above items do you impute the highest stockout cost?
11. Why is it desirable to classify items into groups as does the ABC classification?
12. What kind of policy or procedure would you recommend to improve the inventory operation in a department store? What advantages and disadvantages does your system have vis-à-vis the department store inventory operation described in this chapter?
13. What types of firms might use IBM's IMPACT program? What functions does the program perform?
14. Discuss, in general terms, the IMPACT startup phase and operating phase.
15. How does the IMPACT system forecast demand?
16. Of what value are the status reports and the suggested order quantities put out by the IMPACT program?

PROBLEMS

1. According to the economic lot size formula, if the annual requirement for an item is 8,000 units, setup costs are $20, and the cost of holding the item in inventory is $0.20 per year, what is the economic lot size to order? Supposing the holding cost doubled to $0.40 per year, what is the percentage effect on the order size?

2. The Educational Toy Company produces a line of dolls with a recorder that accepts a variety of tape cassettes. ETC anticipates annual sales of 10,000 dolls of this particular type. There is a small reduction in price for the recorders: less than 800 units, $10.00 per unit; 800 through 2,499 units, $9.90 per unit; and 2,500 or more units, $9.80 per unit.

   If the cost of ordering is $50 and the carrying cost is 20 percent of the price paid, what is the optimum number of units to order each time?

3. To produce the tape recorder doll, Educational Toy Company purchases all the doll material from the same vendor. With an annual demand of 10,000 units, a purchase ordering cost of $10, and storage costs of 20 percent of the unit cost, what is the optimal order size for the following price breaks: 0–499 units, $2.00 per unit; 500–999 units, $1.75 per unit, and 1,000 or more units, $1.50 per unit?

4. Magnetron Inc. manufactures microwave ovens for the commercial market. Currently, Magnetron is producing part 2104 in its fabrication shop for use in the adjacent unit assembly area. Next year's requirement for part 2104 is estimated at 20,000 units. Part 2104 is valued at $50 per unit, and the combined storage and handling cost is $8 per unit per year. The cost of preparing the order and making the production setup is $200. The plant operates 250 days per year. The assembly area operates every working day, completing 80 units, and the fabrication shop produces 160 units per day when it is producing part 2104.

   a. Compute the economic order quantity.

   b. How many orders will be placed each year?

   c. If part 2104 could be purchased from another firm with the same costs as above, what would the order quantity be? (The order is received all at once.)

   d. If the average lead time to order from another firm is 10 working days and a safety stock level is set at 500 units, what is the reorder point?

5. Garrett Corporation, a turbine manufacturer, works an 18-hour day, 300 days a year. Titanium blades can be produced on its turbine blade machine number 1, TBM1, at a rate of 500 per hour, and the average usage rate is 5,000 per day. The blades cost $15 apiece, and storage costs $0.10 per day per blade because of insurance, interest on investments, and space allocation. TBM1 costs $250 to set up for each run. Lead time requires production to begin after stock drops to 500 blades. What is the optimum production run for TBM1?

6. A popular item stocked by the Fair Deal Department Store has an expected demand for next year of 600 units. The cost to purchase these units from a supplier is $20 per unit and $12 to prepare the purchase order. The annual carrying cost is $4 per unit.

a. Show graphically (cost versus order quantity) the various costs involved in this problem.
b. Mathematically, determine the economic order quantity.
c. If Fair Deal is currently ordering 100 units at a time, how much could it save by using the EOQ?
d. Show graphically how this problem would change if the supplier offered Fair Deal the following quantity discounts: 0–49 units, no discount; 50–99 units, 1 percent; 100–199 units, 2 percent; 200–299 units, 3 percent; and 300 units or more, 4 percent.

7. Instead of producing part 2104 for its microwave oven, Magnetron Inc. is contemplating the purchase of this part from another vendor. Although Magnetron is confident that it will always receive its ordered parts at the specified time, it has one concern: if its stock of part 2104 runs out on the assembly line and is installed later, there is an additional cost, which it estimates at an annual rate of $40 per unit.

The cost to prepare and release a part order to the vendor is $50. Magnetron requires 20,000 units per year and the annual carrying cost per part is $8.
a. Compute the economic order quantity.
b. What is the maximum number of units that will be on hand?

8. Sunrise Baking Company is trying to determine the number of doughnuts it should make each day. From an analysis of its past demands, Sunrise estimates the demand for doughnuts as

Demand	Probability of demand
1,800 dozen	0.05
2,000	0.10
2,200	0.20
2,400	0.30
2,600	0.20
2,800	0.10
3,000	0.05

Each dozen sells for $0.69 and costs $0.49, which includes handling and transportation, as well as the mix. Doughnuts that are not sold at the end of the day are reduced to $0.29 and sold the following day as day-old merchandise.
a. Construct a table showing the profit or losses for each possible order quantity.
b. What is the optimum number of doughnuts to make?
c. Solve this problem by using marginal analysis.

9. Apples that are not sold during the season for immediate consumption by eating, canning, or freezing are used to make cider, and a food broker is trying to decide how many apples he should buy from the orchards in order to maximize his profit. He estimates his potential sales to be normally distributed with a mean of 10,000 bushels and a standard deviation of 1,000 bushels. He can buy the apples for $3 per bushel, and will receive $5 per bushel for those he sells. Unsold apples to be used for cider are worth $2 per bushel for that purpose.

Using marginal analysis and Appendix D at the end of the book, how many apples should the broker buy? Do the problem both by marginal analysis and in the tabular form for a range of purchase levels.

10. Visit a service establishment, such as a hospital pharmacy, central supply, or food service, or a butcher shop, grocery store, bank, restaurant, or supermarket. Determine how they maintain their inventory—what records they keep, how they establish their safety stock level, and what procedure they use for ordering stock.

11. The following items are carried in a firm's inventory and have the indicated annual dollar usage. How would you group them into an ABC classification? What percentage falls in each category?

Item number	Annual usage	Item number	Annual usage
14..............	$ 1,200	63..............	$ 92,000
23..............	37,000	45..............	28,000
07..............	32,000	77..............	8,300
36..............	108,000	29..............	11,000
84..............	65,000	31..............	35,000
26..............	14,000	42..............	18,000
53..............	19,000	15..............	29,000
37..............	3,700		

12. The text described how one department store conducted its inventory ordering for a housewares department and a linen and domestic items department. How could you apply the theory and models in this chapter to enhance the operation of the system?

13. From your own knowledge or from data gathered from a marketing-oriented firm, illustrate how the IMPACT system may be introduced.

SELECTED BIBLIOGRAPHY

Hadley, G., and Whitin, T. M.   *Analysis of Inventory Systems.* Englewood Cliffs, N.J.: Prentice-Hall, 1963.

International Business Machines Corporation   *Basic Principles of Wholesale IMPACT.* Publication E20–8105–1.

———   *Introduction to IBM Wholesale IMPACT.* Publication E20–0278–0.

———   *Inventory Control.* Publication 520–14491.

———   *Wholesale IMPACT—Advanced Principles and Implementations Manual.* Publication E20–0174–0.

Plossl, G. W., and Wight, O. W.   *Production and Inventory Control.* Englewood Cliffs, N.J.: Prentice-Hall, 1967.

9

Design of inventory systems for dependent demand: Material requirements planning

I n the previous chapter, we presented models that were useful to determine order quantities and order points for items facing independent demand. The term independence was used to imply distinct demands for each item, thus allowing separate inventory quantity calculations. Dependent demand items, on the other hand, were defined as those items for which demand is a direct result of the demand for a "higher level" item. (In our introductory example in Chapter 8, the higher level item was cars and the dependent items were wheels.)

We also saw, through the various models in Chapter 8, that independent demand tends to fluctuate because of random elements. When this takes place over an extended time period, a description of the demand may be made in statistical terms such as a mean, standard deviation, trend line, regression line, autocorrelation, and cyclical time series. Dependent demand, in contrast, is usually not dispersed throughout the time period but rather tends to occur at specific points. Thus, dependent demand is called *lumpy*. Lumpy demand is caused by the way the production process is operated. Most manufacturing occurs in lots and all the items needed to produce the lot are usually withdrawn from inventory at the same time, not unit-by-unit.

In addition to the demand for units created through dependent demand, the timing of their need is also crucial. The main topic of this chapter, Material Requirements Planning,[1] deals directly with this scheduling problem. After discussing the logic of Material Requirements Planning and presenting an example, we will comment on various aspects of the procedure and then follow this with a brief description of the Production Information and Control System (PICS), which incorporates the same logic, and the Communications Oriented Production Information and Control System (COPICS), which is still in the developmental stage.

BENEFITS OF A MATERIAL REQUIREMENTS PLANNING (MRP) SYSTEM

At the present time (1976), more than a thousand companies are using computerized Material Requirements Planning.[2] Among the benefits stated by these users are the following:

Increased sales.

Reduced sales price.

Reduced inventory.

Better customer service.

Better response to market demands.

---

[1] The current popularity of Materials Requirements Planning is due in great part to the campaigning of Dr. Joseph Orlicky of IBM, the American Production and Inventory Control Society with its large number of publications and teaching aids, and the highly successful lectures, consulting assignments, and writings of men such as Oliver Wight and George Plossl. Much of the material in this chapter has been influenced by the authors' attendance at MRP workshops hosted by Dr. Orlicky and IBM.

[2] Statements made by Oliver Wight of Oliver Wight Associates, Inc., and Joseph Orlicky of IBM.

Ability to change the master schedule.

Reduced set-up and tear-down costs.

Reduced idle time.

In addition, the MRP system:

Gives advance notice so managers can see the planned schedule before actual release of orders.

Tells when to de-expedite as well as expedite.

Delays or cancels orders.

Changes order quantities.

Advances or delays order due dates.

Aids Capacity Planning.

Some users have claimed as much as a 40 percent reduction in inventory investment.

A SIMPLE MRP EXAMPLE

Before we develop the subject of material requirements planning in detail, let us give a very brief illustration of what MRP is all about.

Suppose that we are to produce a product called T, which is made of two parts U and three parts V. Part U, in turn, is made of one part W and two parts X. Part V is made of two parts W and two parts Y. Figure 9.1 shows the product structure tree of product T. By simple computation, then, we can calculate that if 100 units of T are required, then we will need:

$$
\begin{aligned}
\text{Part } U: &\quad 2 \times \text{number of } T\text{'s} &=&\quad 2 \times 100 &=& 200 \\
\text{Part } V: &\quad 3 \times \text{number of } T\text{'s} &=&\quad 3 \times 100 &=& 300 \\
\text{Part } W: &\left\{\begin{array}{l} 1 \times \text{number of } U\text{'s} \\ +2 \times \text{number of } V\text{'s} \end{array}\right\} &=& \left\{\begin{array}{l} 1 \times 200 \\ +2 \times 300 \end{array}\right\} &=& 800 \\
\text{Part } X: &\quad 2 \times \text{number of } U\text{'s} &=&\quad 2 \times 200 &=& 400 \\
\text{Part } Y: &\quad 2 \times \text{number of } V\text{'s} &=&\quad 2 \times 300 &=& 600
\end{aligned}
$$

Now, consider the time element to obtain these items. This time can pertain either to the time needed to produce the part internally or to the time needed to obtain the part from an outside vendor. Assume, now, that T takes one week to make; U, 2 weeks; V, 2 weeks; W, 3 weeks; X, 1 week;

FIGURE 9.1

Product structure tree for product T

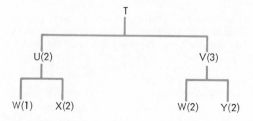

FIGURE 9.2

Material requirements plan for completing 100 units of product T in period 7

		Week							
		1	2	3	4	5	6	7	
T	Required Date							100	T Lead Time = 1 Week
	Order Placement						100		
U	Required Date						200		U Lead Time = 2 Weeks
	Order Placement				200				
V	Required Date						300		V Lead Time = 2 Weeks
	Order Placement				300				
W	Required Date				800				W Lead Time = 3 Weeks
	Order Placement	800							
X	Required Date				400				X Lead Time = 1 Week
	Order Placement			400					
Y	Required Date				600				Y Lead Time = 1 Week
	Order Placement			600					

and Y, 1 week. If we know when product T is required we can create a time schedule chart specifying when all materials must be ordered and received to meet the demand for T. Figure 9.2 shows which items are needed and when they are needed. We have thus created a materials requirements plan based on the demand for product T and the knowledge of how T is made and the time needed to obtain each part.

From this simple illustration, it is apparent that developing a materials requirements plan manually for thousands, or even hundreds of items would be impractical—a great deal of computation is needed and a tremendous amount of data must be available about the inventory status (number of units on hand, on order, etc.) and about the product structure (how the product is made and how many units of each material are required). Because of this, we are compelled to use a computer, and hence our emphasis from here on in this chapter is to discuss the files that are needed for a computer program and the general make-up of the system. However, *the basic logic of the program is essentially the same as that which we have just gone through for our simple example.*

MATERIAL REQUIREMENTS PLANNING (MRP)

Based on the forecasted demand for an end item, a material requirements planning system generates a complete list of parts and subassemblies required to produce the end item along with the required amounts and the correct timing to release orders for these items. Thus, *Material Require-ments Planning creates schedules identifying the specific parts and ma-terials required to produce an end item, the exact numbers needed, and the dates when orders for these materials should be released and be received or completed within the production cycle.* Current use of the term material requirements planning, or MRP, implies the use of a large computer pro-gram (usually one that was produced by a major computer manufacturer) to carry out the foregoing operations.

Material requirements planning is not new in concept. Logic dictates that the Romans probably used it in their construction projects, the Venetians in their shipbuilding, and the Chinese in building the Great Wall. Building contractors have always been forced into planning for ma-terial to be delivered when needed and not before, because of space re-quirements. What is new is the larger scale and the more rapid changes that can be made by the use of high capacity computers. This allows ma-terial requirements planning to be used in firms that produce many prod-ucts involving thousands of parts and materials.

Purposes, objectives, and philosophy of MRP

The main purposes of an MRP system are to control inventory levels, operating priorities for items, and capacity planning to load the production system. These may be briefly expanded as follows:[3]

Inventory
  Order the right part.
  Order in the right quantity.
  Order at the right time.
Priorities
  Order with the right due date.
  Keep the due date valid.
Capacity
  Plan for a complete load.
  Plan an accurate load.
  Plan for an adequate time to view future load.

We could state that the *theme* of MRP is "getting the right materials to the right place at the right time."

The *objectives* of inventory management under an MRP system are to improve customer service, to minimize inventory investment, and to max-imize production operating efficiency.

The *philosophy* of material requirements planning is that materials should be expedited (hurried) when their lack would delay the overall production schedule and de-expedited (delayed) when the schedule falls behind and postpones their need. Inventories tie up finances, take space, clutter up areas, prohibit design changes, and prevent the cancellation or delay of orders.

---

[3] Joseph Orlicky, *Material Requirements Planning* (New York: McGraw-Hill Book Company, 1975) p. 158.

MATERIAL REQUIREMENTS PLANNING
SYSTEM STRUCTURE

As mentioned earlier, the term Material Requirements Planning (MRP) refers to a computer program that generates schedules to meet material needs. Often, however, MRP is also used to imply the total system of materials planning, which includes the inputs to the computer program as well, and is shown in Figure 9.3.

Each facet of Figure 9.3 will be explained in more detail in the following sections, but essentially the MRP system works as follows: Orders for products that arise both from known customers and from random sources are used to create a Master Production Schedule, which states the number of items to be produced during specific time periods. A Bill of Materials file identifies the specific materials that are used to make each item and the correct quantities of each. The Inventory Records file contains data such as the number of units on hand and on order. These three sources—Master Production Schedule, Bill of Materials file, and Inventory Records file— become the data sources for the Material Requirements Program, which expands the production schedule into a detailed order schedule plan for the entire production sequence.

FIGURE 9.3

Overall view of the inputs to a Material Requirements Planning program and the reports generated by the program

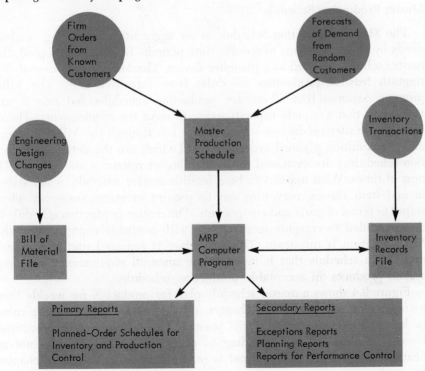

Demand for products

Product demand stems from two main categories: regular customer orders and orders that occur randomly. In the normal course of operation, businesses usually receive orders from customers for specific items in specific amounts. These orders, usually generated by salesmen, include promised delivery dates. These constitute firm orders, and their sizes may need only slight adjustment based on experience (some percentage due to cancellation, for example).

In addition to these orders from known customers, there are random orders from other sources, which may be forecasted through traditional statistical analysis. This independent demand may then be subjected to further analytical procedures to determine safety stock levels, order points, and order quantities to satisfy a specific service level.

The regular customer demand and the independent demand for end products are combined to become the input for the master production schedule.

Demand for repair parts and supplies. In addition to their demand for end products, customers also order specific parts and components either as spares or for service and repair. These demands for items less complex than the end product are usually not part of a master schedule but are fed directly into the Material Requirements Planning (MRP) program at the appropriate levels.

Master Production Schedule

The Master Production Schedule is an aggregate plan stating product needs by classes of items in specific time periods. Before it is adopted, the master schedule is used as a planning device. The MRP system cannot distinguish feasible production schedules from infeasible ones. The MRP program assumes that all master production schedules fed into it are feasible in that adequate capacity exists to meet the requirements. Therefore, trial master production schedules are run through the MRP program, and the resulting planned order releases (which are the detailed production schedules) are examined for availability of resources and reasonableness of times. What appears to be a feasible master schedule, when stated in end item classes, may turn out to require excessive resources when stated in terms of parts and components. The master production schedule is then modified to coincide more closely with available capacity, and the MRP program is run again. This procedure is repeated until the master production schedule that is input to the material requirements planning system produces an acceptable production schedule.

Figure 9.4 shows a master schedule plan for product X for weekly time periods. (For clarity in this chapter, all figures are presented in ruled tables. Actual computer output is presented as columns or rows without lines, with some output extending to overlapping rows. Though not as neatly displayed, computer output is read almost as easily as the chapter figures.)

FIGURE 9.4

Master production schedule for product X

	Week Number									
Product X	1	2	3	4	5	6	7	8	9	10
Required Quantity	200			400		200	100			900

Once the master production schedule is produced, it must be broken down into demands for the parts and materials that go into making this end product. The file that contains the complete product description and the sequence in which it is created is called the Bill of Materials File. This Bill of Materials File (BOM) is one of the three main inputs to the MRP program, the other two being the Master Schedule and the Inventory Status file.

Bill of Materials File

The Bill of Materials File (BOM) is often called the product structure file or product tree since it shows how a product is put together. It contains the information to identify each item and the quantity used per unit of the item of which it is a part. To illustrate this, consider product A shown in Figure 9.5. Product A is made of two units of part B and three units of part C. Part B, in turn, is made of one unit of part D and four units of part E. Part C is made of two units of part F, five units of part G, and four units of part H.

In the past, bill of material files have often listed parts as an "indented" file. This clearly identifies each item and the manner in which it is assembled since each indentation signifies the components of the item. A comparison of the indented parts in Figure 9.6 with the item structure in 9.5 shows the ease of relating the two displays. From a computer standpoint, however, storing items in indented parts lists is very inefficient. In order to compute the amount of each item needed at the lower levels, each item would need to be expanded ("exploded") and summed. A more efficient procedure is to store parts data in a single-level explosion. That is, each item and component is listed showing only its parent, and the number of units that are needed per unit of its parent. Figure 9.6 shows both the single level parts list and the indented parts list for product A.

FIGURE 9.5

Product structure tree for Product A

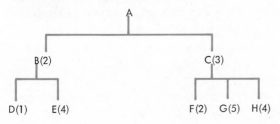

FIGURE 9.6

Parts list shown both in an indented format and in a single level list

Indented parts list	Single level parts list
.A	.A
.B(2)	.B(2)
.D(1)	.C(3)
.E(4)	.B
.C(3)	.D(1)
.F(2)	.E(4)
.G(5)	.C
.H(4)	.F(2)
	.G(5)
	.H(4)

FIGURE 9.7

Product L hierarchy in (a) expanded to the lowest level of each item in (b).

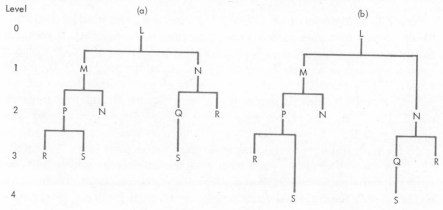

A data element (called a "pointer" or "locator") is also contained in each file to identify the parent of each part and allow a retracing upward through the process.

Leveling. The single explosion procedure in the bill of materials file allows each sub-part to be totalled easily when all identical parts occur at the same level for each end product. Consider product L shown in Figure 9.7 (a). Notice that item N, for example, occurs both as an input to L and as an input to M. Item N is lowered to level 2 (part b) to bring all Ns to the same level. By placing all identical items at the same level, it then becomes a simple matter for the computer to scan across each level and summarize the number of units of each item required.

Inventory Records File

The inventory records file under a computerized system can be quite lengthy. Each item in inventory is carried as a separate file. Although records of each item are not usually kept in complete detail, it is possible for each item in the inventory record file to contain the data shown in Table 9.1.

Items are carried in the *status* segment of the file according to specific time periods (termed time "buckets" in MRP slang). These files are accessed by the MRP program as needed during the program run. Figure 9.8 (page 431) shows an illustration of an inventory record file with some of the optional data inputs.

The MRP program performs its analysis from the top of the product structure downward, exploding requirements level-by-level. There are times, however, when it is desirable to identify the parent item that caused the material requirement. The MRP program allows the creation of a *peg record* file either separately or as part of the inventory record file. The pegging of requirements allows one to retrace a material requirement upward in the product structure through each level, identifying each parent item that created the demand.

Inventory Transactions File. The Inventory Status File is kept up to date by posting inventory transactions as they occur. These changes occur because of stock receipts and disbursements, scrap losses, wrong parts, cancelled orders, etc.

MRP Computer Program

The Material Requirements Planning program operates on the inventory file, the master schedule, and the bill of materials file. It works in this way: a list of end items needed by time periods is specified by the master schedule. A description of the materials and parts needed to make each item is specified in the bill of materials file. The number of units of each item and material currently on hand and on order is contained in the inventory file. The MRP program "works" on the inventory file (which is segmented into time periods) while continually referring to the bill of materials file to compute the quantities of each item needed. The number of units of each item required is then corrected for on-hand amounts and the net requirement is "offset" (set back in time) to allow for the lead time needed to obtain the material.

(One obstacle that many potential users of an MRP program have found is that their bill of materials file and inventory records file are not adequate to provide the data in the format required by the program. Thus they must modify these files prior to installing an MRP system.)

As noted previously, the MRP program presumes that any master production schedule fed to it is a feasible schedule. The MRP system alone makes no allowance for the capacity of the production system to produce the quantities specified within the time periods stated in the master schedule. Therefore, the master scheduler (a person) uses an iterative process in which a tentative master schedule is fed into the MRP system (along with other items requiring the same resources) and the output examined for production feasibility. The master schedule is adjusted to try

TABLE 9.1

Inventory record file and the range of possible data elements

1. Item master data segment
    Item identity
    Item characteristics
    Planning factors
    Safety stock
    Pointers to other files
2. Inventory status segment
    Gross requirements
        Control balance or past-due field
        Time-phased data fields
        Total
    Scheduled receipts
        Control balance or past-due field
        Time-phased data fields
        Total
    On hand
        Current on hand
        Allocated on hand
        Projected on-hand fields
        Total (ending inventory or net requirements)
    Planned-order releases
        Control balance or past-due field
        Time-phased data fields
        Total
3. Subsidiary data segment
    Order details
        External requirements
        Open (shop and purchase) orders
        Released portion of blanket orders
        Blanket order detail and history
        Other (user's choice)
    Records of pending action
        Purchase requisitions outstanding
        Purchase-order changes requested (quantity, due date)
        Material requisitions outstanding
        Shop order changes requested (rescheduled due dates)
        Planned (shop) orders held up, material shortage
        Shipment of item requested (requisition, etc.)
        Other (user's choice)
    Counters, accumulators
        Usage to date
        Scrap (or vendor rejects) to date
        Detail of demand history
        Forecast error, by period
        Other (user's choice)
    Keeping-track records
        Firm planned orders
        Unused scrap allowance, by open shop order
        Engineering change action taken
        Orders held up, pending engineering change
        Orders held up, raw material substitution
        Other interventions by inventory planner

Source: Joseph Orlicky, *Material Requirements Planning* (New York: McGraw-Hill, 1975), pp. 181–83.

FIGURE 9.8

The inventory status record for an item in inventory

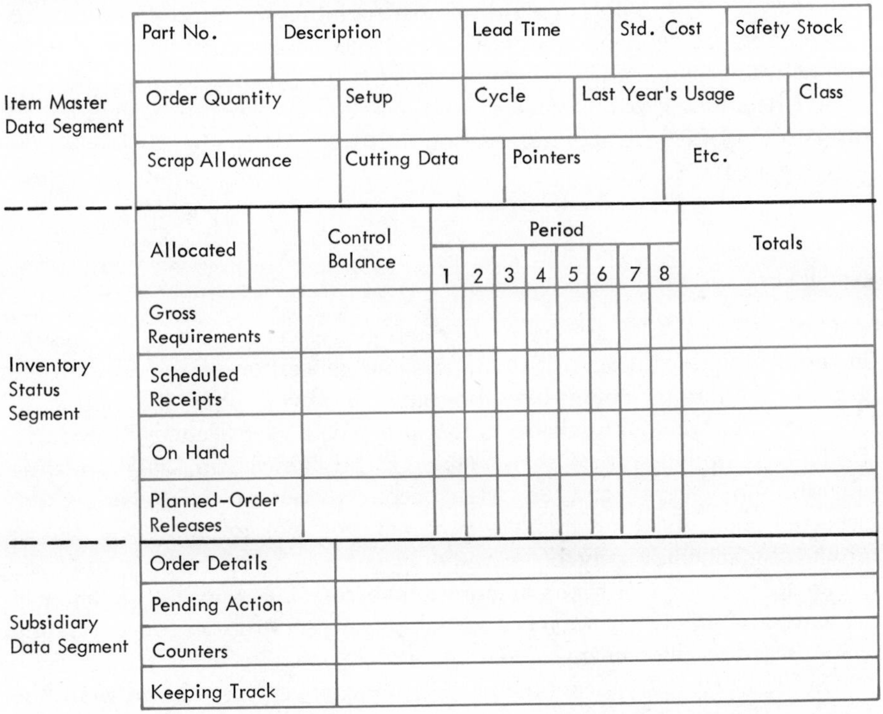

Item Master Data Segment	Part No.		Description			Lead Time		Std. Cost		Safety Stock		
	Order Quantity		Setup		Cycle		Last Year's Usage			Class		
	Scrap Allowance		Cutting Data		Pointers			Etc.				
Inventory Status Segment	Allocated		Control Balance		Period								Totals
					1	2	3	4	5	6	7	8	
	Gross Requirements												
	Scheduled Receipts												
	On Hand												
	Planned–Order Releases												
Subsidiary Data Segment	Order Details												
	Pending Action												
	Counters												
	Keeping Track												

Source: Joseph Orlicky, *Materials Requirements Planning* (New York: McGraw-Hill Book Company, 1975), p. 182.

to correct any imbalances and the program is executed again. This process is repeated until the output is acceptable.

Output reports

Since the MRP program has access to the bill of materials file, the master production schedule, and the inventory records file, outputs can take on an almost unlimited range of format and content. These reports are usually classified as primary reports and secondary reports.

Primary Reports. Primary reports are the main or "normal" reports used for inventory and production control. These reports consist of:

1. *Planned orders* to be released at a future time.
2. *Order release notices* to execute the planned orders.
3. *Changes in due dates* of open orders due to rescheduling.
4. *Cancellations or suspensions* of open orders due to cancellation or suspension of orders on the master production schedule.
5. *Inventory status data.*

Secondary Reports. Additional reports, which are optional under the MRP system, fall into the following main categories:

1. *Planning reports* to be used, for example, in forecasting inventory and specifying requirements over some future time horizon.

2. *Performance reports* for purposes of pointing out inactive items, and determining the agreement between actual and programmed item lead times and between actual and programmed quantity usages and costs.

3. *Exceptions reports*, which point out serious discrepancies such as errors, out-of-range situations, late or overdue orders, excessive scrap, or nonexistent parts.

Net change systems

Ordinarily an MRP system is operated every week or two. This results in the complete explosion of items and the generation of the normal and exception reports. Some MRP programs, however, offer the option of generating intermediate schedules that are called "Net Change" Schedules. Under this option, rather than making a full-blown run, only updating quantities are entered, and the system accounts solely for those changes that occurred since the last complete program run. For example, the master production schedule may be updated by adding or subtracting only the differences from its previous amounts. Inventory files may be modified to take account of such factors as a lost shipment, scrap losses, or a counting error. Based on these changes, new reports are generated.

On the surface, it appears that a daily net change program run would be highly satisfactory. In practice, however, few companies are electing to use the net change option, and most are relying instead on their weekly or biweekly complete MRP schedule run. The reasons are not completely known as yet, but it seems that the more frequent net change runs may not be worth the added effort required to perform them, and too-frequent runs cause overreaction or "system nervousness."

We will now present a more elaborate example to show the operation of an MRP system.

EXAMPLE OF AN MRP SYSTEM

Ampere, Inc., produces a line of electric meters installed in residential buildings by electric utility companies to measure power consumption. Meters used on single family homes are of two basic types for different voltage and amperage ranges. In addition to complete meters, some parts and subassemblies are sold separately to be used for repair or to facilitate a changeover to a different voltage or power load. The problem for the MRP system, then, is to determine a production schedule that would identify each item, the period in which it is needed, and the appropriate quantities. This schedule is then checked for feasibility, and the schedule modified if necessary.

Forecasting demand

Demand for the meters and components originates from two sources: regular customers that place firm orders and unidentified customers that make the normal random demands for these items.

Table 9.2 shows the requirement for meters A and B, subassembly D, and Part E for a six month period. The known requirements were firm customer orders and the random requirements were forecasted using one of the usual classical techniques and past demand data.

TABLE 9.2

Future requirements for meters A and B, subassembly D, and part E stemming from specific customer orders and from random sources

Month	Meter A Known	Meter A Random	Meter B Known	Meter B Random	Subassembly D Known	Subassembly D Random	Part E Known	Part E Random
3...............	1,000	250	400	60	200	70	300	80
4...............	600	250	300	60	180	70	350	80
5...............	300	250	500	60	250	70	300	80
6...............	700	250	400	60	200	70	250	80
7...............	600	250	300	60	150	70	200	80
8...............	700	250	700	60	160	70	200	80

Developing a master production schedule

For the meter and component requirements specified in Table 9.2, assume that the quantities to satisfy the known demands are to be delivered according to customers' delivery schedules throughout the month, but that the items to satisfy random demands must be available during the first week of the month.

The first schedule that we will develop will assume that *all* items are to be available the first week of the month. This trial is reasonable since management prefers to produce meters in single lots each month rather than continuously throughout the month.

Figure 9.9 shows the first trial master schedule under these conditions, with demands for months 3 and 4 shown as the first week of the month, or as weeks 9 and 13. For brevity, we will work only with these two demand periods.

FIGURE 9.9

A Master Schedule to satisfy demand requirements as specified in Table 9.2

	Week								
	9	10	11	12	13	14	15	16	17
Meter A	1,250				850				550
Meter B	460				360				560
Subassembly D	270				250				320
Part E	380				430				380

Bill of materials (product structure) file

The product structure for Meters A and B are shown in Figure 9.10 in the typical way using low-level coding, in which each item is placed at the lowest level at which it appears in the structure hierarchy. Meters A and B consist of two Subassemblies, C and D, and two parts, E and F. Quantities in parentheses indicate the number of units required per unit of the parent item.

FIGURE 9.10

Product structure for Meters A and B showing the subassemblies and parts that make up the meters and the numbers of units required per unit of parent shown in parentheses

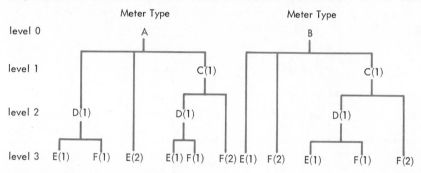

FIGURE 9.11

Indented parts list for Meter A and Meter B, with the required number of items per unit of parent listed in parentheses

Meter A	Meter B
.A	.B
.D(1)	.E(1)
.E(1)	.F(2)
.F(1)	.C(1)
.E(2)	.D(1)
.C(1)	.E(1)
.D(1)	.F(1)
.E(1)	.F(2)
.F(1)	
.F(2)	

Figure 9.11 shows an indented parts list for the structure of Meters A and B. As mentioned earlier in the chapter, the bill of materials file carries all items without indentation for computational ease, but the indented printout clearly shows the manner of product assembly.

Inventory records (item master) file

The inventory records file would be similar to the one that was shown in Figure 9.8. The differences, as stated earlier in this chapter, are that the in-

TABLE 9.3

Number of units on hand and lead time data
that would appear on the Inventory Record File

Item	On-hand Inventory	Lead time (weeks)
A.............	50	2
B.............	60	2
C.............	40	1
D.............	30	1
E.............	30	1
F.............	40	1

ventory record file also contains much additional data, such as vendor identity, cost, lead times, etc. For this example, the pertinent data contained in the inventory records file are the on-hand inventory at the start of the program run and the lead times. These data are taken from the inventory records file and shown in Table 9.3.

Running the MRP program

The correct conditions are now set to run the MRP computer program—end-item requirements have been established through the master production schedule, the status of inventory and the order lead times are contained in the inventory item master file, and the bill of materials file contains the product structure data. The MRP program now explodes the item requirements according to the BOM file, level by level, in conjunction with the inventory records file. A release date for the net requirements order is offset to an earlier time period to account for the lead time. Orders for parts and subassemblies are added through the inventory file, bypassing the master production schedule, which, ordinarily, does not schedule at a low enough level to include spares and repair parts.

Figure 9.12 shows the planned order release dates for this particular run. The program logic can best be understood by following the analysis below. (We will confine our analysis to the problem of meeting the gross requirements for 1,250 units of meter A, 460 units of meter B, 270 units of subassembly D and 380 units of Part E, all in week 9.)

The 50 units of A on hand results in a net requirement of 1,200 units of A. To receive meter A in week 9, the order must be placed in week 7 to account for the two-week lead time. The same procedure follows for item B, resulting in a planned 400-unit order released in period 7.

The rationale for these steps is that for an item to be released for processing, all of its components must be available. The planned order release date for the parent item therefore becomes the same gross requirement period for the sub-items.

Referring to Figure 9.10, level 1, one unit of C is required for each A and each B. Therefore, the gross requirements for C in week 7 are 1,600 units (1,200 for A and 400 for B). Taking into account the 40 units on hand and the one week lead time, 1,560 units of C must be ordered in week 6.

FIGURE 9.12

Material Requirements Planning Schedule for Meters A and B, subassemblies C and D, and parts E and F

Item		4	5	6	7	8	9	10	11	12	13
							Week				
A	Gross Requirements						1,250				850
	On Hand 50						50				
	Net Requirements						1,200				
(LT=2)	Planned–Order Receipt						1,200				
	Planned–Order Release				1,200						
B	Gross Requirements						460				360
	On Hand 60						60				
	Net Requirements						400				
(LT=2)	Planned–Order Receipt						400				
	Planned–Order Release				400						
C	Gross Requirements				1,600						
	On Hand 40				40						
	Net Requirements				1,560						
(LT=1)	Planned–Order Receipt				1,560						
	Planned–Order Release			1,560							
D	Gross Requirements			1,560	1,200		270				250
	On Hand 30			30	0		0				
	Net Requirements			1,530	1,200		270				
(LT=1)	Planned–Order Receipt			1,530	1,200		270				
	Planned–Order Release		1,530	1,200		270					
E	Gross Requirements		1,530	1,200	{2,400 / 400}	270	380				430
	On Hand 30		30	0	0	0					
(LT=1)	Net Requirements		1,500	1,200	2,800	270	380				
	Planned–Order Receipt		1,500	1,200	2,800	270	380				
	Planned–Order Release	1,500	1,200	2,800	270	380					
F	Gross Requirements		1,530	{3,120 / 1,200}	800	270					
	On Hand 40		40	0	0						
(LT=1)	Net Requirements		1,490	4,320	800	270					
	Planned–Order Receipt		1,490	4,320	800	270					
	Planned–Order Release	1,490	4,320	800	270						

Level 2 of Figure 9.10 shows that one unit of D is required for each A and each C. The 1,200 units of D required for A are gross requirements in week 7, and the 1,560 units of D for item C are the gross requirements for week 6. Using the on-hand inventory first and the one-week lead time results in the planned order releases for 1,530 units in week 5 and 1,200 units in week 6.

Level 3 contains items E and F. Because E and F are each used in several places, Table 9.4 is presented to identify more clearly the parent item, the number of units required for each parent item, and the week in which it is required. Two units of item E are used in each item A. The 1,200-unit planned order release for A in period 7 becomes the gross requirement for 2,400 units of E in the same period. One unit of E is used in each B, so the planned order release for 400 units of B in period 7 becomes the gross requirement for 400 units of E in week 7. Item E is also used in item D at the rate of one per unit. The 1,530-unit planned order release for D in period 5 becomes the gross requirement for 1,530 units of E in period 5, and a 1,500-unit planned order release in period 4 after accounting for the 30 units on hand and the one-week lead time. The 1,200-unit planned order release for D in period 6 results in gross requirements for 1,200 units of E in week 6 and a planned order release for 1,200 units in week 5.

TABLE 9.4

The identification of the parent of items C, D, E, and F and item gross
requirements stated by specific weeks

Item	Parent	Number of units per parent	Resultant gross requirement	Gross requirement week
C	A	1	1,200	7
C	B	1	400	7
D	A	1	1,200	7
D	C	1	1,560	6
E	A	2	2,400	7
E	B	1	400	7
E	D	1	1,530	5
E	D	1	1,200	6
F	B	2	800	7
F	C	2	3,120	6
F	D	1	1,200	6
F	D	1	1,530	5

Item F is used in B, C, and D. The planned order releases for B, C, and
D become the gross requirements for F for the same week, except that the
planned order release for 400 units of B and 1,560 of C become gross requirements for 800 and 3,120 units of F since the usage rate is two per unit.

The independent order for 270 units of subassembly D in week 9 is
handled as an input to D's gross requirements for that week. This is then
exploded into the derived requirements for 270 units of E and F. The 380-
unit requirement for part E to meet an independent repair part demand is
fed directly into the gross requirements for part E.

The independent demands for week 13 have not been expanded as yet.

The bottom line of each item in Figure 9.12 is taken as a proposed load
on the productive system. The final production schedule is developed
manually or with the firm's computerized production package. If the schedule is infeasible or the loading severely unbalanced, the master production
schedule is revised and the MRP package is run again with the new master
schedule.

Most beneficial areas for applying MRP

The following comments were made by participants at a Requirement
Planning Workshop[4] in discussing the best conditions for MRP system installation:

"MRP is most valuable in assembly type manufacture."

"MRP cannot be used for services."

"MRP is most valuable when there . . ."

     . . . are long assembly lead times."

---

[4] *Inventory Management in the Real World,* Joint Meeting of AIDS, APICS, TIMS,
and AIIE. Cincinnati, Ohio, November 5, 1975.

. . . are short lead times for parts."

. . . are reliable lead times for parts."

. . . is a frozen Master Schedule."

. . . are lot sizes which are small compared with variability."

One speaker stated that his firm did not have success when it tried to use existing MRP systems. He viewed the existing programs and data processes as too inflexible to meet the company's needs. His firm found it preferable to develop its own programs completely from scratch. (Note: The firm in this case was a manufacturer of varied and highly complex products.)

Material requirements planning for services

As mentioned above, it has been asserted that MRP cannot be used for services. The reasoning is that MRP is limited to systems having inventoriable items. Although little has been done on the issue to the present time, it appears quite likely that MRP can be a very valuable asset in the production of services. It seems to us that one need only consider the producing elements as inventory (equipment, space, personnel) and the procedure would be valid. Consider, for example, an open heart surgery operation. The Master Schedule can establish a time for the surgery (or surgeries if there are several scheduled). The Bill of Materials could specify all required equipment and personnel—MD's, nurses, anesthesiologist, operating room, heart/lung machine, defibrillator, etc. The Inventory Status file would show the availability of the resources and commit them to the project. The MRP program could then produce a schedule showing when various parts of the operation are to be started, expected completion times, required materials, etc. Checking this schedule would allow "Capacity Planning" in answering such questions as: "Are all the materials and personnel available?" and "Does the system produce a feasible schedule?"

For more complicated service systems—that is, those that perform many and varied services simultaneously—the use of MRP seems worthy of consideration.

MISCELLANEOUS ISSUES ON MRP

Safety stock

Ordinarily, safety stock is not advised in an MRP system that is based on derived demand. There is some feeling, however, that when the availability of parts could suffer from a long and inflexible lead time, or is subject to strikes or cancellation, a safety stock offers protection against production delays. A safety stock is sometimes intentionally created by overplanning. One of the main arguments against using safety stock is that the MRP system considers it a fixed quantity and the safety stock will never actually be used.

Production lot sizes

Utilizing lot sizes for convenience in production runs or in economic order quantities is practical only for lower-level items (basic parts or raw materials). The difficulty in using a lot size at a higher level is that the discrepancy between actual demand and the lot size becomes exaggerated for the sub-items. Consider the following illustration:

Item A is made of one unit of B, which is made of one unit of C, and the lot sizes of A, B, and C are equal to 100, 150, and 200 respectively. If there are no units currently in inventory, then a demand for 75 units of A will cause 200 units of C to be ordered—the 25-unit excess in A leads to a 125-unit excess of C.

$$.A \qquad\qquad \text{lot size of } A = 100$$
$$.B(1) \qquad\qquad \text{lot size of } B = 150$$
$$.C(1) \qquad \text{lot size of } C = 200$$

The higher the product-structure level of lot sizing, the greater the potential exaggeration of demand at low levels.

Accuracy of records

Maintaining accurate records is critical to the success of an MRP system. Some of the inaccuracies that find their way into the major files are discussed below.

Bill of materials file. Often the Bill of Materials File does not accurately represent either the product or the manufacturing procedure. Original product designs are usually modified based on production and use experience, and operating personnel usually modify the process or assembly procedure. These changes may not have been entered into the BOM file.

Inventory records file. Many companies have made a practice of having an "open stockroom." Any person needing inventory supplies could simply walk in, take whatever he needed, make the appropriate entries if necessary, and leave. Periodic inventory counting and replenishment would bring stocks back to an acceptable level. In a Materials Requirement Planning system, however, open stockrooms cannot be tolerated. Inventory count must be accurate for MRP to function correctly since, in most cases, there is no safety stock and every unit must be accounted for. In order to maintain the integrity of the inventory stock, firms using MRP restrict entry into the stockroom and keep the area locked. So important is inventory accuracy that some firms have even resorted to high fencing around every inventory stock area to prohibit unauthorized use of material.

The Inventory Records File must also contain the true inventory status. There should be assurance that daily transactions are entered.

Master production schedule. The entire MRP system is founded on the objective of satisfying the Master Production Schedule. Schedules change, however, because of increases in orders, delays, cancellation of orders, etc. It is critical, therefore, that the master production schedule be updated to reflect the true demands for products and realistic due dates.

ONE FIRM'S EXPERIENCE IN INSTALLING AN MRP SYSTEM

The following article reports the experience of a firm that introduced MRP into its operating system.[5] It was written by the vice-president of Moog Automotive, Inc., and provides an interesting perspective of MRP in practice.

Coping With the Materials Crunch

MRP, in conjunction with a new computer, is making it possible for this company and, importantly, its suppliers, to outmaneuver today's critical materials crunch.

In a period of critical shortages, material and inventory control at Moog Automotive, Inc., has actually been improving. The situation has been caused by a new computer-managed Material Requirements Planning (MRP) system. It is run on an IBM System/370 Model 145 computer. Moog produces steering and suspension replacement parts, totaling about 4,200. Its customers number about 450, ranging from wholesale distributors to tire store outlets.

Essentially, our Material Requirements Planning system is based on time-phased scheduling, and is a vast improvement over order-point systems of the past. MRP provides information which enables each Moog inventory analyst to closely follow the critical element or problem in his area of responsibility and take effective action.

As one example: each day we run a Fillable/Non-Fillable Report for planners, with full information on each order that can be filled and each order that cannot be filled. For the orders that cannot be filled, the report tells the planner what components are missing, in what quantity, and the planner who is responsible for the missing items. Similarly, the planners receive a daily Component Allocation Analysis showing them the demands against their assigned parts.

If an order is listed as fillable, the planner merely releases it, and the computer generates the paperwork necessary for manufacturing or packaging. But if a ball joint, for instance, requires six components, we no longer schedule it onto the machines to later find out that only five components are available. Instead, based on the commonality of some of these components, we allocate them to another ball joint which can be assembled.

In 1972, we decided that MRP provided the facilities Moog needed because it is time-phased and permits us to plan farther into the future. We also decided to install the following companion computer-managed programs: forecasting, capacity planning, allocation, and shop floor control.

Under our system, the inventory control manager develops finished goods forecasts by part number and product group. He reviews them with a forecast committee, then enters the refined figures into the computer. Input are both the current and the following years' forecasts. He enters a base index percentage to divide the forecast into monthly increments. The monthly forecasts are based on seasonal demand, on inventory and production levels desired, and so forth.

This data, which is stored in the computer, then is the basis for MRP. The System/370 calculates weekly gross requirements for each item. It then produces

---

[5] Robert A. Dennis, Vice President, Moog Automotive, Inc., St. Louis, Mo. "Coping With the Materials Crunch," *Factory*, August, 1974, pp. 50–51.

a summary report, by product group, which is a "rough cut" monthly Master Schedule for the coming year. This is reviewed in detail to ensure we have a level master schedule. If it is not level, the basic assumptions are altered, and the Master Schedule is rerun.

The MRP system generates a weekly Master Requirements Planning Report—which develops requirements weekly for the quarter, then monthly for the rest of the year. It is regenerated weekly. The report shows production planners, for each part number, the weekly gross requirement for both the end item and all its components, all lead times, and ordering policy guidelines for each item. Such comprehensive data helps the planner to avoid overplanning and under-planning. Also, when a part is needed, the system generates the order quantity and date needed.

A similar report is produced for Purchasing, and includes sufficient data to alert the suppliers to our long-range needs. Each week, too, Purchasing receives a list of parts that are scheduled for order release in the current month. This is an action report indicating what components and materials to order, the date the order is to be released, when it is due at Moog, and if we need it in less than the normal lead time. We also run an exception report for planners flagging problems with inventory, checking misscheduled orders and other problems.

On a daily basis, the firm-planned orders are analyzed by the allocation system that assigns inventory to manufacturing orders and packaging. Also produced daily are the Fillable/Non-Fillable Report and the component allocation analysis.

Expediting is much improved. Now, when the computer prints an expedite list for Purchasing, they know it is 100 percent valid and can expedite the required items more effectively. Supplier performance has been improved, too, because suppliers know that when we give them our requirements, they are honest requirements. With MRP we know exactly what we need and when we have to have it.

Before installing MRP, members of the MRP project team visited key suppliers to brief them on the program, including projected benefits to each supplier. For example, we can now tell a supplier Moog's long-range requirements to let him better plan his own production procurement, and capacity. We told our suppliers that we felt that this then entitled Moog to preferential treatment.

Generally, we have been able to convince our suppliers both of MRP's importance and the need for accurate information. They now provide more realistic lead times and updating as their situations change, and also can better differentiate between procurement lead times and production lead times. Cooperation of suppliers is vital in the success of MRP, of course. Incidentally, one of our largest suppliers is now installing his own MRP system.

As an additional control factor, we established a central stores area where all raw materials are now received, except steel bars. Stores checks all materials and components for proper identity, makes counts, and issues to the manufacturing departments as scheduled.

Capacity planning system

Released orders and orders to be released are used to update the capacity planning system which generates a weekly report showing the load by work center, by hours available, machine load, and amount over or under capacity. It includes manpower figures. The first quarter workload is itemized by week, and each subsequent quarter by month. The work center summary provides enough short-range data to enable us to determine whether additional production time needs to be scheduled on a weekly basis.

In contrast, our previous systems generally considered only each quarter, which was too gross a segment to provide the level of detail necessary for adequate priority scheduling. This resulted in numerous problems, such as the wrong mix of components and materials, excess inventory, and little or no time-phasing for lead times.

Looking into the near term: We expect to have shop floor control operational within a few months. We are now researching data collection and data transmission equipment to support the control aspects of our MRP plans and making appropriate cost justification studies.

Today, a Moog planner can quickly determine that on the third week of the month he should package, say, 1000 specific ball joints, based on the Master Schedule; and he can find out with equal speed if the order is fillable—and if not, why. Consequently, if he dispatches an order to the Packaging Department, personnel there can know its status immediately.

Similarly, if a component is missing and we have to contact a vendor for expedited service, most of the time we are able to do so in time to meet the schedule. The expedite is further supported by the vendor's realization that any request from Moog for rush service is based on genuine need.

PRODUCTION AND INFORMATION
CONTROL SYSTEM (PICS)

Many of the topics that have been presented in this book thus far are integrated in the computer system described in this section.

The Production and Information Control System (PICS) is designed for fabrication and assembly types of manufacturing.[6] PICS was prompted by two necessities: (1) the recognized need for a central information system in a fabrication and assembly plant and (2) the desire for a framework to facilitate computerization of the information system. A major problem in any production system is that data and information about the system are dispersed throughout the entire operation. PICS would provide a central location for data files containing accurate current data easily accessible to a variety of users.

The PICS system is based on *dependent demand*. A forecast for product demand is fed into the system from some external source, usually an analysis made by the marketing department. The data contained in this forecast for specific time periods is then available to the PICS program.

The Material Requirements Program (MRP) is a significant part of the PICS program. Although MRP and PICS were developed separately, they are quite similar, and now parts of the MRP system have been incorporated in PICS, as some of the findings from experience in using PICS have been included in MRP. The major differences between PICS and MRP are first, that PICS can be installed as a complete system whereas MRP is a software program dependent on other files, and second, that PICS extends the in-

---

[6] IBM, *The Production Information and Control System*, GE20–0280–2.

FIGURE 9.13

Integrated Production and Information Control System (PICS) with access to central data files

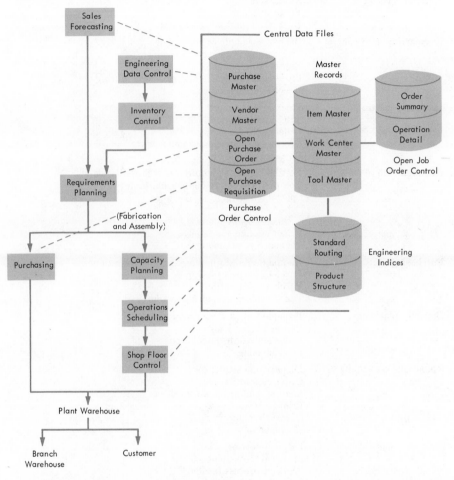

ventory control system to include scheduling. In addition to computing the required materials in the right amounts according to time periods as needed, PICS also contains a job scheduling or shop loading routine. While MRP stops, leaving the actual scheduling and routing to human personnel, PICS routes each job to specific work centers. (It does this through a simulation procedure that tests alternative routings until a satisfactory load balance is achieved.) PICS is also able to provide information about machine and labor utilization and the exact location of jobs in the system at any point in time.

Figure 9.13 shows the basic structure and information flow of the PICS system. The entire system is linked together by immediate access to a common data file that contains the firm's operational records. With only a part number, for example, the product description, standard routing, purchase

TABLE 9.5

Features of PICS subsystems

Sales forecasting	Model selection
	Forecast plans
	Evaluation and measurement
Engineering data control	Basic records file organization
	Engineering drawings
	Engineering changes
	Production structure and standard routing
	Records maintenance
Inventory control	Stock status report
	ABC inventory analysis
	Order policy
	Inventory maintenance and update
	Physical inventory
Requirements planning	Finished product requirements gross to net
	Component requirements gross to net
	Special features:
	Lot sizing
	Offset requirements
	Net change
	Pegged requirements
Purchasing	Requisition and purchase order preparation
	Purchase order followup
	Purchase evaluation
	Vendor evaluation and selection
Capacity planning	Projected work center load report
	Planned order load
	Order start date calculations
	Load leveling
Operations scheduling	Dispatching sequence
	Order estimator
	Load summary by work center
	Priority rules
	Queue time analysis
	Tool control
Shop floor control	Labor reporting
	Material movement
	Work-in-process feedback
	Creation of control forms
	Machine utilization

order status, job order summary, and even the work center in which the job is being performed may be identified.[7]

In PICS, each functional area has been developed as an independent subsystem. Not only is this more practical from a computer system development aspect, but it is highly beneficial for implementation into an ongoing production system. The user can, at his own discretion, decide which subsystems he would like to incorporate first and in what sequence. In practice, the user would not try to put all products and all functional areas into use

---

[7] Each file contains varied data of interest. The "item master" is the master file, and it contains 117 fields that tell all about the item: its description, cost, structure, routing, order policy, forecast, lead time, usage history, stock on hand, projected orders, committed units, items on order, and engineering change status. The master file directs further search to specific files for more detailed information.

at the same time; he gradually builds this up with a small number of products and develops one area at a time.

Information flows from two sources: (1) sales forecasting and (2) engineering data control. Table 9.5 lists the subsystems, along with some of the main features of each.

The sales forecasting subsystem analyzes historical data and employs a sales forecast as input to requirements planning. The mission of engineering data control is to organize and maintain the basic records: item master, product structure, standard routing, and work center master. The inventory control subsystem computes inventory on hand, on order, and usage rates. The inputs from inventory control and sales forecasting are combined to project future requirements of finished goods. Product structure records then break this requirement down into components to be directed to the purchasing, assembly, and fabrication departments.

The flow continues as purchasing prepares purchase orders and receiving cards, based on item identification and the vendor master. An open purchase order is created so that the order will be followed up.

Assembly and fabrication order requirements are used in capacity planning for facility and manpower needs. Order start times are computed from the standard routing records and the available capacity as given by the work center master record. Operations scheduling takes the orders released by capacity planning and makes short-range schedules for work centers. An analysis of work loads and completion dates is then conducted, based on various dispatching sequences and priority rules. The tools needed in production are designated in this step.

Shop floor control is the last phase of this system. It prepares shop packets and other factory documentation, open job order summaries, and operation detail records for monitoring and reporting work progress. The output of purchasing, assembly, and fabrication converges at the plant warehouse.

COPICS—COMMUNICATIONS ORIENTED PRODUCTION INFORMATION AND CONTROL SYSTEM

PICS (Production and Information Control System) was developed by IBM on the basis of an idea or concept of how a manufacturing firm might function under a computer-processing software system. This concept finally came to realization as was described in the preceding section of this chapter.

COPICS is a similar case. The Communication Oriented Production Information and Control System is not now a working system. Figure 9.14, which shows the functional flow of COPICS, is hypothetical. Many individual parts of the proposed COPICS system, however, do currently exist. There are programs for forecasting, inventory control, engineering data management, etc. What remains to be done on this system is to link and integrate the various existing independent programs into an efficient operating system. This will entail modifying existing programs and writing some new programs. Overall, this is likely a decade-long project.

In concept, COPICS is intended to evolve into a dynamic on-line manu-

FIGURE 9.14

Communications Oriented Production Information and Control System structure

COPICS Manufacturing - Functional Flow

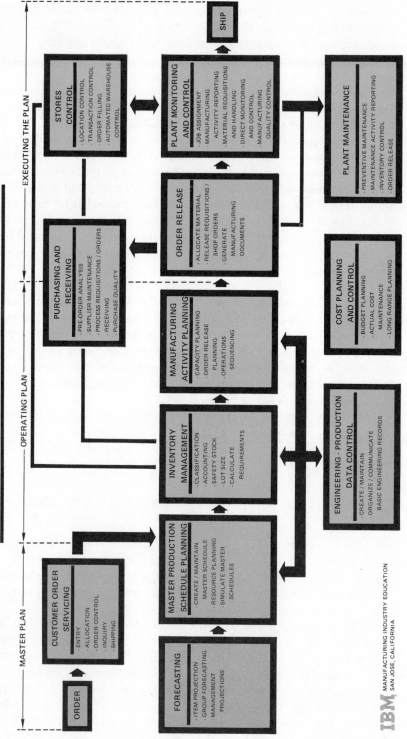

IBM MANUFACTURING INDUSTRY EDUCATION
SAN JOSE, CALIFORNIA

facturing control system. Its extensive and common data base is accessible for problem solving, planning, and control purposes through a network of computer terminals. It is concerned with the entire scope of the manufacturing system, from forecasting demand, through materials and processing control, on to plant maintenance. Additional features of COPICS include simulation capabilities to test alternative strategies.

The Material Requirements Planning program presented in this chapter, along with its required Bill of Materials file, Master Production Schedule, and Inventory Status file, will eventually become integrated parts of the COPICS system. When completed, COPICS is expected to provide many benefits. Some of these are: reduced inventories, improved customer service, better utilization of production facilities, reduced work in-process, greater productivity, higher quality, fewer shortages, reduced costs, elimination of redundant data, reduced risks, and faster information processing for planning.

CONCLUSION

Historically, research and writings on inventory theory have emphasized models and techniques that were most appropriate in independent demand situations. Meanwhile, practitioners struggled with the conceptually simple but time-consuming common-sense methods to deal with dependent demand situations. In the past few years, however, inventory practice has changed in many organizations primarily because of the capability of computers to

TABLE 9.6

Six most widely used procedures in 1973 (based upon 1,846 usable responses out of 8,000 surveyed)

Procedure	Usage
"ABC" principle	62
Economic order quantity	56
MRP	47
Statistical re-order point calculation	32
Exponential smoothing	30
Capacity planning	30

automate the heavy data-handling chores inherent in dependent demand cases. We are now, in fact, confronted with the interesting phenomenon of practice leading theory—MRP is a *fait accompli*, doing the job without a body of scientific theory to support it.

A 1973 survey by the American Production and Inventory Control Society indicated that six techniques were particularly widely used by its members (see Table 9.6).[8] The survey also asked respondents what tech-

---

[8] Edward W. Davis, "A Look at the Use of Production-Inventory Techniques: Past and Present," *Production and Inventory Management*, vol. 16, no. 4, December, 1975, pp. 1–19.

niques they planned to use in the future, and 26 percent answered MRP. "On this basis an impressive 73% eventual usage would be indicated for MRP!"[9] Findings such as this lend support to the MRP advocates' assertion that "the MRP Revolution is upon us!"

REVIEW AND DISCUSSION QUESTIONS

1. Since material requirements planning appears so reasonable, discuss reasons why its popularity was delayed until the past several years.
2. Traditionally, inventory terminology has referred to the number of units "on hand" and "on order." Discuss the significance of MRP terms such as "planned order release" and "scheduled order receipts."
3. Most practitioners currently run an MRP program weekly or biweekly. Would it be more valuable if it were run daily? Discuss.
4. What is the role of safety stock in an MRP system?
5. Discuss the concept of dependent and independent demand.
6. Contrast the significance of the term "lead time" both in the traditional EOQ context and in an MRP system.
7. Discuss the importance of the master production schedule in an MRP system.
8. What are the sources of demand in an MRP system? Are these dependent or independent and how are they used as inputs of the system?
9. State the types of data that would be carried in the Bill of Materials file and the Inventory Record file.
10. Distinguish between the intended uses of the IMPACT system presented in Chapter 8 and the Production and Information Control System (PICS).
11. What are the PICS subsystems and what functions do they perform?

PROBLEMS

1. In the following material requirements plan for Item J, indicate the correct net requirements, planned order receipts and planned order releases to meet the gross requirements. Lead time is one week.

Week number

Item J	0	1	2	3	4	5
Gross requirements.....		50	75		50	70
On hand 40........						
Net requirements......						
Planned order receipt...						
Planned order releases..						

---

9 Ibid., p. 2.

2. Product A consists of 2 units of subassembly B, 3 units of C, and 1 unit of D. B is composed of 4 units of E and 3 units of F. C is made of 2 units of H and 3 units of D. H is made of 5 units of E and 2 units of G.
   a. Construct a simple product structure tree.
   b. Construct a product structure tree using low level coding.
   c. Construct an indented bill of materials.
   d. In order to produce 100 units of A, determine the numbers of units of B, C, D, E, F, G, and H required.

3. Old C.B. Radios, Inc. produces two automatic scanner citizens'-band models for mobile installation, a standard model and a deluxe model of its "Good Buddy" line. The two radio models are internally identical, but the enclosures and finish trims differ.

   Old C.B. handles the production in the following way: The chassis (radio unit) is produced by Old C.B. to meet expected demand and has a manufacturing lead time of two weeks. The enclosures are purchased from a sheet steel company and have a three-week lead time. The trim is purchased from an electronics company as pre-packaged units consisting of knobs, trim pieces, and mounting hardware. Trim packages have a two-week lead time. Final assembly time may be disregarded since the addition of the trim package as well as the mounting are performed by the customer.

   Old C.B. supplies wholesalers and retailers who place specific orders for both models up to eight weeks in advance. These orders, together with enough additional units to satisfy the small number of individual sales, are summarized in the following demand schedule:

Week	1	2	3	4	5	6	7	8
Deluxe model.......				300				400
Standard model......					200			100

   There are currently 50 radio unit chassis on hand but no trim packages or enclosures.

   Prepare a material requirements plan to meet the demand schedule exactly. Specify the gross and net requirements, on-hand amounts and the planned order release and receipt periods for the radio chassis, the deluxe trim, standard trim, deluxe enclosure, and standard enclosure.

4. Repeat the example in the section titled "Example of an MRP system" given in this chapter. However, assume that unexpected changes have caused the lead time for Item C to be 2 weeks instead of 1 week. Construct a new modified MRP schedule to account for the new lead time.

5. White and Peters, Inc., are manufacturers of electrical tools for the home handyman. One of the items in W & P's hand drill line is a quarter-inch drill. Demand for this quarter-inch drill is randomly distributed with an annual amount estimated to be 100,000 units. The manufacturing cost of this drill is $7.50 and its suggested retail price is $19.95.

   Each operating unit of White and Peters is operated as a separate cost center. The organizational structure assigns to the marketing and sales department the responsibility for finished goods inventory, which is stored in a factory warehouse. Marketing personnel have computed that the cost of holding units in inventory is $16\frac{2}{3}$ percent of manufacturing cost. This amount is the total due to allocated warehouse space, the firm's pro-rated cost of capital, and miscellaneous costs. Marketing personnel have further estimated that the cost to place each order with manufacturing is $100 since they perform an inventory count and records check each time an order is placed.

Each quarter-inch drill consists of five subassemblies: the motor assembly, chuck assembly, switch and cord assembly, housing assembly (consisting of a left and a right half), and the packaging assembly (consisting of a styrofoam pack, operating instructions, warranty card, chuck key, and the enclosing carton). Manufacturing lead time of the motor assembly and chuck assembly is 4 weeks, and the lead times for the switch and cord assembly and the housing assembly are 2 weeks. Lead time for the packaging assembly is 1 week and lead time for final assembly is also one week.

The drills are put together and packaged on an assembly line, so all subassembly units must be available at the same time. Assembly time is 15 seconds per drill, so the assembly line is used for other drill sizes and models when it is not assembling the quarter-inch drill. Scheduling the various products accounts for the one-week lead time for the assembly process. W & P closes down the entire manufacturing operation during a two-week vacation period each year.

a. In view of the costs involved, compute the order quantity that marketing should submit to manufacturing.

b. For manufacturing, determine a Master Schedule to meet the orders which can be met for the next eight weeks. Develop a material requirements plan for each subassembly, specifying gross and net requirements and planned order-release and order-receipt dates. Identify the soonest that a lot can be completed. Assume that there are no subassembly units currently in stock.

SELECTED BIBLIOGRAPHY

American Production and Inventory Control Society   *APICS Special Report: Materials Requirement Planning by Computer,* American Production and Inventory Control Society, 1971.

International Business Machines Corporation   *Communications Oriented Production Information and Control System.* Publications G320–1974 through G320–1981.

———   *The Production Information and Control System.* Publication GE20–0280–2.

Journal of American Production and Inventory Control Society   (Numerous articles on MRP appear. Most of these cite the difficulties and experiences of practitioners.)

Journal of American Institute of Decision Science   (Several articles on MRP that are more analytical, examining some foundations of MRP.)

Orlicky, Joseph   *Materials Requirements Planning,* New York: McGraw-Hill, 1975.

———, **Plossl, G. W., and Wight, O. W.**   *Materials Requirements Planning Systems,* IBM publication, G320–1170, 1971.

Proceedings of APICS and AIDS   (Many papers on all aspects of Materials Replenishment Planning Systems are usually presented at the annual society meetings and reprinted in the proceedings.)

Tersine, Richard J.   *Materials Management and Inventory Systems.* New York: North-Holland, Inc., 1976.

Thurston, Phillip H.   "Requirements Planning for Inventory Control," *Harvard Business Review*, May–June 1972, pp. 67–71.

Wight, Oliver W.   *Production and Inventory Management in the Computer Age,* Boston: Cahners Books, 1974.

Section three

Manning the system

10

Job design

Perhaps the most challenging (and perplexing) design activity encountered by the productive system is the development of the jobs that each worker and work group are to perform. This is so for at least three reasons:

1. There is often an inherent conflict between the needs and goals of the worker and work group and the requirements of the transformation process.
2. The unique nature of each individual results in a wide range of attitudinal, physiological, and productivity responses in performing any given task.
3. The changing character of the work force and the work itself lays open to question the traditional models of worker behavior and the efficacy of standard approaches to work development.

In this chapter we will explore these and other issues in job design and present some guidelines for carrying out the job-design function.

JOB DESIGN AS A NATIONAL (AND INTERNATIONAL) CONCERN

The landmark report, *Work in America* (published in 1973), described in detail the problems confronting workers in the United States and discussed the urgent need to restructure work across the entire spectrum of jobs. In essence, the report contended that extreme job specialization and the lack of opportunity to be one's own boss were the major sources of wide-ranging worker dissatisfaction. The message of the report has been echoed by popular writers such as Studs Terkel (*Working*) and Paul Dickson (*The Future of the Workplace*), who have provided graphic examples of unfulfilling jobs as personal and organizational problems. A management consultant, Roy Walters, periodically issues a list of the "Ten Worst Jobs," which is continually changed because so many people feel that their jobs should be included.[1] Two psychologists,[2] D. A. Bernstein and T. M. Alloway, have gone so far as to advocate the use of animals to perform jobs that are beneath the intellectual capacity of humans, and concluded their article by suggesting that man's existence will be enhanced "when we learn when to 'send a bird to do a bird's job.' "[3]

From Europe (as well as the United States) has come increasing evidence that poorly designed jobs are a pervasive societal problem, affecting the mental and physical health of the worker both on and off the job.[4] The

---

[1] A 1975 list has, in no special order, the following boring jobs: assembly-line worker, highway toll collector, car-watcher in a tunnel, pool typist, bank guard, copy-machine operator, bogus typesetter (those who set type that is not to be used), computer-tape librarian (a person who rolls up spools of tape all day), housewife (not to be confused with mother), automatic elevator operator.

[2] D. A. Bernstein and T. M. Alloway, "On the Use of Alternative Organisms," *Journal of Applied Psychology*, vol. 53, no. 6, 1969, pp. 506–9.

[3] Ibid., p. 509.

[4] See, for example, L. E. Davis and A. B. Cherns, *Quality of Working Life: Problems, Prospects, and State of the Art* (Glencoe, Ill.: Free Press, 1975).

general problem was succinctly stated several years ago by Jerome M. Rosow, Assistant Secretary of Labor for Policy, Evaluation, and Research:

> The fact is that millions of workers, who earn between $5,000 and $10,000 a year, are getting increasingly frustrated. Despite steady labor they cannot attain the quality of life for themselves or their families that is expected from conscientious job performance.
>
> Their paychecks do not cover legitimate basic family needs.
>
> Their work life is unsatisfactory but they see no way of breaking out.
>
> Their total life pattern is discouraging. In short, they are caught in a three-way squeeze: an economic squeeze, a workplace squeeze and a socio-environmental squeeze.[5]

Other authorities have also expressed concern over the diminished quality of the average individual's work life.[6] Obviously, such considerations are highly relevant to the topic of job design; and, just as obviously, if we concur with the notion of a "workplace squeeze," we have been doing something wrong in our job design activities.

Job design defined

Job design may be defined as the function of specifying the work activities of an individual or group in an organizational setting. Its objective is to develop work assignments that meet the requirements of the organization and the technology and that satisfy the personal and individual requirements of the job holder. The term *job* (in the context of nonsupervisory work) and the activities subsumed under it are defined below.

1. *Micromotion:* the smallest work activities, involving such elementary movements as reaching, grasping, positioning, or releasing an object.
2. *Element:* an aggregation of two or more micromotions, usually thought of as a more or less complete entity, such as picking up, transporting, and positioning an item.
3. *Task:* an aggregation of two or more elements into a complete activity, such as wiring a circuit board, sweeping a floor, cutting a tree.
4. *Job:* the set of all tasks that must be performed by a given worker. A job may consist of several tasks, such as typing, filing, and taking dictation, as in secretarial work, or it may consist of a single task, such as attaching a wheel to a car, as in automobile assembly.

Job design is a complex function because of the variety of factors that enter into arriving at the ultimate job structure. Decisions must be made as to who is to perform the job, where it is to be performed, and how it is to be performed. And, as can be seen in Figure 10.1, each of these factors may have additional considerations.

---

[5] News release of the U.S. Department of Labor, USDL 71–051, February 1971.

[6] See Judson Gooding, "Blue-Collar Blues on the Assembly Line," *Fortune,* July 1970, pp. 69–78, and Wickham Skinner, "The Anachronistic Factory," *Harvard Business Review,* vol. 49, no. 1 (January–February 1971), pp. 61–70.

FIGURE 10.1

Factors in job design

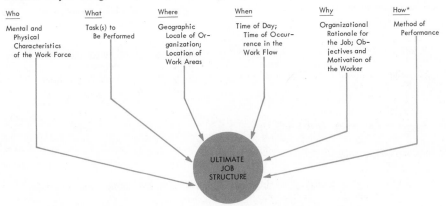

Who	What	Where	When	Why	How*
Mental and Physical Characteristics of the Work Force	Task(s) to Be Performed	Geographic Locale of Organization; Location of Work Areas	Time of Day; Time of Occurrence in the Work Flow	Organizational Rationale for the Job; Objectives and Motivation of the Worker	Method of Performance

ULTIMATE JOB STRUCTURE

° See Chapter 11, "Methods, Measurement, and Wage Payment."

PSYCHOSOCIAL CONSIDERATIONS IN JOB DESIGN

Degree of labor specialization

Specialization of labor is the two-edged sword of job design. On the one hand, specialization has made possible high-speed, low-cost production, and, from a materialistic standpoint, has greatly enhanced our standard of living. On the other hand, it is well known that extreme specialization, such as that encountered in mass production industries, often has serious adverse effects on the worker, which in turn are passed on to the production system. In essence, the problem is the determination of how much specialization is enough; that is, at what point do the disadvantages outweigh the advantages? (See Table 10.1.)

Recent research suggests that the disadvantages dominate the advantages much more commonly than was thought in the past. However, simply stating that, for purely humanitarian reasons, specialization should be avoided is a risky assertion. The reason, of course, is that people differ in what they want from their work and what they are willing to put into it. Some workers prefer not to make decisions about their work, some like to daydream on the job, and others are simply not capable of performing more complex work. Still, as was pointed out earlier, there is a good deal of frustration on the part of the work force with the way many jobs are structured, leading researchers and thoughtful businessmen to try different approaches to job design. The more common of these approaches are job rotation, worker participation, and job enlargement. Of these, job enlargement has received a good deal of attention in the production literature.

Job enlargement

Job enlargement generally entails making adjustments to a specialized job so as to make it more interesting to the job holder. A job is said to be

TABLE 10.1

Advantages and disadvantages of specialization of labor

Advantages of specialization

To management:
1. Rapid training of the work force
2. Ease in recruiting new workers
3. High output due to simple and repetitive work
4. Low wages due to ease of substitutability of labor
5. Close control over work flow and work loads

To labor:
1. Little responsibility for output
2. Little mental effort required
3. Little or no education required to obtain work

Disadvantages of specialization

To management:
1. Difficulty in controlling quality since no one person has responsibility for entire product
2. "Hidden" costs of worker dissatisfaction, arising from
   a. turnover
   b. absenteeism
   c. tardiness
   d. grievances
   e. intentional disruption of production process

To labor:
1. Boredom stemming from repetitive nature of work
2. Little gratification from the work itself because of small contribution to each item.
3. Little or no control over the work pace, leading to frustration and fatigue (in assembly line type situations)
4. Little opportunity to progress to a better job since significant learning is rarely possible on fractionated work
5. Little opportunity to show initiative through developing better methods or tools
6. Local muscular fatigue due to use of the same muscles in performing the task
7. Little opportunity for communication with fellow workers due to layout of the work area

enlarged *horizontally* if the worker performs a greater number or variety of tasks, and it is said to be enlarged *vertically* if the worker is involved in planning, organizing, and inspecting his own work. Horizontal job enlargement is intended to counteract oversimplification and to permit the worker to perform a "whole unit of work." Vertical enlargement (often termed *job enrichment*) attempts to broaden the worker's influence in the transformation process by giving him certain "managerial powers" over his own activities.

A brief example of horizontal job enlargement, undertaken by IBM's French affiliate in the subassembly of counters used on tabulators, follows:

The jobs originally had been divided among 13 workers, each doing a fragmentary operation. These were semi-skilled men who were bored with their jobs and were anxious to advance. The jobs were enlarged by successively consolidating the 13 stages into 7, and then into 4 jobs. As an ancillary part of the program the workers were given theoretical and practical training on Saturdays for a period of six weeks. Because of the enlarged jobs and the week-end training, the workers were initiated into the lowest order of the skilled class. Also, the workers were reported to like having fuller jobs and feeling responsible to the customer for the quality of their work.[7]

As is apparent from this fairly representative application, job enlargement has some appealing features. On the other hand, a number of theoretical and practical questions must be raised with regard to this concept:

How many operations are enough? If two are good, are four better?

What are the criteria for determining when a job should be enlarged? Job enlargement is based upon the following cause-and-effect chain, in which every link is subject to debate by behavioralists: Repetition → Monotony → Boredom → Job dissatisfaction → Poor job performance. (The implication sign, →, is to be interpreted as "leads to").

What about individual differences? (Studies have shown that cultural background plays a large part in determining how workers will respond to enlarged jobs.)

What about organizational differences? (Some organizations have a "climate" that discourages any sort of behavioral change.)[8]

What is the long-term effect on output and quality? (While good results often have been reported for several months following the introduction of job enlargement, its long-run value may be contested. In one of the better-known "successful" applications, the work output never reached the pre-enlarged level.)

What is the long-term effect on the worker? (While some workers may respond positively at first, the long-run measures of satisfaction, such as reduced turnover, grievances, and transfer rates [which are usually given as justification for job enlargement], often are not achieved.)

Perhaps the most serious question surrounding the application of job enlargement (as well as other narrow structural experimentation with work) is the lack of a clear understanding of what a job should be—to use Davis's terms—"in an ecological framework."[9] For instance, as he pointed out in several studies, local culture plays a substantial part in the worker's perception of his job and therefore in his desire to perform it well. Likewise, the nature of the work group, the nature of supervision, and the worker's perceived role in the scheme of things mediate his performance.

It should be apparent that job enlargement is only one tack that may be taken in the design of jobs, and some theorists, including Davis, have attempted to reconcile these factors with the demands of technology to arrive at a different approach to work design. This approach, termed *sociotechnical systems*, and some of its key concepts will now be considered.

---

[7] Georges Friedmann, *The Anatomy of Work* (New York: Free Press of Glencoe, 1960), p. 48.

[8] W. E. Reif and F. Luthans, "Does Job Enrichment Really Pay Off?" *California Management Review*, vol. 15, no. 1, Spring 1972, pp. 30–37.

[9] Louis E. Davis, *Job Satisfaction—A Socio-Technical View*, Report 575–1–69 (Los Angeles: University of California, 1969), p. 8.

Socio-technical systems

According to A. K. Rice,

The concept of a production system as a socio-technical system designates a general field of study concerned with the interrelations of the technical and socio-psychological organization of industrial production systems. . . . The concept of a socio-technical system arose from the consideration that any production system requires both a technological organization—equipment and process layout—and work organization relating to each other those who carry out the necessary tasks. The technological demands place limits on the type of work organization possible, but a work organization has social and psychological properties of its own that are independent of technology. . . . A socio-technical system must also satisfy the financial conditions of the industry of which it is a part. It must have economic dimensions, all of which are interdependent but all of which have independent values of their own.[10]

The operational implication of this concept is that the job designer must recognize the fact that there are two dimensions to any productive system —the technical system and the accompanying social system—and that attempting to optimize one system in isolation from the other may be expected to lead to inferior total performance by the organization.

The concept of socio-technical systems was first elucidated by Eric Trist and his colleagues at the Tavistock Institute of Social Research in London and was developed from their study of different work arrangements in mining coal. From their studies, a number of interesting ideas about the relationship of man to technology emerged. Among these are:

1. Man's role in the socio-technical system.
2. The nature of task boundaries.
3. Degree of work-group autonomy.

Man's role in the socio-technical system. When we think of why a person is hired for an industrial job we usually assume that he is to produce something by using tools, operating a machine, or otherwise performing some physical activity. While this is undoubtedly true for many if not the majority of jobs, a surprisingly large number of work activities do not require the worker to use direct productive skills. Rather, they entail monitoring and/or adjusting some process whose motive power is not initiated by the worker. In essence, his function is often that of a variance controller rather than a producing entity. "His relationship to the process shifts from the mainstream to that of standby concerned with startup and reducing downtime by anticipating faults and developing strategies for corrective action."[11] In a steel mill, this variance control function would fall to the worker who monitors the temperature of a heat of ingots; in a refinery, to the worker who tracks the speed of flow of gasolines through the pipes, and in a manufacturing plant, to the worker who monitors the automatic equipment.

---

[10] A. K. Rice, *Productivity and Social Organization: The Ahmedabad Experiment* (London: Tavistock, 1958), p. 4.

[11] Davis, *Job Satisfaction,* p. 11.

The distinction between man operating as a variance controller as opposed to a producing entity is significant because it dictates the key attributes that should be specified in filling the position, as well as providing an accurate conception of the task itself. For example, it may be that a skilled machinist may be less suited for monitoring the operation of an automatic lathe than a nonmachinist who has experience in, say, monitoring a radar scope.

Nature of task boundaries.   The way in which we describe the boundaries of a task can have significant implications for the success of the socio-technical system.[12] Any task may be defined in at least one of three ways: by its technological attributes, by its territorial location, and by its time of performance. Thus we could variously describe a task as drilling a hole in a piece of steel (technology), performed in a corner of the drilling department (territory), and on the night shift (time).

Specifying these several dimensions of task boundaries is useful in job design for several reasons. First of all, it enhances the likelihood that factors peculiar to the task environment will not be overlooked; for example, two tasks that otherwise have the same technological characteristics may be markedly different by virtue of the fact that they are performed in different locations. Second, it aids in understanding the interaction a particular task has with another task and hence the necessary coordination that the worker or work group performing the task must have with other workers or work groups. For example, if we consider a task in just the technological dimension, we may miss the fact that it may have to be performed by two different people on different shifts (time) and may be moved—while partially completed—to a different machine (territory). Third, attention to each of these three dimensions helps distinguish the most appropriate supervisory structure for overseeing the task performance. In some cases it may be desirable to group divergent tasks under the direction of one supervisor to take advantage of the fact that he is in the territory where they are performed. In other cases tasks might be grouped according to time, as in the case of a night foreman, who might be in charge of a totally different set of tasks than a day foreman.

Work-group autonomy.   An autonomous work group may be defined as an organizational arrangement in which decisions are arrived at by the same persons who put them into action. The need for autonomy arises because of the inherent variability in many work situations, which either precludes complete task specification by management or makes such specification less effective than on-the-spot decisions by the work group. Such variability may take the form of defects in materials, special characteristics of the work locale, or eccentricities in the process itself.

The ways in which autonomy may be manifested are several. The work group may decide the bases upon which tasks are allocated, that is, by seniority, skill, or variety. It may carry out the task allocation; that is, deter-

---

[12] For further discussion of techniques for describing socio-technical systems, see Richard B. Chase, "A Review of Models for Mapping the Socio-Technical System," *AIIE Transactions*, vol. 7, no. 1, March 1975, pp. 48–55.

mine who gets each task and when tasks are to be reallocated. And where the group is paid on the basis of its total output, it may even select the method of sharing its compensation, with certain tasks perhaps being paid at a higher rate than others.

From the point of view of job design, what is required for such groups is not detailed task design but some minimal critical specification as to how the work group can become self-maintaining and self-adjusting. This, of course, is the problem for management since it must specify the general technology-territory-time constraints within which the group must operate. And in addition it must provide the enabling conditions—the policies and resources—to allow the group to carry out its work.

The development of these enabling conditions is itself no small problem. For while work-group autonomy has been practiced throughout history in hunting, farming, and crafts, and is currently encountered in process industries, maintenance departments, etc., the setting of goals and boundaries varies greatly, according to the environment and mission of the parent organization. To utilize autonomous groups effectively, the organization must specify what it wants in the way of performance in terms of output and quality, and it must assure that the group has the requisite technical skills for achieving these goals. In addition it must be sure that the social organization that evolves in the group shares the broader goals of the organization and treats its members fairly in terms of task allocation and compensation.

Socio-technical guidelines for job design. The increased understanding of man's role in a socio-technical system, the need for careful delineation of task boundaries, and the potential for enhanced performance embodied in group (as well as individual) autonomy have led to the development of several hypotheses for job requirements:

1. The need for the content of a job to be reasonably demanding for the individual in terms other than sheer endurance and yet provide some variety (not necessarily novelty)
2. The need for being able to learn on the job and to go on learning
3. The need for some minimal area of decision making that the individual can call his own
4. The need for some minimal degree of social support and recognition at the work place
5. The need to be able to relate what the individual does and what he produces to his social life
6. The need to feel that the job leads to some sort of desirable future.[13]

Consistent with these requirements, the following guidelines for job design may be offered at the level of the individual:

1. *Optimum variety of tasks within the job.* Too much variety can be inefficient for training and production, as well as frustrating for

---

[13] These six hypotheses are drawn from Davis, *Job Satisfaction*, p. 14.

the worker. However, too little variety can be conducive to boredom or fatigue. The optimum level would allow the operator to take a rest from a high level of attention or effort or a demanding activity while working at another activity and, conversely, allow him to stretch himself and his capacities after a period of routine activity.

2. *A meaningful pattern of tasks that gives each job a semblance of a single, overall task.* The tasks should be such that, although involving different levels of attention or degrees of effort of different kinds of skill, they are interdependent. That is, carrying out one task makes it easier to get on with the next or gives a better end result to the overall task. Given such a pattern, the worker can help to find a method of working suitable to his requirements and can more easily relate his job to that of others.

3. *Optimum length of work cycle.* Too short a cycle means too much finishing and starting; too long a cycle makes it difficult to build up a rhythm of work.

4. *Some scope for setting standards of quantity and quality of production and a suitable feedback of knowledge of results.* Minimum standards generally have to be set by management to determine whether a worker is sufficiently trained, skilled, or careful to hold the job. Workers are more likely to accept responsibility for higher standards if they have some freedom in setting them, and are more likely to learn from the job if there is feedback. They can neither effectively set standards nor learn if there is not a quick enough feedback of knowledge of results.

5. *Inclusion in the job of some of the auxiliary and preparatory tasks.* The worker cannot and will not accept responsibility for matters outside his control. Insofar as the preceding criteria are met, the inclusion of such "boundary tasks" (e.g., make-ready activities, inspection of completed work) will extend the scope of the workers' responsibility for and involvement in the job.

6. *Inclusion in the job of some degree of care, skill, knowledge, or effort that is worthy of respect in the community.*

7. *Perceivable contribution of the job to the utility of the product for the consumer.*

Some *group-level* guidelines are:

8. *Providing for "interlocking" tasks, job rotation, or physical proximity where there is a necessary interdependence of jobs* (for technical or psychological reasons). At a minimum, this helps sustain communication and create mutual understanding between workers whose tasks are interdependent, and thus lessens friction, discrimination, and "scapegoating." At best, this procedure will help create work groups that enforce standards of cooperation and mutual help.

9. *Providing for interlocking tasks, job rotation, or physical proximity where the individual jobs entail a relatively high degree of stress.*

Stress can arise from apparently simple things, such as physical activity, concentration, noise, and isolation, if these persist for long periods. Left to their own devices, people will become habituated, but the effects of the stress will tend to be reflected in more mistakes, accidents, and the like. Communication with others in a similar plight tends to lessen the strain.

10. *Providing for interlocking tasks, job rotation, or physical proximity where the individual jobs do not make an obvious, perceivable contribution to the utility of the end product.*

11. *If a number of jobs are linked together by interlocking tasks or job rotation, they should, as a group,*

    a. Have some semblance of an overall task that makes a contribution to the utility of the product;

    b. Have some scope for setting standards and receiving knowledge results; and

    c. have some control over the "boundary tasks."[14]

Following a socio-technical approach to job design by implementing some of the more controversial guidelines may create a certain amount of malaise in the typical organization. For example, if one accepts the notion that groups may be able to self-organize and function autonomously more successfully if their activities are not completely prescribed, production management personnel and industrial engineers who are charged with the job design function must be able to adjust to such a loose-rein situation. And whether they will be able to do so depends jointly on management's philosophy toward such an approach and their own security in their changed organizational role. Indeed, this is more than a small challenge to industrial engineers because, historically, they have been weaned on a "one best way" philosophy—that is, for every job there is a "preferred" structure and it is the *industrial engineer's* function to find it and implement it. Similarly, management may perceive that it is relinquishing some of its power to direct and control its work force and therefore may do so with great reluctance—a response which is not lost on the average worker.

Still, where the guidelines have been applied (though perhaps in some other form), the results have been extremely encouraging,[15] and a number of job-design experiments currently in progress should lend further support to their validity. To operationalize these ideas for the broad spectrum of organizations, however, requires a good deal more work in developing basic concepts and tools for socio-technical analysis. In particular, more systematic methods of describing the socio-technical interface are needed and more discriminating terms for describing the attributes of jobs must be found. The first point requires inclusion of such variables as workers' task

[14] These eleven guidelines are drawn from F. E. Emery, E. Thorsud, and K. Lange, *The Industrial Democracy Project,* Report No. 2 (Trondheim: Institute for Industrial and Social Research, Technical University of Norway, 1965).

[15] See Paul Dickson, *The Future of the Workplace* (New York: Weybright and Talley, 1975), and L. E. Davis and A. B. Cherns, *Quality of Working Life: Problems, Prospects, and State of the Art* (Glencoe, Ill.: Free Press, 1975).

goals and task and social interdependencies into the descriptions of the work-place layout and the jobs themselves. From this, job designers would be able to see more clearly how the technology and the social systems interrelate and thereby move toward improved work structures. As for the second point, terms such as *monitoring, controlling,* and *adjusting,* for example, are too imprecise for distinguishing among tasks in those industries where the majority of the work force performs activities which could be variously described by any one of these terms. (Petroleum processing would be such an industry.) Hence a set of terms and definitions should be developed that are discriminating enough for job design in a variety of industries.

EXPERIMENTS IN JOB DESIGN

Table 10.2, reproduced from *Work in America,* provides a concise summary of some experiments in job restructuring and management in a variety of firms in several countries; in most of the cases cited the changes took hold and are no longer viewed by the companies as "trial runs." Examination of "Techniques Used" (item 5 on the table) indicates a diversity in design approaches used, yet underlying all of the innovations is a provision for increased independence on the part of the worker in doing his or her job.

PHYSICAL CONSIDERATIONS IN JOB DESIGN

Beyond the psychosocial aspects of job design, another aspect of the topic warrants consideration, namely, the physical side. Indeed, while motivation and work-group structure strongly influence worker performance, they may be of secondary importance if the job is too demanding or is otherwise ill-designed from a physical standpoint. In this section we will examine the physical side of work in terms of its demands on the individual and then consider one approach to job design utilizing physiological criteria.

Work task continuum

One way of viewing the general nature of the physical requirements inherent in work is through the rough continuum in Figure 10.2. In this typology, *manual tasks* are defined as tasks that entail stress on large muscle groups in the body and lead to overall fatigue, as measured by increases in the vital functions. In this context, the body is viewed as a heat engine that is supplied by fuel—food and liquids—and uses oxygen for its transformation into energy. *Motor tasks* are controlled by the central nervous system and their measure of effectiveness is the speed and precision of movements. While these tasks lead to fatigue, the effect is localized in the smaller muscle groups such as the fingers, hands, and arms and hence cannot be adequately measured by indices of *general* fatigue. (In measuring the physiological stress of motor tasks, researchers are investigating the

TABLE 10.2
Experiments in Job Design

		Organization		
	Netherlands PTT	*Kaiser Aluminum Corporation Ravenswood, W. Va.*	*Bankers Trust Company New York*	*Operations Division, Bureau of Traffic— Ohio Department of Highways*
1. Establishment(s) or employee groups	Clerical workers— data collection.	Maintenance workers in reduction plant.	Production typists in stock transfer operations.	Six field construction crews.
2. Year initiated	Not specified.	1971	1969	Not specified.
3. Number Employees affected	100	60	200	Not specified.
4. Problem	Jobs were routine. Workers and supervisors were both "notably uninterested" in their work.	Productivity was low. There were walkouts and slowdowns.	Production was low and quality poor. Absenteeism and turnover were high and employee attitudes were poor . . . Jobs were routine, repetitive and devoid of intrinsic interest . . . Too much overseeing.	Low productivity and poor quality of performance.
5. Technique used	Jobs were enlarged to comprise a whole collaborative process (e.g., listing, punching, control punching, corrections, etc.) instead of a single stage of this process.	Time clocks were removed and supervision virtually eliminated. Workers now decide what maintenance jobs are to be done and in what priority and keep their own time cards.	Typists were given the opportunity (1) to change their own computer output tapes, (2) to handle typing for a specific group of customers, (3) to check their own work, and (4) to schedule their own work. Training was given in these areas.	Three experimental groups were established, each with a different degree of self-determination of work schedules. Crews were unaware that they were participating in an experiment.
6. Human results	88% of the workers in the experimental group said the work had become more interesting.	"Morale has improved along with pride in workmanship," says the maintenance chief.	A quantitative survey disclosed improved attitudes and greater satisfaction.	Data showed that as participation increased, so did morale.
7. Economic results	There was a 15% increase in output per man-hour.	Tardiness is now "nonexistent." Maintenance costs are down 5.5%. Maintenance work is done with more "quality."	Absenteeism and tardiness were reduced while production and quality increased. Job enrichment programs were extended.	There was no significant change in productivity.
8. Reference(s)	Wilson, N. A. B., *On the Quality of Working Life*, A Personal Report to the NATO Committee on Challenges of Modern Society, p. 36	Thompson, Donald B., "Enrichment in Action Convinces Skeptics," *Industry Week*, Feb. 14, 1971	Detteback, William W., Assistant Vice Pres. Bankers Trust, and Kraft, Philip, Partner; Roy W. Walters Associates, "Organization Change Through Job Enrichment," *Training and Development Journal*, August 1971	Powell, Reed M., and Schlacter, John L., "Participative Management: A Panacea?" *Academy of Management Journal*, June 1971, pp. 165–73

TABLE 10.2 (*continued*)

		Organization		
Monsanto-Textiles Co. Pensacola, Fla.	*Alcan Aluminum Corp. Oswego, N.Y.*	*Micro Wax Department —Shell Stanlow Refinery, Ellesmere Port; Cheshire, England*	*Philips Electrical Industries— Holland*	*Ferado Company United Kingdom*
Production workers of nylon tire yarn.	Rolling mill operators.	Chemical operators.	Assembly workers.	Production workers making brake linings.
1971	1965	1963	1960	Not specified.
6,000	Not specified.	Not specified.	240–300	Not specified.
Not specified.	High rates of absenteeism and tardiness.	Low productivity, low morale, and possibility of "shutdown."	Not specified.	Not specified.
Four-day classroom sessions were held to involve production workers in problemsolving. Also, employees set production goals and rotated jobs.	Time clocks were removed and production jobs designed to give workers unusual freedom and decisionmaking responsibilities. Salaries were guaranteed during absences or layoffs.	Operators formed group teams that provided both more flexibility within shift teams and rotation in jobs. Time clocks were also removed.	Independent work groups were formed and made responsible for job allocations, material and quality control, and providing delegates for management talks.	Groups of six men were trained to use all machines involved in the process and allowed to move from one machine to the other. Each group sees the batch of marketable products they have made.
"For the employee the program means 'humanized' working conditions," the plant manager reported.	"Monotony is relieved," says the plant manager.	"It is well known that absence and sickness may be symptomatic of alienation . . . from the work situation. Thus . . . [these] statistics are partly an indication of morale," said that plant manager.	The members of semi-autonomous groups derived more satisfaction from their work compared with workers in the old situation.	Job satisfaction in the plant has been found to increase.
"The cost of the program more than pays for itself in higher productivity through fewer idle machines and lower repair costs —a possible gain of 100,000 pounds of yarn a year," says the plant manager.	Absenteeism decreased to about 2.5% compared to an industry average of about 10%. Productivity increased.	"Output" in three sections increased by 35%, 40%, and 100% over 1965. Absence and sickness decreased from 4.3% in 1963 to 3.3% in 1969.	By 1967, waste and repairs decreased by 4% and there was an unspecified savings of lower managerial personnel.	There is less turnover' and original delivery times have been cut by seven-eighths.
U.S. News and World Report, op. cit. at p. 52	"The Honor System," *Wall Street Journal*, May 22, 1970 "Alcan Hails in Dumping Time Clock," *The Plain Dealer*, Sept. 29, 1969	Burden, Derek, *A Participative Approach to Management*, Shell U.K., April 15, 1970	Davis & Trist—*Work In America*, Approaches to Improving Quality of Working Life, June 1972, p. 18	Wilson, N. A. B., *op. cit.* at p. 40

Source: *Work in America*, Appendix—Case Studies in the Humanization of Work.

FIGURE 10.2

Physical task continuum

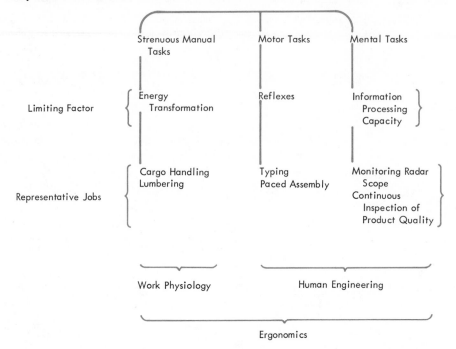

use of electromyography, which records the changes in electrical potential in the involved muscular extremity, i.e., the hands, arms, and fingers.) *Mental tasks* involve rapid decision making based upon certain types of stimuli, such as "blips" on a radar screen or defects in a product. Here the measure of effectiveness is generally some combination of time to respond and number and kind of error. Research into this type of work is usually predicated on concepts from the discipline of information theory, and, as might be expected by the nature of the tasks, much of the source work has been provided by military agencies.

As noted in Figure 10.2, motor tasks and mental tasks fall under the heading *human engineering* while the study of the physical aspects of work in general is called *ergonomics* (from the Greek noun for "work" and the Greek verb for "to manage"). Of the three categories, the analysis of strenuous manual work, approached through the discipline of work physiology, seems to be most complete in terms of theoretical development and practical application, and we will therefore devote the remainder of this section to its discussion.

Before we get into the "how" of designing strenuous work, we will give some justification for *why* it should be studied. In this regard, an argument often put forth in discussion of strenuous work is that it is becoming less widespread in the developed countries, thanks to mechanization, and therefore is of diminished importance in modern organizations. This point, of course, is difficult to dispute, yet there are some compelling reasons that the nature of such activities should be clearly understood by the job designer.

First, it is unlikely, for economic reasons, that we will ever succeed in eliminating all strenuous (or heavy) work. In many instances, manpower is far less costly and far more versatile than machine power.

Second, even though we now engage in fewer heavy tasks, the ones that remain may be critical to the functioning of certain production systems. For example, a worker may be in charge of loading and unloading a bank of machines that may represent a sizable investment, and if he does not adequately perform his function, the resulting loss in output could be just as great as if the work were inefficiently performed by hand by a large number of workers.

Third, space and weight limitations often make mechanization impossible, as in mining operations, cargo handling aboard aircraft, and in certain types of construction work.

Finally, it is a fact that large numbers of people in parts of the United States, as well as the rest of the world, are employed in predominantly heavy manual work. Inefficiency in their use can be a grave waste of human resources.

Work physiology

Work physiology is essentially the application of physiological techniques to manual work. The techniques are predicated on the assumption that certain physiological changes take place during work and that, by observing these changes, the level of physical stress can be determined. Unlike traditional industrial engineering practice, where performance time is the criterion of work intensity (e.g., the faster the work the more fatiguing it is to the worker), work physiology attempts to determine directly, and express by physiological indices, the true fatigue engendered by the work.

The physiological indices most widely used by work physiologists are heart rate and oxygen consumption rate, converted to calories per unit of time. Other indices, such as sweat rate, lactic acid concentration in the blood, and body temperature, have also been used, but for various reasons are impractical for industrial application. The remainder of this discussion focuses on how heart rate and oxygen consumption can be employed in work-stress evaluation.

Heart rate (in beats per minute) is a familiar way of gauging physiological stress, and we have some reliable guidelines for its use. One is that the maximum sustainable heart rate for an eight-hour work day is about 115 beats per minute for the "average" worker. He could exceed this level for a short period of time, but then would have to cease working to permit his body to recover. Of prime importance in this recovery process is the need for the working muscles to get a fresh supply of oxygen through the blood and rid themselves of the body's main waste product, carbon dioxide.

Oxygen consumption, converted to calories per unit of time, is the basic

TABLE 10.3

Calorie requirements for various activities

Type of activity	Typical energy cost in calories per minute
Sitting at rest............	1.7
Writing.................	2.0
Typing.................	2.3
Medium assembly work.....	2.9
Shoe repair..............	3.0
Machining..............	3.3
Ironing.................	4.4
Heavy assembly work......	5.1
Chopping wood...........	7.5
Digging.................	8.9
Tending furnace..........	12.0
Walking upstairs..........	12.0

Source: *Bioastronautics Data Book,* Paul Webb, ed. (Washington, D.C.: Scientific and Technical Information Division, National Aeronautics and Space Administration, 1964).

measure for determining the energy expended by the body at work. Expressing oxygen consumption as calories has become common practice even in underdeveloped countries because of the need to establish the minimum amount of food required to enable a worker to function effectively. Thus calories provide the basis for an input-output equation for broad-scale nutritional planning. With respect to the maximum sustainable calorie consumption level, most authorities agree that five calories per minute represents a conservative upper limit. The approximate number of calories required per minute for various activities is shown in Table 10.3. Table 10.4 is a rough grading of work difficulty in terms of calories and heart rate. It bears repeating that work physiology techniques are of greatest value when the work is of moderate to heavy intensity and involves large muscle masses. Clerical or assembly tasks, which may entail a high level of localized fatigue, are not well suited for heart rate or oxygen consumption analyses.

Procedure for using work physiology in job design. Assuming that the worker who is to perform the job has been trained in similar work activities,

TABLE 10.4

Grading of work by physiological measurements

Work load	Energy expenditure (calories/minute)	Heart rate (beats/minute)
Very light.............	less than 2.5	less than 75
Light.................	2.5– 5.0	75–100
Moderate.............	5.0– 7.5	100–125
Very hard.............	7.5–10.0	125–150
Extremely hard........	10.0–12.5	150–175

Source: E. H. Christensen, "Heart Rate and Body Temperature as Indices of Metabolic Rate during Work," *Arbeitsphysiologie* (March 1950).

understands what is required by the job at hand, and is correctly fitted with heart rate and energy expenditure rate data-gathering equipment, the first step in the work physiology design procedure is to obtain the worker's resting values for heart rate and energy expenditure rate. These values are important in that they permit determination of the time it takes to recover from strenuous activity. The next step is to have the worker perform the specified task at a prescribed rate for some specified period of time, say 15 minutes, followed by a resting period of adequate duration to allow complete recovery. (This time is of course variable, but recovery from most industrial tasks is complete after 15 to 20 minutes of seated rest.) This procedure is repeated for different configurations of the job under study.

By way of example, suppose we wish to determine if the task of loading 25-pound cartons onto a conveyor can be performed at a sustained rate of 10 cartons per minute. We would attempt to determine if this work pace is too demanding—that is, entails greater than five calories or 115 heart beats per minute.[16] If either level is exceeded, the work rate would be reduced until the worker's physiological responses are roughly equal to (or less than) these values. If reducing the pace is not practicable, thought might be given to testing another worker, installing material handling devices (such as floor lifts or hoists), or even changing the weight of the cartons. If any of these adjustments entails strenuous activity, the worker would be tested again following the same procedure.

The work environment

Several factors in the work environment may affect job performance—such as illumination, noise, temperature and humidity, and composition of the air. Though each is worthy of discussion, space does not permit thorough treatment of these topics and the interested reader is therefore referred to the A.S.H.R.A.E., Chapanis, and McCormick works listed at the end of the chapter. It should be pointed out also that these factors have a strong bearing on the safety and general health of the worker, and therefore have been subjected to legal regulation through the Occupational Safety and Health Act of 1970.

CONCLUSION

In 1972, the First International Conference on the Quality of Working Life was held, and since that time, the tempo of research in the area has quickened, both in the United States and abroad. Such recognition that job design is a priority issue for society and the organization as a whole means that the topic is, or will become, a priority concern for the production

---

[16] It is not necessary to use both heart and energy expenditure rate in every situation. However, while heart rate determinations are generally easier to make, this index is highly sensitive to environmental factors such as temperature and humidity. Therefore, unless these factors are relatively constant over the work day, it may prove difficult to obtain a true picture of job stress by heart rate alone.

manager. It should be apparent from the foregoing that achieving a good job design may be a complex undertaking; it demands more than a little understanding of human behavior and knowledge of technology and production economics. Neither finding individuals with such diverse skills nor training them is easy, but the problem, both for social and economic reasons, cannot be ignored. Indeed, wherever people are used for jobs beneath their level of intellectual endowment or their physical capabilities are incorrectly employed, the enemy of all productive systems—waste— prevails.

PROPOSITIONS

Propositions contrasting services and manufacturing relative to job design

Product: Because most service jobs require frequent exchange of information with the customer, verbal communication skills are often a primary consideration in service system job design. In manufacturing, exchange of information is generally less frequent and/or executed by nonverbal means (specifications, written procedures, drawings).

Technology of transformation: In manufacturing systems, the technology of transformation is tangible and is generally perceived as fixed by job designers. In service systems, the technology of transformation is at least partially intangible, and is generally perceived as variable by job designers.

Operating-control system: Because of the inherent variability in the service product, the primary task requirement may vary from minute to minute and indeed, may not even be known to the job incumbent. In manufacturing, the primary task requirement rarely varies and is generally clearly understood.

Workforce: In most service systems, the skills of the workforce are sold directly to the customer. In manufacturing, workforce skills are embodied completely in the physical product.

REVIEW AND DISCUSSION QUESTIONS

1. Have you ever had a job that you would nominate for inclusion on the "Ten Worst Jobs" list? What are some of the ways in which that job might be enriched?

2. In 1974, a group of assembly-line workers from an American auto firm worked for several weeks on an "enriched" auto assembly operation in Sweden. On their return, they expressed generally negative feelings about

the Swedish line. What do you think might have been the cause of this dissatisfaction?

(Hint: See N. Foy and H. Gadon, "Worker Participation: Contrasts in Three Countries," *Harvard Business Review,* May–June 1976, pp. 71–83.)

3. What is the effect of a more sophisticated work force on the job of the industrial engineer?

4. What is a socio-technical system? It has been suggested that most managers view their operations as technical-social systems. Do you agree?

5. What are the pros and cons of job enlargement? Can it be applied where it is most needed? Discuss.

6. Where would you put the following tasks on the work task continuum: piloting an airplane, playing a piano, operating a cash register?

7. Stanley Student comes home at night and collapses in a chair in front of the TV set, claiming that he's "bushed from studying all day." To this his wife responds tenderly: "Bullfeathers! I've been ironing and washing and climbing up and down stairs all day while all you've been doing is listening to lectures and typing term papers. *You* make dinner and wash the dishes, and let *me* rest!" Could Stanley get out of this by using work physiology data to show how tired he is, or should he resort to some other ploy?

8. "Heavy manual work is really such a small component of modern American industry that further study of it is not really necessary." Comment.

PROBLEMS

1. For any job you have held,
    a. Describe your role in the socio-technical system, the nature of task boundaries, and the extent of work-group autonomy.
    b. Determine how well it matched each of the 11 socio-technical guidelines for job design (listed in pages 462–64). We suggest that you do this formally, using the scale shown below:

1	2	3	4	
(None)	(Little)	(Some)	(Much)	Not relevant

    For example, suppose that you wish to score the match between your job and criterion 3 (optimum length of work cycle). If you conclude that your job permitted no opportunity to build a comfortable rhythm of work, you would circle 1 on the scale for this criterion. Proceeding this way for each of the 13 criteria (criterion number 11 has three parts) permits the calculation of an average score for the entire job, which can then be compared to other class members' jobs. If a particular criterion is not relevant to your job, it should not be included in deciding the average job design score. (Obviously, 13 scales such as the one shown above are required for this assignment.)

2. Take a brisk walk around a quarter-mile track. After completing your walk, remain standing and take your pulse (at your wrist), immediately and about a minute later. From this decide whether you are physiologically suited to moderate to heavy work.

SELECTED BIBLIOGRAPHY

A.S.H.R.A.E. Guide and Data Book, 1960: Fundamentals and Equipment. New York: American Society of Heating, Refrigeration, and Air Conditioning Engineers, 1961.

Chapanis, Alphonse   *Man-Machine Engineering.* Belmont, Calif.: Wadsworth Publishing Co., 1965.

Chase, Richard B.   "A Review of Models for Mapping the Socio-Technical System," *AIIE Transactions,* vol. 7, no. 1, March 1975, pp. 48–55.

————.   "Work Physiology: A New Selection Tool," *Personnel Administration* (November–December 1969), pp. 47–53.

Davis, Louis E.   "Readying the Unready: Postindustrial Jobs," *California Management Review,* vol. 3, no. 4 (Summer 1971), pp. 27–36.

Dickson, Paul   *The Future of the Workplace,* New York: Weybright and Talley, 1975.

Herbst, P. G.   *Socio-technical Design, Strategies in Multidisciplinary Research,* London: Tavistock Publications, 1974.

McCormick, E. J.   *Human Engineering.* New York: McGraw-Hill, 1957.

Miller, E. J.   "Technology, Territory and Time: The Internal Differentiation of Complex Production Systems," *Human Relations,* vol. 12, no. 3 (1959), pp. 243–72.

Susman, Gerald I.   "The Concept of Status Congruence as a Basis to Predict Task Allocations in Autonomous Work Groups," *Administrative Science Quarterly,* vol. 15, no. 2 (June 1970), pp. 164–75.

Thorsrud, E., and Emery, F.   "Industrial Democracy in Norway," *Industrial Relations,* vol. 9, no. 2 (February 1970), pp. 187–96.

Trist, E. L., Higgin, G. W., Murray, H., and Pollack, H. P.   *Organizational Choice.* London: Tavistock, 1963.

Terkel, Studs   *Working.* New York: Pantheon Books, 1972.

Upjohn Institute for Employment Research   *Work in America.* Cambridge, Mass.: MIT Press, 1973.

Foy, N. and Gadon, H.   "Worker Participation: Contrasts in Three Countries," *Harvard Business Review,* vol. 54, no. 3 (May–June 1976), pp. 71–83.

Van Der Zwaan, A. H.   "The Sociotechnical Systems Approach: A Critical Evaluation," *International Journal of Production Research,* vol. 13, no. 2, 1975, pp. 149–163.

11

Methods, measurement, and wage payment

". . . brook no idleness. Stand over them (the fieldworkers) during their work, and brook no interruptions. Do not distract your field-workers." *

I n this chapter, as in the previous one, the concern is with the man in the system and the work he performs. Now, however, our focus shifts from delineating the boundaries and general character of the job to the specifics of job performance. In particular, we wish to consider

1. How the work should be accomplished (work methods)
2. How performance may be evaluated (work measurement)
3. How workers should be compensated (wage payment plans)

These three areas—methods, measurement, and wage payment—received a great deal of attention in the late 19th and early 20th century. A considerable amount of research and study was conducted and many innovations were made. Since then, improvements have been slight and the state of the art today is much as it was twenty or thirty years ago. For this reason, a large part of this chapter is historical in nature. History is especially important in this field since it had much to do with the way in which production management is perceived today.[1]

HISTORICAL BACKGROUND

The field of production management was born in the factory environment of the late 19th century. During this time factory work was characterized by a large proportion of direct labor with little mechanization. It was therefore natural that attention focused on the man in the system—on the methods he used and the time he required to perform his work.

The problem of time, or more specifically, its efficient utilization, was of primary interest to Frederick W. Taylor. In his book *Principles of Scientific Management,* he observed that most people were aware of the waste of natural resources—forests, water power, land—because these were visible losses. The waste of human resources, which he considered more important, was not obvious. After extensive research, he considered that such waste of human effort was avoidable if management approached the study of work scientifically—choosing the right man for the job and developing the best method of performance and timing it exactly. Taylor recognized that to implement his notions of efficiency required that both labor and management must benefit from their application. He also assumed—quite correctly in the context of his era—that workmen wanted high wages and that employers wanted low labor cost (high productivity from their workers). Unfortunately, many businessmen were not as skilled or careful as Taylor in applying the scientific management concepts of time study and the wage

---

* Samuel N. Kramer, *Sumerians: Their History, Culture and Character* (Chicago: University of Chicago Press, 1963).

[1] Production management has an "image" problem in that, to the uninitiated, the term conjures up a picture of dusty shop floors, stopwatches, and worker abuse. We hope the reader has obtained a truer picture of the field as it is today.

payment plans that Taylor developed. Extensive industrial turmoil was the result. Nevertheless, much of what Taylor proposed was correctly applied and much of our nation's abundant production is due in part to Taylor's insight into work.

WORK METHODS

In our development of the productive system we have defined the tasks that must be done by workers. But *how* should they be done? Years ago, production workers were craftsmen who had their own (sometimes secret) methods for doing work. However, as products became more complicated, as mechanization of a higher order was introduced, and as output rates increased, the responsibilities for work methods were necessarily transferred to management. It was no longer logical or economically feasible to allow individual workers to produce the same product by different methods.[2] Further, work specialization brought much of the concept of craftwork to an end as less skilled workers were employed on the simpler tasks.

In contemporary industry, the responsibility for developing work methods in large firms is typically assigned to a staff department that is designated "methods analysis" or to industrial engineering. In small firms this activity is often performed by individual specialists who report to the chief industrial engineer or to the production manager.

The degree of flexibility in work methods design varies with the level of technology. The less sophisticated the technology (either through less precise requirements or greater manual inputs), the greater the input of the methods department. When the labor input is highly constrained by a rigid process design or a high mechanization-to-labor ratio, there may be little opportunity to do much more than try to fit the man to the job as best as can be done.

Because manufacturing firms have become highly mechanized, the most rewarding applications of methods design and improvement now often lie outside the factory. The high labor content of service industries, for example, makes them a fertile field for the application of work methods analysis. The use of simple charting techniques such as flow process charts, is almost guaranteed to bring immediate results when applied to hospitals, financial institutions, retailing establishments, etc., even though such organizations tend to perceive themselves as being "nonproduction" in character.

The principal approach to the study of work methods is the construction of charts (such as operations charts, man/machine charts, activity charts) in conjunction with time study or standard time data. The choice of which charting method to use depends on the activity level of the task; that is, whether the focus is on (1) the overall productive system, (2) the stationary worker at a fixed work place, (3) a worker interacting with equipment,

---

[2] It has been claimed that the failure of the Stanley Steamer automobile was due directly to its production by individual craftsmen. Neither parts nor methods were standardized, and therefore the original craftsmen had to be sought out for needed repairs.

TABLE 11.1

Work methods design aids

Activity	*Objective of study*	*Study techniques*
Overall productive system	Eliminate or combine steps; shorten transport distance; identify delays	Flow diagram, process chart
Stationary worker at fixed work place	Simplify method; minimize motions	Operations charts, simo charts; apply principles of motion economy
Worker interacts with equipment	Minimize idle time; find number or combination of machines to balance cost of man and machine idle time	Activity chart, man-machine charts
Worker interacts with other workers	Maximize productivity; minimize interference	Activity charts, gang process charts

or (4) a worker interacting with other workers (see Table 11.1). (Several of these charting techniques were introduced in Chapter 3, where they were used to aid process selection.)

Overall productive system

The objective in studying the overall productive system is to identify delays, transport distances, processes, and processing time requirements in order to simplify the entire operation. Once the process has been charted, the following questions may be asked.

What is done? Must it be done? What would happen if it were not done?
Where is the task done? Must it be done at that location or could it be done somewhere else?
When is the task performed? Is it critical that it be done then or is there flexibility in time and sequence? Could it be done in combination with some other step in the process?
How is the task done? Why is it done this way? Is there another way?
Who does the task? Can someone else do it? Should the worker be of a higher or lower skill level?

These thought-provoking questions usually lead to elimination of much of the unnecessary work, as well as to simplifying the remaining work, by combining a number of processing steps and changing the order of performance.

Use of the *process chart* is valuable in studying an overall system, though care must be taken to follow the same item throughout the process. The subject may be a product being manufactured, a service being created, or a person performing a sequence of activities.

Common notation in process charting is shown in Figure 11.1.

A process chart may be used in an office to follow the flow of any form —an application, a claim, or a requisition form, for example. A description

FIGURE 11.1

Common notation in process charting

○   Operation. Something actually is being done. This may be work on a product, some support activity or anything that is directly productive in nature.

▷   Transportation. The subject of the study (product, service, or person) moves from one location to another.

□   Inspection. The subject is observed for quality and correctness.

D   Delay. The subject of the study must wait before starting the next step in the process.

▽   Storage. The subject is stored, such as finished products in inventory or completed papers in a file. Frequently, a distinction is made between temporary storage and permanent storage by inserting a T or P in the triangle.

of each step in the form's flow is noted in the chart along with the chart symbol.

Figure 11.2 shows the flow of a purchase order with the layout and work method. By concentrating on simplifying the method and shortening the number of steps involved, the new method shown in Figure 11.3 was devised. Further improvement may be possible by authorizing the supervisor to sign any orders up to some specified limit, thereby relieving the purchasing agent of some of the work load.

Stationary worker at fixed work place

Many work tasks require the worker to remain at the same place. When the nature of his work is primarily manual (e.g., sorting, inspecting, making entries, or assembly operations), the focus of work design is on simplifying the work method and making the required operator motions as few and as easy as possible.

There are two basic ways to determine the best method when studying a single worker who is performing an essentially manual task. The first is to search among the workers and find the one who performs the job best. His method is then accepted as the standard and others who would work on that job are trained to perform it in the same way. This was basically Taylor's approach, though after determining the best method he searched for "first-class men" to perform according to the method. (A "first-class man" possessed the natural ability to do much more productive work in a particular task than the average. Men who were not "first class" were transferred to other jobs.) The second way to determine the best method is to observe the performance of a number of workers, analyze in detail each step of their work, and pick out the superior features of each worker's performance. This results in a composite method that combines the best elements of the group studied. This was the procedure used by Frank Gilbreth, the "father of motion study," to determine the "one best way" to perform a work task.

FIGURE 11.2

Flow diagram and process chart of an office procedure—present method[*]

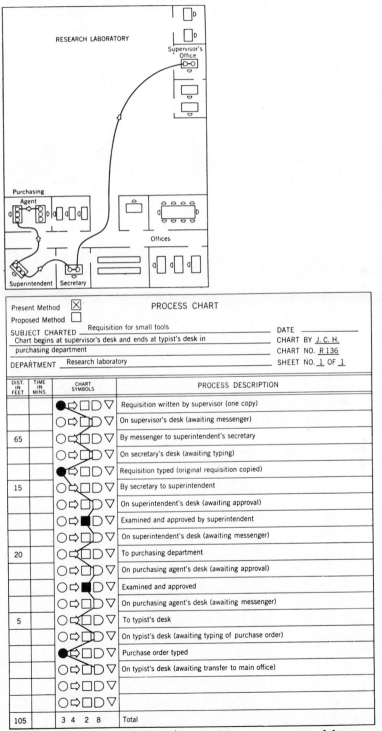

Requisition is written by supervisor, typed by secretary, approved by super-intendent, and approved by purchasing agent; then a purchase order is prepared by a stenographer.

From Ralph M. Barnes, *Motion and Time Study* (New York: John Wiley & Sons, 1968) pp. 76–79.

FIGURE 11.3

Flow diagram and process chart of an office procedure—proposed method*

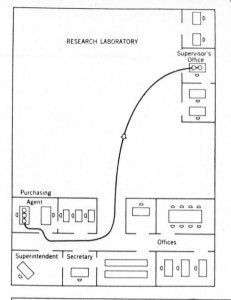

Present Method ☐	PROCESS CHART
Proposed Method ☒	

SUBJECT CHARTED ___Requisition for small tools___

___Chart begins at supervisor's desk and ends at purchasing agent's desk___

DATE _____

CHART BY _J. C. H._

CHART NO. _R 149_

DEPARTMENT ___Research laboratory___

SHEET NO. _1_ OF _1_

DIST. IN FEET	TIME IN MINS.	CHART SYMBOLS	PROCESS DESCRIPTION
		●⇨☐D▽	Purchase order written in triplicate by supervisor
		○⇨☐D▽	On supervisor's desk (awaiting messenger)
75		○⇨☐D▽	By messenger to purchasing agent
		○⇨☐D▽	On purchasing agent's desk (awaiting approval)
		○⇨■D▽	Examined and approved by purchasing agent
		○⇨☐D▽	On purchasing agent's desk (awaiting transfer to main office)
		○⇨☐D▽	
		○⇨☐D▽	
		○⇨☐D▽	
		○⇨☐D▽	
		○⇨☐D▽	
		○⇨☐D▽	
		○⇨☐D▽	
		○⇨☐D▽	

SUMMARY

	PRESENT METHOD	PROPOSED METHOD	DIFFER-ENCE
Operations ○	3	1	2
Transportations ⇨	4	1	3
Inspections ☐	2	1	1
Delays D	8	3	5
Distance Traveled in Feet	105	75	30

| 75 | 1 1 1 3 | Total |

* Requisition is written in triplicate by supervisor and approved by purchasing agent.
From Ralph M. Barnes, *Motion and Time Study* (New York: John Wiley & Sons, 1968).

Whereas Taylor observed actual performance to find the best method, Frank Gilbreth and his wife Lillian relied on movie film. Through "micromotion analysis"—observation of the filmed work performance frame by frame—the Gilbreths studied work very closely and defined its basic elements, which were termed *therbligs* (Gilbreth spelled backward, with the *t* and *h* transposed). Their study led to the rules or principles of motion economy listed in Table 11.2.

Once the motions for performing the task have been identified, an *opera-

TABLE 11.2

Principles of motion economy (checksheet for motion economy and fatigue reduction)

Use of the human body	*Arrangement of the work place*	*Design of tools and equipment*
1. The two hands should begin as well as complete their motions at the same time.	10. There should be a definite and fixed place for all tools and materials.	18. The hands should be relieved of all work that can be done more advantageously by a jig, a fixture, or a foot-operated device.
2. The two hands should not be idle at the same time except during rest periods.	11. Tools, materials, and controls should be located close to the point of use.	19. Two or more tools should be combined wherever possible.
3. Motions of the arms should be made in opposite and symmetrical directions, and should be made simultaneously.	12. Gravity feed bins and containers should be used to deliver material close to the point of use.	20. Tools and materials should be pre-positioned whenever possible.
4. Hand and body motions should be confined to the lowest classification with which it is possible to perform the work satisfactorily.	13. Drop deliveries should be used wherever possible.	21. Where each finger performs some specific movement, such as in typewriting, the load should be distributed in accordance with the inherent capacities of the fingers.
5. Momentum should be employed to assist the worker wherever possible, and it should be reduced to a minimum if it must be overcome by muscular effort.	14. Materials and tools should be located to permit the best sequence of motions.	22. Levers, crossbars, and hand wheels should be located in such positions that the operator can manipulate them with the least change in body position and with the greatest mechanical advantage.
6. Smooth continuous curved motions of the hands are preferable to straight-line motions involving sudden and sharp changes in direction.	15. Provisions should be made for adequate conditions for seeing. Good illumination is the first requirement for satisfactory visual perception.	
7. Ballistic movements are faster, easier, and more accurate than restricted or "controlled" movements.	16. The height of the work place and the chair should preferably be arranged so that alternate sitting and standing at work are easily possible.	
8. Work should be arranged to permit easy and natural rhythm wherever possible.	17. A chair of the type and height to permit good posture should be provided for every worker.	
9. Eye fixations should be as few and as close together as possible.		

From Ralph M. Barnes, *Motion and Time Study* (New York: John Wiley & Sons, 1968), p. 220.

FIGURE 11.4

SIMO chart for assembly of variable resistor

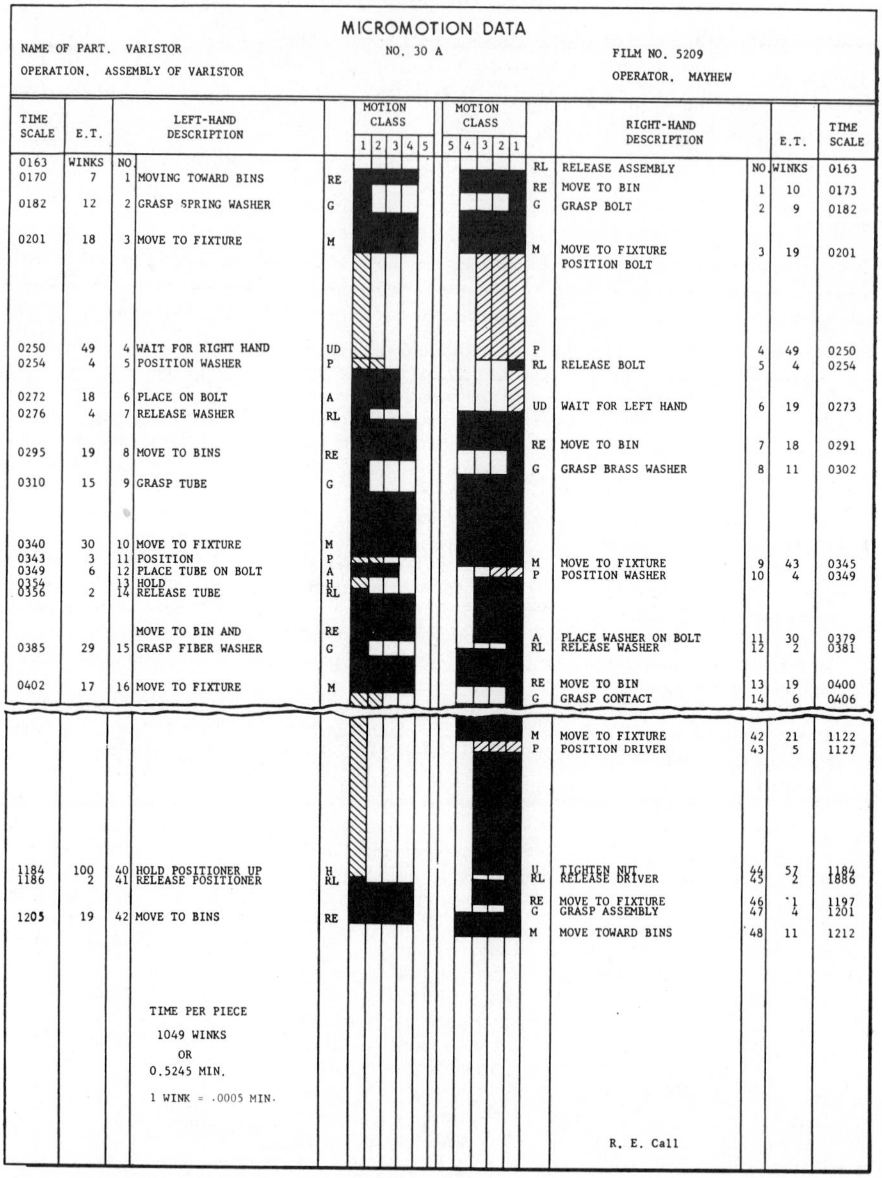

MICROMOTION DATA

NAME OF PART. VARISTOR   NO. 30 A

OPERATION. ASSEMBLY OF VARISTOR

FILM NO. 5209

OPERATOR. MAYHEW

TIME SCALE	E.T.	NO.	LEFT-HAND DESCRIPTION	MOTION CLASS		RIGHT-HAND DESCRIPTION	NO.	WINKS	TIME SCALE
0163	WINKS				RL	RELEASE ASSEMBLY	NO.	WINKS	0163
0170	7	1	MOVING TOWARD BINS	RE	RE	MOVE TO BIN	1	10	0173
0182	12	2	GRASP SPRING WASHER	G	G	GRASP BOLT	2	9	0182
0201	18	3	MOVE TO FIXTURE	M	M	MOVE TO FIXTURE POSITION BOLT	3	19	0201
0250	49	4	WAIT FOR RIGHT HAND	UD	P		4	49	0250
0254	4	5	POSITION WASHER	P	RL	RELEASE BOLT	5	4	0254
0272	18	6	PLACE ON BOLT	A			6	19	0273
0276	4	7	RELEASE WASHER	RL	UD	WAIT FOR LEFT HAND			
0295	19	8	MOVE TO BINS	RE	RE	MOVE TO BIN	7	18	0291
0310	15	9	GRASP TUBE	G	G	GRASP BRASS WASHER	8	11	0302
0340	30	10	MOVE TO FIXTURE	M	M	MOVE TO FIXTURE	9	43	0345
0343	3	11	POSITION	P	P	POSITION WASHER	10	4	0349
0349	6	12	PLACE TUBE ON BOLT	A					
0354		13	HOLD	H					
0356	2	14	RELEASE TUBE	RL					
			MOVE TO BIN AND	RE	A	PLACE WASHER ON BOLT	11	30	0379
0385	29	15	GRASP FIBER WASHER	G	RL	RELEASE WASHER	12	2	0381
0402	17	16	MOVE TO FIXTURE	M	RE	MOVE TO BIN	13	19	0400
					G	GRASP CONTACT	14	6	0406
					M	MOVE TO FIXTURE	42	21	1122
					P	POSITION DRIVER	43	5	1127
1184	100	40	HOLD POSITIONER UP	H	U	TIGHTEN NUT	44	57	1184
1186	2	41	RELEASE POSITIONER	RL	RL	RELEASE DRIVER	45	2	1886
					RE	MOVE TO FIXTURE	46	1	1197
1205	19	42	MOVE TO BINS	RE	G	GRASP ASSEMBLY	47	4	1201
					M	MOVE TOWARD BINS	48	11	1212

TIME PER PIECE

1049 WINKS

OR

0.5245 MIN.

1 WINK = .0005 MIN.

R. E. Call

From Benjamin W. Niebel, *Motion and Time Study*, 6th ed. (Homewood, Ill.: Richard D. Irwin, Inc., 1976), p. 201.

tions chart may be made, listing the operations and their sequence of performance. For greater detail, a *simo (simultaneous motion) chart* may be constructed, which lists not only the operations but also the times for both left and right hands. This chart may be assembled from data collected with a stopwatch, from analysis of a movie film of the operation, or from predetermined motion time data (discussed later in this chapter). Many aspects of poor design will be immediately obvious: a hand being used as a holding device (rather than a jig or fixture), an idle hand, or an exceptionally long time for positioning.

Figure 11.4 is an extract of a simo chart for the assembly of a variable resistor. This chart is more detailed than the usual chart since it was constructed from a filmed sequence and contains the identifying motion notation and degree of difficulty (motion class).

Worker interacting with equipment

When a person and equipment operate to perform the productive process, interest focuses on the efficient utilization of the man's time and the equipment. When the working time of the operator is less than the equipment run time, a *man-machine chart* is a useful device in analysis. If the operator can operate several pieces of equipment, the problem is to find the most economical combination of man and equipment. This optimum point occurs when the combined cost of the idle time of a particular combination of equipment and the idle time for the worker is at a minimum.

Man-machine charts are always drawn to scale, the scale being time as measured by length. Figure 11.5, gives an example of a man-machine chart for one operator running two machines. Note that the operator is busy all the time and therefore could not be assigned a third machine. The decision of whether the operator should operate one or two machines is made by comparing the lost value due to the idle time of the two machines with the value of the idle time of the operator if he operates only one machine (in which case this one machine would have full attention and no idle time).

Workers interacting with other workers

A great amount of our productive output in manufacturing and service industries is performed by teams. The degree of interaction may be as simple as one operator handing a part to another—or as complex as a cardiovascular surgical team of doctors, nurses, anesthesiologist, operator of an artificial heart machine, X-ray technician, standby blood donors, and pathologist (and perhaps a priest or minister to pray a little).

An *activity* or a *gang process chart* is useful in plotting the activities of each individual on a time scale similar to that of the man-machine chart. A gang process chart is usually employed to trace the interaction of a number of men with machines of a specified operating cycle with the objective of finding the best combination of men and machines. An activity chart is less restrictive and may be used to follow the interaction of any group of operators, with or without equipment being involved. In addition, they are often used for the study and definition of each operator in an ongoing repetitive process, and they are extremely valuable in developing a standardized procedure for the accomplishment of a specific task. Figure 11.6, for example, shows an activity chart for a hospital's emergency routine in performing a

FIGURE 11.5

Man and machine process chart for milling machine operation

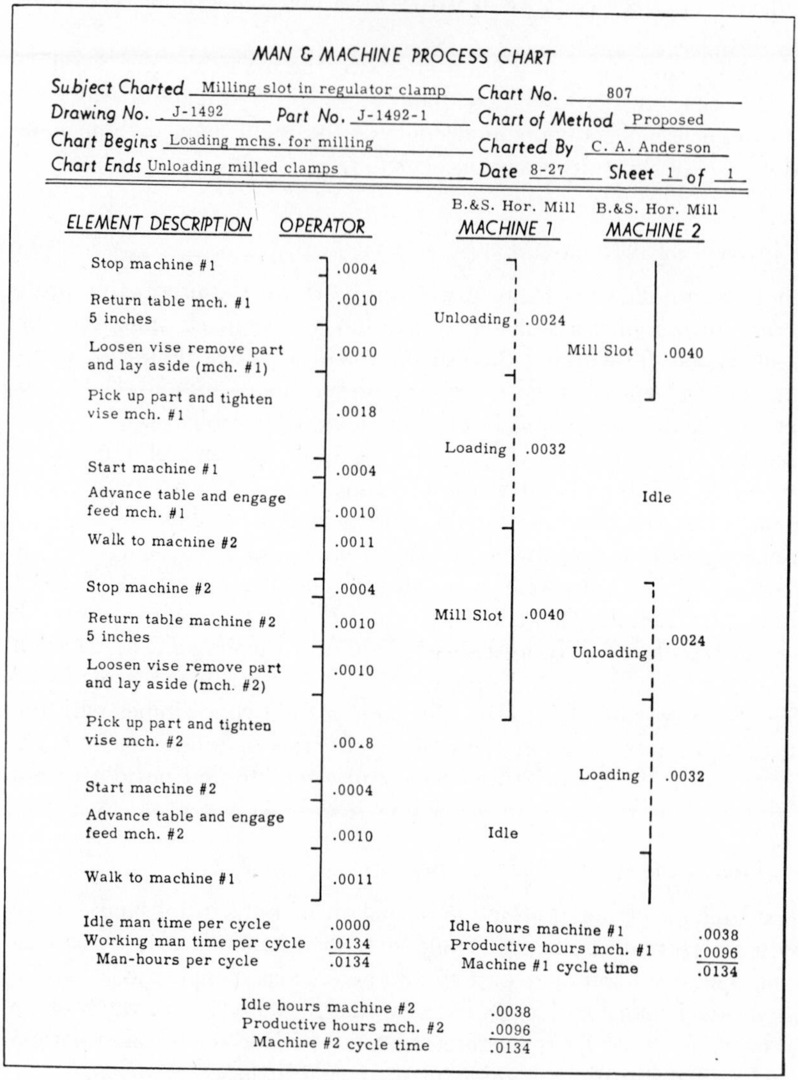

MAN & MACHINE PROCESS CHART

Subject Charted _Milling slot in regulator clamp_   Chart No. ___807___
Drawing No. _J-1492_   Part No. _J-1492-1_   Chart of Method _Proposed_
Chart Begins _Loading mchs. for milling_   Charted By _C. A. Anderson_
Chart Ends _Unloading milled clamps_   Date _8-27_   Sheet _1_ of _1_

ELEMENT DESCRIPTION	OPERATOR	B.&S. Hor. Mill MACHINE 1	B.&S. Hor. Mill MACHINE 2
Stop machine #1	.0004		
Return table mch. #1 5 inches	.0010	Unloading .0024	
Loosen vise remove part and lay aside (mch. #1)	.0010		Mill Slot .0040
Pick up part and tighten vise mch. #1	.0018		
Start machine #1	.0004	Loading .0032	
Advance table and engage feed mch. #1	.0010		Idle
Walk to machine #2	.0011		
Stop machine #2	.0004		
Return table machine #2 5 inches	.0010	Mill Slot .0040	Unloading .0024
Loosen vise remove part and lay aside (mch. #2)	.0010		
Pick up part and tighten vise mch. #2	.00.8		
Start machine #2	.0004		Loading .0032
Advance table and engage feed mch. #2	.0010	Idle	
Walk to machine #1	.0011		

Idle man time per cycle	.0000	Idle hours machine #1	.0038
Working man time per cycle	.0134	Productive hours mch. #1	.0096
Man-hours per cycle	.0134	Machine #1 cycle time	.0134

Idle hours machine #2	.0038
Productive hours mch. #2	.0096
Machine #2 cycle time	.0134

Source: Benjamin W. Niebel, *Motion and Time Study,* 6th ed. (Homewood, Ill.: Richard D. Irwin, Inc., 1976), p. 124.

tracheotomy (opening a patient's throat surgically to allow him to breathe), where detailed activity analysis is of major importance and any delay could be fatal.

Work methods techniques and socio-technical systems

Figure 11.7 illustrates how the graphical and charting techniques just discussed come into play when the factory is viewed as a socio-technical

FIGURE 11.6

Activity chart of emergency tracheotomy

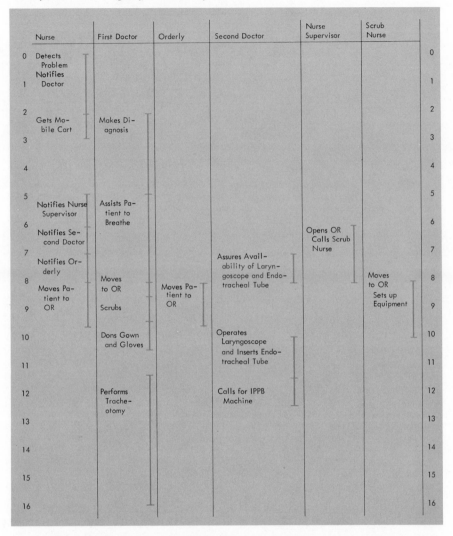

Data taken from Harold E. Smalley and John Freeman, *Hospital Industrial Engineering* (New York: Reinhold Publishing Co., 1966), p. 409.

system. Note in particular the role of the techniques in bringing together the three basic elements of a socio-technical system—individuals, machines and materials—at successive levels of aggregation.

WORK MEASUREMENT

"When you can measure it, you know something about it."—Lord Kelvin. The efficient operation of any firm is predicated on some knowledge of

FIGURE 11.7

Structural elements of a socio-technical system

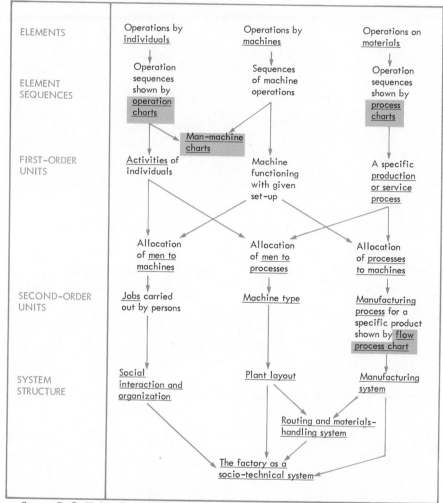

Source: P. G. Herbst, *Socio-technical Design: Strategies in Multidisciplinary Research* (London: Tavistock Publications, 1974), p. 119.

how long it takes to make a product or perform a service. Without some indication of the time requirements,

1. Costs could not be estimated and therefore prices could not be quoted.
2. Budgets could not be made.
3. Evaluation of performance would be impossible since there would be no basis for comparison.
4. Incentive plans and merits increases could not be offered.

There are five accepted ways to derive the time required in the performance of a human task:

1. Time study (stopwatch and micromotion analysis)
2. Elemental standard time data
3. Predetermined motion-time data
4. Work sampling
5. Work physiology

Each of these methods has some advantages over the others and has particular areas of application. Table 11.3 lists these methods and relates them to a general class of jobs. The arbitrary use of historical records to estimate future performance is generally bad practice. Experience has shown that tasks which are performed without any formal analysis range very widely in "fairness." Some tasks are very easy (allowed times are too long) and some are too difficult (inadequate time is allowed). Therefore good practice requires that production tasks be measured formally, using one of the five methods stated.

TABLE 11.3

Types of work measurement applied to differing tasks

Type of Work	Major methods of determining task time
Very short interval, highly repetitive...........	Film analysis
Short interval, repetitive....................	Stopwatch time study; predetermined motion-time data
Task in conjunction with machinery or other fixed-processing-time equipment.......	Elemental data
Infrequent work or work of a long cycle time..................................	Work sampling
Moderate to strenuous work.................	Physiological measurement (primarily the determination of heart rate and oxygen consumption)

Time study

Time study was formalized by Frederick W. Taylor in 1881. Since Taylor's time, volumes have been written on time study, and the technique is undoubtedly the most widely used of the quantitatively based methods of work measurement. The pervasiveness of the technique is borne out in a survey in which Ralph M. Barnes found that 74 out of 75 companies having incentive plans used time study to set work standards.[3]

A time study is generally made with a stopwatch, although in some instances film analysis or a timed recording device may be used. Procedurally, the job or task to be studied is separated into measurable parts or elements and each element is timed individually. After a number of repetitions, the collected times are averaged. (The standard deviation may be computed to give a measure of variance in the performance times.) The averaged times for each element are added and the result is the performance time for that operator. However, to make this operator's time usable for all workers,

[3] Ralph M. Barnes, "Industrial Engineering Survey," *Journal of Industrial Engineering*, vol. 18, no. 12 (December 1967), pp. 11–14.

a measure of speed or "performance rating" must be included. Rating will be treated later in this chapter, but its purpose is to attach a factor to account for an operator's working faster or slower than "normal." For example, if an operator performs a task in 2 minutes and the time study analyst estimates him to be performing about 20 percent faster than normal, the normal time would be computed as 2 minutes + 0.20(2 minutes), or $1.2(2) = 2.4$ minutes. In equation form,

Normal time = Observed operator performance time × Performance rating

In the above example, denoting normal time by NT,

$$NT = 2(1.2) = 2.4 \text{ minutes}$$

When an operator is observed for a period of time, the number of units he produces during this time, along with his performance rating, give the normal time as

$$NT = \frac{\text{Time worked}}{\text{Number of units produced}} \times \text{Performance rating}$$

"Standard time" is derived by adding allowances to "normal time" for personal needs (washroom and coffee breaks, etc.), unavoidable work delays (equipment breakdown, lack of materials, etc.), and worker fatigue (physical or mental). Two such equations are

Standard time = Normal time + (Allowances × Normal time)

or

$$ST = NT(1 + \text{Allowances}) \tag{1}$$

and

$$ST = \frac{NT}{1 - \text{Allowances}} \tag{2}$$

The first equation is most often used in practice. If one presumes that allowances should be applied to the total working period, then equation 2 is the correct one. To illustrate, suppose that the normal time to perform a task is one minute and that allowances for personal needs, delays, and fatigue total 15 percent; then, by equation 1,

$$ST = 1(1 + 0.15) = 1.15 \text{ minutes}$$

In an eight-hour day, a worker would produce $8 \times 60/1.15$, or 417 units. This implies 417 minutes working and $480 - 417$ (or 63) minutes for allowances.

With equation 2,

$$ST = \frac{1}{1 - 0.15} = 1.18 \text{ minutes}$$

In the same eight-hour day, $8 \times 60/1.18$ (or 408) units are produced with 408 working minutes and 72 minutes for allowances.

As mentioned previously, preparatory to making a time study the task is

broken down into elements or parts. Some general rules for this breakdown are:

1. Define each work element short in duration but long enough so each
   can be timed with a stopwatch and the time can be written down.
2. If the operator works with equipment that runs separately—that is,
   the operator performs a task and the equipment runs independently
   —separate the actions of the operator and of the equipment into
   different elements.
3. Define any delays by the operator or equipment into separate elements.

Figure 11.8 shows a stopwatch time study of a core-making operation.
Note that the operator was rated on his performance for each element separately, although some analysts will simply give a single overall rating. The
times are summed and the result is the normal time for the task. Converting
this normal time to standard time will be discussed below, but first some
consideration should be given to the number of observations that are required in a time study. Should the operator be observed through 10 performances of the task, or through 30, or 100?

Table 11.4 gives a suggested number of observations based on cycle time
and the number of times the cycle occurs annually.[4]

Elemental standard-time data

Elemental standard-time data tables contain performance times for
operations that are common to many applications. The time data within
each table are generally single-time entries that summarize more detailed
analysis obtained through time study, as in the following example.

Suppose a company produces nozzles and we are concerned with establishing time standards for drilling the orifice in each nozzle. There are many
sizes of nozzles, a variety of materials, varied openings with both single and
multiple holes and different-size holes, and a range in the precision of hole
sizes. The number of possible combinations is overwhelming. It should be
obvious that each possible nozzle configuration need not be studied. There
are many similarities among the various nozzles, so that common time-data
tables may be compiled.

The basic procedure for drilling all nozzles may be:

1. Place nozzle in jig, tighten, and position.
2. Insert drill into chuck and prepare to drill hole.
3. Drill hole.
4. Raise drill.
5. Reposition jig.
6. Drill second hole.
7. Repeat 4, 5, and 6 until required holes are drilled.

---

[4] For more precise methods for determining sample sizes, see Barnes, *Motion and
Time Study* reference, p. 359.

FIGURE 11.8

Stopwatch time study of a core-making operation

STUDY NO. 8765

OBSERVATION SHEET

SHEET 1 OF 1 SHEETS

ELEMENTS	SPEED	FEED	UPPER LINE: SUBTRACTED TIME / LOWER LINE: READING 1	2	3	4	5	6	7	8	9	10	11	12	13	14	15	MIN. TIME	AV. TIME	SELECTED TIME	OCC. PER CYCLE	RATING	NORMAL TIME
1. Fill core box with 3 handfuls of sand. Press sand down each time.			.09	.09	.09	.08	.08	.08	.10	.07	.08	.08	.09	.07	.08	.09	.06	.06	.081	.081	1	115	.093
			.09	.41	.71	1.07	.38	.67	.98	.28	.57	.87	.18	.46	.76	4.05	.32						
2. Press sand down with one trowel stroke. Strike off with one trowel stroke.			.06	.05	.08	.06	.05	.05	.06	.05	.05	.06	.06	.05	.05	.06	.06	.05	.059	.059	1	125	.074
			15	.46	.79	.13	.43	.72	2.04	.33	.62	.93	.24	.51	.81	.11	.38						
3. Get and place plate on core box, turn over, rap, and remove box.			.13	.13	.15	.14	.13	.13	.14	.13	.14	.13	.14	.12	.13	.13	.13	.10	.126	.126	1	135	.170
			.28	.59	.94	.27	.56	.85	.18	.46	.76	3.06	.36	.65	.93	.24	.51						
4. Carry plate with core 4 feet. Dispose on oven truck.			.04	.03	.04	.03	.03	.03	.03	.03	.03	.03	.03	.03	.03	.02	.03	.02	.032	.032	1	125	.040
			.32	.62	.98	.30	.59	.88	.21	.49	.79	.09	.39	.68	.96	.26	.54						
(1)			.07	.10	.08	.08	.08	.08	.07	.08	.08	.08	.07	.07	.08	.09	.09						
			.61	.95	.25	.53	.83	.12	.41	.71	7.01	.28	.55	.84	.16	.48	.77						
(2)			.05	.05	.05	.06	.06	.06	.06	.06	.05	.06	.06	.07	.06	.05	.05						
			.66	5.00	.30	.58	.89	.18	.47	.77	.06	.34	.61	.91	.22	.53	.82						
(3)			.14	.13	.12	.13	.12	.13	.13	.12	.11	.12	.13	.13	.14	.13	.13						
			.80	.13	.42	.71	6.01	.31	.60	.89	.17	.46	.74	8.04	.36	.66	.95						
(4)			.05	.04	.03	.04	.03	.03	.03	.04	.03	.02	.03	.04	.03	.02	.03						
			.85	.17	.45	.75	.04	.34	.63	.93	.20	.48	.77	.08	.39	.68	.98						
(1)			.07	.07	.08	.08	.07	.08	.07	.08	.09	.08	.08	.08	.08	.08	.09						
			9.05	.34	.64	.93	.21	.50	.78	11.07	.39	.69	.99	.29	.59	.89	.19						
(2)			.05	.06	.05	.06	.06	.06	.06	.07	.08	.07	.06	.06	.07	.06	.08						
			.10	.40	.69	.99	.27	.57	.84	.14	.47	.76	12.05	.35	.66	.95	.27						
(3)			.14	.13	.13	.11	.12	.11	.11	.12	.10	.12	.12	.13	.12	.12	.11						
			.24	.53	.82	10.10	.39	.68	.95	.26	.57	.88	.17	.48	13.07	.78	.38						
(4)			.03	.03	.03	.04	.03	.03	.03	.04	.04	.03	.03	.03	.03	.03	.03						
			.27	.56	.85	.14	.42	.71	.99	.30	.61	.91	.20	.51	.81	.10	.41						

FOREIGN ELEMENTS:

Tally-by elements

No. 1	No. 2	No. 3	No. 4
.06-J	.05-ЖЖЖJ	.10-J	.02-Ж
.07-ЖЖ	.06-ЖЖЖ-JJ	.11-ЖЖJ	.03-ЖЖЖ-J
	.07-Ж	.12-ЖЖJ	.04-ЖЖЖ-J
	.08-J	.13-ЖЖЖ-J	.05-J
.08-ЖЖ-J/		.14-ЖЖJ	
.09-ЖЖ-J		.15-J	
.10-"			

TOOLS, JIGS, GAUGES, PATTERNS, ETC. ✓

Core box No. C-1D-7253, Size 1⅞"x 3½"x8½", Wt. 1 lb.; 5"Molder's trowel

Plates 4 x 9 ; weight with core 3½ lb. Core sand No. A16

OVERALL RATING	BEGIN	END	ELAPSED	UNITS FINISHED	ACTUAL TIME PER PIECE
125	9:18	9:32	14:00	45	0.31 Min.

From Ralph M. Barnes, *Motion and Time Study* (New York: John Wiley & Sons, 1968), p. 401.

8. Raise drill and remove from chuck.
9. Remove nozzle from jig.

Also, a detailed time study of item 1, "Place nozzle in jig, tighten, and position," may contain the studied elements of

a. Clean jig.
b. Pick up nozzle and place in jig.
c. Tighten right set screw.

d. Tighten front set screw.
e. Position jig under drill.
f. Tighten clamp.

Practice may show that the resulting standard time for placing all nozzles in the jig can be adequately described by three or four size categories. Therefore a standard data table for item 1, "Place nozzle in jig, tighten, and position," may be reduced to a single line with the standard time for each of the three or four sizes.

The time required for element 3, "Drill hole," will depend on three factors: material composition (e.g., brass, steel), drill size and type, and hole depth. Each material composition would constitute a separate part of the table, the vertical column would list drill descriptions and sizes, and the horizontal lines would list hole depths. Thus to find the standard time to drill a hole, one would identify the material, find the appropriate drill size and hole depth, and read off the standard time.

The same procedure is followed for the remainder of the required operations. The standard time for each operation is obtained from a table that has been compiled from earlier time studies. Given the existence of these

TABLE 11.4

Guide to number of cycles to be observed in a time study

	Minimum number of cycles to study (activity)		
When time (hours) per cycle is more than	*Over 10,000 per Year*	*1,000 to 10,000*	*Under 1,000*
8.000............	2	1	1
3.000............	3	2	1
2.000............	4	2	1
1.000............	5	3	2
0.800............	6	3	2
0.500............	8	4	3
0.300............	10	5	4
0.200............	12	6	5
0.120............	15	8	6
0.080............	20	10	8
0.050............	25	12	10
0.035............	30	15	12
0.020............	40	20	15
0.012............	50	25	20
0.008............	60	30	25
0.005............	80	40	30
0.003............	100	50	40
0.002............	120	60	50
under 0.002............	140	80	60

From Benjamin W. Niebel, *Motion and Time Study,* 6th ed. (Homewood, Ill.: Richard D. Irwin, Inc., 1976), p. 325.

standard data tables, the time for drilling any nozzle (whether or not previously produced) may be derived by describing the nozzle configuration and extracting the time from the tables. Such elemental-data tables may be compiled for any series of operations that have commonality among various tasks. This avoids the need for separate time studies.

Predetermined motion-time data systems

To set a standard time for performing a task by using predetermined motion-time systems (PMTS), one divides the total task into elements, rates the difficulty of each element, looks in the tables for the time allowed for each element, and then adds all the element times together. PMTS systems are based on three assumptions:

1. That the time required by many individuals performing the same work element will fall into the bell-shaped normal distribution.
2. That the times required for performance of the separate elements are additive; that is, the expected time required for completion of the total task is equal to the sum of the times required to complete the separate elements.
3. That the time study analyst has the ability to describe accurately the procedure to do the work task, to break down the task into appropriate elements, and to apply the degree of difficulty that correctly determines the allowable fatigue rest time.

The three most often used predetermined motion-time data systems are *methods time measurement* (MTM), *basic motion time study* (BMT), and *work factor*.

To illustrate PMTS data, Table 11.5 presents a sample of MTM data. This table describes the element "reach," stipulating the different times allowed for varying conditions. Companies that are in the consulting business and use PMTS to set time standards for their customers state that their systems are more accurate than stopwatch time study. Their reasoning stems from the fact that PMTS data have been accumulated through observing many individuals and, therefore, each element of data (the time it takes to extend the arm a specified distance, for example) is the average of a large number of observations and highly accurate.

However, there are several challenges to PMTS accuracy. First, the workforce in a specific location may not be the same as the workforce population from which the PMTS data were derived. Second, to set a time standard, the analyst must break down the task into elements and identify them correctly. Different analysts, using the same PMTS system, perceive the job differently and will therefore come up with different element descriptions and, consequently, different times. Third, along with the element breakdown, the analyst must stipulate the degree of difficulty involved in performing that work element. (In the work factor system, this is called a *work factor*, and it indicates the amount of control or weight needed for performance of the task; in the MTM system, this is stated as "cases," which

TABLE 11.5

MTM predetermined motion-time data for the hand and arm movement "reach"

REACH—R							
Distance Moved Inches	Time TMU				Hand In Motion		CASE AND DESCRIPTION
	A	B	C or D	E	A	B	
¾ or less	2.0	2.0	2.0	2.0	1.6	1.6	A Reach to object in fixed location, or to object in other hand or on which other hand rests.
1	2.5	2.5	3.6	2.4	2.3	2.3	
2	4.0	4.0	5.9	3.8	3.5	2.7	
3	5.3	5.3	7.3	5.3	4.5	3.6	B Reach to single object in location which may vary slightly from cycle to cycle.
4	6.1	6.4	8.4	6.8	4.9	4.3	
5	6.5	7.8	9.4	7.4	5.3	5.0	
6	7.0	8.6	10.1	8.0	5.7	5.7	
7	7.4	9.3	10.8	8.7	6.1	6.5	
8	7.9	10.1	11.5	9.3	6.5	7.2	C Reach to object jumbled with other objects in a group so that search and select occur.
9	8.3	10.8	12.2	9.9	6.9	7.9	
10	8.7	11.5	12.9	10.5	7.3	8.6	
12	9.6	12.9	14.2	11.8	8.1	10.1	
14	10.5	14.4	15.6	13.0	8.9	11.5	D Reach to a very small object or where accurate grasp is required.
16	11.4	15.8	17.0	14.2	9.7	12.9	
18	12.3	17.2	18.4	15.5	10.5	14.4	
20	13.1	18.6	19.8	16.7	11.3	15.8	
22	14.0	20.1	21.2	18.0	12.1	17.3	E Reach to indefinite location to get hand in position for body balance or next motion or out of way.
24	14.9	21.5	22.5	19.2	12.9	18.8	
26	15.8	22.9	23.9	20.4	13.7	20.2	
28	16.7	24.4	25.3	21.7	14.5	21.7	
30	17.5	25.8	26.7	22.9	15.3	23.2	

Source: Copyrighted by the MTM Association for Standards and Research. No reprint permission without written consent from the MTM Association, 9–10 Saddle River Road, Fair Lawn, New Jersey 07410.

give the particular times allowed, depending on the precision needed to perform the task or the degree of performance difficulty.) Studies have shown that analysts vary in their ratings of job difficulty. In summary, the combined effects of these factors often result in a significant variation in the standard times derived—differences in the description of what is involved in the job and differences in the difficulty perceived by the analysts.

In practice, many companies use both predetermined motion time analysis and stopwatch time study and compare the results. A practical sequence that is used in industry is to plan operations by using predetermined motion-time data and to follow up with stopwatch time study after the operations have been in existence for a while and operators have become experienced.

Work sampling

As the name suggests, work sampling involves observing a portion or sample of the work activity. Then, based on the findings in this sample, some statements can be made about the activity. For example, if we were to observe a fire department rescue squad at 100 random times during the day and found it to be involved in a rescue mission for 30 of the 100 times (en route, on site, or returning from a cell), we would estimate that the rescue squad spends 30 percent of its time directly on rescue mission calls. (The time it takes to make an observation depends on what is being observed.

Many times only a glance is needed to determine the activity, and the majority of studies require only several seconds' observation.)

Observing an activity even 100 times may not, however, provide the accuracy desired in the estimate. In order to refine this estimate, three main issues must be decided (These points will be discussed later in this section, along with an example):

1. What level of statistical confidence is desired in the results?
2. How many observations are necessary?
3. Precisely when should the observations be made?

The three primary applications for work sampling are

1. *Ratio delay:* to determine the activity-time percentage for personnel or equipment. For example, interest may be in the amount of time a machine is running or idle.
2. *Performance measurement:* to develop a performance index for workers. When the amount of work time is related to the quantity of output, a measure of performance is developed. This is useful for periodic performance evaluation.
3. *Time standards:* to obtain the standard time for a task. When work sampling is used for this purpose, however, the observer must be experienced since he must attach a performance rating to his observations.

The number of observations required in a work sampling study can be fairly large, ranging from several hundred to several thousand, depending on the activity and the desired degree of accuracy. Although the number of observations required in a work sample can be computed from formulas, the easiest way is to refer to a table such as Table 11.6, which gives the number of observations needed for a 95 percent confidence level in terms of absolute error. *Absolute error* is the actual range of the observations. For example, if the percentage of time a clerk is idle is 10 percent and the designer of the study is satisfied with a 2.5 percent range (or the true percentage lies within 7.5 to 12.5 percent), the number of observations required for the work sampling study is 576. A 2 percent error (or an interval of 8 to 12 percent) would require 900 observations.

The steps involved in making a work sampling study are:

1. Identify the specific activity or activities that are the main purpose for the study. For example, a study may be made to determine the percentage of time equipment is working, idle, or under repair.
2. Estimate the proportion of time of the activity of interest to the total time (e.g., that the equipment is working 80 percent of the time). These estimates can be made from the analyst's knowledge, past data, reliable guesses from others, or a pilot work-sampling study.
3. State the desired accuracy in the study results.
4. Determine the specific times when each observation is to be made.
5. At two or three intervals during the study period, recompute the required sample size by using the data collected thus far. Adjust the number of observations as deemed appropriate.

TABLE 11.6: Determining the number of observations required for a given absolute error at various values of p, with a 95% confidence level*

Percentage of total time occupied by activity or delay, p	Absolute error					
	±1.0%	±1.5%	±2.0%	±2.5%	±3.0%	±3.5%
1 or 99.........	396	176	99	63	44	32
2 or 98.........	784	348	196	125	87	64
3 or 97.........	1,164	517	291	186	129	95
4 or 96.........	1,536	683	384	246	171	125
5 or 95.........	1,900	844	475	304	211	155
6 or 94.........	2,256	1003	564	361	251	184
7 or 93.........	2,604	1157	651	417	289	213
8 or 92.........	2,944	1308	736	471	327	240
9 or 91.........	3,276	1456	819	524	364	267
10 or 90.........	3,600	1600	900	576	400	294
11 or 89.........	3,916	1740	979	627	435	320
12 or 88.........	4,224	1877	1056	676	469	344
13 or 87.........	4,524	2011	1131	724	503	369
14 or 86.........	4,816	2140	1204	771	535	393
15 or 85.........	5,100	2267	1275	816	567	416
16 or 84.........	5,376	2389	1344	860	597	439
17 or 83.........	5,644	2508	1411	903	627	461
18 or 82.........	5,904	2624	1476	945	656	482
19 or 81.........	6,156	2736	1539	985	684	502
20 or 80.........	6,400	2844	1600	1024	711	522
21 or 79.........	6,636	2949	1659	1062	737	542
22 or 78.........	6,864	3050	1716	1098	763	560
23 or 77.........	7,084	3148	1771	1133	787	578
24 or 76.........	7,296	3243	1824	1167	811	596
25 or 75.........	7,500	3333	1875	1200	833	612
26 or 74.........	7,696	3420	1924	1231	855	628
27 or 73.........	7,884	3504	1971	1261	876	644
28 or 72.........	8,064	3584	2016	1290	896	658
29 or 71.........	8,236	3660	2059	1318	915	672
30 or 70.........	8,400	3733	2100	1344	933	686
31 or 69.........	8,556	3803	2139	1369	951	698
32 or 68.........	8,704	3868	2176	1393	967	710
33 or 67.........	8,844	3931	2211	1415	983	722
34 or 66.........	8,976	3989	2244	1436	997	733
35 or 65.........	9,100	4044	2275	1456	1011	743
36 or 64.........	9,216	4096	2304	1475	1024	753
37 or 63.........	9,324	4144	2331	1492	1036	761
38 or 62.........	9,424	4188	2356	1508	1047	769
39 or 61.........	9,516	4229	2379	1523	1057	777
40 or 60.........	9,600	4266	2400	1536	1067	784
41 or 59.........	9,676	4300	2419	1548	1075	790
42 or 58.........	9,744	4330	2436	1559	1083	795
43 or 57.........	9,804	4357	2451	1569	1089	800
44 or 56.........	9,856	4380	2464	1577	1095	804
45 or 55.........	9,900	4400	2475	1584	1099	808
46 or 54.........	9,936	4416	2484	1590	1104	811
47 or 53.........	9,964	4428	2491	1594	1107	813
48 or 52.........	9,984	4437	2496	1597	1109	815
49 or 51.........	9,996	4442	2499	1599	1110	816
50.............	10,000	4444	2500	1600	1111	816

* Number of observations is obtained from the formula for the distribution of a proportion:

$$Sp = 2 \sqrt{\frac{p(1-p)}{N}} \quad \text{or, in terms of } N, \quad N = \frac{4p(1-p)}{Sp^2}$$

where
Sp = Desired absolute accuracy
p = Percentage occurrence of activity or delay being measured
N = Number of random observations (sample size)
2 = Number of standard deviations to give desired confidence level (95% $\cong$ 2 standard deviations)

From a procedural standpoint, the number of observations to be taken in a work sampling study is usually divided equally over the study period. Thus if 500 observations are to be made over a 10-day period, the observations are usually scheduled at 500/10, or 50 per day. Each day's observations are then assigned a specific time by using a random number table.

Work sampling applied to nursing. There has been a long-standing argument that a large amount of nurses' hospital time is spent on non-nursing activities. This, the argument goes, creates an apparent shortage of well-trained nursing personnel, a significant waste of talent, a corresponding loss of efficiency, and increased hospital costs, since nurses' wages are the highest single cost in the operation of a hospital. Further, pressure is growing for hospitals and hospital administrators to contain costs. With the above in mind, let us use work sampling to test the hypothesis that a large portion of nurses' time is spent on nonnursing duties.

Assume at the outset that we have made a list of all the activities that are part of nursing and will make our observations in only two categories: nursing and nonnursing activities. (An expanded study could list *all* nursing activities to determine the portion of time spent in each.)[5] Therefore when we observe a nurse during the study and find her performing one of the duties on the nursing list, we simply place a tally mark in the nursing column. If we observe her doing anything besides nursing, we place a tally mark in the nonnursing column.

We can now proceed to plan the study. Assume that our estimate (or the estimate of the nursing supervisor) is that nurses spend 60 percent of their time in nursing activities. Assume, further, that we would like to be 95 percent confident that the findings of our study will be within the absolute error range of plus or minus 3 percent; that is, that if our study shows nurses spend 60 percent of their time on nursing duties, we are 95 percent confident that the true percentage lies between 57 and 63 percent. From Table 11.6, we find that 1,067 observations are required for 60 percent activity time and ±3 percent error. If our study is to take place over 10 days, we will start with 107 observations per day.

In order to determine when each day's observations are to be made, we use a random number table in a manner similar to the example in the simulation supplement to Chapter 6. If the study extends over an eight-hour shift, we can assign numbers to correspond to each consecutive minute.[6] The list in Table 11.7 shows the assignment of numbers to corresponding minutes. For simplicity, since each number corresponds to one minute, a three-number scheme is used wherein the second and the third number correspond to the minute of the hour. A number of other schemes would also be appropriate.[7]

---

[5] Actually, there is much debate on what constitutes nursing activity. For instance, is talking to a patient a nursing duty?

[6] For this study, it is likely that the night shift (11 P.M. to 7 A.M.) would be run separately since the nature of nighttime nursing duties is considerably different from daytime duties.

[7] If a number of studies are planned, a computer program may be used to generate a randomized schedule for the observation times.

TABLE 11.7

Time	Assigned numbers
7:00– 7:59 A.M.	100–159
8:00– 8:59 A.M.	200–259
9:00– 9:59 A.M.	300–359
10:00–10:59 A.M.	400–459
11:00–11:59 A.M.	500–559
12:00–12:59 A.M.	600–659
1:00– 1:59 P.M.	700–759
2:00– 2:59 P.M.	800–859

If we refer to a random number table and list three-digit numbers, we can assign each number to a time. The random numbers shown in Table 11.8 demonstrate the procedure.

This procedure is followed to generate 107 observation times, and the times are rearranged chronologically for ease in planning. Rearranging the times determined in Table 11.8 gives the total observations per day shown in Table 11.9.

TABLE 11.8

Random number	Corresponding time from the preceding list
669	nonexistent
831	2:31 P.M.
555	11:55 A.M.
470	nonexistent
113	7:13 A.M.
080	nonexistent
520	11:20 A.M.
204	8:04 A.M.
732	1:32 P.M.
420	10:20 A.M.

To be perfectly random in this study, we should also "randomize" the nurse we observe each time (the use of various nurses minimizes the effect of bias). In the study, our first observation is made at 7:13 A.M. for nurse X. We walk into her area and, on seeing her, check either a nursing or a nonnursing activity. Each observation need be only long enough to

TABLE 11.9

Observation	Scheduled time	Nursing activity (√)	Non-nursing activity (√)
1	7:13 A.M.		
2	8:04 A.M.		
3	10:20 A.M.		
4	11:20 A.M.		
5	11:55 A.M.		
6	1:32 P.M.		
7	2:31 P.M.		

determine the class of activity—in most cases only a glance. At 8:04 A.M. we observe nurse Y. We continue in this way to the end of the day and the 107 observations. At the end of the second day (and 214 observations), we decide to check for the adequacy of our sample size.

Let's say we made 150 observations of nurses working and 64 of them not working, which gives 70.1 percent working. From Table 11.6, this corresponds to 933 observations. Since we have already taken 214 observations, we need take only 719 over the next eight days, or 90 per day.

When the study is half over, another check should be made. For instance, if days 3, 4, and 5 showed 55, 59, and 64 working observations, the cumulative data would give 328 working observations of a total 484, or a 67.8 percent working activity. Table 11.6 shows the sample size to be about 967, leaving 483 to be made—at 97 per day—for the following five days. Another computation should be made before the last day to see if another adjustment is required. If after the tenth day several more observations are indicated, these can be made on day 11.

If at the end of the study we find that 66 percent of nurses' time is involved with what has been defined as nursing activity, there should be an analysis to identify the remaining 34 percent (actually, the 95 percent confidence limits are from 63 to 69 percent as the true value). Approximately 12 to 15 percent is justifiable for coffee breaks and personal needs, which leaves 20 to 22 percent of the time that must be justified and compared to what the industry considers ideal levels of nursing activity. To identify the nonnursing activities, a more detailed breakdown could have been originally built into the sampling plan. Otherwise, a follow-up study may be in order.

Setting time standards using work sampling.

As mentioned earlier, work sampling can be used to set time standards. To do this, the analyst must record the subject's performance rate (or index) along with working observations. The additional data required and the formula for calculating standard time are given in Figure 11.9.

FIGURE 11.9

Deriving a time standard using work sampling

Information	*Source of data*	*Data for one day*
Total time expended by operator (working time and idle time)	Time cards	480 min.
Number of parts produced	Inspection Department	420 pieces
Working time in percent	Work sampling	85%
Idle time in percent	Work sampling	15%
Average performance index	Work sampling	110%
Total allowances	Company time-study manual	15%

$$\text{Standard time per piece} = \frac{\binom{\text{Total time}}{\text{in minutes}} \times (\text{Working time}) \times (\text{Performance index})}{\text{Total number of pieces produced}} \times \frac{1}{1 - \text{Allowances}}$$

$$= \left(\frac{480 \times 0.85 \times 1.10}{420}\right) \times \left(\frac{1}{1 - 0.15}\right) = 1.26 \text{ minutes}.$$

Source: R. M. Barnes, *Work Sampling,* 2d ed. (New York: John Wiley & Sons, 1966), p. 81.

Advantages of work sampling over time study.

1. Several work sampling studies may be conducted simultaneously by one observer.
2. The observer need not be a trained analyst, unless the purpose of the study is to determine a time standard.
3. No timing devices are required.
4. Work of a long cycle time may be studied with fewer observer hours.
5. The duration of the study is longer, so that the effects of short period variations are minimized.
6. The study may be temporarily delayed, at any time, with little effect.
7. Since work sampling needs only instantaneous observation (made over a longer period), the operator has less chance to influence the findings by changing his work method.

When the cycle time is short, time study, rather than work sampling, is more appropriate. One drawback of work sampling is that it does not provide as complete a breakdown of elements as time study. Another difficulty with work sampling is that observers, rather than follow a random sequence of observations, tend to develop a repetitive route of travel. This may allow the time of the observations to be predictable and thus invalidate the findings. A third factor—a potential drawback—is that the basic assumption in work sampling is that all observations pertain to the same static system. If the system is in the process of change, work sampling may give misleading results.

Work physiology

In addition to its use in job design, work physiology, using the indices of energy expenditure and heart rate, is equally applicable to setting time standards for moderate to heavy tasks. To show the procedure involved, we will use a carton-handling example similar to the one discussed in Chapter 10. This work task involves stacking 25-pound cartons from a waist-high level to a 66-inch height. To set a standard for this task using the index of energy expenditure in calories per minute, we would take energy expenditure readings over a range of work speeds for each operator who is to perform the task. From this data we would compute the individual and average energy expenditure for all operators at each work pace. Then that carton-handling rate that corresponds to five calories per minute (the generally acceptable level of sustainable work activity) would be selected as the standard pace. This pace, in turn, would be converted to minutes per carton, which, when personal and delay allowances are added, becomes the time standard.[8]

Figure 11.10 illustrates the individual and average data for six workers performing the task at three different paces. As can be seen from the graph, the energy requirements for each worker are almost linearly correlated with work pace, which permits accurate caloric estimation for work paces

---

[8] An identical procedure would be followed if we use heart rate data with 115 heart beats per minute as the sustainable level of work activity.

FIGURE 11.10

Energy expenditure versus work pace in waist-high table to head-high
table study (25-pound carton)

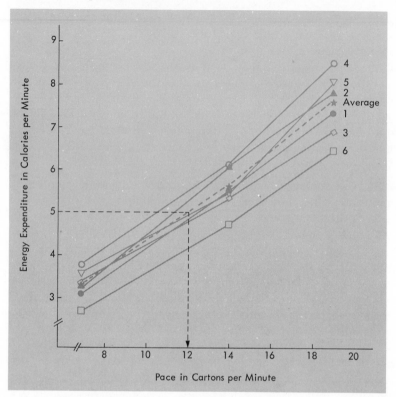

that have not actually been tried. The standard pace is obtained by extending a horizontal line from the 5-caloric point on the ordinate to the
average line, and by dropping a vertical line to the abscissa. This indicates
a pace of 12 cartons per minute, or a standard time (exclusive of personal
and delay allowances) of 0.083 minutes per carton.

While work physiology has been employed to some extent in setting time
standards, its real potential has yet to be recognized by a number of industries that could benefit by its use, because industrial engineers who set
standards are not generally exposed to work physiology in their training,
and because the equipment required to perform work physiology studies is
expensive and sophisticated. Nevertheless, the future should see more widespread application of the techniques—if only because there is no other
scientific way of ascertaining the physical cost of work.[9]

---

[9] One of the authors performed a study to test the validity of stopwatch time study
and two predetermined motion-time data systems when applied to moderate and strenuous work. When the tasks were performed at standard times, energy expenditure levels of
the workers varied widely, ranging from about half to more than double the recommended physiological levels. See Nicholas J. Aquilano, "A Physiological Evaluation of
Time Standards for Strenuous Work as Set by Stopwatch Time Study and Two Predetermined Motion Time Data Systems," *Journal of Industrial Engineering*, vol. 19,
no. 9 (September 1968), pp. 425–32.

Unresolved problems

Over the years since time study was first introduced, there has been continual debate on several aspects of work measurement. The most controversial aspects are (1) rating performance, (2) time allowance, and (3) machine-controlled operations.

Rating performance.   When a time study analyst observes an operator performing a work task, he notes two measurements: the time the operator takes to do the work and the speed at which he does it. The first is purely an objective measurement; times are read from a clock or stopwatch. The second measurement is mostly subjective; while the operator is performing the work task, the analyst estimates his speed as compared to a "normal" speed. On the basis of 100 percent as normal performance, an operator performing at 25 percent greater than normal would be given a performance rating of 125 percent. If he is 10 percent below normal, he would be rated at 90 percent. There are two questions here: What is "normal"? and How can the analyst judge how well an operator performs against this "normal"?

Any definition of normal performance is filled with ambiguity, but perhaps this concept can be clarified somewhat. There is variation in nature and among men, so that performance capabilities vary, but these variations can be plotted so as to yield the statistical normal distribution. Further—if we disregard the few extreme cases—there is about a two-to-one ratio; that is, the best performances are about twice as good as the poorest. Figure 11.11 shows a normal distribution of what would be expected if a large number of workers performed a particular work task. Some would be slow, and some fast, but the large majority would perform at about the average, and the output of the fastest would be about twice that of the slowest.

Given this phenomenon, what should we consider normal output? Intuitively, it would seem that "normal" should correspond to average performance, but this is not the case. Convention has established normal speed as the pace that can be exceeded by 96 or 97 percent of the worker popu-

FIGURE 11.11

Expected performance of a large number of workers

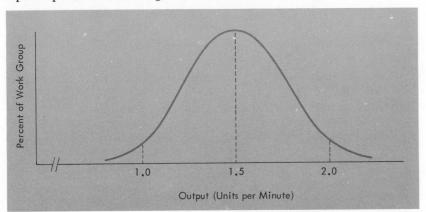

Output (Units per Minute)

FIGURE 11.12

Comparison of average standard times for each time study engineer (data grouped
by companies from which the time study engineers came)

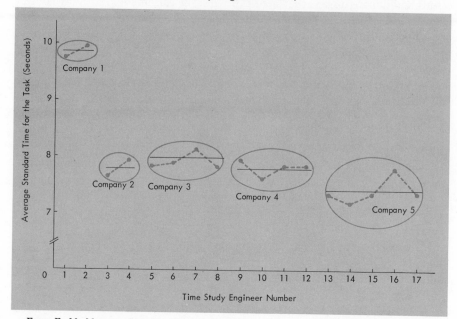

From E. M. Mansoor, "An Investigation into Certain Aspects of Rating Practice," *Journal of
Industrial Engineering,* vol. 12, no. 2 (February 1967), p. 188.

lation (although the workers must be qualified for the job and work according to the prescribed method).

The mechanics of establishing the normal time is a real problem. While
the analyst is observing an operator and noting performance time, he must
also judge how fast or how slowly that operator is working compared to
"normal." The accuracy of this rating depends to a great extent on the
ability and experience[10] of the analyst. Some companies have established a
policy of having their time study analysts, as a group, periodically rate
several operations and compare their ratings. This gives them a chance to
"rezero" their concept of normal time. Another approach is to have short
retraining programs in which the analysts view films that show various
operations and specify the accepted normal time to perform them.

It is interesting to note that the concepts of normal and standard time
vary among companies. This is undoubtedly due to training within the
company and analysts' working closely with each other. Figure 11.12 shows
the standard time developed for a task by 17 time study analysts from
five different companies. Each analyst had observed 15 repetitions by eight

---

[10] Experience is no guarantee, however. A study involving experienced time-study
analysts from the United Kingdom and Israel showed that highly trained specialists
were unable to detect partially trained workers or differences in small motion sequences.
(See H. Gershoni, "An Analysis of Time Study Based on Studies Made in the United
Kingdom and Israel," *AIIE Transactions,* vol. 1, no. 3, September 1969, pp. 244–51.

operators, for a total of 120 observations of the same task. Notice that *within* each company the analysts more or less agreed on the standard time, but the differences *among* companies are significant.

Time allowance. To the normal time an analyst determines for a task, he adds "allowances" to account for the personal needs of the individual and variation in the system. Although there are differences throughout industry, the total allowances typically amount to about 15 percent. This includes personal time (washup, coffee breaks, etc.), a moderate delay in obtaining work materials, and some rest time (more as diversion from boredom rather than from fatigue). The standard time for average, light industrial tasks is therefore about 115 percent of normal time.

When the environment in which the worker performs has some adverse elements, or when the work is physically demanding, additional time is needed by the worker for recovery.

The kinds of activities that would warrant physiologically based rest allowances are visually demanding or mentally fatiguing, entail uncomfortable body position, require special devices or protective clothing, are physically fatiguing for the total body (generalized) or physically fatiguing through repeated use of specific body members[11] (localized, as fingers in typing or arms in reaching).

When the work task is moderate to heavy in physical demand, the determination of rest allowance for fatigue becomes crucial. Many jobs are sufficiently demanding to require the worker to spend half or more of the time just recovering from fatigue. The methods that currently are used to determine this rest time are quite arbitrary, and analysts use a table such as Table 11.10, which is purported to allow proper rest time. Tables such as this have been developed on a trial-and-error basis and offer allowances that seem to be satisfactory. However, since this table is based on averages, many applications will result in standard times that are too long (loose) or too short (tight). The most accurate method for determining appropriate rest allowance for work that is physically fatiguing seems to be the measurement of heart rate and oxygen consumption (as described in this chapter under "Work Physiology").

Machine-controlled operations. When a worker performs manual or mental tasks independently and with a continual supply of available work at his work station, his performance is left to his own discretion. When he is committed to interact with equipment, however, his rate of output also depends on the equipment with which he is working. If an operator inputs data to a time-sharing computer terminal, a time standard can be derived for the operator in developing and inputting data and for readout, but he has no control of the speed of the computer's portion of the operation. Thus any attempt to rate the performance of the operator/terminal system may do injustice if this is to be used as the basis of a wage incentive plan. Simi-

---

[11] Science marches on: A study of 181 female right-handed operators in the electromechanical and confectionary industries showed that long, thick fingers are related to high productivity. See G. Salvendy, "Hand Size and Assembly Performance," *AIIE Transactions,* vol. 3, no. 1, March 1971, pp. 32–36.

TABLE 11.10

Rest allowances (in percentage) for various classes of work

1. Constant allowances:
   - a. Personal allowance...................................... 5
   - b. Basic fatigue allowance.......................... 4
2. Variable allowances:
   - A. Standing allowance................................. 2
   - B. Abnormal position allowance:
     - a. Slightly awkward.............................. 0
     - b. Awkward (bending)............................ 2
     - c. Very awkward (lying, stretching)............... 7
   - C. Use of force, or muscular energy (lifting, pulling, or pushing:
       Weight lifted (pounds):

5	0
10	1
15	2
20	3
25	4
30	5
35	7
40	9
45	11
50	13
60	17
70	22

   - D. Bad light:
     - a. Slightly below recommended................... 0
     - b. Well below................................ 2
     - c. Quite inadequate........................... 5
   - E. Atmospheric conditions (heat and humidity):
       Variable...................................... 0–10
   - F. Close attention:
     - a. Fairly fine work............................. 0
     - b. Fine or exacting............................ 2
     - c. Very fine or very exacting.................... 5
   - G. Noise level:
     - a. Continuous
     - b. Intermittent—loud.......................... 2
     - c. Intermittent—very loud...................... 5
     - d. High pitched—loud.......................... 5
   - H. Mental strain:
     - a. Fairly complex process....................... 1
     - b. Complex or wide span of attention.............. 4
     - c. Very complex............................... 8
   - I. Monotony:
     - a. Low...................................... 0
     - b. Medium................................... 1
     - c. High..................................... 4
   - J. Tediousness:
     - a. Rather tedious.............................. 0
     - b. Tedious................................... 2
     - c. Very tedious............................... 5

From Niebel, *Motion and Time Study*, p. 380.

larly, consider the machinist who loads work into a numerically controlled machine tool: once he pushes the button and the tape or card drive takes over, he no longer can affect output. The question, then, is How, on an incentive basis, should the operators in such situations be paid?

Three practices that have been used are (1) pay the operator at his incentive rate when he works and at his base rate while the equipment operates; (2) pay the operator for the entire time at the incentive rate he attained during his work time; (3) develop time standards for the entire man-machine operation and pay the operator on an incentive basis.

The problem with plan 1 is that the operator's incentive rate is diluted. For example, if the time is distributed equally between operator and machine control, to obtain a 25 percent premium pay the operator would have to work at a 150 percent rate, or 50 percent above normal during his half of the cycle. While he can do some planning, preparation, and resting during the machine cycle, which would allow him some advantage in performing above 25 percent, it would be an injustice to expect him to perform fully 50 percent faster.

Under plan 2, to pay the operator for the entire cycle at his performance level during his work portion gives him an unfair advantage. A standard rate includes personal time, fatigue time, and some delay time. While the equipment is operating, he has time to rest as well as prepare for his next operation, and under these conditions he would be expected to be able to perform at a higher rate. The criticism of plan 3 is similar to that of plan 1: the operator may not be able to increase his output significantly during the equipment portion of the cycle.

The best plan to use when there is a significant machine control portion of the cycle is a *multi*factor system. Such systems pay the operator on the bases of his speed of performance, accuracy, and machine or equipment utilization. The more expensive the equipment, the greater the weight given to keeping the equipment running.[12]

WAGE INCENTIVE PLANS

For the majority of people in our workforce, money remains a strong—if not the strongest—motivator. In this section we will consider some of the common wage incentive plans that attempt to relate man's desire for additional income to the firms' need for productive efficiency.

There is no clear-cut way to categorize wage incentive plans. One possibility is to classify plans into those that are established by management and into participative plans, in which workers play a large part. The first includes the traditional plans, which have time or unit production as the basis. The participative plans may use the same measurements, but they differ in that worker committees perform a great deal of the design and analysis. Plans in each category will now be examined more closely.

---

[12] For a discussion of incentive standards based upon reducing downtime, see C. F. James, "Incentives for Machine Paced Operations, *Industrial Engineering,* vol. 7, no. 9, September 1975, pp. 52–55.

Plans established by management

Four subcategories of plans under this heading are:

1. Plans based on time worked.
2. Plans based on work output.
3. Plans based on either (1) or (2) that have some provision for gain sharing or bonuses.
4. Plans based on general performance of the worker or the firm over an extended time period, that is, indirect payment plans and "fringe benefits."

Table 11.11 lists each of these subcategories with several of the best-known plans.

Time-based plans. In this class, the straight pay rates (hourly, daily, or weekly) are payments to the worker in direct relationship to time spent on the job. Thus if the hourly rate is $4.50 per hour and a worker puts in a 40-hour week, he receives his week's pay of 40 × $4.50, or $180. Variations of this plan, now rarely used, had rates hinged to productivity and incorporating different hourly rates for different levels of output.

Piece rate plans. Here a worker is paid strictly on the basis of performance. A straight piece rate pays for the number of units completed. If a worker completes 100 units a day and the rate is $0.30 per unit, his earnings are $0.30 × 100, or $30.

Of historical interest is the "differential piece rate" plan developed by Frederick W. Taylor. This plan has two piece rates: a low rate and a high rate. Its objective is to encourage workers to produce at a level above an established breakpoint by paying a higher piece rate for such production. To illustrate, the standard output might be 80 units per day; the rate below 80 might be $0.275 per unit and, above 80, $0.35 per unit. Thus if a worker produced 70 units, his pay would be $19.75. A worker producing 90 units would earn $31.50. The increase of 20 units from 70 to 90 (about 29 percent) results in a greater than proportionate increase in pay ($19.75 to $31.50, or about 65 percent). Taylor's plan had no "bottom" wage, whereas other plans, such as the Manchester plan, guaranteed the worker a minimum daily wage.

TABLE 11.11

Wage payment plans for direct labor

Type of plan	Method of payment
Time based..........	Straight hourly or day rate, straight salary
Piece rate............	Straight piece rate, Taylor differential piece rate, Manchester plan
Gain sharing or bonus...........	Halsey plan, Rowan plan, Gantt task and bonus plan, measured day rate, 100 percent bonus (most used)
Indirect payments (fringe benefits)....	Yearly bonus, profit sharing, pension plans, stock distribution, paid insurance, holidays, vacations

A minimum wage plan (Manchester type) is in common use today. Such plans are desirable where, for example, a new employee is learning his job or where conditions beyond the worker's control often prevent production (through a lack of materials, power, etc.). To illustrate, assume a worker's base hourly rate is $3 per hour and during the week he works on a variety of jobs, each with a different piece rate. On each of these jobs he is guaranteed at least his base rate. If he makes the rate, he is paid at the piece rate. Now suppose the worker completes a job consisting of 25 pieces, at a rate of $0.60 per piece, in four hours. His wages would be the larger of his base rate ($4 \times \$3 = \$12$) or his piece rate ($25 \times \$0.60 = \$15$). Thus in this case he would be paid $15 for the four hours' work.

Gain sharing or bonus plans. Plans in this category guarantee a base rate and divide any amount in excess of this base between management and the worker. Among such plans are the Halsey plan, which guarantees the standard rate and shares higher output on a 50–50 or ⅓–⅔ basis between the worker and management; the Rowan plan, which is similar to the Halsey plan, except that it pays at a decreasing rate and has an upper limit of twice the standard rate; and the Gantt task and bonus plan, which pays a man a guaranteed day rate as a minimum, with a 20–50 percent premium for higher performance. Although quite popular around the turn of the century, these plans are no longer widely used.

Measured day work is used today and is gaining in popularity. It is similar to other plans in rewarding increased production, but the major difference is a longer period for measurement—one to three months. If the policy is to measure work over a two-month period, for example, a worker's performance is tabulated and this establishes his pay rate for the next two-month period. His performance during the next two-month period determines his pay rate for the third two-month period, etc. The advantage of this plan, from a worker's standpoint, is that his paycheck remains relatively constant and a few bad days during the period may be made up.

Indirect payments. Most of the entries in this category are familiar fringe benefits: extra holidays, vacations, company-paid insurance premiums, relocation allowances, company contributions to pension plans, etc. When nonproductive time is included (rest breaks, coffee breaks, washup, and so forth), fringe benefits throughout industry average about 25 percent of each employee's wages.

There are a variety of other incentive plans, such as stock options, stock warrants, bonuses, interest-free loans, etc., but in general they are not worker oriented; rather, they are intended to attract and hold top management.

Participative plans

There has been a long-standing attitude on the part of some companies that employees should participate in matters that affect their pay, such as work methods design, job evaluation, wage rates, and evaluation of output.

A number of approaches have been made so as to involve workers. The Scanlon and Kaiser plans are the best known; the Eastman Kodak plan is the most recent (though not yet widely publicized).

Scanlon plan.   In the late 1930s the Lapointe Machine and Tool Company was on the verge of bankruptcy, but through the efforts of union president Joseph Scanlon and company management, a plan was devised to save the company by reducing labor cost. In essence, this plan starts with the normal labor cost within the firm. Workers are rewarded as a group for any reductions in labor cost below this "normal" base cost. The plan's success depends on the formation of committees of workers throughout the firm whose purpose is to search out areas for cost saving and to devise or suggest ways for improvement. Highly successful results have led to the adoption of this plan by a wide variety of firms.[13]

Kaiser plan.   The Kaiser plan was introduced in 1963[14] and was revised in 1967. The basic approach of the plan is a sharing not only of labor cost savings, as in the Scanlon plan, but also of savings from any reductions of material and supply costs. Material and supply cost savings are divided 32.5 percent to the workers and 67.5 percent to the firm. A large number of committees are formed throughout the plant to search out and investigate cost-saving methods. Rewards are distributed on a companywide basis, even though adopted suggestions come from individual workers. The observed results for workers range from a 10.6 to a 35 percent premium over their base wage. Additionally, there was a reduction in absenteeism and wildcat strikes.

Eastman Kodak plan.   Barnes describes the premium payment plan used at Eastman Kodak Company.[15] In this plan, a stable wage is paid to workers, replacing the traditional wage incentive plans. Its objective is to bring workers into the discussion of what the goals should be for the individual and the department, how the goals might be attained, and what constitutes a reasonable measure of performance. Wage rates are set at the premium level. Workers, having helped determine the methods, standards, and measures of performance, are expected to produce at that premium rate with less direction. As a result, supervision and paper work have been reduced, incentive rates have been sustained, and there is more satisfaction for each worker through greater participation and self-direction.

CONCLUSION

Despite the fact that work methods and measurement in many schools have been eclipsed in popularity by other topics in operations management, they still have critical importance to the functioning of most productive systems. Certainly, all production planning is based directly or indirectly

---

[13] See A. J. Geare, "Productivity from Scanlon-type Plans," *Academy of Management Review*, Vol. 1, No. 3, July 1976, pp. 99–108.

[14] See "The Kaiser Sharing Plan's First Year," *Conference Board Record*, vol. 1, no. 7 (July 1964).

[15] Barnes, *Motion and Time Study*, pp. 688–701.

on "standards," and even the most democratic work arrangements must achieve some specified output rate if the supporting organization is to compete effectively. In this chapter, we have gone into some detail on concepts that in most manufacturing firms, at least, would lie within the purview of industrial or manufacturing engineers. Nevertheless, it is our strong belief that an understanding of work methods, time study, work sampling, and incentive plans is essential to the practice, if not the theory, of operations management.

PROPOSITIONS

Propositions contrasting services and manufacturing relative to methods, measurement, and wage payment

Product: Because service per unit of time is only weakly associated with service system effectiveness, standards of performance are generally based upon output effectiveness of the service as opposed to the efficient use of inputs. In manufacturing, time is directly related to performance and hence efficient use of inputs as measured by time is the common basis of work standards.

Technology of transformation: In service systems, work methods generally define a portion of the service product and are often variable (as a function of the customer). In manufacturing, work methods can be completely prescribed prior to production and therefore can be fixed across a number of products.

Operating-control system: Because of the points made above, service system work tasks can rarely be as completely rationalized (i.e., precisely specified in terms of work content and work time) as manufacturing work tasks.

Workforce: Because service jobs must include some discretion in task time and work method, service system pay plans are difficult to relate solely to unit output. In manufacturing, it is possible to specify task time and work methods completely; hence, pay plans can be directly related to unit output.

REVIEW AND DISCUSSION QUESTIONS

1. Briefly describe the purposes and main features of a flowchart, operations chart, Simo chart, activity chart, man-machine chart, and gang process chart.
2. Name five ways in which a standard time may be determined for a work task.
3. Which method or methods would you elect to use to develop a time standard for
    A clerk typist?
    A foundry worker?
    An airline pilot flying a plane?

An airline stewardess?

A surgeon performing an operation?

A salesperson selling clothing?

A stock boy restocking shelves in a supermarket?

4. One of the objections workers have to being timed for purposes of setting standards is the process of rating. Do you think this objection is valid?

5. Of four ways to pay workers—based on (1) time worked, (2) amount of output, (3) gain sharing or bonus plans, and (4) fringe benefits—which would be most suitable for: Industrial engineers? Auto mechanics? Sales clerks? Fishermen? Cattle-ranch hands?

6. Summarize what you feel are the good and the bad features of employee participative plans.

7. Comment on the following statements.

   a. "All of our people work at 125 percent of normal pace. In fact, it's a company policy."

   b. "Now that we've introduced job enrichment, we are going to let the workers worry about work methods."

   c. "We don't worry about performance rating since we introduced MTM."

   d. "We feel our policy on fatigue allowances is quite fair. Our material handlers and our lathe operators both get 10 percent."

   e. "Rate cutting is a thing of the past in our shop. If a man produces more than 150 percent of standard, we of course assume that there has been a change in method, and adjust the standard accordingly."

   f. "We're very lucky in our plant: we don't have one worker out of 300 who produces at a rate less than 90 percent of our fastest man."

   g. "Frederick W. Taylor had a great idea when he put his stopwatch inside a hollowed-out book in order to take time studies without being observed. In fact, I think we ought to try it to save hassling with the union over how we set our time standards."

PROBLEMS

1. Visit an auto service shop—either a franchised agency or an independent dealer and, using a flow diagram or process chart, follow several automobiles through the repair facility. Can you make any suggestions on how to reduce handling time, or travel distance?

2. Study a university's mail handling system and construct a flow diagram or flow process chart for incoming and outgoing U.S. mail and for the handling and distribution of campus mail. What improvements might you recommend?

3. At a local hospital, pick a subject and follow it through the system using a flow diagram. The subject may be an incoming patient, an employee going through the hiring and indoctrination process, food or supplies, or a hospital employee's request for vacation. Make suggestions for improvement.

4. Analyze and suggest an efficient procedure for each of the following:

   a. Changing a tire on a car

   b. Making a pot of coffee as rapidly as possible (electric percolator) and putting out the cream, sugar, cups, saucers, etc.

5. Using the principles of motion economy, design a method for a typist to make an original and one carbon copy of a letter, address an envelope, sign and fold the letter, insert it into the envelope, and stamp and seal it. Draw a diagram of the work-place layout.

6. From the standpoint of reducing time, think of the entire procedure for getting out of bed in the morning, showering, getting dressed, eating breakfast, etc. How might you complete the process faster?

7. In keeping with its policy, an insurance office would like to perform a work sampling study to analyze the performance of clerks as to the percentage of time they spend in direct contact with customers. Last year's analysis showed that clerks were in contact with customers by phone or in person for 45 percent of the time.

   a. At a 95 percent confidence level, how many observations would you make to determine the clerk-customer contact for 3 percent absolute error (37–43 percent)?

   b. If you found the new percentage to be 50 percent, would you be content with your sample size in (*a*)?

8. In making a time study of a laboratory technician performing an analysis of processed food in a canning factory, the following times were noted for a particular operation.

Run	Seconds	Run	Seconds
1..........	21	11..........	40
2..........	21	12..........	20
3..........	16	13..........	18
4..........	20	14..........	19
5..........	19	15..........	23
6..........	16	16..........	15
7..........	22	17..........	18
8..........	20	18..........	20
9..........	19	19..........	19
10..........	19	20..........	21

It is your judgment that the technician is working faster than normal at about 120 percent. If company policy for allowances (personal, fatigue, etc.) stipulates 10 percent,

   a. Determine the normal time.

   b. Determine the standard time.

   c. If the technician is paid at $3.00 per hour, what would the earned rate be under a 100 percent plan?

9. The accounting department of a hospital wishes to set a standard for its billing clerks. A study has been performed on the job resulting in the information presented below. Develop a standard providing for 20 percent allowances. (The study was performed using the *continuous* method of timing and readings are in 100ths of minutes)

Element	Cycle				Performance rating in percent
	1	*2*	*3*	*4*	
Get envelopes..........	10		68		90
Get/insert bills........	20	44	78	100	100
Enclose bill and seal envelope........	32	56	89	115	95

10. A work sampling study was made of an order-clerk in order to estimate the percentage of the total week that she spent on each activity (results listed below). In addition to classifying the order-clerk's activity, the observer rated her performance level whenever a sampling observation found her doing one of the productive activities. Since all order forms carried consecutive preprinted numbers, it was an easy matter to determine how many orders the order-clerk wrote. Assume that such a check revealed that the order-clerk under study wrote 583 orders during the week of the sampling study. Further assume that on the basis of the sampling study, it is determined that the averages of the performance ratings made of her working pace for the four productive activities are those given above. The company policy is to give a personal allowance of 10 percent of the normal time for all office work. From the results of the sampling study, the assumptions given above and the fact that the order-clerk worked a total of 40 hours during the week covered by the sampling study, determine the standard time (minutes per order) for the order writing operations.

Activity	Actual percentage of week	Average performance rating (normal = 100%)
Order writing	52.5%	80%
Filing	12.5%	90%
Walking	15.0%	75%
Receiving instructions	9.6%	100%
Idle	10.4%	—
	100.0%	

11. It is estimated that a bank teller spends about 10 percent of her time in a particular type of transaction. The bank manager would like a work sampling study performed that will show, within plus-or-minus 3 percent, whether the clerk's time is really 10 percent (i.e., from 7 to 13 percent). The manager is well satisfied with a 95 percent confidence level.

   From Table 11.6 you observe that, for the first "cut" at the problem, a sample size of 400 is indicated for the 10 percent activity time and plus-or-minus 3 percent absolute error.

   State how you would perform the work sampling study. If the study were to be made over a five-day week from the hours of 9 to 5, specify the exact time (in minutes increments) that you would make Monday's observations.

12. Sample observations of an industrial job were obtained over a 40-hour week. During the week the worker produced a total of 280 assemblies and was rated at 135 percent performance. Further, the sample showed that the worker was working during 80 percent of the time. Allowances for this type of work total 10 percent.

   a. Determine the normal time for the task.

   b. Determine the standard time.

13. A worker's base rate is $4 per hour. If he produces 120 units above the standard of 480 units, determine his earnings for an eight-hour day under

   a. A 50–50 gain sharing plan.

   b. A 100 percent premium payment plan.

SELECTED BIBLIOGRAPHY

Aquilano, Nicholas J. "A Physiological Evaluation of Time Standards for Strenuous Work as Set by Stopwatch Time Study and Two Predetermined Motion-Time Data Systems," *Journal of Industrial Engineering*, Vol. 19, No. 9 (September 1968), pp. 425–32.

————. "Why IE's Can't Measure Fatigue," *Industrial Engineering* (March 1970), pp. 51–53.

Barnes, Ralph M. *Motion and Time Study: Design and Measurement of Work.* 6th ed. New York: John Wiley & Sons, 1968.

Dunn, J. D., and F. M. Rachel *Wage and Salary Administration,* New York: McGraw-Hill, 1971.

Fitzgerald, Thomas H. "Why Motivation Theory Doesn't Work," *Harvard Business Review* (July–August 1971), pp. 37–44.

Geare, A. J. "Productivity from Scanlon-type Plans," *Academy of Management Review,* Vol. 1, No. 3, July 1976, pp. 99–108.

Hamilton, Bernard J., and Chase, Richard B. "A Work Physiology Study of the Relative Effects of Pace and Weight in a Carton Handling Task," *AIIE Transactions,* Vol. 1, No. 2 (June 1969), pp. 106–11.

Herzberg, F., Mausner, B., and Snyderman, B. B. *The Motivation to Work.* 2nd ed. New York: John Wiley & Sons, 1959.

Hettenhouse, George W. "Compensation Cafeteria for Top Executives," *Harvard Business Review* (September–October 1971), pp. 113–19.

Mundel, Marven E. *Motion and Time Study.* Englewood Cliffs, N.J.: Prentice-Hall, 1960.

Niebel, Benjamin W. *Motion and Time Study.* 6th ed. Homewood, Ill.: Richard D. Irwin, Inc., 1976.

Section four

Startup of the
system

12

System startup

T he period of transition between design of a system and its steady state operation is commonly referred to as the *startup period*. This period is often a "traumatic" time in the life cycle of a productive system since it is here that the separate elements considered in design must be brought together and begin to function as a system. Indeed, not only must such technological components as processing equipment and material handling devices be integrated into an operational whole, but the management subsystems for planning and controlling production, inventory, quality, etc., must be made to articulate properly as well.

In this chapter we will discuss some of the factors that must be considered in achieving the integration of these subsystems and we will present some concepts and techniques that have proved useful for this purpose in the past. In particular, we will consider some alternative organizational arrangements for managing startup, as well as the use of critical path techniques in planning it and learning curves for predicting and monitoring its progress.

STARTUP CONTRASTED WITH DESIGN AND STEADY STATE

Figure 12.1 illustrates the relationship of the startup period to design and steady state operations in terms of product output for a hypothetical productive system.

As a rule, the objective in managing the installation phase is to minimize

FIGURE 12.1

Relationship between design, startup, and steady state and system output for a hypothetical productive system

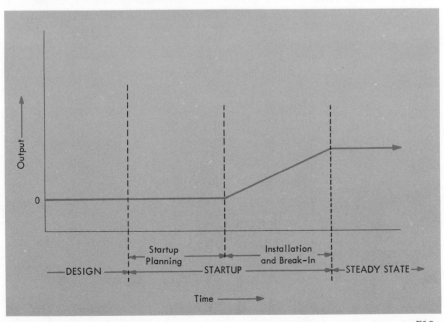

the transition time; that is, to reach full-scale production as soon as possible. However, in certain instances it is desirable to go slowly—so as to permit more careful study of the performance of the system over different output ranges, to allow management and the work force to learn to cope with operating problems when errors are less costly, or to achieve a particular production-inventory balance.

Table 12.1 summarizes some of the key differences between design and startup and steady state operations in terms of workforce skills and the focus of production subsystems. Looking first at the *workforce* entries in the table, we see that management is generally concerned with planning during the design stage, coordinating the work flow and information flow during startup, and monitoring operations during the steady state period. The dashed line in the *labor* row means that operatives rarely participate in the formal design process. Later on, however, during startup, operative skill in handling unforeseen problems and debugging the system is generally required, even though the worker generally is hired to meet the more restricted demands of steady state production activities.

The entries under *focus of the production subsystems* are examples of the key differences in managing design, startup, and steady state activities. As far as startup is concerned, the general emphasis is on dealing with many of the detailed decisions that are only implied by the system design. For example, each machine will have its own peculiarities, and identifying the tolerances that each can achieve and relating these tolerances to quality control limits must be carried out on the basis of shop-floor experimentation. Likewise, establishing specific lot sizes, order points, and

TABLE 12.1

Key differences between design, startup, and steady state

<table>
<tr><th colspan="2"></th><th>DESIGN</th><th>STARTUP</th><th>STEADY STATE</th></tr>
<tr><td rowspan="3">Work Force</td><td colspan="4">Primary Skills of Work Force</td></tr>
<tr><td>Management</td><td>Planning</td><td>Coordinating</td><td>Monitoring</td></tr>
<tr><td>Labor</td><td>------</td><td>Trouble Shooting</td><td>Producing</td></tr>
<tr><td rowspan="8">Subsystems</td><td colspan="4">Focus of Production Subsystems</td></tr>
<tr><td>Processes</td><td>Economic Mix of Equipment</td><td>Identification of Tolerances</td><td>Equipment Maintenance</td></tr>
<tr><td>Facilities</td><td>Layout</td><td>Relocation of Components</td><td>Smooth Flow of Goods</td></tr>
<tr><td>Quality</td><td>Specification of Quality Measures</td><td>Identification of Control Limits</td><td>Economic Sampling Plans</td></tr>
<tr><td>Production Planning</td><td>Information Require-ments and Procedures</td><td>Data Gathering and Information Feedback</td><td>Testing Alternative Strategies</td></tr>
<tr><td>Scheduling</td><td>Methods for Scheduling</td><td>Sequence of Operations</td><td>Determination of Priority</td></tr>
<tr><td>Inventory</td><td>Procedures</td><td>Order Rates, Records, etc.</td><td>Optimal Inventory Level</td></tr>
<tr><td>Task</td><td>Specification of Jobs and Workers</td><td>Selection and Training</td><td>Increasing Output</td></tr>
</table>

buffer stocks for inventory control depend upon observation of actual demand, cost, and production figures. The concept of steady state production of course assumes that the bugs have been worked out of the design, and the emphasis shifts to keeping the system running smoothly.

STARTUP PLANNING

Organizing for implementation

Sometime during the planning period, management must decide on the organizational arrangement whereby it will implement the startup. The broad strategies available to management for this purpose are:

1. Have the same personnel who are to run the system initiate it, following the steady state organization structure.
2. Organize a special startup team composed of representatives of various parts of the operating system and allow it to break the system in.
3. Obtain the services of outside specialists who would either direct operating personnel during the startup period or perform all startup activities with their own personnel.

We will now consider the pros and cons of each of these approaches.

Use of regular personnel.   One advantage of having regular personnel handle startup activities is that they will be learning about the system as it takes shape and thereby will acquire insight into its particular foibles, which will be of great value later on. Of equal or even greater importance is the idea that since operating personnel are responsible for the success of the system in the long run, they should be allowed to "bend and shape" the system during the transition period as well.

The main disadvantage in having operating personnel perform this function is that the skills required during startup may differ substantially from those required during steady state. In many instances the difference between startup and steady state is so vast that we might be viewing two distinct organizations rather than one at different points in time. From this observation it may be argued that completely dissimilar organizational arrangements should be employed for each phase, depending of course upon the nature of the firm and industry being considered. For example, in the steady state operation of an oil refinery, the ability to cut costs and monitor technological processes is paramount, and operating management would likely be selected on the basis of these skills. In contrast, the startup period for a refinery entails a good deal of "fire fighting," demanding fast reactions on the part of management. Hence dissimilar types of organization structures and managerial teams may very well be in order for a refinery, depending upon its stage in the life cycle.

Organizing specific startup teams.   One difference between this approach and the strategy outlined above is that special attention is given to support activities such as maintenance and quality control. This emphasis reflects the obvious truth that equipment problems and product defects are inevitable in any new undertaking. Another difference is that it is typical in certain industries, such as chemicals and petroleum, for the chief operating engineer to assume the directorship of the startup operation—rather than, say, the production manager, who will assume control during steady state operations. This organizational arrangement also reflects the significance of the technological aspects of the startup problem.

The exact composition of the startup team varies with the organization. In starting a chemical plant, for example, it has been suggested that the startup team should consist of the following four groups, under the direction of the chief operating engineer.

1. A technical operating group, composed primarily of graduate engineers chosen especially for the startup
2. A plant management group, which is expected to maintain supervisory and line control over the nontechnical operating personnel and which will assume technical control of the plant when the startup phase is over
3. A maintenance group, which may be part of the normal plant staff but which may be supplemented with additional engineering members for the startup phase
4. A laboratory group, which will be part of the normal plant staff but will be reinforced with additional technical advisers during the startup[1]

Use of outside specialists. A number of construction firms specialize in what are termed *turn-key operations,* in which they assume total responsibility for breaking in, as well as building, a new plant. Their services include hiring and training operating personnel and performing pilot runs in the completed facility. When they turn over the "key" to permanent management, the system—theoretically at least—is ready for full-scale production.

Another approach, also using outside specialists, involves development of mixed startup teams, in which certain skills not possessed by in-house personnel are provided by consulting firms. For example, systems engineering capability is generally required to initiate a computerized control system in a steel plant, but it might be unnecessary or too costly for a steel company to retain systems engineering specialists on a permanent basis.

Developing a startup schedule

Preparation for startup is usually begun during the later phases of design and consists of placing orders for productive resources, installing these resources, and testing the performance of key parts of the productive system. Regarding the order-placing aspects, requests for equipment, supplies, and raw materials must be placed with suppliers; orders for plant services such as water, heat, and electricity must be placed with local utilities; and manpower needs must be filled by transferring personnel from another company plant or recruiting new personnel. Each of these components, in turn, must

---

[1] Manfred Gans and Frank A. Fitzgerald, "Plant Start-Up," Chap. 12 in *The Chemical Plant from Process Selection to Commercial Operation,* Ralph Landau and Alvin S. Cohan, eds. (New York: Reinhold Publishing Corp., 1966), pp. 270–89.

be installed; or in the case of the labor force, it must be trained to operate the equipment and perform the necessary support functions. As far as testing is concerned, the equipment must be debugged, the labor force must be integrated into the work flow, and the production control system must undergo dry runs to check its capability to provide accurate and timely information and to take corrective action.

While it is easy to broadly define these activities, the actual scheduling of a startup is often an extremely complex task, if for no other reason than the sheer volume of order placing, installation, and testing that must be performed. To deal with its complexity, some formal mechanism of planning and control must be employed, and Gantt charts and simple precedence diagrams historically have been used for this purpose. In recent years, however, critical path networks of various types[2] have become increasingly popular and now are considered *de rigueur* in administering startups of even modest complexity.

A number of examples of hypothetical critical path network applications, including three dealing with different plant startup situations, have been published by *Factory* magazine. One of these illustrated a network that might be used by a food processor in making a short-distance move from an urban to a suburban location; another illustrated a network that might be used by a machine tool manufacturer in consolidating several obsolete plants into one new plant; and a third (shown in Figure 12.2) illustrated a network that might be used by an electronics firm in making a cross-country relocation of an existing plant.

In looking at the network properties of this example, we see that it is a PERT-type network since the arrows denote activities and the nodes, events, and the start and completion of certain activities are explained separately.[3] (As mentioned in the supplement, this additional information is required because the PERT technique, unlike the critical path method, may not always indicate the relationship between the completion of one activity and the start of a subsequent one.) Further, a number of dummy time lines are used to preserve proper sequences when one activity does not depend directly on another. Finally, we note that the critical path is not depicted, although applying time estimates to this network should be a straightforward (though perhaps tedious) operation.

Turning to the startup aspects, we observe that this network displays layout, site selection, and building construction, in addition to new plant startup planning and production startup. These phases reflect the special features of this startup situation and, of course, reflect its added complexity over a simple cross-country move or the construction of a new plant. Note that the startup planning phase is under the direction of a project manager who has several "coordinators" reporting to him; so it is essentially the same as the startup team strategy mentioned earlier in the chapter.

---

[2] See the supplement to this chapter for an explanation of the theory and mechanics of these methods.

[3] These starts and completions could be shown as individual nodes in the network, but would increase its size substantially.

FIGURE 12.2

Startup PERT chart

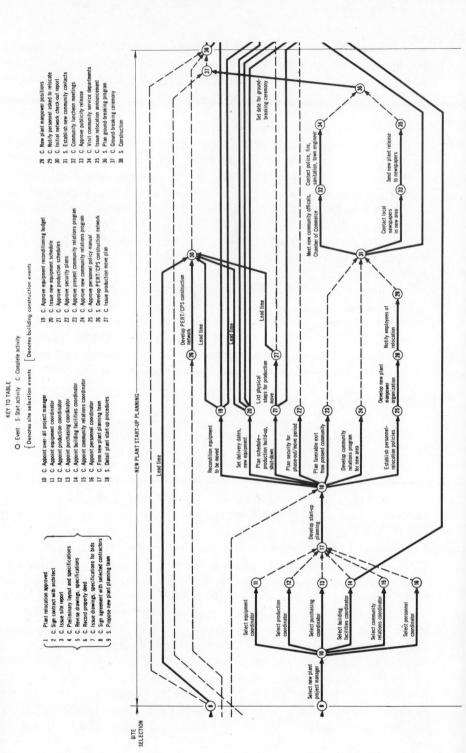

KEY TO TABLE

O - Event   S - Start activity   C - Complete activity

{ Denotes site selection events   [Denotes building construction events

{ Denotes site selection events

1   Plant relocation approved
2   C. Sign contract with architect
3   C. Issue site report
4   C. Preliminary layout and specifications
5   C. Revise drawings, specifications
6   C. Record property deed
7   C. Issue drawings, specifications for bids
8   C. Sign agreement with selected contractors
9   S. Propose new plant planning team

10   C. Appoint over-all project manager
11   C. Appoint equipment coordinator
12   C. Appoint production coordinator
13   C. Appoint purchasing coordinator
14   C. Appoint building facilities coordinator
15   C. Appoint community relations coordinator
16   C. Appoint personnel coordinator
17   C. Form new plant planning team
18   S. Detail plant start-up procedures

19   C. Approve equipment reconditioning budget
20   C. Issue new equipment schedule
21   C. Approve production schedules
22   C. Approve security plans
23   C. Approve present community relations program
24   C. Approve new community relations program
25   C. Approve personnel policy manual
26   S. Develop PERT/CPS construction network
27   C. Issue production move plan

28   C. New plant manpower positions
29   C. Notify personnel asked to relocate
30   C. Initial network check-out report
31   S. Establish new community contacts
32   C. Community luncheon meetings
33   C. Approve publicity release
34   C. Visit community service departments
35   C. Issue relocation announcement
36   S. Plan ground-breaking program
37   C. Ground-breaking ceremony
38   S. Construction

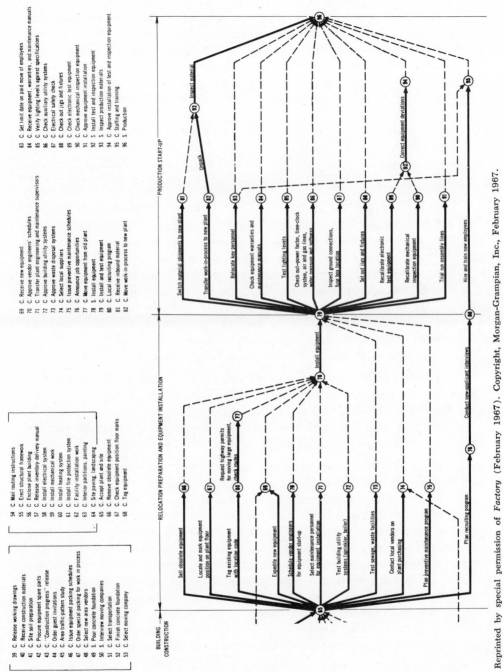

Reprinted by special permission of *Factory* (February 1967). Copyright, Morgan-Grampian, Inc., February 1967.

Also, the importance of lead time in placing orders for equipment, supplies, and internal and external services is reflected in the network by the number of lead-time activity arrows. Further, we can see that the developer of the network was careful to keep the various activities at the same level of abstraction, showing just the primary stages of the project. The development of subnetworks would probably be left to the various coordinators, with the exception of the construction network (activity 26–10), which would probably be developed by the architect with some member of management.

PREDICTING STARTUP PROGRESS: LEARNING CURVES

Determining when steady state and specific transient production levels will be achieved is of great importance in breaking in a productive system. Clearly, the ability to fill customers' orders, build inventory, coordinate transportation services, and perform a number of other vital production functions depends upon a realistic appraisal of production progress over time. A common approach to making this appraisal is the development and analysis of *learning curves*. A learning curve, in its basic form, is simply a line displaying the relationship between unit production time and the number of consecutive units of production.

Learning curve theory is based upon three assumptions:

1. The amount of time required to complete a given task or unit of a product will be less each time the task is undertaken.
2. The unit time will decrease at a decreasing rate.
3. The reduction in time will follow a specific and predictable pattern, such as an exponential function.[4]

Each of these assumptions was found to hold true in the airframe industry, where learning curves were first applied. Specifically, it was observed that, as output doubled, there was a 20 percent reduction in direct production man-hours per unit between doubled units. Thus if it took 100,000 hours for plane 1, it would take 80,000 hours for plane 2, 64,000 hours for plane 4, etc. Since the 20 percent reduction meant that, say, unit 4 took only 80 percent of the production time required for unit 2, the line connecting the coordinates of output and time was referred to as an "80 percent learning curve." (By convention, the percentage learning rate is used to denote any given learning curve.)

A learning curve may be developed from an arithmetic tabulation or by logarithms, depending upon the amount and form of the available data.

Arithmetic tabulation

In following an arithmetic tabulation approach, the number of units produced (proposed or actual) is listed and the corresponding man-hours

---

[4] W. J. Fabrycky, and P. E. Torgersen, *Operations Economy: Industrial Applications of Operations Research* (Englewood Cliffs, N.J.: Prentice-Hall, 1966), p. 100.

TABLE 12.2

Unit, cumulative, and cumulative average direct labor man-hours required for an 80 percent learning curve

(1) Unit number	(2) Unit direct labor man-hours	(3) Cumulative direct labor man-hours	(4) Cumulative average direct labor man-hours
1......	100,000	100,000	100,000
2......	80,000	180,000	90,000
4......	64,000	314,210	78,553
8......	51,200	534,591	66,824
16......	40,960	892,014	55,751
32......	32,768	1,467,862	45,871
64......	26,214	2,392,453	37,382
128......	20,972	3,874,395	30,269
256......	16,777	6,247,318	24,404

Source: W. J. Fabrycky and Paul E. Torgersen, *Operations Economy: Industrial Applications of Operations Research,* © 1966, Prentice-Hall, Inc., p. 100. Reprinted by permission of the publisher.

for each doubled unit level are calculated by multiplying the unit's direct labor man-hours by the selected learning percentage. Thus if we are developing an 80 percent learning curve, we would arrive at the figures listed in column 2 of Table 12.2. Since it is often desirable for planning purposes to know the cumulative average direct labor man-hours, column 4, which lists this information, is also provided. The calculation of these figures is straightforward; for example, for unit 4, cumulative average direct labor man-hours would be found by dividing cumulative direct labor man-hours by 4, yielding the figure given in column 4. These values are plotted in Figure 12.3.

In practice, learning curves are plotted on log-log paper, which results in the unit curves' becoming linear throughout their entire range and the cumulative curve's becoming linear after the first few units. The property of linearity is desirable because it facilitates extrapolation and permits a more accurate reading of the cumulative curve. Figure 12.4 shows the 80 percent curve on logarithmic paper.

While the arithmetic tabulation approach is useful, direct logarithmic analysis of learning curve problems is generally more efficient since it does not require a complete enumeration of successive time-output combinations. Moreover, where such data are not available, an analytical model that uses logarithms may be the most convenient way of obtaining output estimates.

Logarithmic analysis

It may be shown that the mathematical expression for the relationship between direct labor man-hour requirements and the number of units produced is[5]

---

[5] This equation says that the number of direct man-hours required for any given unit is reduced exponentially as more units are produced.

FIGURE 12.3

Arithmetic plot of an 80 percent learning curve

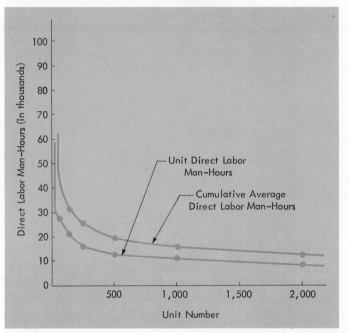

Source: W. J. Fabrycky and Paul E. Torgersen, *Operations Economy: Industrial Applications of Operations Research*, © 1966, Prentice-Hall, Inc., p. 101. Reprinted by permission of the publisher.

$$Y_x = Kx^n$$

where

x = the unit number
Y_x = the number of direct labor man-hours required to produce the xth unit
K = the number of direct labor man-hours required to produce the first unit
n = log b/log 2
b = learning factor

Thus to find the man-hour requirement for the eighth unit in our example (Table 12.2), we would substitute as follows:

$$Y_8 = (100,000)\ (8)^n$$

This may be solved by using logarithms, as follows:

$$Y_8 = 100,000(8)^{\log 0.8/\log 2}$$
$$= 100,000(8)^{-0.322}$$
$$= \frac{100,000}{(8)^{0.322}}$$
$$= \frac{100,000}{1.9535}$$
$$= 51,200$$

FIGURE 12.4

Logarithmic plot of an 80 percent learning curve

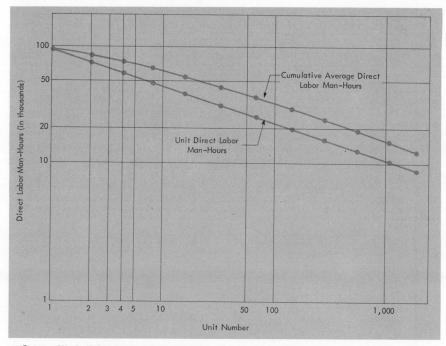

Source: W. J. Fabrycky and Paul E. Torgersen, *Operations Economy: Industrial Applications of Operations Research,* © 1966, Prentice-Hall, Inc., p. 101. Reprinted by permission of the publisher.

Therefore it would take 51,200 hours to make the eighth unit.

Where the learning percentage is known, the table of coefficients originally published by Conway and Schultz can be used to estimate the man-hours required to produce selected units. Use of the table requires that an estimate of man-hours for some base unit be made (Conway and Schultz term this the *ultimate unit,* or ULT) and that a learning percentage be selected. This ultimate unit is then used to estimate the man-hours required for any unit, regardless of whether it is made before or after the ultimate unit.

To illustrate, suppose we want to estimate the time required to produce the 8th and the 32nd units, given that it takes 40,960 hours to produce the 16th unit and that the learning percentage is 80 percent. The first step is to find what percentage the 8th and 32nd units are of the ultimate unit, unit number 16:

$$8/16 = 50 \text{ percent}$$
$$32/16 = 200 \text{ percent}$$

The next step is to multiply these figures by their corresponding coefficients (from Table 12.3). Since the learning percentage is 80 percent, these coefficients, or F values in the table, would be 1.250 for unit number

TABLE 12.3

Coefficients for learning curves with rates from 70 to 98 percent

%ULT	70% F	72% F	74% F	76% F	78% F	80% F	82% F	84% F	86% F	88% F	90% F	92% F	94% F	96% F	98% F	%ULT
2	7.486	6.386	5.469	4.706	4.065	3.523	3.065	2.675	2.343	2.058	1.812	1.601	1.418	1.259	1.121	2
4	5.240	4.596	4.047	3.576	3.170	2.818	2.514	2.247	2.015	1.811	1.631	1.473	1.333	1.209	1.098	4
6	4.253	3.792	3.394	3.046	2.742	2.473	2.238	2.029	1.844	1.680	1.534	1.403	1.286	1.180	1.085	6
8	3.658	3.309	2.995	2.718	2.473	2.255	2.061	1.888	1.733	1.593	1.468	1.355	1.253	1.160	1.076	8
10	3.270	2.977	2.718	2.489	2.283	2.098	1.933	1.785	1.651	1.529	1.419	1.319	1.228	1.145	1.069	10
12	2.977	2.730	2.511	2.315	2.139	1.978	1.835	1.704	1.586	1.479	1.380	1.290	1.208	1.133	1.064	12
14	2.751	2.538	2.349	2.178	2.023	1.883	1.756	1.640	1.534	1.437	1.348	1.267	1.192	1.123	1.059	14
16	2.568	2.383	2.217	2.066	1.929	1.804	1.690	1.586	1.490	1.402	1.321	1.247	1.178	1.114	1.055	16
18	2.420	2.253	2.106	1.972	1.849	1.737	1.634	1.539	1.452	1.372	1.298	1.229	1.165	1.106	1.051	18
20	2.290	2.144	2.012	1.891	1.781	1.679	1.585	1.499	1.420	1.346	1.277	1.214	1.155	1.100	1.048	20
22	2.179	2.049	1.930	1.821	1.721	1.628	1.542	1.463	1.390	1.322	1.259	1.200	1.145	1.093	1.045	22
24	2.084	1.966	1.858	1.759	1.668	1.583	1.505	1.432	1.364	1.301	1.242	1.187	1.136	1.088	1.042	24
26	2.000	1.893	1.795	1.705	1.621	1.542	1.471	1.403	1.341	1.282	1.227	1.176	1.128	1.083	1.040	26
28	1.925	1.827	1.738	1.655	1.578	1.506	1.440	1.377	1.319	1.265	1.213	1.165	1.120	1.078	1.038	28
30	1.858	1.769	1.687	1.611	1.540	1.473	1.412	1.354	1.300	1.249	1.201	1.156	1.113	1.074	1.036	30
32	1.798	1.715	1.640	1.570	1.504	1.443	1.386	1.332	1.281	1.234	1.189	1.147	1.107	1.070	1.034	32
34	1.742	1.667	1.597	1.533	1.472	1.415	1.362	1.312	1.265	1.220	1.178	1.139	1.101	1.066	1.032	34
36	1.692	1.622	1.558	1.498	1.442	1.389	1.340	1.293	1.249	1.207	1.168	1.131	1.095	1.062	1.030	36
38	1.645	1.583	1.522	1.467	1.415	1.365	1.320	1.275	1.235	1.195	1.158	1.123	1.090	1.059	1.029	38
40	1.602	1.543	1.489	1.437	1.389	1.343	1.300	1.259	1.221	1.184	1.149	1.116	1.085	1.055	1.027	40
42	1.562	1.507	1.458	1.410	1.365	1.322	1.282	1.244	1.208	1.173	1.141	1.110	1.081	1.052	1.026	42
44	1.526	1.475	1.430	1.384	1.342	1.303	1.265	1.229	1.196	1.163	1.133	1.104	1.076	1.050	1.024	44
46	1.491	1.444	1.401	1.360	1.321	1.284	1.249	1.216	1.184	1.154	1.125	1.098	1.072	1.047	1.023	46
48	1.459	1.416	1.375	1.337	1.301	1.266	1.234	1.203	1.173	1.145	1.118	1.092	1.068	1.044	1.022	48
50	1.429	1.388	1.351	1.316	1.282	1.250	1.220	1.190	1.163	1.136	1.111	1.087	1.064	1.042	1.020	50
55	1.360	1.327	1.296	1.267	1.240	1.212	1.187	1.162	1.139	1.117	1.095	1.074	1.055	1.036	1.017	55
60	1.300	1.273	1.248	1.224	1.201	1.178	1.158	1.137	1.118	1.099	1.081	1.063	1.047	1.031	1.015	60
65	1.248	1.226	1.205	1.186	1.167	1.148	1.132	1.114	1.098	1.083	1.068	1.053	1.039	1.026	1.013	65
70	1.201	1.184	1.167	1.152	1.137	1.121	1.108	1.094	1.081	1.068	1.056	1.044	1.032	1.021	1.010	70
75	1.159	1.145	1.133	1.121	1.109	1.097	1.086	1.075	1.065	1.054	1.045	1.035	1.026	1.017	1.008	75
80	1.122	1.111	1.101	1.092	1.083	1.074	1.066	1.058	1.050	1.042	1.034	1.027	1.020	1.013	1.007	80
85	1.088	1.080	1.073	1.066	1.060	1.054	1.048	1.042	1.036	1.030	1.025	1.020	1.015	1.010	1.005	85
90	1.056	1.051	1.047	1.043	1.039	1.034	1.031	1.027	1.023	1.020	1.016	1.013	1.010	1.006	1.003	90
95	1.027	1.024	1.022	1.020	1.019	1.016	1.015	1.013	1.011	1.010	1.008	1.006	1.005	1.003	1.001	95
100	1.000	1.000	1.000	1.000	1.000	1.000	1.000	1.000	1.000	1.000	1.000	1.000	1.000	1.000	1.000	100
110	.9521	.9557	.9593	.9628	.9665	.9696	.9731	.9764	.9796	.9827	.9855	.9885	.9916	.9945	.9973	110
120	.9105	.9167	.9239	.9300	.9369	.9428	.9492	.9551	.9610	.9670	.9726	.9783	.9839	.9894	.9947	120
130	.8737	.8827	.8921	.9015	.9104	.9200	.9279	.9359	.9447	.9528	.9609	.9689	.9769	.9848	.9923	130
140	.8410	.8522	.8640	.8749	.8864	.8974	.9084	.9188	.9294	.9399	.9501	.9603	.9704	.9805	.9903	140
150	.8117	.8248	.8381	.8514	.8645	.8776	.8905	.9029	.9156	.9280	.9402	.9523	.9645	.9765	.9882	150
160	.7852	.8000	.8152	.8303	.8452	.8595	.8744	.8885	.9028	.9170	.9309	.9450	.9590	.9727	.9864	160
170	.7611	.7773	.7938	.8105	.8270	.8428	.8591	.8752	.8910	.9067	.9225	.9381	.9538	.9693	.9847	170
180	.7390	.7566	.7746	.7926	.8103	.8274	.8452	.8624	.8798	.8974	.9144	.9316	.9489	.9660	.9830	180
190	.7187	.7374	.7568	.7759	.7947	.8133	.8322	.8510	.8698	.8885	.9070	.9257	.9443	.9630	.9815	190
200	.7000	.7197	.7398	.7598	.7801	.7996	.8202	.8401	.8600	.8801	.8999	.9200	.9401	.9601	.9800	200
220	.6665	.6879	.7098	.7319	.7540	.7759	.7981	.8201	.8423	.8646	.8870	.9095	.9321	.9548	.9772	220
240	.6373	.6601	.6835	.7071	.7306	.7543	.7783	.8022	.8265	.8508	.8754	.8999	.9249	.9498	.9748	240
260	.6116	.6355	.6602	.6848	.7103	.7349	.7607	.7863	.8123	.8384	.8649	.8914	.9182	.9453	.9726	260
280	.5887	.6137	.6392	.6650	.6915	.7177	.7447	.7717	.7992	.8270	.8550	.8834	.9122	.9412	.9704	280
300	.5682	.5939	.6203	.6471	.6743	.7019	.7301	.7586	.7875	.8161	.8462	.8761	.9066	.9374	.9684	300

Source: R. W. Conway and Andrew Schultz, Jr., "The Manufacturing Progress Function," *Journal of Industrial Engineering*, vol. 10, no. 1 (January–February 1959), pp. 39–54.

8 and 0.8000 for unit number 32, and the estimates would be obtained as follows.

Unit	Percent of ULT	F	ULT	F × ULT (= estimate)
8......	50	1.250	40,960	51,200 man-hours
32......	200	0.800	40,960	32,710 man-hours

Reference to Table 12.2 shows that these estimates closely follow the values derived from the exact arithmetic tabulation approach. The value of the Conway and Schultz method is in its ability to permit calculation of man-hour estimates for a wide range of learning percentages without having to take logs, graph a learning curve, or perform an extensive series of multiplications.

Estimating the learning percentage

If production has been under way for some time, statistical regression analysis can be employed to find the learning percentage. Thus the equation $Y_x = Kx^n$ is converted to a straight-line function by using logs, and estimates of b and K are made from raw production data by using the method of least squares. And, as in any statistical analysis, the accuracy of the estimation becomes a function of the number of observations.

If production has not started, estimating the learning percentage becomes enlightened guesswork. In these cases the options open to the analyst are:

1. Assume that the learning percentage will be the same as it has been for previous applications within the same industry.
2. Assume that it will be the same as it has been for the same or similar products.
3. Analyze the similarities and differences between the proposed startup and previous startups and develop a revised learning percentage that appears best to fit the situation.

In selecting the option, the decision turns on how closely the startup under consideration approximates previous startups in the same industry or with the same or similar products. In any case, while a number of industries have used learning curves extensively, uncritical acceptance of the industry norm (such as the 80 percent figure for the airframe industry) is risky, and therefore, an analysis of the similarities and differences should be undertaken even though it may ultimately lead to the industry improvement percentage. The reasons for disparities between a firm's learning rate and that of its industry are two. First, there are the inevitable differences in operating characteristics between any two firms, stemming from the equipment, methods, product design, plant organization, etc. Second, procedural differences are manifested in the development of the learning percentage itself, such as whether the industry rate is based upon a single product or on a product line, and the manner in which the data were aggregated.

Using the learning curve

In addition to the care required in using the industry rate of learning, certain other factors should be noted before applying this concept to a given situation. Briefly, these are

1. Built-in production bias through suggesting any learning rate. If a manager expects an 80 percent improvement factor, he may treat this percentage as a goal rather than as an unbiased measure of actual learning. In short, it may be a "self-fulfilling prophecy."

2. Preproduction versus postproduction adjustments. The amount of learning shown by the learning curve depends both on the initial unit(s) of output and on the learning percentage. If there is much preproduction planning, experimentation, and adjustment, the early units will be produced more rapidly than if improvements are made after the first few units—other things being equal. In the first case, therefore, the apparent learning will be less than in the second case, even though subsequent "actual" learning may be the same in each instance.

3. Changes in indirect labor and supervision. Learning curves represent direct labor output, but if the mix of indirect labor and supervision changes, it is likely that the productivity of direct labor will be altered. We would expect, for example, that more supervisors, repairmen, and material handlers would speed up production whereas a reduction in their numbers would slow it down.

4. Changes in purchasing practices, methods, and organization structure. Obviously, significant adjustments in any of these factors will affect the production rate and hence the learning curve. Likewise, the institution of incentive systems, preventive maintenance programs, zero defect programs, and other schemes designed to improve efficiency or product quality generally would have some impact on the learning phenomenon.

5. Contract phaseout. Though not relevant to all startup situations, the point should be made that the learning curve may begin to turn upward as a contract nears completion. This may result from transferring trained workers to other projects, nonreplacement of worn tooling, and reduced attention to efficiency on the part of management.

Range of application.   While the learning curve is most commonly thought to be appropriate for primarily manual work, such as assembly, it is generally applicable to any situation where deliberate efforts are made to improve a productive process. In airframe manufacture, the 80 percent learning factor is derived not only from increasing experience on the part of direct labor but also from various staff and service groups that contributed improvements in methods, tooling, material handling, and so forth. Thus the general improvement phenomenon depicted by learning curves really reflects the results of the constellation of activities performed by organization personnel whose function is to enhance production.[6] This point

---

[6] The terms *manufacturing progress function, progress acceleration curve,* and *performance curve* are alternative designations used to emphasize the fact that the learning curve describes more than worker learning.

is underscored when we note that learning curves have been successfully applied in a number of industries that exhibit highly dissimilar production processes, such as petroleum, construction, textiles, candy making, and metal working.

FURTHER CONSIDERATIONS IN STARTUP

In addition to such basic techniques as PERT and learning curve derivation in the implementation of the startup process, attention must be given to other pertinent considerations. *Maintenance, quality control, budgeting, information flow, personnel training,* and *testing* programs must also be regarded as major areas of concern in getting a new facility operational.

To explore these factors in context, we draw upon a comprehensive article by Gans and Fitzgerald[7] describing the startup activities required in commissioning a first-of-a-kind chemical plant.[8]

Maintenance. Maintenance programs are run on records; so early in the planning phase department files should be set up for each process area. These files should include such information as construction and equipment specifications, spare parts and provisioning lists (including availability), and operating instructions. In addition, maintenance schedules specifying time intervals for inspection and parts replacement should be prepared and manuals detailing maintenance procedures and reliability features of the equipment should be developed. Further, maintenance personnel should become familiar with the equipment, perhaps through training at the manufacturers' facilities. Also, schedules should be developed to assure maintenance personnel availability during both production startup and preoperational testing.

Quality control. Steady state quality control in chemical plants is performed in a laboratory, and generally by technicians. However, during startup it is desirable to have trained chemists assist not only in the setting up of quality control methods but in the actual sampling of process output as well. (It bears mention that startup is a poor time to "shake down" a testing laboratory; hence, whenever possible, laboratory equipment and procedures should be debugged during the planning phase.)

Budgeting. Budgets for startup can be divided into three types: (1) budgets for "normal" expenditures for equipment, material, and personnel; (2) contingency budgets for changes and additions; and (3) contingency budgets for equipment breakdowns. The first type is developed from the startup schedule and can be calculated with good accuracy. The second type varies according to the amount and quality of engineering and research that has been invested in plant design. Previous experience in plant startup provides a good basis for this budget, assuming, of course, that adjustments are made for the technological differences between the

---

[7] "Plant Start-Up," pp. 270–89.

[8] In their introduction, the authors emphasize the difficulty of this startup situation and note that it "presents the most exciting and demanding challenge to the chemical engineer" (p. 270).

new plant and the existing facilities upon which the budget is predicated. Gans and Fitzgerald note that it is not unusual to find provision in a startup budget for a sum of money equal to 5 to 10 percent of plant capital investment for alterations and additions.

Budgets for equipment breakdown (the third type) are the most difficult to derive because of uncertainty about their occurrence. Care in selecting manufacturers and thorough testing of equipment are the best steps to take to minimize the amount of funds allocated for this purpose.

Information systems. Since operating problems and questions are bound to arise during startup, it is essential that an information system be set up that can permit adjustments in real time. Gans and Fitzgerald urge the establishment of an information center, which may range from a simple filing system to a sophisticated computer-based information retrieval operation. They also recommend that the system be instigated at the beginning of the project and that it be readily accessible to all responsible personnel on a 24-hour basis.

The information center should have a wide range of source material. A partial listing would include data on the standards used in designing pipes, electrical equipment, etc.; process flow characteristics in the form of process flowsheets, process descriptions, etc.; an engineering data file containing information on equipment, vendors, and purchase order numbers; plant layout data, such as drawings and plot plans; operating instructions describing the plant, testing procedures, preparation and startup procedures, shutdown procedures, and steady state operating procedures; analytical procedures data detailing quality control methods from raw materials through finished goods; and calculation instructions for evaluating plant performance, production, and yield. In practice, the value of the information retrieval system increases tremendously with maturity of the overall facility.

Personnel training. Gans and Fitzgerald suggest that a three-phase training program be provided for chemical operators and maintenance and laboratory personnel. These phases consist of (1) general classroom training, (2) specific classroom training, coupled with work in pilot plants, on laboratory equipment, and special training devices, and (3) plant instructions and in-plant training during testing and pre-operational activities. Regarding the third phase, the special nature of chemical processing enables training to progress with the product; that is, by operating safety interlocks between different parts of the process, the early sections of the plant can operate as a training ground for subsequent sections as the latter are taken over.

Testing programs. The testing actions required before a chemical plant becomes operational are quite extensive. Among these are pressure tests on piping and equipment, dry runs on pumps, furnaces, etc., "hot tests" to ensure leak-tightness at high temperatures, and closed-loop dynamics testing with safe fluids to check the facility as a total flow system.

Some of the principles developed for planning testing procedures in the chemical industry are relevant to other technologies. One is that tests should be run for several days to give all shifts a chance to conduct the same test and to allow repetition of the test if the results are not as expected. A second is that critical instruments must be calibrated over their full range to enable accurate feedback under all output levels. A third is that equipment should be run at all levels to test its limits. If a valve is "destined" to burst, having it burst during a test period is usually far less costly than during actual production.

STARTUP IN NONMANUFACTURING ORGANIZATIONS

Retailing organizations

It is usually difficult to determine the length of the startup period in retailing operations. This is so because achievement of the steady state level of service is in large part dependent upon the amount of customer demand, which in turn can be only partially controlled by the system. Department stores, for instance, often experience their highest demand for service during their first few days of operation, and hence the long-run steady state level of demand may be lower than it is during startup. (Manufacturing systems, in contrast, can negotiate order delivery dates and order quantities to permit a smooth break-in period.) Steady state achievement in retail outlets, therefore, must often be defined in subjective terms, such as "that point in time at which the store runs smoothly" or "when people know their jobs," rather than by achievement of a particular output goal. Further, when ancillary services such as credit accounts and home delivery are being developed, the determination of when steady state has been achieved may become even more difficult since each of these services also is subject to a break-in period.

Clerical operations

In insurance companies, brokerage houses, and other service systems that have a large volume of posting, typing, and filing, it is sometimes possible to describe the attainment of steady state in terms of output. In these situations, learning curves also may be derived for clerical personnel performing such tasks as filling out forms and sorting mail. On the other hand, when a clerical staff grows as a function of demand, total output may be inappropriate as a measure of steady state achievement. In these cases, management would have to examine the general performance level of the office to gauge whether or not the system has made the transition from startup to steady state.

Hospitals

Hospitals have startup characteristics that are common to both manufacturing and retailing operations. They are similar to manufacturing systems in that they build up to their steady state level in increments, rather than by permitting full use of their available physical capacity from the day they first open their doors. The University of Arizona Medical Center, for example, offered limited out-patient care and permitted the use of only 40 of its 300 beds in its first few months of operation. This enabled its staff to become familiar with the layout of the facility and refine its medical and support procedures. Hospitals, while they may refuse to meet demands for their services, are similar to retailing operations in that they cannot achieve a full-capacity steady state level without customer demand.

Hospital startups vary substantially in degree of difficulty. Convalescent hospitals, small private hospitals, and other hospitals offering a limited range of health services encounter far fewer startup problems than medical centers, which also engage in teaching and research. Thus planning for startup in the latter type of institutions must be more extensive, and implementation often requires special organizational arrangements. The University of Arizona Medical Center employed a startup team approach wherein a planning committee, consisting of the director of nursing, director of pharmacy and supplies, manager of systems engineering, and administrator of business and finance, reported to the hospital administrator, who acted as a program manager. During the planning phase, the planning committee developed an inventory of hospital functions that were translated into activities and assigned to members of the group. To keep track of the progress in each of these activities, a critical path network, similar to that used in the critical path method (described in the supplement to this chapter), was employed. The administration was generally satisfied with this approach, and the six-month transition from startup to steady state went fairly smoothly.

OTHER TYPES OF STARTUP SITUATIONS

The issues discussed thus far relate mainly to the startup of a new facility. However, equivalent situations can arise after the plant has been established. Some of these may be plantwide in impact, such as those which occur after a drawn-out strike, a major technological change, or a shift in product line. Others may be limited in scope, such as reopening a department after the installation of a new piece of equipment or performing extensive maintenance or repair. Indeed, it could be argued that a startup situation arises after any production hiatus.

Startups after a plant shutdown present problems different from those that accompany new-plant startups. The main reason for such differences is that, in the latter situation, achieving design integrity of the plant is paramount while, in the former, reversing the procedures required to shut down operations is the central undertaking. In other words, new-plant startup inevitably entails tinkering with processes, equipment, management controls, and even the product itself in order to get the productive system on line. In contrast, the problems encountered in a startup after a shutdown derive primarily from the way in which production was terminated and the extensiveness of the "mothballing" process. The kinds of problems that occur in these types of startups initially revolve around the acquiring of resources: raw materials supply lines must be reestablished, plant utility services must be reactivated, and, most importantly, operating personnel must be regrouped.

In startups associated with product changes of intermittent production situations, such as batch production, worker relearning time is of great interest, and some research has been done on the topic. Citing empirical data, Nicholas Bayloff observed "a definite relearning phenomenon taking place after the initial run of a new product," and hypothesized that "the amount of readaptation or relearning that is encountered during subsequent production runs is inversely and geometrically related to the length of the initial run; as the length of the initial run increases, the relearning required in subsequent runs decreases rapidly."[9] The rationale is that since relearning time is in effect a setup-type cost, it should tend to favor fewer production runs.[10]

THE ROLE OF RESEARCH AND DEVELOPMENT IN STARTUP

Daniel Roman has listed several purposes of research and development[11] (several of which have been previously noted in Chapter 2):

1. Discovering and furthering knowledge
2. Developing new products
3. Improving existing products
4. Finding new uses for existing products
5. Improving production processes
6. Finding potential uses for byproducts or waste products generated by present production
7. Analyzing and studying competitors' products
8. Providing technical service to functional departments in the organization

The relationship between R&D and production depends upon which of these purposes is being considered, though all of them ultimately affect production operations. In general, the primary area of concern for the production manager in his dealings with the R&D function (aside from improving existing processes or requesting assistance) is transferring new products and process ideas from development to production. In handling this problem, Gerstenfeld proposes five basic transfer models and suggests

---

[9] Nicholas Bayloff, "Start-up Management," *I.E.E.E. Transactions on Engineering Management,* vol. EM 17, no. 4 (November 1970), pp. 132–41.

[10] Economic batch-size models, incorporating learning functions, are currently being developed.

[11] Daniel Roman, *Research and Development Management: The Economics and Administration of Technology* (New York: Appleton-Century-Crofts, 1968), p. 18.

TABLE 12.4

Product transfer models

MODEL	FEATURES	ADVANTAGES/DISADVANTAGES	WHEN APPROPRIATE
A Product Specifications and Drawings R&D — Product Specifications and Drawings — Mfg	Drawings Prepared by R&D and Then Sent to Manufacturing, Communication Is in the Form of Interpreting the Documents	Simple Procedure No Multifunctional Personnel Needed Manufacturing Engineers Do Not Have to Understand Job Requirements of R&D and Vice Versa Manufacturing Has Little Influence on Product Design R&D May Not be Aware of Production Capabilities or the Impact of the New Product Lack of Enthusiasm by Manufacturing Personnel "Just A Package of Papers"	1. Uncomplicated Product 2. Flexible Production 3. Transfer Time Not Critical 4. Little Need to Reduce Production Costs 5. Skilled Multifunctional People Not Needed to Make Transfer 6. R&D and Manufacturing Operate Independently
B Manufacturing Participation in R&D R&D —— Mfg	A Manufacturing Engineer Is Assigned to the R&D Laboratory Final Design an Integration of R&D and Manufacturing Contributions Manufacturing Planning Parallels Product Design	Interaction Results in Decreased Production Costs The Manufacturing Engineer Is Involved and Interested in the New Product The Manufacturing Engineer Knows Who to Contact in R&D if Problems Arise Manufacturing Specifications Are Ready When Product Design Is Finished	1. Production Cost Reduction Is Essential 2. Transfer Time Is Critical 3. Product Is of Average Complexity for Company 4. A Manufacturing Engineer Is Available 5. Production Quantity High Enough to Justify Additional Expense
C R&D Participation In Manufacturing R&D —→ Mfg	R&D Personnel Who Design a Product Transfer It to Manufacturing	Requires Less Time because No Manufacturing Engineers Are Trained Initially Relatively High Costs of Production because R&D Engineers Lack Manufacturing Skills There Is a Tendency to Overdesign Transfer Time Long because Manufacturing May Resent R&D Interference and Not Cooperate Manufacturing Depends on R&D Phase-Out of R&D Timing Is Delicate	1. New Product Complex 2. Product Process Continuous 3. Transfer Timing Not Too Critical 4. Production Costs Are Not a Major Factor 5. Manufacturing Dependent on R&D Engineering 6. An R&D Engineer with Manufacturing Skill Is Available
D Corporate Coordinator R&D — Corporate Coordinator — Mfg	One Man Follows a New Product through All Its Phases from R&D through Manufacturing Coordinator Has Authority from Corporate Offices	Coordinator Has Authority to Get Prompt Action to Move Project across Functional Interfaces New Product Transfer Time Is Minimal Location of Manufacturing and R&D Not Critical because Only Coordinator Has to Move There May Be Fierce Competition among Coordinators of Different Products Coordinator Must Be Skilled In Many Areas	1. Transfer Time Is a Very Important Factor 2. A Man with the Required Skills Is Available 3. New Product of Moderate Complexity 4. Frequency of New Products Is Low 5. Manufacturing Plant and Development Lab Are Separated
E Transfer Team R&D — Transfer Team — Mfg	Specialists from R&D and Manufacturing Are Formed into a Team Members Must Have Authority and Technical Knowledge	Team Must Be Able to Reach Consensus Each Team Member Has His Own Interests Absenteeism, Changing Membership, and Lack of Understanding May Limit Effectiveness Decisions Tend to Be Slow Members Must Be Close Geographically So They Can Meet as Required Obtaining Members with Both Technical and Communications Skills Is Difficult	1. New Product Complex 2. Production Quantity High 3. Minimum Production Cost Desired 4. Transfer Time May Be Slow 5. Laboratory Located near Plant 6. Personnel for Team Is Available

Source: Arthur Gerstenfeld, *Effective Management of Research and Development* (Menlo Park, Calif.: Addison-Wesley Publishing Co., 1970), pp. 41–53.

the conditions under which each is applicable.[12] These models are summarized in Table 12.4.

The liaison between R&D and manufacturing is often critical in achieving a smooth transfer to production. As Burns discovered in studying the organization of some 20 electronics firms in England and Scotland, "the translation of jobs to be done from the language and methods appropriate to R&D engineers into terms manageable by draftsmen, production engineers, production supervisors, and, ultimately, operatives remains a central task of the organization." Burns notes further that the reverse is also true: the language of the shop has to be translated into the language of the laboratory; and these "linguistics" problems in turn have sometimes led management to the creation of "special intermediaries, whose job it is to interpret." However, when such a function is perceived as necessary, there is a likelihood that it will grow into a department that depends on continual communication problems for its survival. In this regard, Burns states that "the fewer the links in the chain from development to production, the more development and production are forced to learn each other's language, and the more effective, speedy, and troublefree is the passage of designs through various stages."[13]

In the United States, Lockheed Aircraft is an example of a firm that was confronted with transfer problems. According to Willis M. Hawkins, the firm's corporate vice president of science and engineering, "there is a great gap between research results (recognition of a new idea) and readiness for it in production." He sees this gap as "actually two chasms, one between research and engineering and another between engineering and manufacturing." The situation exists "in spite of all the interdivision discussions, the symposia, and all the other technological interdivision activities." The problem stems in part from the fact that every division is a profit center and each division manager uses his technical people to make divisional profits. "This results in the situation where an abundance of talent is present in some places and badly needed in others."[14] Hawkins feels that a better allocation of manpower could be achieved by the establishment of a corporate office with a talent inventory and a training program or a rotating assignment program.

PROBLEMS IN STARTUP

The problems that arise during startup are as varied as the systems. However, the following excerpts from *Plant Relocation: A Case History of a Move*, describing some of the pitfalls encountered by General Foods in

---

[12] Arthur Gerstenfeld, *Effective Management of Research and Development* (Reading, Mass.: Addison-Wesley, 1970), pp. 41–53.

[13] Tom Burns, "Research, Development, and Production: Problems of Conflict and Cooperation," in *Operations Management Selected Readings*, G. K. Groff and J. F. Muth, eds. (Homewood, Ill.: Richard D. Irwin, 1969), pp. 157–71.

[14] Willis M. Hawkins, "Technology Transfer Programs at Lockheed," *Transactions of the I.E.E.E.*, vol. 16, no. 3 (August 1969), pp. 121–25.

opening a new plant, are indicative of the types of problems encountered by other firms.

The start-up of production lines did not always go smoothly. . . . For example, in some production areas the dust collection system proved to be inadequate, and a consulting firm was retained to correct the problems. . . . Start-up operations almost always revealed minor—but important—problems in electrical systems, drainage systems, pumps, valves, and so forth, which had to be corrected before full-scale production could begin.

One major problem occurred in the start-up of rice production. This was caused not by in-plant troubles but by a delay in completion of a secondary sewage-treatment plant being constructed for the city. Rice production was scheduled to begin in the summer of 1964. However, with the additional sewage treatment capacity not available, the starchy effluent of the rice would have been released into a nearby river where it would have created an odor problem, particularly during warm weather. Therefore, production of rice was delayed until late fall [with another plant producing rice inventory].[15]

Some other problems encountered by General Foods included maintaining the required level of sanitation, the training and indoctrination of new employees, and coping with insufficient warehousing and shipping space.

In addition to the above types of problems, which for the most part are unavoidable even with the best planning, management may encounter problems arising from its own mistakes. In the previously cited article on startup management, Nicholas Bayloff observed that such mistakes fall into four major categories: (1) changes in production design and production factors, (2) discontinuous manufacturing policies, (3) insufficient provision of technical supervision and assistance, and (4) ineffective motivation and compensation programs.

A product design change, such as a switch from hot rolled to cold rolled steel, may require substantial retraining of the work force and yield a minimal amount of learning transfer. A production factor change, such as the substitution of a plastic component for a metal one, may impede operation of the system by necessitating new quality control procedures, new tooling, and new suppliers. In a similar vein, Woods and Elgie, in a study of 106 Canadian manufacturing firms found that start-up problems were enhanced when a firm was an early adopter of a new manufacturing technology.[16]

Discontinuous manufacturing, in which the initial run of a new product is interrupted, can entail significant relearning costs during subsequent production runs. This point is illustrated by Bayloff in an example in which the rate of output for a second production run of television tubes of six weeks averaged only about half that achieved at the end of an initial eight-week run. Of particular interest here is the fact that the break between

---

[15] E. S. Whitman and W. J. Schmidt, *Plant Relocation: A Case History of a Move* (New York: American Management Association, 1966), p. 85.

[16] Albert R. Wood and Richard J. Elgie, "Problems in Early versus Late Adoption of Manufacturing Innovations," *Proceedings of 35th Annual Meeting, Academy of Management*, August 1975, pp. 92–94.

FIGURE 12.5

Steel plant startup

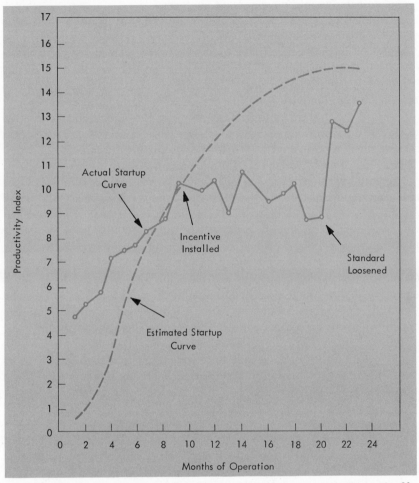

Source: Nicholas Bayloff, "Start-up Management," *I.E.E.E. Transactions on Engineering Management,* vol. EM 17, no. 4 (November 1970), p. 139.

the two runs was only one month, illustrating how rapidly a system "forgets."

Insufficient technical supervision may lead to delays in decision making and reduced production during startup, or, even worse, to incorrect decisions that may stop production entirely. While necessary for all types of startup, good technical supervision is of key importance in industries where technological innovation is a natural concomitant of the startup operation. Steel mills, chemical plants, and oil refineries, for example, are often confronted with technical problems that require research and development personnel to design customized processes or oversee operation of advanced sensing and control devices. Unfortunately, management does not always recognize the fact that the startup of such advanced technological systems represents "the final stage of an engineering development effort—not merely a reduction to efficient operating practice—and therefore demands the involvement of design and development engineers."[17]

Motivation and compensation problems during startup often stem from improper design and administration of incentive systems. As was noted in Chapter 11, incentives are tricky under the best circumstances, and therefore it is not surprising that they can be especially troublesome during startup, when there is uncertainty about the process and about what constitutes a fair productivity level.

A very serious hazard is that labor may use the uncertainty about the true steady state production level to obtain loose output standards for an incentive plan. Again, Bayloff provides a useful illustration.

Figure 12.5 shows two curves: (1) an estimated start-up curve made by the company (without reference to learning curve analysis), and (2) the actual production history of the start-up. Compensation was . . . based upon the past average earnings in the early stage of the start-up and this period was marked by steady productivity increases at a level exceeding management expectations. When the permanent incentive was installed, however, the increases ceased and productivity remained essentially constant for approximately 10 months at well below the projected level. Management needed production and consequently "bought out" the workers by loosening the production standard. The immediate and significant jump in productivity that followed indicates the degree to which the operating crew was able to bargain for a higher incentive rate.[18]

Clearly, it is up to management to avoid falling into such situations as this by "designing compensation systems that motivate workers to perform —not bargain—during start-up."[19]

CONCLUSION

Despite the fact that every productive system encounters some transition period between design and steady state operation, there is nothing like a complete body of literature on the topic. Indeed, management theory and operations research—the disciplines from which we would expect a good deal of research on startup—have yielded little in the way of empirical findings, and even less in the way of theoretical analysis.[20] Instead, it has been the technology-oriented disciplines, notably chemical and petroleum engineering, that—by necessity—have considered the managerial aspects of the problem. This is not to say that management researchers and operations research specialists are not generally aware of the startup problem; rather, they have preferred to focus their efforts on design and steady state prob-

---

[17] Ibid., p. 136.

[18] Ibid., p. 139.

[19] Ibid.

[20] Even learning curves, which have been studied extensively, provide information only on the progress of a startup; they do not provide guidance on *how* the startup should be accomplished.

lems. Unfortunately, the effect of this emphasis is that startup is treated as a special case and its existence is noted simply as something that is *not* covered by the particular theory or model that is under discussion.

PROPOSITIONS

Propositions contrasting service and manufacturing relative to system startup

Product: Service system startup approximates completion when productive capacity first becomes available for use. In manufacturing, startup is not completed until productive capacity is utilized approximately at its long-run output rate.

Technology of transformation: The startup period in service systems is often used to refine both the product and process specifications. In manufacturing startup, refinements are usually limited to process specifications since the product design is typically completely specified prior to production.

Operating-control system: In service systems, peak demand is often achieved during the startup period, and hence operating-control procedures must be appropriate to handle complete capacity utilization. In manufacturing, peak demand on the productive facility can usually be deferred, and hence operating-control procedures have time to evolve.

Workforce: In service systems startup, workforce training focuses on learning procedures. In manufacturing system start-up, workforce training focuses on sharpening skills.

REVIEW AND DISCUSSION QUESTIONS

1. What are three strategies for the implementation of a new productive system? What are the pros and cons of each?
2. List some production management tools that might be useful in planning and controlling startups.
3. How would you determine when startup is completed and steady state operations begin for the following organizations?
    a. An international airline
    b. A university
    c. A nightclub
    d. A television station
4. What are the basic assumptions of learning curve theory? What are the operational limitations of the theory?
5. What are the major differences between startup in manufacturing and startup in nonmanufacturing operations?

6. What types of management errors did Bayloff observe in his study of startup?
7. Does labor generally have the upper hand during startup? Discuss.
8. As a manager, which learning percentage would you prefer (other things being equal), 80%, 70%, or 60%? Explain.
9. Which product transfer model would be appropriate for each of the following situations?
    a. A toy company wants to get a new toy into production in a hurry. The toy is not complex, and the R&D lab is geographically separated from the plant.
    b. A new plastic is discovered by a company's researchers and it is necessary to adjust the existing process in order to make it. ·
    c. An aerospace firm is developing a new gyro for a communications satellite. It has already received an order for 1,000 gyros. The R&D facility is located near the plant.
    d. A ballpoint pen company is developing a new line of pens it wants to have on the market in time for Christmas.

PROBLEMS

1. Captain Nemo, owner of the Sub-optimum Underwater Boat Company (SUB), is puzzled. He has a contract for 11 boats and has completed four of them. He has observed that his production manager, young Mr. Overick, has been reassigning more and more men to torpedo assembly after the construction of the first four boats. The first boat, for example, required 225 men, each working a 40-hour week, while 45 fewer men were required for the second boat. Overick has told him that "this is just the beginning" and that he will complete the last boat in the current contract with only 100 men!

    Help Captain Nemo out. Explain to him what is going on and, based on the data at hand, refute or justify Overick's assertion.

2. SUB has produced the first unit of a new line of minisubs at a cost of $500,000, $200,000 of which was for materials and the remaining $300,000 was for labor. It has agreed to accept a 10 percent profit, based upon cost, and is willing to contract on the basis of a 70 percent learning curve. What will be the contract price for three minisubs?

3. After completing a total of six minisubs, SUB receives an order for one sub from the Swiss navy. Given the fact that a 70 percent learning curve prevailed for the previous order, what price should they quote the Swiss navy, assuming that they wish to make the same percentage profit as before?

4. Assuming a "learning rate" of 75 percent, what would be the expected direct labor man-hours required in making the 128th item, given that the fourth item took 50,000 direct labor man-hours?

SELECTED BIBLIOGRAPHY

Abernathy, William J., and Rosenbloom, Richard S. "Parallel and Sequential R&D Strategies: Application of a Simple Model," *I.E.E.E. Transactions on Engineering Management,* vol. 15, no. 1 (March 1968), pp. 1–12.

———— **and Wayne, Kenneth** "Limits of the Learning Curve," *Harvard Business Review,* vol. 52, no. 5 (September–October 1974), pp. 109–19.

Bayloff, Nicholas "Start-up Management," *I.E.E.E. Transactions on Engineering Management,* vol. EM 17, no. 4 (November 1970), pp. 132–41.

Gans, Manfred, and Fitzgerald, Frank A. "Plant Start-up," *The Chemical Plant,* ed. Ralph Landau, Chap. 12. New York: Reinhold Publishing Corp., 1966.

Gerstenfeld, Arthur *Effective Management of Research and Development.* Reading, Mass.: Addison-Wesley Publishing Co., 1970.

Henderson, R. *Plant Start-Up Productivity* (unpublished, Ph.D. Dissertation, School of Business Administration, University of Western Ontario, London, Ontario, 1974).

Whitman, Edmund S., and Schmidt, W. James *Plant Relocation: A Case History of a Move.* New York: American Management Association, 1966.

Wood, Albert R., and Richard J. Elgie "Problems in Early versus Later Adoption of Manufacturing Innovations," *Proceedings of 35th Annual Meeting, Academy of Management,* August, 1975, pp. 92–94.

Supplement to chapter twelve

Critical path scheduling

CRITICAL PATH SCHEDULING refers to a set of graphical techniques used in planning and controlling projects. In any given project there are three factors of concern: *time, cost,* and *resource availability,* and critical path techniques have been developed to deal with each of these, individually and in combination. The organization of this supplement follows the lines of these three factors, with major sections focusing on time-based models, time cost models, and limited resource models.

PERT (*Program Evaluation and Review Technique*) and CPM (*Critical Path Method*), the two best-known techniques, were both developed in the late 1950s. PERT was developed under the sponsorship of the U.S. Navy Special Projects Office in 1958 as a management tool for scheduling and controlling the Polaris missile project.[1] CPM was developed in 1957 by J. E. Kelly of Remington-Rand and M. R. Walker of du Pont to aid in scheduling maintenance shutdowns of chemical processing plants. Since their development, a number of variants have been devised, which, though little different on basic concept, have raised the invention of acronyms almost to an art form.[2]

---

[1] Which it did with notable success, being credited for reducing the project length by 18 months.

[2] Acronyms of some of the better-known techniques are SPERT, HEP, ICONS, PEP, LESS, and GERT.

By and large, critical path scheduling techniques attempt to display a project in graphical form and relate its component tasks in such a way as to focus attention on those which are crucial to the project's completion.

In Chapter 7 we defined a project as *a series of related jobs usually directed toward some major output and requiring an extensive period of time to perform.* For critical path scheduling techniques to be most applicable, a project must have the following characteristics:

1. It must have well-defined jobs or tasks whose completion marks the end of the project.
2. The jobs or tasks are independent in that they may be started, stopped, and conducted separately within a given sequence.
3. The jobs or tasks are ordered in that they must follow each other in a given sequence.
4. A job or task, once started, must continue without interruption until completion.

Construction, aerospace, and shipbuilding industries commonly meet these criteria, and hence critical path techniques find wide application within them. "Big business" in general, made substantial use of PERT and CPM as far back as 1965, with 44 percent of a sample of 186 (from the *Fortune 500*) indicating such use.[3] A breakdown of specific applications derived from the same survey is given in Table S.12.1.

TABLE S.12.1

Areas of application of PERT and CPM

Areas of application	*Respondents using techniques*
Construction	53.3%
Research and development	48.1
Product planning	37.0
Maintenance	29.6
Computer installation	25.9
Marketing	7.4
Other	29.6

Source: Modified from Peter B. Schoderbek, "A Study of the Applications of PERT," *Academy of Management Journal* (September 1965), p. 203.

TIME-ORIENTED TECHNIQUES

The basic forms of PERT and CPM focus on finding the longest time-consuming path through a network of tasks as a basis for planning and controlling a project. As will be observed in the ensuing discussion, there are some differences in the way the networks of the two techniques are structured and in their terminologies. However, the basic difference lies in the fact that PERT permits explicit treatment of probability in its time estimates whereas CPM does not. This distinction reflects PERT's origin in

---

[3] Peter B. Schoderbek, "A Study of the Applications of PERT," *Academy of Management Journal* (September 1965), pp. 199–206.

scheduling advanced development projects that are characterized by uncertainty and CPM's origin in the scheduling of the fairly routine activity of plant maintenance.

In a sense, both techniques owe their development to their widely used predecessor, the Gantt chart.[4] While the Gantt chart is able to relate activities to time in a usable fashion for very small projects, the interrelationship of activities, when displayed in this form, becomes extremely difficult to visualize and to work with for projects greater than 25 or 30 activities. Moreover, the Gantt chart provides no direct procedure for ascertaining the *critical path,* which, despite its theoretical shortcomings, is of great practical value.[5]

PERT

The following steps are required in developing and solving a PERT network.

1. *Identify each activity to be done in the project.* Assuming that the PERT analyst has an understanding of the technical aspects of the program, the output from this step is simply a listing of activities. While it is important that all activities required to complete the project are included, care should be taken to ensure that they are presented at a constant level of detail. For example, in building a house an activity such as *nail down front step* would not be shown on the same PERT chart as *lay foundation.* In network terminology, they are at different levels of *indenture,* and hence such a mixture of major and minor activities would be inappropriate.

2. *Determine the sequence of activities and construct a network reflecting the precedence relationships.* This is a valuable step, even if a complete PERT analysis is not performed, since it forces the analyst to consider the interrelationships of activities and present them in visual form. PERT networking follows an *activity on arrow, event on node* structure; that is, arrows denote activities and nodes denote events. Activities consume time and resources, and events mark their start or completion. Thus *write book* would be an activity and *book completed* would be an event.

In the network segment illustrated in Figure S.12.1, we have specified three events and two activities, although each event node signifies two events: the end of one event and the beginning of another. That is, event 2 marks not only the completion of the book but the start of printing the book. Event 3 signifies the completion of printing, and perhaps the start of the distribution, and so on.

In the construction of a network, care must be taken to assure that the activities and events are in the proper order and that the logic of their relationships is maintained. For example, it would be illogical to have a situation where event A precedes event B, B precedes C, and C precedes A. Also, in many projects problems arise in showing the precise form of dependencies, and the networking device termed a *dummy activity* must be

---

[4] A Gantt chart is illustrated in Chapter 7.

[5] See "Picking on PERT and CPM", page 569.

FIGURE S.12.1

Start Writing   Book Completed   Printing Completed
         Write Book   Print Book
→————————①—————————→②————————→③————————→

employed. Dummy activities consume no resources and are typically depicted as dashed arrows. A summary of some of the situations in which
dummies are used is provided in Figure S.12.2.

3. *Ascertain time estimates for each activity.* The PERT algorithm requires that three estimates be obtained for each activity:

a = optimistic time: the minimum reasonable period of time in which
   the activity can be completed. (There is only a small probability,
   typically assumed to be 1 percent, that the activity can be completed in a shorter period of time.)

m = most likely time: the best guess of the time required. (This would
   be the only time estimate submitted if one is using CPM). Since m
   would be the time thought most likely to appear, it is also the mode
   of the beta distribution, discussed in step 4.

b = pessimistic time: the maximum reasonable period of time the activity would take to be completed. (There is only a small probability, typically assumed to be 1 percent, that it would take longer
   to complete the activity.)

Typically, this information is gathered from those people who are to perform the activity.

4. *Calculate the expected time (ET) for each activity.* The formula for
this calculation is as follows:

$$\text{ET} = \frac{a + 4m + b}{6}$$

This is based upon the beta statistical distribution and weights the most
likely time (m) four times more than either the optimistic time (a) or the
pessimistic time (b). The beta distribution was selected by the PERT
research team because it is extremely flexible; that is, it can take on the
variety of forms that typically arise in project activity durations, it has
finite end points, which limit the possible activity times to the area between
a and b (see Figure S.12.3), and in the simplified version used in PERT, it
permits straightforward computation of the activity mean and standard
deviation. Four "typical" beta curves are illustrated in Figure S.12.3.

5. *Calculate the variances (σ^2) of the activity times.* Specifically, this is
the variance, σ^2, associated with each ET, and is computed as follows:

$$\sigma^2 = \left(\frac{b - a}{6}\right)^2$$

As can be seen, the variance is the square of one-sixth the difference between the two extreme time estimates, and of course the greater this
difference, the larger the variance.

FIGURE S.12.2

The use of dummy activities in network construction

1. Partial Dependence

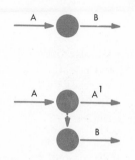

Implies A Must Be Completely Finished
before B Can Start.

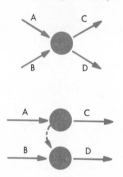

Indicates That B Can Start When A Is
Partially Completed.

2. Clarify Precedence Relationships

Implies That C and D Are Dependent on
A and B.

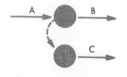

Indicates That D Depends on A and B;
C Depends Only on A.

3. Existence of Competing Resource
Requirements

Indicates That C Cannot Start (in This
Case) Until Equipment Becomes Available
from A.

4. Clarify Event Numbers for
Computer Use

Conceptually Correct but Two Activities
Have Identical Event Numbers.

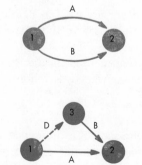

Enables Separate Activity Designations
That Is, for Activity D, 1-3; A, 1-2;
and B, 3-2.

FIGURE S.12.3

Typical beta curves

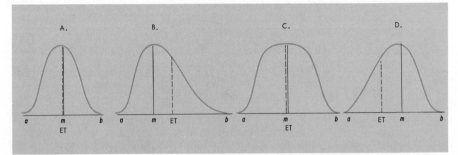

Curve A indicates very little uncertainty about the activity time, and since it is symmetrical, the expected time (ET) and the most likely or modal time (m) fall along the same point.

Curve B indicates a high probability of finishing the activity early, but if something goes wrong, the activity time could be greatly extended.

Curve C is almost a rectangular distribution, which suggests that the estimator sees the probability of finishing the activity early or late as equally likely, and $m \cong ET$.

Curve D indicates that there is a small chance of finishing the activity early, but it is more probable that it will take an extended period of time.

6. *Determine the critical path.* The critical path is the longest sequence of connected activities through the network and is defined as the path with zero *slack* time. *Slack time* (T_S), in turn, is calculated for each event and is the difference between the earliest expected completion time and the latest expected completion time for an event. Slack may be thought of as the amount of time the start of a given event may be delayed without delaying the completion of the project.

7. *Determine the probability of completing the project on a given date.* A unique feature of PERT is that it enables the analyst to assess the effect of uncertainty on project completion time. The mechanics of deriving this probability are as follows:

    a) Sum the variance values associated with each activity on the critical path.

    b) Substitute this figure, along with the project due date and the project expected completion time, into the Z transformation formula. This formula is as follows:

$$Z = \frac{D - T_E}{\sqrt{\Sigma \sigma_{cp}^2}}$$

where

        D = Due date for project
        T_E = Earliest expected completion time for last activity
      $\Sigma \sigma_{cp}^2$ = Sum of the variances along critical path

    c) Calculate the value of Z, which is the number of standard deviations the project due date is from the expected completion time.

    d) Using the value for Z, find the probability of meeting the project due date (using a table of normal probabilities—see Table S.12.2).

The *earliest expected completion time* (T_E) for an event is found by starting at the beginning of the network and summing the expected times (ETs) for each event preceding the event of interest. If two or more arrows converge on an event node, use the largest computed figure. The *latest expected completion time* (T_L) for an event is found by starting at the end of the network and working toward the beginning, subtracting the expected completion time (ET) for each event from the value of the T_L for each successor event. To begin the process requires the establishment of some T_L for the last event. This value is typically set equal to T_E for that event, or to the desired project completion time (D). If two or more arrows converge on an event node, take the smallest computed figure as the T_L value.

TABLE S.12.2

Values of the standard normal distribution function

Z	Probability	Z	Probability	Z	Probability
−3.0	0.0013	−0.9	0.1841	1.1	0.8643
−2.9	0.0019	−0.8	0.2119	1.2	0.8849
−2.8	0.0026	−0.7	0.2420	1.3	0.9032
−2.7	0.0035	−0.6	0.2743	1.4	0.9192
−2.6	0.0047	−0.5	0.3085	1.5	0.9332
−2.5	0.0062	−0.4	0.3446	1.6	0.9452
−2.4	0.0082	−0.3	0.3821	1.7	0.9554
−2.3	0.0107	−0.2	0.4207	1.8	0.9641
−2.2	0.0139	−0.1	0.4602	1.9	0.9713
−2.1	0.0179	0	0.5000	2.0	0.9772
−2.0	0.0228	0.1	0.5398	2.1	0.9821
−1.9	0.0287	0.2	0.5793	2.2	0.9861
−1.8	0.0359	0.3	0.6179	2.3	0.9893
−1.7	0.0446	0.4	0.6554	2.4	0.9918
−1.6	0.0548	0.5	0.6915	2.5	0.9938
−1.5	0.0668	0.6	0.7257	2.6	0.9953
−1.4	0.0808	0.7	0.7580	2.7	0.9965
−1.3	0.0968	0.8	0.7881	2.8	0.9974
−1.2	0.1151	0.9	0.8159	2.9	0.9981
−1.1	0.1357	1.0	0.8413	3.0	0.9987
−1.0	0.1587				

The theoretical justification for the probability determination procedure is as follows. It may be shown mathematically that the sum of the variances associated with a series of events following any distribution (for example, the beta) may be treated as the variance estimate for the entire series if two conditions are met: (1) the events are independent and (2) the variation around the mean of the series is normally distributed. Invoking this relationship in PERT time estimating permits summing of the variances associated with each activity on the critical path to arrive at an estimate of variance for the entire project since it is assumed that the network activities are (a) independent (condition 1), and (b) that the variation around the project completion time is normally distributed (condition 2).

The standard deviation of the total project is the square root of this sum.

Applying the PERT procedure: A sample problem. In order to meet the exhaust emissions standards, an automobile manufacturing company must modify the design of the antismog device on all its cars. In order to install the device on next year's models, the vice president of manufacturing can allow only 35 weeks' time to build a prototype, along with specifying the required changes in tooling and methods to produce it. The vice president assigns this project to the manager of development engineering and requests him to "PERT chart" the problem and to provide an estimate of the likelihood of completing the project in the time allowed. Let's follow the steps listed above and show how the manager might proceed.

1. Activity identification. The research manager decides that the following activities are the major components of the project: redesign of the antismog device, prototype construction, prototype testing, methods specification (summarized in a report), new tooling evaluation studies, a tooling report, and a final report summarizing all aspects of the design, tooling, and methods.

2. Activity sequencing and network construction. On the basis of discussion with his staff of engineers, the research manager develops the precedence table and sequence network shown in Figure S.12.4. Note that he must add a "dummy" time line to permit unique activity designations for the writing of the tooling report and methods report. In this example the table reflects this adjustment, even though it is presumed to be identified before the network was developed. In practice, the manager would be unlikely to recognize the need for dummy activities before at least a rough network is drawn.

3 and 4. Establish time estimates and calculate activity time variances. Once he decides on the activities to be performed, the manager would ask

FIGURE S.12.4

Precedence relationships

Activity	Activity Designation	Immediate Predecessors
Redesign	0-1	---
Build Prototyoe	1-2	0-1
Evaluate Tooling	1-3	0-1
Test Prototype	2-3	1-2
Dummy	3-4	1-3, 2-3
Write Tooling Report	4-5	3-4, 2-3
Write Methods Report	3-5	1-3, 2-3
Write Final Report	5-6	3-5, 4-5

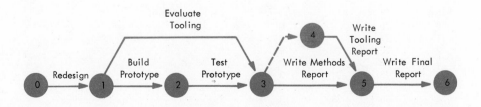

TABLE S.12.3

Activity expected times and variances

Activity	Activity designation	Time estimates a	m	b	Expected times (ET) $\dfrac{a + 4m + b}{6}$	Activity variances (σ^2) $\left(\dfrac{b-a}{6}\right)^2$
Redesign..............	0–1	10	22	28	21	9
Build prototype.......	1–2	4	4	10	5	1
Evaluate tooling.......	1–3	4	6	14	7	$2\frac{7}{9}$
Test prototype........	2–3	1	2	3	2	$\frac{1}{9}$
Dummy..............	3–4	–	–	–	–	–
Write tooling report....	4–5	1	5	9	5	$1\frac{7}{9}$
Write methods report...	3–5	7	8	9	8	$\frac{1}{9}$
Write final report......	5–6	2	2	2	2	0

his staff to estimate the optimistic, most likely, and pessimistic times for those activities under their control. He would then calculate ET and σ^2 for each activity and list it in a form such as that shown in Table S.12.3.

5. *Determine critical path.* Figure S.12.5 is a "working" PERT chart in that it is in the form an analyst would use to arrive at the critical path and expected completion time for the project. Each T_E is found first by summing from event 0 forward; each T_L is found next by setting T_L and T_E equal to 38 and subtracting, moving backward through the network. Slack times are calculated below the chart. Examining the slack values, we see that events 0, 1, 2, 3, 5, and 6 are critical and that part of the network shows two critical paths, since the events associated with parallel activities 1–3 and 1–2, 2–3 each has zero slack.

FIGURE S.12.5

Identification of critical path

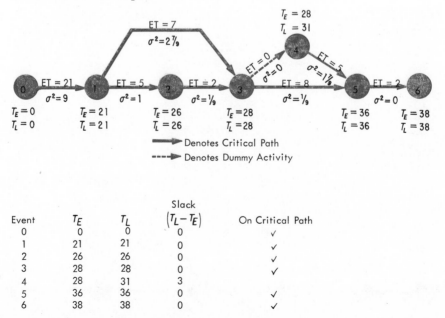

Denotes Critical Path
Denotes Dummy Activity

Event	T_E	T_L	Slack $(T_L - T_E)$	On Critical Path
0	0	0	0	✓
1	21	21	0	✓
2	26	26	0	✓
3	28	28	0	✓
4	28	31	3	
5	36	36	0	✓
6	38	38	0	✓

6. Probability of completion. Since there are two critical paths in the network, a decision must be made as to which variances to use in arriving at the probability of completion. A conservative approach dictates that the path with the largest total variance be used since this would focus management's attention on those activities that are most likely to exhibit broad variations. On this basis, the variances associated with activities 0–1, 1–3, 3–5, and 5–6 would be used to find the probability of completion. Thus $\Sigma\sigma_{cp}^2 = 9 + 2\frac{7}{9} + \frac{1}{9} + 0 = 11\frac{8}{9}$. (We will round this to 12.) The due date (D) was given as 35 weeks and the earliest expected completed time $(T_E$ for the last event) was found to be 38. Substituting into the Z equation and solving, we obtain

$$Z = \frac{D - T_E}{\sqrt{\Sigma\sigma_{cp}^2}} = \frac{35 - 38}{\sqrt{12}} = \frac{-3}{3.46} \cong -0.9$$

Looking at Table S.12.2, we see that a Z value of -0.9 yields a probability of 0.18, which means that the research manager has only about an 18 percent chance of completing the project on time.

CPM

As mentioned earlier, the major distinction between CPM and PERT is the use of statistics in the latter. Otherwise, despite some differences in network construction and terminology, the approaches are similar.

The following steps are required in developing and solving a CPM network (Figure S.12.6).

1. *Identify each activity to be done in the project.* In CPM, the term *job* is often used to refer to the task being performed, rather than separating out activities and events as in PERT. However, since current practice seems to be to treat the terms as synonymous, we will refer to the CPM tasks to be done as *activities*.

2. *Determine the sequence of activities and construct a network reflecting precedence relationships.* CPM is activity oriented with arrows denoting precedence only. A typical segment in using the book-writing example from PERT (step 2) would show the activity above the node rather than on the arrow. To restate, nodes in CPM represent activities in the PERT sense, not events.

3. *Ascertain time estimates for each activity.* This is the "best guess" time and can be thought of as equivalent to expected time (ET), which is derived statistically in PERT (step 4). While the CPM procedure has no provision for statistical estimation of this value, the individual who provides the estimate may employ a simple statistical model in arriving at a figure. For example, he may feel that two times are equally likely and therefore take their average as his estimate.

4. *Determine the critical path.* As in PERT, this is the path with zero slack. To arrive at slack time requires the calculation of four times values for each activity:

Early start time (ES), which is the earliest possible time that the activity can begin

FIGURE S.12.6

Steps to develop and solve a CPM network

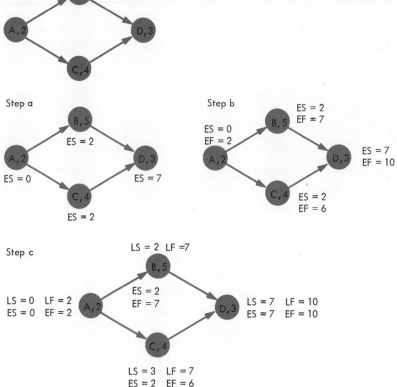

Step a

Step b

Step c

Early finish time (EF), which is the early start time plus the time needed to complete the activity

Late start time (LS), which is the latest time an activity can begin without delaying the project.

Late finish time (LF), which is the latest time an activity can end without delaying the project.

The procedure for arriving at these values and for determining slack and the critical path can best be explained by reference to the simple network shown (Figure S.12.6). The letters denote the activities and the numbers the activity times.

    a. Find ES time. Take zero as the start of the project and set this equal to ES for activity A. To find ES for B, we add the duration of A (which is 2) to zero and obtain 2. Likewise, ES for C would be 0 + 2, or 2. To find ES for D, we take the larger ES and duration time for the preceding activities: since B = 2 + 5 = 7 and C = 2 + 4 = 6, ES for D = 7. These values are entered on the diagram (Figure S.12.6, step a). The largest value is selected since activity

D cannot begin until the longest time-consuming activity preceding it is completed.

b. Find EF times. The EF for A is its ES time, 0, plus its duration of 2, or 2. B's EF is its ES of 2 plus its duration of 5, or 7. C's is 2 + 4, or 6, and D's is 7 + 3, or 10 (Figure S.12.6, step b). In practice, one computes ES and EF together while proceeding through the network. Since ES plus activity time equals EF, the EF becomes the ES of the following event, etc.

c. Find late start and late finish times. While the procedure for making these calculations can be presented in mathematical form, the concept is much easier to explain and understand if it is presented in an "intuitive" way. The basic approach is to start at the end of the project with some desired or assumed completion time. Working back toward the beginning, one activity at a time, we determine how long the starting of this activity may be delayed without affecting the start of the one that follows it.

In reference to the sample network, let us assume that the late finish time for the project is equal to the early finish time for activity D, that is, 10. If this is the case, the latest possible starting time for D will be 10 − 3, or 7. The latest time C can finish without delaying the LS of D is 7, which means that C's LS is 7 − 4, or 3. The latest time B can finish without delaying the LS of D is also 7, which means that B's LS is 7 − 5, or 2. Since A precedes two activities, the choice of LS and LF values depends upon which of those activities must be started first. Clearly, B determines the LF for A since its LS is 2, whereas C can be delayed one day without extending the project. Finally, since A must be finished by day 2, it cannot start any later than day 0, and hence its LS is 0. These LS and LF values are entered in the network (Figure S.12.6, step c).

d. Determine slack time for each activity. Slack for each activity is defined as either LS − ES or LF − EF. In this example, only activity C has slack (1 day); therefore the critical path is A, B, D.

Applying CPM to the design modification project. For the sake of brevity, we have summarized the results of the various steps of the CPM procedure in the form shown in Figure S.12.7. Note that the CPM network appears greatly different from the PERT network even though the activities and the critical path(s) are the same. Also note that no dummy arrows are required for this problem. (In general, CPM uses fewer dummies than PERT because an activity is designated only by a node, rather than by an arrow connecting two events.)

TIME-COST MODELS

In practice, project managers are as much concerned with the cost to complete a project as with the time to complete the project. For

FIGURE S.12.7

CPM network for Antismog Device Redesign Project

CPM Activity Designations and Time Estimates

Activity	Designation	Immediate Predecessors	Time in Weeks	(ET Values of PERT
Redesign	A	--	21	Used for Comparison)
Build prototype	B	A	5	
Evaluate tooling	C	A	7	
Test prototype	D	B	2	
Write tooling report	E	C,D	5	
Write methods report	F	C,D	8	
Write final report	G	E,F	2	

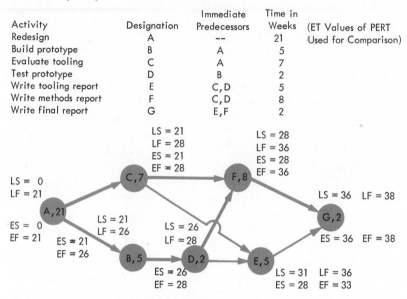

Slack Calculations and Critical Path Determinations

Activity	LS - ES	Slack	On Critical Path
A	0-0	0	✓
B	21-21	0	✓
C	21-21	0	✓
D	26-26	0	✓
E	31-28	3	
F	28-28	0	✓
G	36-36	0	✓

this reason, extensions of PERT and CPM have been devised that attempt to develop a minimum-cost schedule for an entire project and to control budgetary expenditures during the conduct of a project. Current usage indicates that the approaches that focus on minimum cost scheduling typically use CPM networks, while those that focus on budgetary control generally fall under the heading PERT–COST. However, it should be emphasized that minimum-cost scheduling has been employed as an option in PERT–COST systems, and budgetary control schemes have been employed in conjunction with CPM scheduling.

Minimum-cost scheduling (time-cost tradeoff)

The basic assumption in minimum cost scheduling of a project is that there is a relationship between activity completion time and the cost of a project. On one hand, it costs money to expedite the completion of an activity, while on the other it costs money to sustain (or lengthen) the project. The costs associated with expediting activities are termed *activity direct costs.* Some of these may be worker-related, such as overtime work, hiring more workers, and transferring workers from other jobs, while others are resource-related, such as buying or leasing additional or more efficient equipment and drawing upon additional support facilities.

The costs associated with sustaining the project are termed *project indirect costs* and consist of overhead, facilities, and resource opportunity costs, and—under certain contractual situations—penalty costs or lost incentive payments. Since these two categories of opposing costs are dependent upon time, the scheduling problem is essentially one of finding that project duration that minimizes their sum, or in other words finding the optimum point in a time-cost tradeoff.

The procedure for finding this point consists of six steps, and it will be explained by using the simple four-activity network employed in the previous section. Figure S.12.8 shows the data.

1. Prepare a CPM-type network diagram. For each activity this diagram should list:

   a) Normal Cost (NC): The lowest expected activity cost (these are the lesser of the cost figures shown under each node below)
   b) Normal Time (NT): The time associated with each normal cost
   c) Crash Time (CT): The shortest possible activity time
   d) Crash Cost (CC): The cost associated with each crash time

2. Determine the cost per unit of time (assume days) to expedite each activity. The relationship between activity time and cost may be shown graphically by plotting CC and CT coordinates and connecting them to the NC and NT coordinates by a concave, convex, or straight line—or some other form, depending upon the actual cost structure of activity performance. For activity A we assume a linear relationship between time and cost. This assumption is common in practice and facilitates the derivation of the cost per day to expedite since this value may be found directly by taking the slope of the line using the formula Slope = (CC − NC) ÷ (NT − CT). (When the assumption of linearity cannot be made, the cost of expediting must be determined graphically for each of the days the activity may be shortened.)

The calculations needed to obtain the cost of expediting the remaining activities are shown in Table S.12.4.

3. Prepare a normal-time, normal-cost schedule. For the simple network we have been using, this schedule would take 10 days and would cost $26. The critical path would be A, B, D. Arriving at the values used to derive the expediting costs and the total cost for the schedule is facilitated by using the tabular format shown in Figure S.12.8, step 3.

4. Prepare a crash-time, crash-cost schedule. This schedule would take five days and would cost $45. It should be noted, however, that the same schedule time could be achieved at a lower cost since activity B could be delayed one more day without delaying the total project. Hence the "rational" crash schedule would appear as shown in Figure S.12.8, step 4, and in this case would yield two critical paths.

FIGURE S.12.8

Example of time-cost trade off procedure

Step 1 Prepare CPM Diagram with Activity Costs

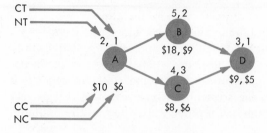

Step 2 Determine Cost per Unit of Time

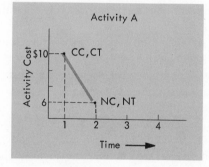

Step 3 Prepare Normal Time, Normal Cost Schedule

	A	B	C	D		
Activity Time	2†	5†	4	3†		
Days Expedited	–	–	–	–		
Expediting Costs	–	–	–	–	=	$ 0
Normal Costs	$6	9	6	5	=	26
Total Costs						$26

† Denotes Activity on Critical Path

5. Prepare intermediate schedules. Once the range of schedule times and costs is known, the next step is to find one or more intermediate schedules that can be used as coordinates to plot the project direct cost curve. In our example, the crash schedule is five days and the normal schedule is 10 days.

An arbitrarily selected intermediate schedule that might provide a clue to the slope of the curve is a seven-day schedule. To arrive at this schedule, we would start a crash schedule and add a total of two days to activity

FIGURE S.12.8 (*continued*)

Step 4　Prepare Crash Cost Schedule

	A	B	C	D		
Activity Time	1†	2	3†	1†		
Days Expedited	1	3	1	2		
Expediting Costs	$4	9	2	4	=	$19
Normal Costs					=	26
Total Costs						$45

Rational Crash Schedule

	A	B	C	D		
Activity Time	1†	3†	3†	1†		
Days Expedited	1	2	1	2		
Expediting Costs	$4	6	2	4	=	$16
Normal Costs					=	26
Total Costs						$42

Step 5　Prepare Intermediate Schedules

	A	B	C	D		
Activity Time	2†	4†	4†	1†		
Days Expedited	–	1	–	2		
Expediting Costs	–	$3	–	4	=	$ 7
Normal Costs					=	26
Total Costs						$33

† Denotes Activity on Critical Path

Step 6　Plot Costs and Find Minimum Cost Schedule

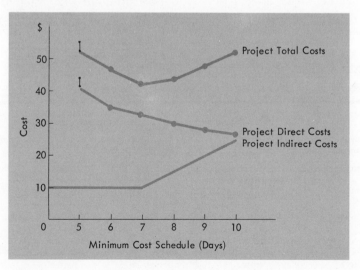

TABLE S.12.4

Calculation of cost per day to expedite each activity

Activity	$CC - NC$	$NT - CT$	$\dfrac{CC - NC}{NT - CT}$	Cost per day to expedite	Number of days activity may be shortened
A.................	$10 - $6	2 − 1	$\dfrac{\$10 - \$6}{2 - 1}$	$4	1
B.................	$18 − $9	5 − 2	$\dfrac{\$18 - \$9}{5 - 2}$	$3	3
C.................	$ 8 − $6	4 − 3	$\dfrac{\$8 - \$6}{4 - 3}$	$2	1
D.................	$ 9 − $5	3 − 1	$\dfrac{\$9 - \$5}{3 - 1}$	$2	2

crash times of those activities on the critical path. Obviously, we would choose the activities that cost the most to expedite as the first ones to be "relaxed." Thus we would add one day to the crash schedule of activity A, saving $4 (this is the maximum for A since this puts it back to its normal time of two days). Activity B has the next highest expediting cost, so we would add two days to its crash time, saving $6 (2 days × $3). This would yield the schedule shown in Figure S.12.8, step 5.

6. *Plot project-direct, indirect, and total-cost curves and find minimum-cost schedule.* For the sake of comparison, all intermediate schedules have been derived for this example (see Table S.12.5). However, as can be seen from the project direct cost curve shown in Figure S.12.8, step 6, connecting just the three cost coordinates associated with 10-, 7-, and 5-day schedules would provide a good estimate of the entire cost curve. To complete the

TABLE S.12.5

Activity direct cost calculations, intermediate schedules

Schedule duration		Activity A	B	C	D	Total expediting costs	Normal costs	Total direct costs per activity
6 days.....	Activity time.......	1*	4*	4*	1*			
	Days expedited.....	1	1	—	2			
	Expediting costs....$4		$3	—	$4	= $11 +	$26 =	$37
7 days.....	Activity time.......	2*	4*	4	1*			
	Days expedited.....	—	1	—	2			
	Expediting costs....	—	$3	—	$4	= 7 +	26 =	33
8 days.....	Activity time.......	2*	5*	4	1*			
	Days expedited.....	—	—	—	2			
	Expediting costs....	—	—	—	$4	= 4 +	26 =	30
9 days.....	Activity time.......	2*	5*	4	2*			
	Days expedited.....	—	—	—	1			
	Expediting costs....	—	—	—	$2	= 2 +	26 =	28

* Denotes activity on critical path.

example requires the inclusion of the indirect project cost curve, which in this case is a constant $10 per day for a 5-, 6-, or 7-day schedule, and increases at a rate of $5 per day for 8-, 9-, and 10-day project durations. (This type of curve would be typical of a situation where penalties are levied for exceeding a due date—or, conversely, where bonuses are awarded for meeting the schedule or for early completion.)

Summing the values for direct and indirect costs for each day yields the project total cost curve. As can be seen from the graph, this curve is at its minimum for a seven-day schedule, which costs $43. It should be noted that the black lines extending upward from the project total cost curve and the project direct cost curve at 5 days reflect the difference in cost between the all-crash and "rational" crash schedules.

PERT–COST

The basic objectives of PERT–COST are (1) to develop a realistic original project cost estimate and (2) to meet or excel this cost estimate through detailed cost monitoring and control. The essential features of a PERT–COST system are:

1. A modified PERT–TIME network
2. A work breakdown structure
3. Work packages
4. A series of reports

Each of these will be discussed using the Antismog Device Redesign Project (introduced earlier).

1. *Modified PERT–TIME network.* The modification consists of adding cost estimates for the completion of each activity, based upon the expected completion time (*ET*) of each activity. (Hypothetical costs for three activities are shown in Figure S.12.9.)

2. *Work breakdown structure.* The work breakdown structure specifies which organizational units are responsible for each activity required by the project. In our example, we might have a design group, a testing group, and a documentation group, each of which would be responsible for one of these three phases of the project. In addition, the work breakdown structure specifies different levels of project reporting. For example, the president of the auto company would be on level 1, the research manager on level 2, and

FIGURE S.12.9

Work packages for three phases of the Antismog Device Redesign Project (data shown for work package *B* only)

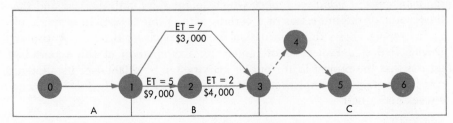

heads of the three groups on level 3. (Naturally, the work breakdown structure for a major project such as a missile system would be much more complex, would cut across organizational lines, and would be under the direction of a project manager who could command resources throughout the firm.)

3. *Work packages.* A work package refers to a group of activities which are combined for purposes of budgetary control. Often termed *cost work packages*, they may be determined on the basis of activity duration time—for example, a work package equals three month's work—or on the basis of expenditure—for example, a work package equals $75,000 in cost. In our example we have three work packages, A, B, and C, which relate directly to the three groups mentioned in the work breakdown structure. Work packages are commonly denoted by blocks around their activities. As can be seen in Figure S.12.9, work package B consists of three activities and is budgeted at $16,000.

TABLE S.12.6

PERT–COST status report (2d summary report for Antismog Device Redesign Project [work package *B*], current date 1/3)

Activity	Budget No.	Cost Status						Time Status							
		Work Performed to Date			Totals at Completion										
		Value	Actual Cost	(Over) or Under	Planned Cost	Latest Revised Estimate	Projected (Over) or Under	Expected Time	Scheduled Time	Scheduled Completion Date	Latest Completion Date	Activity Slack	Percent Completed	Scheduled Percent	Percent Ahead or (Behind)
1–2	B–1	6	8	(2)	9	12	(3)	5	5	1/5	1/5	0	40	60	(20)
1–3	B–2	2	2	—	3	3	—	7	7	1/7	1/7	0	42.8	42.8	—
2–3	B–3	—	—	—	4	4	—	2	2	1/7	1/7	0	—	—	—

4. *Reports.* The more elaborate PERT–COST systems use a number of reports that go to different levels of the work breakdown structure, as well as to certain functional areas of the firm, such as finance, accounting, and personnel. Information provided by these reports includes manpower availability and use, the general financial status of the project, and trends and prediction of deviations of cost and time from plan (the latter often in graphical form). A key report, which goes to the project manager, is the *management summary report,* which summarizes both the cost and the time status of the project as of a certain date. Table S.12.6, an example of such a report, shows this information for work package B on the Antismog Device Redesign Project as of January 3. Examination of this report indicates that the project is in trouble: activity 1–2 is $2,000 over its allotted cost for its stage of completion and is 20 percent behind schedule, or about a week and a half.

Problems with PERT–COST. Although PERT–COST is subject to the same criticisms as PERT–TIME (which are considered later in the supplement), its emphasis on budgeting subjects it to additional problems as well. In particular, the use of work packages generally requires new cost accounting codes, some adjustments in handling overhead, some means of determining allocation of indirect costs, and some way of pro-rating materials costs between work packages. Moreover, the sheer volume of accounting and budgetary data that are required to support an effective PERT–COST system can present a real information problem, even if the firm has good capability in data processing.

In summary, PERT–COST must be classified as an expensive technique, at least in comparison with the other techniques discussed in this supplement. And while it has been used with good success, it is not something that an organization should attempt without a good deal of prior research and planning.[6]

LIMITED RESOURCE MODELS

PERT and CPM implicitly assume that sufficient resources are always available to perform each activity. In practice, however, there is often competition for resources, especially manpower, between projects and between concurrently scheduled activities. Ideally, project managers would like to be able to incorporate into their network scheduling some mathematical way of assuring that resources will be optimally used and their availability never exceeded. Unfortunately, these goals are difficult to achieve, especially when other scheduling criteria, such as minimizing project duration or project cost, are also being considered. The complexity of the problem centers on the fact that for every possible starting time of an activity there are generally several possible resource combinations, and therefore for a project of even modest size there is usually a vast number of combinations to evaluate.

To illustrate how we might schedule a project to manpower constraints, consider the following diagrams. Figure S.12.10A is a small CPM-type network; the numbers in the circles denote both job number and crew size requirement and the number above the circle denotes the activity time in days. In Figure S.12.10B, a schedule graph of this project, the activities are plotted against a time scale. The number above each arrow represent's the job number and daily crew size requirement. The dashed line represents slack time (defined here as a job's early start minus its late start time). If there is no limitation on crew size this project can be completed in eight days.

Minimizing schedule time given limited manpower

Now suppose that there is a five-man-per-day resource limitation. Clearly, the project duration must be extended, and we would like to find a schedule

---

[6] The fact that the first full-scale application of PERT–COST was on the controversial TFX airplane development program offers further evidence in support of this admonition.

FIGURE S.12.10

CPM network and schedule graph—no resource limitation

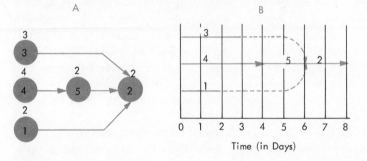

Time (in Days)

that will minimize the additional time required. As mentioned above, problems of this type have many possible schedules, and while an optimizing technique (such as linear programming) might be used for a small project such as this one, it is more useful to consider a heuristic method, which more likely would be employed in practice. In this regard, Weist has developed a procedure using three simple heuristic rules that would be applied on a day-by-day basis:

1. Allocate resources serially in time. That is, start on the first day and schedule all jobs possible; then do the same for the second day; and so on.
2. When several jobs compete for the same resources, give preference to the jobs with the least slack.
3. Reschedule noncritical jobs, if possible, in order to free resources for scheduling critical or nonslack jobs.[7]

Applying these rules yields the 11-day schedule shown in Figure S.12.11. Note that the dashed lines no longer unequivocally denote slack since only job 1 can be delayed without extending the project. Is this the shortest schedule given the five-man resource limitation? The answer is yes—based upon comparing it to all possible schedules. However, while the heuristic rules "worked" in this case, recall from our discussion of layout techniques (in Chapter 4) that heuristic methods do not guarantee optimum solutions; they only increase the likelihood of a better one. Thus following these rules for a different problem might result in a poor solution.

Other heuristic rules for deciding on job priority (subject to manpower limitations and technological ordering) are:

a. Schedule the job with the shortest duration first.
b. Schedule the job with the longest duration first.
c. Schedule the jobs for a particular organizational department first.
d. Schedule the job with the least technical uncertainty first.

[7] J. Weist, "Heuristic Programs for Decision Making," *Harvard Business Review* (September–October 1966), pp. 129–43.

FIGURE S.12.11

Schedule graph—five man resource limitation, 11 day schedule

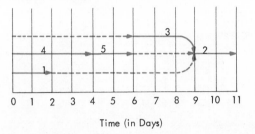

Time (in Days)

Manpower leveling given a fixed schedule date

The above example focused on the allocation of resources in order to minimize schedule time; however, a different sort of problem arises in resource leveling. In this situation the project completion date is fixed and management wants to smooth out or balance resource requirements throughout the project so as to minimize the costs involved in acquiring or releasing resources. Consider the following example, in which four days are available for the project and the appropriate crew size (i.e., number of men per day) must be determined. For the sake of presentation we have assumed that there are no sequence restrictions and no job 4. A schedule for this situation, in which all jobs are performed as soon as possible (termed *a left-justified schedule*), and the manpower loading chart for this solution appear in Figure S.12.12. By inspection, it is obvious that the work load could be better balanced and the crew size reduced. One way to proceed would be to try pushing all slack jobs over to their late start time to derive a "right-justified" schedule (Figure S.12.13).

This does not help the situation particularly, other than defer peak manpower requirements until the end of the project. (Such a schedule is sometimes desirable for long projects where management is concerned with the

FIGURE S.12.12

Schedule graph and manpower loading chart for left-justified schedule

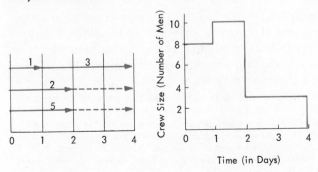

Time (in Days)

FIGURE S.12.13

Schedule graph and manpower loading chart for
right-justified schedule

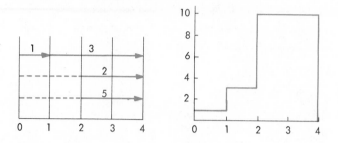

FIGURE S.12.14

Schedule graph and manpower loading chart for
trial and error schedule

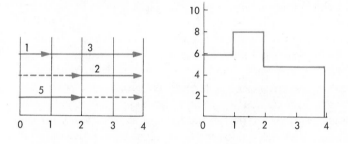

time value of money and would prefer to forestall expenditures. Incidentally, right-justified schedules will always result in achieving peak loads toward the end of the project if slack exists.)

The third solution developed by trial and error (Figure S.12.14) is the best one possible, and we note that the work load is better balanced and has a lower peak load than the other two. An ideal solution, in general, would be one yielding a rectangular manpower loading chart.[8]

CRITICAL PATH SCHEDULING AND THE COMPUTER

The rapid growth of critical path scheduling techniques has been accompanied by the development of computer programs to handle such tedious chores as calculating slack times, combining and updating networks, time-cost tradeoffs, statistical estimates, and resource allocations. The decision whether or not to use a computer depends, in general, upon the number of activities, the number of performance reviews, and the amount of updating

---

[8] Whether this is true in a given situation depends, of course, on the costs involved. The problem of minimizing the sum of all cost elements associated with a project, and a computer scheduling program designed to do it, is discussed in E. S. Buffa and W. H. Taubert, *Production and Inventory Systems Planning and Control,* rev. ed. (Homewood, Ill.: Richard D. Irwin, Inc., 1972), pp. 510–50.

required for the project. A common rule of thumb is that when the number of arrows exceeds 100, a computer program should be seriously considered for the basic PERT and CPM models. Computers are generally considered a must for minimum-cost scheduling, PERT–COST, and limited resource problems. A listing of some of the available computer programs and their features is presented in the Davis and Phillips bibliographical references.

PICKING ON PERT AND CPM

The widespread application of critical path techniques has generated a number of theoretically oriented writings that challenge certain underlying assumptions of the models in general and PERT and CPM in particular. Some of the more significant assumptions and their criticisms are summarized in Table S.12.7.

In addition to theoretical questions, there are some practical problems in applying critical path techniques. One that is of particular relevance to the PERT method is the difficulty encountered by operating personnel in understanding the statistical underpinnings of the model. The beta distribution of activity times, the three time estimates, the activity variances, and the use of normal distribution to arrive at project completion probabilities are all potential sources of misunderstandings, and with misunderstanding come distrust and obstruction. Thus if PERT is to be applied, management must be sure that the people charged with monitoring and controlling activity performance have a general understanding of the statistical features of PERT as well as the general nature of critical path scheduling. A trend in recent applications of PERT is to do away with the three time estimates in favor of one "best estimate." This modification however, at once removes some of the complexity from PERT and alleviates some of the theoretical problems in Table S.12.7. However, with this simplification comes a loss of the traits that set PERT apart and enable it to deal with statistical problems of project scheduling often in a better, though perhaps imperfect, way.

A second problem, recently investigated by Britney,[9] relates to the cost of over- and underestimating activity duration times. "Underestimates precipitate reallocations of resources and, in many cases, cause costly project delays. Overestimates, on the other hand, result in inactivity and tend to misdirect management's attention to relatively unfruitful areas causing planning losses."[10] (Britney recommends a modification of PERT called BPERT (which employs concepts from Bayesian decision theory) to explicitly consider these two categories of cost in deriving a project network plan.)

Another problem that sometimes arises, especially when PERT is used by subcontractors working with the government, is the attempt to "beat" the network in order to get on or off the critical path. Many government

---

[9] Robert R. Britney, "Bayesian Point Estimation and the PERT Scheduling of Stochastic Activities," *Management Science*, vol. 22, no. 9, May 1976, pp. 938–48.

[10] Ibid., p. 939.

TABLE S.12.7

Significant PERT/CPM assumptions and their criticisms

Assumption	*Criticisms*
1 Project activities can be identified as entities (that is, there is a clear beginning and ending point for each activity).	Projects, especially complex ones, change in content over time, and therefore a network made at the beginning may be highly inaccurate later on. Also, the very fact that activities are specified and a network formalized tends to limit the flexibility that is required to handle changing situations as the project progresses.
2 Project activity sequence relationships can be specified and "networked."	Sequence relationships cannot always be specified beforehand. In some projects, in fact, the ordering of certain activities is conditional on previous activities. (PERT and CPM, in their basic form, have no provision for treating this problem, although some other techniques have been proposed that present the project manager with several contingency paths, given different outcomes from each activity.)
3 Project control should focus on the critical path.	It is not necessarily true that the longest time-consuming path (or the path with zero slack) obtained from summing activity expected time values will ultimately determine project completion time. What often happens as the project progresses is that some activity not on the critical path becomes delayed to such a degree that it extends the entire project. For this reason it has been suggested that a critical activity concept replace the critical path concept as focus of managerial control. Under this approach, attention would center on those activities that have a high potential variation and lie on a "near-critical path." A near-critical path is one that does not share any activities with the critical path and, though it has slack, could become critical if one or a few activities along it become delayed. Obviously, the more parallelism in a network, the more likely that one or more near-critical paths will exist. Conversely, the more a network approximates a single series of activities, the less likely it is to have near-critical paths.

contracts provide cost incentives for finishing a project early or on a "cost-plus-fixed-fee" basis. The contractor who is on the critical path generally has more leverage in obtaining additional funds from these contracts since he has a major influence in determining the duration of the project. On the other hand—for political reasons we won't go into here—some contractors deem it desirable to be less "visible" and therefore adjust their time estimates and activity descriptions in such a way as to ensure that they *won't* be on the critical path. This criticism of course reflects more on the use of the method than on the method itself, but PERT (and CPM, for that matter), by virtue of its focus on the critical path, enables such ploys to be used.

Finally, the cost of applying critical path methods to a project is some-

TABLE S.12.7 *(continued)*

Assumption	*Criticisms*
4 The activity times in PERT follow the beta distribution, with the variance of the project assumed to be equal to the sum of the variances along the critical path	As was mentioned in the discussion on PERT, the beta distribution was selected for a variety of good reasons. Nevertheless, each component of the statistical treatment in PERT has been brought into question. First, the formulas are in reality a modification of the beta distribution mean and variance, which, when compared to the basic formulas, could be expected to lead to absolute errors on the order of 10 percent for ET and 5 percent for the individual variances. Second, given that the activity time distributions have the properties of unimodality, continuity, and finite positive end points, other distributions with the same properties would yield different means and variances. Third, obtaining three "valid" time estimates to put into the PERT formulas presents operational problems—it is often difficult to arrive at one activity time estimate, let alone three, and the subjective definitions of a and b do not help the matter. (How optimistic and pessimistic should one be?)

times used as a basis for criticism. However, the cost of applying PERT–TIME rarely exceeds 2 percent of total project cost, and PERT–COST rarely exceeds 5 percent of total project costs. Thus, this added cost is generally outweighed by the savings from improved scheduling and reduced project time.

CONCLUSION

The critical path techniques of PERT and CPM have proven themselves in the past decade and promise to be of continued value in the future. Certainly the fact that management has a tool that allows it to structure complex projects in an understandable way, to pick out possible sources of delay before they occur, to isolate areas of responsibility, and of course to save time in the performance of costly projects are sufficient to justify this assertion. It also seems likely that the various techniques employing cost features will become increasingly applied, especially in the construction industries, which are feeling a growing pressure to keep costs down.[11] Finally, limited resource models that use heuristic methods will continue to be applied, abetted by practical observations as to which heuristic rules lead to better schedules. In this regard, Davis suggests that a likely mechanism for find-

---

[11] As of 1971, cost-minimizing models in construction were not widely used. A survey of 33 major construction firms showed that while 68 percent of the companies used critical path methods, only one reported using PERT–COST. See C. Warren Neel, "Evaluation of Network Models Use in Industrial Construction," *I.E.E.E. Transactions on Engineering Management,* EM 18–18, no. 1 (February 1971), pp. 7–11.

ing such heuristics is man-machine interactive procedures that can take advantage "of the full heuristic power of the computer much more imaginatively than has hitherto been realized."[12]

REVIEW AND DISCUSSION QUESTIONS

1. What characteristics must a project have in order for critical path scheduling to be applicable? What types of projects have been subjected to critical path analysis?
2. What is the major difference between PERT and CPM?
3. Why was the beta distribution chosen by PERT developers to represent activity time variation?
4. What are the underlying assumptions of minimum cost scheduling? Are they equally realistic?
5. What is meant by a "rational" crash schedule?
6. Define or describe the following: work breakdown structure, work package, and management summary report.
7. What does the term *slack* refer to in limited resource scheduling? Compare it to the slack concept as used in CPM.
8. Compare the objectives of resource allocation models and manpower loading models.
9. "Project control should always focus on the critical path." Comment.
10. Why would a subcontractor for a government project want his activities on the critical path? Under what conditions would he try to avoid being on the critical path?

PROBLEMS

1. Your wife has decided that you will build a patio and barbecue grill during your vacation. Since your annual vacation starts next week, you must have a plan in order to complete the patio on time. And because your wife wants an enclosed patio, you will have to hire some help. Listed below are the activities and events involved.

   Prepare a PERT network for the patio project, including any additional events and activities you deem necessary to portray your plan adequately.[13]

---

[12] E. W. Davis, "Project Scheduling under Resource Constraints—Historical Review," *AIIE Transactions*, vol. 5, no. 4, December 1973, pp. 297–311. Quote on page 311.

[13] Drawn from "PERT Exercise Manual," DOD 1.6/:P 94/6, PERT Orientation and Training Center, Washington, D.C. (1965).

Events	*Activities*
Wife's approval of design	
Building permit applied for	Apply for building permit
Building materials ordered	Order building materials
Ground leveled	Level ground
Help hired	Hire help
Concrete forms laid out	Lay out concrete forms
Structure fabricated	Fabricate structure
Building inspection approved	Receive building permit
Lighting installed	Install lighting
Concrete work finished	Finish cement
Project completed	
Materials received	Receive materials
Help paid	Pay help
Ready-mix concrete ordered	Order concrete
Barbecue completed	Build barbecue
Painting completed	Paint
Building permit received	Building inspection
	Receive concrete

2. A wagon train of settlers is going to California and is due to leave Saint Joseph, Missouri, in the spring of 1849. According to Bart Whipwielder, the wagon boss, the trip will take the train through Fort Leavenworth, Kansas, and Reno, Nevada, en route to Sacramento. Competition for settlers is keen, so Bart is optimistic in his advertising. He says the first leg of the trip will take two weeks, the second leg three weeks, and the third leg two weeks. Harvey Weakwill, an irresolute settler, fears the worst. He says that the first leg will take four weeks, the second leg 11 weeks, and the third leg, 10 weeks. However, Trotting Turkey, the trusty Indian guide who has made twelve trips and is considered the expert, indicates the most likely times for the trip are: first leg, three weeks; second leg, four weeks, and third leg, three weeks. How many weeks' provisions must be stocked so that the settlers can be 95 percent sure that they will arrive in Sacramento before their food is gone?

3. Using the PERT network shown, which shows three times estimates (in weeks) for all activities, find the following:

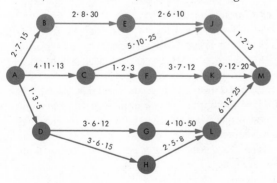

   a. The critical path.
   b. The variances of activities along the critical path.
   c. The probability of completing the project in 36 weeks.

4. The home office billing department of a chain of department stores prepares monthly inventory reports for use by the stores' purchasing agents. Given the information below, use the critical path method to determine

a. how long the total process will take.

b. which jobs can be delayed without delaying the early start of any subsequent activity.

Job and Description		Immediate Predecessors	Time (in hours)
a	Start..	–	0
b	Get computer printouts of customer purchases......	a	10
c	Get stock records for the month....................	a	20
d	Reconcile purchase printouts and stock records.......	b,c	30
e	Total stock records by department..................	b,c	20
f	Determine reorder quantities for coming period.......	e	40
g	Prepare stock reports for purchasing agents..........	d,f	20
h	Finish...	g	0

5. Zapp Inc. is nearly finished with a project to produce a small warning-signal generator. Because of a reduction in performance characteristics required, the remainder of the work is simpler than was originally planned and a new estimate of time to completion must be made. The following is known:

Activity	Time (days)	Immediate predecessors	Description
a	1	—	Check total weight and approve
b	2	—	Check power consumption
c	2	—	Check temperature requirements
d	2	a,b	Choose connecting plug
e	4	b,c	Fix resistors' final values
f	1	c	Choose encapsulating foam
g	4	d	Ensure hermetic seal
h	8	g,e,f	Perform final test

a. Draw a critical path scheduling diagram and indicate the critical path.

b. What is the minimum time to completion?

c. If the starting day is day zero, what is the early start time for activity *d*?

d. What is the slack time for activity *d*?

e. During the second day of work (day 1) it is discovered that activity *f* (Choose encapsulating foam) will take four days instead of one. Will this delay the project? If the activity takes six days, will the project be delayed?

f. Zapp Inc. has a limited number of men available to work on the project, and only two activities can be under way at the same time. Will this delay the project beyond what the time would have been with unlimited resources (activity *f* takes six days to complete)? If you are interested, try creating a schedule with this limited resource restriction.

6. For the CPM network shown:

a. Determine the critical path and the early completion time for the project.

b. Using the data shown, reduce the project completion time by four weeks. Assume a linear cost per day shortened and show, step by step, how you arrived at your schedule. Also indicate the critical path.

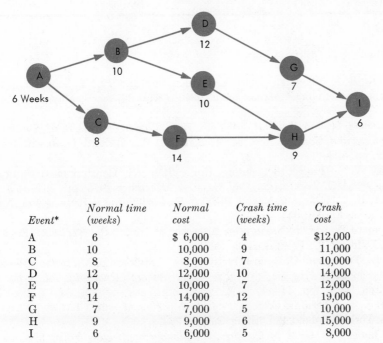

Event*	Normal time (weeks)	Normal cost	Crash time (weeks)	Crash cost
A	6	$ 6,000	4	$12,000
B	10	10,000	9	11,000
C	8	8,000	7	10,000
D	12	12,000	10	14,000
E	10	10,000	7	12,000
F	14	14,000	12	19,000
G	7	7,000	5	10,000
H	9	9,000	6	15,000
I	6	6,000	5	8,000

° An activity cannot be shortened to less than its crash time.

7. The following network depicts the activity sequence required to complete
   a small project. The time to complete each activity is shown next to each
   activity designation, and for simplicity it is assumed that the resource
   requirements for each job are the same as the job time; for example,
   activity *d* requires four days to complete using four men each day.

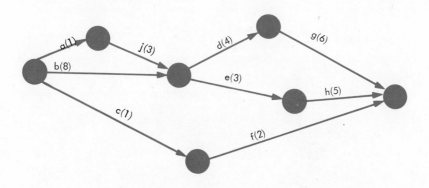

   a. Assuming a condition of unlimited resources, develop an early start
   (that is, left-justified) schedule using a schedule graph.

   b. Now, assuming that only 10 men are available each day, develop
   a late start (that is, right-justified) schedule.

   c. Sketch the manpower loading charts for the solutions derived in (*a*)
   and (*b*).

SELECTED BIBLIOGRAPHY

Britney, R. R.   "Bayesian Point Estimation and the PERT Scheduling of Stochastic Activities," *Management Science*, vol. 22, no. 9, May 1976, pp. 938–948.

Buffa, Elwood S. and Taubert, William H.   *Production-Inventory Systems: Planning and Control.* Rev. ed. Homewood, Ill.: Richard D. Irwin, Inc., 1972, pp. 303–66.

Davis, E. W.   "Project Scheduling Under Resource Constraints—Historical Review," *AIIE Transactions*, vol. 5, no. 4, December 1973, pp. 297–311.

Dooley, A. R.   "Interpretations of PERT," *Harvard Business Review*, Vol. No. 2 (March–April 1964), pp. 160–62.

Hein, Leonard W.   *The Quantitative Approach to Managerial Decisions.* Englewood Cliffs, N.J.: Prentice-Hall, 1967.

Levy, F. K., Thompson, G. L., and Weist, J. D.   "Multi-Ship, Multi-Shop Workload Smoothing Program," *Naval Logistics Research Quarterly*, vol. 9, no. 1 (March 1962), pp. 34–44.

Moder, J. J., and Phillips, C. R.   *Project Management with CPM and PERT.* New York: Reinhold Publishing Corp., 1964.

O'Brien, James J.   *CPM in Construction Management.* New York: McGraw-Hill, 1965.

Phillips, C. R.   "Fifteen Key Features of Computer Programs for CPM and PERT," *Journal of Industrial Engineering*, vol. 15 (January–February 1964), pp. 14–20.

Weist, Jerome D., and Levy, Ferdinand K.   *A Management Guide to PERT/CPM.* Englewood Cliffs, N.J.: Prentice-Hall, 1969.

Section five

The system in
steady state

OVERVIEW

THE STEADY STATE period is the longest phase of the typical system's life cycle. The production manager's job during this period consists of maintaining adequate performance of the system and searching out ways in which that performance can be improved.

Chapter 13 deals with maintaining performance by focusing on some of the day-to-day problems (or malfunctions) encountered by the system and describes the ways in which these problems can be corrected.

Chapter 14 considers the ways in which the production manager can make an already satisfactory system perform even better.

Together, these two chapters highlight the routine and not-so-routine problems and opportunities faced by the production manager in a going concern.

13

Malfunctions and corrections

W hile the achievement of a steady state level of system performance implies that design and startup problems have been solved, it does not mean that the pressure is off the production manager. Regardless of how careful the planning, few systems of any complexity can be expected to operate indefinitely without encountering some type of malfunction that must be corrected. This is true not only for the physical production process but for the production management system that monitors that process as well. Indeed, while machinery may produce scrap or break down, thus necessitating repairs, the operating and control system that governs the use of that machinery may provide faulty information and incorrect decisions, requiring that it, too, be overhauled.

In this chapter we will examine the types of malfunctions that may disrupt the production system and look at the two production management functions—production control and maintenance—that are most vitally concerned with interruptions of the production process. In addition, we will discuss the concept of a control system, the existence of which is essential to detect and correct malfunctions. Finally, we will consider the growing problem of environmental pollution and its effect on the activities of the production manager.

SOURCES OF MALFUNCTIONS

Malfunctions in the production system arise from sources internal and external to the system. Those sources within the production system are production processes, production personnel, and production operating and control systems. Some of those sources that are external to the system are corporate policy, other functional areas of the firm, suppliers, unions, governmental policies and actions, competitors, and customers.

The distinction between internal and external sources is significant for two reasons. First, external sources are beyond the production manager's sphere of influence, and therefore malfunctions arising from them cannot be dealt with unilaterally; the production manager and his staff must reach solutions to the problems with a second party, such as a union representative, a customer's agent, or a legal counselor. Second, formal and often highly sophisticated control systems can be employed for handling malfunctions that arise internally, whereas the variety of potential malfunctions arising from external sources is so broad that it precludes development of refined control procedures to deal with every eventuality. Indeed, it is one thing to develop a system for correcting machine malfunctions, but it is quite another undertaking to keep the workforce operating in the face of—say—a wildcat strike.

CONTROL

Control may be broadly defined as the process of measuring, evaluating, and adjusting system performance so that it meets system goals. Within this definition we have isolated five phases of control: sensing, comparing, analyzing, decision making, and corrective action. These phases, along with the required information inputs, their sources, and some key considerations, are presented in Figure 13.1. Although the inclusion of information inputs in any discussion of control is necessary since no control system can operate without data, its inclusion here is doubly useful because it provides a consistent framework for treating the variety of topics that bear upon the general nature of malfunctions and corrections.

Sensing (phase 1) is essentially data gathering so as to determine the status of the system. This status information comes from operating data, which are found in written documents such as reports, accounting statements, control charts, and time cards, or from mechanical devices such as heat sensors, gauges, and dials, or from observations by individuals in the system, such as workers, engineers, supervisors, and production control personnel.

Comparing (phase 2) entails matching the operating data with the predetermined standards of performance, derived from time standards, company goals, equipment manuals, etc. Standards of performance might include product specifications, desired output levels, allowable temperature ranges, and the like. If the control system is designed correctly, the malfunction should come to light at this point, but in any case the control process would continue through each subsequent phase.

Analyzing (phase 3) is concerned with detecting the cause of a malfunction. Possible sources of the malfunction should be made available

FIGURE 13.1

Phases of control

CONTROL PHASE	REQUIRED INFORMATION	TYPICAL INFORMATION SOURCES	KEY CONSIDERATIONS
1. Sensing	Operating Data	Control Charts / Reports	Relevant Data
2. Comparing	Standards	Company Goals / Equipment Manuals / Time Statistics	Timeliness
3. Analyzing	Error Sources	Staff Specialists / Work Force / Customers / Records	Error Detection
4. Decision Making	Alternatives	Staff Specialists / Work Force / Consultants	Development of Responses
5. Corrective Action	Responsible Element	Organization Chart / Process Specifications / Staff Specialists / Work Force	Information Feedback

to be used for fault finding. (We will consider several fault-finding methods below.) Customers, design engineers, output reports, and profit and loss statements are common sources of information on product and organization problems. Flight recorders and ships' logs often provide the clues in determining why airplanes and ships were lost.

Decision making (phase 4) entails selecting the appropriate corrective action from among some specified set of alternatives. This step can become quite involved, depending upon the complexity of the system and the degree of uncertainty within the environment in which the system operates. (A more lengthy discussion of this topic is provided in Chapter 16.) Data for the development of alternatives may come from product designers, production management personnel, sales personnel, repair manuals, and trade journals—to name but a few. The decision maker can be either an individual or a component of some physical system that has been programmed to alter the system's status when some specific deviation is noted; for example, a numerically controlled machine may be programmed to shut down when a drill bit breaks.

Corrective action (phase 5) implements the adjustment decision and may consist of just one action, such as a water sprinkling system being activated when heat is sensed, or several actions, such as a worker's stopping, repairing, and restarting a machine. The "responsible element" may be a switch in a mechanical device, or an individual who is given the responsibility for adjusting performance on the basis of his position in an organization.

Follow-up (though not shown as a specific phase in control) is a common feature in production management control systems where people are the dominant element. In complex production systems, such as a large job shop, the follow-up function is often performed by an expediter who traces the progress of specific orders and attempts to assure that they will be out on time.

In passing, we might note that extensive use of an expediter can raise more problems than it solves, because by trying to get his job to the "head of the line," the expediter may foil a master schedule that has been designed to optimize the completion time for all jobs in the system. On the basis of a large computer simulation study of a job shop, Hottenstein concluded (among other things) that "The use of expediting significantly increases the average time a job spends in the shop by increasing waiting time per job" and that "Shops with expediting, with few exceptions, do a poorer job in meeting delivery date commitments than do their counterpart shops which do not employ expediting."[1] This general undesirability of expediting is supported by Plossl, who on the basis of extensive industrial experience avers that "if a little expediting is good, a little less will be better."[2]

---

[1] M. P. Hottenstein, "A Simulation Study of Expediting in a Job Shop," *Production and Inventory Management* (Second Quarter, 1969), pp. 9–10.

[2] G. W. Plossl, "Common Sense: Help or Hindrance in Production Control?" *Production and Inventory Management* (Second Quarter, 1969), p. 13.

Key considerations

In developing the control process, one should be attuned to certain factors, or key considerations, that arise during each phase.

Relevant data. During the sensing phase it is often important to exclude as much extraneous data as possible from the control process. It will be recalled from Chapter 6 that data are not information, and moreover that too much data can clutter up the sensing activity to the degree that real information cannot be discerned. Application of the exception principle may help in such situations, if the sensing element is capable of distinguishing between significant variations and events that are simply unusual.

Timeliness. When the comparing phase takes place is often as important as *what* it compares. This point can be clarified by distinguishing between two general approaches to control in the context of time. One is "current control," which is concerned with controlling performance while it is still taking place, and the other is "post control," which occurs after the fact and attempts to determine whether events turned out as planned. While there is a need for both types of control in all organizations, problems arise when management makes its comparisons after the fact (post control) when they really are needed during operations (current control).

The type of control that is employed also implies the type of control "tool" that is used. In current control we would employ "tools of adjustment," consisting of time-based devices such as control charts, while in post control we would use "tools of evaluation," such as productivity reports, scrap reports, and accounting documents.

Error detection. During the analysis phase, error detection (also known as fault finding or trouble shooting) can be a substantial challenge because finding out what went wrong (especially in complex systems) may be as difficult and time consuming as deciding upon the appropriate corrective action. Scientists and engineers have been particularly interested in the topic of problem location, and a good deal of sophisticated research has been done in developing error detection methods (especially in dealing with electrical circuitry malfunctions). Table 13.1 summarizes several of these trouble-shooting approaches.

Development of responses. A key consideration in dealing with malfunctions at the decision-making phase is the development and selection of alternative responses; that is, deciding what options are available and which is the best one to select. In dealing with these questions, the technique of sequential analysis can be of great value. Sequential analysis, in this context, consists of breaking down a problem area into its constituent parts to show cause-and-effect, or cause-and-solution, relationships.

Figure 13.2, an example of sequential analysis, illustrates some of the general sources of production system malfunctions, focusing in this case on the causes of high direct labor costs. Note that this is just a partial "tree" (which is indicated by the lines extending outward from the nodes). If we were to continue the analysis, we might hypothesize, for example, that loose time standards are caused by poor methods study, which in turn might be caused by inexperienced methods analysts, and so on. There is no limitation

TABLE 13.1

Trouble-shooting approaches

Approach	*Basic concept*	*Example*
Detection at a glance	Individual looks at process operation directly or reads meters, trouble lights, etc., which are part of the system	Miner checks gas meter for toxic fumes in mine shaft. Mechanic listens to engine idle. Physician observes patient's walk for signs of general illness
Short and continuity checks	Check interconnections and components of system one at a time	Television repairman tests each transistor tube and circuit
a. Signal tracing	A standard signal is inserted into input of a multistage system and successive components within the system are systematically monitored for prescribed outputs	TV, stereo, radio repair procedure; technician monitors test points in systematic (typically back-to-front) sequence
b. Signal substitution	Prescribed signal is inserted into subsystem or independent component of system and individual stage is monitored for prescribed output	Signal introduced to test the audio section of a faulty TV or stereo
Creating independence	Testing dependent components independently of operating system, according to separate test specifications	Assembler is removed from assembly line and time studied
Binary splits	Successive halving of a system to reduce number of checks. (The maximum and average number of checks by this method is $\log_2 N$, where $N =$ number of components. The maximum for a sequential approach is $N - 1$, and the average is $$\frac{1}{N}\left[\frac{(N-1)N}{2}+(N^{-1})\right]$$	Determining the bottleneck in a 16-station assembly line by measuring output of the 8th assembly station first: if its output is sufficient, go to the 12th; if it is sufficient, go to 14th. (The maximum number of checks required by this procedure is 4 versus the 15 that would be the maximum required by a sequential approach)
Stress methods	This approach is generally applied to avoid malfunctions and consists of overloading or underloading a system to "weed out" weak components	Performing "figure 8s" with a "prototype" airliner; physical and mental tests of soldiers; vibration testing of car radios
Block substitution	Successive replacement of a block or "module," consisting of interrelated components, with a new block or module. This procedure enables simultaneous fault finding and correction	Substitution of new wired circuit panel for existing panel in a malfunctioning computer; substitution of work group or team for one that has been ineffective

Source: Summarized in part from Van Court Hare, *Systems Analysis: A Diagnostic Approach* (New York: Harcourt Brace Jovanovich, 1967), pp. 259–72.

FIGURE 13.2

Two segments of a sequential analysis diagram focusing on the causes of high direct labor costs for a hypothetical system

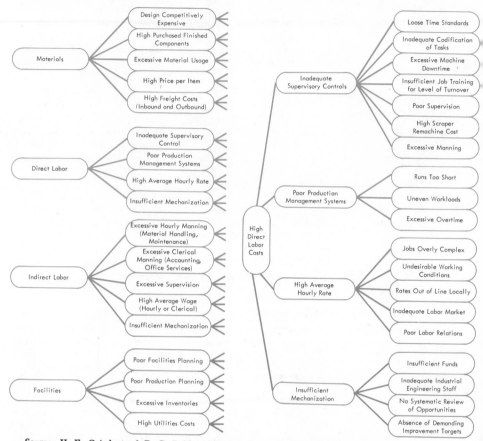

Source: H. E. Geissler and P. C. Buhler, "Zeroing in on Cost Savings," *Modern Manufacturing* (November 1970), p. 84. Reprinted by special permission of *Factory*, November 1970. Copyright, Morgan-Grampian, Inc., November 1970.

to how many branches and nodes are considered; the important thing is that the likely source of the problem is ultimately pinpointed.

Figure 13.3 illustrates sequential analysis applied to finding the most costly source of excess scrap and rework in the production of turbine blades. In this example the procedure entails isolating the relevant factors at each stage of the process and then costing out each stage by summing from the "probable cause" backward to "grouping." Since the path leading to *tooling setup wrong* has the highest total cost, this would be taken as the probable cause, and therefore would receive first attention.

In addition to using cost in selecting an area for correction, sequential analysis can employ statistical probability to aid in selection. For example, in reference to the heading *type of discrepancy* in the turbine blade case (Figure 13.3), we might hypothesize that for Dept. 100 there is a 60 percent probability that *drilled hole–off location on size* is the real discrepancy, and

FIGURE 13.3

Sequential analysis applied to finding the most costly source

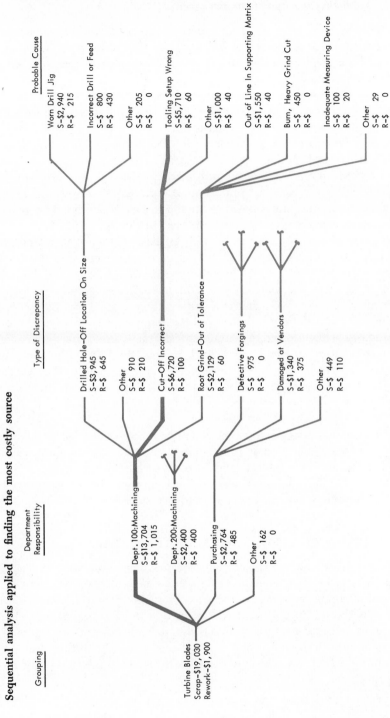

Source: H. E. Geissler and P. C. Buhler, "Zeroing on Cost Savings," *Modern Manufacturing*, November 1970, p. 84.

that there is only a 20, 15, and 5 percent probability that *other, cut-off incorrect,* and *root grind–out of tolerance* are the true causes. Thus on the basis of highest probability, corrective action would be centered initially on the first alternative.[3]

Information feedback. Information feedback is both a key consideration and a vital component of a control system. In simplest terms, feedback is information about the output or status of a system that is used to affect the input and therefore the performance of that system. Feedback may be either positive or negative.

Feedback is positive when the information carried by the feedback loop adds to and reinforces the input signal and thereby results in an even greater output. And since positive feedback causes continual increase in output, some form of limitation must exist to constrain its effect. An example of positive feedback can be seen in the operation of a maintenance program, where the greater the success of the program, the greater the demand for preventive maintenance service. In this case the limitation would be the size and availability of the maintenance crew.

Feedback is negative when the information carried by the feedback loop opposes and therefore diminishes the input signal. An example is the operation of a thermostat that automatically activates a furnace to bring room temperature to the desired level, so that the higher the room temperature, the greater the signal to decrease furnace output. (*Positive* feedback, in this case, would cause an increasingly higher demand for furnace output as the room temperature rises, and the limitation would be the ultimate heating capacity of the furnace.)

When there is a significant time delay in the feedback loop, the system output may oscillate for some time while trying to achieve stability. This is common in business systems, and is epitomized in production-inventory systems, where information delays arising from the production-distribution process alternately lead to stockouts and overstock.[4]

PRODUCTION CONTROL AND MAINTENANCE

Though all production departments deal with malfunctions at one time or another, production control and facilities maintenance are most often involved in coping with these problems. Production control is involved because it is the focal point of daily production decisions, and maintenance is involved because its specific organizational role is to avert (as well as repair) failures in the physical aspects of the system. With this observation as an introduction, we will now examine the general activities of each of these functions.

---

[3] For a different approach to diagramming system problems and solutions, see Michael S. Inoue and James L. Riggs, "Describe Your System with Cause and Effect Diagrams," *Industrial Engineering* (April 1971), pp. 26–31, and James L. Riggs and Michael S. Inoue, *Introduction to Operations Research and Management Science* (New York: McGraw-Hill, 1975).

[4] See the discussion on industrial dynamics in the supplement to Chapter 6.

Activities of production control departments

As was discussed in Chapter 3, production management activities are often diffused throughout service organizations and therefore production control departments are rarely included in the formal organization structures of banks, hospitals, universities, etc. Manufacturing and process industries, on the other hand, typically have such departments, which are formalized under the heading "production planning," "production planning and inventory control," or simply "production control." A survey by the American Production and Inventory Control Society shows that the activities which generally fall under the jurisdiction of production control department are: (1) aggregate production planning, (2) production scheduling, and (3) inventory control. And, as can be seen from Table 13.2, the survey indicates that production control departments are often involved in many other production management and peripheral activities.

In terms of its role in the organization structure, production control is a coordinative staff function—one that serves the line organization by correlating the work of specialized staff departments (for example, product and process design, personnel, maintenance, and quality control) and the line organization.

The manager of production control commonly reports to either the plant manager or the production manager, though in some firms he may report directly to the president.

In handling malfunctions (as well as day-to-day operations), production control generally has autonomy up to the point where its decisions affect the operating budgets of departments other than those under the line manager to whom production control reports. That is, in dealing with an "outside" department, production control would not authorize overtime work, additional manpower, or new inventory items without the former's formal consent since such action would have to be charged against the budget of a different line manager.

A wide variety of malfunctions are of concern to production control. Among the more easily recognizable are failures in the production process, such as equipment breakdowns, extremely high scrap rates, and work stoppages. Less visible, but often of major consequence, are malfunctions in the production control system itself. The following excerpt from Plossl and Wight (p. 338) summarizes some of the more common symptoms and the probable underlying causes of a malfunctioning production control system:

1. *The forecasts are inaccurate*—this usually indicates an inflexible production control system and a lack of communication between production control and marketing or sales (along with a great deal of buck-passing). There is often room for considerable improvement in the marketing forecast, however, and this should start with a real understanding of the use that will be made of the forecast and of the consequences of poor forecasting.

2. *Nothing gets through our plant unless it is expedited*—this generally indicates that the plant is not operating at the proper capacity and that production control is forcing more and more work into the plant. Instead of recognizing

TABLE 13.2

Responsibilities of production and inventory control

Activity		Others also responsible	
Production planning			
Levels of production	77%	Production manager	8%
Plant capacity studies	50	Chief industrial engineer	15
Release new products for production	50	Chief product engineer	24
Participate in sales forecast	35	Sales manager	36
Authorize new product tooling	18	Chief industrial engineer	24
Levels of inventories for:			
Work in process	88	Plant manager	3
Production materials	81	Procurement	5
Finished goods	70	Sales manager	9
Decide to manufacture new products	25	Top management	11
Customer service			
Delivery schedules	76	Sales manager	10
Delivery promises	76	" "	11
Answers for customer follow-ups	48	" "	28
Order records	46	" "	26
Instructions to ship	44	" "	28
Shipping department			
Control of physical quantities of finished goods	65	Shipping foreman	5
Traffic			
Routing shipments	27	Traffic department	36
Routing purchased goods	23	Procurement	32
		Traffic	26
Production control			
Product routing	55	Chief industrial engineer	9
Make-or-buy decisions	37	Chief product engineer	11
Production orders			
Preparation and issue	91	Production manager	1
Order frequency (number of runs)	90	Plant manager	1
Quantity determination	90	Sales manager	2
Scheduling product through factory	87	Plant manager	2
Estimating manufacturing lead time	87	Production manager	2
Machine loading scheduled products	77	" "	3
Scrap allowances	68	Chief product engineer	3
Dispatching			
Schedules and instructions	91	Production manager	2
Follow-up reporting	87	" "	2
Expediting in plant	87	" "	2
Control quantity of work in process	82	Plant manager	5
Intraplant traffic	66	" "	3
Controlling raw material inventories			
Control quantity of production material	78	Procurement director	7
Placing purchase requisition	77	" "	11
Record keeping	75	Procurement director	9
Determine item inventory level	75	" "	9
Determine order frequency	73	" "	14
Determine inventory reserves	71	" "	10
Determine order quantity	70	" "	16
Control operating supplies inventory	53	" "	10
Control operating supplies quantities	48	" "	11
Determine purchase lead time	36	" "	51

Source: James H. Greene, *Production Control: Systems and Decisions* (Homewood, Ill.: Richard D. Irwin, Inc., 1965), p. 589.

and curing the real problem—*capacity*—they are attempting to cure the symptom (poor control over individual orders) by expediting.

3. *We never have enough lead time*—this indicates too much work-in-process. Ironically, allowing longer lead times will probably generate a higher level of work-in-process and compound the problem.

4. *We never seem to have the right items in production*—this is common in a company making complex assemblies, where the component inventory is replenished via order points rather than material plans using the latest forecast of assembly requirements, or where requirements are not generated frequently enough to relate component schedules to changing assembly requirements.

5. *We don't have time to follow production control system routines—there are too many crises*—production control people seem to enjoy fire-fighting more than fire-prevention. The longer that planning is postponed, the more fire-fighting becomes a way of life. As systems deteriorate, patchwork subsystems develop, which compound the problems further and expand production control's job to the point where it can't possibly be handled properly by the available personnel.[5]

Although rectifying such situations requires that a thorough study be made of the system in which they are found, several guidelines might be applied to the scheduling aspects of these problems.[6]

1. *Keep backlogs off the shop floor.* In job shop situations it is tempting to start orders as soon as possible, regardless of whether they will be delayed until the completion of other orders at various points in the process. These excess physical inventories create a space problem by cluttering up work areas, generate more expediting, make engineering changes more difficult to implement, and create general inefficiency in work flow scheduling.

2. *Schedule only items the factory can make.* Releasing orders for production when materials, components, or tools are not available during the schedule period creates problems similar to those in (1), and in addition results in a lack of confidence in the production control department on the part of operating personnel. Therefore production schedulers should be made to keep careful tabs on the status of all resources and they should not release orders until they know that they can be completed during the schedule period.

3. *Schedule to a short cycle.* Frequent scheduling (weekly or even daily) generally permits greater efficiency in the production flow by reducing in-process inventories and providing up-to-date information to departments up and down the production stream.

4. *Sequence orders according to latest requirements rather than according to the required dates that were established when the order was first released.* The status of orders often varies between the time the orders are placed by the customer and the time at which they are released for production. This variation may be caused by other orders' progressing

---

[5] Source: G. W. Plossl and O. W. Wight, *Production and Inventory Control: Principles and Techniques* (Englewood Cliffs, N.J.: Prentice-Hall, 1967). By permission of the publisher.

[6] The first four principles are drawn from Plossl and Wight, *Production and Inventory Control*, pp. 251–53.

faster or slower than anticipated, inventory stockouts, revisions in order specifications, etc. Therefore, so that adjustments may be made for the most recent changes in output requirements, it is advisable to wait until the last possible moment to release an order for production.

5. *Accept some periods of worker inactivity in monitoring the production schedule.* The fact that workers fear the consequences of inactivity (for example, layoffs) leads them to either to "stockpile" work or to slow down, to make sure that they are never out of work. This practice of building backlogs causes management to add to the inefficiency by authorizing overtime work, hiring more workers, etc.

This self-defeating behavior pattern, which has been termed the *backlog syndrome,*[7] insidiously eats away at the firm's profits. To deal with this problem requires that management reduce the workers' reliance on the physical presence of inventory and that management be willing to accept short periods of work force inactivity in setting up and monitoring the production schedule.

The maintenance function

The maintenance function may be thought of as a second production system operating in parallel with the firm's product manufacturing system. That is, in maintenance, as in direct productive activities, work must be scheduled, inventories of spare parts maintained, prescribed quality standards met, and labor standards and wage payment systems established. On one hand, the significance of this similarity is that the quantitative techniques employed in direct production are generally applicable to maintenance, and therefore it is theoretically possible to have a highly effective maintenance operation. On the other hand, the fact that maintenance must have access to the physical components of the production system means that there is always a potential for conflict between the two systems.

To develop the latter point it may be, for example, that the *most desirable maintenance policy* dictates that preventive maintenance be performed after the 2,000th hour of a machine's operation, while the *most efficient production rate* dictates that a production run consuming 2,500 hours be completed. Clearly, there are strong arguments on both sides—maintenance holding that extended operation will lead to more extensive repair and a less efficient work schedule and production arguing that it has a deadline to meet and must "get the product out." The ideal way of resolving such a problem is to boil the issue down to relative costs and decide on the least expensive alternative. Unfortunately, attaching a price tag to late deliveries (if maintenance is permitted to delay production) or to the possible additional repairs and inefficiencies of a new maintenance schedule (if production is allowed to proceed) can be extremely difficult. Thus the issue more often than not is decided by relative organizational power, organizational "log rolling," or an intuitively based managerial decree.

---

[7] Earl R. Gommersall, "The Backlog Syndrome," *Harvard Business Review* (September–October) 1964, pp. 105–15.

Another problem arising from this "second system" status of maintenance is crew size determination. Maintenance skills can be expensive, and union restrictions often limit the type of work that can be performed by any one maintenance man. Hence we are faced with another tradeoff—this time balancing the cost of retaining a given number of maintenance service personnel against the cost of equipment downtime. This problem has been analyzed by the use of queuing theory and simulation, but here too the problem of costing intangibles often arises. One such intangible is maintenance worker idle time. Ideally, management would like to have enough maintenance men to enable immediate repair of any breakdown and to perform preventive maintenance at the exact time prescribed by its maintenance policy. In most companies, however, complete coverage would result in substantial nonmaintenance time, and would become prohibitively expensive unless there is some interim job for the men to do. Moreover, even if there is work to be done, it may not be suitable (e.g., skilled repairmen having to perform material handling work). Thus even before a queuing or simulation analysis is undertaken, considerable investigation may be required to determine just how much idle time costs, and in some instances it may even be necessary to develop an idle-time work schedule to evaluate the feasibility of a supplemental work routine.

Organizationally, the maintenance manager may report to the production manager, the plant manager, or, perhaps the plant engineer. His responsibility typically includes machine and equipment maintenance and building and building service maintenance. (Building and building services would be the maintenance supervisor's only concerns in the vast majority of service systems). With regard to the physical location of the maintenance function in a plant, it may be centralized, with workers assigned to different parts of the facility as need arises, or it may be decentralized into particular areas of the plant. Whether it is decentralized depends on several factors: whether there is sufficient demand for maintenance services, the time required to travel from a central shop, the degree of specialization required of the maintenance men, and the seriousness of downtime to the operation of a particular plant activity.

Focusing on machine and equipment maintenance, the major operational question is whether to fix equipment before it malfunctions (preventive maintenance) or wait and fix it after it malfunctions (remedial maintenance). Again, we are confronted with a tradeoff situation. In this case the tradeoff appears as shown in Figure 13.4, where preventive maintenance costs consist of those costs arising from inspecting and adjusting equipment, replacing or repairing parts, and the loss of production time engendered by these activities. Corrective maintenance costs are those that arise when the equipment fails, or cannot be operated at a reasonable cost. These costs also include lost production time, the costs of performing the maintenance, and in some instances the part of the cost of replacement equipment which, with better maintenance, would have been deferred.

The objective in dealing with this cost tradeoff is to find that point in time and that amount of maintenance that minimize the total cost of the

FIGURE 13.4

Amount of preventive maintenance

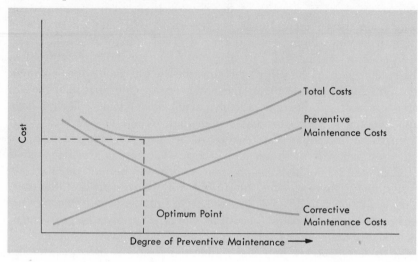

maintenance operation, as well as those productive operations that are affected by maintenance activities. Finding the optimum time and level of maintenance activities is often a complex task because the probable break-down times for various parts of pieces of equipment must be known, the repair times must be known, and—if maintenance personnel and resources are limited—maintenance priorities among machines and among depart-ments must be determined.

Moreover, even if these factors are known, evaluating and choosing from the broad range of possible maintenance policies present a sticky decision problem. Table 13.3 summarizes the possible policies available under three general approaches to maintenance: remedial maintenance, preventive maintenance, and conditional maintenance. The check marks denote various alternatives that can be used in each policy. *Remedial maintenance* refers to either a complete overhaul or replacement or repair of a piece of equip-ment when it breaks down. Such work can be performed immediately after a breakdown occurs or be placed in a queue of work that is performed at set intervals, such as every week or month. The latter policy might be fol-lowed where there is standby equipment and maintenance crews follow a specified schedule of rounds. (By definition, remedial maintenance would not be performed at the end of *n* hours of equipment operation unless the equipment breaks down at exactly that point in time, and hence no such possibility is provided in Table 13.3.)

Preventive maintenance refers to maintenance performed prior to break-down and may be either minor in nature, such as a simple repair, or major, such as a complete overhaul or replacement. A preventive maintenance *program* may include provision for immediate repair or overhaul after a breakdown as well as for repairs or overhaul at predetermined time periods.

TABLE 13.3

Maintenance policies and alternatives

	Maintenance alternatives			
Maintenance policies	*Repair, overhaul, or replace at the end of* n *hours of operation*	*Repair, overhaul, or replace at set time periods*	*Repair, overhaul, or replace after breakdown*	*Inspect and measure need for repair, overhaul, or replacement*
Remedial maintenance.....			✓	
Preventive maintenance.......	✓	✓		
Conditional maintenance.......				✓

A *conditional maintenance* policy refers to overhaul or repair that is performed on the basis of inspecting and measuring the state of the equipment. If the equipment passes the test, it might be allowed to operate until it breaks down or until it has reached a certain number of operating hours, after which it is replaced, overhauled, or repaired.

Policy selection: An example. Suppose an electronics firm has 100 laser etching machines and management wants to determine whether it should follow a remedial policy, in which overhauls are performed only after a machine breaks down, or whether it should employ a preventive maintenance policy, in which overhauls are performed on all equipment at the end of specified periods and breakdowns are repaired as they occur.

To determine which policy to use, we must know the cost of preventive maintenance, the cost of breakdown repairs, and the probability of breakdown after an overhaul or repair as a function of time since the previous repair. Assume that we have this information and it is as follows:

Cost of providing preventive maintenance for one machine $(C_1) = \$20$
Cost of servicing a breakdown $(C_2) = \$100$

Probability distribution, as a function of time since previous repair or overhaul (we'll take months as our units of time), is shown in Table 13.4.

The probabilities shown in this table are the results of "life testing." Data of this type are derived by subjecting a sample to a test and observing what happens to all the units over the passage of time. For example, if we

TABLE 13.4

Month after maintenance (j)	*Probability of breakdown* (p_j)
1.............................	0.25
2.............................	0.15
3.............................	0.10
4.............................	0.10
5.............................	0.15
6.............................	0.25

FIGURE 13.5

Life cycle testing showing the number of machines that broke down period by period

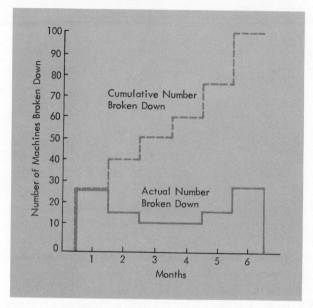

subjected 100 machines to a test until they broke down and found the results as: 25 breakdowns in the first month, 15 in the second, 10 in the third, 10 in the fourth, 15 in the fifth, and 25 in the sixth, these data could be plotted as a histogram shown in Figure 13.5.

The average life of the machines, then, is derived by computing the total number of months all machines lasted, divided by the number of machines, or:

Number of machines	Time (months) before breakdown		Number of months operated
25	× 1	=	25
15	× 2	=	30
10	× 3	=	30
10	× 4	=	40
15	× 5	=	75
25	× 6	=	150
Total months for 100 machines		=	350

Average life = 350/100 = 3.5 months before breakdown

The average number of breakdowns in one month, then, would be 100/3.5, or 28.57.

Life testing data are generally plotted as a probability distribution and care should be taken to interpret the meaning correctly. For example, Table 13.4 shows that within two months 40 percent of the *original* machines will break down. There is a strong but erroneous tendency to express the number of breakdowns as $0.25N + 0.15(N - 0.25N)$, where N is the original number of units (100 machines in our example). The number of breakdowns calculated this way is only 36.25 instead of the correct number, 40.

We are now ready to evaluate and compare the remedial policy of repairing breakdowns and the preventive maintenance policy.

Remedial policy. The total cost of this policy (TC_R) is determined simply by dividing the cost of repairing all machines (N) by the expected number of months between breakdowns, or

$$TC_R = \frac{NC_2}{\sum_{i=1}^{j} i p_i} = \frac{(100)(\$100)}{1(0.25) + 2(0.15) + 3(0.10) + 4(0.10) + 5(0.15) + 6(0.25)}$$

$$= \frac{\$10,000}{3.50} = \$2,857.14$$

Preventive policy. This policy should be viewed as consisting of six subpolicies, each corresponding to a given number of months between maintenance operations. That is, we must determine the cost of a preventive maintenance program involving maintenance every one month, every two months, every three months, and so on. To do this, we must first calculate the expected total number of breakdowns for each alternative.

The expected number of breakdowns, if preventive maintenance is performed on all machines each month, may be designated B_1, and is simply the number of machines times the probability of a breakdown within one month after maintenance (p_1), or

$$B_1 = Np_1 = (100)(0.25) = 25$$

The total number of breakdowns occurring by the end of period 2 is $N(p_1 + p_2)$ plus B_1p_1 (to account for the machines that were repaired in the first period and will need repair in the second). Hence

$$\begin{aligned} B_2 &= N(p_1 + p_2) + B_1p_1 \\ &= 100(0.25 + 0.15) + 25(0.25) \\ &= 46.25 \end{aligned}$$

The expected number of breakdowns for maintenance every three months is:

$$\begin{aligned} B_3 &= N(p_1 + p_2 + p_3) + B_2p_1 + B_1p_2 \\ &= 100(0.25 + 0.15 + 0.10) + 46.25(0.25) + 25(0.15) \\ &= 65.31 \end{aligned}$$

And for every four months:

$$B_4 = N(p_1 + p_2 + p_3 + p_4) + B_3p_1 + B_2p_2 + B_1p_3$$

$$= 100(0.25 + 0.15 + 0.10 + 0.10) + 64.31(0.25) + 46.25(0.15) + 25(0.10)$$

$$= 85.77$$

And for every n months:

$$B_n = N(p_1 + p_2 + p_3 + \cdots + p_n) + B_1p_{n-1} + B_2p_{n-2} + \cdots + B_{n-1}p_1$$

Proceeding this way, we obtain

$$B_5 = 113.36$$
$$B_6 = 156.12$$

Given these values, we may derive the total monthly cost of maintenance for each subpolicy as shown in Table 13.5. Examination of the total cost column (f) indicates that the best subpolicy is to perform preventive maintenance every four months. Such an approach is also less costly than the remedial policy by $213.14 ($2,857.14 − $2,644.00).

In evaluating this problem there are certain features worth noting. First, it may be surprising to discover that the expected breakdown cost for a one-month policy is greater than for any of the other policies considered. This point may be easily clarified, however, when we check back to the breakdown probabilities given at the beginning of the discussion and note the high failure rate in the first month after maintenance. In maintenance situations this phenomenon is known as *infant mortality,* and reflects the common occurrence of malfunctions associated with break-in operations. Such malfunctions may arise because new parts are coupled with worn

TABLE 13.5

Calculation of monthly maintenance costs for six different maintenance periods

(a) *Preventive maintenance every* M *months*	(b) *Total expected breakdowns in* M *months* (B)	(c) *Mean number of breakdowns per month* (b ÷ a)	(d) *Expected breakdown cost per month* (c × $100)	(e) *Expected preventive maintenance cost per month* $\left(\dfrac{1}{M} \times \$20 \times 100\right)$	(f) *Expected total monthly cost of maintenance subpolicy* (d + e)
1............	25	25	$2,500	$2,000	$4,500
2............	46.25	23.12	2,312	1,000	3,312
3............	65.81	21.77	2,177	667	2,844
4............	85.77	21.44	2,144	500	2,644
5............	113.36	22.67	2,267	400	2,667
6............	156.12	26.02	2,602	333	2,935

parts, gaskets and fittings are slightly rearranged during repair, or the repair or overhaul was incorrectly performed. Incidentally, even though the breakdown percentage after six months is the same as after the first month (25 percent), the "tampering effect" has been watered down by the maintenance activities of the preceding five months.

Second, if the breakdown probabilities were graphed, they would yield a dish-shape curve depicting—in addition to an infant mortality period at the beginning—a normal operating period in the center and a wear-out period toward the end. This configuration reflects the fact that equipment breakdown is typically a function of age. This is, if a machine survives its break-in period, it will probably operate satisfactorily for a relatively extended period of time, until it ultimately shows signs of wear and is again overhauled or replaced.

Maintenance as a system reliability problem

Hardy and Krajewski[8] suggest that the major purpose of maintenance is to maintain the reliability of the operating system at a reasonable level and still maximize profits or minimize costs. They point out that maintenance acts that tend to improve system reliability fall under two broad policy categories: (1) policies that tend to reduce the frequency of failures and (2) policies that tend to reduce the severity of failures. Their listing of such policies includes the following:

1. Policies tending to reduce the frequency of failures
    a. Preventive maintenance (including conditional maintenance)
    b. Proper instruction of operators
    c. Overbuilding-underutilization
    d. Simplification of the operation
    e. Early replacement
    f. Designing reliability into the components of the system
2. Policies tending to reduce the severity of failures
    a. Speeding the repair service (e.g., increase size of repair crews)
    b. Easing the task of repair (e.g., modular design of equipment)
    c. Providing alternative output during repair time (e.g., redundant equipment)

For purposes of maintenance planning, they suggest that different policies be tested via simulation to determine their effect on total annual cost. Their approach differs from the one shown in the previous example by explicitly including policies that reduce the *severity* of failures (as well as those that reduce the frequency of failures). Our example dealt with but a few frequency of failure policy alternatives, and hence does not capture all of the policy considerations that affect most maintenance decisions.

Maintenance information systems

A large amount of data is required to support a comprehensive maintenance program even in a moderate-size plant. And not only must this information be accurate, but to be of real value it must be timely as well. For these reasons it is not surprising that many companies have turned to the computer as the nucleus of their maintenance information system. To get an idea of the type of information required for such a system and the way in which it is used, we have reproduced a comprehensive system developed by Efraim Turban.[9] As Turban points out, this is a hypothetical system, and most organizations use only various segments of it. Nevertheless, it is particularly useful for our purposes because it shows the full range of information options that could be employed for any maintenance situation.

[8] S. T. Hardy and L. J. Krajewski, "A Simulation of Interactive Maintenance Decisions," *Decision Sciences*, vol. 6, no. 1, January 1975, pp. 92–105.

[9] Efraim Turban, "The Complete Computerized Maintenance System," *Industrial Engineering* (March 1969), pp. 20–27.

FIGURE 13.6

The major parts of a completely computerized maintenance system

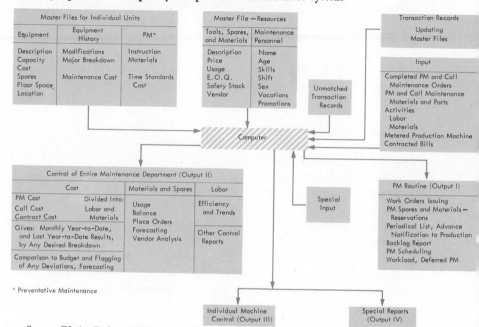

* Preventative Maintenance

Source: Efraim Turban, "The Complete Computerized Maintenance System," *Industrial Engineering* (March 1969), p. 20.

The essential features of this system, as shown in Figure 13.6, will now be described.

Inputs. The input to the computer can be divided into routine and special data. The routine data include completed work orders, specifying the amount of labor, parts, and materials used, and a description of the maintenance activity. Special input data might consist of cost comparisons with other plants, breakdown distributions, time study data, etc., which would be the bases for special output reports shown in Figure 13.6 and discussed below.

Files. This diagram separates two types of files: master files for individual units and master files for resources.

The master files for equipment are usually kept on magnetic tape and they contain such data as specifications, capacity, cost, economic age, setup costs, location, and floor space for all major pieces of equipment. The master files for resources contain information on workers (skills, wages, etc.) and on such resources as spare parts, optimal order quantities for maintenance materials, preferred vendor, and the like.

Outputs. The *preventive maintenance routine (output I)* issues work orders for various machines on the basis of programmed priority rules that are based upon file data. It may also prepare a list of materials and parts to be reserved for a particular job, as well as a list of upcoming jobs, in order to notify production departments of planned maintenance. Likewise, it may provide backlog reports of jobs waiting to be completed and may generate a revised schedule in which, for example, overdue jobs are given first priority in the next period.

Maintenance control (*output II*) is a key control feature of this system, and it could be programmed to provide printouts of efficiency ratios, breakdown repair costs, preventive maintenance costs, budget overruns, and even trends in these factors in graphical form.

Individual machine control (*output III*), as used here, refers simply to developing the types of reports shown in output II for a specific machine rather than for all machines. This would enable detailed analysis of poorly functioning machines and provide valuable information on the effectiveness of the preventive maintenance policy.

Special reports (*output IV*) refers to the output from simulations, critical path studies, inventory models, and other output report tools that would be useful in carrying out the maintenance function. Also in the special report category would be completely automated maintenance activities, such as automatic sensing, analysis, and action (i.e., shutdown), of a malfunctioning machine. (In the future, it is possible that computerized trouble shooting and repair will be included as part of the complete maintenance system.)

FAME—A computer program for maintenance scheduling. The FAME (Facilities Maintenance Engineering)[10] program is one of several commercial computer programs for maintenance scheduling that implements many of the elements of the generalized system proposed by Turban (described above). The FAME program provides maintenance managers with a preventive maintenance data base that in turn can be conveniently used to develop preventive maintenance schedules and labor requirements. The program, developed by General Electric, will:

Accept up to 10,000 equipment records.

Store up to 72,000 maintenance records, identifying, by craft, the required inspection procedures.

Generate upon request preventive maintenance schedules.

Accumulate and report craft man-hour requirements in support of maintenance schedules.

Automatically log preventive maintenance completions.

The data base used by FAME is composed of two record types—equipment records and maintenance records. A typical equipment record with two associated maintenance records is graphically illustrated as follows:

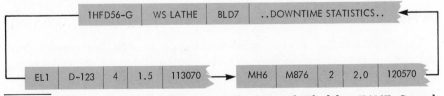

_____

[10] *User's Guide to Preventive Maintenance Planning and Scheduling FAME*, General Electric Company, 1973.

FIGURE 13.7

A sample FAME preventive maintenance schedule

LIST PMØFILE

```
PMØFILE        12:05

1000 MAINTENANCE SCHEDULE THRU 123170
1010      1 CATALØGUE#1   ANNEX     PMINST#1 MACH       3.3  52270 ......
1020      1 CATALØGUE#1   ANNEX     PMINST#1 MACH       3.3  52970 ......
1030      1 CATALØGUE#1   ANNEX     PMINST#1 MACH       3.3  60570 ......
1040      1 CATALØGUE#1   ANNEX     PMINST#1 MACH       3.3  61270 ......
1050      1 CATALØGUE#1   ANNEX     PMINST#1 MACH       3.3  61970 ......
1060      1 CATALØGUE#1   ANNEX     PMINST#1 MACH       3.3  62670 ......
1070      1 CATALØGUE#1   ANNEX     PMINST#1 MACH       3.3  70370 ......

1360      1 CATALØGUE#1   ANNEX     PMINST#1 MACH       3.3 122570 ......
1370      6 EQUIP NØ 17   DEPT-137  PM#1003  MASN      56.0  71470 ......
1380      5 EQUIP NØ 17   DEPT-137  PM#173   INST      24.0  92570 ......
1390      5 EQUIP NØ 17   DEPT-137  PM#173   INST      24.0 122570 ......
1400 99999
1410**TØTAL-HØURS**                                            DATE
1420 CRAFT   MAN/HRS                                           HOURS
1430  MACH    105.6                                            CRAFT CODE
1440  PLMR     10.0                                            PM INSTRU. NO.
1450  ELEC      4.9                                            EQUIP. LOCATION
1460  CPTR     16.0                                            EQUIPMENT NAME
1470  MASN     56.0                                            LINE NUMBER
1480  INST     48.0                                            CRAFT HOURS REQUIREMENTS
```

READY

Source: General Electric Company, *Preventive Maintenance Planning and Scheduling, FAME,* User's Guide (1973), p. 4.

The computer, when reading the equipment record, notes that the equipment is a Warner Swasey Lathe with an equipment tag number of 1HFD56-G located in building 7. Upon inspecting the two associated maintenance records, the computer further recognizes that two types of preventive maintenance are performed on the equipment. The first is electrical maintenance (craft code EL1) performed every four weeks and requiring 1.5 hours. The specific procedure for this maintenance may be found in company instruction D-123. The next scheduled date for preventive maintenance is November 30, 1970. (Not shown in the illustration is the last inspection date.) The second type of maintenance performed on the equipment is mechanical maintenance (craft code MH6). It is performed every two weeks and requires 2.0 hours. The next scheduled date for this maintenance is December 5, 1970.

The actual preventive maintenance schedule is initiated in response to the user's keyboard request (FAME is an interactive program). A schedule such as the one shown in Figure 13.7 can be made for a week, a month, or a year.

ENVIRONMENTAL POLLUTION AND THE PRODUCTION SYSTEM

Through the pollution of air and waterways was once considered a normal concomitant of production, governmental edicts and societal values have now cast it as a major malfunction in the production system. While undoubtedly the primary effect of pollution laws is felt by the process engineer, the design engineer, and other scientific personnel, the production manager must also recognize the consequences of such laws and adjust his operations accordingly. Indeed, in some industries not only must the production manager cope with these new constraints on his production process and the product itself, he must also operate in light of an uncertain technology wherein the physical devices of pollution control are themselves prone to malfunctions.

The general sequence of events in coping with pollution problems is depicted in Figure 13.8. By far the principal focus of antipollution laws and public concern has been in the areas of air and water pollution, which in turn are forcing significant changes in products and processes. In the product-change category, the automobile industry is probably the one most severely affected by antipollution efforts. Automobile manufacturers must reduce engine exhaust emissions to satisfy the requirements of the 1970 Clean Air Act. Indicative of the wide range of industries that are feeling the effect of antipollution legislation in regard to their product, soap manufacturers must reduce the amount of phosphates to prescribed levels in certain states, and container manufacturers, in response to public pressure, have been experimenting with biodegradable bottles.

FIGURE 13.8

General sequence of events in coping with pollution problems

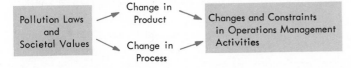

In the process-change category, the Environmental Protection Agency has invoked the venerable Refuse Act of 1899, which makes it unlawful to discharge refuse (except liquid discharges from municipal sewers) into navigable waterways and their tributaries without a permit from the Army Corps of Engineers. And the 1965 Water Quality Act requires states to set water quality standards for interstate waterways and to develop implementation procedures. Some of the most powerful firms in the United States are greatly affected by these laws, including the major steel producers, chemical processors, and paper manufacturers.

Some companies have the misfortune of having pollution problems with both their product and their production process. The oil industry, for example, beset by oil spillage problems in the oceans, has been zealously pressured to remove noxious emittants from its end-product fuels. Some companies are not only confronted with product and process pollution controls but—in addition—are found in violation of one pollution law in their effort to comply with another law.

The full influence of pollution abatement process changes on the production manager's activities is not well documented, but by looking at the typical responses by a firm, or even an industry, we can deduce the areas that are most severely affected. Table 13.6 summarizes the reactions of

TABLE 13.6

Production management activities affected by pollution control in the steel industry

Typical steel company reaction to anti-pollution enforcement	*Significantly affected production management activities*					
	Inventory	*Workforce*	*Scheduling*	*Layout*	*Quality*	*Maintenance*
Reduce production levels............	x	x	x			x
Add antipollution devices...........	x	x	x	x	x	x
Modernize...........	x	x	x	x	x	x
Recycle of wastes....		x	x	x	x	x
Change product mix..............	x	x	x			x

companies and involved production management activities in the steel industry.

While the force of technology limits the types of adjustments that can be made in production management activities in process industries (e.g., steel), this is not the case in mass production industries. In the automobile industry, for example, the addition of a smog control device on a car can entail a new set of scheduling, layout, quality control, and inventory problems that fall directly under the jurisdiction of the production manager, who must solve them.

As might be expected, the degree to which production management activities are affected by antipollution efforts depends upon the extent of the adjustment to the production process. In reference to the continuum shown in Figure 13.9, we would expect that the impact of antipollution strategies on the production manager's activities would increase as company actions move from *reduce production levels* to *adopt new technology*.

The milder forms of adjustment would involve a simple varying of decision rules, such as changing inventory reorder points to correspond to reduced production levels or changes in the product mix. Somewhat stronger forms would be the inclusion of additional operations, such as more inspections to ensure that each product meets antipollution standards, or that the process is not producing excessive wastes. Of greater impact would be the addition of antipollution devices or equipment that sig-

FIGURE 13.9

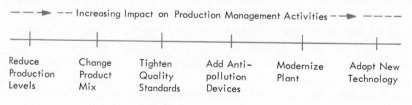

Antipollution Strategies

nificantly extend the production process, such as Dow Chemical's system for sensing and removing contamination in cooling water. This type of change often results in realignments of organizational responsibilities, as well as marked adjustments in decision rules and operator tasks. Modernization of the plant would lead to similar types of adjustments. The extreme case of adopting a new technology would undoubtedly require redesign of all the production subsystems, and hence revision of the production management activities.

While antipollution efforts have centered on six industries—chemicals, iron and steel, electrical utilities, pulp and paper, petroleum, and rubber—a variety of other industries are also affected. In the food industry, for example, the requirement that a company obtain a permit to use a waterway for waste disposal has led certain dairy companies, sugar beet processors, pet food manufacturers, and beer companies (is nothing sacred?) to seek new techniques for getting rid of sewage. Clearly very few of the industries that contribute to a nation's economy will remain untouched by the problems of pollution, and the production manager will find the topic constantly entering into his day-to-day decision making.

CONCLUSION

In this chapter we have examined some of the malfunctions that arise in the production system and we have discussed some of the techniques and organizational groups that help the production manager cope with them. In the ideal situation, malfunctions would be minimized or averted through effective design and continual monitoring. However, the very fact that the production system is dynamic means that malfunctions are unavoidable. Indeed, most production managers would agree that handling day-to-day problems is primarily what they are paid for.

PROPOSITIONS

Propositions contrasting services and manufacturing relative to malfunctions and corrections

Product: In service systems, a major malfunction will generally have an immediate and direct effect on the customer in the system. In manufacturing, a malfunction in the system will have no effect on the customer unless it is inadvertently embodied in the end product, or affects the environment.

Technology of transformation: With the exception of transportation services, maintenance activities in service systems focus on the environment or surroundings of the service facility and are "housekeeping" in nature. In manufacturing (and transportation) the primary focus of maintenance activities is equipment.

Operating-control system: In service systems, production control is usually a shared responsibility. In manufacturing, it is commonly given departmental status and assigned specific responsibilities.

Workforce: In service systems, a malfunction often arises from the interaction between the customers and the employees, and hence its severity can be directly affected by the employees' interpersonal skills. In manufacturing, a malfunction usually arises from a failure in a physical process, and hence its severity is more dependent upon the employees' manual or analytical skills.

REVIEW AND DISCUSSION QUESTIONS

1. "Into each life a little rain must fall." How does this axiom relate to the nature and purpose of this chapter?

2. Why is the distinction between an internal and an external malfunction significant?

3. What is control? Is control possible without any of the five phases cited in the chapter?

4. Distinguish between *current control* and *post control* and between *tools of adjustment* and *tools of evaluation.*

5. Which trouble-shooting techniques are used in the following situations?
    a. On the basis of a blonde hair on your lapel, your wife claims that you weren't "out with the boys."
    b. A ballet coach makes Rudolf dance with a broomstick in order to determine if he blew the *pas de deux* when dancing with Margot.
    c. A radiologist observes barium sulphate going through your system with a fluoroscope to see if you have stomach trouble.
    d. A basketball coach sends in five new players to cut down on "turnovers."
    e. A manager calculates the learning percentage from historical data in order to estimate the completion time for a sizable number of items.
    f. An operations management instructor administers a "pop" quiz the first week of the semester.

6. What is the role of production control in dealing with malfunctions? How does it differ from that of quality control?

7. What is a coordinative staff function?

8. Develop a responsibility "profile" of the typical production control manager. (Use Table 13.2 as a guide.)

9. What are some of the organizational problems faced by production control?

10. What are some of the underlying causes of malfunction in a production control system? How can the scheduling aspects of these problems be corrected?

11. What problems are caused by maintenance's "second system" status?

12. What are the main features of the completely computerized maintenance system proposed by Turban? What elements of the system could be viewed as dependent demand items in the MRP sense?

13. What antipollution regulations have particular impact on the industries in your locale? How do local production managers adjust their operations in light of these regulations?

14. How does the preventive maintenance example on page 593 and the Hardy and Krajewski's simulation model relate to the Turban and FAME systems?

15. What maintenance policies do you follow with respect to:
    a. Your automobile (or other form of transportation)?
    b. Your physical health?
    On which of the two systems above do you spend the most money in preventive maintenance?

PROBLEMS

1. Perform a sequential analysis to determine the root cause(s) of either of the following.
   a. Your not getting an "A" on a recent examination
   b. Your not getting a promotion (or a raise) on your job
   Given this hindsight, would you have done anything differently?

2. For the policy selection example, suppose that the probability of breakdown for the laser etching machines has changed and is now as follows. What is the new optimum policy?

Month after maintenance (j)	Probability of breakdown (p_j)
1..................................	0.30
2..................................	0.20
3..................................	0.10
4..................................	0.10
5..................................	0.10
6..................................	0.20

3. As was noted in this chapter, queuing theory is often used to analyze maintenance problems. Using Table S.7.5 apply finite queuing theory to the following situation.

    An electronics firm has just purchased four super-etcher machines. These machines have greater capacity and speed than the other models currently in service, but they need adjustment periodically. At present, management has two men available to perform these adjustments but thinks it may need another man. Given the following data, determine if the additional man should be hired.
    a. The need for adjustment is Poisson distributed, with a mean of one adjustment every hour for each super-etcher.
    b. Adjustments take an average of 30 minutes each, although the actual time is exponentially distributed.
    c. Adjusters are paid $4 per hour. (A etcherman union requirement is that adjusters work only on super-etchers.)
    d. Downtime for a super-etcher is estimated at $50 per hour.

4. Simulation is also commonly used to study maintenance problems; try your hand at applying Monte Carlo simulation to the following situation.

Minnie's Massage Parlor has become automated with the introduction of Vibromats. A Vibromat is a motorized vibrating board that has the capability of performing a total massage on all muscles of the body simultaneously. A vibromat has three vibrators, each of which is subject to breakdown according to the following probability distribution. In order to repair any vibrator,

Hours of operation	Probability of failure
50	0.20
100	0.15
150	0.10
200	0.07
250	0.13
300	0.15
350	0.20

it is necessary to remove the massage board, which takes $1\frac{1}{2}$ hours. Disassembling a vibrator takes $\frac{1}{4}$ hour, overhauling a vibrator takes one hour, and reassembling a vibrator takes $\frac{1}{3}$ hour. Putting the massage board back in place takes $1\frac{1}{2}$ hours. Although a Vibromat has to be shut down while it is being repaired, there is no downtime cost as the massage parlor has standby Vibromats.

Minnie, who does all the repairs herself, wants to know which of three policies to adopt: (I) repair a vibrator only when it fails, (II) repair all three vibrators if one fails, or (III) repair the vibrator that fails plus all vibrators on the Vibromats that have been in use longer than the expected service life of 100 hours.

Suggested procedure. A convenient way of making the best policy determination is to use a table such as that shown below, in which *number* refers to the number of times an operation was observed to take place. *Time* is simply *hours per operation number*. Summing these values, obtained from the simulation, gives a total repair time for the policy under con-

		Policy I		II		III	
Operation	Hours per operation	Number	Time	Number	Time	Number	Time
Remove massage board	$1\frac{1}{2}$						
Disassemble	$\frac{1}{4}$						
Overhaul	1						
Reassemble	$\frac{1}{3}$						
Replace massage board	$1\frac{1}{2}$						
Total time							

sideration, and the best policy would be the one that has the lowest total time.

To obtain the data for this table, we suggest that a 900-hour simulation history be derived for each policy. This means that each vibrator's history covers 900 hours. To make the comparisons equivalent, use the same stream of random numbers for vibrators 1, 2, and 3 in all three policies. Procedurally, this entails generating about 10 figures for *hours of operation* for each vibrator.

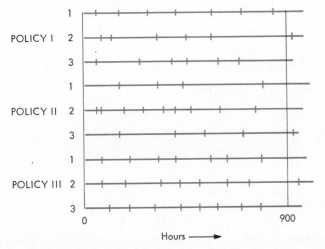

To facilitate the counting of operations and to gain an insight into how each policy affects vibrator running time, display your hours of operation data on a diagram such as that shown. The horizontal lines represent vibrators and the short vertical lines represent points at which a repair is made. In your simulation, of course, there will be some relationship between the vertical lines if, for example, all vibrators are repaired when one breaks down. (The lines in the sketch are merely for illustrative purposes and do not represent values obtained from any particular simulation.)

SELECTED BIBLIOGRAPHY

General Electric Company   *Preventive Maintenance Planning and Scheduling, FAME,* User's Guide (Bethesda, Md.: 1973).

Greene, James H.   *Production and Inventory Control: Systems and Decisions,* Rev. ed. Homewood, Ill.: Richard D. Irwin, Inc., 1974.

Hardy, S. T., and Krajewski, L. J.   "A Simulation of Interactive Maintenance Decisions," *Decision Sciences,* vol. 6, no. 1 (January 1975), pp. 92–105.

Morrow, L. C.   *Maintenance Engineering Handbook.* 2d ed. New York: McGraw-Hill, 1966.

Plossl, G. W., and Wight, O. W.   *Production and Inventory Control Principles and Techniques.* Englewood Cliffs, N.J.: Prentice-Hall, 1967.

Turban, E.   "The Complete Computerized Maintenance System," *Industrial Engineering* (March 1969), pp. 20–27.

Wilkinson, John J.   "How to Manage Maintenance," *Harvard Business Review* (March–April 1968).

14

Areas and techniques for improvement

The importance of improvement was brought to national attention in 1970 through the creation of the National Commission on Productivity. This agency did not really get under way until 1974 because of insufficient funding. In November, 1975, Congress approved the present version of the agency, renaming it The National Center on Productivity and Quality of Working Life. In its first report to Congress, the newly created agency summarized the primary goal given to it as:

The Center will act as a catalyst and focal point for national efforts to stimulate increased productivity growth and improve quality of working life throughout the economy. It will be a central reference source for information, data, methods, and techniques for productivity improvement. It will actively encourage selected segments of the economy to pursue new or expanded productivity improvement programs. It will stimulate, review, and help coordinate Federal efforts to improve productivity. It will work to help inform decision makers and the public at large about productivity issues and their importance to the economy.[1]

It seems quite fitting to start off this chapter on identifying areas and techniques for improvement with Congressional recognition of the significance of the subject.

Within the life cycle of a productive system, improvement, as a major effort, takes place during the steady state period. By this time, the major problems in product design, production processes, etc., will have been ironed out and attention can now be focused on refining the system—performing some specialized studies and examining operations for cost reduction opportunities and ways for improvement.

While various improvement efforts and programs tend to overlap, it is useful to categorize them under the same four areas we have used for our propositions—

Improvement in the *product*.
Improvement in the *technology of transformation*.
Improvement in the *operating-control system*.
Improvement in the *workforce*.

In this chapter we will explore each of these categories in some detail, relating the techniques and guidelines that have been employed by practitioners to facilitate the improvement process. By necessity, coverage of such a diversity of topics requires a certain amount of outlining and listing, and therefore the interested reader is encouraged to consult the original sources cited for elaboration on particular topics.

IMPROVEMENT IN THE PRODUCT

The design of a product commits the productive system to specific processing methods; therefore the greatest opportunity for cost savings occurs during the initial design phase. Once the manufacturing process is under

---

[1] Matthew Heyman, "Productivity: Washington Update," *Industrial Engineering*, vol. 8, no. 4 (April 1976), p. 22.

way, however, cost reduction may be possible through redesign, changes in the processing methods, and the selection of components and materials. Value engineering and value analysis are useful techniques in the investigation.

Value engineering

Briefly, value engineering is defined as the systematic identification of the function of a product or service, establishment of a value for that function, and assurance that the required function is provided at the lowest total cost. The Department of Defense, which has done much to promote value engineering through defense contracting, defines a value engineering study as

an intensive appraisal of all the elements of the design, manufacture, or construction, procurement, inspection, installation, and maintenance of an item and its components, including the applicable specifications and operational requirements, in order to achieve the necessary performance, maintainability, and reliability of the item at minimum cost.[2]

The purpose of value engineering is to make certain that every element of cost (for example, labor, materials, supplies, styling, and service) contributes proportionately to the function of the item. These objectives may also be stated in different ways, depending on the intent and audience. One way is to state that value engineering has two fundamental goals: (1) to provide better value in delivered products and (2) to improve the company's competitive position. Another way is to state that value engineering includes a tradeoff decision—that is, to improve the product for a given cost, or to provide the same or better performance at lower cost without reducing quality or reliability. In any situation, however, the approach of value engineering is the same; that is

1. Break down the product into separate parts and operations.
2. Determine the production cost for each part and operation.
3. Determine the relative value of each part or operation in the end product.
4. For the high-cost, low-value items, search for a new approach.

The concept of value is difficult to express. Value depends on the usefulness to the user, which is supposedly based on the value of the function performed by the product or service. But how does one go about determining the value of a bolt on the wing of an airplane, without which the plane cannot fly? Or how much quality and reliability does one build into an automobile tire to lessen the chances of a blowout and possible accident? Clearly, the idea of relative costs is part of the analysis procedure. Whether it is recognized directly or indirectly, automobile manufacturers, for example, establish the "cost" of human life through a tradeoff between vehicle design and reliability and the amount of court settlements.

---

[2] Armed Services Procurement Regulation, Section 3–406.3.

As an illustration, the methodology of the value engineering plan or program is demonstrated by the use of six elementary steps that were developed primarily for high-production consumer products. These elementary steps can be outlined as follows.

1. Item selection. High-volume items are preferred for study because of their greater potential savings. The product or process should be in the earliest possible stage of production planning in order to reduce the implementation costs of design changes.

2. Information phases. Pertinent information and the relevant facts surrounding the product or process should be collected to estimate the possible cost savings. Then the item should be studied to determine its specific function. All aspects of the item should be challenged and simple tests for value should be made, as follows.

Questions	*Tests for value*
What is it?	Is cost proportionate to value?
What does it do?	Does the object need all these features?
Is it necessary?	Is there anything better for the same
What does it cost?	use?
What else can do the same job?	Can any component be made by a lower cost method?
	Can a standard part be used?
	Is the object made with the proper tooling and materials?

3. Development of alternatives. In the speculative or creative phase of the study, "brainstorming" sessions are held and "cloud 9" thinking is encouraged. The primary or basic functions of the product are listed in detail. The methods used to provide each function are examined and alternative ways to provide the same functions are proposed. The emphasis in this phase is on creativity; criticism and evaluation of ideas are barred. The value engineer is simply seeking a large number of unique and unusual ideas as feasible alternatives.

4. Cost analysis of alternatives. Cost comparisons and analyses are made of all alternatives that appear to be feasible. The lowest-cost methods are chosen for further scrutiny and analysis.

5. Testing and verification. All promising alternatives are evaluated to assure economic and technical feasibility.

6. Proposal submission and follow-up. The alternatives that have survived 4 and 5 (above) are formally submitted to the engineering staff for final evaluation. Also included are the assumptions, cost estimates of materials, labor, tooling, and design sketches, and any other relevant data that may be helpful in the evaluation.[3]

In a survey of firms that have been using value engineering for some years, Mobley and Schwetter found that the most popular method of measuring success is in net dollar savings (total cost reduction less cost of

---

[3] Carl Heyel, *The Encyclopedia of Management* (New York: Reinhold Publishing Co., 1963), p. 1025.

implementation). Also popular is the ratio of return—that is, the net savings divided by the cost. In the survey, the ratios ran between 8 and 10 to 1; that is, a $10,000 investment in value analysis effort returned a net savings of $80,000 to $100,000!

They particularly noted the requirements for a successful value engineering/value analysis program:

1. It must have strong management backing.
2. It must be led by qualified personnel.
3. It should have wide employee participation.

Many intangible benefits had also been reported as a result of a value engineering program. Among these are

1. The product designers question new designs.
2. The philosophy of cost reduction encourages people to become cost conscious.
3. Customer relations are better.
4. Internal communications and teamwork improve.
5. The individual has a feeling of participation.[4]

A value engineering program should continually review all products, services, and processes for design value. In a design organization, it has been found that one value engineer to 30 technical engineers is sufficient to gain good cost reductions through value engineering techniques.[5] In many organizations the value engineer chairs a group known as the *value engineering task force*. Persons with different functional backgrounds, such as accounting, purchasing, engineering, and production, while acting under the guidance of the value engineer, apply the basic value-engineering methods to selected areas or products for possible cost improvements. Rotating the membership and the functional areas in the value engineering group is an effective way to provide a high level of creativity, as well as train personnel in value engineering techniques.

Value analysis

Similar to the idea of value engineering is the concept of value analysis. The distinction between the two is that value analysis is typically used in conjunction with the cost analysis of purchased items. It is generally conceded that a lucrative place to save is on the cost of parts purchased, and that the purchasing department is the most authoritative source for the cost analysis of components and materials.

The major economic gains of value analysis lie in the design stages. A well-applied program can eliminate costly redesign and result in a product with "designed-in" value. The value analyst functions as both a catalyst and

---

[4] Norman V. Mobley and Joseph P. Schwetter, "Value Engineering Practice," *Journal of Industrial Engineering*, vol. 18, no. 11 (November 1967), pp. xii–xiii.

[5] H. B. Maynard, *Handbook of Business Administration* (New York: McGraw-Hill, 1967), p. 6.

a coordinator in bringing the proper technical skills to bear on problem areas. He seeks to assure maximum economy and reduction in the cost of purchased items through

1. Establishing methods to analyze and measure basic values inherent in design, materials and method of manufacture,
2. Collaborating with purchasing personnel to determine the priority status of parts and materials to be studied,
3. Analyzing items scheduled for procurement to ascertain possible material substitution, revisions in design modifications in manufacturing methods, or changes in methods of selecting suppliers.[6]

Through the application of value engineering and analysis techniques in the purchasing function, preproduction design cost reductions may be achieved. A typical sequence of questions that may be asked is as follows:

Does the item have any design features that are not necessary?

How much does it weigh? Can any section be changed or eliminated to cut weight?

Is the finish better than needed? Are any sections finished that need not be?

Are all tolerances essential for the function?

Can the part be redesigned so as to be made by a lower-cost process?

Can two or more parts be made as one?

Can any holes be eliminated by using less costly fasteners?

Are there any nonstandard parts that can be eliminated?

The firm's suppliers should also be consulted for suggestions and ideas. Since he is a specialist in his own area, a supplier is likely to contribute many feasible and practical recommendations to aid in the reduction of product, tools, or equipment costs.

Deliberate change

Closely allied with value engineering/value analysis is the concept of *deliberate change* used by the Procter and Gamble Company.[7] Production costs may be reduced in two ways: (1) by controlling the costs of existing methods through better performance and (2) through a *deliberate change* of methods.

Deliberate change is quite different from cost improvement. Improvement techniques frequently smack of "efficiency" or budget-cutting strategies, which encounter psychological resistance from management and labor alike. This is particularly true if the operation is well run and improvements

---

[6] H. B. Maynard (ed.), *Industrial Engineering Handbook* (2d ed.; New York: McGraw-Hill, 1963), pp. 107–9.

[7] See Arthur Spinanger, "Increasing Profits through Deliberate Methods Change," *Proceedings of Seventeenth Annual Industrial Engineering Institute* (Berkeley: University of California Press, 1965), pp. 33–37.

are difficult to achieve. On the other hand, the How-can-the-methods-of-work-be-changed? approach is often much better received, and its advocates claim it has greater potential savings. This approach takes the philosophy that

1. *Perfection is no barrier to change.* This implies that where further improvement to an existing work method is nearly impossible, there is probably a different and superior method that may be feasible.
2. *Every dollar of cost should contribute its share of the profit.* Because each dollar that is invested in anything is done so with the idea of making a profit, the investment should not be made if it does not have this result.
3. *The savings potential is the full existing cost.* This attitude does not consider any item of cost as necessary. An example is the procedure of using a liner and a carton to package shampoo. The liner was omitted first, and then the carton, and the shampoo sold better unpackaged. In another example a storage-tank roof required high maintenance costs, but upon investigation it was determined that neither evaporation into the air nor dilution through rainfall significantly affected the tank's contents. Thus there was no need for the roof, and it was eliminated.

IMPROVEMENT IN THE TECHNOLOGY OF TRANSFORMATION

When the production facility was first designed, it was done so based upon assumptions and incomplete information. Once the system is operating, however, experience and new data usually will show where improvements may be made. In the sections to follow, we will briefly discuss refinements and cost reduction in the areas of plant layout, work methods, quality control, maintenance, inventory, and scheduling.

Plant layout

The degree of attention given to any type of planned relayout varies directly with "(1) the frequency of product and material changes, (2) the frequency of process and methods improvements, (3) the ease of moving machinery and equipment, and (4) the permanency of the buildings relative to the life of products, processes and equipment."[8]

Trubshaw has 10 steps to follow for plant relayout (Table 14.1).

When relayout of an area has been decided upon, two important steps should be followed in order to have it accepted by both management and workers.

First, encourage participation by all the people involved. A relayout is often disruptive—it causes inconveniences, changes job assignments, and destroys social relationships. To assure that it will be accepted, affected

---

[8] Richard Muther, "The Importance of Plant Layout in Cost Reduction," in *How to Reduce Production Costs* (New York: American Management Association, 1956), p. 7.

TABLE 14.1

Ten steps for plant relayout

1. *Make long-range plans.*
2. *Establish layout limits.*
3. *Chart line flow.*
4. *Study current problems.*
5. *Review legal phases.*
6. *Investigate cost reduction sources.*
7. *Obtain equipment descriptions.*
8. *Examine feasibility of change.*
9. *Verify existing information.*
10. *Maintain the master plan.*

Source: Louis F. Trubshaw, "New Plants are Fine, but—It Pays to Consider Re-Layout," *Factory* (March 1966), pp. 64–67.

personnel should be convinced that it is necessary and they should be given a say in its planning.

Second, make the proposed relayout clear. So that there are no misunderstandings, a layout should be clearly drawn and adequately described.

Muther notes that some additional benefits offered by relayout are.

A layout change affords an opportunity to get rid of a lot of bad habits. Here is an ideal time to sweep clean, to break with tradition, to shake off any bad practices, to change a lot of things you may have wanted to do but have been holding back. A company should take advantage of this fresh start to streamline the operation of the area involved to get a psychological new start.

A layout change permits re-organization or modification of procedures. Management may really want a change in supervision, in the inspection procedure, or in the method of ordering material. By making a re-layout, the desired changes can be incorporated as a necessary part of the physical re-arrangement.[9]

Work methods

There are two approaches to improving work methods. The first, generally termed *work simplification,* seeks to gain the cooperation of employees and train them in some basic principles so as to simplify their own work. Work improvement, then, comes from workers' suggestions. The second method is usually called *methods analysis* or *methods engineering,* which in its full-blown application becomes a formal study to reduce costs.

Work simplification. The motto "Work smarter—not harder" was first proclaimed by Allan H. Mogensen, a pioneer in work simplification. He believed that every person in an organization should participate in the effort to magnify the returns from work simplification programs. As a consultant, he would set up formal classes, which were open to all employees. The duration of classes was variable, but they usually met once or twice a week for 10 or 12 weeks. The class instructor would lecture on work simplification

---

[9] Richard Muther, "Managing the Plant Layout Function," *Advanced Management* (April 1955), pp. 7–8.

FIGURE 14.1

Opportunities for savings in a typical work task through application of methods engineering and time study

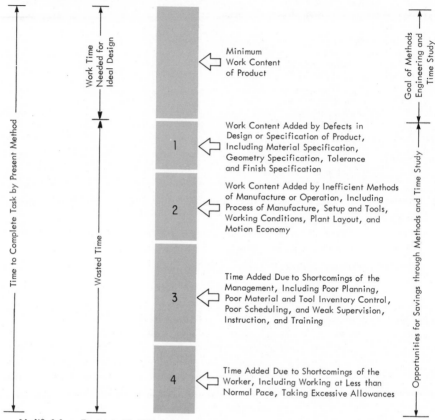

Modified from Benjamin W. Niebel, *Motion and Time Study* 6th ed. (Homewood, Ill.: Richard D. Irwin, Inc., 1976), p. 4.

concepts, including principles of motion economy, time study, procedures for flow, process and man-machine charting, and work place layout. These lectures were then supplemented with workshop projects and movies showing representative "successes" in applying work simplification. Participants were encouraged to bring their own projects to be worked on. Over the years, this type of program achieved a good deal of success, and many large manufacturing concerns have adopted Mogensen's approach and developed their own in-house staffs to administer their programs. Such programs have also spread into service industries, with numerous major hospitals, for example, routinely conducting such training programs.

Methods engineering.   Methods engineering, the more technical approach to cost reduction, has been defined by Niebel as "the systematic procedure for subjecting all direct and indirect operations to close scrutiny in order to introduce improvements that will make work easier to perform and will allow work to be done in less time and with less investment per unit."[10]

One of the objectives of methods engineering is to eliminate unnecessary processing time. While every task has some technologically defined minimum time to perform, in practice a host of delays are added to this basic time requirement. These delays are attributable to flaws in product design, defective materials, shortages of materials, inefficient methods, poor management practice, and worker inefficiencies. Figure 14.1 shows that the time actually needed to perform a job task takes less than one-third of the total time used. Thus, a completely effective application of methods engineering and time study could save more than two-thirds of the time taken by the existing method.

When the intent of a methods study is to improve the current method of work, experience has shown that the best procedure is to use a systematic study similar to that used during the initial work center design. Westinghouse Electric Corporation advocates the following steps[11] to assure the most favorable results.

1. Make a preliminary survey.
2. Determine the extent of analysis justified.
3. Develop process charts.
4. Investigate the approaches to operations analysis.
5. Make a motion study when justified.
6. Compare the old and new method.
7. Present the new method.
8. Check the installation of the new method.
9. Correct time values.
10. Follow up the new method.

IMPROVEMENT IN THE OPERATING-CONTROL SYSTEM

Quality control

As mentioned in Chapter 5, quality control enters the productive system at various levels—at the executive level in determining product lines and corporate policy, at the operating level in assuring product conformance to specifications, and at the customer contact level in quality assurance. While the system is running smoothly, reexamination is in order to determine

1. Whether the quality of the products accurately evokes the desired corporate image.
2. Whether the existing products, and those presently in research, are consistent with long-range plans.

---

[10] Benjamin W. Niebel, *Motion and Time Study*, 6th ed. (Homewood, Ill.: Richard D. Irwin, Inc., 1976), p. 6.

[11] Ibid.

Frequently a company that has built its reputation on precision products tries to enter a new market with low-cost, competitive-quality merchandise or service, and its corporate image suffers. Customers will initially buy such products sight unseen, based on the known-quality name. In a short time, however, there is realization that the product is no better than that of the other competitors. The resulting damage to the company's reputation often affects customers for its precision products. The reverse is also true: a company that begins business in a low-price, moderate-quality line will have great difficulty bringing out a line of high-quality, high-price products. When a company's name becomes associated with moderate- or low-level goods, the transition to high-quality products is possible, but it takes a great deal of time and public relations effort.

In Chapter 5, sampling and inspection were treated in terms of the consequences of bad quality. There, the original system design was being considered, but looking at the system in its steady state condition, one has an opportunity to sharpen the original cost estimates. Quite often the production output of a process turns out better than in the original process design. Therefore some inspection points may be eliminated or moved elsewhere in the system.

It is quite likely that the inspection procedures of the quality control function may be improved. Two costs are related to the products inspected: (1) the cost of passing bad items as good and (2) the cost of discarding good items as bad. For the inspecting personnel, important characteristics that affect these costs are perception (the defect must be recognized) and reaction (the act of rejection must be performed, such as removal of the part from the system or marking it in some way). Since individuals differ in their ability to perceive variations and in speed of response, it is commonplace to test the visual acuity and reaction time of applicants for inspectors' jobs.

One increasingly popular way to heighten the quality of inspection is to identify the inspector. When an inspector's output changes from unidentifiable to directly traceable (for example, by using an identifying stamp), quality levels increase dramatically. To carry this backward a step in the productive process, when the worker who produces a part identifies it as his by using a stamp, the inspection point sometimes may be completely eliminated. This supports the finding that the employee's pride (or self-consciousness) in his work is a very strong motivating force. Any simple identifying device that ties the worker with his output can be very effective. Also effective in increasing quality levels is "job enlargement," which often increases job interest.

Maintenance

Maintenance has historically been viewed as low-level work, trailing most other operating functions in importance—a necessary evil, to be tolerated at best. This downgrading is unfortunate since the maintenance function, if properly run, can greatly enhance the operation of the production system. Nevertheless, an efficient maintenance operation is the exception rather than the rule, and as a result, maintenance problems abound. In discussing potential areas for maintenance improvement, Newbrough lists symptoms of maintenance neglect[12] as

> Excessive machine breakdowns.
> Frequent emergency work.
> Domination of maintenance by production.
> Lack of an equipment replacement program.
> Insufficient preventive maintenance.
> No planned selection of maintenance supervisors and managers.
> Inadequate training of maintenance personnel.
> Poor shop facilities.

Newbrough further points out that cost reduction possibilities exist in many significant areas, such as[13]

> Reduction in unnecessary work through preventive action, better methods, and improved tools
> Better labor productivity through better planning, scheduling, and performance evaluation
> Better control of excess costs, such as overtime, machine downtime, materials and supplies, etc.

As was mentioned in Chapter 13, maintenance, in a sense, is a parallel production system, and therefore many of the managerial and analytical techniques that have proven successful in other areas of production may be applied to it. This indicates that the place to start in developing an effective maintenance program is in the selection of qualified managers to run the program. However, the importance of selecting good maintenance managers has only recently begun to be recognized. Historically, a man was promoted to a maintenance foreman or management position because he was a good mechanic—a practice that often meant the addition of a poor manager and the loss of a good mechanic.

There is a wide variety of areas in which maintenance improvement efforts can be quite rewarding. We will very briefly comment on just two of them: The analysis of repair records for equipment breakdown, and the stocking of maintenance spare parts.

Good maintenance management includes a standard policy for the review of equipment repair records. Analysis of maintenance repair cards may show:

1. An operator is working incorrectly and causing breakdowns;
2. Maintenance repairmen are doing poor work, resulting in repeated breakdowns; and
3. Machines or equipment either are being used for the wrong purposes or contain design weaknesses that should be corrected.

---

[12] E. T. Newbrough, *Effective Maintenance Management* (New York: McGraw-Hill, 1967), pp. 2–3.

[13] Ibid., p. 4.

A rather interesting area in maintenance is the stocking of spare parts to maintain equipment operation. While the same type of analysis may be used here as in conventional inventory control, the probabilities of breakdown and the assignment of downtime costs are far more difficult to estimate. Because of this, manufacturers of equipment offer prepared packages of maintenance parts and supplies, along with programmed procedures. From data gathered from its various customers, the manufacturer determines the most frequent causes of breakdowns and assembles appropriate parts packages that are available at the time equipment is purchased. Frequently, manufacturers also compile a second or third list of items with lower breakdown probabilities, to be stocked by users for whom machine downtime is very costly. As a company gains experience with this equipment in its own application, the maintenance recommendations and spare parts supplies are revised.

Preventive maintenance programs.   The cost of maintenance may be significantly reduced through the introduction of a preventive maintenance program. The feasibility of such a program, however, requires careful investigation. Chapter 13 described preventive maintenance and presented an example showing one approach to determining maintenance policy. Briefly, it was concluded that preventive maintenance procedures are warranted when

1. On a cost tradeoff basis it is more economical to service the equipment while it is still operable (as opposed to letting it run until it breaks down).
2. The probabilities of component breakdown can be adequately predicted.

Figure 14.2 shows three breakdown frequency distributions. Component A shows no trend; therefore a policy cannot be established for its routine replacement. Component B is relatively constant during its initial usage, but expectation of breakdown increases rapidly. Component C has a high breakdown rate during its break-in period, followed by a relatively stable period, and then an increasing fatality rate with age. Thus two components,

FIGURE 14.2

Breakdown frequency as a function of the amount a component has been used

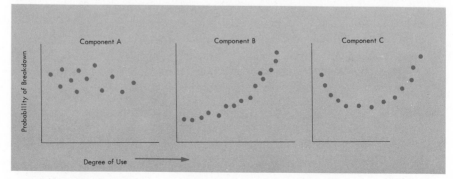

B and C, have breakdown predictability and therefore would be candidates for a preventive maintenance program.

Inventory system

Insuring an adequate supply of materials. The normal routine of purchasing materials from vendors is occasionally upset as a consequence of energy, fuel, and raw material shortages. Such shortages disrupt the production schedule and raise such questions as: Should the firm curtail production and wait out the shortage? Should the firm bid up prices for the existing supply to assure meeting its market? Should the firm try to find another firm to produce its product (perhaps a firm with its own supply source or a foreign firm not facing supply problems)?

In order to insure an adequate supply of materials, a firm should, first, determine which of the materials it purchases are critical to its operation; second, examine the sources of supply to find how reliable they would be during times of shortage; third, develop alternate supply strategies such as (*a*) offering assistance to present suppliers to increase their reliability, (*b*) purchase a plant capable of producing the material that may be in short supply, or (*c*) integrate vertically to include producing the material as an integral part of the firm's operation. As a general rule, for those cases when material does become in short supply, the firm should develop a strategy to allocate what supply there is to those products that have the greatest benefit to the firm.[14]

Table 14.2 lists each of the above topics along with a procedure to examine the materials shortage problem.

Reducing lead times, holding costs, and ordering costs. Some of the more common objectives in improving an inventory system are to reduce lead times, holding costs, and ordering costs. The following strategies describe six practical ways of bringing about these reductions. It must be noted, however, that some of these alternatives may not be available to the firm.

1. Select suppliers near the plant. In many situations it is worth paying a higher unit cost to ensure having the vendor near enough to the plant to provide local delivery. Besides the reduction in delivery lead times, tangible savings can be obtained through a reduction in safety stocks because they are, in effect, maintained by the supplier. Moreover, closeness to the supplier allows a smaller quantity of items to be received at any one time, thereby cutting down on material handling and initial storage charges.

2. Enter contract purchase agreements with local distributors. This approach usually involves daily supplier deliveries and requires that a special catalog be prepared by the company's purchasing department. (In effect, this action is the purchase of inventory capacity from the vendor; the capacity is translated into items as they are needed.) The main savings

---

[14] For a more detailed discussion, see A. A. Meitz and Breaux B. Castleman, "How to Cope with Supply Shortages," *Harvard Business Review*, vol. 53, no. 1 (January–February 1975), pp. 91–96.

TABLE 14.2

Determining a firm's critical inventory of purchased materials, and alternate strategies to assure adequate supply

Operation	Procedure	Explanation
Screen to identify critical materials	Examine total purchased list; develop critical list and final super-critical list	An item may be termed critical if: the item is a significant portion of final product; the item is essential to the production of several different products; the product is a significant market share; product loss would lose market share or diminish profit; or if alternate materials have high cost.
Analyze vendors to determine risk	Assess present vendors, alternate vendors of substitutable materials	Identify high-risk situations such as availability of items from very few vendors, recent rapid price increases, and recent lengthening of delivery times. Examine suppliers also to determine *their* material suppliers.
Develop alternate supply strategies	Assistance programs	Increase the reliability of a supplier through programs such as financial support and managerial and technical assistance.
	"Insurance policy investments"	Purchase a marginal or uneconomic facility producing a critical item to be used in case of shortages.
	Vertical integration	Expand the firm, creating its own production of critical items.
Decide how to use materials in short supply	Examine product data for market share, profit ratios, life-cycle positions.	Allocate materials in short supply to high-profit products and those in rapid growth phases. Omit high-risk products and mature, declining products.

Source: Table adapted from A. A. Meitz and Breaux B. Castleman, "How to Cope With Supply Shortages," *Harvard Business Review*, vol. 53, no. 1 (January–February 1975), pp. 91–96.

stems from a clear understanding of the specifications of the inventory items supplied, which allows phoning in orders and thereby eliminates purchase order preparation. The main additional cost to the company is the preparation and maintenance of the catalog.

3. *Negotiate for "set-aside" stocks at the supplier's warehouse or plant.* This approach is designed to guarantee that a certain amount of stock will always be available for company needs. Also, it eliminates the need to consider the supplier's production or delivery lead time, as well as the time it takes the company to receive the goods from the supplier.

4. *Have the supplier stock partially processed material that he can finish upon demand.* Some suppliers are reluctant to stock a finished item, but they may be willing to stock semiprocessed material that can be used for other customers' orders. The advantage of this approach is that it enables the supplier to anticipate the long-lead-time portion of his production cycle and thus shorten his lead time after the receipt of an order.

5. *Negotiate lead time reductions with the supplier.* This requires a certain amount of investigation if lead time appears to be unusually long.

Emphasis should be placed on discovering low-price items that have a long lead time, since it is likely that these extended lead times can be reduced.

6. *Purchase from the vendor by economic-order quantity analysis but contract for several partial deliveries.* Although transportation and receiving costs are higher, significant savings may be realized through reduced holding costs. The usual EOQ model is modified to reflect the changed costs. The model is solved for the optimum number of deliveries, and the economic delivery quantity may be obtained. The procedure is somewhat involved, but significant savings may be realized.[15]

Scheduling system

At the aggregate level, scheduling can be improved in some cases simply by revising the review period. (Too often the aggregate plan is accepted as a rigid plan of action.) There must be frequent reviews, using the most recent data. The scheduling function also can be improved by smoothing the demands placed on the production system. Some of the following ways to reduce overall costs have been mentioned in previous chapters, in which the designs of the planning and scheduling systems were at issue.

Warehousing. A common strategy is to level production rates by producing for inventory during slack or slow periods and depleting these inventories during periods of high demand. This strategy, which is common when seasonal or cyclical variations are highly predictable, has the effect of establishing a stable production rate throughout the year. Inventory building creates a more efficient use of capacity, and, in the long run, labor costs are reduced through a stable employment level. However, the costs of carrying inventory in periods of slack demand and the possibility of obsolescence must be carefully measured before such a strategy can improve overall costs and output.

Strike protection programs. An aggregate plan can be effective only if it provides for all major contingencies. A labor strike or work stoppage by any one supplier may bring about a material shortage that can have the effect of completely halting production. Strike protection programs have proven to be effective in reducing the probability of material shortages due to a supplier's labor problems.

Such a program begins with a compilation of the expiration dates of the labor contracts of all suppliers. At least six months in advance of the termination of each contract, the probability of a strike and its likely duration are estimated. On the basis of these estimates, stockpiling of the affected material may be initiated by increasing orders. The list of materials to be stockpiled should be determined from an analysis to identify the critical and super-critical items, as in Table 14.2. There is no doubt that

---

[15] For derivation of the modified EOQ model, see "Computer-Maker Upgrades Inventory System," *Industrial Engineering* (June 1969), pp. 16–23. (Proper application of the method is limited to independent-demand items.)

strike protection programs are costly in terms of excess inventories, but they must be measured in terms of large potential losses.

Multiple suppliers.   To assure a constant materials flow, and to hedge against an individual supplier's labor or production problems, many firms prefer to split their material requirements among different suppliers. The advantage is that if one supplier should fail to deliver the goods, those ordered from another will permit partial operation. Further, the alternate supplier may be able to provide the additional goods to make up for the shortage.

Capacity constraints.   If capacity is inadequate for the coming period, a portion of the production process, or at least the bottleneck operations, may be subcontracted to a firm that has the required capacity. Another alternative may be to rent additional equipment for a short period of time. A third way is to enter into cross-production agreements with competitors. In cross-production, two or more firms enter into an agreement to produce certain items exclusively. Each firm produces the others' requirements for given products, which helps create economies of scale, longer production runs, and reductions in setup time.

Short-interval scheduling.   The basic idea of short interval scheduling is to force tight supervisory control over production through frequent (usually hourly) checks on output. The benefits from this practice arise from identifying lagging production quickly and thereby taking corrective action more rapidly than under typical scheduling practices. The use of the methodology is predicated on well defined output standards and a generally constant product demand.

IMPROVEMENT IN THE WORKFORCE

Earlier in this chapter we looked at the potential for improvement through redesign of the product and new work place layouts. Now the concentration is on the man in the system: how to motivate him for greater and higher-quality production while at the same time assuring his contentment with the job. In this section we will examine two methods of motivation—variable work week schedules and zero defects programs.

Variable work week schedules

Since higher wages are not always adequate motivation to improve labor performance a variety of other ways have been tried, with varying degrees of success. One of these, the variable work schedule, was first tried on a national scale in 1970. Many firms replaced their normal 5-day, 8-hour work week with a 4-day, 10-hour schedule. The belief was that employees with three days off each week would be happier. The results of this schedule are still inconclusive; while some firms continue to adopt the 4-day work week, others who have used it are switching back to their former 5-day schedule.

The most recent variant of work schedules is the variable work week, which is often termed the flexible work schedule. Flexible working hours started in West Germany in 1967 and the idea is now in wide use in Europe. The method allows workers to put in their required number of hours within a wider period of time. For example, an employee working an 8-hour day in a firm operating from 8 A.M. to 10 P.M. may choose his own time of day for the 8 hours. The flexibility varies widely. Some firms require the presence of employees for some specific periods and then allow them to choose the remainder. Others even allow a wide latitude of variation by weeks, so long as at the end of each month each employee fulfills his required number of working hours.

The flexible work week schedule is now being tried by many firms in the United States and the number of workers under such plans seems to be growing. Experience in Europe has shown that when a flexible work hour plan is installed in a compatible managerial environment, productivity improves, morale rises, labor turnover drops, absenteeism decreases, and overtime declines.[16]

Zero defects programs

Numerous programs for employee motivation have been adopted in recent years with the objective of seeking improvement through company-wide employee participation. Titles of such programs are ZERO DEFECTS, PRIDE (Personal Responsibility in Daily Effort), and "accent on quality." Zero defects programs have had a particularly strong push because the Department of Defense has incorporated them into its contract requirements.

The zero defects philosophy creates an "attitude of defect prevention." It relies entirely on moral suasion since there are no direct monetary rewards. Zero defects is neither a production design goal nor a quality control design feature; that is, the selection and method of the production process were not chosen with the objective of zero or very low defective output. Nor are the sampling plans and inspection procedures designed to assure 100 percent acceptable output. Rather, the system is designed for, say, 95 to 98 percent good quality, and the workers seek to eliminate the normally expected 2 to 5 percent bad output. This improvement, in essence, is viewed as "all gravy" since a higher than designed output quality is drawn from the system without incurring additional costs.

For example, consider two machines that are available for purchase. The more expensive machine may produce at higher quality, though at a high cost. To hold the product cost down, however, the lower-cost machine may be bought. Now if through "babying" this machine and frequently "tweaking it up" the output quality can be increased beyond what would be its normally expected output, we have the idea of the zero defects approach. The machine operator must be encouraged to get the best that he

---

[16] Alvar O. Elbing, Herman Gadon, and John R. M. Gordon, "Flexible Working Hours, It's About Time," *Harvard Business Review*, vol. 52, no. 1 (January–February 1974), p. 154.

can out of the machine without significantly reducing output or increasing cost.[17]

In order for a firm to benefit from zero defects–type motivational programs, there must be

1. Intensive communication—constant reminders of the importance of the effort through signs, stickers, contests, posters, etc. This is aimed at instilling pride in workmanship and extolling the importance of the job.
2. Plantwide recognition—publicly granting rewards, certificates, and plaques.
3. Problem identification. Employees point out areas that in their opinion may be improved but they need not suggest how the improvements might be achieved.
4. Employee goal setting. Employees participate in establishing their own goals because there is more motivation to achieve these goals if one has participated in their creation. Generally, employees set their goals higher than others might set them.

One of the secrets of success is constant promotion of the program to assure that interest will not die down. This means a variety of promotional efforts, such as rotating the areas of attention and inter- and intraplant competition. The results of such programs have been highly satisfying when they have been conducted with management's sincere intent to achieve organizational objectives without sacrificing the needs of the work force.[18]

CONCLUSION

In many respects the steady state period is a precarious one. For the energetic firm, it can be a time in which new ideas and higher achievements can be sought. If management does its job in motivating the work force the period can be a springboard to new products, new production methodologies, and new operating procedures, bringing greater success to the firm. For other firms, unfortunately, the steady state becomes an achievement in itself and is followed by only a sustained period of stagnation.

By and large, operating in the daily environment of relatively static conditions is routine, hard work. Few great feats are realized. Rather, the goal is one of making a large number of small accomplishments—finding a way to save a few minutes' productive time, changing the design of a product so that it may be made of different materials, or getting together with employees so as to promote a more harmonious system.

---

[17] For some products, a product output of zero defects is a system design constraint and not a motivational program. Consider the importance of heart pacemakers or components for our space program. The goal of close to 100 percent quality output is achieved through high-cost production methods and repeated inspections.

[18] D. A. Snyder, "Motivational Programs, Their Development and Function," *Journal of Industrial Engineering*, Vol. 19, No. 6 (June 1968), pp. 274–78.

PROPOSITIONS

Propositions contrasting services and manufacturing relative to improvement of the system

Product: In service systems, improvement of the productive *system* generally has a direct effect on the service product. In manufacturing, improvement of the productive system generally has little, if any effect on the nature of the manufactured product.

Technology of transformation: Because of the subjective nature of services, it is often impossible to quantify the value of the improvement to the service system. In manufacturing, the value of an improvement is almost always quantifiable.

Operating-control system: In services, a common objective of improving the operating-control system is to enhance the service product in the eyes of the customer. In manufacturing, the customer is often unaware of the elements of the operating-control system and hence the general objective of improvement is to reduce cost.

Workforce: Improvement in service systems is typically associated with greater specialization of the workforce; in a manufacturing environment, workforce improvement generally involves broadening of worker skills.

REVIEW AND DISCUSSION QUESTIONS

1. From the aspect of cost saving opportunities, why is it especially important that the product be well designed in the first place?
2. What is value engineering and what does it seek to achieve?
3. From a value engineering standpoint, what questions might you ask about a new cordless electrical can opener that has just been designed by your company?
4. Using value analysis, what questions might a purchasing agent ask and what factors might he examine prior to ordering materials to produce a product?
5. How might you improve quality control in
   An automobile factory?
   A hospital?
   A university classroom?
   A university's curriculum?
6. What reasons might a company give in defending its attempts to keep all its products or services at relatively the same level of quality?
7. What are the goals of an effective maintenance program?
8. Define preventive maintenance. Would a preventive maintenance program be appropriate for the following cases:

Keeping a car's brakes in order?

Preventing an appendectomy?

Making your clothing last longer?

9. How might you increase likelihood that materials needed by the production system will be available?

10. What are some of the ways to improve the scheduling of activities?

11. "We should always strive to produce goods completely free of defects." Comment on this statement and its implications.

12. "As I see it, improvement is a responsibility of management, not the work force. Moreover, most workers don't have time to think about improving things if their jobs are completely specified and they are busy all the time." Comment.

PROBLEMS

1. How would you apply the deliberate change approach to cost reduction in the following:
   a. The structure of your classroom chair?
   b. The operation of a hospital and its various departments?
   c. The operation of a police department and its various functions?

2. Visit an establishment such as a department store, pharmacy, laundry, supermarket, or business office and
   a. Make a sketch of the existing layout.
   b. Determine the criteria by which it evaluates performance (e.g., time to serve customer, quickest time to complete the product or service, maximum product exposure time).
   c. Propose a new layout.
   d. Given your new layout, how would you suggest it be implemented?

3. Select a product and analyze it to determine
   a. Whether it is satisfactory for its intended use.
   b. Whether it is maintainable (cleanable, its parts easily replaced, etc.).
   c. How it might be improved functionally.
   d. How the cost of its manufacture might be reduced.

4. Alpha-Numerics manufactures a line of computer circuit module boards that are used in several of the large-scale computers. Because of recent modifications to improve these systems, Alpha-Numerics must improve the quality of its circuit modules by about 15 percent to meet the new requirements. What suggestions would you make to meet this new quality level?

5. Consider the physical plant and resources of your college or university— buildings, air conditioning, plumbing, trees, shrubbery, roads, equipment, etc. What improvements would you suggest in maintaining this system?

6. Fisher Ordnance Inc. has obtained a government contract to provide munitions to be used in the peace-keeping efforts that we have been involved in during the past 20 or so years. Several components it purchases from vendors are very critical to meeting delivery schedules, so Fisher wants to be quite sure that they will be available when needed. At the same time, however, Fisher does not want to stock excessive quantities of these purchased

components. What alternatives might Fisher explore to meet its inventory needs?

7. In an effort to upgrade its entire corporate image, Timely Watch Company has instituted a "quality in worksmanship" program. What methods or alternatives should it consider as feasible ways of improving labor performance?

8. Electro-Magnetics, Inc., was the winner of a contract to produce a newly developed powerful magnet that, it is said, will revolutionize the motor and propulsion industry in much the same way that transistors revolutionized the electronics industry. The contract contains a relatively standard clause attaching a penalty to late deliveries of finished magnets. EMI, however, is a relatively small firm and would not be able to survive such penalties for any extended period. Management has great confidence that their workforce will stay with them throughout the contract, but they feel that they are susceptible to material shortages that could shut down their production.

   Recognizing that EMI cannot purchase all of the material at once for this long-term contract, how would you suggest they approach this potential problem of material shortage?

9. Universal Insurance, Inc., is essentially a financial institution acting as a money broker for its subsidiary companies. Approximately 80 percent of the revenue of these subsidiaries comes from casualty insurance premiums. A Department of Productivity Improvement (DPI) has just been formed and is now staffed with several relatively young business school and engineering school graduates. Because of the large amount of clerical help, data processing analysts, policy writers, and claims adjusters involved, DPI is seeking ways to improve the labor force. There are several subsidiaries, and the results of their work improvement programs will be implemented at each of these companies.

   Question: What alternatives would you suggest they look at in their work improvement efforts?

SELECTED BIBLIOGRAPHY

Blanchard, B. B., and Lowery, Edward E.   *Maintainability: Principles and Practice.* New York: McGraw-Hill, 1969.

Dearden, John   "How to Make Incentive Plans Work," *Harvard Business Review* (July–August 1972), pp. 117–24.

Elbing, Alvar O., Gadon, Herman, and Gordon, John R. M.   "Flexible Working Hours, It's About Time," *Harvard Business Review,* vol. 52, no. 1 (January–February 1974), pp. 18–33.

Greve, J. W., and Wilson, F. W. (eds.)   *Value Engineering in Manufacturing.* Englewood Cliffs, N.J.: Prentice-Hall, 1967.

Heyman, Matthew   "Productivity: Washington Update," *Industrial Engineering,* vol. 8, no. 4 (April 1976), pp. 20–23.

Lastra, Frank T.   "Comparative Review of Cost Reduction Programs in Manufacturing," *Journal of Industrial Engineering,* vol. 16, no. 5 (September–October 1965), pp. 340–45.

Lehrer, Robert N.   *The Management of Improvement*. New York: Reinhold Publishing Co., 1965.

Meitz, A. A., and Castleman, Breaux B.   "How to Cope with Supply Shortages," *Harvard Business Review*, vol. 53, no. 1 (January–February 1975), pp. 91–96.

Newbrough, E. T.   *Effective Maintenance Management*. New York: McGraw-Hill, 1967.

Smith, Martin R.   *Short Interval Scheduling A Systematic Approach to Cost Reduction*, New York: McGraw-Hill, 1968.

Spinanger, Arthur   "Increasing Profits through Deliberate Methods Change," *Proceedings of Seventeenth Annual Industrial Engineering Institute UCLA* (1965).

Vollmann, T. E., and Buffa, E. S.   "The Facilities Layout Problem in Perspective," *Management Science*, vol. 12, no. 10 (June 1966), pp. 450–68.

Section six

Revision of the system

OVERVIEW

Changing environmental conditions should stimulate the production manager to consider alternative procedures and technologies to ensure that the productive system remains competitive. The chapters in this section deal with two dimensions of this issue.

Chapter 15 focuses on the evaluation of production policies to determine whether they are consistent with the organization's current and emerging primary task.

Chapter 16 examines a variety of factors and techniques that should be considered in executing major productive system revisions in response to significant environmental changes.

15

Evaluation of production policies

As the production system evolves, it often happens that the policies that it follows with respect to product, technology, operating-control system, and workforce are not the policies it should be following to help the organization perform its primary task. In this chapter, we will elaborate on this critical problem and present two questionnaires for examining production policies in manufacturing and service organizations. To illustrate the use of the questionnaires, we will apply them to short case examples. We will begin our discussion by reexamining the concept of "primary task."

PRIMARY TASK OF THE FIRM

As mentioned in the context of product selection in Chapter 2, the organization has a primary task that it must perform if it is to survive and thrive. A firm's primary task is a function of its competitive environment[1] and may be composed of several elements. A classic example is a teaching hospital, which must recruit medical students, train them, and graduate an acceptable portion of them as qualified doctors. It also must be available to the public to meet routine and emergency health needs of the community. A firm's primary task may differ from its stated objectives. The objectives are essentially what it *wishes* to do; the primary task is what it *must* do. (Unless otherwise stated, however, we will assume that a firm's stated objectives are consistent with its primary task.)

PRIMARY TASK OF THE PRODUCTION FUNCTION

The primary task of the production function should be supportive of the primary task of the firm. Conflicts, of course, inevitably arise. For example, the internally developed primary task of the manufacturing unit might be to maximize production for stock; from the perspective of the organization, however, a greater profit might be obtained by limiting stock output and holding capacity available to fill special orders.

Skinner[2] has observed that few factories can or should try to excel on every measure of performance. (We believe this statement holds true for most service systems as well.) If one adopts this view, it forces production managers to recognize that there is a limited set of factors that constitute the true primary task of their area. A way of delineating these factors is to answer Skinner's question, "What must we be especially good at? Cost, quality, lead times, reliability, changing schedules, new product introduction, or low investment?"[3] Once this delineation is made, production policies can be specified and evaluated on a rational basis. (Example primary tasks for different types of organizations are listed in Table 15.1.)

---

[1] The role of the environment is developed in Chapter 16.

[2] Wickham Skinner, "The Focused Factory," *Harvard Business Review,* May–June 1974, pp. 113–21.

[3] Ibid., p. 115.

TABLE 15.1

Typical primary tasks of sample organizations and their production

Type of organization	*Primary task of firm*	*Resultant primary task of production*
Electronics company	1. Make customized products 2. Advance product features 3. Introduce products rapidly	1. Produce specialized products 2. Master problems of new product design and production 3. Operate effectively with short lead times
Feeder airline	1. Service all required routes 2. Be perceived by customers as friendly and efficient 3. Maintain outstanding safety record	1. Maintain an efficient scheduling system for all aircraft 2. Develop worker attitudes and competence 3. Employ advanced maintenance procedures and personnel
Firefighting units of the forest service	1. Put out fires rapidly 2. Keep firefighting costs at a minimum 3. Keep fire related casualties at a minimum	1. Be able to organize and arrive at fire scene in a minimum number of hours 2. Utilize project planning to organize support services 3. Deploy personnel and equipment according to latest principles of fire safety
Small oil producer	1. Meet regional demands for oil rapidly 2. Maintain a competitive return on investment 3. Provide a variety of petroleum products at a low cost relative to competition	1. Keep oil inventory levels high 2. Utilize production capacity at its optimal level 3. Maintain a flexible refinery operation

PRODUCTION POLICIES

A policy is a general guide to action and (theoretically) is derived from enterprise objectives. Policies are defined in various ways, even within the same organization. At one extreme, a policy may be formally stated and codified in a policy manual. At the other extreme, it may be an unstated norm that is followed habitually by individuals performing their jobs and making decisions. While it is usually desirable to have all policies explicitly defined, it is rare that an organization can foresee all eventualities that require a policy statement. Thus, many policies are inferred from other policies or corporate objectives, and/or are developed ad hoc to meet the demands of a new situation. In the treatment of production policies that follows, we will assume that policies are generally known to the organizations in question, but will not dwell on how they would be defined formally in a policy manual. Our interest is in the general intent of the policy—not the specific terminology in which it is worded.

Production policies can be classified under the four headings we have used in contrasting manufacturing and services: product, technology of transformation, operating-control system, and workforce. Within each classification are specific policy decision areas that are of concern to the production area of most firms. These are shown in Table 15.2.

TABLE 15.2

General production policy areas

Product	Technology of transformation	Operating- control system	Workforce
Design	Facilities	Inventory	Skills
Producibility	Equipment	Scheduling	Job design
Introduction	Supplies	Quality	Compensation
Stability		Organization	

EVALUATION OF PRODUCTION POLICIES

In Chapter 2, the tradeoffs made in policy development and the process of policy determination were illustrated in Table 2.4 and Figure 2.8, respectively. At this point, however, our emphasis shifts to evaluating specific policies in a going concern. In particular, we are interested in answering the following questions:

a. Given the primary task of the firm and production function, what is the "correct" emphasis for each production policy alternative?
b. How close is the match (or alignment) between currently existing policy alternatives and the correct alternatives?

Once these questions have been answered, the production manager is in a better position to interpret past performance of the production area, and more importantly, to take remedial action by altering current policy to bring it into line with the primary tasks of the firm and production function. To perform this evaluation, however, requires that management have some mechanism that enables classification of policy alternatives and permits some measurement of the degree of alignment between current and correct policy. One approach that we have found to be useful for these purposes is to apply production policy questionnaires that act as both a checklist and a rough measuring device. Two such questionnaires—one for manufacturing and one for services—are provided in Tables 15.3 and 15.4. To use them, the person evaluating the production system simply notes what appears to be the current policy alternative and then what he believes to be the correct alternative. The degree to which there is overall policy agreement is measured by calculating the percentage of items in agreement out of the total items which were scored.[4] A rough interpretation of the alignment percentage is as follows: 90 or more, excellent; 80–89, good; 70–79, average; 60–69, poor; less than 60, very poor.

A question that commonly arises with respect to the questionnaire is "What does it mean if the firm is doing poorly despite a high alignment percentage?" The answer to this could be any of the following:

1. The firm has not recognized its primary task.
2. The production function has not recognized its primary task.

---

[4] In the case examples, it is not always possible to identify all current and/or correct policy alternatives. Therefore, a percentage score is used rather than a straight numerical count of items in agreement.

3. Policies are not being properly executed (a policy is simply a form of plan and hence is only a part of the management process).

Of course, too, the questionnaires shown here are highly compressed for instructional purposes, weight each item equally, and no doubt omit certain items that are important to a particular firm in a particular industry.

CASES AND APPLICATION OF QUESTIONNAIRES

The Tucson Toy Company and Big Jim's Gym cases are juxtaposed with policy questionnaires for manufacturing and service organizations, respectively. The reader is encouraged to analyze these cases using the questionnaires and answer the questions posed at the end of the cases.[5] The objectives of the exercise are first, to practice taking a systematic approach to analyzing the admittedly fuzzy, but highly important issue of production policy; second, to develop a heightened awareness of the interaction between primary task and policy; and third, to deduce from limited data what policy alternatives are appropriate and inappropriate for a given productive system. Our ultimate goal is for the reader to gain "a new set of eyes" for viewing the subtle dynamics among the many factors that define production operations.

Tucson Toy Company

The Tucson Toy Company (TTC) views its primary task as making for stock a standardized line of high quality, unique toys that "last from pablum to puberty." As a rule, they introduce one or two new toys a year. In August of this year, the owner and manufacturing manager, Dwight Smith, has been informed by his toy inventors that they have designed a "King Kong Robot Doll." This doll will stand two feet high and is capable of climbing walls using its suction cup "hands" and make bellowing sounds from a continuous tape voice box. One of the company's three manufacturing staff departments, design engineering, states that the product can be made primarily from molded plastic using the firm's new all-purpose molders (now used for making small attachments to the firm's wooden toys). TTC in its previous initial production of new toys has relied heavily on its skilled work force to "de-bug" the product design as they make the product, and to perform quality inspections on the finished product. Production runs have been short runs to fill customer orders. If the King Kong doll is to go into production, however, the production run size will have to be large and assembly and testing procedures will have to be more refined. Currently, each toy maker performs almost all processing steps at his workbench. The production engineering department believes that the assembly of the new toy is well within the skill levels of the current workforce, but that the voice box and battery-operated movement mechanism will have

---

[5] Our scoring and interpretation of the two cases is given in problems 3 and 4 at the end of the chapter.

TABLE 15.3
Manufacturing policy questionnaire

Product
  A. *Design*
  1. Breadth of product line (standardized/mixed/customized)   A B C
  2. Allowable variability in component specifications (little/some/much)   A B C
  3. Coordination among engineering, marketing, and manufacturing (little/some/much)   A B C
  4. Design from scratch rather than around existing components (usually/sometimes/rarely)   A B C
  5. Concern for producibility (little/some/much)   A B C
  B. *Introduction*
  6. Use of specialized start-up procedures (little/some/much)   A B C
  7. Stability of design after production release (little/some/much)   A B C
Technology of Transformation
  8. Degree of mechanization of product assembly (little/some/much)   A B C
  9. Degree of automatic inspection and testing (little/some/much)   A B C
  10. Degree of mechanization of materials handling (little/some/much)   A B C
  11. Degree of equipment specialization (little/some/much)   A B C
  12. Flexibility of equipment to meet changes in volume, run length, and product mix (little/some/much)   A B C
  13. Number of plants (one/few/many)   A B C
  14. Plants located to be near (suppliers/markets/labor pools)   A B C
  15. Plants specialized by (product/both/process)   A B C
  16. Extent of production-related R & D (little/some/much)   A B C
  17. Extent of subcontracting (little/some/much)   A B C
Operating-control system
  18. Investment in production and inventory control system (low/medium/high)   A B C
  19. Use of inventory to decouple production stages (little/some/much)   A B C
  20. Production to order vs. production for stock (order/mixed/stock)   A B C
  21. Production strategy (level production/mixed/adjust with demand)   A B C
  22. Emphasis on quality control (little/moderate/much)   A B C
  23. Amount of inspection throughout the manufacturing process (little/some/much)   A B C
  24. Organization of manufacturing (functional/project/product)   A B C
  25. Number of supervisory levels in manufacturing (few/several/many)   A B C
  26. Number of staff departments to support manufacturing (few/several/many)   A B C
Workforce
  27. Range of worker skills (narrow/medium/broad)   A B C
  28. Job content of most jobs (short cycle/medium/long)   A B C
  29. Extent of worker control over work pace (little/some/much)   A B C
  30. Extent of worker or group discretion in work planning (little/some/much)   A B C
  31. Wage payment system (salary/salary + output/output)   A B C
Instructions for scoring
  1. Circle either A, B, or C to identify what you believe to be the *correct* policy alternative (A, B, and C correspond to the order of the descriptive terms in the parentheses.)
  2. Place an X over either A, B, or C to identify what appears to be the policy *currently* being used.
  3. Calculate the percentage of items in agreement out of the total items that you were able to score (i.e., the items that have both a circle and an X associated with them). This gives an alignment percentage.
      General scoring guide: 90–100% = excellent; 80–89% = good; 70–79% = fair; 60–69% = poor; below 60% = very poor.

This questionnaire is based upon a questionnaire entitled "Choices and Alternatives in Production System Design," developed by Wickham Skinner and his associates at the Harvard Graduate School of Business Administration.

to be subcontracted. TTC has always had good relations with subcontractors primarily because the firm has placed its orders with sufficient lead time so that its vendors could optimally sequence TTC's orders with those of some larger toy producers in Tucson. Dwight Smith has always favored long range production planning so that he can keep his 50 toy makers busy all year. (One of the reasons he set up the factory in Tucson was so that he could draw upon the large population of toy makers from the "old country" who lived there.) The supervisors of the firm's three production departments—castles, puppets, and novelties—have been perceived by Dwight Smith to be favorable to the new product. The novelty department supervisor, Fred Avide, has stated "my men can make any toy—you give us an output incentive and we'll produce around the clock."

The marketing department has forecast a demand of 5,000 King Kong robots for the Christmas rush. They should sell for $29.50. A preliminary cost analysis made by the process engineering department is that they will cost no more than $7.00 apiece to manufacture. The company is currently operating at 70 percent capacity. Financing is available and there is no problem with cash flow. Dwight Smith is wondering if he should go into production of King Kong dolls.

QUESTIONS FOR THE READER:

a. Indicate the correct and current policy choices on the manufacturing policy questionnaire. Calculate the percentage of items that are in agreement.

b. Based upon your findings, should TTC introduce the King Kong doll? Explain.

Big Jim's Gym

Big Jim has been in the body building business for many years in Glendale, California. His gymnasium, originally for men, now consists of separate facilities for men and women located beneath a pizza parlor in downtown Glendale. Jim views the primary task of his business as "providing a full range of body building and weight reduction services for upper and middle class men, women and children in the Glendale area."

Currently, he has 20 employees who work with the customers in designing their health programs. At present, his gym has separate weight-lifting and exercise rooms for men and women, a pool, a sauna bath, and a small running track behind the building. While Jim states that every customer is different, he makes men go through his 23-step conditioning course and women follow the diet in "Big Jim's Energy Diet" pamphlet. (Customers are usually enrolled in a ten-week introductory course, and then left to advance at their own pace.)

The gym is modeled after the one Jim first managed on an army base in Pennsylvania "right down to the olive-drab walls." Jim maintains that the

TABLE 15.4

Service systems policy questionnaire

Product
1. Ratio of customer direct contact time with system to service creation time (low/medium/high)   A B C
2. Extent of direct labor input in creating service product (small/medium/large)   A B C
3. Primary service is viewed as (professional/trade/artistic)   A B C
4. Breadth of service (standard/mixed/customized)   A B C
5. Variability of customer service demands (low/medium/high)   A B C
6. Number of major elements defining service product (few/some/many)   A B C
7. Range of supplementary services (narrow/medium/wide)   A B C
8. Uniqueness of service relative to regional competition (little/some/much)   A B C
9. Introduction of major new services (rare/occasional/frequent)   A B C
10. Concern with legal restrictions in performing service (little/some/much)   A B C

Technology of transformation
11. Capability to alter service capacity rapidly (little/some/much)   A B C
12. Degree of mechanization of service (little/some/much)   A B C
13. Amount of preparatory work prior to providing a unit of service (little/some/much)   A B C
14. Average number of processing stages customer goes through in obtaining service (few/several/many)   A B C
15. Emphasis on efficiency in layout of facility (little/moderate/major)   A B C
16. Emphasis on aesthetics in layout of facility (little/moderate/major)   A B C
17. Extent of equipment specialization (little/some/much)   A B C
18. Number of service centers (one/few/many)   A B C
19. Size of service center relative to direct competitors (small/medium/large)   A B C
20. Specific service centers located primarily for (convenience of customer/convenience of owner/other)   A B C
21. Reliance upon suppliers (little/some/much)   A B C

Operating-control system
22. Investment in inventory control system (low/medium/high)   A B C
23. Extent of use of supplies to produce service (little/some/much)   A B C
24. Primary inventory viewed as (space/people/supplies)   A B C
25. Service strategy (level/mixed/adjust with demand)   A B C
26. Allowed variability in service scheduling (little/some/much)   A B C
27. Ability to backlog service orders (little/some/much)   A B C
28. Number of supervisory levels (few/several/many)   A B C
29. Number of staff departments to support service (none/some/many)   A B C
30. Method of assignment of service personnel (customer selects/mixed/system selects)   A B C

Workforce
31. Size of workforce relative to competition (small/medium/large)   A B C
32. Required range of worker skills (narrow/medium/broad)   A B C
33. Use of certified professionals in creating service produce (none/some/much)   A B C
34. Job content of most jobs (short cycle/medium/long cycle)   A B C
35. Work pace controlled by (customer/worker/system)   A B C
36. Wage payment system based primarily on (fees/hourly/output or sales)   A B C

Instructions for scoring
1. Circle either A, B, or C to identify what you believe to be the *correct* policy alternative (A, B, and C correspond to the order of the descriptive terms in the parentheses).
2. Place an X over either A, B, or C to identify what appears to be the policy *currently* being used.
3. Calculate the percentage of items in agreement out of the total items that you were able to score (i.e., the items that have both a circle and an X associated with them). This gives an alignment percentage.
   General scoring guide: 90–100% = excellent; 80–89% = good; 70–79% = fair; 60–69% = poor; below 60% = very poor.

spartan atmosphere is necessary "to build mental and physical toughness." With some pride, Jim notes that he has all of the latest barbells and slant-board apparatus. Jim has always viewed his major inventory items as liniments and bandages, which are ordered periodically from a wholesaler or are purchased from a nearby drug store if stockouts occur. (Other items are purchased from a local sporting goods store.)

Jim is very concerned about keeping all of his staff busy and keeping the equipment in constant use so he requires that customers follow a specific hour-by-hour schedule on equipment use. If the equipment is scheduled to capacity, he requests that his customers come at slow periods during the day or evening. (This procedure has met with some resistance on the part of customers but Jim tells them that that is the price they must pay if he is to provide the most up-to-date health center services.)

Jim has done a survey of the prices charged by the other four health centers in the area and his fees are about average.* The other health centers have about the same number of employees although two of them use licensed beauty consultants. Jim considers this an "unnecessary frill" and tells all of his customers that anybody who works for him is an expert on all aspects of body maintenance. Jim has instituted a policy of job rotation whereby each member of the staff, with the exception of the clerk-typist, changes activities each hour. Employees are paid by the hour and are primarily college graduates who are interested in athletics. Turnover has not been a problem, even though Jim pays only slightly more than the minimum wage.

Although Jim's capacity is fully utilized, the number of memberships has dropped off from 500 to about 300 in the last six months, and profits have dropped proportionately. His accountant is looking into the possibility of raising membership fees.

ASSIGNMENT FOR THE READER:

a. Use the Service Policy Questionnaire (Table 15.4) to determine the alignment percentage between current policy and correct policy in light of Big Jim's primary task.

b. Based upon your analysis, what steps do you recommend Jim take to reverse the trend in memberships?

CONCLUSION

To managers and students alike, identifying the primary task of the firm and selecting the appropriate production policy alternatives to support it

---

* Within this market segment Jim is competing with, among others, the Glendale Athletic Club. GAC's facilities include ten handball-racquetball courts, eight tennis courts, a 50-meter pool, sauna and steam rooms, a weight room with five $5,000 Nautilus weight lifting machines, and a fully equipped health bar. GAC's staff includes a trainer, five masseuses, five instructors, and ten other staff members.

seldom provides the feeling of satisfaction one obtains from a crisp, clean solution to a mathematical production problem. Nevertheless, a correct reading of the task of the firm (or production system) and then the identification of appropriate production policies can greatly enhance the performance of the organization, and help assure that subsequent quantitative analyses will be "on target."

PROPOSITIONS

Propositions contrasting services and manufacturing relative to evaluation of production policies

Product: Because the customer is directly involved in creation of the service product, production policies constitute a major portion of the product itself. In manufacturing, the customer is involved at most, only indirectly in product creation and hence production policies are not perceived as part of the product.

Technology of transformation: Because service systems tend to be more labor-intensive than manufacturing, production policies in services are less bound by equipment limitations and hence can be more flexible than production policies in manufacturing.

Operating-control system: Because of the inherent variability in the service product, service system production policies tend to be more difficult to evaluate objectively than production policies for manufacturing.

Workforce: Because a member of the direct workforce in services is often responsible for communicating production policies affecting the customer at several different points in the process, a service worker must often be aware of production policies guiding other members of the workforce. In manufacturing, a direct worker is rarely in contact with the customer and hence need not know production policies affecting other parts of the production system.

REVIEW AND DISCUSSION QUESTIONS

1. How does the primary task of the organization relate to the primary task of the production function?
2. Can you identify any policy areas in services that do not exist in manufacturing, and vice versa?
3. What is the distinction between a firm's primary task and its objectives? Present an example from your own experience in which the primary task of a firm was at odds with the objectives set for it by management.

4. Using your college or university as an example, refute or support the assertion that a production system cannot excel on every measure of performance.

5. Propose another method for scoring the policy questionnaires that would permit a more extensive quantitative measurement of the difference between correct and current policy.

6. What additional policy choices might one wish to consider in dealing with a processing organization such as a chemical plant?

PROBLEMS

(Problem assignments are given at the end of the cases.)

1. Schuette Sound Systems of Palo Alto, California wishes to audit its manufacturing policy to determine whether its technology-of-transformation and operating-control system policies are in alignment with the primary task of the firm. Schuette, which has been in business for ten years, views its primary task as producing electronic sound components for both military and civilian customers. Management is of the opinion that the long-run success of the firm is dependent upon its ability to produce a wide variety of customized products at a low cost (relative to its competition).

Currently, the firm devotes about sixty percent of its capacity to an Air Force order for an electronic jungle surveillance system. Twenty percent of its capacity is devoted to developing a prototype sound system for a "wristwatch" television set called the "watch TV." (Schuette's management believes that this may be a major area of sound system demand in the future.) The remaining capacity is now being utilized in filling orders from 20 different customers.

Schuette has been able to vary greatly its capacity primarily by using general purpose equipment in all phases of its operations and because of its highly flexible management team which is able to change "hats" from line to staff quite easily. The company has prided itself on its ability to manufacture virtually all of its components and to save money by purchasing its raw materials from suppliers as far away as Japan. Inventory control is handled by the purchasing agent and a production control clerk. A Kardex file is used to keep track of inventory purchases and a complete inventory count is made at least every six months. The company has favored buying in volume to obtain price breaks and keeps raw material inventory in a warehouse located next to the manufacturing facility. Work in process inventory is kept at a high level to "keep flexible," while finished goods inventory is kept low for tax avoidance purposes.

Because of its dealings with the military, Schuette is highly conscious of quality and performs one-hundred percent inspections on all incoming raw materials and finished goods. The company's return on investment is about the same as its dozen major competitors in the bay area.

Assignment:

a. Use the Manufacturing Policy Questionnaire (Table 15.3) to determine the alignment percentage for items under *Technology of transformation* (items 8 through 17), and *Operating-control system* (items 18 through 26).

b.   What changes in the above two policy areas seem to be in order if Schuette is to efficiently produce the wristwatch television set in volume?

2.   The Walker Wire Products Company is a small firm manufacturing a wide assortment of resistance-welded wire products. Of the company's average annual business of $500,000, approximately fifty percent is accounted for by racks for holding dishes and glassware in commercial dishwashing machines, forty percent by point-of-purchase advertising display stands, and ten percent by miscellaneous special orders for many different purposes. Mr. Brown, the owner, states his primary task as "to make a profit every year."

The company's plant is located in an industrial district near its workforce, and consists of two floors of an old manufacturing building. The building is so laid out that, the first floor being suitable only for storage, the second floor is used for all manufacturing operations. Equipment includes a general purpose wire-straightening machine to straighten and cut to size the coils of wire that supply 90 percent of the raw materials needed; two forming machines to bend the wire to desired shapes before assembly; 10 spot-and butt-welders for assembly; and miscellaneous equipment used in dowelling, painting, and crating the finished products. Materials are transported by hand in roller bins.

The personnel of the company, exclusive of salesmen, numbers about forty people. Most of the management functions are handled by Mr. Brown and his secretary. All production management, from the time a worker order is transmitted from the office, is under the supervision of a salaried foreman, who has almost complete supervision of the workforce of thirty-five men. The foreman is a man of "the old school," who carries a heavy work load but does not believe in modern production-management practices. At times he has been reprimanded by the owner for unfair treatment of the workers in trying to increase production in rush times. He is, however, a valuable man who knows the business well. No logical successor to him has been found, and no assistant foreman is being trained.

Operations are, for the most part, handled on a job-order basis. For example, when an order for dish racks is received, the secretary date-stamps the order and places it in the "Order Pending" basket. Shop orders are written up daily by Mr. Brown, usually after the morning mail is received. Because of the varying sizes and types of racks required for different washing machines, some technical knowledge is required to write up the orders. Moreover, customers are often not clear in stating their needs. The order is transmitted to the foreman, who is usually in a position, through his general knowledge of the progress of other orders in the shop, to give a fair estimate of when the order will be started and finished. From this point forward, the foreman is responsible for the routing, scheduling, dispatching, and inspection of the order.

Few records are kept. The workers do turn in time slips, but little utilization is made of them. Workers are paid a straight hourly rate, and, as most of the work is of a semi-skilled nature and the workers are highly unionized, advancements in wages are usually made on an overall negotiated basis. Although the foreman has a rough idea of who the best workers are, he has no figures of productivity to give him definite knowledge. Most workers do a variety of tasks including getting their own materials. No attempt has been made to specialize workers beyond allocating the most difficult welding operations to those men that are obviously the most skillful.

Mr. Brown has long appreciated the advantages that would accrue to the company if some of the company's production could be carried on continuously rather than on a job-lot basis. He realizes that certain sizes and models of the dish racks sell in larger volume than others, but, because of tieing up working capital in finished inventory that may move slowly, he hesitates to produce much for stock. About half of the dish rack sales is for original equipment, that is, to the manufacturers of dishwashing machines. The other half goes to hotels and restaurants for replacement of racks that are broken or damaged in use.

Display stands are always of special design, and usually orders are placed for several thousand or more to be delivered on rather short notice. This is quite profitable, but on the other hand, because of the piling up of work-in-process, it disrupts plant operations and clutters floor areas. Moreover, dish rack orders are sidetracked, delivery promises are not met, and steady customers become displeased. In fact, the display stand business is so difficult to handle that, upon occasion, very large orders have been refused because the present organization and plant simply could not handle them.

Another problem that frequently confronts the management is the control of wire-forming and welding fixtures. A set of permanent fixtures is used for the fabrication of dish racks, but display stands require special fixtures. Often, when repeat orders are received for display racks, the foreman finds that he cannot locate the special fixtures or that they have been rebuilt to make new fixtures. There have been some customer complaints about the welds breaking. In general, the conduct of the business is characterized by a lack of record-keeping, which has been excused by the management on the grounds of the company's small size and its inability to assume the additional overhead expense of adding "non-productive" workers to the organization.

Assignment:

    a. Evaluate Mr. Brown's statement that the primary task of his firm is "to make a profit." Propose an alternative primary task based upon the information in the case.

    b. Complete the Manufacturing Policy Questionnaire (Table 15.3), indicating current policy and correct policy for each item. Base your answers to correct policy on *your* definition of Walker's primary task.

    c. Based upon your questionnaire results, specify one important policy under *Product, Technology of transformation, Operating-control system,* and *Workforce* that should be changed. Justify your choice.

    d. Identify the most critical problem from question c above and develop a plan to solve it.

  3. Use the manufacturing policy questionnaire to answer the questions at the end of the "Tucson Toy Company" case. Compare your analysis with the one given below.

Scoring and interpretation of the Tucson Toy Company:

Scoring: Our application of the manufacturing policy questionnaire yielded only eight items in alignment (items 1, 3, 13, 19, 23, 24, 25, and 26). This gives an alignment percentage of 26.

Interpretation: The primary task of TTC has been to produce items that apparently are traditional toys, characterized by durability and simplicity. Little effort goes into standardization of design or into production procedures, since the toy makers seemingly design as they produce. The King Kong doll, however, will require a good deal more in the way of planning and co-ordination because it is a radical departure for TTC in terms of toy technology. (The company's "distinctive competence" seems to be in wooden toys, whereas the King Kong doll is plastic and mechanical.) The technology of transformation will have to be changed from a quasi-craft operation to a production line. This in turn implies mechanization to some degree for parts handling and inspection; and probably the use of special purpose equipment at various stages of the process. The company has done little in the way of process engineering and the equipment is general-purpose. TTC will have to engage in more subcontracting than it currently does and will have to consider carefully the extent of inventory it will keep on hand. The firm currently does not use inventory to decouple production stages since the work is not specialized by department. (If a production line type operation is undertaken, such decoupling will still not be mandatory if care is taken to balance workloads across operations.) A major problem, if the King Kong doll is introduced, will be the change in work procedures required on the part of the workforce. Currently, the workers have a great deal of freedom in performing their jobs, but a switch to a line technology will no doubt eliminate much of it. Fred Avide indicates, however, that the workers are anxious to make more money, but it remains to be seen how they would take to specialized jobs. In summary, the King Kong doll is ill-suited to TTC's current policies and primary task. Other, more compatible toys should be investigated.

4. Use the Services Policy Questionnaire to answer the questions at the end of the Big Jim's Gym case. Compare your analysis with the one given below. Scoring and interpretation of Big Jim's Gym:

   Scoring: Our application of the questionnaire for service system policy yielded only six items in alignment (items 1, 3, 21, 19, 31, and 32). This gives an alignment percentage of 16.

   Interpretation: Jim defined the task of his firm in terms of providing services to people in the "glamour" health market, yet the product provided is an old-line weight-lifter's gym. (In fact it is primitive compared to the GAC product.) Jim's competitors are offering a product that is highly customized and includes a wide range of supplementary services. The technology of transformation used by Jim is simple, but unnecessarily inflexible. Aesthetics, equipment specialization, and convenience to the customer are low. In short, Jim has adopted an assembly line approach, which is in direct conflict with his primary task. (Note the similarity to the Tucson Toy Company in this regard.) The operating-control system obviously is designed from the point of view of maximizing the use of physical facilities and worker skills. This may be appropriate for a military base, but is hardly appealing to the clientele that Jim wishes to attract. Jim also has a narrow view of inventory, and apparently takes little advantage of wholesale sources for supplies and equipment. Jim's workforce is not professional or committed to the field, in contrast to his competitors, who have professionals on their staffs. In summary, Jim must either redefine his primary task—perhaps focusing on his natural constituency, weight-lifters—or make a large investment in upgrading his production system.

SELECTED BIBLIOGRAPHY

Herbst, P. G.   *Socio-technical Design: Strategies in Multidisciplinary Research.* London: Tavistock Publications, 1974.

Skinner, Wickham   "Choices and Alternatives in Production System Design," *POM Perspectives* (Academy of Management), George Gore, editor, September, 1974.

————   "The Focused Factory," *Harvard Business Review* (May–June, 1974), pp. 113–21.

16

Response to environmental change

All organizations are confronted with challenges and opportunities from their environment, which must be effectively dealt with if the firms are to prosper. In this chapter we will explore these challenges and opportunities and examine how they give rise to effective adaptive action on the part of the production system.

One pivotal factor in this discussion is the locus of the production function in the scheme of things. Simply stated, What discretion does the production manager have to carry out change in light of the role of the production function in the total organization? To deal adequately with this issue requires that the total organization be placed in perspective relative to its environment. A discussion of open systems theory is provided as a groundwork for this effort.

A second factor of importance is the determination of how the firm decides on a particular response to an event, given that it has several options. This issue can be cast as a problem in decision making, and accordingly we will introduce two quantitative approaches of proven value in deciding upon a course of action.

A third significant consideration concerns the actual implementation of a change in the production system. A superior technological system is useless if the supporting operating and control systems are not suitable or if the work force does not want it to succeed. Thus we will give some attention to these factors and offer some guidelines along with an example showing the effects of a major change in a production system is described.

OPEN SYSTEMS THEORY

Open systems theory is more a way of viewing organizations than a precise theory. The underlying idea is that organizations are not static structures whose design and activities are fixed, but viable organisms that carry on a continual interplay (or more correctly an ongoing exchange of materials, personnel, manpower, and energy) with their environment. Open systems are characterized by several other features as well. Among these are negative entropy, dynamic equilibrium, negative feedback, and input coding.[1]

Negative entropy

Entropy refers, among other things, to the tendency inherent in all physical systems to run down. Open systems, by virtue of their constant interchange with the environment, can acquire *negative* entropy (i.e., defeat the process) by drawing more energy from their environment than they expend. For example, the accumulation of monetary reserves by a business firm can help arrest the entropic process perhaps indefinitely.

---

[1] "Differentiation" and "equifinality" are also cited as characteristics of open systems, however, they are somewhat peripheral to a discussion of production function adaptation and will not be considered here.

Dynamic equilibrium

This term refers to the preservation of the character of the system in light of changes in the system's environment. To put it another way, it is the ability of a system to utilize varying inputs by selecting the appropriate compensatory actions. Such actions might include product modifications, organizational restructuring, and vertical and horizontal integration.

Negative feedback

This refers to the utilization of information to correct a system's deviation from course. In quality control this might be statistical data that signal that a process is tending to go out of control. For an organization, it might be a consumer survey that indicates that the firm's product is missing its desired market.

Input coding

This refers to the selective mechanisms by which incoming data are translated into usable or compatible information. An organization might set up a coding mechanism for decision rules that would result in funneling all information on a key competitor directly to the sales manager, provide his staff assistant with summary information on relevant tariffs, and circulate trade publications to all members of his sales staff.

THE ENVIRONMENT

The way in which one conceives of the organization's environment is of prime importance to open systems theory.[2] In a pioneering article, Emery and Trist recognized this fact and noted that an understanding of organizational behavior requires some knowledge of (*a*) the nature of the interdependencies between elements in the environment and elements in the firm and (*b*) the processes through which parts of the environment become related to each other. They hypothesized that there are laws that determine the effects of the interdependencies or exchanges, which they termed the *causal texture* of the environment. Thus some action by a firm might be expected to lead not only to a response from, say, a competitor, but also on the part of some supplier to that competitor, who might have no direct interaction with the firm.[3]

Extending Emery's and Trist's work, Shirley Terreberry observed that organizational environments are becoming increasingly turbulent (i.e., more complex and changing), that organizations are becoming increasingly

---

[2] Environment may be defined as the surroundings of an organization or the "climate" in which the organization functions. See William R. Dill, "The Impact of Environment on Organizational Development," in *Readings in Organization Theory: Open Systems Approaches,* John G. Maurer, ed. (New York: Random House, 1972), pp. 81–106.

[3] F. E. Emery and E. L. Trist, "The Causal Texture of Organizational Environments," ibid., pp. 46–57.

FIGURE 16.1

Illustration of a firm (system X) in
a turbulent environment

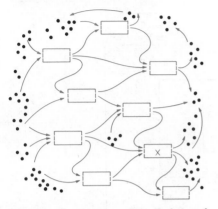

Source: Shirley Terreberry, "The Evolution of
Organizational Environments," in *Readings in
Organizational Theory: Open Systems Ap-
proaches,* John G. Maurer, ed. (New York:
Random House, 1972), p. 67.

less autonomous (i.e., rules and regulations limit their activities), and that
other organizations are becoming increasingly important components of a
given organization's environment.[4] Her conception of the complex nature of
the relationship between an organization and its turbulent environment is
reproduced in Figure 16.1.

The rectangles in Figure 16.1 represent formal organizations and the
dots represent individuals (for example, consumers) and *non*formal social groups (for example, communities). The arrows represent inputs to,
and outputs from, the various elements in the environment. The key point
in this illustration is that an action taken by some apparently unrelated part
of the environment may ultimately become an input to system X. Thus system X is really part of a complex interrelated network, or a subsystem of a
large (and often undefined) environmental system. The effect of this causal
chain on the firm is increased uncertainty about the predictability of its inputs and hence about the validity and suitability of its long-range plans. In
short, the turbulent environment is ill defined and unpredictable.

These characteristics of a turbulent environment lead to a central tenet
of open system theory; namely, that a system's adaptability (and ultimate
survival) rests on its ability to learn about and to adjust to changing environmental conditions. To enable such learning and adjustment to occur,
not only must effective direct information links be set up between the firm
and its environment but an active search for areas of potential change must
be continually undertaken.

At this point one might ask how the foregoing concepts affect the pro-

---

[4] Shirley Terreberry, "The Evolution of Organizational Environments," *Readings in
Organization Theory: Open System Approaches,* John G. Mauer, ed. (New York:
Random House, 1972), pp. 58–74.

FIGURE 16.2

Relationship between production function, other organization functions, and the environment

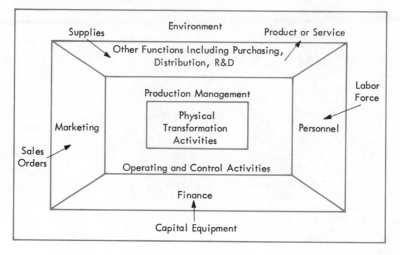

duction function. If a firm is an open system operating in a turbulent environment, is it the responsibility of the production function to establish direct links with elements in the environment, anticipate environmental changes, etc.? In general, the answer is no. The production function, at least in traditional manufacturing organizations, establishes few direct links with its external environment. By and large it is "buffered" by other functional parts of the firm. For example, if we look at the internal structure of a typical "system X" we would observe that the production function is conceptually the inner core of the organization, with little formal structural contact with the external environment.

Consider the relationship between the production and other organization functions and the environment shown in Figure 16.2. Orders are received by the sales department, which is an arm of the marketing function; supplies and raw materials are obtained through the purchasing function; capital for equipment purchases comes from the finance function; the labor force is obtained through the personnel function; and the product is delivered by the distribution function. Thus while there may be a good deal of interaction between the firm and its environment, the production function is rarely involved in it directly: As was mentioned in Chapter 2, it is an *internal* function in most organizations.

Buffering the production function from direct environmental influence is desirable for several reasons:[5]

1. Interaction with environmental elements (e.g., customers and salesmen on the production floor) can be a disturbing influence on the transformation process.

---

[5] The first three points are based upon propositions in J. D. Thompson's *Organizations in Action* (New York: McGraw-Hill, 1967), pp. 14–24.

2. The technological transformation process is often more efficient than the processes required in obtaining inputs and disposing of finished goods.[6]
3. In certain technologies (for example, assembly lines, petroleum) maximum productivity can be achieved only by operating as if the market could absorb all of the product being manufactured and at a continuous rate. This means that the transformation process must shift at least some of the input and output activities to other parts of the firm.
4. The managerial skills required for successful operation of the transformation process are often different from those required for successful operation of the boundary systems, for example, marketing and personnel.

Of course not all production functions are sealed off from their environment, nor do all those that are designed to be sealed off have impermeable boundaries. Custom-product industries, which must meet unique product specifications, often have customers who interact with production function personnel, and service organizations such as fire and police departments must carry out their production functions *in* the environment. Nevertheless, isolation of the technical core (or the transformation process) is the rule in manufacturing and process industries.

In view of the production function's unique organizational role, the production manager is limited to certain types of actions. While on the one hand he can obtain limited amounts of equipment, make certain adjustments in the work force, and alter the layout, production sequence, and work methods, he must generally treat product output, product mix, and product specifications as given quantities or constraints that can be altered only with the concurrence of the other functional areas of the firm. For example, the production manager cannot change a quality specification without the approval of the marketing department, which first negotiated the contract with the buyer. Similarly, he usually cannot exceed his inventory budget without the approval of the finance function.

The effect of these organizational checks and balances is that any major revision in the production function becomes a policy decision, involving not only production personnel but representatives from top management and the other affected functional areas.

THE ADAPTATION PROCESS

Most organizations have special departments whose *primary* job is drawing information from the environment and translating it into planning premises for adaptation.[7] Research and development, market research, long-

---

[6] In this regard, Thompson notes that medical technology can determine if an appendectomy is in order but it "contains no cause/effect statements about bringing sufferers to the attention of medical practitioners, or about the provision of specified equipment, skills, and medications." Ibid., p. 19.

[7] Marketing and finance, while they interact with the environment, are typically geared for steady state operation, so they too rely on special "sensing" agents (for example, market research) to signal the need for change within their domains.

range planning, and operations research groups are common examples. Thus when we refer to adaptation by the production function, even in an open systems context, we are referring to a derivative effect induced by activities on the part of those organizational functions that directly interact with the environment, and most particularly to those whose mission is to search for and generate change. Figure 16.3 illustrates the broad features of the adaptation process.

Briefly, what transpires is that a significant change in the environment is anticipated or observed by one of the adaptive subsystems—market research, R&D, long-range planning, and so forth—which translates or "encodes" this change into information for the production function. The production function, with the aid of the other organizational functions, develops alternative courses of action, selects the most desirable, and then implements it, and this constitutes the adjustment.

FIGURE 16.3

Broad features of the adaptation process

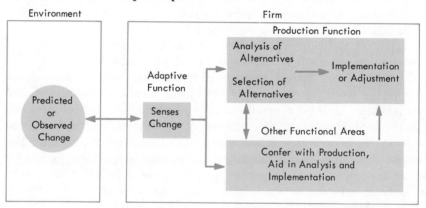

Types of environmental change

Some of the categories of environmental change that may ultimately lead to major adjustment by the production function are

1. Substantial change in product volume demand
2. Substantial shift in product mix demand
3. Major technological innovations
4. Major changes in sources of supply
5. Collective bargaining agreements
6. Legal decisions
7. Shifts in societal values

Table 16.1 presents some examples of these changes and some possible (derivative) production function responses.

Examples of environmental changes and production function adjustments

Environmental change	Example	Production function response
Substantial change in product demand..........	Newspaper publisher's subscriptions expected to increase due to a competitor's going out of business	Purchase and installation of new equipment
Substantial shift in product mix demand.......	Furniture manufacturer experiences high demand for low-cost stereo cabinets and little demand for custom cabinets	Change production process from process layout to product layout
Major technological innovation..............	Firm switches from vacuum tubes and hand wiring to transistors and printed circuit boards	Shift from largely manual to largely mechanized manufacturing
Changes in sources of supply.................	Razor blade manufacturer is cut off from Rhodesian chrome suppliers and must use lower-grade Turkish chrome	Additional metal treatment, more quality control checks
Collective bargaining agreements..............	Shipping company agrees to guaranteed annual wage in return for eliminating certain jobs	Introduction of containerization
Legal decisions..............	Paper manufacturer forced to purify water discharged into lake	Installation of purification equipment and redesign of paper processing operations
Shift in societal values.......	Movie studio shifts from shooting epic pictures in Hollywood to art movies filmed on location	Size of permanent production staff reduced and local personnel recruited as needed

ANALYSIS AND SELECTION OF ALTERNATIVES

Once it has been decided that a revision of the productive system should be considered, the question becomes one of selecting the appropriate course of action. There are, of course, numerous approaches to the general decision-making process, ranging from purely subjective judgments to highly quantified analyses. While space precludes a complete survey, two quantitative approaches are commonly found in the production management literature that merit development in some detail; namely, decision theory and cost-effectiveness analysis.

Decision theory

Decision theory may be defined as a set of general concepts and techniques that assist a decision maker in choosing among alternatives. De-

TABLE 16.2

Sample decision matrix

Strategies (S)	States of nature (N) and probabilities of occurrence (Pr)				
	N_1 Pr_1	N_2 Pr_2	N_3 Pr_3	... ...	N_n Pr_n
S_1	O_{11}	O_{12}	O_{13}	...	O_{1n}
S_2	O_{21}	O_{22}	O_{23}	...	O_{2n}
.	.	.	.	...	.
.	.	.	.	...	.
.	.	.	.	...	.
S_m	O_{m1}	O_{m2}	O_{m3}	...	O_{mn}

cision theory problems are commonly cast in a standard framework, termed a *decision matrix* (see Table 16.2), which consists of the following components.

1. *Strategies* or *alternatives* (S), available to the decision maker. For example "make" and "buy" would be two strategies in a make-or-buy decision problem. Strategies are within the control of the decision maker, and may be active or passive—that is, the possibility of "no action" may be considered a strategy.
2. *States of nature* (N), which are characteristics of the environment and are beyond the control of the decision maker. The term derives from the weather, where we might observe, say, three states of nature: sunshine, rain, or snow. In business decisions, states of nature might be various levels of demand for a product, the number of competitors, governmental actions, etc. (if they cannot be controlled by the firm).
3. *Predictions of likelihood* (Pr), or the probability associated with the occurrence of each state of nature. If a particular state of nature is sure to occur ($Pr = 1.0$), the decision situation is termed one of *certainty*. If the decision maker can assign probability of occurrence to one or more states of nature, with no one state given a value of one, it is termed a *risk* situation. Finally, if the decision maker has no idea of the probabilities of occurrence of any state of nature, the situation is defined as decision making under *uncertainty*. Thus in the sample decision matrix there would be an entry for probability if the situation is one of certainty or risk, and no entry if it is one of uncertainty.
4. *Payoffs* or *outcomes* (O), which represent the value associated with each combination of strategy and state of nature. In Table 16.2 the payoff when S_1 is employed and N_2 occurs is the real value given to O_{12}. This value may be stated in terms of utility, cost, profit, satisfaction, etc.

Solving a decision theory problem obviously requires that some choice be made from among the alternatives, and thus some rule or *decision criterion* must be selected for this purpose. In certainty situations, the decision criterion is to select the single strategy with the highest payoff. Since only one state of nature is relevant, this entails a simple scanning of the payoff column under the "certain" *N* and picking the best one.

In risk situations, two or more *N*s are relevant, and therefore the decision maker should include probability of occurrence in his decision. The two most common criteria are "expected value" and "maximum likelihood." For expected value, the procedure is to take the probability-weighted average of each strategy over all states of nature and select the one with the highest payoff. (This method is shown in the example described below.) The maximum likelihood approach consists of treating the state of nature with the highest probability of occurrence as certain to occur, and then the procedure is identical to the certainty case.

Choosing a decision criterion for use in uncertainty problems presents special problems because the decision maker (theoretically) has no clue as to which state of nature is likely to occur and therefore cannot rely on the powerful concept of expected value in making his choice. As a result, he is thrust into the situation of having to formulate his own philosophy of choice. Resolving this dilemma has occupied decision theorists for many years, and a number have proposed different techniques to reflect various decision-making philosophies.

There are techniques for solving uncertainty problems when the decision maker wants to act "rationally"; or views himself as an "optimist," a "pessimist," or a "regret minimizer"; or where he feels "lucky" or "unlucky"; or wants to avoid the problem altogether and use chance as the decision criterion. For example, if a decision maker wants to behave rationally, the approach offered by Laplace dictates that, since he has no knowledge to the contrary, he should assume that all states of nature are equally likely to occur and weight each outcome for a given strategy by $1/n$. Thus if we are talking about a problem with three states of nature, each outcome for a given strategy would be weighted by ⅓ or 0.33.

Decision making under risk: A sample problem. A newspaper publisher is anticipating a large increase in demand, we will say, because of the failure of a competing paper and an influx of new residents into the community. In light of this, the management of the newspaper has decided to move out of its antiquated building and into a larger one. In addition, the management has decided to increase newspaper production by purchasing one of the three systems listed below. (Making this selection constitutes the decision problem.)

1. New conventional presses (CP)
2. Offset presses (O)
3. Computerized system (C) that ties special presses into a digital computer

A preliminary study by the newspaper's management has yielded the probability distribution for average daily demand for the next 10 years as shown in Figure 16.4.

The investment costs of each alternative, adjusted for salvage value, cost

FIGURE 16.4

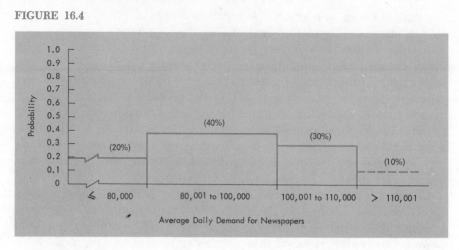

of capital, depreciation, and taxes, are: conventional presses, $400,000; off-set presses, $600,000; and computer system, $750,000. The annual operating costs associated with each alternative for the four different levels of demand are shown in Table 16.3.

TABLE 16.3

Daily demand	Conventional presses	Offset presses	Computer system
≤80,000	$350,000	$200,000	$200,000
80,001–100,000	370,000	250,000	200,000
100,001–110,000	475,000	250,000	400,000
>110,000	510,000	300,000	600,000

Decision theory analysis. At this point we observe that the states of nature are the four levels of possible demand and the decision problem is one of risk since it is felt that probabilities can be attached to the occurrence of each state of nature. And since we have isolated and quantified the relevant alternatives, we may proceed to develop a decision matrix and calculate expected values. We complete our decision matrix for the average annual operating cost for four levels of average daily demand $(\bar{D})$ as shown in Table 16.4. Thus our calculation of expected values yields

$$E.V.CP = (0.2)(\$350,000) + (0.4)(\$370,000) + (0.3)(\$475,000)$$
$$+ (0.1)(\$510,000) = \$411,500$$
$$E.V.O = (0.2)(\$200,000) + (0.4)(\$250,000) + (0.3)(\$250,000)$$
$$+ (0.1)(\$300,000) = \$245,000$$
$$E.V.C = (0.2)(\$200,000) + (0.4)(\$200,000) + (0.3)(\$400,000)$$
$$+ (0.1)(\$600,000) = \$300,000$$

Since these expected value figures represent annual expenditures for the firm, each one must be adjusted by the firm's cost of capital. Assuming a discount rate of 10 percent, the present value factor for an annuity is 6.2

TABLE 16.4

Decision matrix for average annual operating cost

	$Pr = 0.2$	$Pr = 0.4$	$Pr = 0.3$	$Pr = 0.1$
	$\bar{D} \leq 80,000$	$80,001 \leq \bar{D} \leq 100,000$	$100,001 \leq \bar{D} \leq 110,000$	$\bar{D} > 110,000$
Conventional presses	$350,000	$370,000	$475,000	$510,000
Offset presses	200,000	250,000	250,000	300,000
Computer system	200,000	200,000	400,000	600,000

(rounded from Table S.3.5). Multiplying the expected values by this figure yields the following adjusted expected operating costs:

$$E.V.CP = (\$411,500)(6.2) = \$2,551,300$$
$$E.V.O = (\$245,000)(6.2) = \$1,519,000$$
$$E.V.C = (\$300,000)(6.2) = \$1,860,000$$

The initial investment cost is added to the adjusted expected value figures to arrive at a total cost for each alternative:

Alternative	Adjusted expected value		Initial investment		Total cost
CP	$2,551,300	+	$400,000	=	$2,951,300
O	1,519,000	+	600,000	=	2,119,000
C	1,860,000	+	750,000	=	2,610,000

And the choice—based solely on cost considerations—is the offset press system.

Cost-effectiveness analysis

Cost-effectiveness analysis is a decision-making methodology that ultimately leads to a comparison of alternatives in terms of their costs and effectiveness in attaining some specific objective. It differs from conventional economic analysis in that it attempts to devise a quantitative criterion that can simultaneously measure both the quantitative and qualitative elements of a decision problem. Because its methodology permits analysis of alternatives with widely ranging physical and operational characteristics, it has been applied in situations where a general objective can be achieved in many ways. In addition to industrial applications, cost-effectiveness analysis has been applied to problems of health care, urban planning, and law enforcement, as well as other complex problems of community and national concern.

Probably the most extensive use of the approach, however, has been in the area of national defense, where it was first developed, and then applied on a broad scale, by the U.S. Department of Defense under Secretary McNamara. In fact, during the Kennedy and Johnson administrations cost-effectiveness analysis, became *the* approved method of choosing among alternative weapon systems. Given its historical antecedents, therefore, it is not surprising that much of the literature on the topic is liberally sprinkled with such military terms as *mission, strategy,* and *tactic,* even when the application being described is as benign as deciding on the location of an orphanage in the suburbs.

The procedure for performing a cost-effectiveness analysis typically includes the following steps.

1. Define objectives that the systems are to fulfill.
2. Identify mission requirements essential to the attainment of the objectives.
3. Develop alternative systems for accomplishing the mission.
4. Establish bases for evaluating alternative systems.
5. Formulate effectiveness model.
6. Formulate cost model.
7. Determine decision criterion.
8. Analyze systems costs versus effectiveness.
9. Perform sensitivity analysis.

To illustrate what is entailed in each of these steps, we will apply them to a slightly modified version of the newspaper process selection problem described in the previous section. The modifications include (1) the simplifying assumption that average daily demand for newspapers is expected to be at least 100,000 papers per day and (2) the addition of production characteristics that affect the output of the alternative systems.

1. *Objective.* Produce a high-quality newspaper in sufficient quantity to meet daily demand for the next 10 years.

2. *Mission requirements.* These are the individual system's goals, which must be met if the overall objective is to be achieved. In this example they are: Meet a specified demand (demand is expected to be at least 100,000 papers per day) and print parts of the paper in at least five colors.

3 and 4. *Alternative systems and evaluation bases.* This is shown in Table 16.5.

5. *Formulate effectiveness model.* Evaluation bases variables X_1, X_2, X_3 can be converted to a single measure, E.

$$E = \text{Salable papers/day} = (X_1)(1 - X_2)(1 - X_3)$$
$$\text{Effectiveness of CP} = (110,000)(1 - 0.02)(1 - 0.05) = 102,410$$
$$\text{Effectiveness of } O = (150,000)(1 - 0.04)(1 - 0.10) = 129,600$$
$$\text{Effectiveness of } C = (175,000)(1 - 0.03)(1 - 0.08) = 156,170$$

TABLE 16.5

Evaluation bases	Alternative systems		
	Conventional presses	Offset presses	Computer system
Maximum output (X_1)........	110,000	150,000	175,000
Expected loss due to paper quality (X_2).............	0.02	0.04	0.03
Expected loss due to downtime (X_3).................	0.05	0.10	0.08
Number of colors that can be printed without additional press runs...............	4	5	4

6. *Formulate cost model.* The cost function should reflect the present value of all associated costs for each alternative, discounted over a 10-year time horizon. The function would be

$$C_T = C_I + C_P + C_F$$

where

C_T = Grand total cost for a proposed plan of action
C_I = Total costs incurred for initial investment
C_P = Total costs incurred for production operations over a 10-year time horizon
C_F = Cost of additional desirable feature(s), for example, color reproduction capability

The costs C_P and C_F are new data inputs and C_I came from the decision theory problem. These are used to derive C_T (see Table 16.6).

TABLE 16.6

Alternative	C_I	C_P	C_F	C_T
Conventional presses...	$400,000	$495,500	$4,500	$ 900,000
Offset presses.........	600,000	250,000	...	850,000
Computer system......	750,000	500,000	...	1,250,000

7. *Select decision criterion.* Several different decision criteria have been employed to rank and select alternatives.

1. Maximize effectiveness divided by cost (max $E \div C$).
2. Maximize effectiveness minus cost (max $E - C$).
3. Maximize effectiveness given a fixed cost (max $E|C$).
4. Minimize cost given a fixed effectiveness (min $C|E$).

For this example, we will choose number 1, although each has its pros and cons.[8]

8. *Analyze systems costs versus effectiveness.* Table 16.7 presents the cost, effectiveness value, and the $E \div C$ ratio for each candidate system.

TABLE 16.7

Cost effectiveness for three printing systems

System	Cost	Effectiveness	$E \div C$
Conventional...........	$ 900,000	102,410	0.114
Offset.................	850,000	129,600	0.152
Computer.............	1,250,000	156,170	0.125

On the basis of the effectiveness ratio criterion, the choice would be the offset process. However, before the decision is finalized, management should go beyond the quantitative evaluation and consider the importance of those factors that could not be quantified—for example, management skill in

---

[8] See *Journal of Industrial Engineering* (July 1968), p. 363, for a comparison of these criteria.

handling the several technologies, operator availability and the training required for each alternative, proven capability of each process in other situations, etc.

A particularly critical factor here is the question of backup offset equipment. The analysis assumed that one offset press would be adequate; however, if problems develop with this equipment, the system must be shut down completely, whereas in the conventional press system, less efficient but serviceable replacement presses might be more readily available.

Finally, there is always a question as to the cost figures provided for a computerized system. Breakthroughs in computer technology are almost daily occurrences and satisfactory computerized systems might become available at a greatly reduced cost, making this alternative much more desirable.

9. *Perform sensitivity analysis.*   In many cost-effectiveness studies the decision is very "sensitive" to the assumptions. In this example it was assumed that demand would be at least 100,000 papers per day; however, if demand reaches 120,000 papers per day, the conventional press system under consideration would be inadequate. Thus a sensitivity analysis might also be made using a variety of conventional press systems.

Similarly, it would be worth considering the effect of changes in the expected loss values on the decision. We might discover, for example, that an increase of a few percentage points in the probability of expected loss due to paper quality would alter our decision.

Finally, the offset press system requires a better-quality paper than the conventional press, and in many locales such paper is provided by only a few suppliers. Thus if there is a problem with a supplier, the expected loss due to paper quality might be much higher than the assumed 4 percent because of having to use a lower-quality paper or having to wait for shipments from a more distant source.

IMPLEMENTING CHANGE

Once the decision has been made that a particular type of adjustment in the transformation process is in order, the focus shifts to implementation. In this section we will discuss the nature of implementation, looking first at the interaction among the three main variables of a productive system: the technology, the operating and control system, and the behavioral system. We will then present some considerations that affect the adaptation of the operating-control and the behavioral system; and finally we will develop an example contrasting two production systems in a change context.

Interaction among productive system variables: A viewpoint

Figure 16.5 depicts the general sequence of events and interactions that occur when an environmental change calls for a change in technology. Note that even though the change in the technology is initiated by a change in the environment, the extent of that change is moderated by the three-way interaction among the technology, the operating and control sys-

FIGURE 16.5

Interactions arising from environmental change

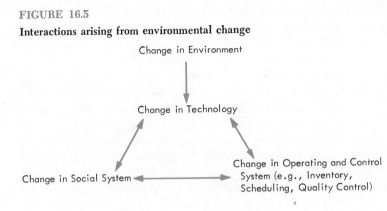

tem, and the social system. Naturally, the extent of this moderation varies according to the flexibility of the three elements and management's willingness to permit the social system and the control system to influence the technology of transformation. For example, a new transformation process may produce most efficiently in production runs of 400 but quality control considerations favor runs of 200. Or perhaps a new assembly line can produce most efficiently when it is a straight line but the desire for worker interaction suggests a circular line. The adoption of the first modification represents an accommodation with the operating and control system; adoption of the second represents an accommodation with the social system.

We hasten to point out, however, that things are not usually looked at in this way. The more typical approach is to view technology as given and then to fit the other systems in as well as possible. And while this approach has the advantage of simplicity—that is, only one system (technology) is to be optimized—the likely result is suboptimization of the entire system. Therefore we propose that in introducing a change (or in the initial design of a production system, for that matter) all three components be viewed as variables, none of which is necessarily more important than the others.

Implementing change: Operating and control considerations

There are several factors that bear mentioning when one is instituting a change in the operating-control system. First, running the new system in parallel with the old—contrary to popular belief—is undesirable because it tends to perpetuate an outmoded system rather than solve problems associated with the new one. Of course, dropping the old system before the new one has been fully tested is not recommended. However, once a system has been proved effective on a pilot basis, the old one may be discarded if procedures are set up to monitor errors carefully and correct them—so production may continue even if the new system requires adjustment.

Second, it is extremely desirable to simulate the new operating-control system before implementing it. For example, simulation can provide answers to such questions as Does the quality control procedure provide sufficiently rapid feedback? Are the inventory record-keeping procedures adequate for the new system? Are the scheduling decision rules operational? If a full-blown computer simulation study is not feasible, at least a hand simulation and a "walk through" test should be performed before the operating and control system is considered established.

Third, revision of a system, like plant startup, is often amenable to project management techniques such as the use of project teams and the planning and control devices of Gantt charts and CPM. Of particular value in using these devices are periodic progress reports that pinpoint problem areas and note what is being done about them. This information would be used by the project manager in controlling the implementation of the system.

Finally, retraining personnel in production control, quality control, and maintenance to enable them to handle the new operating and control system should be considered as important as retraining the direct labor force. Though this point is an obvious one, it is nonetheless often overlooked. For example, changing an inventory system from periodic to order point may require that production control personnel become skilled in working with lot size models and safety-stock concepts, which may entail some classroom instruction. Likewise, the scheduling notions required in running a job shop are substantially different from those demanded for balancing an assembly line, and therefore appropriate training of production personnel is in order if a switch from one to the other is made.

Introducing change: Behavioral considerations

While technological problems of change will ultimately yield to the laws of science, there are no formulas to assure that work force problems will be overcome. Indeed, as we have mentioned several times before, people problems are often the most difficult problems confronting the production manager, and they become more challenging in the face of change.

Sources of behavioral problems during change. Problems during change situations commonly arise from alterations in one or more of the following factors.

1. The work itself
2. Work group relationships
3. Wage payment
4. Working conditions
5. Unions

The work itself. For many individuals, the requirement that they must perform a new or different set of tasks is a traumatic experience. A classic case in point is switching a worker from a work bench job involving many tasks performed at his own pace to an assembly line job requiring but a few tasks that, however, must be completed within the time dictated by the line cycle time. The "de-skilling" aspect of this type of change, coupled with the forced-pacing aspect of assembly line work, often generates strong overt resistance on the part of the work force when it is first installed and characteristically leads to such dysfunctional consequences as absenteeism, turnover, and grievances once it becomes permanent. However, it should be borne in mind that any significant job change is likely to encounter resistance.

Work group relationships. Technological change, especially, often has a profound effect on work groups. In some instances a work group may be broken up completely, while at other times the formal authority and informal leadership patterns may be disrupted. Sometimes something as seemingly minor as a change in the noise level that accompanies the introduction of a new piece of equipment may greatly affect work group relationships. Interestingly enough, a *decrease* in noise may in some instances be as detrimental to established group relationships as an *increase,* since the group may be most comfortable in a nonverbal environment.

Wage payment. Shifting from a basically manually controlled job to a machine-controlled job can lead to sticky compensation problems. In manual operations (for example, machining parts on a conventional lathe) the worker has direct control over the amount of work he completes, and it is common to find wage incentives applied to such jobs. However, when the work is semiautomatic (the worker merely feeds a lathe that performs all the cutting automatically), the control of the work pace is partially removed from the operator, and an output-based incentive system is unlikely to apply. For such cases, compromise schemes must be developed, such as payment of average incentive earnings; or a completely new plan, based perhaps upon minimizing equipment downtime, must be developed. And, of course, worker uncertainty about the wage adjustment is obviously a potential source of resistance.

Work hours. Automated production processes often dictate that longer shifts be worked so that work breaks come at intervals different from those in simpler technologies. Obviously, both contingencies would be of concern to the worker.

Unions. In view of the fact that much technological innovation is introduced to reduce labor costs, it is small wonder that union opposition is often the major obstacle to effectuating a change. To counter such opposition, management typically agrees to provide such features as retraining, early retirement benefits, transfer provisions, and job guarantees in its labor contracts.

Guides to implementing change. Dealing with resistance to change is a subject of controversy among behavioral scientists. However, since it is a common problem faced by the production function, we will venture the following observations, which seem to be fairly representative of current expert thinking on the topic.

First of all, approaches to change introduction can be viewed as a continuum ranging from a traditional management approach to a behavioral science approach.[9] In the traditional approach, management decides every aspect of the change from the initial planning to the specifications of new tasks; in the behavioral approach, these issues are left up to the workers

---

[9] This conceptualization is drawn from Edwin B. Flippo, *Management: A Behavioral Approach* (New York: Allyn & Bacon, 1970).

themselves, who are limited only by the operating requirements of the technology. Between these two extremes are such approaches as suggestion systems and direct consultation with workers. While not recommending one particular approach as the most desirable, the least we should say is that the traditional approach almost inevitably leads to some hostility, for the simple reason that people like to have some influence on the way their work is to be performed. Or, short of this, people at least like to know the logic behind a change and let management know their feelings on the matter—considerations that are excluded in the extreme traditional approach. Beyond this general assertion, the most desirable strategy of change introduction can be determined only after considering the organization, the technology, and the work force in context.

As far as general guidelines for introducing change are concerned, the following suggestions, summarized from Edwin Flippo,[10] make good sense.

1. Where possible, hold the disturbance of existing customs and informal relationships to a minimum. For example, if it is customary to rotate the responsibility for cleanup when workers are performing bench work, permit the same procedure when an assembly line is introduced. This may create some labor allocation problems in the short run but it may avoid potential status problems in the long run.

2. Provide information in advance about the change. This should include the logic behind the change, its nature and extent, planned timing, impact upon the productive system, and, most importantly, its impact upon each worker. Misinformation about the effects of change should be scrupulously avoided.

3. Encourage employee participation in instituting the change. Not only are employees more likely to go along with the change if participating in it, but they are likely to make suggestions that will be of value in and of themselves.

4. Attempt to minimize the cost to the employee of making the change. For example, management can develop retraining programs, guarantee maintenance of the employees' present salary, or even share the benefits of the change with the work force. From a purely economic standpoint, such protection can be justified as an investment in future labor cooperation and stability.

5. Provide the opportunity for the employee to register his concern about the change. Resentment is often unavoidable, and if the worker is allowed to air his grievances without punitive actions on management's part, the probability that he will ultimately accept the change is greatly increased.

Effect of change on a hypothetical production system

The following example is provided to illustrate the combined effects on production management activities that occur when a firm changes both its production throughput strategy and its transformation technology.

Suppose that a firm produces internal combustion engines to customers' order and the production is performed in four departments—Department 1: components machining (valves, gaskets, flywheels, etc.); Department 2: engine block machining; Department 3: assembly; and Department 4: engine testing. Since the flow of materials between departments is unidirectional while the flow within departments may be multidirectional, the

---

[10] Ibid., pp. 482–86.

FIGURE 16.6

Nonautomated hybrid job shop

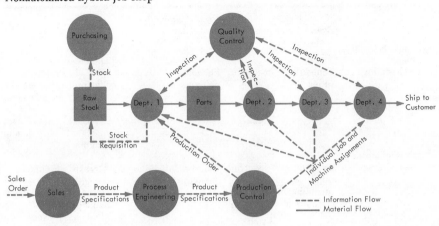

FIGURE 16.7

Partly automated flow shop

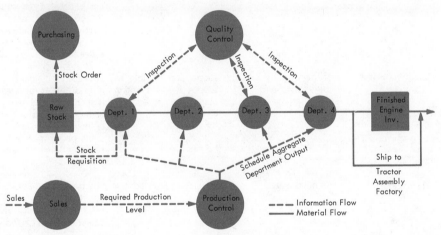

entire operation may be classified as a hybrid job shop.[11] The material flow and the information flow for this mode of production are shown in Figure 16.6.

Now suppose that the firm is bought out by a tractor company and limits its production to the manufacture of tractor engines. And suppose, finally, that while the job of each department remains essentially the same, the homogeneity of the product line justifies the introduction of adaptive numerical control machine tools for machining the engine block.[12] We may

[11] See Chapter 7.

[12] *Adaptive control* (in this discussion) refers to the ability of a numerically controlled machine tool to automatically adjust for changes in feed and speed rates. Without adaptive control, numerically controlled equipment (i.e., equipment operated by digital input from a tape or computer) must be programmed to stop production when tool wear causes damage to the product. This requires human intervention in the process and reduces production.

TABLE 16.8

Comparison of machine-shop system features before and after change

Activity	Nonautomated hybrid job shop	Partly automated flow shop	Effect of change
Production Control Master scheduling....	Schedule to customer order	Schedule to annual demand	Greatly simplified. Output requirements known; process engineering step can be bypassed after first units of each model engine
Job & machine scheduling....	Production control must schedule each machine, taking account of job priorities	Can be left to each department	Greatly simplified, especially in automated Dept. 2. Production control is left free to deal with exceptions
Inventory control.......	Periodic system	Reorder point	Probable reduction in required safety stock since there is less uncertainty in type and quantity of demand. Little or no finished-goods inventory required
Quality control....	Inspection by lots in all departments	Inspection by lots in Depts. 1, 3, 4. Dept. 2 inspection performed by machine	Adaptive control eliminates in-process inspection. General reduction in number of inspection stations since product characteristics are well-known
Maintenance......	As need arises	Strictly scheduled	Greater maintenance effort required since failure of one machine can shut down system
Product costing....	Each order assessed its direct cost plus overhead	Direct and overhead cost allocated over all products	Simplifies product costing. Management can now use cost variances more effectively as a control device

now ask: What is the nature of the differences in the information flows, the production management activities, and the behavioral system between this partially automated system (Figure 16.7) and the nonautomated system?

We have attempted to answer this question in summary form in Table 16.8, which breaks down the production activities and behavioral requirements of both systems. As a general comment, it is apparent that the narrowing of the product line and the institution of automated equipment have

TABLE 16.8 (*continued*)

Activity	Nonautomated hybrid job shop	Partly automated flow shop	Effect of change
Wage payment....	Output-based in all departments	Dept. 2 based upon continual operation of machinery	Dept. 2 wage payment becomes tricky since workers have little influence on output rate. A wage system must be developed that assures that machine is kept operating to capacity
Behaviorial factors Social relationships..	Much interaction required since workers must confer on many jobs	Little interaction required	Probably a reduction in general job satisfaction because of reduced interaction
Intrinsic nature of work.........	Wide variety of tasks required by each individual, e.g., machine setup, operation, blueprint reading	Little variety in tasks performed by each individual and complete change in tasks in Dept. 2—from machine operators to console operators	Increased output due to job specialization but probable reduction in job satisfaction. Dept. 2 workers are limited to watching panels of lights

a profound, though not unexpected, effect on the production management activities and the work force. However, while these changes are extreme, even less drastic revisions may lead to sizable adjustments in the operating and control activities, the magnitude of which may come as a surprise to the unwary manager. The lesson is clear: Management must take time to plan not only for the technological aspects of change but for the operating and control system alterations as well. Indeed, even though the process flow itself is greatly simplified, there is no guarantee that the management of the process also will be simplified—or, of course, that the transition from one system to the next will be smooth.

Adaptation in the Automobile Industry

We turn from hypothetical examples to a real-world example of adaptation, citing Abernathy, who provides an interesting summary of product innovations and their concomitant production process innovations (or adaptations) relative to engines in the automotive industry. (See Table 16.9.)

The two largest firms competing in the auto industry have adopted almost completely different innovation strategies. As shown below, Ford has generally developed major innovations in process technology, while General Motors has generally developed major innovations in components that add

TABLE 16.9

Thirty-three technological innovations in mass-production of engines

Decade	Product Innovation	Process Innovation
1900–1909	Simple and reliable engine (Model T)	Multiple simultaneous machining
1910–1919	V-8 engine design	Continuous pouring of molten iron
1920–1929	Aluminum alloy pistons	Cemented carbide cutting tools
	Crank case ventilation	Dynamic crankshaft balancing
	Special exhaust valve materials	
1930–1939	Down draft carburetors	Cast crankshafts and camshafts
	Automatic choke	Precision boring
	Low-cost V-8 engine	Surface tunnel broaching
1945–1954	Short-stroke, high-compression V-8	Integration of engine plants with transfer lines
	New combustion chamber design— OHV engine	Dynamic engine balancing
	12-volt electrical system	Automatic air gauges in machining
1955–1964	Aluminum engines	High-tolerance iron-casting methods
	Thin-wall cast gray iron cylinder block engines	Automatic crankshaft grinding with measurement
	Multi-barrel carburetors	Segmented transfer lines for block and head
		Ceramic boring
1965–1974	Advances in electronic ignition	Programmable controller for machining systems
	Overhead cam engine on mass-production cars	Electronic sensors and automated testing in engine line
	Stratified charge engine	

Source: William J. Abernathy, *The Productivity Dilemma—Roadblocks to Innovation in the Automobile Industry,* Chapter 5. Division of Research, Harvard Graduate School of Business, 1976.

performance features to the car. Abernathy points out that "The trace of this tendency extends up to recent years."[13]

Ford	*General Motors*
Mechanized moving assembly	Electric starter
Welding in body and chassis assembly	V-8 engine design
Cast crankshafts and camshafts (1934 and 1952)	Cemented carbide cutting tools
Economical V-8 engine production	Independent front suspensions
Integration of engine plants with transfer lines	Automatic transmission advances
	Electronic ignition systems
High-speed automated stamping	Energy-absorbing steering columns
Thin-wall gray cast iron engines	Aluminum engines

CONCLUSION

In order to simplify the coverage of some rather complex issues, the discussion of adaptation in this chapter has focussed on systems that produce tangible products rather than services. Hospitals and penitentiaries, for instance, would provide interesting contrasts in the way adaptation is carried out in service industries. However, in these systems the social issues dominate the technological and operating and control aspects to such a

---

[13] William J. Abernathy, *The Productivity Dilemma—Roadblocks to Innovation in the Automobile Industry.* Division of Research, Harvard Graduate School of Business, 1976. The quotation and the lists following it are taken from Chapter 5.

degree as would force us to go beyond production management and into behavioral science for a meaningful discussion.

Further, space limitations necessitate the omission of those industries that are characterized by recurring major adjustments. In aerospace, for example, revision is a way of life, with each new contract representing a potential catalyst for change. But the procedures spelled out in our newspaper and machine shop examples generally pertain, although in reality, many more variables enter into the decision-making process.

As a final note, we would like to reemphasize the point that the production manager must be aware of the interrelationships among technology, behavior, and operating and control systems. Examples abound of firms that, despite elegant technological innovations, ran into severe production and personnel problems because they tried to optimize the technical system without simultaneously considering the requirements of the other two systems. Admittedly, joint optimization of three systems is far more difficult than optimizing one, especially since the required conceptual tools are far from developed. Nevertheless, simply recognizing the problem in and of itself may help management to avoid some errors and encourage the making of minor adjustments in technology for the sake of improving the performance of the entire operation.

PROPOSITIONS

Propositions contrasting services and manufacturing relative to response to environmental change

Product: Because the service product is primarily intangible, a service system can often adapt to environmental change by simply redefining its product. In manufacturing, the characteristics and end use of the product are fixed and hence a physical change in the product is generally required for purposes of product adaptation.

Technology of transformation: Because most service systems are labor intensive, service systems can often adapt to major environmental change by adjusting procedures. In manufacturing, which is typically capital intensive, major environmental change usually leads to introducing new equipment.

Operating-control system: Because of the subjective nature of the service product, operating-control system adaptation in response to environmental change may be carried out even if it is recognized that the adaptation reduces service system efficiency. In manufacturing (where the product is clearly defined), adaptations are always instituted to increase the efficiency of the system. (Exceptions to both cases exist when the adaptation is made in response to legal requirements.)

Workforce: In services, the production system is not sealed off from the customer and hence the direct production workforce may both sense and adapt immediately to a change in the environment. In manufacturing, the production system is buffered by other parts of the organization and hence sensing and immediate adaptation to a change in the environment is not required of the direct production workforce.

REVIEW AND DISCUSSION QUESTIONS

1. Distinguish between open and closed systems.
2. What problems are presented by the fact that the production function is buffered by other functional areas of the firm?
3. Contrast the adaptation process with the five phases of control discussed in Chapter 13. What similarities and differences do you find?
4. Distinguish between certainty, risk, and uncertainty in decision making.
5. It has been asserted that complete certainty and complete uncertainty rarely, if ever, exist in a real-world decision problem. Drawing upon your own experience, support or reject this assertion.
6. "Decision making under certainty rarely presents a difficult problem because all the decision maker is required to do is scan the payoffs under the certain *N* and pick the highest one." Comment.
7. "Cost-effectiveness analysis may work for government decision making but it is not needed to make a sound business decision." What do you think is the rationale for this statement? Do you agree with it?
8. How might adaptation be included in defining the primary task of an electronics firm? Give two examples of production policies that would support an adaptive primary task statement for such a firm.
9. Manufacturers of appliances often issue warranty cards that are to be returned to the factory rather than, say, the marketing department. What do you suppose is the reason for this practice?

PROBLEMS

1. The Great Desert University (G.D.U.) is interested in cutting down on its teaching costs in its basic management classes. It is currently using professors to staff the courses, but the administration feels that the use of teaching machines or teaching assistants should be investigated as alternative means of instruction. Presently there are four management professors engaged full-time in teaching these courses, and if a change is made to either teaching machines or teaching assistants, three will be let go.[14] A senior professor will be left to administer the program, although this activity will be incidental to his new job as Assistant Dean (if either of the new approaches is adopted). Ten percent of his salary will be applied to administration of the course. Enrollment is constant at 300 students per year.

---

[14] The three professors have been offered positions in the Athletics Management Department at Arid State University.

Given the following data, use cost-effectiveness analysis to determine which teaching alternative G.D.U. should select.

Professors:

Maximum number of students per year per professor = 120
Average number of class hours missed as a percentage of total hours = 5 percent
Annual salary = $15,000
Proportion of graduates satisfied with past instruction in the course = 95 percent

Teaching machines:

Estimated number of machines required to meet enrollment of 300 students per year = 30
Repair and maintenance downtime as a percentage of total class hours = 20 percent
Annual cost to lease and service a machine = $1,000
Percentage of students satisfied with instruction (based upon a national survey) = 80 percent
Annual incremental administrative costs incurred because professors are not available for curriculum development, counseling, etc. = $10,000

Teaching assistants: (five would be required):

Maximum number of students per year per assistant = 70
(All enrolled students must be taught this course on schedule.)
Annual salary = $4,000
Percentage of students satisfied with instruction (based upon a survey of recent graduates from other colleges of G.D.U.) = 60 percent

2. How would the following statements by the G.D.U. administration affect your analysis and choice of alternatives in Problem 1?
   a. "We want the best teaching possible for our budgeted amount of $50,000 for next year's classes."
   b. "Let's spend the minimum amount we can just so long as every student who wishes can take the course."
   c. "The professors' union is threatening legal action if we dismiss three faculty members. We should win the case, but it will cost about $20,000 in attorneys' fees."

SELECTED BIBLIOGRAPHY

Abernathy, William J.   *The Productivity Dilemma—Roadblocks to Innovation in the Automobile Industry.* Division of Research, Harvard Graduate School of Business, 1976.
Flippo, Edwin B.   *Management: A Behavioral Approach.* New York: Allyn & Bacon, 1970.
Hitch, C. J., and McKean, R. N.   *The Economics of Defense in the Nuclear Age.* Cambridge, Mass.: Harvard University Press, 1960.

Litterer, Joseph A.   *The Analysis of Organizations.* New York: John Wiley & Sons, 1965.

Maurer, John G. (ed.)   *Readings in Organization Theory: Open Systems Approaches.* New York: Random House, 1972.

Miller, E. J., and Rice, A. K.   *Systems of Organizations.* London: Tavistock Publications, 1967.

Robertson, Thomas S., and Chase, Richard B.   "The Sales Process: An Open Systems Approach," *Business Topics,* vol. 16, no. 8 (Autumn 1968), pp. 45–52.

Rudwick, Bernard H.   *Systems Analysis for Effecting Planning: Principles and Cases.* New York: John Wiley & Sons, 1969.

Thompson, James D.   *Organizations in Action.* New York: McGraw-Hill, 1967.

Section seven

Termination of the system

17

Termination, rebirth, and conclusions

I n this final chapter we will first discuss the termination and the rebirth of the productive system. Then we will engage in termination of the book —offering some conjecture about the future of production and operations management.

TERMINATION AND REBIRTH

The productive system is terminated when (1) production ceases permanently or (2) when a system is so greatly revised that the major portion of the original design is no longer relevant to its subsequent operations. The first view reflects the common conception of termination—that of a company, and hence its productive system, ceasing operations. The second reflects the orientation of the text—that the system design derives from a particular product objective and that this objective may change over time, rendering that system obsolete. This view conveys the idea that termination of the productive system can occur without termination of the firm of which it is a part, and it underscores the fact that a viable firm will normally phase out old systems and introduce new ones throughout the course of its existence.

Product and system life cycles

The distinction between the two views of termination, as well as the long-term relationship between a productive system and its product, can be developed by considering the interrelationship of system life cycles and product life cycles.

Product life cycles. This concept is widely used in marketing to describe the sales performance of a product over time. The basic idea is that products go through five stages:

1. *Introduction:* the product is put on the market and awareness and acceptance are minimal.
2. *Growth:* the product begins to make rapid sales gains because of the cumulative effects of introductory promotion, distribution, and word-of-mouth influence.
3. *Maturity:* sales growth continues but at a declining rate, because of the diminishing number of potential customers who remain unaware of the product or who have taken no action.
4. *Saturation:* sales reach and remain on a plateau (marked by the level of replacement demand).
5. *Decline:* sales begin to diminish absolutely as the product is gradually edged out by better products or substitutes.[1]

Figure 17.1 illustrates the general relationship between sales volume and these stages over time.

Productive system life cycles. As was described throughout the book, the productive system has four general phases: design, startup, steady state,

---
[1] Taken from Philip Kotler, *Marketing Management, Analysis, Planning, and Control* (Englewood Cliffs, N.J.: Prentice-Hall, 1967), p. 291.

FIGURE 17.1

Stages in the product life cycle

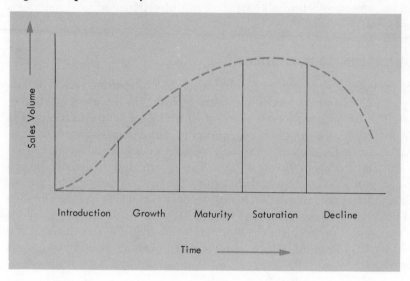

and termination. The generalized relationship between these phases and system output is shown in Figure 17.2.

If we combine the product and the productive system life cycles and assume a hypothetical one-product firm, we get the graph shown in Figure 17.3. Examining these combined cycles, we see that the initial phases of the product life cycle continue past the point at which the productive system has achieved steady state output levels. What we have presumed here is that a typical system produces more than it sells during the product's growth phase since the system is usually designed to meet forecast maturity and saturation phase demands.

The difference between output and sales (shown by the light area in the

FIGURE 17.2

Productive system life cycle

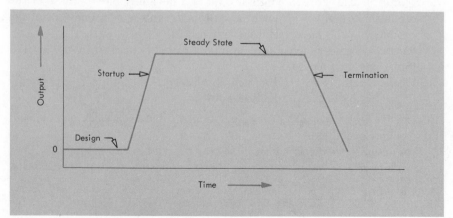

FIGURE 17.3

Product and productive system life cycles

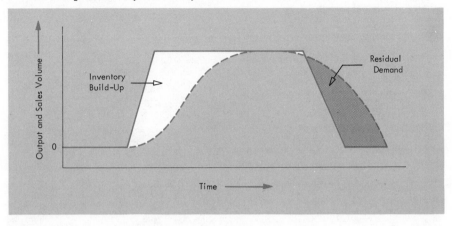

graph) represents inventory which is built up because output exceeds demand. During steady state operations at the product maturity stage, supply
and demand for the product have reached equilibrium, so that a replacement is available for each item sold. When the product begins to decline in
sales, some excess inventory is again built up, but then is eliminated as the
system cuts back production. During the final stage of the system's life cycle,
residual demand for the product at last exceeds production (by the amount
depicted by the dark area in the graph). Theoretically, the amount of
this demand is equal to the amount of the previous inventory build-up,
since management would plan to stop production at that point in time
when existing inventory stocks would satisfy all remaining demand.

If we stopped here—that is, if we assumed that the system was shut
down, the resources sold off, and the work force sent home—we would
label this an example of *permanent termination.* On the other hand, if management decides to produce a new product and engages in a complete
overhaul of the original system, we would consider it an example of *temporary termination,* and our product and system life cycles might take the
form shown in Figure 17.4.

In this illustration we have assumed that redesign of the system is undertaken during the steady state and termination phases of the initial system's
life cycle. This might be a reasonable strategy in that it permits startup of
the revised system to begin as soon as operations of the initial system are
terminated. We have also assumed (for simplicity) that only one new
product is to be produced by the redesigned system and that the life cycle
curves for both product and system are roughly equivalent to those of their
original counterparts. In actuality, of course, these assumptions are highly
restrictive since most manufacturing firms produce several products rather
than one, and we would not expect any two system life cycles or any two
product life cycles to be identical. With this as a background, we will consider both types of termination in more detail.

FIGURE 17.4

Temporary termination with design and startup of revised system begun during latter phases of original system

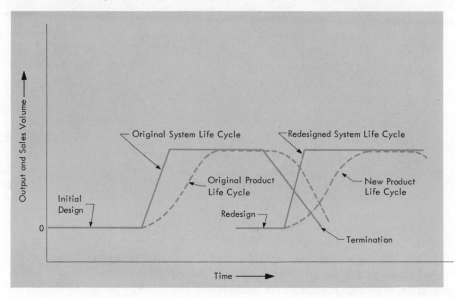

Temporary termination

To repeat, temporary termination refers to a situation in which a system is so greatly revised that the major portion of the original design is no longer relevant to its subsequent operations. Common reasons that the original design would no longer be relevant are: Major technological changes, vertical integration, and major changes in output requirements.

Major technological changes. Shifting from nonautomated to automated processes in a factory, changing from table to cafeteria service in a restaurant, or converting from a clinic to a nursing home entail massive redesign of the production system. The procedures for scheduling, maintaining inventories, controlling quality, and performing maintenance would have to be specified anew and the tasks of direct labor and management adjusted accordingly. In terms of life cycle curves, if we take the introduction of automation as an example, it is quite probable that the change from the initial system to the revised system would appear as shown in Figure 17.5.

In this instance, product demand is seen as growing throughout the operation of the initial system and automation is chosen as a way of meeting long-run future demand. The termination of the initial system would be instantaneous and there would be a short production hiatus until the redesigned system became operational. It would be reasonable to expect that the automated system would be redesigned during the latter stages of the initial system's operation, and familiarity with the product would allow rapid achievement of steady state operations for the redesigned system.

FIGURE 17.5

Life cycles before and after a major technological change

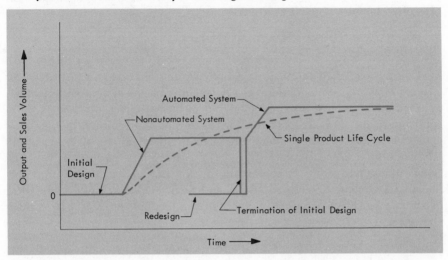

Vertical integration. Vertical integration refers to the growth of a firm by its extension backward—so to speak—so as to incorporate its source of supply or by its extension forward so as to incorporate its distribution or retailing activities. Under certain conditions, therefore, vertical integration can lead to a major redesign of the productive system. For example, a small company might become integrated with a larger one and therefore be required to concentrate on producing only certain models of its existing line. This could compel a system redesign in order to take advantage of the potential production economies that derive from a narrowed product line. Similarly, a system redesign might be desirable when a firm, through integration, obtains a stable source of supply that permits a higher production rate.

Major changes in output requirements. A common cause of temporary system termination is an increase in product output requirements that necessitates the expansion of existing facilities or the introduction of a new facility. In the latter case, especially, production may become "a brand new ballgame" since a new plant would undoubtedly tend to incorporate the latest advances in operating technology and management. Also, the desirable features of the old system would be included and the undesirable excluded, and even if the basic process is the same, the supporting activities are likely to be altered so greatly that the revised system would bear little resemblance to the original.

In contrast to meeting increased output requirements, temporary termination and redesign can occur because a manufacturing firm decides to reduce output at one of its facilities. In this situation, the firm might sell its equipment, or transfer it to another plant, and restructure its production process in such a way that a smaller work force could operate efficiently at a smaller-scale plant. It might also rent out the newly available space or (as often happens) use it as a warehouse.

System blending

Closely related to the issue of temporary termination is the problem of *system blending,* which denotes the dovetailing of one system with another. This problem is most often encountered in business mergers, and is probably most acute in mergers of the horizontal type. A *horizontal merger* combines companies whose products are virtually identical and that operate in the same geographic market.[2] Consider, for example, a merger of two local newspapers that results in combining the two productive systems into one. Beyond the marketing, distribution, and financial issues involved, critical decisions must be made regarding the production system itself. Among these are:

Who will be in charge of production operations? Each newspaper presumably has a production manager, and now there is need for only one.

Which production employees will remain? Union regulations will apply to most direct labor—printers, stereotypers, linotype operators, etc.—but what about clerical personnel and non-union supervisory people?

Which equipment is to be transferred from the vacated plant? Which is to be sold?

What new equipment is to be purchased? (The combining of operations is often an ideal situation in which to introduce new technologies.)

What about maintenance policies? Introducing new equipment and transferring old equipment will undoubtedly alter maintenance operations and schedules.

What about the changeover period? Will production cease? If so, for how long?

As far as actually making these decisions is concerned, the methods covered in the literature on organizational change and summarized in Chapter 16 of this book are highly relevant to the personnel issues. Conventional economic analysis would most certainly be employed for the equipment-related decisions, and critical path methods would be highly useful in planning and controlling the activities of the changeover period.

From a broader standpoint, however, the key requirement is objectivity, which means that the management of the acquiring company should eschew some rather common misconceptions about management policies and procedures. Three of these misconceptions have been identified by

---

[2] Other types are *vertical mergers* and *conglomerate mergers.* A vertical merger is one in which the firms involved have had a buyer-seller relationship. (In these cases the comments made regarding vertical integration pertain.) A conglomerate merger covers all other cases, and includes mergers to extend the product line or to enter new markets. (These types of mergers often have no effect on the production systems of the combining firms.)

Searby,[3] and the first one is the "halo assumption"—which holds that because the acquiring company was bigger and more successful before the merger, its people and policies should be retained and adopted after the merger. The flaw here, of course, is that no company is always correct in its handling of personnel and procedures, nor is any company completely lacking in these areas. Then there is the "small world assumption," which holds that one of the companies must be doing things the right way and so the decision should boil down to picking one approach from two alternatives. Clearly, this overlooks other alternatives that might be even better. Finally, there is the "compromise assumption," which holds that decisions can be made by choosing one company's approach one time, another's the next time, and a combination of approaches at other times.[4] Again, this overlooks new alternatives that may be superior.

Permanent termination

Permanent termination—the permanent closing of a production system—can be further broken down into general and local termination.

General termination. *General termination* refers to the dissolution of a productive system as a result of a firm's going out of business.[5] The causes for this type of termination include product failures, marketing failures, misallocation of capital, governmental rulings, and production inefficiencies. Quite often, however, these causes are closely interrelated and it is therefore difficult to isolate the production system's role in a firm's termination. Nevertheless, whether the production system remains healthy and contributes to the firm's stability or becomes weak and contributes to its demise depends on how well it responds to a variety of pressures. In this regard, Wickham Skinner has identified three classes of pressure that affect operations on the production side of the manufacturing firm. These are[6]

1. New pressures from outside the firm.
2. New problems within the firm.
3. The impact of accelerating technology.

Outside pressures. According to Skinner, the primary sources of pressure from outside the firm are new trends in industry and in the market-

---

[3] F. W. Searby, "Controlling Postmerger Change," *Harvard Business Review* (September–October 1969), pp. 154–55.

[4] Searby gives this a more colorful title—"the Henry Clay assumption," because it reflects this famous legislator's approach to settling disputes.

[5] Permanent general termination is fairly common in American industry. In 1969, for example, there were 9,154 business failures out of roughly 2.5 million businesses, which means that 37 out of every 10,000 businesses ceased operation. This, incidentally, was the best year for business survival during the decade 1959–69, which averaged about 50 failures per 10,000 businesses per year.

[6] Wickham Skinner, "Production under Pressure," *Harvard Business Review* (November–December 1966), pp. 137–46.

place. There is increasing competition not only because of the trend on the part of U.S. firms to diversify and enter new markets but because foreign firms have developed products that compete on the basis of quality as well as price. Indeed, the inroads made by Japan and West Germany in electronics, textiles, and automobiles are ample evidence of this.

In addition to competing in product quality and price, production systems have been forced to provide more rapid output and greater product variety in order to fulfill the marketing objectives necessitated by competition. Obviously, the production manager who must satisfy each of these criteria simultaneously is confronted by a substantial challenge.

Internal pressures. Cost control, manning the operation, and handling paper work are three areas that create internal pressures. Cost control has become a greater problem than in the past primarily because mechanization, shorter production runs, and higher quality have increased the proportion of indirect workers to direct workers. Indirect jobs, such as maintenance and material handling, are generally harder to measure and consequently more difficult to improve than most direct labor activities. Direct jobs are often partly machine controlled and less repetitive, and therefore determining their contribution to cost and output for purposes of enhancing efficiency is also a greater problem than ever before.

Manning the operation also has become a bigger problem because the shift from direct to indirect work and from manual tasks to machine monitoring makes worker selection and training more complicated and more important. In the past the dividing line between jobs requiring skilled workers and those suited to unskilled or semiskilled workers was fairly clear. Now, however, with the development of more sophisticated machinery (and workers to operate it), the distinction has become blurred.

Handling paper work is a widely discussed problem of contemporary industry—and one that tends to grow as the productive system produces a wider range of products, increases its output, and speeds up its deliveries. Certainly the amount and kind of information and the way in which it is used tell much about the health of the production function and the enterprise as a whole.

Accelerating technology. Technological innovations in equipment, products, and materials have in many respects complicated production management decision making. The introduction of numerically controlled machinery, for example, not only entails a sizable investment of capital but may alter the operation and scheduling of every part of the production process. Innovations in product design and materials also can change the whole character of the transformation process, and if incorrectly handled can be sources of trouble for the production system. Further complicating the issue of innovation is the fact that management has only imperfect knowledge of the technological possibilities in any of these areas. A company may select a state-of-the-art process one week and find it is out of date the next. Thus a firm might find itself being forced out of business because it chose to increase capacity by adopting a new but less efficient process than the one that was adopted by its competitor only a week or a month later.

Local termination. In *local termination* a firm closes down one of two or more productive systems but otherwise continues in business. Unlike general termination, local termination may be undertaken by a healthy or even an expanding firm. An organization may initiate this type of termination for several reasons: (1) it wishes to combine productive facilities, (2) it desires to buy components it previously made, (3) it has exhausted the market or resource supply in a particular locale, or (4) a combination of factors has raised its costs too high to permit continued operation at its present location. Also, a number of terminations have been the direct result of firms' taking advantage of the special taxation and labor benefits offered by some states and foreign countries that are anxious to increase their industrial base.

The manner in which firms conduct local terminations has changed substantially in recent years, and especially with regard to the handling of their employees. For example, it used to be common practice to keep employees in the dark as long as possible about an imminent plant closing. The presumption was that the workers would either curtail their production or, if they were on incentive, try to overproduce in order to make a "killing" on their last few paychecks. However, while these fears were sometimes borne out in situations where employees were forewarned, an even more chaotic state of affairs often developed in those situations where they were not forewarned. Moreover, management's "strategy of silence" commonly resulted in an abiding bitterness after the plant closed its doors.

But, as we said, things have changed. In the first place, there are restrictions on the conditions under which a plant may be closed down. By way of example, in 1965 textile workers at one of a company's plants organized a union, which was duly recognized as a legitimate bargaining agent by the National Labor Relations Board. As a result of this unionization, the company management elected to close down the plant and move elsewhere, and the union thereupon filed suit with the NLRB, which found in the union's favor and decreed that a plant could not shut down for anti-union reasons. This ruling was then appealed by the company to the U.S. Supreme Court, which concluded that a plant could be shut down for any reason provided the *entire firm* is terminated. However, in what was to become a landmark decision, it also ruled that the closing of a specific plant solely for purposes of "chilling the union" was illegal.

In the second place, management has become more sensitive to the loss of goodwill engendered by a cavalier attitude toward the welfare of its workforce and the effects on the surrounding community when faced with a plant termination. This has led large organizations (especially) to give ample warning that a plant is to be closed down and to spend rather substantial sums in arranging personnel transfers and establishing retraining programs.

System phase-out

Despite the fact that the phase-out period is generally unpleasant for management, it is nonetheless amenable to planning. Indeed, the decisions

FIGURE 17.6

Four patterns of output reduction

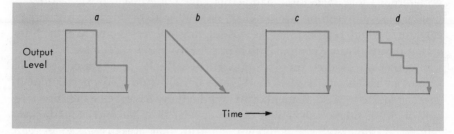

made regarding output reduction can have a marked effect on the ultimate financial position of the firm.

To get an insight into the problem, consider four of the many possible patterns of output reduction shown in Figure 17.6.

Pattern *a* shows a two-stage decrease in production, and would be typical of a system that requires large chunks of capacity to operate. An example would be a company that uses two identical assembly lines to make its product, so that the first drop in output would be associated with closing down one line and the second drop with closing down the other line.

Pattern *b* indicates a gradual linear termination, and would be typical of a system that can reduce output in small increments. An example of this would be a job shop that can handle product orders on a variety of different machines, and therefore the elimination of one machine at a time would have relatively small influence on output.

Pattern *c* represents an instantaneous termination, and would be typified by a small system that simply cannot operate at reduced capacity—or by a system of any size that cannot obtain enough revenue to cover its variable costs. An example of the first case would be a restaurant that closes due to lack of business; an example of the second would be an ocean liner's being sold for scrap because of its high operating costs.

Pattern *d*, exhibiting a stairstep decrease, is probably the most common phase-out pattern. Certainly most process industries would close down by incremental steps, as would certain service systems, such as hospitals and schools.

System phase-out: General termination. Finding the optimum termination point. Even when an entire firm is going out of business, the rational production manager would like to choose that phase-out pattern that meets residual demand at the lowest cost. In most respects this becomes an aggregate planning problem similar to those encountered during steady state operations. That is, demand must be forecast, production levels must be set in light of existing inventories, and the size of the work force must be established to meet output requirements. There are some differences, however, and—depending upon the system under consideration—they can make the problem more complex.

Consider a company that finds that its main product is no longer demanded in sufficient quantity for it to make a profit and whose facilities are so specialized that it cannot effect a changeover to some other product. In this situation termination is probably not unexpected, and management would therefore have some discretion over the rate at which it phases out its operations. If we assume that demand from retailers will be gradually reduced to zero by some time period (T), the problem would be to find the point (t_i) during that period when the system should be terminated. To see how this determination might be made, consider the modified break-even chart in Figure 17.7.

Here we see that fixed costs are reduced in steps, reflecting the fact that assets are being sold off piecemeal. This phasing of liquidation is also reflected in the curve labeled *income from asset selloff*. With each reduction in assets comes a reduction in production capability, which we have considered by reducing the total variable cost of production. In this example the point of optimum termination would be at one of two times, depending upon whether there is an income obtainable from asset selloff. If there is, termination should take place where total revenue intersects total variable costs—at point a (time t_1). If there is none, the system should continue in operation until total revenue intersects total variable cost—at point b (time t_2). Obviously, if termination occurs at time t_1, the fixed-cost line would no longer exist; also, the remaining assets would be immediately sold, so the *income from asset selloff* line would no longer be relevant.

To generalize from this illustration is risky, but it seems fair to say that the key problem in finding the optimum termination point is deciding when

FIGURE 17.7

Modified break-even chart for termination analysis

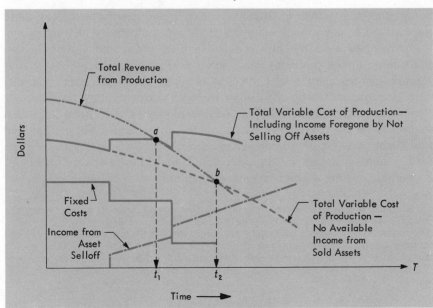

to sell off resources. The factors that must be weighed in this decision are the cost savings from asset liquidation (e.g., maintenance, obsolescence, depreciation, and opportunity costs) versus the foregone revenue from a loss of productive capacity. From an operational standpoint, obtaining accurate projections of all these costs would pose a severe problem, which would be compounded if management wished to consider alternative patterns of output reduction.

System phase-out: Local termination. The number of options available to the branch plant production manager regarding output levels, disposition of equipment, and work force levels varies according to the role of the phased-out system in the total organization. If the terminated facility is a supplier to other facilities in the organization, production might be expected to continue at the steady state level right up to the closing day. This

FIGURE 17.8

Termination classification

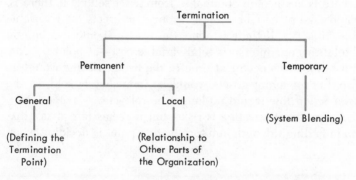

would tend to eliminate some of the sticky timing decisions, such as those encountered in equipment selloff in phase-out under general termination.

On the other hand, if central management adopts a "total systems" viewpoint, these timing problems could increase during a local phase-out. For example, management might want to consider the desirability of transferring equipment to one of its other facilities versus selling it in the used-equipment market. To make this decision requires the consideration of a whole host of related factors, including the anticipated state of the used equipment over the phase-out period, the likely effect on output at both the terminating facility and the remaining plants, the forecast demand for the output, and the desired inventory position of the organization.[7]

---

[7] Roodman and Schwarz have developed a mathematical approach to minimizing discounted costs from phasing out facilities as demand shifts and declines over a specified planning horizon. The costs considered are the variable operating cost at each facility, the transportation costs between facilities and demand centers, and the costs to operate and close each facility. (See G. M. Roodman and L. B. Schwarz, "Optimal and Heuristic Facility Phase-out Strategies," *AIIE Transactions*, vol. 7, no. 2, February 1975, pp. 177–84.)

Summary on termination

Termination is a relatively unexplored phase in the system life cycle, and in order to analyze it we were forced to develop our own classification scheme. This scheme, along with some of the key considerations (in parentheses), is illustrated in Figure 17.8.

In this chapter we have attempted to show that there is a good deal more to termination than sending the work force home and putting a "closed" sign on the front door. We have also tried to convey the fact that there are good reasons why termination should be attended to as carefully as startup and steady state operations. What remains to be done, however, is to develop guidelines for managing this final phase of a system's life cycle.

CONCLUSION: FUTURE TRENDS IN PRODUCTION AND OPERATIONS MANAGEMENT

A major component of production and operations management is forecasting, and it seems only reasonable that forecasting can also be applied to the field itself. Thus, relying on a general trend analysis, the following observations about the near future of production and operations management are offered.[8]

Increased study of the nature of production and operations management in services

We have attempted throughout the book to illustrate production management applications in service industries. And, as we also indicated, service systems differ among themselves (as well as from manufacturing) along several dimensions. The next question, which we believe will be investigated in the near future, is "What differences affect the actual design and operation of service systems?" (Perhaps this will lead to the development of a "theory of services," which was alluded to in Chapter 1.)

Greater emphasis on socio-technical factors in system design

The changing attitudes of the work force, coupled with increasing technological sophistication, have not been accompanied by a growth in predictive models which treat man and technology simultaneously. Many of the models used in layout, scheduling, and work measurement are highly sophisticated in their dealing with things but are very naive and/or incomplete in dealing with people.

It is our opinion, however, that the need to enrich such models so they

---

[8] Since the first edition of this book appeared, a number of the items in this section have been discussed by other writers. See for example, R. D. Smith and D. Robey "Research and Applications in Operations Management: Discussion of a Paradox, *Academy of Management Journal,* vol. 16, no. 4, December, 1973, pp. 647–57.

can consider the effect of the work group, total task completion, job discretion, etc., will be recognized to a greater degree by workers in the field.
In fact, we expect to see a blending of the skills of the production researcher with those of the behavioral scientist to develop models that
encompass social and psychological variables, along with technological
factors, in order to move toward true total optimization in system design.

Increased use of production capability outside the firm

The high cost of maintaining in-house production specialists, coupled
with the development of specialized consulting firms, will lead many
medium- and small-size companies to look outside their own organization
for certain production management services. We expect to see a growth of
firms that offer—on a continuing basis—such services as quality control,
maintenance, inventory control, work design and measurement, and layout.
In addition, the large computer manufacturers that now offer specialized
skills in these areas as part of the services provided to users of their computers will probably continue to expand their abilities along these lines.

Increased use of external computer services

The combination of convenience and low relative cost of computer terminals will lead more and more companies to purchase computer time on a remote system rather than maintain their own computers. While an elaborate
computer installation will probably remain the ultimate corporate status
symbol, the fact that extensive computer capability can be purchased as
needed from outside sources at a reasonable cost will compel even large
organizations to reevaluate the desirability of a highly sophisticated in-
house system.

Increased use of commercial computer programs

The number and variety of "packaged" programs developed by computer
firms are impressive, to say the least. Indeed, several computer service
offices could not tell us exactly how many different program packages they
had in the areas of shop scheduling and project scheduling. No doubt, this
vagueness reflects the fact that these firms are continually developing new
programs in response to, or anticipation of, industry demand. Certainly,
using an existing program rather than developing one from scratch has
tremendous appeal. Thus, given that program rental or sales costs are within
reason (and the programs do what they are intended to do), we predict
that the established upward trend in their use will continue.

Greater concern with the environment

It has become increasingly recognized that "this spaceship earth" is a
finite and surprisingly fragile resource, and that society's interest in con-

trolling pollution and conserving resources of all kinds is becoming more pronounced. This means that productive systems will face tighter and tighter constraints in their operations, and that the production manager will be required to deal with them more carefully than ever before. Thus, the ultimate effect of this trend is to make imperative the training and development of truly professional production managers.

Greater emphasis on management as opposed to mathematical techniques

In the 1960s production management entered what might be termed its "mathematical technique period." Any mathematical tool that had any potential for aiding production management decision making was considered a candidate for inclusion in the field. This preoccupation with mathematics, however, had positive *and* negative effects. On the positive side, it gave the field a certain amount of academic respectability, which justified its being offered by quantitatively oriented business schools. This, in turn, exposed a generation of potential managers to the value of quantitative techniques in their decision making. But on the negative side, it tended—in those same schools—to move attention *away* from the managerial or organizational problems encountered by the practicing production manager.

Moreover, the development of quantitative techniques outstripped their range of likely application. That is, though models were sound in theory, the problems associated with implementing them (incomplete or inaccurate data, extensive time to set problems in the appropriate form, etc.) often exceeded the benefits derived from their use.[9]

In light of these problems, a number of schools have begun to reevaluate what they need from their production management courses. It is our feeling that, when all is said and done, this reevaluation will lead to putting "management" back into production management.

We hope, finally, that another trend will emerge—interest in the study of productive systems over time. Whether one calls this a "life cycle" approach is really immaterial; the point is that by viewing a productive system in this way, the total picture is more likely to come into focus, and hence the simple but elusive goal of better decision making is more likely to be achieved.

REVIEW AND DISCUSSION QUESTIONS

1. Define general termination, local termination, system blending.
2. How does the decision problem of selling off equipment in the face of termination differ from equipment selloff during steady state operations?

---

[9] Morris hypothesizes that ". . . The most favorable cost-effectiveness relationships are associated with the simple, basic, quantitative methods, rather than with those which are complex, exotic, and sophisticated." William T. Morris, "Quantitative Methods —A Management Perspective," *Industrial Engineering*, vol. 7, no. 6, June 1975, p. 47.

3. How does local termination differ from a temporary shutdown (as described in Chapter 12) with respect to the managerial problems posed by each?

4. What managerial problems are encountered by merging two systems for the purpose of combining production operations?

5. Graph the system and product life cycle curves you would expect to characterize the following organizations. (Use the same time scale for all.)
   a. A general hospital
   b. A restaurant
   c. A Broadway stage show
   d. A Christmas tree farm

6. What is involved in finding the optimum termination point? How might break-even analysis be used in this determination?

7. What are some of the pressures currently confronting the production side of a manufacturing firm? Do you see similar pressures confronting service firms in the next decade? Discuss.

Appendixes

Appendix A

Uniformly distributed random digits

56970	10799	52098	04184	54967	72938	50834	23777	08392
83125	85077	60490	44369	66130	72936	69848	59973	08144
55503	21383	02464	26141	68779	66388	75242	82690	74099
47019	06683	33203	29603	54553	25971	69573	83854	24715
84828	61152	79526	29554	84580	37859	28504	61980	34997
08021	31331	79227	05748	51276	57143	31926	00915	45821
36458	28285	30424	98420	72925	40729	22337	48293	86847
05752	96065	36847	87729	81679	59126	59437	33225	31280
26768	02513	58454	56958	20575	76746	40878	06846	32828
42613	72456	43030	58085	06766	60227	96414	32671	45587
95457	12176	65482	25596	02678	54592	63607	82096	21913
95276	67524	63564	95958	39750	64379	46059	51666	10433
66954	53574	64776	92345	95110	59448	77249	54044	67942
17457	44151	14113	02462	02798	54977	48340	66738	60184
03704	23322	83214	59337	01695	60666	97410	55064	17427
21538	16997	33210	60337	27976	70661	08250	69509	60264
57178	16730	08310	70348	11317	71623	55510	64750	87759
31048	40058	94953	55866	96283	40620	52087	80817	74533
69799	83300	16498	80733	96422	58078	99643	39847	96884
90595	65017	59231	17772	67831	33317	00520	90401	41700
33570	34761	08039	78784	09977	29398	93896	78227	90110
15340	82760	57477	13898	48431	72936	78160	87240	52710
64079	07733	36512	56186	99098	48850	72527	08486	10951
63491	84886	67118	62063	74958	20946	28147	39338	32109
92003	76568	41034	28260	79708	00770	88643	21188	01850
52360	46658	66511	04172	73085	11795	52594	13287	82531
74622	12142	68355	65635	21828	39539	18988	53609	04001
04157	50070	61343	64315	70836	82857	35335	87900	36194
86003	60070	66241	32836	27573	11479	94114	81641	00496
41208	80187	20351	09630	84668	42486	71303	19512	50277
06433	80674	24520	18222	10610	05794	37515	48619	62866
39298	47829	72648	37414	75755	04717	29899	78817	03509
89884	59651	67533	68123	17730	95862	08034	19473	63971
61512	32155	51906	61662	64430	16688	37275	51262	11569
99653	47635	12506	88535	36553	23757	34209	55803	96275
95913	11085	13772	76638	48423	25018	99041	77529	81360
55804	44004	13122	44115	01601	50541	00147	77685	58788
35334	82410	91601	40617	72876	33967	73830	15405	96554
57729	88646	76487	11622	96297	24160	09903	14047	22917
86648	89317	63677	70119	94739	25875	38829	68377	43918
30574	06039	07967	32422	76791	30725	53711	93385	13421
81307	13114	83580	79974	45929	85113	72268	09858	52104
02410	96385	79067	54939	21410	86980	91772	93307	34116
18969	87444	52233	62319	08598	09066	95288	04794	01534
87863	80514	66860	62297	80198	19347	73234	86265	49096
08397	10538	15438	62311	72844	60203	46412	65943	79232
28520	45247	58729	10854	99058	18260	38765	90038	94209
44285	09452	15867	70418	57012	72122	36634	97283	95943
86299	22510	33571	23309	57040	29285	67870	21913	72958
84842	05748	90894	61658	15001	94005	36308	41161	37341

Appendix B

Normally distributed random digits

1.98677	1.23481	-.28360	.99427	-.87919	-.21600
-.59341	1.54221	-.65806	1.08372	1.68560	1.14899
.11340	.19126	-.65084	.12188	.02338	-.61545
.89783	-.54929	-.03663	-1.89506	.15158	-.20061
-.50790	1.14463	1.30917	1.26528	.09459	.16423
-1.63968	-.63248	.21482	-1.16241	-.60015	-.55233
1.14081	-.29988	-.48053	-1.21397	-.34391	-1.84881
-.43354	-.32855	.67115	.52289	-1.42796	-.14181
.05707	.35331	.20470	.01847	1.71086	-1.44738
.77153	.72576	-.29833	.26139	1.25845	-.35468
-1.38286	.04406	-.75499	.61068	.61903	-.96845
1.60166	-1.66161	.70886	-.20302	-.28373	2.07219
-.48781	.02629	-.34306	2.00746	-1.12059	.07943
-1.10632	1.18250	-.60065	.09737	.63297	1.00659
.77000	-.87214	-.63584	-.39546	-.72776	.45594
-.56882	-.23153	-2.03852	-.28101	.30384	-.14246
.27721	-.04776	.11740	-.17211	1.63483	1.34221
-.40251	-.31052	-1.04834	-.23243	-1.52224	.85903
1.27086	-.93166	.03766	1.21016	.13451	.81941
1.14464	.56176	.89824	1.54670	1.48411	.14422
.04172	1.49673	-.15490	.77084	-.29064	2.87643
-.36795	1.22318	-1.05084	-1.05409	.82052	.09670
1.94110	1.00826	-.85411	-1.31341	-1.85921	.74578
.14946	-2.75470	-.10830	1.02845	.69291	-.78579
.32512	1.11241	.45138	.79940	-.91803	-1.35919
.66748	-.55806	.27694	.80928	-.18061	1.26569
-1.23681	-.49094	.34951	1.66404	.30419	-1.32670
-.57808	-.04187	2.01897	.92651	.10518	-.34227
1.24924	-.98726	-.24277	-.48852	1.14221	-.43447
.38640	-.26990	-.21369	.65047	.27436	-2.30590
.47191	.52304	-1.16670	1.11789	-.10954	1.17787
-1.12401	.24826	.03741	-.72132	-.44131	-1.10636
-.04997	-1.19941	-.63591	1.27889	.69289	-.27419
-.08265	1.08497	.12277	-.61647	-2.74235	1.10660
.28522	.04496	-1.53535	.42616	-.54092	-1.99089
-.60318	-.00926	-1.57852	-.68966	-1.07899	-2.26274
1.66247	-.94171	-1.84672	.14506	-1.79616	-.03350
-.06993	.82752	-1.79937	-.58224	.38834	1.17421
.22572	-.23812	1.38760	.97453	-.48264	.42092
2.12500	.18124	.22034	1.06353	-.84988	-1.40673
-.51185	-1.35882	1.34636	-.03440	.31133	1.63670
.35724	-1.45402	.16793	1.16726	-.76094	-.38834
-1.29352	-.28185	-.86607	.68714	2.16262	1.82108
.34521	1.16515	-.11361	-1.35778	.16051	.93119
-1.33783	-.28278	-.09756	1.38268	-1.74537	.76566

Appendix C

Areas of the standard normal distribution

An entry in the table is the proportion under the entire curve which is between $z = 0$ and a positive value of z. Areas for negative values of z are obtained by symmetry.

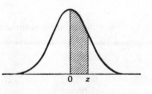

z	.00	.01	.02	.03	.04	.05	.06	.07	.08	.09
0.0	.0000	.0040	.0080	.0120	.0160	.0199	.0239	.0279	.0319	.0359
0.1	.0398	.0438	.0478	.0517	.0557	.0596	.0636	.0675	.0714	.0753
0.2	.0793	.0832	.0871	.0910	.0948	.0987	.1026	.1064	.1103	.1141
0.3	.1179	.1217	.1255	.1293	.1331	.1368	.1406	.1443	.1480	.1517
0.4	.1554	.1591	.1628	.1664	.1700	.1736	.1772	.1808	.1844	.1879
0.5	.1915	.1950	.1985	.2019	.2054	.2088	.2123	.2157	.2190	.2224
0.6	.2257	.2291	.2324	.2357	.2389	.2422	.2454	.2486	.2517	.2549
0.7	.2580	.2611	.2642	.2673	.2703	.2734	.2764	.2794	.2823	.2852
0.8	.2881	.2910	.2939	.2967	.2995	.3023	.3051	.3078	.3106	.3133
0.9	.3159	.3186	.3212	.3238	.3264	.3289	.3315	.3340	.3365	.3389
1.0	.3413	.3438	.3461	.3485	.3508	.3531	.3554	.3577	.3599	.3621
1.1	.3643	.3665	.3686	.3708	.3729	.3749	.3770	.3790	.3810	.3830
1.2	.3849	.3869	.3888	.3907	.3925	.3944	.3962	.3980	.3997	.4015
1.3	.4032	.4049	.4066	.4082	.4099	.4115	.4131	.4147	.4162	.4177
1.4	.4192	.4207	.4222	.4236	.4251	.4265	.4279	.4292	.4306	.4319
1.5	.4332	.4345	.4357	.4370	.4382	.4394	.4406	.4418	.4429	.4441
1.6	.4452	.4463	.4474	.4484	.4495	.4505	.4515	.4525	.4535	.4545
1.7	.4554	.4564	.4573	.4582	.4591	.4599	.4608	.4616	.4625	.4633
1.8	.4641	.4649	.4656	.4664	.4671	.4678	.4686	.4693	.4699	.4706
1.9	.4713	.4719	.4726	.4732	.4738	.4744	.4750	.4756	.4761	.4767
2.0	.4772	.4778	.4783	.4788	.4793	.4798	.4803	.4808	.4812	.4817
2.1	.4821	.4826	.4830	.4834	.4838	.4842	.4846	.4850	.4854	.4857
2.2	.4861	.4864	.4868	.4871	.4875	.4878	.4881	.4884	.4887	.4890
2.3	.4893	.4896	.4898	.4901	.4904	.4906	.4909	.4911	.4913	.4916
2.4	.4918	.4920	.4922	.4925	.4927	.4929	.4931	.4932	.4934	.4936
2.5	.4938	.4940	.4941	.4943	.4945	.4946	.4948	.4949	.4951	.4952
2.6	.4953	.4955	.4956	.4957	.4959	.4960	.4961	.4962	.4963	.4964
2.7	.4965	.4966	.4967	.4968	.4969	.4970	.4971	.4972	.4973	.4974
2.8	.4974	.4975	.4976	.4977	.4977	.4978	.4979	.4979	.4980	.4981
2.9	.4981	.4982	.4982	.4983	.4984	.4984	.4985	.4985	.4986	.4986
3.0	.4987	.4987	.4987	.4988	.4988	.4989	.4989	.4989	.4990	.4990

Source: Paul G. Hoel, *Elementary Statistics* (New York: John Wiley & Sons, 1960), p. 240.

Appendix D

Areas of the cumulative standard normal distribution

z	G(z)	z	G(z)	z	G(z)
−4.00	0.00003	−3.60	0.00016	−3.20	0.00069
−3.99	0.00003	−3.59	0.00017	−3.19	0.00071
−3.98	0.00003	−3.58	0.00017	−3.18	0.00074
−3.97	0.00004	−3.57	0.00018	−3.17	0.00076
−3.96	0.00004	−3.56	0.00019	−3.16	0.00079
−3.95	0.00004	−3.55	0.00019	−3.15	0.00082
−3.94	0.00004	−3.54	0.00020	−3.14	0.00084
−3.93	0.00004	−3.53	0.00021	−3.13	0.00087
−3.92	0.00004	−3.52	0.00022	−3.12	0.00090
−3.91	0.00005	−3.51	0.00022	−3.11	0.00094
−3.90	0.00005	−3.50	0.00023	−3.10	0.00097
−3.89	0.00005	−3.49	0.00024	−3.09	0.00100
−3.88	0.00005	−3.48	0.00025	−3.08	0.00104
−3.87	0.00005	−3.47	0.00026	−3.07	0.00107
−3.86	0.00006	−3.46	0.00027	−3.06	0.00111
−3.85	0.00006	−3.45	0.00028	−3.05	0.00114
−3.84	0.00006	−3.44	0.00029	−3.04	0.00118
−3.83	0.00006	−3.43	0.00030	−3.03	0.00122
−3.82	0.00007	−3.42	0.00031	−3.02	0.00126
−3.81	0.00007	−3.41	0.00032	−3.01	0.00131
−3.80	0.00007	−3.40	0.00034	−3.00	0.00135
−3.79	0.00008	−3.39	0.00035	−2.99	0.00139
−3.78	0.00008	−3.38	0.00036	−2.98	0.00144
−3.77	0.00008	−3.37	0.00038	−2.97	0.00149
−3.76	0.00008	−3.36	0.00039	−2.96	0.00154
−3.75	0.00009	−3.35	0.00040	−2.95	0.00159
−3.74	0.00009	−3.34	0.00042	−2.94	0.00164
−3.73	0.00010	−3.33	0.00043	−2.93	0.00169
−3.72	0.00010	−3.32	0.00045	−2.92	0.00175
−3.71	0.00010	−3.31	0.00047	−2.91	0.00181
−3.70	0.00011	−3.30	0.00048	−2.90	0.00187
−3.69	0.00011	−3.29	0.00050	−2.89	0.00193
−3.68	0.00012	−3.28	0.00052	−2.88	0.00199
−3.67	0.00012	−3.27	0.00054	−2.87	0.00205
−3.66	0.00013	−3.26	0.00056	−2.86	0.00212
−3.65	0.00013	−3.25	0.00058	−2.85	0.00219
−3.64	0.00014	−3.24	0.00060	−2.84	0.00226
−3.63	0.00014	−3.23	0.00062	−2.83	0.00233
−3.62	0.00015	−3.22	0.00064	−2.82	0.00240
−3.61	0.00015	−3.21	0.00066	−2.81	0.00248

Source: Bernard Ostle, *Statistics in Research*, 2d ed. (Ames, Iowa: Iowa State University Press, 1967), pp. 517–22.

z	G(z)	z	(Gz)	z	G(z)
−2.80	0.00256	−2.30	0.01072	−1.80	0.03593
−2.79	0.00264	−2.29	0.01101	−1.79	0.03673
−2.78	0.00272	−2.28	0.01130	−1.78	0.03754
−2.77	0.00280	−2.27	0.01160	−1.77	0.03836
−2.76	0.00289	−2.26	0.01191	−1.76	0.03920
−2.75	0.00298	−2.25	0.01222	−1.75	0.04006
−2.74	0.00307	−2.24	0.01255	−1.74	0.04093
−2.73	0.00317	−2.23	0.01287	−1.73	0.04182
−2.72	0.00326	−2.22	0.01321	−1.72	0.04272
−2.71	0.00336	−2.21	0.01355	−1.71	0.04363
−2.70	0.00347	−2.20	0.01390	−1.70	0.04457
−2.69	0.00357	−2.19	0.01426	−1.69	0.04551
−2.68	0.00368	−2.18	0.01463	−1.68	0.04648
−2.67	0.00379	−2.17	0.01500	−1.67	0.04746
−2.66	0.00391	−2.16	0.01539	−1.66	0.04846
−2.65	0.00402	−2.15	0.01578	−1.65	0.04947
−2.64	0.00415	−2.14	0.01618	−1.64	0.05050
−2.63	0.00427	−2.13	0.01659	−1.63	0.05155
−2.62	0.00440	−2.12	0.01700	−1.62	0.05262
−2.61	0.00453	−2.11	0.01743	−1.61	0.05370
−2.60	0.00466	−2.10	0.01786	−1.60	0.05480
−2.59	0.00480	−2.09	0.01831	−1.59	0.05592
−2.58	0.00494	−2.08	0.01876	−1.58	0.05705
−2.57	0.00508	−2.07	0.01923	−1.57	0.05821
−2.56	0.00523	−2.06	0.01970	−1.56	0.05938
−2.55	0.00539	−2.05	0.02018	−1.55	0.06057
−2.54	0.00554	−2.04	0.02068	−1.54	0.06178
−2.53	0.00570	−2.03	0.02118	−1.53	0.06301
−2.52	0.00587	−2.02	0.02169	−1.52	0.06426
−2.51	0.00604	−2.01	0.02222	−1.51	0.06552
−2.50	0.00621	−2.00	0.02275	−1.50	0.06681
−2.49	0.00639	−1.99	0.02330	−1.49	0.06811
−2.48	0.00657	−1.98	0.02385	−1.48	0.06944
−2.47	0.00676	−1.97	0.02442	−1.47	0.07078
−2.46	0.00695	−1.96	0.02500	−1.46	0.07215
−2.45	0.00714	−1.95	0.02559	−1.45	0.07353
−2.44	0.00734	−1.94	0.02619	−1.44	0.07493
−2.43	0.00755	−1.93	0.02680	−1.43	0.07636
−2.42	0.00776	−1.92	0.02743	−1.42	0.07780
−2.41	0.00798	−1.91	0.02807	−1.41	0.07927
−2.40	0.00820	−1.90	0.02872	−1.40	0.08076
−2.39	0.00842	−1.89	0.02938	−1.39	0.08226
−2.38	0.00866	−1.88	0.03005	−1.38	0.08379
−2.37	0.00889	−1.87	0.03074	−1.37	0.08534
−2.36	0.00914	−1.86	0.03144	−1.36	0.08691
−2.35	0.00939	−1.85	0.03216	−1.35	0.08851
−2.34	0.00964	−1.84	0.03288	−1.34	0.09012
−2.33	0.00990	−1.83	0.03362	−1.33	0.09176
−2.32	0.01017	−1.82	0.03438	−1.32	0.09342
−2.31	0.01044	−1.81	0.03515	−1.31	0.09510

z	$G(z)$	z	$G(z)$	z	$G(z)$
−1.30	0.09680	−0.85	0.19766	−0.40	0.34458
−1.29	0.09853	−0.84	0.20045	−0.39	0.34827
−1.28	0.10027	−0.83	0.20327	−0.38	0.35197
−1.27	0.10204	−0.82	0.20611	−0.37	0.35569
−1.26	0.10383	−0.81	0.20897	−0.36	0.35942
−1.25	0.10565	−0.80	0.21186	−0.35	0.36317
−1.24	0.10749	−0.79	0.21476	−0.34	0.36693
−1.23	0.10935	−0.78	0.21770	−0.33	0.37070
−1.22	0.11123	−0.77	0.22065	−0.32	0.37448
−1.21	0.11314	−0.76	0.22363	−0.31	0.37828
−1.20	0.11507	−0.75	0.22663	−0.30	0.38209
−1.19	0.11702	−0.74	0.22965	−0.29	0.38591
−1.18	0.11900	−0.73	0.23270	−0.28	0.38974
−1.17	0.12100	−0.72	0.23576	−0.27	0.39358
−1.16	0.12302	−0.71	0.23885	−0.26	0.39743
−1.15	0.12507	−0.70	0.24196	−0.25	0.40129
−1.14	0.12714	−0.69	0.24510	−0.24	0.40517
−1.13	0.12924	−0.68	0.24825	−0.23	0.40905
−1.12	0.13136	−0.67	0.25143	−0.22	0.41294
−1.11	0.13350	−0.66	0.25463	−0.21	0.41683
−1.10	0.13567	−0.65	0.25785	−0.20	0.42074
−1.09	0.13786	−0.64	0.26109	−0.19	0.42465
−1.08	0.14007	−0.63	0.26435	−0.18	0.42858
−1.07	0.14231	−0.62	0.26763	−0.17	0.43251
−1.06	0.14457	−0.61	0.27093	−0.16	0.43644
−1.05	0.14686	−0.60	0.27425	−0.15	0.44038
−1.04	0.14917	−0.59	0.27760	−0.14	0.44433
−1.03	0.15150	−0.58	0.28096	−0.13	0.44828
−1.02	0.15386	−0.57	0.28434	−0.12	0.45224
−1.01	0.15625	−0.56	0.28774	−0.11	0.45620
−1.00	0.15866	−0.55	0.29116	−0.10	0.46017
−0.99	0.16109	−0.54	0.29460	−0.09	0.46414
−0.98	0.16354	−0.53	0.29806	−0.08	0.46812
−0.97	0.16602	−0.52	0.30153	−0.07	0.47210
−0.96	0.16853	−0.51	0.30503	−0.06	0.47608
−0.95	0.17106	−0.50	0.30854	−0.05	0.48006
−0.94	0.17361	−0.49	0.31207	−0.04	0.48405
−0.93	0.17619	−0.48	0.31561	−0.03	0.48803
−0.92	0.17879	−0.47	0.31918	−0.02	0.49202
−0.91	0.18141	−0.46	0.32276	−0.01	0.49601
−0.90	0.18406	−0.45	0.32636	0.00	0.50000
−0.89	0.18673	−0.44	0.32997	0.01	0.50399
−0.88	0.18943	−0.43	0.33360	0.02	0.50798
−0.87	0.19215	−0.42	0.33724	0.03	0.51197
−0.86	0.19489	−0.41	0.34090	0.04	0.51595

z	$G(z)$	z	$G(z)$	z	$G(z)$
0.05	0.51994	0.50	0.69146	0.95	0.82894
0.06	0.52392	0.51	0.69497	0.96	0.83147
0.07	0.52790	0.52	0.69847	0.97	0.83398
0.08	0.53188	0.53	0.70194	0.98	0.83646
0.09	0.53586	0.54	0.70540	0.99	0.83891
0.10	0.53983	0.55	0.70884	1.00	0.84134
0.11	0.54380	0.56	0.71226	1.01	0.84375
0.12	0.54776	0.57	0.71566	1.02	0.84614
0.13	0.55172	0.58	0.71904	1.03	0.84850
0.14	0.55567	0.59	0.72240	1.04	0.85083
0.15	0.55962	0.60	0.72575	1.05	0.85314
0.16	0.56356	0.61	0.72907	1.06	0.85543
0.17	0.56749	0.62	0.73237	1.07	0.85769
0.18	0.57142	0.63	0.73565	1.08	0.85993
0.19	0.57535	0.64	0.73891	1.09	0.86214
0.20	0.57926	0.65	0.74215	1.10	0.86433
0.21	0.58317	0.66	0.74537	1.11	0.86650
0.22	0.58706	0.67	0.74857	1.12	0.86864
0.23	0.59095	0.68	0.75175	1.13	0.87076
0.24	0.59483	0.69	0.75490	1.14	0.87286
0.25	0.59871	0.70	0.75804	1.15	0.87493
0.26	0.60257	0.71	0.76115	1.16	0.87698
0.27	0.60642	0.72	0.76424	1.17	0.87900
0.28	0.61026	0.73	0.76730	1.18	0.88100
0.29	0.61409	0.74	0.77035	1.19	0.88298
0.30	0.61791	0.75	0.77337	1.20	0.88493
0.31	0.62172	0.76	0.77637	1.21	0.88686
0.32	0.62552	0.77	0.77935	1.22	0.88877
0.33	0.62930	0.78	0.78230	1.23	0.89065
0.34	0.63307	0.79	0.78524	1.24	0.89251
0.35	0.63683	0.80	0.78814	1.25	0.89435
0.36	0.64058	0.81	0.79103	1.26	0.89617
0.37	0.64431	0.82	0.79389	1.27	0.89796
0.38	0.64803	0.83	0.79673	1.28	0.89973
0.39	0.65173	0.84	0.79955	1.29	0.90147
0.40	0.65542	0.85	0.80234	1.30	0.90320
0.41	0.65910	0.86	0.80511	1.31	0.90490
0.42	0.66276	0.87	0.80785	1.32	0.90658
0.43	0.66640	0.88	0.81057	1.33	0.90824
0.44	0.67003	0.89	0.81327	1.34	0.90988
0.45	0.67364	0.90	0.81594	1.35	0.91149
0.46	0.67724	0.91	0.81859	1.36	0.91309
0.47	0.68082	0.92	0.82121	1.37	0.91466
0.48	0.68439	0.93	0.82381	1.38	0.91621
0.49	0.68793	0.94	0.82639	1.39	0.91774

z	$G(z)$	z	$G(z)$	z	$G(z)$
1.40	0.91924	1.85	0.96784	2.30	0.98928
1.41	0.92073	1.86	0.96856	2.31	0.98956
1.42	0.92220	1.87	0.96926	2.32	0.98983
1.43	0.92364	1.88	0.96995	2.33	0.99010
1.44	0.92507	1.89	0.97062	2.34	0.99036
1.45	0.92647	1.90	0.97128	2.35	0.99061
1.46	0.92785	1.91	0.97193	2.36	0.99086
1.47	0.92922	1.92	0.97257	2.37	0.99111
1.48	0.93056	1.93	0.97320	2.38	0.99134
1.49	0.93189	1.94	0.97381	2.39	0.99158
1.50	0.93319	1.95	0.97441	2.40	0.99180
1.51	0.93448	1.96	0.97500	2.41	0.99202
1.52	0.93574	1.97	0.97558	2.42	0.99224
1.53	0.93699	1.98	0.97615	2.43	0.99245
1.54	0.93822	1.99	0.97670	2.44	0.99266
1.55	0.93943	2.00	0.97725	2.45	0.99286
1.56	0.94062	2.01	0.97778	2.46	0.99305
1.57	0.94179	2.02	0.97831	2.47	0.99324
1.58	0.94295	2.03	0.97882	2.48	0.99343
1.59	0.94408	2.04	0.97932	2.49	0.99361
1.60	0.94520	2.05	0.97982	2.50	0.99379
1.61	0.94630	2.06	0.98030	2.51	0.99396
1.62	0.94738	2.07	0.98077	2.52	0.99413
1.63	0.94845	2.08	0.98124	2.53	0.99430
1.64	0.94950	2.09	0.98169	2.54	0.99446
1.65	0.95053	2.10	0.98214	2.55	0.99461
1.66	0.95154	2.11	0.98257	2.56	0.99477
1.67	0.95254	2.12	0.98300	2.57	0.99492
1.68	0.95352	2.13	0.98341	2.58	0.99506
1.69	0.95449	2.14	0.98382	2.59	0.99520
1.70	0.95543	2.15	0.98422	2.60	0.99534
1.71	0.95637	2.16	0.98461	2.61	0.99547
1.72	0.95728	2.17	0.98500	2.62	0.99560
1.73	0.95818	2.18	0.98537	2.63	0.99573
1.74	0.95907	2.19	0.98574	2.64	0.99585
1.75	0.95994	2.20	0.98610	2.65	0.99598
1.76	0.96080	2.21	0.98645	2.66	0.99609
1.77	0.96164	2.22	0.98679	2.67	0.99621
1.78	0.96246	2.23	0.98713	2.68	0.99632
1.79	0.96327	2.24	0.98745	2.69	0.99643
1.80	0.96407	2.25	0.98778	2.70	0.99653
1.81	0.96485	2.26	0.98809	2.71	0.99664
1.82	0.96562	2.27	0.98840	2.72	0.99674
1.83	0.96638	2.28	0.98870	2.73	0.99683
1.84	0.96712	2.29	0.98899	2.74	0.99693

z	G(z)	z	G(z)	z	G(z)
2.75	0.99702	3.20	0.99931	3.65	0.99987
2.76	0.99711	3.21	0.99934	3.66	0.99987
2.77	0.99720	3.22	0.99936	3.67	0.99988
2.78	0.99728	3.23	0.99938	3.68	0.99988
2.79	0.99736	3.24	0.99940	3.69	0.99989
2.80	0.99744	3.25	0.99942	3.70	0.99989
2.81	0.99752	3.26	0.99944	3.71	0.99990
2.82	0.99760	3.27	0.99946	3.72	0.99990
2.83	0.99767	3.28	0.99948	3.73	0.99990
2.84	0.99774	3.29	0.99950	3.74	0.99991
2.85	0.99781	3.30	0.99952	3.75	0.99991
2.86	0.99788	3.31	0.99953	3.76	0.99992
2.87	0.99795	3.32	0.99955	3.77	0.99992
2.88	0.99801	3.33	0.99957	3.78	0.99992
2.89	0.99807	3.34	0.99958	3.79	0.99992
2.90	0.99813	3.35	0.99960	3.80	0.99993
2.91	0.99819	3.36	0.99961	3.81	0.99993
2.92	0.99825	3.37	0.99962	3.82	0.99993
2.93	0.99831	3.38	0.99964	3.83	0.99994
2.94	0.99836	3.39	0.99965	3.84	0.99994
2.95	0.99841	3.40	0.99966	3.85	0.99994
2.96	0.99846	3.41	0.99968	3.86	0.99994
2.97	0.99851	3.42	0.99969	3.87	0.99995
2.98	0.99856	3.43	0.99970	3.88	0.99995
2.99	0.99861	3.44	0.99971	3.89	0.99995
3.00	0.99865	3.45	0.99972	3.90	0.99995
3.01	0.99869	3.46	0.99973	3.91	0.99995
3.02	0.99874	3.47	0.99974	3.92	0.99996
3.03	0.99878	3.48	0.99975	3.93	0.99996
3.04	0.99882	3.49	0.99976	3.94	0.99996
3.05	0.99886	3.50	0.99977	3.95	0.99996
3.06	0.99889	3.51	0.99978	3.96	0.99996
3.07	0.99893	3.52	0.99978	3.97	0.99996
3.08	0.99897	3.53	0.99979	3.98	0.99997
3.09	0.99900	3.54	0.99980	3.99	0.99997
3.10	0.99903	3.55	0.99981	4.00	0.99997
3.11	0.99906	3.56	0.99981		
3.12	0.99910	3.57	0.99982		
3.13	0.99913	3.58	0.99983		
3.14	0.99916	3.59	0.99983		
3.15	0.99918	3.60	0.99984		
3.16	0.99921	3.61	0.99985		
3.17	0.99924	3.62	0.99985		
3.18	0.99926	3.63	0.99986		
3.19	0.99929	3.64	0.99986		

Indexes

Author index

Subject index

This book has been set in 10 and 9 point Caledonia, leaded 2 points. Section titles and chapter numbers are in 24 point Scotch Roman; chapter titles and section numbers are in 18 point Scotch Roman. The size of the type page is 28 x 48½ picas.